THE WORKS OF ALLEN GINSBERG 1941–1994

Self Portrait 8/c/85 Boulder
Allen Ginsberg

THE WORKS OF ALLEN GINSBERG 1941–1994

A Descriptive Bibliography

BILL MORGAN

With a Foreword by Allen Ginsberg

Bibliographies and Indexes in American Literature,
Number 19

GREENWOOD PRESS
Westport, Connecticut • London

Library of Congress Cataloging-in-Publication Data

Morgan, Bill, 1949–
    The works of Allen Ginsberg, 1941–1994 : a descriptive
bibliography / Bill Morgan ; with a foreword by Allen Ginsberg.
       p.   cm.—(Bibliographies and indexes in American literature,
ISSN 0742–6860 ; no. 19)
    Includes bibliographical references and index.
    ISBN 0–313–29389–9 (alk. paper)
    1. Ginsberg, Allen, 1926– —Bibliography. I. Title.
II. Series.
Z8342.5.M67   1995
[PS3513.I74]
016.811′54—dc20   94–41266

British Library Cataloguing in Publication Data is available.

Library of Congress Catalog Card Number: 94–41266
ISBN: 0–313–29389–9
ISSN: 0742–6860

First published in 1995

Greenwood Press, 88 Post Road West, Westport, CT 06881
An imprint of Greenwood Publishing Group, Inc.

Printed in the United States of America

The paper used in this book complies with the
Permanent Paper Standard issued by the National
Information Standards Organization (Z39.48–1984).

10 9 8 7 6 5 4 3 2 1

For Judy

kind gentle tender-hearted love

Contents

Thoughts on Bill Morgan's Bibliography

Bill Morgan spent two decades in close examination of my work, cataloguing publications and also archives. His familiarity with information in private papers as well as formal publications enriched the intelligence accessible to him as bibliographer of a vast unruly mass of books, translations in several dozen languages, interviews cross country & round the planet, blurbs and other intense ephemera.

In addition he's accounted late XX Century extensions of bardic energy into music, audio recordings, films and photography. As of Fall 1993, there were over ten thousand entries registering half a century's poetical activity.

"Ten thousand things of the world" summed up cosmos for old Taoist philosophers. Chuang-tze questions such voluminous literature, "Better not to move, but to let things be." So why such workaholic exuberance?

Eros accounts for much of the record, even the author's political, narcotic or meditative divagations. Decades ago poets visioned that we were entering a strange period of human history. Might the "American Century" end in hypertechnologic police state, suppression of feeling-awareness, ecological disaster or mechanical gridlock, & possible loss of our planet? I recorded these considerations as poet among poets Kerouac, Corso, Burroughs & Orlovsky, a core group in the literary movement later labeled "Beat Generation."

Our literature sacramentalized some ground of human sympathy, intelligent "adhesiveness," Eros at home. Walt Whitman prescribed "candor" as the skillful means for signaling this friendliness. Many of the main themes, motifs, proclamations or strands of sense in this artistic play — from individual spiritual liberation to communal liberation movements — are described in various detail in writings itemized by Mr. Morgan. These individualist manifestoes begin with self-published pamphlets — rare 1955 pre-publication ditto'd copies of Howl typed by Robert Creeley, & my own 1956 pamphlet "Siesta in Xbalba" mimeo'd on a ship in the Arctic.

I'm grateful to Bill Morgan for making this enormous meticulous catalogue. As Senior Citizen still mining my own uncollected work and accumulating more poems, he's made my own tasks of research and retrieval much easier. I hope his vast labors will serve researchers other than myself.

Allen Ginsberg
Oslo 10/30/93

Acknowledgments

The compiler wishes to thank Allen Ginsberg for his cooperation in making this bibliography possible. Without his patience during the past 15 years this project could not have been completed. If there is any success in the completeness of this book, it is due to his own great cares as a collector and preserver of the word.

Special thanks to Judy Matz who has faithfully supported my work for longer than she cares to remember. I'll never forget her loyalty and confidence in the work.

For their decades-long help the following people must be separately acknowledged: Bob Rosenthal, secretary to Allen Ginsberg and co-inventor of the FYPC files [faded yellow press clippings]; Jack Hagstrom, fellow bibliographer and sounding board, whose suggestions were always frustratingly correct; and the entire staff of the Columbia University Rare Book Room where Allen's archive has been on loan for the past 25 years; they treated me as a welcome guest instead of an eternal pest.

Collective praise to Allen Ginsberg's staff over the years (Dave Breithaupt, Althea Crawford, Jacqueline Gens, David Greenberg, Peter Hale, Helena Hughes, Juanita Lieberman, Gina Pellicano, Ben Schafer, Victoria Smart, Vicki Stanbury), the staff at Columbia University (John Albrey, Jean Ashton, Mimi Bowling, Bernard Crystal, Rudolph Ellenbogen, Patrick Lawlor, Kenneth A. Lohf, Kevin O'Connor, Henry Rowen, Ellen Scaruffi, Allison Scott, Jane Siegel, Marvin Taylor, Brad Westbrook, Hugh Wilburn) and the staff of City Lights Books (Lawrence Ferlinghetti, Nancy Peters, Bob Sharrad, Anne Janowitz, Pamela Mosher) and a one-man staff in and of himself, Bob Wilson of the Phoenix Bookshop. Thanks to Greenwood Press and editors George F. Butler and Jane C. Lerner for guidance along the way.

The compiler thanks the staff members of the following libraries, which he visited over the past 14 years: *California:* San Francisco Public, Univ. of California, Berkeley; *Connecticut:* Univ. of Connecticut, Yale Univ.; *Delaware:* Univ. of Delaware, Newark; *Illinois:* Northwestern Univ.; *Maryland:* National Library of Medicine; *Massachusetts:* Amherst College, Harvard Univ., Univ. of Mass.; *New Jersey:* Princeton Univ., Rutgers; *New York:* New York Public Library, NYU, SUNY Buffalo, Syracuse Univ.; *Pennsylvania:* Temple Univ., Univ. of Pittsburgh; *Rhode Island:* Brown Univ.; *Texas:* Univ. of Texas, Austin; *District of Columbia:* Library of Congress.

Frequent reference was made to George Dowden's *A Bibliography of Works by Allen Ginsberg* published by City Lights, 197 and to Michelle P. Kraus' *Allen Ginsberg : An Annotated Bibliography, 1969-1977* published by the Scarecrow Press, 1980. Both of these were very important checklists of the early works and made this researcher's work much easier.

And heartfelt thanks to the following organizations and individuals who helped in the pursuit of information:

Abbeville Press; Keith Abbott; About Books; Harry N. Abrams, Inc. (Ellen Rosefsky); Sam Abrams; Bob Adamshick; Albatross Book Co.; Daisy Aldan; Alfred Van Der Marck

Editions; All-Union State Order of the Red Banner of Labour Library of Foreign Literature
(E. Pereslegina); Donald Allen; W.H. Allen, Ltd. (Claire Watts); Allison & Busby;
Alternative Orange (Philip Goff); Alternative Press (Ken Mikolowski); Oleg Alyakvinsky;
American Academy and Institute of Arts and Letters (Nancy Johnson, Kathryn
Talalay)American Library Associations Publications; Amherst College (Joanne C.
Dougherty, John Lancaster); David Amram; Anacapa Books (Jane Willsea); Michael Andre;
Olav Angell; Alan Ansen; Görgen Antonsson; Aperture; Appalachian Literary League
(Joanie Barrett); A-L Books (Deborah Applefield); Archon Books (James Thorpe III); Ardis
Publishers (L. Karpor); Arion Press (Claire Ewing, Glenn Todd); Arizona Daily Star
(Elaine Raines); Asbury Park Press (Chris Matkorish); John Ashbery; Asphodel Book
Shop (Jim Lowell); Atticus Books (Ralph Cook); Audrey Cohen College (Hibbert Moss);
Avon Books (Lisa Considine); Fadil Bajraj; Ballantine (Jane Bess); Gordon Ball; Allen
Bank; Amiri Baraka; Bärenreiter-Verlag (Martin Weyde); Mary Beach; Beacon Press (Beth
McGillicuddy); Bennington College (John Swan); John Berendt; Bertram Rota Ltd.
(Anthony Rota); Biblioteca Nacional-Buenos Aires (Julio Oscar Zolezzi); Biblioteca
Nacional de Bolivia (Josep M. Barnadas); Biblioteca Nacional del Peru (Ana Maria
Maldonado); Biblioteca Nazionale Centrale Vittorio Emanuele II-Rome (Biblioteca
Nacional-Madrid (Concha Lois); Bibliotheque de la Sorbonne (Yannick Nexon);
Bibliotheque Nationale (Jean-Louis Pailhes); Bibliotheque Nationale-Alger (Medhar
Kenza); Bibliotheque Nationale Suisse; Bibliotheque Royale Albert Ier (Frans Van
Wijnsberghe); Big Fish (Sparrow); Mary Biggs; Edition Galerie Bruno Bischofberger
(Regula Haffner); Gordon Bishop; George Bixby; Black Ace Books; Black Sparrow Press
(John Martin); Bloodaxe Books (Neil Astley); B.C. Bloomfield; Robert Bly; Victor
Bockris; Jim Bogan; Boss (Reginald Gay); Christian Bourgois Editeur; George Bowering;
Boz Publishing (Richard D. Simonds, Jr.); The British Library; Eugene Brooks; Brown
University, John Hay Library (Rosemary Cullen, Samuel A. Streit); Bunny and the
Crocodile Press (Grace Cavalieri); William Burroughs; Busyhaus (Robert Hauser); George
Butterick; Cadmus Editions (Jiffrey Miller); Cainero, Steven Eddy; Calgary Herald (Jackie
Trosch); Cappelen (Inga Bostad); Carleton University Press; Carnivorous Arpeggio Press
(George Messo); Carolyn Cassady; Annie Charters; Cherry Valley Editions (Pam Plymell);
Chicago Historical Society (Judy Sponsler, Claudia Lamm Wood); Chronicle Books;
Citadel Press; Tom Clark; Cleveland Public Library (Evelyn M. Ward); Cleveland State
University; Alan Clodd; Coach House Press; Andrei Codrescu; Coffee House Press
(Michael L. Wiegers, Lisa Janssen); Larry Collins; Columbia University (Paul R. Palmer);
Cooper Street Publications (John J. Dorfner); David Cope; Country Publishers (Garrison
Ellis); Cover (Jeff Wright); Crawdaddy; Creative Arts Book Co. (Don Ellis); Creative
Living (Robert H. Spencer); Crossing Press; Crown Publishers (David Groff); Dahlberg,
R'lene Howell; Dalkey Archive Press (Steven Moore); Dell Publishing (Daniel Levy);
Andreas Deutsch Ltd. (Kate Morris, J.M. Simpson); Devil/Paradis (Thierry Tillier); Didier
Erudition (Jean Didier); John Dinsmore; Diane di Prima; Dirty Goat (Joe Bratcher); Elsa
Dorfman; Doubleday (C. Christiansen, Robert Radick); Nicky Drumbolis; Prabhat K.
Dutta; E.P. Dutton (Trent Duffy); Les Ecrits des Forges Inc. (Bernard Pozier); End Times
(Craig Taatjes); David Engel; Istvan Eorsi; Esquire; Europa Könyvkiado Budapest (Varady
Szabolcs); Faber and Faber (Jane Feaver); Fahey, William A. Fahey; Fantome Press (C.M.
James); Farrar, Straus & Giroux; Chris Felver; Jeff & Brenda Ferris; Leslie Fiedler; Firefly
Press (Carl Kay); First Line (Ai Wei Wei); Fischbach Gallery (Beverly Zagor); Folger
Shakespeare Library (Jean Nordhaus); Follett Publishing (Elaine Goldberg); Forever
Young (Bernard Froidefond); Fort Worth Art Museum (Susan Colegrove); Fort Worth
Star-Telegram (Kristin Sandefur); Brian Foye; Raymond Foye; Robert Frank; Frank (David
Applefield); Ted Frederick; Friction (Randy Roark); From Here Press (William J.
Higginson); Fundacao Biblioteca Nacional (Eliane Perez); Christopher Funkhauser;
Gagosian Gallery; Gale Research (Rick Layman); Galeria Bonino, Ltd. (Osvaldo Gomariz);
Galerie Watari; Donald Gallup; Gay Sunshine Press (Winston Leyland); George Mason
University (Ruth Kerns); Hartmut H. Gerdes; Glide Publications; David Glotzer;
Gloucester Lyceum and Sawyer Free Library (Judith Clark); Victor Gollancz (Hugo Cox);
Josh Gosciak; Gotham Book Mart (Andreas Brown); Grand Forks Public City-County
Library; Grove Weidenfeld (Abigail Cheever, Leslie Keenan, Anne Sikora); George
Gruntz; HackerArt Books; Jon Halper; Hammond Inc. (C. Koch); Hammond Music
Enterprises (Beth Greer, Hank O'Neal); Hampshire College (Susan A. Dayall); Hanging

Loose (Robert Hershon); Carl Hanser Verlag (Margarete Grusling); Reinhard Harbaum; Gunnar Harding; HarperCollins (Charlotte Abbott, Ashley Chase, Mary Lou Dorking, Peggy Jeanes, Terry Karten, Lisa M. Vitiello); Harris County Department of Education (Susan J. Sheridan); Richard Harteis; Harvard University (Susan Halpert, Gordon Hylton); Gerald S. Hawkins; Heartwood (June Cable); Helsinki University Library (Kristina Nyman); Joanne & Gordon Henderson; Martin Hill; Hill & Wang (Elisabeth Dyssegaard); Jack Hirschman; Albert Hofmann Foundation (Virginia D. Berg); Anselm Hollo; David J. Holmes Autographs (Mark W. Sullivan); Henry Holt and Co.; Holy Cow! Press; Lita Hornick; Houghton Mifflin Co.; Jo House; Howling Mantra (Daniel Marcou); Andrew Hoyem; Vicki Hudspith; Humana Press (Margaret Jacobs, Thomas Lanigan); Lewis Hyde; Indiana University (Joel Silver, Saundra Taylor); Tim Inkster; Instituto da Biblioteca Nacional e do Livro; Jewish National & University Library (Libby Kahane); John Hill School (Mildred Ringer); Hettie Jones; Peter M. Jones; Godfrey Jordan; Pierre Joris; Kanawha County Public Library System (Susan H. Harper); Eliot Katz; Michael Kellner; Kendall/Hunt Publishing Co.; Kenosha Public Library (Lynn Hagen); Kent State University Press (Flo Cunningham); William Keogan; Basil King; King Features (Penny Elie); King Saud University (Saad A. Al-Dobaian); King's College London (Eric Mottram); KLIM (Inger Kristensen); Arthur & Kit Knight; Alfred A. Knopf Inc. (Ashbel Green); Michael Köhler; Det Kongelige Bibliotek (Jacob Thomsen); Koninklijke Bibliotheek Albert I (J.P. van Loon); Kraus Reprint Co. (Caryl P. Dreiblatt, Jodi Piazza); Rochelle Kraut; Kunsthalle-Basel; James Laughlin; Robert LaVigne; Lawrence Public Library; Todd Lawson; Jean-Jacques Lebel; Eileen Leeds; Lehman College (Janet Butler Munch); LeMoyne College (Gretchen E. Pearson); Elbert Lenrow; Leon County Commissioners (Ronald Kanen); LePellec, Yves; Harry Lewis; Limberlost Press (Rick Ardinger); Little, Brown and Co. (Brenda Taylor); Long Shot (Danny Shot); Lovely Jobly; Michael McCurdy; Fred McDarrah; McGill University (Margaret Monks); Laurence McGilvery; Macmillan Co. of Australia (Lisa Highton, Roger Williamson); John S. McWhinnie; Mai Hors Saison; Maisonneuve Press (Robert Merrill); Judith Malina; Man Alive! (David Kirschenbaum); Manic D Press (Jennifer Joseph); Männer Vogue (Andreas Fischer); Paul Mariah; Marin County Free Library (Gail Haar); Greg Masters; Anne Matz; Taylor Mead; Jonas Mekas; Jack Micheline; Midwest Quarterly (Debbie Ware); Miles; Jeffrey Miller; George Robert Minkoff; Wolfgang Mohrhenn; Moment (Eric Lyden); Peter Money; John Montgomery; Steven Moore; Ted Morgan; William Morrow & Co. (Steven Wilson); Museum of Fine Arts, Houston (Kathleen Robinson); Museum of Modern Art (Nancy Kranz); Nacionalna i Sveucilisna Biblioteka (Biserka Dunda); NAMBLA Journal; Napalm Health Spa (Jim Cohn); Narodni Knihovna (Ulrika Horakova); Naropa Institute (Cecily Alexander, Rebecca Bush, David Gansz); National Diet Library, Tokyo (Y. Morita); National Foreign Language Library (Zdenka Kaposvari); National Lampoon; National Library of Greece (Panayotis G. Nicolopoulos); National Library of the Philippines (Redempta A. Francia); National Library of China (Cheng Zhen); National Library of Thailand (Thara Kanakamani); National Poetry Foundation (Marie Alpert, Gail Sapiel, Carroll Terrell); F.A. Nettelbeck; Maurice F. Neville, Rare Books; New Censorship (Ivan Suvanjieff); New Directions (Fred Martin); New Haven Free Public Library (David M. Hinkley); New Jersey State Library (Doris Murphy); New Letters (Janice Woolery); New Press (Bob Alramion); New York Public Library (Mimi Bowling, Sharon Frost); New York Quarterly (William Packard); New York University (Sherlyn Abdoo, Theodore Grieder, Frank Walker); New York Woman (Phyllis Freeman); Dirk Nishen GmbH & Co. (Michael Meyer); North Atlantic Books (Jim Bogan); Northern Lights Publishing Co. (C.F. Terrell); Northouse & Northouse (Cameron Northouse); Northwestern University Library (R. Russell Maylone); Off the Wall (Wes Wilson); Lars Ohlerich; Ojai Foundation (Ann Hammond); Omega Institute (Sarah Priestman); Onondaga Community College (Frank Doble); Onondaga County Public Library (Mark E. Allnatt); Organisation Mondiale des Poetes (Nelleke Oostveen); Peter Orlovsky; Österreichische Nationalbibliothek (Bettina Kann); Other Publishers; Ottawa Public Library (Diana Hall); Ron Padgett; Paideuma; Nam June Paik; Paragon House (Donald Kennison); Parallax Press; Paris Review; Passaic County Historical Society (Kate Gordon); Paterson Public Library (Leo Fickleberg); Simon and Rose Pettet; Peace Press (Warren Peace); Richard Peabody; Peckerwood Magazine; Claude Pelieu; Penguin Books Ltd. (Vanessa Terry); Penguin Books India (David Davidar); Penmaen Press (Michael McCurdy); Pennsylvania State University (Charles Mann); Otto

Penzler; Peregrine Smith Books; James E. Perrizo; Persea Books (Michael Braziller); Pharos Books (Matthew Jennett); Pinched Nerves Press (Steven Hartman); Pepper & Stern; Fernanda Pivano; Charles Plymell; Poetry Center (Larry Price); Poetry Magazine; The Poetry Project (Ed Friedman, Eileen Myles); Poetry Society; Poets & Writers (Elliot Figman); Poets Reading Inc. (Michael Logue); Portable Lower East Side (Kurt Hollander); Penn Posset; Princeton University (Scott Carlisle); Provincetown Arts (Chrisopher Busa); Provine Press (Jeffrey Bartlett); Quill & Brush (Richard Peabody); Quorum (Branko Cegec); Random House (Samantha Chang); Red Ozier Press (Steve Miller); William Reese Co. (Terry G. Halladay); Regent Press (Joe Weber); Rhino Records (Shari Overend); Paul Rickert; Pamela Robinson; Eriko Kamio Rowe; Rumor (Timothy G. Merello); Rutgers University; S Press Tonbandverlag; Ruth and Marvin Sackner Archvie; Sacramento Public Library (Ruth Ellis); The Sacred and the Profane (Sue Fox); St. Martin's Press (Garrett Kiely); Salve Regina University (John T. Anderson); San Francisco Public Library; San Francisco Review of Books (Donald Paul); Ed Sanders; Santa Cruz City-County Public Library; Tom Savage; Scarecrow Press (Norman Horrocks); Ron Schick; Andrew Sclanders; Michael Schumacher; Second Coming Magazine (A.D. Winans); Shambhala Publications (Helen Martineau); Shiny; Jack Shu Shuai; Sierra Club Books (Kin Nishida); Brent Sikkema Fine Art (Matthew Aquilone); Barry Silesky; Simon & Schuster (Cassie Jones, Carolyn Reidy); Simon Fraser University (Gene Bridwell), Vojo Sindolic; Rani Singh; Skidmore College (Peggy Seiden); Skyline Books (James Musser); Holly Solomon Gallery; Carl Solway Gallery; Sotheby's (N.D. Stanley); Sounds True (Claude Frank); Spao & Spassiba (Lukas Moodysson); Staatsbibliothek zu Berlin (A. Schubarth); Stanford University Libraries (Margaret J. Kimball); Starscrewer (Lucien Suel); State Historical Society of Wisconsin (Geraldine Strey); SUNY at Buffalo (Robert Bertholf); SUNY at Oneonta (Elaine L. Downing); SUNY at Stony Brook (Evert Volkersz, Paul B. Wiener); Sulfur (Clayton Eshelman); Robert and Patricia Sutherland-Cohen; Yu Suwa; Syracuse University Library (Carol Parke); Szivarvany (Ferenc J. Mozsi); Talking Head (Leif Owen Klein); G. Thomas Tanselle; Teachers & Writers Collaborative; Tel Aviv Review (Lea Hahn); Temple University (Thomas M. Whitehead); Thinker Review (Ron Whitefield); Third Rail (Uri Hertz); Thomas Crane Public Library; Thunder's Mouth Press (Eliza C. Galaher, Anne Stillwaggon); Time-Life Books (Linda Lee); Toronto Public Library (Leena M. Oraw); Tribu (Bertrand Tochme); Turret Books; Twayne Publishers (Mark Zadrozny, Sarah B. Zobel); Twelvetrees Press (Lynn O'Connor); John Tytell; Underground Forest; Underwood-Miller; USIS (K. Prem); Universitetet i Oslo (Tove D. Johansen); University of Arkansas Press (Scot Danforth, David Sanders); University of California at Berkeley (Anthonly Bliss, William M. Roberts); University of California at Irvine (Kevin Fredette); UCLA (Doris Curran); University of Chicago Press; University of Colorado (Bruce P. Montgomery); University of Connecticut (George Butterick); University of Iowa Press (Holly Carver, Edie Roberts); University of Kentucky (Robert A. McGill-Aken); University of Liverpool (Catherine Rees); University of Michigan Press (Christine Slovey); University of Minnesota Libraries (Dennis Lien); University of Missouri-Kansas City (Marilyn Burlingame); University of Nebraska (G.A. Rudolph); University of New Mexico (Terry A. Gugliotta); University of North Carolina (Bernice Bergup); University of Puerto Rico (Irma N. Ramirez); University of Sydney (A.E. Cahill); University of Texas at Austin (Kathy Henderson, Richard W. Oram, Tom Staley); University of Toronto (Harold Averill); University of Tulsa (Lori N. Curtis); University of Virginia (Martin Davis, Carol Rossi); University of Wisconsin (Mary Freymiller); University of Wyoming (Diana Shelton); Unmuzzled Ox (Michael Andre); Unwin Hyman (Frances Dedrick); Vajradhatu (Ned Nisbet); Vajradhatu Sun; Vanity Press; Viking Press; Walker Art Center (Margaret O'Neill-Ligon); Wanted Man (John Bauldie); Warner Books (Diane Stockwell); Shizuko Watari; Water Row Books (Jeffrey Weinberg); Steve Watson; Dean Faulkner Wells; George Beach Whitman; Wichita Public Library (Larry Vos); Bernhard Widder; Mary Helen Wiesel; Eleanor Wilderman; Ted Wilentz; Jonathan Williams; Words Etcetera (Julian Nangle); Workers Press; Jeffrey Wright; Andrew Wylie; Yale University; Marie Zabranova; Ali Zarrin; Zeitgeist (Bruce K. Isaacson).

Introduction

For the past fifteen years I have been making the trek to Allen Ginsberg's office, opening the drawer in the desk with my name on it, and discovering the feast of newly arrived books and magazines that lie there, awaiting my cataloguing. Never have I found that drawer empty; often the meal ends with more publications than I can digest. Day after day publications arrive, passing from Allen's hand and eye, through that drawer and on to the shelves of his huge archive. This is a menu of those items, listing all the possible choices on the bill of fare of Allen's poetic table. I can't imagine that drawer ever being empty, and until it is, this bibliography will serve as a guide to a life-long work in progress.

In the late 1960s I began working with Lawrence Ferlinghetti on the book which eventually became *Lawrence Ferlinghetti: A Comprehensive Bibliography to 1980* published by Garland in 1982. In the course of that work I visited countless collections and libraries across the country and nowhere did I find a better private resource than Allen Ginsberg's own archive. If I couldn't locate a scarce copy of *Beatitude* magazine in any public collection, I could be assured that Allen had it on his own shelves. If I needed to find a copy of an obscure flyer, I could count on the Ginsberg Archive. The only obstacle to using his collection was that it consisted of more than a thousand boxes of unsorted paper. Once work was completed on the Ferlinghetti bibliography, I decided, with Allen's permission, to catalogue the contents of the Ginsberg Archive, to enable access by future researchers. This bibliography has grown quite naturally out of that organizational work.

Allen Ginsberg must surely be one of the most prolific writers of our times. He has been widely published and is a generous contributor to underground magazines and small press anthologies. His loyalty to City Lights Books for 25 years is only one example of his commitment to independent publishing, helping to establish City Lights as one of the most influential small presses in the world. His active support of many causes over the years has lent itself to the publication of numerous position papers, petitions and open letters, most of which are uncollected. The subject range of publications is vast for a single author, from Buddhist studies to drug research to gay rights issues to tireless support of fellow writers. His works may be found in the music corner of the bookstore just as easily as the photography, political and religion sections, sometimes even in the occult and history departments. And just as soon as you say "but not the cookbook section of the store," there he is with a recipe for savory oatmeal.

Since childhood he has maintained working journals and from these come ideas for poems and prose that develop into major works. Poems are often published which are in progress between initial inspiration and finished draft. Ginsberg tends to tinker with his poetry much more than his dictum "First Thought Best Thought" would suggest, and the publication histories of each poem are a log of those adjustments.

This bibliography, intended as a complete, comprehensive guide to the work of Allen Ginsberg, is designed to present a history of his published works and to trace the evolution of his writings over a period of publications and revisions. Found here are the production details and descriptions of the physical qualities of Ginsberg's books. For those interested in works about Allen Ginsberg and his writings, this bibliography will be followed next year by a secondary bibliography of criticism and biography. Although often found in primary bibliographies, the translations of Allen Ginsberg's works will be found in that volume. In only a few special instances, where the bilingual printing of the poem is the true first appearance, are translations included here.

Everyone must have models. For Allen Ginsberg it was Walt Whitman, William Blake and William Carlos Williams. For this bibliographer I have followed the outstanding research as set forth in the works of B.C. Bloomfield and Edward Mendelson in their *W.H. Auden: A Bibliography,* second edition (Charlottesville, VA: University Press of Virginia, 1972), Jack W.C. Hagstrom and George Bixby in their *Thom Gunn: A Bibliography, 1940—1978* (London, England: Bertram Rota, 1979) and Donald Gallup in his *Ezra Pound: A Bibliography* (Charlottesville, VA: University Press of Virginia, 1983).

All writings by Allen Ginsberg listed in the bibliography are poems unless otherwise indicated. It must be mentioned that it is often difficult to distinguish poetry from prose in Ginsberg's work. Indeed, one of the major contributions of Ginsberg's writing has been to break down the distinction between poetry and prose. Many of his works were originally found in his journals in simple prose format, later restructured to create poems on the page. His poem, "The Bricklayer's Lunch Hour" is an excellent example of something which he originally set down as a prose journal entry and then later recognized it as the elegant poem that it is. For purposes of indexing this bibliography, the compiler has made a distinction between prose and poetry, but such labels should not be considered as the poet's own judgments.

Chronological order always prevails. Descriptions are based upon the compiler's examination of the items. Items not seen by the compiler have been indicated by an asterisk immediately following the entry number. Please note that in some cases clippings from Ginsberg's own collection have been difficult to verify, but are included here with as complete citation as possible in an attempt to be comprehensive. Sometimes page numbers of clippings could not be verified and in those cases they are blank.

All printing is in black ink on white paper unless otherwise noted. Standard practice is observed when transcribing upper and lower-case letters. Throughout the text "AG" refers to Allen Ginsberg. The very rare cases of anonymous works and those with pseudonyms are noted. Items signed by Ginsberg but not written by him are identified in chronological sequence as "Related Items" within each section, i.e. open letters signed by Ginsberg and many other authors but were not composed by Allen.

Section A contains complete publication histories for all English-language books and pamphlets by Allen Ginsberg. Due to the large number of broadsides created by Ginsberg, a special section AA for those items follows the A section. This will enable the researcher to get a realistic picture of the frequency and range of monograph publications. Special attention has been given to the numbering system in order to differentiate the various editions, issues and states of each title. Modern publishing techniques are quickly eroding the usefulness of terms such as edition. In a conversation with the compiler, G.T. Tanselle once defined an edition as that which is "created by an original typesetting or keystroking of the letters onto the plates, etc. for the production of the book." This is a very helpful method for determining editions. We aren't as likely to be confused by booksellers' terms such as paperback edition or limited edition, which frequently only reflect a variation in cover materials. With the universal use of computers, word processors and scanners in publishing, the creation of true second and subsequent editions becomes more and more uncommon. It is not necessary to re-key an entire document once it has been converted to a machine-readable format. Variations in type size, font and layout are endless with even the simplest of computers. Hence, issues and states become more and more important. Author's corrections are embedded in the new printings with only a few adjustments to the entire text. These are problems for future bibliographers to wrestle with, but here it must be pointed out that a strict adherence to the term edition as described above has been followed. The first impression is fully described, with reprintings merely enumerated except where a substantial change in content or format occurs. All subsequent states are identified as such, except where treated as new editions or issues. In my numbering system, for example, A3a1.1 stands for A3 = *Howl and Other Poems;* a = first edition; 1 = first issue; and .1 stands for first impression (printing).

Title page transcription comes first in each citation with collation, binding and publication histories following that. Colors of inks, papers and bindings are designated as suggested by G.T. Tanselle in his "A System for Color Identification for Bibliographical Description" (*Studies in Bibliography*, vol. 20 (1967) pp. 203-234). ISCC-NBS Color numbers are identified only in their first use in a citation and afterwards are referred to by descriptive name only. Inks have sometimes not been described by this method if they were not printed on white paper and if a large enough area was not covered by ink. For example, a thin layer of red ink on a green paper produces a color greatly different from that of the same ink on white paper, making ink color identification difficult.

The dimensions given are those of the cover height preceding width, to the nearest tenth of a centimeter. All watermarks and special papers are noted. Dust jackets and wrappers are described.

In cases where limited, cloth and paper issues were all published on the same day, preference is given to them in that order. Numbers, etc., for limited issues which appear in holograph are noted here for example only; other copies may vary but this describes the arrangement of the issues this compiler has examined. Notes have been added where confusion may exist because of photocopy and mimeograph printings. Where substantial additions and deletions have been made to a text, they are noted even if the publisher does not identify them.

The title page descriptions are standard, with editorial interpolations always enclosed in square brackets. Within each collation I have followed the examples of the above-mentioned bibliographies and of Fredson Bowers in his *Principles of Bibliographical Description* (Princeton, NJ: Princeton University Press, 1949).

Binding descriptions follow standard practice with no attempt to identify materials beyond general terms. Papers are described as fully as possible but varying shades of white are all identified as white.

Items written by Allen Ginsberg are identified completely and indexed by first line and title. By checking the index each work's first publication can be discovered. Publication data is from correspondence with the publisher and/or copyright offices unless otherwise noted. Some research produced conflicting data; this is also noted. As a matter of policy, many publishers would not divulge the number of copies printed of their publications; some would not even release publication dates. The price listed is the original list price for a work; price changes have usually not been listed, unless such listing helps identify various impressions. Throughout the bibliography the notes will point out any unusual features.

Section AA contains broadsides and portfolios containing broadsides by Allen Ginsberg. Traditionally these would be included in the A Section of the bibliography, but due to the large number of items in both sections, a separate section has been created for additional clarity. Programs, flyers and handouts are included here only if they include first appearances of work. Other such publications are to be found in the miscellaneous section E. Descriptions follow the standards set forth in the A section.

Section B contains descriptions of all books by other authors and editors that contain first book appearances of Ginsberg's works, including works previously published in periodical form. This section follows an abbreviated form of the style used in the A section. Descriptions of bindings as well as collation information have been shortened. All contents attributed to Ginsberg are fully listed and indexed. Books that contain only photographs by Ginsberg without written text other than their legends are not included here, but are found in Section D. Anthologies which reprint works from previously published books are excluded. Please note that due to this restriction several popular anthologies do not appear in the bibliography, such as Penguin's *Ferlinghetti, Ginsberg, Corso* which was an early best seller in England. Occasionally reprint histories for items in this section have not been located or would not be released by the publisher, but the compiler has included all information that was available to him.

Section C includes all first appearances of works by Allen Ginsberg in periodical form, including poems, prose and letters as well as drawings, translations and reviews written by Ginsberg. Periodicals containing photographs taken by Ginsberg are not listed here, but are found in Section D. Entries from the same issue of a periodical are prioritized by page number. Chronological order is followed here. Items with month-only or seasonal dates are listed as if published on the first day of the month or season unless the publisher could supply a more accurate or official publication date, i.e. (Winter [Dec. 1955] 1956). In those cases the dates are included within square brackets. Therefore a date of Feb. 1980 is filed as if it appeared on Feb. 1, 1980, and Spring 1980 is filed as if appeared on March 22, 1980. Items with only a year designation are listed as if the publication date were after December 31 of that year. Where two periodicals have the same date, the order is alphabetical by periodical title. Publication dates which the compiler has found to be different from or more exact than the issue date on the periodical are given in square brackets and arranged according to that date. Occasionally these differences are significant. The title for a poem or prose piece is listed, with a note to a more common title if they are not the same. All items are signed as "Allen Ginsberg" unless otherwise noted. The place of publication of each periodical, where known, is listed in the index. Once an item has appeared in book form, periodical reprintings are listed only if revisions to the text were made. For untitled works reference is made to the first line of text.

Some items which appeared in foreign-language periodicals before appearing in English-language periodicals are listed here only if they are bilingual in format and include Ginsberg's original English words. All other translations will appear in a secondary bibliography of works about Allen Ginsberg to be published next year by Greenwood Press.

Section D lists books, periodicals and miscellaneous published materials which reproduce photographs taken by Allen Ginsberg. A photographer since the forties, Ginsberg has seriously followed these talents to produce a large body of work which chronicles his life, his friends and his travels. The publications are in chronological order and include only the first appearance of either the photographs or the legends with references to earlier printings of the same photograph with different legends. Regardless of whether it appears in book or periodical, the photograph/legend is listed here only in its first published form.

Ginsberg spends a great amount of time polishing the legends to the photographs and considers each one to be a small essay. Occasionally the holograph legend is identical to an earlier appearance in wording but is not identical in handwriting and for the sake of completeness, both items are entered, treating the handwriting as an object in and of itself, and therefore the variation is noted. Publications in this section may or may not have appeared in earlier sections of the bibliography.

Section E lists miscellaneous appearances of Ginsberg's work, including but not limited to dust jacket blurbs, printed postcards, advertising flyers, catalogs, posters, librettos, petitions and programs for readings which contain the writings and drawings of Ginsberg. Many of these materials are ephemeral and in a few instances the poet's entire contribution is quoted. Because of the elusiveness of this type of material, there is no way to judge how complete this section is; the compiler had unlimited access to Ginsberg's extensive collection of ephemera, but there will always be undiscovered items in this category.

Section F lists commercially-produced and distributed recordings of Ginsberg's readings. Only works which contain Ginsberg's voice are included here; not included are readings of his work by others. Included here are also Ginsberg's readings of other poets' works, most notably William Blake. No attempt has been made to list private recordings of his readings of which there are thousands in his own archive alone.

Section G lists commercially-produced films and videotapes of appearances by Allen Ginsberg and adaptations of his work for those media. No attempt has been made to list private films. Subsection GG lists only a few selected TV and radio appearances; a more complete list could be produced of these appearances, but there is no way to research those citations or even verify that the broadcasts were aired. Certainly many may never have been recorded or retained, but Ginsberg has been broadcast widely over the years.

Two indexes are included which list all proper names and titles mentioned in the bibliography. The first index lists titles and first lines of Ginsberg's poetry and prose. When the articles *a, an* or *the* appear as the first word, they are ignored. This is a common alphabetical convention, but since the advent of computer-generated indexes, it must be restated. Here the alphabetical filing rules as set by the Library of Congress are followed. The second index is a general index to the contents of the bibliography. In addition, all people portrayed in photographs taken by Allen Ginsberg are indexed here, but no attempt has been made to index writings or photographs by any other subject, location or date.

Use this bibliography as a traveler would a map. Let it take you to the works but never replace those works. Let Allen Ginsberg's words speak for themselves and enjoy the banquet served up by him.

I have relied greatly on the help of others along the way and hope that the preceding acknowledgments will in a small way thank them for that help.

Bill Morgan
New York City 8/1/94

BIBLIOGRAPHY

A

Books and Pamphlets by Allen Ginsberg

a1. *First edition*

HOWL | for | Carl Solomon | by | Allen Ginsberg | "Unscrew the locks from the doors! | Unscrew the doors themselves from their jambs!"

Seventeen single (8 1/2 x 11 in.) sheets, printed on rectos only, ll. [i-ii] 1-15. [i]: title page. [ii]: 'Dedicatory Page | To | Jack Kerouac newBuddha of American prose who spit forth intelli- | gence into eleven books written in half the number of years (1951-1956) | ---ON THE ROAD, VISIONS OF NEAL, DR. SAX, SPRINGTIME MARY, THE SUBTER- | RANEANS, SAN FRANCISCO BLUES, SOME OF THE DHARMA, BOOK OF DREAMS, WAKE | UP, MEXICO CITY BLUES, & VISIONS OF GERARD---creating a spontaneous bop | prosody and original classic literature. Several phrases and the title | of <u>Howl</u> are taken from Him. | William Seward Burroughs, author of NAKED LUNCH, an endless novel | which will drive everybody mad. | Neal Cassady, author of THE FIRST THIRD, an autobiography 1949, | which enlightened Buddha. All these books are published in Heaven. | Lucien Carr, recently promoted to Night Bureau Manager of New York | United Press.' 1-15: text.

27.8 x 21.5 cm. Stapled once in the upper left corner so that the title page forms the cover. All edges trimmed. White wove paper unwatermarked. Entirely printed in dark purple (224) ink.

Contents: Howl — A Supermarket in California — Sunflower Sutra — America

Distributed free to friends. Published May 16, 1956 in an impression of 25 copies.

Note: A copy from the library of Robert LaVigne with the history of this publication set forth in an autograph inscription by AG as follows: "This copy one of twenty five paid for by me with pure human blood costed [sic] $10.00 typed by poet Robert Creely [sic] dittoed by Martha Rexroth transported by me to the hands of Robert Lavigne[sic] in exchange for several drawings--self portraits on the bed and the incredible plans with Circle for water and floers [sic] May 16, 1956 S.F. adios Robert till N.Y. fame fortune history and big private black cockly sad woes shared and grave to come. Love, Allen."

a2. *Re-issue (unauthorized, 1979)*

HOWL | for | Carl Solomon | by | Allen Ginsberg | "Unscrew the locks from the doors! | Unscrew the doors themselves from their jambs!" | GOTHAM BOOK MART, INC. | 41 WEST 47TH ST. | NEW YORK, N.Y. 10036

Seventeen single (8 1/2 x 11 in.) sheets, printed on rectos only, ll. [i-ii] 1-15. [i]: title page. [ii]: 'Dedicatory Page | To | Jack Kerouac newBuddha of American prose who spit forth intelli- | gence into eleven books written in half the number of years (1951-1956) | ---ON THE ROAD, VISIONS OF NEAL, DR. SAX, SPRINGTIME MARY, THE SUBTER- | RANEANS, SAN FRANCISCO BLUES, SOME OF THE DHARMA, BOOK OF DREAMS, WAKE | UP, MEXICO CITY BLUES, & VISIONS OF GERARD---creating a spontaneous bop | prosody and original classic literature. Several phrases and the title | of <u>Howl</u> are taken from Him. | William Seward Burroughs, author of NAKED LUNCH, an endless novel | which will drive everybody mad. | Neal Cassady, author of THE FIRST THIRD, an autobiography 1949, | which enlightened Buddha. All these books are published in Heaven. | Lucien Carr, recently promoted to Night Bureau Manager of New York | United Press.' 1-15: text.

27.9 x 21.5 cm. Stapled once in the upper left corner so that the title page forms the cover. All edges trimmed. White wove paper unwatermarked. Entirely printed in moderate violet (211) ink.

Never released but printed ca. 1979 in an impression of approximately 100 copies, most copies are believed to have been destroyed.

Note: This was intended to be a facsimile edition, it was printed by Gotham Book Mart from the original ditto masters used for the first printing which had been saved by Allen Ginsberg. About 100 copies were printed, but it is not known whether all were stamped with the Gotham Book Mart imprint or not. If any were not stamped the only difference between the original and the facsimile is the color of the ditto ink used. The original ink was close to dark purple (224) ink and the reproduction was closer to moderate violet (211) ink. All the pages in the facsimile edition are perfectly aligned on the page, while many copies of the original seem to have been printed at an angle or off-center. The following note from the publisher was sent to Ginsberg. "After considerable searching in our storage rooms...we did find the early mimeo HOWL "masters" <u>and</u> the box of copies which had been made from the masters. ... I do not remember the details and it appears that none of them were sold. ... I am returning to you the master mimeos and a few copies of the "reprint" which we made. Shall we destroy the remaining copies (about 100)? If not, I feel strongly that they should be imprinted in some way (the Gotham Book Mart rubberstamp?). It would be too easy to confuse them with the original which now sells for a great deal of money. I can assure you we have not sold any of these since they were made." No one is quite certain what happened to them after that point, but they are believed to have been destroyed. Three copies with the Gotham Book Mart rubberstamp are known to exist.

A2   SIESTA IN XBALBA   1956

SIESTA IN XBALBA | and | Return To The States | by | ALLEN GINSBERG | dedicated to | Karena Shields | As | Published By The Author | July 1956 | Near | ICY CAPE, ALASKA | At the Sign of the Midnight Sun

Single gathering of twelve leaves, pp. [i] 1-22 [23]. [i]: title page. 1-22: text. [23]: blank.

20.3 x 16.5 cm. Stapled twice on the left side so that the title page forms the front cover. All edges trimmed. White wove paper unwatermarked.

Contents: [prefatory note] — Siesta in Xbalba

Distributed free to friends. Published July 28-29, 1956 in an impression of 52 copies.

Note: In a letter to Kerouac from AG at the time of publication he states that 52 copies were printed.

A3   **HOWL AND OTHER POEMS**   **1956**

a1.1 *First edition, first printing*

HOWL | AND OTHER POEMS | BY | *ALLEN GINSBERG* | 'Unscrew the locks
from the doors! | Unscrew the doors themselves from their jambs!' | THE POCKET
POETS SERIES: Number Four | The City Lights Pocket Bookshop | San Francisco

Single gathering of twenty-two leaves, pp. [1-6] 7-44. [1]: title page. [2]: 'Library of
Congress Catalog Card Number: 56-8587 | Copyright, 1956 | by | Allen Ginsberg |
The City Lights Pocket Bookshop, Publishers | 261 Columbus Avenue | San Francisco
11, California'. [3]: 'DEDICATION | To — | [13 lines] | Lucien Carr, recently
promoted to Night Bureau Manager | of New York United Press. | —A.G.' [4]:
'PRINTED AT THE PRESS OF VILLIERS PUBLICATIONS | HOLLOWAY,
LONDON, ENGLAND'. [5]: contents page. [6]: blank. 7-8: introduction. 9-44: text.

15.7 x 12.4 cm. Stapled once in stiff black paper wrappers on which a white wraparound
label, 11.4 x 22.4 cm. has been attached. Across the front cover: '[in light blue] THE
POCKET POETS SERIES | [all on label] HOWL | AND OTHER POEMS | *ALLEN
GINSBERG* | Introduction by | William Carlos Williams | [below the label in light
blue] NUMBER FOUR'. Across the back cover: '[in light blue] 75 cents | [all the rest
on the label] *HOWL* AND OTHER POEMS is Allen Ginsberg's | first published book
and the fourth in the POCKET | POETS SERIES which is designed to fill the need for |
low-priced, pocket-size editions of works by contem- | porary poets, both American and
foreign, known and | unknown. Previously published in the Series are the | following:
Lawrence Ferlinghetti, PICTURES OF | THE GONE WORLD; Kenneth Rexroth,
THIRTY | SPANISH POEMS OF LOVE AND EXILE; Kenneth | Patchen, POEMS
OF HUMOR & PROTEST. | ALLEN GINSBERG was born June 3, 1926, the son of |
Naomi Ginsberg, Russian émigré, and Louis Ginsberg, | lyric poet and schoolteacher, in
Paterson, N.J. To these | facts, Ginsberg adds: 'High school in Paterson till 17, |
Columbia College, merchant marine, Texas and Denver, | copyboy, Times Square,
amigos in jail, dishwashing, | book reviews, Mexico City, market research, Satori in |
Harlem. Yucatan & Chiapas 1954, West coast since | then. Carl Solomon, to whom
HOWL is addressed, is | an intuitive Bronx Dadaist and prose-poet.' All edges trimmed.
White wove paper unwatermarked.

Contents: Howl — Footnote to Howl — A Supermarket in California — Transcription of
Organ Music — Sunflower Sutra — America — In the Baggage Room at Greyhound —
An Asphodel — Song — Wild Orphan — In Back of the Real — [prose blurb on back
cover]

75¢. Published Nov. 1, 1956 in an impression of 1,000 copies.

a1.2 *Second printing (April 1957):*

HOWL | AND OTHER POEMS | BY | *ALLEN GINSBERG* | 'Unscrew the locks
from the doors! | Unscrew the doors themselves from their jambs!' | THE POCKET
POETS SERIES: Number Four | The City Lights Pocket Bookshop | San Francisco

Single gathering of twenty-two leaves, pp. [1-6] 7-44. [1]: title page. [2]: 'Library of
Congress Catalog Card Number: 56-8587 | © 1956 | by | Allen Ginsberg | *The
Pocket Poets Series is published* | *by the City Lights Pocket Bookshop,* | *261 Columbus
Avenue, San Francisco* | *11, and distributed nationally by the* | *Paper Editions
Corporation.*' [3]: 'DEDICATION | To — | [13 lines] | —A.G.' [4]: 'Printed in
England at the Press of Villiers Publications, Holloway, | London.' [5]: contents page.
[6]: blank. 7-8: introduction. 9-44: text.

15.4 x 12.4 cm. Stapled once in stiff black paper wrappers on which a white wraparound label, 11.8 x 21.9 cm. has been attached. Across the front cover: '[in light blue] THE POCKET POETS SERIES I [on label] HOWL I AND OTHER POEMS I *ALLEN GINSBERG* I Introduction by I William Carlos Williams I [in light blue below the label] NUMBER FOUR'. Across the back cover: '[in light blue] 75 cents I [on label] HOWL AND OTHER POEMS is Allen Ginsberg's I [19 lines] I [in light blue below the label] Second Edition'. All edges trimmed. White wove paper unwatermarked.

Contents: As first edition, first issue.

75¢. Published April 1957 in an impression of 1,500 copies.

Note: This is the printing from which 520 copies were seized by U.S. Customs officials on March 25, 1957.

a1.3 *Third printing (May 1957):*

HOWL I AND OTHER POEMS I BY I *ALLEN GINSBERG* I 'Unscrew the locks from the doors! I Unscrew the doors themselves from their jambs!' I THE POCKET POETS SERIES: Number Four I The City Lights Pocket Bookshop I San Francisco

Single gathering of twenty-two leaves, pp. [1-6] 7-44. [1]: title page. [2]: 'Library of Congress Catalog Card Number: 56-8587 I *All Rights Reserved I The Pocket Poets Series is published I by the City Lights Pocket Bookshop, I 261 Columbus Avenue, San Francisco I 11, and distributed nationally by the I Paper Editions Corporation I Manufactured in the United States of America*'. [3]: 'DEDICATION I To — I [13 lines] I —A.G.' [4]: blank. [5]: contents page. [6]: blank. 7-8: introduction. 9-44: text.

15.7 x 12.3 cm. Stapled once in stiff black paper wrappers. Across the front cover: '[in white] THE POCKET POETS SERIES I [on a white rectangle simulating the wraparound label] HOWL I AND OTHER POEMS I *ALLEN GINSBERG* I Introduction by I William Carlos Williams I [in white below the rectangle] NUMBER FOUR'. Across the back cover: '[in white] 75 cents I [on the rectangle continued from the front cover] HOWL AND OTHER POEMS is Allen Ginsberg's I [19 lines] I [in white below the rectangle] Third Printing'. All edges trimmed. White wove paper unwatermarked.

Contents: As first edition, first issue.

75¢. Published May 1957 in an impression of 2,500 copies.

Note: This printing was produced in the United States so that the Customs Department would not have jurisdiction in preparation for further obscenity attacks.

a1.4 *Fourth printing (Oct. 1957):*

HOWL I AND OTHER POEMS I BY I *ALLEN GINSBERG* I 'Unscrew the locks from the doors! I Unscrew the doors themselves from their jambs!' I THE POCKET POETS SERIES: Number Four I The City Lights Pocket Bookshop I San Francisco

15.7 x 12.5 cm. Stapled twice in stiff black paper wrappers. Front cover as first edition, third printing. Across the back cover: '[in white] 75 cents I [on the rectangle continued from the front cover] Allen Ginsberg's *HOWL* is the most significant single I [18 lines] I [in white below the rectangle] Fourth Printing'.

Contents: As first edition, first issue.

75¢. Printed October 1957 in an impression of 5,000 copies.

a1.5 *Fifth printing (April 1958):*

As first edition, fourth issue, with printing notice updated on the back cover. Printed April 1958 in an impression of 5,000 copies

a1.6 *Sixth printing (Sept. 1958):*

HOWL | AND OTHER POEMS | BY | *ALLEN GINSBERG* | 'Unscrew the locks from the doors! | Unscrew the doors themselves from their jambs!' | THE POCKET POETS SERIES: Number Four | CITY LIGHTS BOOKS | San Francisco

Single gathering of twenty-two leaves, pp. [1-6] 7-44. [1]: title page. [2]: 'Library of Congress Catalog Card Number: 56-8587 | *First printing: October, 1956* | *Second printing: April, 1957* | *Third printing: May, 1957* | *Fourth printing: October, 1957* | *Fifth printing: April, 1958* | *Sixth printing: September, 1958* | *Copyright 1956 by Allen Ginsberg* | *All Rights Reserved* | *The Pocket Poets Series is published* | *by City Lights Books, 261 Columbus* | *Avenue, San Francisco 11, and distrib-* | *uted nationally by the Paper Editions* | *Corporation.* | *Manufactured in the United States of America*'. [3]: 'DEDICATION | To — | [13 lines] | —A.G.' [4]: blank. [5]: contents page. [6]: blank. 7-8: introduction. 9-44: text.

15.7 x 12.3 cm. Stapled twice in stiff black paper wrappers. Front cover as first edition, fifth issue. Across the back cover: '[in white] 75 cents | [on the rectangle continued from the front cover] Allen Ginsberg's *HOWL* is the most significant single | [19 lines]'. All edges trimmed. White wove paper unwatermarked.

75¢. Printed September 1958 in an impression of 5,000 copies.

a1.7 *Seventh printing (Jan. 1959):*

As first edition, sixth issue with printing note updated on the verso of the title page. Printed January 1959 in an impression of 5,000 copies

a1.8 *Eighth printing (Sept. 1959):*

HOWL | AND OTHER POEMS | BY | *ALLEN GINSBERG* | 'Unscrew the locks from the doors! | Unscrew the doors themselves from their jambs!' | CITY LIGHTS BOOKS | San Francisco

Single gathering of twenty-four leaves, pp. [1-6] 7-44 [45-48]. [1]: title page. [2]: 'Library of Congress Catalog Card Number: 56-8587 | *First printing: October, 1956* | *Second printing: April, 1957* | *Third printing: May, 1957* | *Fourth printing: October, 1957* | *Fifth printing: April, 1958* | *Sixth printing: September, 1958* | *Seventh printing: January, 1959* | *Eighth printing: September, 1959* | *Copyright 1956 by Allen Ginsberg* | © *1959 by Allen Ginsberg* | *The Pocket Poets Series is published* | *by City Lights Books, 261 Columbus* | *Avenue, San Francisco 11, and distrib-* | *uted nationally by the Paper Editions* | *Corporation. Overseas distributors:* | *W. S. Hall & Co.* | *Manufactured in the United States of America*'. [3]: 'DEDICATION | To — | [13 lines]'. [4]: blank. [5]: contents page. [6]: blank. 7-8: introduction. 9-44: text. [45-46]: blank. [47]: publisher's advertisements. [48]: blank.

15.7 x 11.9 cm. Stapled twice in stiff black paper wrappers. Front cover as first edition, seventh issue. Across the back cover: '[in white] 75 cents | [on the rectangle continued from the front cover] Allen Ginsberg's *HOWL AND OTHER POEMS* was origi- | [22 lines]'. All edges trimmed. White wove paper unwatermarked.

Contents: As first edition, first issue with an addition to the prose blurb on the back cover.

75¢. Printed September 1959 in an impression of 5,000 copies.

Note: No additional changes in text occur after this printing, although some changes occur in the binding, etc. All subsequent printings are identified on the verso of the title page and listed below are the reprintings.

a1.9 *Ninth printing (Feb. 1960)*

a1.10 *Tenth printing (Jan. 1961)*

a1.11 *Eleventh printing (Sept. 1962)*

a1.12 *Twelfth printing (July 1963)*

a1.13 *Thirteenth printing (June 1964)*

a1.14 *Fourteenth printing (April 1965)*

a1.15 *Fifteenth printing (Oct. 1965)*

a1.16 *Sixteenth printing (May 1966)*

a1.17 *Seventeenth printing (Sept. 1966)*

a1.18 *Eighteenth printing (Dec. 1966):* 20,000 copies printed.

Note: This issue was incorrectly dated as 1967 on the verso of the title page.

a1.19 *Nineteenth printing (June 1967)*

a1.20 *Twentieth printing (June 1968)*

a1.21 *Twenty-first printing (April 1969)*

a1.22 *Twenty-second printing (Nov. 1969)*

a1.23 *Twenty-third printing (July 1970)*

a1.24 *Twenty-fourth printing (May 1971):* 30,000 copies printed.

a1.25 *Twenty-fifth printing (Jan. 1973):* 22,000 copies printed.

a1.26 *Twenty-sixth printing (printing date unknown)*

a1.27 *Twenty-seventh printing (June 1974)*

a1.28 *Twenty-eighth printing (between April 1976 -April 1977):* 15,000 copies.

a1.29 *Twenty-ninth printing (June 1978):* 15,000 copies.

a1.30 *Thirtieth printing (printing date unknown)*

a1.31 *Thirty-first printing (printing date unknown)*

a1.32 *Thirty-second printing (Feb. 1982):* 10,000 copies.

a1.33 *Thirty-third printing (Sept. 1983):* 10,000 copies.

a1.34 *Thirty-fourth printing (June 1985):* 10,000 copies.

a1.35 *Thirty-fifth printing (Dec. 1986):* 10,000 copies.

a1.36 *Thirty-sixth printing (Feb. 1988):* 10,000 copies.

a1.37 *Thirty-seventh printing (Feb. 1989):* 10,000 copies.

a1.38 *Thirty-eighth printing (March 1990):* 10,000 copies.

a1.39 *Thirty-ninth printing (April 1991):* 10,000 copies.

a1.40 *Fortieth printing (Feb. 1992):* 20,000 copies.

a1.41 *Forty-first printing (July 1993):* 20,000 copies.

a2. *First edition, twenty-third printing, re-issue (Jan. 28, 1974):*

THE I POCKET POETS I SERIES I Volume 1 I Numbers 1-7 I KRAUS REPRINT CO. I Millwood, New York I 1973

$[1-10]^{16}$ $[11]^4$ $[12]^{16}$, pp. [1-360]. [1]: title page. [2]: '[8 lines of LC cataloging data] I *Reprinted with the permission of* I *City Lights Booksellers and Publishers* I KRAUS REPRINT CO. I A U.S. Division of Kraus-Thomson Organization Limited I Printed in Germany'. [3-6]: introduction by Kenneth Rexroth. [7-356]: text. [357-360]: blank.

22.4 x 14.4 cm. Bound in dark purplish red (259) cloth covered boards, lettered across the spine in gold: '[3 rules 2.6 cm. long] I THE I POCKET I POETS I SERIES I [3 rules 2.6 cm. long] I 1 I KRAUS I REPRINT'. All edges trimmed. White endpapers. White wove paper unwatermarked.

Contents: Howl and Other Poems [as first edition] pp. [149-196].

$23.75 or sold as a four volume set at $95.00. Published Jan. 28, 1974 in an impression of 250 copies.

Note: Kraus Reprint Co. collected all the books comprising the Pocket Poets Series and re-issued them in a four volume set primarily for the library trade. No effort was made to reprint the first printings of many of the books in the series and here they have reprinted the 23rd printing of the City Lights paperback.

A4   KADDISH AND OTHER POEMS   1961

a1.1 *First edition, first printing*

KADDISH I AND OTHER POEMS I 1958-1960 I *ALLEN GINSBERG* I '—Die, I If thou wouldst be with that which thou dost seek!' I [publisher's device] I CITY LIGHTS BOOKS

Fifty single leaves, pp. [1-6] 7-100. [1]: title page. [2]: 'Library of Congress Catalog Card Number: 60-14775 I *Copyright © 1961 by Allen Ginsberg* I *All Rights Reserved* I *The Pocket Poets Series is published* I *by City Lights Books, 261 Columbus* I *Avenue, San Francisco 11, Cali-* I *fornia, and distributed nationally to* I *bookstores by the Paper Editions* I *Corporation. Overseas distributors:* I *The Scorpion Press, 11 Rofant Rd.,* I *Northwood, Middlesex, England.*' [3]: dedication page. [4]: acknowledgments page. [5]: contents page. [6]: blank. 7-99: text. 100: '100 I [4 line note]'.

15.8 x 12.0 cm. Perfect bound in stiff black paper wrappers with covers printed so that it appears that a white label has been wrapped around the front to the back covers. Across the front cover: '[in white above the panel] THE POCKET POETS SERIES I [on panel]

KADDISH | AND OTHER POEMS | 1958-1960 | [star] | *ALLEN GINSBERG* | [below panel in white] NUMBER FOURTEEN'. Down the spine: '[on panel] KADDISH ALLEN GINSBERG'. Across the back cover: '[above the panel in white] $1.50 | [7 lines on panel]'. All edges trimmed. White wove paper unwatermarked.

Contents: [acknowledgment note] — Kaddish — Poem Rocket — Europe! Europe! — To Lindsay — Message — To Aunt Rose — At Apollinaire's Grave — The Lion for Real — Ignu — Death to Van Gogh's Ear! — Laughing Gas — Mescaline — Lysergic Acid — Magic Psalm — The Reply — The End — [prose note]

$1.50. Published February 1961 in an impression of 2,500 copies.

Note: The first issue has been identified based upon an inscription in a copy dated April 29, 1961 and signed in Paris.

a1.2 *Second printing (Feb. 1964):*

KADDISH | AND OTHER POEMS | 1958-1960 | *ALLEN GINSBERG* | '—Die, | If thou wouldst be with that which thou dost seek!' | [publisher's device] | CITY LIGHTS BOOKS

Fifty single leaves, pp. [1-6] 7-100. As first issue with the following exceptions. 100: '100 | [4 line note] | Printed at the Press of Villiers Publications Ltd. | Ingestre Road, London, N.W.5, England'.

15.8 x 12.2 cm. Perfect bound in stiff white paper wrappers with covers printed as the first issue with the following exceptions. Across the back cover: '[above the panel in white] $1.50 | [10 lines on panel]'.

$1.50. Published February 1964 in an impression of 2,000 copies.

a1.3 *Third printing (1965):*

KADDISH | AND OTHER POEMS | 1958-1960 | *ALLEN GINSBERG* | '—Die, | If thou wouldst be with that which thou dost seek!' | [publisher's device] | CITY LIGHTS BOOKS

As first issue with the following exceptions. [2]: 'Library of Congress Catalog Card Number: 60-14775 | *Copyright © 1961 by Allen Ginsberg | All Rights Reserved | Third Printing | The Pocket Poets Series is published by City Lights | Books, 261 Columbus Avenue, San Francisco, Cali- | fornia 94111, USA. New York distributors: Bookazine, | 43 East 10th Street, New York, N.Y. 10014, Overseas | distributors: Mandarin Books Ltd., 22 Notting Hill | Gate, London, W.11, England.'*

15.8 x 12.2 cm. Perfect bound in stiff white paper wrappers with covers printed as the first issue with the following exceptions. Across the back cover: '[above the panel in white] $1.50 | [25 lines on panel]'.

Contents: As the first edition with the addition of a prose blurb on the back cover.

$1.50. Published 1965 in an impression of 2,500 copies.

Note: No additional changes in text occur after this printing, although some changes occur in the binding, etc. All subsequent printings are identified on the verso of the title page and listed below are the reprintings.

a1.4 *Fourth printing (March 1966):* 4,000 copies.

a1.5 *Fifth printing (April 1966):* 10,000 copies.

a1.6 *Sixth printing (Oct. 1966):* 10,000 copies.

a1.7 *Seventh printing (April 1967):* 10,000 copies.

a1.8 *Eighth printing (Oct. 1967):* 15,000 copies.

a1.9 *Ninth printing (Feb. 1969):* 10,000 copies.

a1.10 *Tenth printing (Sept. 1969):* 10,000 copies.

a1.11 *Eleventh printing (Feb. 1970):* 10,000 copies.

a1.12 *Twelfth printing (April 1971):* 10,000 copies.

a1.13 *Thirteenth printing (Sept. 1972):* 10,000 copies.

a1.14 *Fourteenth printing (March 1974):* 10,000 copies.

a1.15 *Fifteenth printing (Jan. 1977):* 5,000 copies.

a1.16 *Sixteenth printing (July 1978):* 10,000 copies.

a1.17 *Seventeenth printing (May 1982):* 3,000 copies.

a1.18 *Eighteenth printing (Feb. 1984):* 3,000 copies.

a1.19 *Nineteenth printing (Jan. 1986):* 3,000 copies.

a1.20 *Twentieth printing (Oct. 1987):* 4,000 copies.

a1.21 *Twenty-first printing (Jan. 1989):* 4,000 copies.

a1.22 *Twenty-second printing (Dec. 1991):* 4,000 copies.

a1.23 *Twenty-third printing (Aug. 1993):* 4,000 copies.

a2. *First edition, eleventh printing, re-issue (Jan. 28, 1974):*

THE | POCKET POETS | SERIES | Volume 2 | Numbers 8-14, Supplement | KRAUS REPRINT CO. | Millwood, New York | 1973

[1-15]^{16} [16]^4 [17]^{16}, pp. [1-520]. [1]: title page. [2]: *'Reprinted with the permission of | City Lights Booksellers and Publishers* | KRAUS REPRINT CO. | A U.S. Division of Kraus-Thomson Organization Limited | Printed in Germany'. [3-516]: text. [517-520]: blank.

22.3 x 14.4 cm. Bound in dark purplish red (259) cloth covered boards, lettered across the spine in gold: '[3 rules 3.8 cm. long] | THE | POCKET | POETS | SERIES | [3 rules 3.8 cm. long] | 2 | KRAUS | REPRINT'. All edges trimmed. White endpapers. White wove paper unwatermarked.

Contents: Kaddish and Other Poems [as first edition] pp. [367-470].

$23.75 or sold as a four volume set at $95.00. Published Jan. 28, 1974 in an impression of 250 copies.

Note: Kraus Reprint Co. collected all the books comprising the Pocket Poets Series and re-issued them in a four volume set primarily for the library trade. No effort was made to reprint the first printings of many of the books in the series and here they have reprinted the 11th printing of the City Lights paperback.

A5   **EMPTY MIRROR**   **1961**

a1.1 *First edition, first printing*

EMPTY MIRROR ∣ EARLY POEMS BY ∣ ALLEN GINSBERG ∣ INTRODUCTION BY WILLIAM CARLOS WILLIAMS ∣ TOTEM PRESS ∣ *in association with* ∣ CORINTH BOOKS ∣ *32 West Eighth Street* ∣ *New York 11, New York*

Single gathering of twenty-four leaves, pp. [1-4] 5-47 [48]. [1]: title page. [2]: 'Copyright © 1961 by Allen Ginsberg ∣ Manufactured in the United States of America ∣ Library of Congress Catalog Number: 61-14983 ∣ [7 lines] ∣ TOTEM PRESS ∣ *in association with* ∣ CORINTH BOOKS ∣ *32 West Eighth Street* ∣ *New York 11, New York*'. [3]: dedication page. [4]: blank. 5-6: introduction. 7-47: text. [48]: 'DIANE DI PRIMA, Dinners and Nightmares. ∣ [38 lines] ∣ CORINTH BOOKS ∣ *distributed by* The Citadel Press, *222 Park Ave. So., N.Y.3*'.

20.2 x 13.4 cm. Stapled twice in stiff white paper wrappers. Across the front cover: 'EMPTY MIRROR ∣ EARLY POEMS BY ∣ ALLEN GINSBERG ∣ INTRODUCTION BY WILLIAM CARLOS WILLIAMS ∣ [drawing] ∣ TOTEM/CORINTH $1.25'. Across the back cover: '[small continuation of drawing from the front cover] ∣ TOTEM PRESS ∣ *in association with* ∣ CORINTH BOOKS ∣ *32 West Eighth Street* ∣ *New York 11, New York*'. All edges trimmed. White wove paper unwatermarked.

Contents: I Feel as if I Am at a Dead — Tonite All Is Well...What A — Psalm I — Cezanne's Ports — After All, What Else is There to Say? — Fyodor — The Trembling of the Veil — A Meaningless Institution — In Society — Metaphysics — In Death, Cannot Reach What is Most Near — This Is about Death — Long Live the Spiderweb — I Attempted to Concentrate — Marijuana Notation — A Crazy Spiritual — I Have Increased Power — Hymn — Sunset — A Ghost May Come — A Desolation — The Terms in Which I Think of Reality — A Poem on America — The Bricklayer's Lunch Hour — The Night-Apple — After Dead Souls — Two Boys Went into a Dream Diner — How Come He Got Canned at the Ribbon Factory [by Allen Ginsberg and Lucien Carr] — A Typical Affair — An Atypical Affair — The Archtype Poem [by Allen Ginsberg and Lucien Carr] — Paterson — I Made Love to Myself — The Blue Angel — I Learned a World from Each — Gregory Corso's Story — Walking Home at Night, — The Shrouded Stranger

$1.25. Published ca. August 20, 1961 in an impression of ca. 1,000 copies.

Note: The publisher has kept no records of dates or quantities printed, each printing is estimated at 1,000 copies. At least three additional issues have been identified as follows:

a1.2 *Second printing*

EMPTY MIRROR ∣ EARLY POEMS BY ∣ ALLEN GINSBERG ∣ INTRODUCTION BY WILLIAM CARLOS WILLIAMS ∣ TOTEM PRESS ∣ *in association with* ∣ CORINTH BOOKS ∣ *32 West Eighth Street* ∣ *New York 11, New York*

As first issue except for the following: p. [48]: 'CORINTH PAPERBOOKS ∣ [8 titles in 14 lines] ∣ In association with TOTEM PRESS/LE ROI JONES: ∣ [8 titles in 9 lines] ∣

In association with JARGON BOOKS/JONATHAN WILLIAM: | [3 titles in 3 lines] | CORINTH BOOKS | *distributed by* The Citadel Press, 222 Park Ave. So., N.Y. 3'.

a1.3 *Third printing*

EMPTY MIRROR | EARLY POEMS BY | ALLEN GINSBERG | INTRODUCTION BY WILLIAM CARLOS WILLIAMS | TOTEM PRESS | *in association with* | CORINTH BOOKS

As second issue except for the title page and the following: p. [48]: [blank].

Across the back is an advertisement for 10 books in 14 lines.

a1.4 *Fourth printing*

EMPTY MIRROR | EARLY POEMS BY | ALLEN GINSBERG | INTRODUCTION BY WILLIAM CARLOS WILLIAMS | TOTEM PRESS | *in association with* | CORINTH BOOKS | *17 West Eighth Street* | *New York, N. Y. 10011*

As third issue except for the above change in title page.

b1.1 *Second edition, first printing (1970):*

EMPTY MIRROR | [2 columns separated by a 5.9 cm. vertical rule] [left column] *early* | *poems* | *by* | *with an* | *introduction* | *by* [right column] ALLEN | GINSBERG | William | Carlos | Williams | [below the columns] A TOTEM/CORINTH BOOK

Thirty-two single leaves, pp. [i-iv] v-vii [viii] 9-62 [63-64]. [i]: title page. [ii]: '*Copyright* | © 1961 Allen Ginsberg | [4 lines] | Newly designed edition 1970 | *Credits* | [8 lines]'. [iii]: contents page. [iv]: blank. v-vii: introduction. [viii]: dedication page. 9-62: text. [63]: 'This new edition of EMPTY MIRROR was designed | by Joan Wilentz and printed by the Profile Press | of New York City. The poems were set in Garamond | type; Baskerville was used for the front matter, | and Caslon 540 Italics was used for display.' [64]: advertisement.

20.3 x 15.1 cm. Perfect bound in stiff white paper wrappers. Across the front cover: '[a photograph of a bearded AG looking at a photograph of a younger clean shaven AG] [above the photograph is a gray irregular panel with hollow printing] EMPTY MIRROR | [on the photograph in an irregular panel 2 lines in hollow printing] early poems by | Allen Ginsberg'. Down the spine: '[in white] Ginsberg EMPTY MIRROR Corinth'. Across the back cover: '[a gray irregular panel at left on a darker gray background on which the following is printed in hollow printing in 2 lines] CORINTH BOOKS | $2.50'. All edges trimmed. White laid paper watermarked: '[in black letter] Sulgrave Text'.

Contents: As first printing except for reversing the order of: In Society / Metaphysics — The Blue Angel / Paterson

$2.50. Published in 1970.

b1.2 *Second edition, second printing*

EMPTY MIRROR | [2 columns separated by a 5.9 cm. vertical rule] [left column] *early* | *poems* | *by* | *with an* | *introduction* | *by* [right column] ALLEN | GINSBERG | William | Carlos | Williams | [below the columns] A TOTEM/CORINTH BOOK

As first issue except for the additional of a new printing statement on the verso of the title page. White wove paper unwatermarked.

$3.50. Publication information unknown.

A6   **REALITY SANDWICHES**   **1963**

a1.1 *First edition, first printing*

REALITY | SANDWICHES | 1953-60 | *ALLEN GINSBERG* | *'Scribbled secret notebooks, and wild* | *typewritten pages, for yr own joy'* | [publisher's device] | CITY LIGHTS BOOKS

[1-5]^8 [6]^{10}, pp. [1-6] 7-98 [99-100]. [1]: title page. [2]: 'Library of Congress Catalog Card Number: 63-12219 | © *1963 by Allen Ginsberg* | *The Pocket Poets Series is published* | *by City Lights Books, 261 Columbus* | *Avenue, San Francisco, California,* | *and distributed nationally by the* | *Paper Editions Corporation. Over-* | *seas distributors: The Scorpion* | *Press, Manor House, Pakefield Street,* | *Lowestoft, Suffolk, England'.* [3]: dedication page. [4]: acknowledgments. [5]: contents page. [6]: blank. 7-98: text. [99]: 'Printed at the Press of Villiers Publications Ltd. | Ingestre Road, London, N. W. 5, England'. [100]: blank.

15.9 x 12.4 cm. Bound in stiff white paper wrappers with covers printed so that it appears that a white label has been wrapped around the front to the back covers. Across the front cover: '[white above the panel] THE POCKET POETS SERIES | [on panel] REALITY | SANDWICHES | [star] | *ALLEN GINSBERG* | [below panel in white] NUMBER EIGHTEEN'. Down the spine: '[on panel] Reality Sandwiches Allen Ginsberg'. Across the back cover: '[above the panel in white] $1.50 | [17 lines on panel]'. Across the inside back cover: '[40 lines of advertisements] | [6.3 cm. rule] | Printed at the Press of Villiers Publications Ltd. | Ingestre Road, London, N. W. 5, England'. All edges trimmed. White wove paper unwatermarked.

Contents: [unsigned acknowledgment note] — My Alba — Sakyamuni Coming Out from the Mountain — The Green Automobile — Havana 1953 — Siesta in Xbalba — On Burroughs' Work — Love Poem on Theme by Whitman — Over Kansas — Malest Cornifici Tuo Catullo — Dream Record: June 8, 1955 — Blessed be the Muses — Fragment 1956 — A Strange New Cottage in Berkeley — Sather Gate Illumination — Scribble — Afternoon Seattle — Psalm III — Tears — Ready to Roll — Wrote This Last Night — Squeal — American Change — 'Back on Times Square, Dreaming of Times Square' — My Sad Self — Funny Death — Battleship Newsreel — I Beg You Come Back & Be Cheerful — To an Old Poet in Peru — Aether — [unsigned blurb on the back cover]

$1.50. Published June 1963 in an impression of 3,000 copies.

a1.2 *Second printing (printing date unknown)*

REALITY | SANDWICHES | 1953-60 | *ALLEN GINSBERG* | *'Scribbled secret notebooks, and wild* | *typewritten pages, for yr own joy'* | [publisher's device] | CITY LIGHTS BOOKS

16.0 x 12.3 cm. As first issue except for the addition of the printing statement on the bottom of the back cover and the deletion of the printer's name and address from the bottom of the inside back cover.

Note: No changes in text occur after this printing, second and subsequent printing are identified as such on the back cover or the verso of the title page and listed below are the reprintings.

a1.3 *Third printing (printing date unknown)*

a1.4 *Fourth printing (printing date unknown)*

a1.5 *Fifth printing (Oct. 1966):* 10,000 copies printed.

Note: This issue identified as "New edition printed in The United States of America © 1966 by Allen Ginsberg" on the verso of the title page.

a1.6 *Sixth printing (April 1967)*

a1.7 *Seventh printing (Oct. 1967)*

a1.8 *Eighth printing (Nov. 1968)*

a1.9 *Ninth printing (March 1969)*

a1.10 *Tenth printing (Feb. 1970)*

a1.11 *Eleventh printing (April 1971)*

a1.12 *Twelfth printing (May 1974)*

a1.13 *Thirteenth printing (March 1979):* 5,000 copies printed.

a1.14 *Fourteenth printing (printing date unknown)*

a1.15 *Fifteenth printing (June 1985)*

a1.16 *Sixteenth printing (July 1988):* 1,500 copies printed.

a1.17 *Seventeenth printing (June 1990):* 2,000 copies printed.

a1.18 *Eighteenth printing (March 1992):* 2,000 copies printed.

a1.19 *Nineteenth printing (July 1993):* 2,500 copies printed.

a2. *Tenth printing, re-issue (Jan. 28, 1974)*

THE | POCKET POETS | SERIES | Volume 3 | Numbers 15-21 | KRAUS REPRINT CO. | Millwood, New York | 1973

[1-18]^{16}, pp. [1-576]. [1]: title page. [2]: *'Reprinted with the permission of* | *City Lights Booksellers and Publishers* | KRAUS REPRINT CO. | A U.S. Division of Kraus-Thomson Organization Limited | Printed in Germany'. [3-570]: text. [571-576]: blank.

22.3 x 14.4 cm. Bound in dark purplish red (259) cloth covered boards, lettered across the spine in gold: '[3 rules 3.7 cm. long] | THE | POCKET | POETS | SERIES | [3 rules 3.7 cm. long] | 3 | KRAUS | REPRINT'. All edges trimmed. White endpapers. White wove paper unwatermarked.

Contents: Reality Sandwiches [as first edition] pp. [203-304].

$23.75 or sold as a four volume set at $95.00. Published Jan. 28, 1974 in an impression of 250 copies.

Note: Kraus Reprint Co. collected all the books comprising the Pocket Poets Series and re-issued them in a four volume set primarily for the library trade. No effort was made to reprint the first printings of many of the books in the series and here they have reprinted the tenth printing of the City Lights paperback.

A7   **THE CHANGE**   **1963**

a.1 *First edition, first state*

[2.2 cm. rule] | THE CHANGE: | poems by | ALLEN GINSBERG | [2.9 cm. rule] | published by WRITERS' FORUM | 29a lichfield grove n3 | november 1963

Twelve single leaves, printed on rectos only, ll. [1-12]. [1]: title leaf. [2-11]: text. [12]: '[bullet] | [2 bullets] | writers' forum poets: | [8 lines] | one shilling each (by post one and sixpence) | from 29a lichfield grove finchley n3 | [2 bullets] | [bullet]'.

22.9 x 17.4 cm. Stapled twice in stiff grayish greenish yellow (105) paper wrappers. Across the front cover: '[woodcut design incorporating the following in facsimile holograph lettering] [in grayish greenish yellow] the change | one shilling | allen | ginsburg'. Front and back covers folded over about 3 cm. to form flaps. All edges trimmed. White wove paper watermarked: '[on arched base line] *SPICERS | Plus | Fabric | Duplicator'*.

Contents: Poem: Upper India Express, May 1, 1963 — The Change

One shilling. Published November 1963 in an impression of between 100 and 232 copies.

Note: This print run was completed before it was discovered that AG's name had been misspelled on the front cover. Several copies (possibly 12 according to Dowden) were released with the incorrect spelling, the remainder were altered with black pen and ink to the correct spelling.

a.2 *First edition, corrected state*

[2.2 cm. rule] | THE CHANGE: | poems by | ALLEN GINSBERG | [2.9 cm. rule] | published by WRITERS' FORUM | 29a lichfield grove n3 | november 1963

Note: This state was identical to the first state but a new cover was printed with the correct spelling of Ginsberg. The number of copies printed is unknown.

A8   **WICHITA VORTEX SUTRA**   **1966**

a.1 *First edition, first printing*

WICHITA | VORTEX SUTRA | by Allen Ginsberg | [13 lines of text] | 1

Single gathering of six leaves, pp. 1-12. 1: title page. 2-12: text.

20.2 x 16.4 cm. Stapled twice in moderate orange (53) paper wrappers. Across the front cover: 'Peace News poetry 2s 6d (50 cents) | Allen | Ginsberg | [12.0 cm. rule] | Wichita | Vortex | Sutra'. Across the back cover: 'Reprinted from *Peace News* and printed for Housmans, Publishers, | 5 Caledonian Road, Kings Cross, London N1, by Goodwin Press (TU) | Ltd, 135 Fonthill Road, London N4'. Across the inside front cover: *'This poem is part of a larger work by Allen Ginsberg. It was | published in the*

American paper, Village Voice, *in May* | *1966, and first published in Britain by* Peace News *in its issue* | *of May 27, 1966.'* Across the inside back cover: 'for books, poetry, records | HOUSMANS | the international booksellers | 5 Caledonian Road London N1 (TER 4473) | Send stamped addressed envelope for current lists | Peace News | an independent weekly | news and articles on: | [12 lines]'. All edges trimmed. White wove paper unwatermarked.

Contents: Wichita Vortex Sutra

2s 6d (or 50¢). Published on or shortly after May 27, 1966 in an impression of approximately 500 copies.

a.2 *First edition, second printing (July 1966)*

Note: Second and subsequent printings are identified as such on the inside front cover.

a.3 *First edition, third printing (June 1967)*

a.4 *First edition, fourth printing (Feb. 1969)*

b.1 *First American edition, first printing (1966):*

WICHITA | VORTEX | SUTRA | [deep reddish orange (36)] ALLEN | [deep reddish orange] GINSBERG

Single gathering of ten leaves, pp. [i-ii] 1-15 [16-18]. [i]: title page. [ii]: 'Copyright 1966 by Allen Ginsberg | Published by COYOTE | Distributed by City Lights Books, | 261 Columbus Ave., San Francisco | WICHITA VORTEX SUTRA, which has | appeared in its entirety in the Village | Voice & the Berkeley Barb (& in part | in Life Magazine), will be included in | a selection of Allen Ginsberg's poems | to be published at the end of this year | by CITY LIGHTS BOOKS'. 1-15: text. [16]: 'This edition has been limited to 500 copies.' [17]: blank. [18]: '[publisher's device] | 85¢'.

21.5 x 15.8 cm. Stapled twice in self-cover so that the first and last pages form the covers. All edges trimmed. White wove paper unwatermarked.

85¢. Published ca. August 2, 1966 in an impression of 500 copies.

b.2 *First American edition, second printing (date unknown)*

Note: Second and third printings are identified as such on the verso of the title page and both have covers printed in vivid purplish blue (194) instead of black.

b.3 *First American edition, third printing (Sept. 1967)*

c. *Second American edition (1966):*

[entire page in facsimile hand lettering] WICHITA | VORTEX | SUTRA | BY | ALLEN GINSBERG | All Rights Reserved by | Allen Ginsberg | with special permission of | KQED for reprint by | Allen Ginsberg

Twelve single (8 1/2 x 14 in.) leaves printed on rectos only, ll. [i] [1] 2-11. [i]: title page. [1]-11: text.

35.3 x 21.4 cm. Stapled once in the upper left corner so that the title page forms the front cover. All edges trimmed. White wove paper unwatermarked.

25¢. Published ca. August 7, 1966 in an impression of approx. 800 copies.

Note: This edition has occasionally be refereed to as the correct first edition by the rare book trade, but that is incorrect. In addition a four page version of the poem was printed as a mimeograph insert for *Scrip* magazine in its Summer 1966 issue and has also been identified incorrectly as a monograph.

A9   **PROSE CONTRIBUTION TO CUBAN REVOLUTION**   **1966**

PROSE CONTRIBUTION | TO CUBAN REVOLUTION | ALLEN GINSBERG | Detroit / Artists' Workshop Press / 1966

Single gathering of ten leaves, pp. [1-20]. [1]: title page. [2-4]: blank. [5-18]: text. [19]: blank. [20]: 'PROSE CONTRIBUTION TO THE CUBAN | REVOLUTION was first printed in PA'LANTE | (copyright 1962, by The League of Militant | Poets) and reprinted in pamphlet form here | with the poet's permission. | Copyright © 1966 by Allen Ginsberg | Printed in an edition of 1000 copies | at the Artists' Workshop Press, 4863 | John Lodge, Detroit, Michigan 48201, | by John & Magdalene Sinclair, November | 1966. The cover photograph of Allen | Ginsberg is by Magdalene Sinclair, | Berkeley, California, 1965.'

21.7 x 17.7 cm. Stapled twice in light gray (264) with darker threads paper wrappers. Across the front cover: '[photograph of AG] PROSE CONTRIBU- | TION TO CUBAN | REVOLUTION | ALLEN GINSBERG'. Across the back cover: 'PROSE CONTRIBUTION | TO CUBAN REVOLUTION | [20 lines] | A GUERRILLA REPRINT | Detroit / Artists' Workshop Press / 50¢.' All edges trimmed. White wove paper with darker threads unwatermarked.

Contents: Prose Contribution to Cuban Revolution

50¢. Published November 1966 in an impression of 1,000 copies.

A10   **T.V. BABY POEMS**   **1967**

a1. *First edition, first printing, signed copies:*

[left title page] [all on a drawing of acrobats and performers in a garden setting in brilliant yellow (83)] [very deep purplish red (257)] *Cape Goliard Press Ltd*

[right title page] [all on a continuation of the drawing from the left title page] [very deep purplish red] *T. V. Baby Poems* | [very deep purplish red] *Allen Ginsberg*

[A-D]⁴ [with photograph tipped in between leaves 1 and 2], pp. [1-34]. [1]: blank. [2]: dedication page. [3]: blank. [4]: photograph of the author. [5]: '[numbered in black ink] | [autographed in black ink] | [drawing of an embryonic figure] [ornamental type] T. V. Baby Poems'. [6-7]: title pages. [8]: Copyright © Allen Ginsberg 1967'. [9-33]: text. 34: '[ornamental type] t. v. baby poems | [ornamental type] allen ginsberg | [ornamental type] london 1967 | This book has been designed, printed, & | published by Cape Goliard Press Ltd., 10a | Fairhazel Gardens, London, N. W. 6; set in | Caslon Old Face type & printed on Glaston- | bury Antique Laid paper; & bound in 3 | editions: 100 hardbound in hardcovers, sig- | ned & numbered by the author, 1500 soft- | cover, & 400 casebound library edition. | Illustrations by Victorien Sardou, Allen Gins- | berg, & The Great Crystal. | Cover photograph by Malcolm Hart. | First Edition September 1967'.

25.5 x 17.4 cm. Bound in brilliant yellow (83) rice paper covered boards. Down the spine in gold: 'T. V. BABY POEMS ALLEN GINSBERG CAPE GOLIARD PRESS'. All edges trimmed. White endpapers. White laid paper watermarked: '[crown] | *glastonbury*'. Issued in white rag paper dust jacket with grayish yellow (90) stripes.

Across the front cover of the dust jacket: '[all in strong orange (50)] ALLEN GINSBERG I T. V. BABY POEMS'. Down the spine of the dust jacket: '[all in strong orange] T. V. Baby Poems Allen Ginsberg Cape Goliard Press'.

Contents: Television Was a Baby Crawling Toward That Death Chamber — Portland Coloseum — First Party at Ken Kesey's with Hell's Angels — Middle of a Long Poem on 'These States' — Uptown — City Midnight Junk Strains for Frank O'Hara — Holy Ghost on the Nod over the Body of Bliss

$12.00. Published September 1967 in an impression of 100 copies.

a2. *First edition, first issue, unsigned copies:*

[left title page] [all on a drawing of acrobats and performers in a garden setting in brilliant yellow (83)] [very deep purplish red (257)] *Cape Goliard Press Ltd*

[right title page] [all on a continuation of the drawing from the left title page] [very deep purplish red] *T. V. Baby Poems* I [very deep purplish red] *Allen Ginsberg*

[A-D]^4, pp. [1-32]. As above but unsigned and lacking the tipped in photograph of the author.

25.4 x 17.5 cm. Bound in pale yellow (89) cloth covered boards. Down the spine in gold: 'T. V. BABY POEMS ALLEN GINSBERG CAPE GOLIARD PRESS'. All edges trimmed. White endpapers. White laid paper watermarked: '[crown] I *glastonbury*'. Issued in white paper dust jacket printed in black and deep yellow (85).

21s. Published September 1967 in an impression of 400 copies.

a3.1 *First edition, first issue, paperbound:*

[left title page] [all on a drawing of acrobats and performers in a garden setting in brilliant yellow (83)] [very deep purplish red (257)] *Cape Goliard Press Ltd*

[right title page] [all on a continuation of the drawing from the left title page] [very deep purplish red] *T. V. Baby Poems* I [very deep purplish red] *Allen Ginsberg*

[A]^2 [B-E]^4 [F]^2, pp. [1-40]. [1-5]: blank. [6]: dedication page. [7]: half title page. [8-9]: title pages. [The rest as above allowing for the additional blank pages]

24.9 x 16.9 cm. Bound in white paper wrappers. Across the front cover: '[in light olive brown (94)] T. V. BABY POEMS I [photograph of the author] I [in light olive brown] ALLEN GINSBERG'. Down the spine in light olive brown: 'T. V. BABY POEMS ALLEN GINSBERG CAPE GOLIARD PRESS'. Across the back cover is a photograph of the author. All edges trimmed. White wove paper watermarked: '[crown] I *glastonbury*'.

13s. 6d. Published in September 1968 in an impression of 1,500 copies.

a3.2 *First edition, second printing, paperbound*

Identical to the first issue except for the following:

Note: Second printing identified as such on page [36]. The second printing also has a newly designed cover with a larger photo of the author with the type in red ink and a new price on the back cover.

15s. Published in an unknown quantity.

a4. *First Grossman edition, hardbound (1968)*

[dark red (16)] T. V. Baby Poems | [10.1 x 7.7 cm. illustration of a baby doll in light greenish blue (172)] | [dark red] Allen Ginsberg | [dark red] GROSSMAN PUBLISHERS INC. IN ASSOCIATION | [dark red] WITH CAPE GOLIARD, LONDON | [dark red] NEW YORK 1968

[1-4]⁴ [with photograph tipped in between leaves 2 and 3], pp. [1-34]. [1]: blank. [2]: dedication page. [3]: half title page. [4]: blank. [5]: photograph of the author. [6]: blank. [7]: title page. [8]: Copyright © 1968 Allen Ginsberg | Library of Congress No. 68-15647'. [9-33]: text. 34: 'T. V. BABY POEMS | ALLEN GINSBERG | NEW YORK 1968 | This book has been designed & printed by Cape Goliard | Press Ltd., London, for joint publication with Grossman | Publishers Inc., 125 A East 19th Street, New York; | in an edition consisting of 1,750 soft cover & 750 case- | bound copies. | Illustrations by Allen Ginsberg & The Great Crystal. | Photograph by Malcolm Hart. | Printed in Great Britain.'

25.3 x 17.2 cm. Bound in brilliant greenish yellow (98) cloth covered boards. Down the spine in silver: 'T. V. BABY POEMS ALLEN GINSBERG CAPE GOLIARD / GROSSMAN'. Light bluish gray (190) endpapers. All edges trimmed. White laid paper unwatermarked. Issued in a white paper dust jacket. Across the front cover: 'T. V. Baby Poems | [in very deep red (14) is an illustration of a baby doll framed by 2 frames with rounded corners] | Allen Ginsberg'. Down the spine: 'T. V. BABY POEMS ALLEN GINSBERG CAPE GOLIARD / GROSSMAN'. Across the inside front flap: '[31 lines about the book] | $4.00 | Grossman Publishers Inc.'

$4.00. Published April 26, 1968 in an impression of 750 copies.

a5. *First Grossman edition, paperbound (1968)*

[dark red (16)] T. V. Baby Poems | [10.0 x 7.6 cm. illustration of a baby doll in light greenish blue (172)] | [dark red] Allen Ginsberg | [dark red] GROSSMAN PUBLISHERS INC. IN ASSOCIATION | [dark red] WITH CAPE GOLIARD, LONDON | [dark red] NEW YORK 1968

[1-4]⁴ [with photograph tipped in between leaves 2 and 3], pp. [1-34].

24.5 x 16.7 cm. Bound in light bluish gray (190) paper wrappers. Across the front cover all on a pattern of silver dots on white background: 'T. V. Baby Poems | [in very deep red (14) is an illustration of a toy doll framed by 2 frames with rounded corners] | Allen Ginsberg'. Down the spine: 'T. V. BABY POEMS ALLEN GINSBERG CAPE GOLIARD / GROSSMAN'. Across the back cover on a pattern of silver dots on a white background: '$2.50'. Light bluish gray endpapers. All edges trimmed. White laid paper unwatermarked.

$2.50. Published April 26, 1968 in an impression of 1,750 copies.

A11 **SCRAP LEAVES** **1968**

[star] SCRAP LEAVES [star] | [leaf] Tasty Scribbles [leaf] | by | Allen Ginsberg | [line with 11 dots underneath] [circle with 7 dots inside] [line with 11 dots underneath] | Containing [arrow with 2 points to right, one of which turns down] [the following three lines are in brackets] these odd small | Compositions old | and new [outside of the brackets] [star] To P.O. | [star] [wavy lettering] HEAT | [star] Growing olde Againe | [star] The Old Village Before I die | [star] Cleveland Airport | [star] Senate News | [star] Consulting I Ching Smoking Pot listening to the Fugs Sing Blake | [star] Inscription to Gavin Arthur | [star] A prophecy | [drawing of three fish which share a common head]

Single gathering of eight leaves, pp. [1-16]. [1]: title page. [2-13]: text. [14]: blank. [15]: '150 | Copies Printed | at Sri Ram | Ashram [arrow to right] MILLBROOK, N.Y. | for the Poet's Press, inspired by | Diane Di Prima Marlowe & Alan Marlowe | Editors & Publishers | of which this is Copy # [number in red ink] | Signed, | [autographed in red ink] | Dedicated to the Soul of Leroi Jones'. [16]: blank.

18.3 x 14.3 cm. Stapled twice in moderate yellow (87) wrappers. Across the front cover: '[design of a plant with leaves and root system below the sun and between the leaves/branches on the left and right of the stalk are the following] SCRAP LEAVES | LITTLE POEMS | Hasty scribbles from Journals [with haloed bird on this branch] | Hither too puzzling | for me to publish | BUT INTER- ESTING NOTATIONS | FOR TH' AKASHIC ARTY RECORDS | [design within the roots of a haloed red skull inside a star of David with a flower in its teeth and at left a haloed snake] Transcribed January 18, 1968 by hand of | ALLEN GINSBERG'. All edges trimmed. White laid paper watermarked: *'Gilbert | Allegro Vellum | 100% COTTON FIBRE | USA'.*

Note: The entire publication with illustrations is a facsimile of an autograph manuscript.

Contents: To P.O. — Heat — Growing Old Again — The Old Village Before I Die — Cleveland Airport — Senate News — Consulting I Ching Smoking Pot Listening to the Fugs Sing Blake — To Gavin Arthur — A Prophecy

$10.00. Published circa Feb. 1968 in an impression of 162 copies, 12 of these were advertised as deluxe "with an additional colored tissue fore and aft" but it is doubtful that these were ever produced. None have been seen by the compiler, and Bob Wilson of the Phoenix Bookshop doubts that they exist based on his very extensive experience in this area.

A12   AIRPLANE DREAMS   1968

a1.1 *First edition, paperbound, first state of cover*

AIRPLANE | DREAMS: | Compositions | from Journals | Allen | Ginsberg | *'All things hang like a drop of dew | Upon a blade of grass.'* [drawing of three fish which share a common head] | ANANSI TORONTO 1968

Twenty-four single leaves, pp. [i-x] 1-38. [i-ii]: blank. [iii]: title page. [iv]: 'Acknowledgments: these scribbles were printed | [8 lines] | *Manufactured in Canada.* | THE HOUSE OF ANANSI TORONTO 1968'. [v]: dedication page. [vi]: blank. [vii]: author's note. [viii]: blank. [ix]: contents page. [x]: blank. 1-35: text. 36-37: blank. 38: 'ABOUT THE BOOK | [publisher's device] *Cover design by Linda Leslie; produced by Arden | Cohen and Doug Fetherling. Published by House | of Anansi Press, 671 Spadina Avenue, Toronto 4, | Ontario, in an edition of 6,000 copies.* | 38'.

22.2 x 14.8 cm. Perfect bound in stiff white paper wrappers. Across the front cover: '[all on a brilliant greenish blue (168) photograph of AG] AIRPLANE DREAMS: | Compositions from | Journals | Allen | Ginsberg | $2.75 | [publisher's device]'. Down the spine all in brilliant greenish blue: 'AIRPLANE DREAMS: COMPOSITIONS FROM JOURNALS ALLEN GINSBERG ANANSI HAP 6'. Across the back cover is a drawing of three fish which share a common head all in brilliant greenish blue. All edges trimmed. White wove paper unwatermarked.

Note: An all brilliant greenish blue cover was printed without any black lettering, but the front cover did not show up well and so the lettering on the front cover was overprinted in black (each black letter has a faint blue shadow) with the spine left blue. Only a very small number of these covers were used in the final binding.

Contents: [introductory note] — History of the Jewish Socialist Party in America [prose] — Understand That This is a Dream — New York to San Fran — Consulting I Ching Smoking Pot Listening to the Fugs Sing Blake

$2.75 Canadian. Published ca. May 31, 1968 in an impression of less than 200 copies.

Note: Sometime before the publication of the hardbound issue an error was found in the printing and errata slips were placed in all remaining copies [see hardbound notes for a description of this enclosure]

a1.2 *First edition, paperbound, second state of cover*

AIRPLANE | DREAMS: | Compositions | from Journals | Allen | Ginsberg | *'All things hang like a drop of dew | Upon a blade of grass.'* [drawing of three fish which share a common head] | ANANSI TORONTO 1968

22.2 x 14.8 cm. Perfect bound in stiff white paper wrappers. Across the front cover: '[all on a brilliant greenish blue (168) photograph of AG] AIRPLANE DREAMS: | Compositions from | Journals | Allen | Ginsberg | $2.75 | [publisher's device]'. Down the spine: 'AIRPLANE DREAMS: COMPOSITIONS FROM JOURNALS ALLEN GINSBERG ANANSI HAP 6'. Across the back cover is a drawing of three fish which share a common head all in brilliant greenish blue. All edges trimmed. White wove paper unwatermarked.

$2.75 Canadian. Published ca. May 31, 1968 in an impression of 5,800 copies.

a2.1 *First edition, hardbound*

AIRPLANE | DREAMS: | Compositions | from Journals | Allen | Ginsberg | *'All things hang like a drop of dew | Upon a blade of grass.'* [drawing of three fish which share a common head] | ANANSI TORONTO 1968

[1-3]^8, pp. [i-x] 1-38.

23.0 x 15.4 cm. Bound in very dark greenish blue (175) cloth covered boards. White endpapers. All edges trimmed. White wove paper unwatermarked. Issued in a white paper dust jacket. Across the front cover: '[all on a brilliant greenish blue (168) photograph of AG] AIRPLANE DREAMS: | Compositions from | Journals | Allen | Ginsberg | $5.00 | [publisher's device]'. Down the spine: 'AIRPLANE DREAMS: COMPOSITIONS FROM JOURNALS ALLEN GINSBERG ANANSI HAP 6'. Across the back cover is a drawing of three fish which share a common head all in brilliant greenish blue. Inside the front flap are 22 lines and inside the back flap are 18 lines.

$5.00 Canadian. Published ca. July 10, 1968 in an impression of 200 copies.

Note: Sometime before the publication of the hardbound issue an error was found in the printing and errata slips were placed in all remaining copies of the paperbound and all copies of the hardbound printings.

Issued with a 24.0 x 6.3 cm. white paper bookmark, printed in strong blue (178) and folded in half. On one half: 'Dear Readers: | The Manufacturing Clause of | the American copyright laws is | an interesting piece of legisla- | tion. Among other things, it provides that the copyright on | an American author's work | published outside the U. S. can | be pirated if more than three | thousand copies of that work | are imported to the States. In | protest of this infringing piece | of legislation, and with Allen | Ginsberg's permission, we are | sending five thousand copies | of Airplane Dreams: Composi- | From Journals to the | United States. | The Editors | House of Anansi Press | Toronto | [publisher's device] | HOUSE OF ANANSI | 671 SPADINA AVE. | TORONTO 4, CANADA'. On the other half: 'PLEASE NOTE | In 'Remember that this is a | Dream' one section of the poem has | been inadvertently transposed. | The passage running from page 6, | line 4 (I dream I) to page 7, line 13 | should appear on page 9, where it | follows line 2 ('after thirty-eight | birthday approaching'). | *The Editors* | [drawing of three fish which share a common head]'.

a3.1 *First edition, first American paperbound,*

AIRPLANE | DREAMS: | Compositions | from Journals | Allen | Ginsberg | *'All things hang like a drop of dew* | *Upon a blade of grass.'* [drawing of three fish which share a common head] | HOUSE OF ANANSI [publisher's device] CITY LIGHTS BOOKS

Twenty-four single leaves, pp. [i-x] 1-38. [i-ii]: blank. [iii]: title page. [iv]: 'Acknowledgments: these scribbles were printed | [9 lines] | *USA Edition* © *1969 Allen Ginsberg'*. [v]: dedication page. [vi]: blank. [vii]: author's note. [viii]: blank. [ix]: contents page. [x]: blank. 1-35: text. 36-37: blank. 38: 'CITY LIGHTS PUBLICATIONS 1969 | [advertisement for 45 titles in 45 lines] | 9-69 | 38'.

20.1 x 13.8 cm. Perfect bound in stiff white paper wrappers. Across the front cover: '[all on a photograph of AG in brilliant greenish blue (168)] AIRPLANE DREAMS: | Compositions from | Journals | Allen | Ginsberg | $1.75 | [publisher's device]'. Down the spine: 'AIRPLANE DREAMS: COMPOSITIONS FROM JOURNALS ALLEN GINSBERG'. Across the back cover is a drawing of three fish which share a common head all in brilliant greenish blue. All edges trimmed. White laid paper unwatermarked.

$1.75. Published ca. Nov. 6, 1969, the publisher is unaware of the number of copies printed.

Note: The original Canadian printings were confiscated by U.S. Customs in 1968 when many hundreds of copies were shipped into the country. This printing was made in the U.S. to avoid customs seizure.

A13   WALES, A VISITATION   1968

a1. *First edition, hors commerce*

[all in dark blue (183)] wales - a visitation july 29 | 1967 allen ginsberg cape | goliard press london 1968

Single gathering of eight leaves, pp. [1-16]. [1]: half title page. [2]: blank. [3]: title page. [4]: '© Allen Ginsberg 1968'. [5-14]: text. [15]: '[all in dark blue] DESIGNED PRINTED & PUBLISHED BY CAPE | GOLIARD PRESS LONDON. | AN OFFERING FOR A PEACEFUL SUMMER FROM | ALLEN GINSBERG & CAPE GOLIARD PRESS. | [ornament] NOT FOR SALE [ornament]'. [16]: blank.

12.5 x 16.9 cm. Sewn into stiff white blank paper wrappers. White laid paper unwatermarked. All edges trimmed. Issued with a light brown (57) rice paper dust wrapper. Across the front cover: '[deep reddish orange (36)] wales - a visitation | [deep reddish orange] allen ginsberg'. Across the back cover: '[deep reddish orange] CAPE GOLIARD [publisher's device]'.

Contents: Wales - A Visitation

Hors commerce. Published Summer 1968 in an impression of 200 copies.

b1. *Second edition, signed copies (1968)*

[illustration in brown and white] | [dark green (146) rule] | [dark green] *Wales - A Visitation July 29th 1967* | [dark green] *ALLEN GINSBERG*

Single gathering of fourteen leaves, pp. [1-28]. [1-2]: blank. [3]: '[numbered and signed in black ink] | [dark green] *Cape Goliard Press London* | [dark green] *Wales - A Visitation July 29th 1967'*. [4]: blank. [5]: title page. [6]: '© Copyright Allen Ginsberg 1968'. [7]: photograph of the author. [8-21]: text. [22]: blank. [23]: photograph. [24]: blank. [25]: photograph. [26]: blank. [27]: '[ornament] | This First Edition has been | Designed, Printed & Published by Cape | Goliard Press, 10a Fairhazel Gardens, | London N.W. 6., & Consists of 300 Copies | Casebound. 100 of these Copies are Signed | & Numbered by the Author, & Include a | Recording of the Poem. | 200 *hors Commerce*. | Photographs by Tom Maschler. | Recording © Art & Sound Ltd 1967. | [ornament]'. [28]: blank.

23.6 x 20.6 cm. Bound in grayish yellowish brown (80) paper covered boards. White endpapers coated with brown fibers. White laid paper unwatermarked. All edges trimmed. White pocket for record attached to the inside back cover. A 7" record, 33 1/3 rpm with small hole in it in a plain white dust jacket. Matrix: RPL GP 1309, on one side with a blank white label; no matrix and no label on the other side. Record in a clear plastic cover within the dust jacket. Book issued in a white dust jacket printed in brown across the front cover: '[photograph of the author] | *Wales - A Visitation July 29th 1967* | *ALLEN GINSBERG'*. *This issued in a frosted glassine dust jacket.*

Contents: As first edition, with the contents of the recording being a greatly revised reading of *Wales - A Visitation.*

Unknown price. Published 1968 in an impression of 100 copies.

b2. *Second edition, unsigned copies (1968)*

[illustration in brown and white] | [dark green (146) rule] | [dark green] *Wales --A Visitation July 29th 1967* | [dark green] *ALLEN GINSBERG*

Single gathering of fourteen leaves, pp. [1-28]. As above without the autograph and numbering on page [3] and without the recording.

Hors commerce. Published 1968 in an impression of 200 copies.

c1. *Third edition (1979)*

[all in deep yellowish brown (75)] *Wales Visitation* | *Allen Ginsberg*

Single gathering of six leaves, pp. [1-12]. [1]: blank. [2]: '© Allen Ginsberg 1968 | Reprinted by permission of the author | & City Lights Books San Francisco | Photographs by Tom Maschler | A first draft entitled WALES — A VISITATION was | printed in a limited edition of 300 copies (200 *hors commerce*) | by Cape Goliard Press London 1968'. [3]: title page. [4]: photograph of the author. [5-8]: text. [9]: photograph of the author. [10]: blank. [11]: '*350 copies hand printed* | *February 1979* | *Five Seasons Press* | *Hereford* | *Five Seasons gratefully acknowledges* | *financial assistance from* | *West Midlands Arts* | [publisher's device]'. [12]: blank.

25.2 x 16.4 cm. Sewn in stiff moderate brown (58) paper wrappers. Across the front cover: '[in dark olive green (126)] Hereford Poems Four | [in deep brown (56)] *Wales Visitation* | [in deep brown] *Allen Ginsberg* | [in dark olive green illustration of the author looking at a rock]'. Across the back cover: '[in dark olive green] £1.00'. All edges trimmed. White laid paper watermarked: '[crown | *glastonbury'*, leaves 1, 3-4, 6. Leaves 2 and 5 are white glossy wove paper unwatermarked.

£1.00. Published February 1979 in an impression of 350 copies.

A14 ANKOR WAT 1968

a1. *First edition, signed copies*

Allen Ginsberg | ANKOR | WAT | *photographs by* | *Alexandra Lawrence* | *FULCRUM PRESS*

[A-C]^8, pp. [1-48]. [1]: *'ALLEN GINSBERG'*. [2]: *'ANKOR-WAT'*. [3]: photograph. [4]: title page. [5]: photograph. [6]: '[numbered and signed in black ink and stamped in red with the author's oriental seal] | *Acknowledgements* | To *Long Hair* (Lovebooks) in which an earlier version of this | poem first appeared. This book is produced by Fulcrum Press | 20 Fitzroy Sq. London W.I. and printed in Great Britain by | Lavenham Press Lavenham Suffolk. Design and typography | by Stuart Montgomery. The photographs of Ankor-Wat are by | Alexandra Lawrence. Text copyright © 1968 Allen Ginsberg | Photographs copyright © 1968 Alexandra Lawrence of this first | edition 100 specially bound copies have been numbered and | signed by the author. | Limited edition number'. [7]: photograph. [8]: blank. [9-47]: text. [48]: blank.

23.4 x 15.5 cm. Bound in moderate yellow green (120) cloth covered boards. Down the spine in gold: 'ALLEN GINSBERG *Ankor Wat* FULCRUM'. Grayish yellow green (122) endpapers. White wove coated paper unwatermarked. All edges trimmed. Issued in a white dust jacket. Across the front cover: '[all on a dark greenish yellow (103) and white photograph of a statue] Allen Ginsberg | ANKOR | WAT | *photographs by* | *Alexandra Lawrence* | *FULCRUM PRESS'*. Down the spine: 'ALLEN GINSBERG [dark greenish yellow] *Ankor Wat* [black] FULCRUM'. Across the front inside flap: '[dark greenish yellow] Allen Ginsberg | [8.0 x 8.8 cm. photograph of the author] | [20 lines] | [the lower right corner has been snipped off by the publisher so that the price for the unsigned copies will not be confused with the price for these signed copies]'.

Contents: Ankor Wat — [drawing of three fish which share a common head]

$25.00. Published ca. Summer 1968 in an impression of 100 copies.

a2. *First edition, unsigned copies*

Allen Ginsberg | ANKOR | WAT | *photographs by* | *Alexandra Lawrence* | *FULCRUM PRESS*

[A-C]^8, pp. [1-48]. As first edition, signed copies except for page [6]: *'Acknowledgements* | To *Long Hair* (Lovebooks) in which an earlier version of this | poem first appeared. This book is produced by Fulcrum Press | 20 Fitzroy Sq. London W.I. and printed in Great Britain by | Lavenham Press Lavenham Suffolk. Design and typography | by Stuart Montgomery. The photographs of Ankor-Wat are by | Alexandra Lawrence. Text copyright © 1968 Allen Ginsberg | Photographs copyright © 1968 Alexandra Lawrence of this first | edition 100 specially bound copies have been numbered and | signed by the author.'

23.4 x 15.5 cm. Bound in grayish olive green (127) cloth covered boards. Down the spine in gold: 'ALLEN GINSBERG *Ankor Wat* FULCRUM'. Grayish yellow green (122) endpapers. White wove coated paper unwatermarked. All edges trimmed. Issued in a white dust jacket identical with the signed copies except that the lower right corner has not been snipped off and has the price of 25/- included.

25/-. Published ca. Summer 1968 in an unknown quantity.

Note: A variant binding in a bright forest green has been reported by not seen, probably one of a few experimental covers for the publisher.

a3. *First edition, paperbound*

Allen Ginsberg | ANKOR | WAT | *photographs by* | *Alexandra Lawrence* |
FULCRUM PRESS

[A-C]^8, pp. [1-48]. As first edition, unsigned copies.

22.8 x 15.3 cm. Bound in stiff white paper wrappers. Across the front cover: '[photograph in moderate yellow green (120) of statue's face over which is printed] Allen Ginsberg | ANKOR | WAT | *photographs by* | *Alexandra Lawrence* | *FULCRUM PRESS*'. Down the spine: 'ALLEN GINSBERG [moderate yellow green] *Ankor Wat* [black] FULCRUM'. Across the back cover: 'ALLEN GINSBERG [moderate yellow green] ANKOR WAT [black] 15/- | [8.0 x 8.8 cm. photograph of the author] | [14 lines]'. Across the inside front cover: 'Allen Ginsberg | [16 lines]'. Across the inside back cover: 'FULCRUM PRESS | *20 Fitzroy Square, London W1* | [19 titles in 19 lines]'. All edges trimmed. White wove coated paper unwatermarked.

15/-. Published ca. Summer 1968 in an unknown quantity.

A15   **PLANET NEWS**   **1968**

a1.1 *First edition, first printing*

PLANET | NEWS | 1961-1967 | *ALLEN GINSBERG* | *'O go way man I can* | *hypnotize this nation* | *I can shake the earth's foundation* | *with the Maple Leaf Rag.'* | [publisher's device] | City Lights Books

Seventy-two single leaves, pp. [1-6] 7-144. [1]: title page. [2]: 'Library of Congress Catalog Card Number: 68-25477 | © 1968 by Allen Ginsberg | All Rights Reserved for the Author | First American Edition: November, 1968 | *Other books by Allen Ginsberg:* | [6 lines] | CITY LIGHTS BOOKS are edited by Lawrence Ferlinghetti | and published at the City Lights Bookstore | 261 Columbus Avenue, San Francisco, California, USA'. [3]: dedication page. [4]: acknowledgments page. [5-6]: contents pages. 7-144: text.

15.7 x 12.4 cm. Perfect bound in stiff white paper wrappers with covers printed so that it appears that a white label has been wrapped around the front to the back covers. Across the front cover: '[in white above the panel] THE POCKET POETS SERIES | [on panel] PLANET | NEWS | 1961-1967 | [star] | *ALLEN GINSBERG* | [below panel in white] NUMBER TWENTY THREE'. Down the spine: '[on panel] Planet News Allen Ginsberg'. Across the back cover: '[above the panel in white] $2 | [on panel] PLANET NEWS collecting seven years' Poesy scribed to 1967 | [25 lines] | A.G. May 26, 1968'. Across the inside back cover: 'CITY LIGHTS BOOKS | [39 lines] | 4-68'. All edges trimmed. White wove paper unwatermarked.

Contents: [acknowledgment note] — Who Will Take over the Universe — Journal Night Thoughts — Television Was a Baby Crawling toward that Deathchamber — This Form of Life Needs Sex — Sunset *S. S. Azemour* — Seabattle of Salamis Took Place off Perama — Galilee Shore — Stotras to Kali Destroyer of Illusions — Describe: The Rain on Dasaswamedh — Death News — Vulture Peak — Patna-Benares Express — Last Night in Calcutta — The Change — Why Is God Love, Jack? — Morning — Waking in New York — After Yeats — I am a Victim of Telephone — Today — Message II — Big Beat — Cafe in Warsaw — The Moments Return — Kral Majales — Guru — Drowse

Murmurs — Who Be Kind To — Studying the Signs — Portland Coloseum — First Party at Ken Kesey's with Hell's Angels — Carmel Valley — A Vision in Hollywood — Chances "R" — Wichita Vortex Sutra — Uptown — To the Body — City Midnight Junk Strains — Holy Ghost on the Nod over the Body of Bliss — Wales Visitation — Pentagon Exorcism — [prose note on back cover]

$2.00. Published November 1968 in an impression of 25,000 copies.

Note: This publication has a rather involved printing history. The true first issue is the one identified as "First American Edition: November 1968" on the verso of the title page. The British letterpress printing which was due to be distributed in May 1968 was not available until Dec. 1, 1968, due to a flood at the bindery. The publisher had already ordered an offset edition printed in a much larger quantity by Edwards Brothers printers in Ann Arbor, MI. This printing was ready for distribution in November. Other bibliographies incorrectly have given priority to the English printing. Although printed in England it was intended to be shipped to the United States and hence not truly a British edition.

The English printing can be identified by the Villiers printer's notice on the bottom of the inside back cover and lack of printing notice on the verso of the title page.

a1.2 *First edition, second printing (Feb. 1970):* **15,000 copies.**

Note: Second and subsequent printings are identified as such on the verso of the title page. No significant changes in text occur after the first printing.

a1.3 *First edition, third printing (May 1974):* 7,000 copies.

a1.4 *First edition, fourth printing (Dec. 1979):* 3,000 copies.

a1.5 *First edition, fifth printing (April 1982):* 3,000 copies.

a1.6 *First edition, sixth printing (April 1988):* 1,500 copies.

a1.7 *First edition, seventh printing (May 1990):* 1,500 copies.

a1.8 *First edition, eighth printing (Nov. 1992):* 1,500 copies.

a2. *First British issue (1968)*

PLANET | NEWS | 1961-1967 | *ALLEN GINSBERG* | *'O go way man I can* | *hypnotize this nation* | *I can shake the earth's foundation* | *with the Maple Leaf Rag.'* | [publisher's device] | City Lights Books

[A-I]^8, pp. [1-6] 7-144. [1]: title page. [2]: 'Library of Congress Catalog Card Number: 68-25477 | © 1968 by Allen Ginsberg | All Rights Reserved for the Author | *Other books by Allen Ginsberg:* | [6 lines] | CITY LIGHTS BOOKS are edited by Lawrence Ferlinghetti | and published at the City Lights Bookstore | 261 Columbus Avenue, San Francisco, California, USA'. [3]: dedication page. [4]: acknowledgments page. [5-6]: contents pages. 7-144: text.

15.8 x 12.4 cm. Bound in stiff white paper wrappers with covers printed so that it appears that a white label has been wrapped around the front to the back covers. Across the front cover: '[in white above the panel] THE POCKET POETS SERIES | [on panel] PLANET | NEWS | 1961-1967 | [star] | *ALLEN GINSBERG* | [below panel in white] NUMBER TWENTY THREE'. Down the spine: '[on panel] Planet News Allen Ginsberg'. Across the back cover: '[above the panel in white] $2 | [on panel] PLANET NEWS collecting seven years' Poesy scribed to 1967 | [25 lines] | A.G. May 26, 1968'. Across the inside back cover: 'CITY LIGHTS BOOKS IN PRINT | [42 lines] | [6.3 cm.

rule] I Printed at the Press of Villiers Publications Ltd. I Ingestre Road, London, NW5, England'. All edges trimmed. White wove paper unwatermarked.

$2.00. Published Dec. 1, 1968 in an impression of 5,000 copies.

a3. *First signed hardbound issue (1969)*

PLANET I NEWS I 1961-1967 I *ALLEN GINSBERG* I *'O go way man I can* I *hypnotize this nation* I *I can shake the earth's foundation* I *with the Maple Leaf Rag.'* I [publisher's device] I City Lights Books

[1-9]^8, pp. [1-6] 7-144. [1]: title page. [2]: 'Library of Congress Catalog Card Number: 68-25477 I © 1968 by Allen Ginsberg I All Rights Reserved for the Author I *Other books by Allen Ginsberg:* I [6 lines] I CITY LIGHTS BOOKS are edited by Lawrence Ferlinghetti I and published at the City Lights Bookstore I 261 Columbus Avenue, San Francisco, California, USA'. [3]: dedication page. [4]: acknowledgments page. [5-6]: contents pages. 7-144: text.

16.9 x 12.5 cm. Bound in black cloth covered boards. Across the front cover in gold: 'PLANET I NEWS I 1961-1967 I [star] I *ALLEN GINSBERG*'. Down the spine in gold: 'Planet News Allen Ginsberg'. Endpapers are light greenish yellow (101) laid paper watermarked '[crown] I Abbey Mills I Greenfield'. On the inside front endpaper facing p. [1] is the following colophon: 'Five Hundred copies of this I Limited Edition have been I numbered and signed I by the Author. I This is number [21 dots with the number and autograph in black ink]'. All edges trimmed. White wove paper unwatermarked. Issued in a black paper covered slip-in case. A 6.5 x 5.7 cm. white paper label is attached to the front of the case on which is printed: 'PLANET I NEWS I 1961—1967 I [star] I *ALLEN GINSBERG*'.

$15.00. Published July 4, 1969 in an impression of 500 copies.

a4. *First edition, second printing, re-issue (Jan. 28, 1974)*

THE I POCKET POETS I SERIES I Volume 4 I Numbers 22-28 I KRAUS REPRINT CO. I Millwood, New York I 1973

[1-14]^{16} [15]^8 [16]^{16}, pp. [1-496]. [1]: title page. [2]: *'Reprinted with the permission of* I *City Lights Booksellers and Publishers* I KRAUS REPRINT CO. I A U.S. Division of Kraus-Thomson Organization Limited I Printed in Germany'. [3-492]: text. [493-496]: blank.

22.3 x 14.4 cm. Bound in dark purplish red (259) cloth covered boards, lettered across the spine in gold: '[3 rules 3.8 cm. long] I THE I POCKET I POETS I SERIES I [3 rules 3.8 cm. long] I 4 I KRAUS I REPRINT'. All edges trimmed. White endpapers. White wove paper unwatermarked.

Contents: Planet News [as first edition] pp. [69-216].

$23.75 or sold as a four volume set at $95.00. Published Jan. 28, 1974 in an impression of 250 copies.

Note: Kraus Reprint Co. collected all the books comprising the Pocket Poets Series and re-issued them in a four volume set primarily for the library trade. No effort was made to reprint the first printings of many of the books in the series and here they have reprinted the 2nd printing of the City Lights paperback.

A16   **T.V. BABY POEM**   **1968**

T.V. BABY | POEM | [3.3 cm. rule] | ALLEN GINSBERG

Single gathering of eight leaves, pp. [1-16]. [1]: title page. [2]: '© 1968 | by Allen Ginsberg'. [3]: '[22.4 x 15.2 cm. photo of the author] Allen Ginsberg. | 1966. | Photo A. Léna.' [4]: blank. [5-15]: text. [16]: 'in print | [17 lines] | soon to appear | Ed Sanders, Jean-Jacques Lebel, Julian Beck (Living Theater), etc. | [publisher's device] | BEACH BOOKS, TEXTS & DOCUMENTS | DISTRIBUTED BY | CITY LIGHTS BOOKS | 1562 GRANT AVENUE SAN FRANCISCO, CALIFORNIA 94133'.

27.9 x 21.5 cm. Stapled twice in light yellowish brown (76) paper wrappers. Across the front cover: 'ALLEN GINSBERG | T. V. BABY | POEM | Number Two $1.25'. Across the back cover: '[publisher's device] | Published by | BEACH BOOKS, [publisher's device] Distributed by | TEXTS & DOCUMENTS CITY LIGHTS BOOKS'. White wove paper unwatermarked. All edges trimmed.

Contents: T. V. Baby Poem — [letter to Claude Pelieu and Mary Beach]

$1.25. Published Nov. or Dec. 1968 in an impression of 1,200 copies.

Note: The entire publication is a facsimile of a corrected typescript.

A17   **SONG & SUNFLOWER SUTRA**   **1969**

ALLEN GINSBERG | [dark reddish orange (38)] SONG & | [dark reddish orange] SUNFLOWER | [dark reddish orange] SUTRA | FERNANDA PIVANO

$[1]^4 [2-3]^8$, pp. [1-10] 11-31 [32-40]. [1-4]: blank. [5]: '<<*Concilium Typographicum* >>'. [6]: blank. [7]: title page. [8]: blank. [9] - [32]: text. [33-34]: blank. [35]: 'SIBI & DOMINICAE SODALIBUS | Le due poesie di Allen Ginsberg: <<Song e Sutra | del Girasole >>, questa nella versione di Fernanda | Pivano, sono state composte a mano e stampate in | torchio da F. Riva, che ne ha contato 69 esemplari | A VERONA NELL'AUTUNNO | DEL MCMLXIX. | [publisher's device in dark reddish orange] NUMERO | [typeset number]'. [36-40]: blank.

27.3 x 18.8 cm. Quarter bound in strong reddish orange (35) leather with yellowish white (92) paper covered board, decorated with a symmetrical pattern in deep red (13) and deep orange yellow (69). Up the spine: '[in gold] GINSBERG [bullet] PIVANO'. Top edges only trimmed and gilt. White wove paper watermarked with the publisher's device. White endpapers. Issued in a clear plastic dust jacket. Issued in a slip-in case covered with paper identical to that on the covers.

Contents: Song [The weight of the world] — Sutra Del Girasole [Sunflower Sutra, translated by Fernanda Pivano]

Published in 1969 in an impression of 69 copies. The publisher was unable to provide any additional information about the publication history of this book.

A18 NOTES AFTER AN EVENING WITH WILLIAM CARLOS WILLIAMS 1970

NOTES AFTER AN EVENING WITH | WILLIAM CARLOS WILLIAMS | [8 lines of text] | ALLEN GINSBERG

Single gathering of two leaves, pp. [1-4]. [1]: title page. [2-4]: text.

15.2 x 22.8 cm. Stapled twice in stiff glossy white paper wrappers. Across the front cover all in facsimile of autograph manuscript: 'Allen Ginsberg I Wishing him the best I William Carlos Williams I 3/12/52 I [type] Portents 17'. Across the back cover: 'Copyright © by Allen Ginsberg I One of 300 copies I Portents are published by Samuel Charters'. Light olive gray (112) wove paper unwatermarked. All edges trimmed.

Contents: Notes after an Evening with William Carlos Williams [prose]

$2.00. Published ca. April-May 1970 in an impression of 300 copies.

Note: Although the publisher provided the publication date of ca. April-May 1969 to the compiler, correspondence was discovered which suggests that the actual publication date was about a year later. In a letter from the publisher to AG dated May 18, 1970 is a note saying that the book is finally ready and that 20 copies are enclosed. In a letter from Mrs. William Carlos Williams dated June 12, 1970 she states that she has just seen Portents 17 with her husband's handwriting on cover.

A19   **INDIAN JOURNALS**   **1970**

a1. *First edition, first issue, hardbound*

ALLEN GINSBERG I INDIAN JOURNALS I MARCH 1962 [the J from the line above extends below this line at this point] — MAY 1963 I NOTEBOOKS I DIARY I BLANK PAGES I WRITINGS I DAVE HASELWOOD BOOKS I CITY LIGHTS BOOKS

$[1-2]^{16}$ $[3]^2$ $[4-8]^{16}$, pp. [1-4] 5-44 [i-vi] 45-100 [vii-xii] 101-140 [xiii-xvi] 141-210 [211-212]. [1]: title page. [2]: '© *1970* Allen Ginsberg I All rights reserved I Published jointly by Dave Haselwood Books and City Lights Books, I 1562 Grant Avenue, San Francisco, California 94133'. [3]: drawing of three fish which share a common head by AG. [4]: dedication page. 5-210: text. [211]: blank. [212]: card page.

20.9 x 13.6 cm. Bound in grayish reddish brown (46) cloth. Across the front cover: 'J I O I U I R I INDIAN I A I L I S'. Down the spine: 'GINSBERG INDIAN JOURNALS'. White endpapers. White wove paper unwatermarked. All edges trimmed. Issued in a white dust jacket. Across the front cover: '[all within single rule frame on a brown and white photograph of Shambu Bharti Baba] ALLEN GINSBERG I J I O I U I R I INDIAN I A I L I S'. Down the spine: 'GINSBERG INDIAN JOURNALS'. Across the back cover: 'INDIAN JOURNALS I *Allen Ginsberg* I [25 lines] I *Allen Ginsberg* I January 24, 1970'. Across the inside front flap: '$6.50 I Allen Ginsberg I [33 lines] I *(Continued on back flap)*'. Across the inside back flap: [38 lines]'.

Contents: [journal entries, drawings, photographs (see also D4)] — Noted on Edge of Bombay Map — Eyes Closed — The Ogre That Goes with the Rose — Any Town Will Do — "As if He Had Read Wystan" — A Whitewashed Room on the Roof — Max Frohman — Now I am Brooding on a Pillow — When I was Young You Came with the — To W.C.W. — Under Howrah Bridge — Kheer — In a Straight Fight, Hey God — Shantiniketan — God Cathedral of Goiters, God — In the Bathroom Mirror Staring at — What Vanity? What Possible Divine — Well, Where Now Me, What Next — Taj Mahal — Tonite on the Riverbank "Krishna — There are Certain Limits-You Can't Push — Saraswati's Birthday — Coming Down the Stairs — All That Happens about Everything — The Policeman Flew in the Black Door — Room Drowse Meditation — Describe: The Rain on Dasaswamedh — Walking at Night on Asphalt Campus — Illustrious Object Balloon Igloo — The Sun Is — Should They Ask Him Back, Where Could He Come — The Beggar All Week under the Green Giant Tree — Gridhakuta Hill — Patna-Benares Express — Last Night in Calcutta — [anonymous blurb on the inside front and back dust jacket flaps] — [anonymous blurb on insdie front and back flaps] — [blurb on back of dust jacket]

$6.50. Published May 1970 in an impression of 1,000 copies.

Note: The publisher reports that he sent out 150 review copies.

a2.1 *First edition, first printing, paperbound*

ALLEN GINSBERG | INDIAN JOURNALS | MARCH 1962 [the J from the line above extends below this line at this point] — MAY 1963 | NOTEBOOKS | DIARY | BLANK PAGES | WRITINGS | DAVE HASELWOOD BOOKS | CITY LIGHTS BOOKS

One hundred fourteen single leaves, pp. [1-4] 5-44 [i-vi] 45-100 [vii-xii] 101-140 [xiii-xvi] 141-210 [211-212].

20.2 x 13.2 cm. Perfect bound in stiff white paper wrappers. Across the front cover: '[all on a brown and white photograph of Shambu Bharti Baba] ALLEN GINSBERG | J | O | U | R | INDIAN | A | L | S'. Down the spine: 'GINSBERG INDIAN JOURNALS'. Across the back cover: 'INDIAN JOURNALS | *Allen Ginsberg* | [25 lines] | *Allen Ginsberg* | January 24, 1970 | *$3*'. White wove paper unwatermarked. All edges trimmed.

$3.00. Published May 1970 in an impression of 10,000 copies.

a2.2 *First edition, second printing, paperbound (June 1971)*

Note: Second and third printings are identified as such on the verso of the title page. There are no significant changes to the text. Publisher's records for the quantitites printed are unavailable.

a2.3 *First edition, third printing, paperbound (Oct. 1974)*

b1. *First Indian edition (1990)*

ALLEN GINSBERG | INDIAN JOURNALS [the J from the word Journals extends below this line to separate the next 2 lines] | NOTEBOOKS DIARY BLANK PAGES WRITINGS | MARCH 1962 — MAY 1963 | [design of three fish which share a common head] | [publisher's device] | PENGUIN BOOKS

One hundred sixteen single leaves, pp. [i-iv] [1-4] 5-108 [i-xvi] 109-210 [211-212]. [i]: 'PENGUIN BOOKS | INDIAN JOURNALS | [13 lines]'. [ii]: blank. [iii]: title page. [iv]: 'Penguin Books India Ltd. 72-B Himalaya House. 23 Kasturba Gandhi Marg. | New Delhi-110 001. India. | [4 lines] | First published by Dave Haselwood Books and City Lights Books. 1970 | Published in Penguin Books 1990 | [17 lines]'. [1]: half title page. [2]: blank. [3]: drawing of three fish which share a common head by AG. [4]: dedication page. 5-108: text. [i-xvi]: photographs. 109-210: text. [211]: publisher's information. [212: advertisement.

19.9 x 12.9 cm. Perfect bound in stiff white paper wrappers. Across the front cover in full color all within vivid purplish blue (194) frame with white border and single rules: 'ALLEN GINSBERG | [9.9 cm. red rule] | [in vivid purplish blue] INDIAN JOURNALS | [photo of Indian holy man smoking] NOTEBOOKS | DIARY | BLANK PAGES | WRITINGS | [publisher's device]'. Down the spine on vivid orange (48): 'ALLEN GINSBERG INDIAN JOURNALS ISBN 0-14-013370-4 [publisher's device across the spine]'. Across the back cover: '[all on bluish white (189) within vivid purplish blue frame with white border and single rules] Allen Ginsberg writes: | [photo of author] *Indian Journals* are notebook writings | sketches dream fragments night thoughts | [26 lines] | Cover photograph by Nirmalendu Samui | Cover design by Sunil Sil | India Rs 55 | [in 3 lines] [publisher's device] | A PENGUIN BOOK | Travel [zebra bar code with 3 sets of numbers all within a white 2.5 x 5.2 cm. rectangle]'. White wove paper unwatermarked. All edges trimmed.

Rs 55. Published April 1990 in an impression of 2,100 copies.

A20   **THE MOMENTS RETURN**   **1970**

a1. *First edition, special copies*

[deep yellowish pink (27)] THE MOMENTS RETURN, a poem by Allen Ginsberg with three drawings by Robert LaVigne | [publisher's device in pale yellow (89) and medium gray (265)] [deep yellowish pink] Grabhorn-Hoyem: San Francisco: 1970

Single gathering of eight leaves, pp. [1-16]. [1-4]: blank. [5]: title page. [6]: '[right in medium gray] Copyright 1970 by Allen Ginsberg & Robert La Vigne.' [7-11]: text. [12]: blank. [13]: '[in deep yellowish pink] 200 copies printed by Robert Grabhorn & Andrew Hoyem at 566 Commercial Street, San Francisco.' [14-16]: blank.

22.8 x 38.0 cm. Quarter bound in strong reddish brown (40) leather with yellowish gray (93) paper covered boards. Across the front cover at bottom is an illustration in very deep red (14) and brilliant orange yellow (67) which includes the partial words: 'THE | MOMEN | RE | TUR' in the design. Down the spine in gold: 'THE MOMENTS RETURN'. Across the back cover the same illustration and coloring as the front cover. White endpapers. White wove paper unwatermarked. All edges trimmed.

Contents: The Moments Return

Sold for an undisclosed amount. Published 1970 in an impression of 14 or 15 copies.

Note: No more specific publication information is available from the publisher.

a2. *First edition, ordinary copies*

[deep yellowish pink (27)] THE MOMENTS RETURN, a poem by Allen Ginsberg with three drawings by Robert LaVigne | [publisher's device in pale yellow (89) and medium gray (265)] [deep yellowish pink] Grabhorn-Hoyem: San Francisco: 1970

Nine single leaves, pp. [1-18]. [1-4]: blank. [5]: title page. [6]: '[in medium gray] Copyright 1970 by Allen Ginsberg & Robert La Vigne.' [7-11]: text. [12]: blank. [13]: '[in deep yellowish pink] 200 copies printed by Robert Grabhorn & Andrew Hoyem at 566 Commercial Street, San Francisco.' [14-18]: blank.

23.4 x 38.5 cm. Quarter bound in pale yellow (89) cloth with yellowish white (92) paper covered boards with vertical yellow stripes. Up the spine on a 8.8 x 0.7 cm. yellowish white paper label: 'THE MOMENTS RETURN'. White endpapers. White wove paper unwatermarked. All edges trimmed.

$15.00. Published 1970 in an impression of 185 copies and possibly another 5 additional hors commerce copies.

A21 HOWL **1971**

a1. *First edition*

Howl I for CARL SOLOMON I *by* I [autograph in black ink]

[1-7] ⁴, pp. [i-viii] [1] 2-43 [44-48]. [i-iv]: blank. [v]: title page. [vi]: 'PUBLISHED 1971 GRABHORN-HOYEM, SAN FRANCISCO I REPRINTED WITH PERMISSION OF CITY LIGHTS BOOKS I COPYRIGHTED © 1956 AND 1959 BY ALLEN GINSBERG'. [vii]: 'NOTE: 1971 PRINTING *HOWL & THE NAMES* I [13 lines] I Allen Ginsberg I July 21, 1971'. [viii]: blank. [1]-43: text. [44]: blank. [45]: 'This book comprises the text of *Howl* as it was I published in 1956 with recent minute revisions I by the author and the addition of a related poetic I fragment *The Names*, written in 1957, published I in the *Paris Review* for Spring 1966 and here first I collected with the poem. The title-page bears the I signature of the poet. The drawing for the cover I is by Robert LaVigne. This edition, limited to I 275 copies, was printed on handmade paper from I Goudy Modern type in the Summer of 1971 by I Robert Grabhorn & Andrew Hoyem I of San Francisco I [ornament]'. [46-48]: blank.

30.0 x 23.6 cm. Bound in linen with design of cityscape by Robert LaVigne in medium gray (265), deep reddish orange (36), deep yellowish brown (75), dark yellowish green (137), deep blue (179), deep yellow (85) and white on the front cover, spine and back cover. White laid paper watermarked: 'WSH & C⁰ I BRITISH I HAND MADE I [design of fleurs de lys] I [ornamental type] WSH & C⁰'. Light gray (264) laid endpapers watermarked: *'Strathmore Charcoal 100% cotton fiber U.S.A.'* Top edges trimmed.

Contents: [prose note] — Howl — Footnote to Howl — The Names

$60.00. Published Summer 1971 in an impression of ca. 255 copies.

Note: The colophon states that 275 copies were produced but several copies were misbound and about 20 sets of sheets were not bound due to a lack of adequate covers since those were produced in a very limited quantity. Publisher also states that "about five copies on a slightly different (creamier) English handmade paper were retained in sheets". The compiler has never seen this paper variant. In 1992 the remaining 20 sets of sheets were bound in a new cover design which does not include the LaVigne illustration [see next entry].

a2. *First edition, Arion rebinding, 1992*

Howl I for CARL SOLOMON I *by* I [autograph in black ink: Allen Ginsberg]

Collation: 29.8 x 23.6 cm. [1-7] ⁴, pp. [i-viii] [1] 2-43 [44-48].

Quarter bound in red goat leather with red and gold silk cloth covered boards. Across the front cover in gold on the leather: 'H I O I W I L'. Down the spine in gold: 'HOWL *by* ALLEN GINSBERG'. Across the back cover in gold on the leather: 'H I O I W I L'. White laid paper watermarked: 'WSH & C⁰ I BRITISH I HAND MADE I [design of fleurs de lys] I [ornamental type] WSH & C⁰'. White laid endpapers watermarked in hollow letters: 'WSH & C⁰ I BRITISH I HAND MADE I [design of fleurs de lys] I [ornamental type] WSH & C⁰'. Top edges trimmed. Issued in a red and gold silk cloth slip-in case with a red leather label inset in the spine on which is the following in gold: 'HOWL *by* ALLEN GINSBERG'.

$500.00. Published Oct. 30, 1992 in an impression of 20 copies.

Note: These are the original sheets printed in 1971 but not bound at that time. They were bound in 1992 by Arion Press and Andrew Hoyem in this edition and since the original cover design by Robert LaVigne was not used and the colophon was not altered, it is confusing.

A22   **IMPROVISED POETICS**   **1971**

a1. *First edition, first (proof) state:*

Ginsberg's | *Improvised Poetics* | [publisher's device] | Edited, with an Introduction, by | MARK ROBISON

Single gathering of thirty leaves, pp. [i-vi] 1-51 [52-54]. [i-ii]: blank. [iii]: title page. [iv]: 'Library of Congress Catalog Card Number: 70-171332 | c 1971 by Allen Ginsberg | [4 lines] | First American Edition: July, 1971 | In a limited edition of One Thousand copies, One Hundred of | which are signed and numbered by the author. | ANONYM BOOKS are published in the United States of | America as part of a continuing series and distributed | internationally by | The ANONYM PRESS | Box 54, Kensington Sta., Buffalo, New York 14215'. [v]: introduction. [vi]: dedication page. 1-51: text. [52]: '—A Selected Bibliography— | [28 lines]'. [53-54]: blank.

17.0 x 12.3 cm. Stapled twice in stiff white paper wrappers. Across the front cover is a photograph of AG holding a brief case. Across the back cover: 'GINSBERG'S | IMPROVISED POETICS | [9 lines] | [publisher's device] ANONYM PRESS | BUFFALO, NEW YORK'. Across the inside back cover: 'OCTOBERGRAPHICS | Buffalo, N.Y.' White wove paper unwatermarked, except for the first and last leaves which are very light greenish blue (171) thin wove paper unwatermarked. All edges trimmed.

Contents: [transcription of prose discussion]

Not for sale. Published July 1971 in an impression of 1,000 copies.

Note: This printing is identified by the lack of words on the front cover was destroyed by the publisher and changes made to the text and cover. Many copies still exist, but it is not known how many have survived, although more than ten have been examined by the compiler. In addition one copy has been seen without the printing on the inside back cover.

a2. *First edition, second state, signed copies (Jan. 1972)*

IMPROVISED POETICS |]ALLEN GINSBERG[| Edited, with an Introduction, by | [in light gray (264)] MARK ROBISON | [publisher's device] | ANONYM

Thirty single leaves, pp. [i-vi] 1-51 [52-54]. [i-ii]: blank. [iii]: title page. [iv]: 'Library of Congress Catalog Card Number: 70-171332 | c 1971 by Allen Ginsberg | [3 lines] | First Printing: January, 1972 | In a limited edition of Two Thousand copies, One Hundred of | which are signed and numbered by the author. | This is copy #____ | [numbered and autographed in black ink] | ANONYM BOOKS are published in the United States of America and | distributed by: | ANONYM PRESS | Box 4338, S.F., Cal. | 94101'. [v]: introduction. [vi]: dedication page. 1-51: text. [52]: '—A Selected Bibliography— | [30 lines]'. [53-54]: blank.

17.8 x 13.3 cm. Bound in deep reddish brown (41) cloth covered boards. Across the front cover in silver: 'I | M | POETICS | R | O | V | I | S | E | D | ALLEN | GINSBERG'. Down the spine in silver: 'GINSBERG IMPROVISED POETICS [across the spine] [publisher's device]'. White wove paper unwatermarked, except for the first and last leaves which are thinner wove paper. All edges trimmed.

Contents: As the first state with many corrections.

$20.00. Published January 1972 in an impression of 100 copies.

Note: Possibly several additional copies were made. One copy has been examined which is marked as "Extra #4" and another copy has been reported identified as number 104; the publisher could not be located for comment.

a3. *First edition, second state, unsigned copies (Jan. 1972)*

IMPROVISED POETICS |]ALLEN GINSBERG[| Edited, with an Introduction, by | [in light gray (264)] MARK ROBISON | [publisher's device] | ANONYM

Thirty single leaves, pp. [i-vi] 1-51 [52-54]. [i-ii]: blank. [iii]: title page. [iv]: 'Library of Congress Catalog Card Number: 70-171332 | c 1971 by Allen Ginsberg | [3 lines] | First Printing: January, 1972 | In a limited edition of Two Thousand copies, One Hundred of | which are signed and numbered by the author. | ANONYM BOOKS are published in the United States of America and | distributed by: | ANONYM PRESS | Box 4338, S.F., Cal. | 94101'. [v]: introduction. [vi]: dedication page. 1-51: text. [52]: '—A Selected Bibliography— | [30 lines]'. [53-54]: blank.

17.7 x 13.2 cm. Bound in light yellowish brown (76) cloth covered boards. Across the front cover in deep reddish brown (41): 'I | M | POETICS | R | O | V | I | S | E | D | ALLEN | GINSBERG'. Down the spine in deep reddish brown: 'GINSBERG IMPROVISED POETICS [across the spine] [publisher's device]'. White wove paper unwatermarked, except for the first and last leaves which are thinner wove paper. All edges trimmed.

$8.00. Published January 1972 in an impression of 200 copies.

a4. *First edition, second state, paperbound (Jan. 1972)*

IMPROVISED POETICS |]ALLEN GINSBERG[| Edited, with an Introduction, by | [in light gray (264)] MARK ROBISON | [publisher's device] | ANONYM

Thirty single leaves, pp. [i-vi] 1-51 [52-54]. [i-ii]: blank. [iii]: title page. [iv]: 'Library of Congress Catalog Card Number: 70-171332 | c 1971 by Allen Ginsberg | [3 lines] | First Printing: January, 1972 | In a limited edition of Two Thousand copies, One Hundred of | which are signed and numbered by the author. | ANONYM BOOKS are published in the United States of America and | distributed by: | ANONYM PRESS | Box 4338, S.F., Cal. | 94101'. [v]: introduction. [vi]: dedication page. 1-51: text. [52]: '—A Selected Bibliography— | [30 lines]'. [53-54]: blank.

17.5 x 12.8 cm. Perfect bound in stiff white paper wrappers. Across the front cover all over a photograph of the author in white: 'I | M | POETICS | R | O | V | I | S | E | D | [in black] ALLEN | [in black] GINSBERG'. Down the spine: 'GINSBERG IMPROVISED POETICS [across the spine] [publisher's device]'. Across the back cover: 'IMPROVISED POETICS |]ALLEN GINSBERG[| [9 lines about the book] | [publisher's device] ANONYM'. White wove paper unwatermarked, except for the first and last leaves which are thinner wove paper. All edges trimmed.

$1.50. Published January 1972 in an impression of 1,700 copies.

A23 **OPEN HEAD/OPEN EYE** **1972**

The Sun Poetry Series | [ornamental type] Allen | [ornamental type] Ginsberg | Open head | Sun Books . Melbourne (i)

Single gathering of twenty-eight leaves, pp. i-iii [iv] [1] 2-17 [18-21] [inverted pages] 27-1 [iv] iii-i. i: title page. ii: 'Sun Books Pty Ltd | 107 Moray Street, South Melbourne, Victoria 3205, Australia | This selection first published by Sun Books 1972 | Copyright 1972 by Allen Ginsberg | National Library of Australia card number & ISBN 0 7251 0140 7 | Printed in Australia by Humphrey & Formula Press | Registered in Australia for | (ii) transmission by post as a book'. iii: contents page. [iv]: blank. [1]-17: text of *Open Head*. [18-21]: blank. 27-1: text of *Open Eye* . [iv]: blank. iii: contents page. ii: acknowledgments. i: 'The Sun Poetry Series | [ornamental type] Lawrence | [ornamental type] Ferlinghetti | Open eye | Sun Books. Melbourne (i)'.

21.6 x 14.0 cm. Stapled twice in stiff white paper wrappers. Across the front cover: '[2 rows of stars down the left side] [ornamental type] Allen | [ornamental type] Ginsberg | [in vivid red (11)] Open head | [photograph of the author in an oval frame]'. Across the back cover, inverted: '[2 vivid red rules down the left side] [ornamental type] Lawrence | [ornamental type] Ferlinghetti | [in vivid red] Open eye | [photograph of the author in an oval frame]'. White wove paper unwatermarked. All edges trimmed.

Contents: Elegy for Neal — On Neal's Ashes — Rain-wet Asphalt Heat, Garbage Cubbed [sic] Cans Over-flowing — Memory Gardens — Friday the Thirteenth — Reading Milarepa — September on Jessore Road

$1.75 Australian. Published March 6, 1972 in an impression of 3,000 copies.

Note: The second pagination sequence is *Open Eye* by Lawrence Ferlinghetti, bound with *Open Head* and printed upside down with the back cover of the volume as its front cover.

A24 **NEW YEAR BLUES** **1972**

NEW YEAR BLUES | BY ALLEN GINSBERG | [deep blue] [10 hollow stars] | THE PHOENIX BOOK SHOP NEW YORK 1972

Single gathering of 10 leaves, pp. [1-20]. [1-2]: blank. [3]: title page. [4]: 'Copyright © 1972 by Allen Ginsberg'. [5-16]: text. [17]: 'This first edition of *New Year Blues* | is limited to twenty-six copies, lettered A to Z, | not for sale, and one hundred copies, | numbered and signed by the author. | This is No. 14 in the Phoenix Book Shop | Oblong Octavo Series, | designed and printed by Ronald Gordon at | The Oliphant Press, New York. | Copy No. [number in red ink] | [autograph in black ink]'. [18-20]: blank.

14.0 x 18.4 cm. Sewn into brilliant greenish blue (168) wrappers with flaps on the front and back. Across the front cover: 'NEW YEARS BLUES | BY ALLEN GINSBERG'. White laid paper unwatermarked. Black endpapers. Some bottom edges untrimmed.

Contents: Christmas Blues — Macdougal Street Blues

$15.00. Published May 3, 1972 in an impression of 150 copies: 100 copies are numbered 1 to 100 for sale; 26 copies are lettered A to Z for subscribers; and 24 unsigned, unnumbered copies were used as samples by the publisher.

A25   **BIXBY CANYON OCEAN PATH WORD BREEZE**   **1972**

a1. *First edition, paperbound*

BIXBY CANYON | OCEAN PATH | WORD BREEZE | ALLEN GINSBERG |
Gotham Book Mart New York 1972

Single gathering of fourteen leaves, pp. [1-28]. [1-2]: blank. [3]: epigraph. [4]:
photograph of a beach. [5]: title page. [6]: 'First Printing | BIXBY CANYON OCEAN
PATH WORD BREEZE. Copyright | © 1972 by Allen Ginsberg. All rights reserved.
Printed in the | [6 lines] | Bixby Canyon Ocean Path Word Breeze first appeared in *The*
| *World,* issue #24, Winter 1972. | ISBN 910664-19-6 (paper) | ISBN 910664-20-x
(cloth) | Library of Congress No. 72-86484'. [7]: dedication page. [8-22]: text. [23]:
'Printed August 1972 in New York City for The Gotham Book | Mart by Profile Press.
Front cover illustration from a paint- | ing of Bixby Canyon by Emil White. Photographs
by William | Webb. Published in paper wrappers, 100 hardcover copies | numbered &
signed by the poet, and 26 hardcover copies | lettered A to Z & signed by the poet.' [24]:
publisher's device. [25-28]: blank.

25.9 x 18.1 cm. Stapled twice in moderate yellow (87) paper wrappers. Across the front
cover: 'BIXBY CANYON | OCEAN PATH | WORD BREEZE | [8.7 x 11.0 cm.
multi-colored picture of the seashore is attached] | ALLEN GINSBERG'. Across the
back cover: '$3.00'. White wove paper unwatermarked, first and last leaves are light
brownish gray (63) laid paper watermarked '[ornamental type] Sulgrave Text'. All edges
trimmed.

Contents: Bixby Canyon Ocean Path Word Breeze

$3.00. Published ca. June 1972 in a quantity not known by the publisher.

a2. *First edition, hardbound, signed copies*

BIXBY CANYON | OCEAN PATH | WORD BREEZE | ALLEN GINSBERG |
Gotham Book Mart New York 1972

Single gathering of twelve leaves, pp. [1-24]. [1]: epigraph. [2]: photograph of a beach.
[3]: title page. [4]: 'First Printing | BIXBY CANYON OCEAN PATH WORD
BREEZE. Copyright | © 1972 by Allen Ginsberg. All rights reserved. Printed in the |
[6 lines] | Bixby Canyon Ocean Path Word Breeze first appeared in *The* | *World,* issue
#24, Winter 1972. | ISBN 910664-19-6 (paper) | ISBN 910664-20-x (cloth) | Library
of Congress No. 72-86484'. [5]: dedication page. [6-20]: text. [21]: 'Printed August
1972 in New York City for The Gotham Book | Mart by Profile Press. Front cover
illustration from a paint- | ing of Bixby Canyon by Emil White. Photographs by William
| Webb. Published in paper wrappers, 100 hardcover copies | numbered & signed by the
poet, and 26 hardcover copies | lettered A to Z & signed by the poet. | [numbered and
signed in black ink]'. [22]: publisher's device. [23-24]: blank.

26.3 x 18.4 cm. Bound in dark reddish orange (38) cloth covered boards. Across the
front cover in gold: 'BIXBY CANYON | OCEAN PATH | WORD BREEZE | [8.8 x
11.1 cm. multi-colored picture of the seashore is attached] | ALLEN GINSBERG'.
White wove paper unwatermarked. Grayish yellowish brown endpapers. All edges
trimmed.

$30.00. Published ca. Dec. 1972 in an impression of 136 copies: 26 copies are lettered A
to Z, 100 copies are numbered 1 to 100, and 10 copies are hors commerce copies.

A26   **THE FALL OF AMERICA**   **1972**

a1.1a *First edition, first printing, white covers*

THE | FALL | OF | AMERICA | poems of these states | 1965-1971 | [star] | ALLEN GINSBERG | '...*same electric lightning South* | *follows this train* | *Apocalypse prophesied* — | *the fall of America* | *signalled from Heaven* —' | City [publisher's device] Lights | the pocket poets series no. 30

One hundred and four single leaves, pp. [i-x] 1-39 [40] [xi-xii] 41-73 [74] [xiii-xiv] 75-105 [106] [xv-xvi] 107-169 [170] [xvii-xviii] 171-188 [189-190]. [i]: title page. [ii]: 'Library of Congress Catalog Card Number: 72-84228 | © *1972 Allen Ginsberg* | CITY LIGHTS BOOKS are published at the City Lights | Bookstore, 261 Columbus Avenue, San Francisco, Cali- | fornia 94133. Editorial & Publishing offices: 1562 Grant | Avenue, San Francisco. Editor: Lawrence Ferlinghetti.' [iii]: dedication page. [iv]: acknowledgments. [v-vii]: contents pages. [viii]: blank. [ix] - 188: text. [189]: bibliographical note. [190]: after words.

15.8 x 12.3 cm. Perfect bound in stiff white paper wrappers with covers printed so that it appears that a white label has been wrapped around the front to the back covers. Across the front cover: '[on panel] THE | FALL | OF | AMERICA | poems of these states | 1965-1971 | [star] | ALLEN GINSBERG'. Down the spine: '[on panel] The Fall of America [star] Ginsberg [across the base of the spine below frame is the publisher's device]'. Across the back cover: '[in white above the panel] $2.50 | [11 lines inside a frame]'. White wove paper unwatermarked. All edges trimmed.

Contents: Beginning of a Poem of These States — Continuation of a Long Poem of These States — These States, into L.A. — Hiway Poesy LA-Albuquerque-Texas-Wichita — Auto Poesy: On the Lam from Bloomington — Kansas City to Saint Louis — Bayonne Entering NYC — Wings Lifted over the Black Pit — Cleveland, the Flats — A Vow — Autumn Gold — Done, Finished with the Biggest Cock — Bayonne Turnpike to Tuscarora — An Open Window on Chicago — Returning North of Vortex — Kiss Ass — Elegy Ché Guévara — War Profit Litany — Elegy for Neal Cassady — Chicago to Salt Lake by Air — Manhattan 'Thirties Flash — Please Master — A Prophecy — Bixby Canyon — Crossing Nation — Smoke Rolling Down Street — Pertussin — Swirls of Black Dust on Avenue D — Violence — Past Silver Durango over Mexic Sierra Wrinkles — On Neal's Ashes — Going to Chicago — Grant Park: August 28, 1968 — Car Crash — Over Denver Again — Rising over Night-blackened Detroit Streets — Imaginary Universes — To Poe: Over the Planet, Air Albany-Baltimore — Easter Sunday — Falling Asleep in America — Northwest Passage — Sonora Desert-Edge — Reflections in Sleepy Eye — Independence Day — In a Moonlit Hermit's Cabin — Rain-wet Asphalt Heat, Garbage Curbed Cans Overflowing — Death on All Fronts — Memory Gardens — Flash Back — Graffiti 12th Cubicle Men's Room Syracuse Airport — After Thoughts — G.S. Reading Poesy at Princeton — Friday the Thirteenth — D.C. Mobilization — Ecologue — Guru Om — "Have You Seen This Movie?" — Milarepa Taste — Over Laramie — Bixby Canyon Ocean Path Word Breeze — Hum Bom! — September on Jessore Road — After Words [prose]

$2.50. Published Dec. 1972 in an impression of 10,000 copies.

a1.1b *First edition, first printing, black cover*

THE | FALL | OF | AMERICA | poems of these states | 1965-1971 | [star] | ALLEN GINSBERG | '...*same electric lightning South* | *follows this train* | *Apocalypse prophesied* — | *the fall of America* | *signalled from Heaven* —' | City [publisher's device] Lights | the pocket poets series no. 30

15.8 x 12.3 cm. Identical to the above white cover issue except that the covers are printed entirely in white on a black background.

Note: According to the publisher's memory, the white cover with black print is the true first printing. Bob Wilson, an authority on modern first editions through his Phoenix Book Shop in New York City, remembers that half the first printing was with the white covers and half with the black. He received both these issues simultaneously. The compiler has found Wilson's memory to be much more accurate than City Lights' records and it seems likely that they had the first 10,000 printed with 5,000 of each cover.

a1.2 *First edition, second printing (April 1973):* **10,000 copies**

Note: This black cover printing is distinguished from the above by the price of $3.00 on the back cover.

a1.3 *First edition, third printing (January 1974):* 10,000 copies

Note: Third and subsequent printings are identified as such on the verso of the title page.

a1.4 *First edition, fourth printing (June 1976):* 7,500 copies

a1.5 *First edition, fifth printing (Oct. 1980):* 3,000 copies

a1.6 *First edition, sixth printing (Dec. 1983):* 3,000 copies

a1.7 *First edition, seventh printing (Dec. 1986):* 2,000 copies

a1.8 *First edition, eighth printing (Nov. 1988):* 2,500 copies

a1.9 *First edition, ninth printing (April 1991):* 2,500 copies

a1.10 *First edition, tenth printing (Feb. 1993):* 2,000 copies

A27   **IRON HORSE**   **1973**

a1.1 *First edition, first printing*

[in vivid purplish blue (194) over a grainy pink photograph of a train crossing the plains] [in ornamental type] IRON HORSE | [in ornamental type] ALLEN GINSBERG | The Coach House Press 1972

Twenty-eight single leaves, pp. [1-6] 7-52 [53-56]. [1]: half title page. [2]: blank. [3]: title page. [4-6]: blank. 7-[53]: text. [54]: '[publisher's device] Copyright © Allen Ginsberg | Printed in an edition of 1000 copies, January, 1973. | The Coach House Press, Toronto, Canada.' [55-56]: blank.

14.3 x 20.2 cm. Perfect bound in stiff white paper wrappers printed on the front and back covers in yellow, red, blue and silver is a picture of a train. Across the front cover: '[in red and black ornamental type] IRON HORSE | [in red and black ornamental type] ALLEN GINSBERG'. Down the spine all on silver: 'ALLEN GINSBERG IRON HORSE [across the spine] [publisher's device]'. White laid paper unwatermarked with a photograph of a train in pink and white printed on each page. The entire publication printed in vivid purplish blue ink. All edges trimmed.

Contents: Iron Horse

$3.00. Published Jan. 1973 in an impression of 1,000 copies.

a1.2 *First edition, second printing (April 1973):* **1,000 copies**

Note: Second and third printings are identified as "Second Edition" on page 54, includes minor corrections to the text.

a1.3 *First edition, third printing:* quantity unknown.

a2.1 *First American issue (1974)*

[in vivid purplish blue (194) over a grainy pink photograph of a train crossing the plains] [in ornamental type] IRON HORSE I [in ornamental type] ALLEN GINSBERG I City [publisher's device] Lights

Twenty-eight single leaves, pp. [1-6] 7-52 [53-56]. [1]: half title page. [2]: blank. [3]: title page. [4]: 'First City Lights Edition I Printed in the United States of America I © 1974 by Allen Ginsberg I Library of Congress Catalog Card Number: 73-93941 I ISBN: 0-97296-077-9 I CITY LIGHTS BOOKS are published I at the City Lights Bookstore I 261 Columbus Avenue, San Francisco 94133 I Editorial and Publishing Offices: 1562 Grant Avenue, San Francisco'. [5-6]: blank. 7-[53]: text. [54-56]: blank.

13.9 x 20.2 cm. Perfect bound in stiff white paper wrappers printed on the front and back covers in yellow, red, blue and silver is a picture of a train. Across the front cover: '[in red and black ornamental type] IRON HORSE I [in red and black ornamental type] ALLEN GINSBERG'. Down the spine: 'ALLEN GINSBERG IRON HORSE'. Across the back cover: 'A CITY LIGHT BOOK I $3'. White laid paper unwatermarked with a photograph of a train in pink and white printed on each page. The entire publication in vivid purplish blue ink. All edges trimmed.

$3.00. Published March 1974 in an impression of 10,000 copies.

A28   **THE GATES OF WRATH**   **1973**

a1.1 *First edition, first printing, paperbound*

Allen Ginsberg I THE GATES OF WRATH I *Rhymed Poems: 1948-1952* I Grey Fox Press I Bolinas: 1972

Thirty-six single leaves, pp. [i-xii] [1-2] 3-56 [57-60]. [i-ii]: blank. [iii]: title page. [iv]: 'Copyright © 1972 by Allen Ginsberg I [8 lines] I ISBN: 0-912516-01-1 I [2 lines] I First Edition I Grey Fox Books are distributed by Book People, I 2940 Seventh Street, Berkeley, California 97140'. [v]: epigraph. [vi]: second epigraph. [vii]: contents page. [viii]: blank. [ix-xi]: prefatory letter. [xii]: blank. [1] -56: text. [57-60]: blank.

20.4 x 13.5 cm. Perfect bound in stiff white paper wrappers. Across the front cover: '[strong reddish purple (237) band at top] [in white on band] Allen Ginsberg I [in white on band] THE GATES OF WRATH I [photograph of the author superimposed on a second photograph of the author]'. Down the spine: '[in white on strong reddish purple] Allen Ginsberg *Gates of Wrath*'. Across the back cover: '[on strong reddish purple] $2.50 0-912516-01-1'. White laid paper unwatermarked. All edges trimmed.

Contents: This Is the One and Only — A Prefatory Letter [letter to William Carlos Williams] — I Dwelled in Hell on Earth to Write This Rhyme — Woe Unto Thee, Manhatten, Woe to Thee — The Eye Altering Alters All — On Reading William Blake's "The Sick Rose" — A Very Dove — Vision 1948 — Do We Understand Each Other? — The Voice of Rock — Refrain — A Western Ballad [includes music notation] — Sweet Levinsky — A Mad Gleam — Psalm — Complaint of the Skeleton to Time — Stanzas: Written at Night in Radio City — Please Open the Window and Let Me In — The Shrouded Stranger — Bop Lyrics — Fie My Fum — Pull My Daisy [by AG, Jack

Kerouac and Neal Cassady] — Sometime Jailhouse Blues — An Eastern Ballad — Epigram on a Painting of Golgotha — A Dream — Ode to the Setting Sun — Crash — An Imaginary Rose in a Book — In Memoriam *William Cannestra 1922-1950* — Ode: My 24th Year — A Further Proposal — A Lover's Garden — Love Letter — Dakar Doldrums — Hindsight [prose]

$2.50. Published Feb. 14, 1973 in an impression of 3,000 copies.

a1.2 *First edition, second printing, paperbound (April 1973):* 3,000 copies

Note: Second and third printings identified as such on the verso of the title page.

a1.3 *First edition, third printing, paperbound (1979):* quantity unknown

a2.1 *First edition, first printing, hardbound (1973)*

Allen Ginsberg | THE GATES OF WRATH | *Rhymed Poems: 1948-1952* | Grey Fox Press | Bolinas: 1972

$[1-2]^8$ $[3]^4$ $[4-5]^8$ with the colophon page tipped in between the 6th and 7th leaves of the last signature, pp. [i-xii] [1-2] 3-56 [57-60]. As first paperbound printing except for the following: [57]: 'Of 100 copies specially bound by the | Schuberth Bookbindery and signed by | the author, this is number [number and autograph in black ink]'. [58-62]: blank.

22.3 x 15.3 cm. Bound in dark grayish yellow (91) cloth covered boards. Down the spine: '[deep red (13)] ALLEN GINSBERG *The Gates of Wrath*'. White laid paper unwatermarked. The colophon page is white wove paper. White endpapers. All edges trimmed.

These were not sold individually by the publisher, instead the whole edition was sold to Serendipity Books in Berkeley, CA. Published Sept. 1, 1973 in an impression of 106 copies; 100 of which are signed and numbered 1 to 100 and 6 of which are overruns and signed and lettered A-E and G.

A29   **"THE FALL OF AMERICA" WINS A PRIZE**   **1974**

a1. *First edition, signed copies*

[2 rules 9.3 cm.] | *"The Fall of America" Wins a Prize* | [2 rules 9.3 cm.] | [inset initial] Poem book *Fall of America* is time capsule | [25 lines of text]

Single sheet folded twice, pp. [1-4]. [1]: title page. [2-3]: text. [4]: 'This is the text of Allen Ginsberg's acceptance | speech for the National Book Award in Poetry, | delivered by Peter Orlovsky on April 18th, | 1974, at Alice Tully Hall, Lincoln | Center, New York City. | This is one of 126 special copies | numbered 1-100 and lettered | A-Z and signed by | the author. | [number and autograph in black ink] | © Allen Ginsberg 1974 | Gotham Book Mart and Gallery | 41 West 47th Street, New York City'.

45.4 x 29.0 cm. sheet folded twice to form a 22.7 x 14.5 cm. booklet. Pale yellow (89) laid paper watermarked 'Beckett'. All edges trimmed. Issued in a white 15.7 x 24.4 cm. envelope with the return address in the upper left corner 'Gotham Book Mart | 41 West 47 | New York, N.Y. 10036'.

Contents: Text of Acceptance Speech for the National Book Award in Poetry [prose]

$25.00 for lettered copies and $3.50 for numbered copies. Published after April 18, 1974 in an impression of 126 copies, 100 of which are numbered 1 to 100 and 26 of which were lettered A to Z.

a2. *First edition, unsigned copies*

[2 rules 9.3 cm.] | *"The Fall of America" Wins a Prize* | [2 rules 9.3 cm.] | [inset initial] Poem book *Fall of America* is time capsule | [25 lines of text]

Single sheet folded twice, pp. [1-4]. [1]: title page. [2-3]: text. [4]: 'This is the text of Allen Ginsberg's acceptance | speech for the National Book Award in Poetry, | delivered by Peter Orlovsky on April 18th, | 1974, at Alice Tully Hall, Lincoln | Center, New York City. | © Allen Ginsberg 1974 | Gotham Book Mart and Gallery | 41 West 47th Street, New York City'.

45.4 x 29.0 cm. sheet folded twice to form a 22.7 x 14.5 cm. booklet. Light brown (57) wove paper unwatermarked. All edges trimmed.

$1.00. Published after April 18, 1974 in an unknown quantity.

A30   **THE VISIONS OF THE GREAT REMEMBERER**   **1974**

a1.1 *First edition, first printing, paperbound (signed copies)*

The Visions | of the | Great Rememberer | by | Allen Ginsberg | With Letters by Neal Cassady | & Drawings by Basil King | Mulch [publisher's device] *Press | A Haystack Book*

Forty-four single leaves, pp. [i-x] 1-71 [72-78]. [i]: drawing. [ii]: photograph of the author. [iii]: title page. [iv]: '*The Visions of The Great Rememberer,* along with Basil King's draw- | ings, first appeared in *Mulch No. 4.* | Copyright © 1974 by Allen Ginsberg | Letters of Neal Cassady Copyright © 1974 by Carolyn Cassady | Drawings Copyright © 1974 by Basil King | [3 lines] | 1st Printing | Manufactured in the U.S.A. | ISBN: 0-913142-03-4 | LC No.: 74-77758 | MULCH PRESS | P.O. Box 426 | Amherst, Mass. 01002'. [v]: contents page. [vi]: list of illustrations. [vii]: half title page. [viii]: '*opposite: Jack Kerouac*'. [ix]: photograph of Jack Kerouac. [x]: drawing. 1-[73]: text. [74]: blank. [75]: '*This edition | consists of one thousand | copies bound in paper covers of | which seventy-five have been numbered | and signed by the author | This is number* | [number and autographs of author and artist in black ink]'. [76-78]: blank.

21.5 x 13.5 cm. Perfect bound in stiff white paper wrappers printed all in white on a moderate blue (182) background. Across the front cover: '*The Visions of the | Great Rememberer | by Allen Ginsberg | With Letters by | Neal Cassady | & | Drawings by | Basil King* | [publisher's device]'. Down the spine: '*Visions of the Great Rememberer Ginsberg Mulch Press*'. Across the back cover: '*A HAYSTACK BOOK $2.50 | Allen Ginsberg's first book since win- | ning The National Book Award for | Poetry in 1974* | [14 lines]'. White wove paper unwatermarked. All edges trimmed.

Contents: The Visions of the Great Rememberer [prose] — Intrapersonal Relations, Notes on Moods for the Story [prose] — [3 photographs (see also D8)]

$10.00. Published July 28, 1974 in an impression 75 copies, signed as above and another 15 copies signed on the title page for sponsors of Mulch Press.

a2.1 *First edition, first printing, paperbound*

The Visions | of the | Great Rememberer | by | Allen Ginsberg | With Letters by Neal Cassady | & Drawings by Basil King | Mulch [publisher's device] *Press | A Haystack Book*

Forty-four single leaves, pp. [i-x] 1-71 [72-78]. As the first issue, except that here page [75] is blank.

21.4 x 13.5 cm. As the first issue.

$2.50. Published July 28, 1974 in an impression 925 copies.

a.2.2 *First edition, second printing, paperbound (late-1974):* 2,000 copies.

Note: Second printing identified as such on the verso of the title page.

a3.1 *First edition, second printing, hardbound (late-1974)*

The Visions | of the | Great Rememberer | by | Allen Ginsberg | With Letters by Neal Cassady | & Drawings by Basil King | Mulch [publisher's device] *Press | A Haystack Book*

[1]^{16} [2]^4 [3]^8 [4]^{16}, pp. [i-x] 1-51 [52] [xi-xii] [53-54] 55-71 [72-76]. [i]: drawing. [ii]: photograph of the author. [iii]: title page. [iv]: *'The Visions of The Great Rememberer,* along with Basil King's draw- | ings, first appeared in *Mulch No. 4.* | Copyright © 1974 by Allen Ginsberg | Letters of Neal Cassady Copyright © 1974 by Carolyn Cassady | Drawings Copyright © 1974 by Basil King | [3 lines] | 2nd Printing | Manufactured in the U.S.A. | ISBN: Paperbound: 0-913142-03-4 | Hardbound: 0-913142-11-5 | LC No.: 74-77758 | MULCH PRESS | P.O. Box 426 | Amherst, Mass. 01002'. [v]: contents page. [vi]: list of illustrations. [vii]: half title page. [viii]: *'opposite: Jack Kerouac'.* [ix]: photograph of Jack Kerouac. [x]: drawing. 1-[73]: text. [74-76]: blank.

22.3 x 14.6 cm. Bound in grayish purplish blue (204) cloth covered boards. Down the spine in gold: *'Visions of the Great Rememberer Ginsberg Mulch Press'.* White wove paper unwatermarked. Yellowish gray (93) endpapers. All edges trimmed. Issued in a white paper dust jacket printed brilliant blue (177).

Contents: Text identical to the first printing but here with an additional 3 photographs and the deletion of one photograph.

$6.00. Published late-1974 in an impression 500 copies.

Note: This is the second printing of the paperbound issue, but rebound as the first hardbound issue. Identified as second printing on the verso of the title page but it is the only printing which was hardbound.

A31 **ALLEN VERBATIM** **1974**

a1. *First edition, hardbound*

ALLEN LECTURES ON | *VERBATIM* [in 2 lines] POETRY, | POLITICS, | CONSCIOUSNESS | by Allen Ginsberg | edited by Gordon Ball | McGRAW-HILL BOOK COMPANY | New York St. Louis San Francisco | Düsseldorf London Mexico | Sydney Toronto

One hundred forty-four single leaves, pp. [i-vi] vii-x [xi-xii] xiii-xv [xvi] [1-2] 3-269 [270-272]. [i]: half title page. [ii]: card page. [iii]: title page. [iv]: 'Book design: Elaine Gongora I Copyright © 1974 by Gordon Ball. I All passages ascribed to Allen Ginsberg copyright © 1974 by Allen Ginsberg. I All passages ascribed to Robert Duncan copyright © 1974 by McGraw-Hill, Inc. I [4 lines] I 123456789BABA7987654 I Library of Congress Cataloging in Publication Data I [5 lines] I ISBN 0-07-023285-7'. [v]: dedication page. [vi]: blank. vii-viii: acknowledgments. ix-x: credits. [xi-xii]: contents pages. xiii-xv: introduction. [xvi]: blank. [1]-269: text. [270-272]: blank.

21.9 x 14.2 cm. Perfect bound in moderate red (15) cloth covered boards. Down the spine in silver: 'ALLEN VERBATIM GINSBERG [bullet] BALL [across the base of spine is the publisher's device]'. Across the back cover in silver: '0-07-023285-7'. White wove paper unwatermarked. White endpapers. All edges trimmed. Issued in a white paper dust jacket, printed in silver, red and black.

Contents: Identity Gossip [prose] — Eternity [prose] — Words and Consciousness [prose] — Addiction Politics, 1922-1970 [prose] — Crime in the Streets Caused by Addiction Politics [prose] — Narcotics Agents Peddling Drugs [prose] — CIA Involvement with Opium Traffic at Its Source [prose] — Advice to Youth [prose] — Manhattan Thirties Flash — Early Poetic Community [prose] — A Western Ballad — Stanzas: Written at Night in Radio City — Two Bricklayers are Setting the Walls — In Society — A Poem on America — Kerouac [prose] — Poetic Breath, and Pound's Usura [prose] — The Death of Ezra Pound [prose] — War and Peace [prose] — Spring 1971 Anti-War Games — Myths Associated with Science [prose] — Epilogue [prose] — What Would You Do If You Lost It? — [music notation to William Blake's *A Dream*] — [music notation to William Blake's *The Lamb*] — [music notation to William Blake's *The Chimney Sweeper*] — [music notation to William Blake's *Spring*]

$8.95. Published September 1974, printing quantities are not available from the publisher, they have verified that it was out of print on July 26, 1976.

a2. *First edition, paperbound (1975)*

ALLEN LECTURES ON I *VERBATIM* [in 2 lines] POETRY, I POLITICS, I CONSCIOUSNESS I by Allen Ginsberg I edited by Gordon Ball I McGRAW-HILL BOOK COMPANY I New York [bullet] St. Louis [bullet] San Francisco [bullet] I Auckland [bullet] Düsseldorf [bullet] Johannesburg [bullet] I Kuala Lumpur [bullet] London [bullet] Mexico [bullet] Montreal [bullet] I New Delhi [bullet] Panama [bullet] Paris [bullet] Sao Paulo [bullet] I Singapore [bullet] Sydney [bullet] Tokyo [bullet] Toronto

One hundred forty-four single leaves, pp. [i-vi] vii-x [xi-xii] xiii-xv [xvi] [1-2] 3-269 [270-272]. Identical to the hardbound issue except the following. [iv]: 'Book design: Elaine Gongora I Copyright © 1974 by Gordon Ball. I All passages ascribed to Allen Ginsberg copyright © 1974 by Allen Ginsberg. I All passages ascribed to Robert Duncan copyright © 1974 by McGraw-Hill, Inc. I [4 lines] I First McGraw-Hill Paperbacks edition, 1975 I Library of Congress Cataloging in Publication Data I [5 lines] I ISBN 0-07-023295-4'.

20.7 x 13.5 cm. Perfect bound in stiff white paper wrappers. Across the front cover: '[all on a photograph of the author] [in white within a circle] $3.95 I [in vivid reddish orange (34)] ALLEN I [in vivid reddish orange] VERBATIM I [5.6 cm. vivid reddish orange rule] I [in white] LECTURES ON I [in white] POETRY, POLITICS, I [in white] CONSCIOUSNESS I [in white] BY ALLEN GINSBERG I [5.6 cm. vivid reddish orange rule] I [in vivid reddish orange] EDITED BY GORDON BALL I [publisher's device in vivid reddish orange] [in white] McGRAW-HILL PAPERBACKS'. Down the spine: '[in vivid reddish orange] ALLEN VERBATIM [in black] GINSBERG [bullet in vivid reddish orange] [in black] BALL [in vivid reddish orange] [publisher's device]

McGraw-Hill Paperbacks'. Across the back cover: 'Literature I [37 lines] I [in vivid reddish orange] [publisher's device] McGraw-Hill Paperbacks I [1 line]'. White wove paper unwatermarked. All edges trimmed.

$3.95. Published Nov. 1975, printing quantities are not available from the publisher.

A32   **SAD DUST GLORIES**   **1975**

a1.1 *First edition, first printing*

ALLEN GINSBERG I SAD DUST I GLORIES I poems during I work summer I in woods I THE WORKINGMANS PRESS I Berkeley [bullet] 1975

Single gathering of sixteen leaves, pp. [i-iv] 1-27 [28]. [i]: title page. [ii]: '[5 lines] I Copyright © 1975 by Allen Ginsberg I THE WORKINGMANS PRESS is edited I by Barry Gifford and Gary Wilkie I and distributed by Serendipity Books, I 1790 Shattuck Avenue, Berkeley, CA 94709'. [iii]: contents page. [iv]: blank. 1-27: text. [28]: '[printer's device] I Printed by I Creative Arts Printing I Berkeley, California'.

21.4 x 14.0 cm. Stapled twice into stiff grayish greenish yellow (105) paper wrappers. Across the front cover: '[all on a photograph of the author working on a house with a hammer] SAD DUST I GLORIES I poems during I work summer I in woods I ALLEN GINSBERG'. Across back cover: '$2.00 I THE WORKINGMANS PRESS I c/o Serendipity Books I 1790 Shattuck Avenue I Berkeley, CA 94709'. White wove paper unwatermarked. All edges trimmed.

Contents: Green Notebook — Writ in Moonbeam — Energy Vampire — Driving Volkswagon — Mr Sharpe the Carpenter from Marysville — Walking Uphill Woolen — Talking about Fairies — Acorn People — The Moon Followed by Jupiter Thru Pinetrees — To the Dead — When I Sit — The Mood — Kenji Miyazawa — Could You be Here? — Wind Makes Sound — For Sale For Sale

$2.00. Published ca. Sept. 18, 1975 in an impression of an unknown number of copies.

a1.2 *First edition, second printing*

ALLEN GINSBERG I SAD DUST I GLORIES I poems written I work summer I in sierra woods I THE WORKINGMANS PRESS I Berkeley [bullet] 1975

Single gathering of sixteen leaves, pp. [i-iv] 1-27 [28]. [i]: title page. [ii]: '[5 lines] I Second edition 1977 I Copyright © 1975 by Allen Ginsberg I THE WORKINGMANS PRESS is distributed I by Serendipity Books Distribution, I 1636 Ocean View Avenue, Kensington, CA 94707'. [iii]: contents page. [iv]: blank. 1-27: text. [28]: '[printer's device] I Printed by I Creative Arts Printing I Berkeley, California'.

21.5 x 13.7 cm. Stapled twice into stiff pale yellow (89) paper wrappers, printed all in dark yellowish green (137). Across the front cover: '[all on a photograph of the author working on a house with a hammer] SAD DUST I GLORIES I poems written I work summer I in sierra woods I ALLEN GINSBERG'. Across back cover: '$2.50 I [11 lines about the book] I THE WORKINGMANS PRESS I c/o Serendipity Books Distribution I 1636 Ocean View Avenue I Kensington, CA 94707'. White wove paper unwatermarked. All edges trimmed.

$2.50. Published sometime after April 6, 1977 in an impression of an unknown number of copies.

A33   **FIRST BLUES**   **1975**

a1.1a *First edition, first printing, hardbound, signed copies*

[entire page in hollow letters] FIRST BLUES | Rags, Ballads | & Harmonium Songs | 1971-74 | Allen Ginsberg | Full Court Press

Forty-nine single leaves, pp. [1-6] i-v [vi-x] 1-74 [75-82]. [1-2]: blank. [3]: title page. [4]: '[7 lines] | Copyright © Allen Ginsberg 1975 | [5 lines] | ISBN 0-916190-04-8 (cloth) | ISBN 0-916190-05-6 (paper) | Full Court Press, Inc. | 249 Bleecker Street | New York, New York 10014 | [2 lines]'. [5]: dedication page. [6]: blank. i-v: introduction. [vi]: blank. [vii]: contents page. [viii]: blank. [ix]: half title page. [x]: blank. 1-[77]: text. [78]: blank. [79]: biographical note. [80]: blank. [81]: '*This first edition* | *is published in simultaneous cloth and paper bindings,* | *with one hundred special cloth copies* | *numbered 1-100 and signed* | *by the author* | *and twelve hors commerce copies* | *lettered A-L and signed* | *by the author.* | [number stamped in black and autographed in black]'. [82]: blank.

21.5 x 14.2 cm. Perfect bound in olive gray (113) cloth covered boards. Down the spine in silver: 'FIRST BLUES Allen Ginsberg [across the base of the spine within the publisher's device] 3'. White wove paper unwatermarked. White endpapers. All edges trimmed. Issued in a white paper dust jacket printed strong pink (2) and white.

Contents: Explanation of First Blues [prose] — Vomit Express — Going to San Diego — Jimmy Berman Rag — Many Loves — 4 AM Blues [includes music notation] — New York Blues [includes music notation] — NY Youth Call Annunciation [includes music notation] — Come Back Christmas [includes music notation] — Macdougal Street Blues — CIA Dope Calypso [includes music notation] — Troost Street Blues — Put Down Yr Cigarette Rag [includes music notation] — Slack Key Guitar [includes music notation] — Flying to Fiji — Postcard to D---- — Reef Mantra — Siratoka Beach Croon — Bus Ride Ballad Road to Suva [includes music notation] — Tear Gas Rag [includes music notation] — Blue Gossip — The House of the Rising Sun — Everybody Sing [includes music notation] — Prayer Blues [includes music notation] — Broken Bone Blues [includes music notation] — "When I Woke up This Morning — On Reading Dylan's Writings — Stay Away from the White House [includes music notation] — 2 AM Dirty Jersey Blues — Hardon Blues — Dope Fiend Blues — End Vietnam War — Guru Blues [includes music notation]

$15.00. Published ca. Dec. 15, 1975 in an impression of 112 copies, 100 of which are numbered 1 to 100 and 12 of which are lettered A to L.

Note: The colophon page is tipped into the book. The dust jacket is the same used on the unsigned copies as well and so here the price is incorrectly marked $7.95.

a1.1b *First edition, first printing, hardbound, unsigned copies*

[entire page in hollow letters] FIRST BLUES | Rags, Ballads | & Harmonium Songs | 1971-74 | Allen Ginsberg | Full Court Press

Forty-eight single leaves, pp. [1-6] i-v [vi-x] 1-74 [75-80]. Identical to the signed copies but without the tipped in pages [81-82].

21.5 x 14.4 cm.

$7.95. Published ca. Dec. 15, 1975 in an impression of 638 copies.

a1.2b *First edition, second printing, hardbound, unsigned copies (1976):* 500 copies.

Note: Second printing identified as such on the verso of the title page.

a2.1 *First edition, first printing, paperbound*

[entire page in hollow letters] FIRST BLUES | Rags, Ballads | & Harmonium Songs | 1971-74 | Allen Ginsberg | Full Court Press

Forty-eight single leaves, pp. [1-6] i-v [vi-x] 1-74 [75-82]. The same as the First edition, first printing, hardbound, unsigned copies with the following exceptions.

21.2 x 13.7 cm. Perfect bound in stiff white paper wrappers printed all on strong purplish pink (247). Across the front cover: '[all within a white rule border] [light blue (181) letters outlined in white] FIRST BLUES | [light blue letters outlined in white] Rags, Ballads | [light blue letters outlined in white] & Harmonium Songs | [light blue numbers outlined in white] 1971-74 | [light blue numbers outlined in white] Allen Ginsberg | [in white] Full Court Press'. Down the spine in white: 'FIRST BLUES Allen Ginsberg [across the base of spine within the publisher's device] 3'. Across the back cover: '[all within a white rule border] *$3.50* | *ISBN 0-916190-05-6*'. White wove paper unwatermarked. All edges trimmed.

$3.50. Published ca. Dec. 15, 1975 in an impression of 1,500 copies.

a2.2 *First edition, second printing, paperbound (1976):* 2,000 copies.

Note: Second and subsequent printings are identified as such on the verso of the title page.

a2.3 *First edition, third printing, paperbound (Dec. 6, 1981):* quantity unknown.

A34   **TO EBERHART FROM GINSBERG**   **1976**

a1. *First edition, first printing, signed copies*

TO EBERHART FROM GINSBERG | A Letter about HOWL 1956 | [the rest in moderate blue (182) until noted] [3 rules 8.4 cm. long] | AN EXPLANATION BY ALLEN GINS- | BERG OF HIS PUBLICATION *HOWL* | AND RICHARD EBERHART'S *NEW* | *YORK TIMES* ARTICLE "WEST COAST | RHYTHMS" TOGETHER WITH COM- | MENTS BY BOTH POETS AND RELIEF | ETCHINGS BY JEROME KAPLAN | [3 rules 8.4 cm. long] | [in black] THE PENMAEN PRESS 1976

[1-6]⁴, pp. [1-6] 7-45 [46-48]. [1]: half title page. [2]: blank. [3]: title page. [4]: '[publisher's device] | "West Coast Rhythms" copyright © 1956 by *The New York Times* | *Company*. Reprinted by permission. Remaining textual matter and | prints copyright © 1976 by the Penmaen Press. All rights reserved. | ISBN: 0-915778-09-2 (signed hardcover) | ISBN: 0-915778-08-4 (unsigned softcover) | ISBN: 0-915778-07-6 (unsigned hardcover) | Penmaen Press Books are published by Michael McCurdy at the Pen- | maen Press, Old Sudbury Road, Lincoln, Massachusetts 01773.' [5]: second half title page. [6]: blank. 7-45: text. [46]: blank. [47]: 'This first edition of *To Eberhart from Ginsberg* was printed | & published by Michael McCurdy at the Penmaen Press | in Lincoln, Massachusetts, and completed in March, | 1976. Of an edition of 1500, 300 are hardbound, numbered | and signed by Richard Eberhart and Allen Ginsberg. | [9 lines] | This is number [number in blue ink] . | [autographs in blue and black ink]'. [48]: blank.

24.0 x 16.1 cm. Quarter bound in dark blue (183) cloth with denim cloth covered boards. Up the front cover along the spine on the binding cloth in silver: 'TO EBERHART FROM GINSBERG'. Down the spine in silver: 'TO EBERHART FROM GINSBERG PENMAEN PRESS'. White laid paper watermarked: 'WARREN'S | OLDE STYLE'. White endpapers. Issued in a clear plastic dust jacket.

Contents: More Explanations Twenty Years Later [prose] — A Letter to Eberhart [prose] — [reproduction of a page of the original holograph letter]

$20.00 later raised to $25.00 for the signed copies, $12.00 for the unsigned copies. Published in early June 1976 in an impression of 338 copies, 300 copies of which are signed and numbered 1 to 300. A few of the original unsigned copies were signed by the author and illustrator and initialed instead of numbered and then given to friends, 'hors commerce' and at least one copy was neither signed nor initialled.

Note: The back cover of the paperback edition incorrectly lists the price of the limited edition as $15.00. Although the colophon gives the date of publication as March 1976 th book was not available until early June 1976. The book was signed by Ginsberg on Feb. 23, 1976. The book went to the bindery May 13, 1976 and on May 31, 1976 the book was still at the bindery, this according to correspondence with the publisher at that time. The limited edition was available for sale with a handmade Plexiglas slipcase but according to the publisher "there were no calls for Hauser's Plexiglas case!" and so none were sold.

a2.1a *First edition, first printing, paperbound*

TO EBERHART FROM GINSBERG | A Letter about HOWL 1956 | [the rest in moderate blue (182) until noted] [3 rules 8.4 cm. long] | AN EXPLANATION BY ALLEN GINS- | BERG OF HIS PUBLICATION *HOWL* | AND RICHARD EBERHART'S *NEW* | *YORK TIMES* ARTICLE "WEST COAST | RHYTHMS" TOGETHER WITH COM- | MENTS BY BOTH POETS AND RELIEF | ETCHINGS BY JEROME KAPLAN | [3 rules 8.4 cm. long] | [in black] THE PENMAEN PRESS 1976

Twenty-four single leaves, pp. [1-6] 7-45 [46-48]. The collation is identical to the signed copies but is not signed or numbered.

23.2 x 15.5 cm. Perfect bound in stiff white paper wrappers. Across the front cover and all in white on black unless noted: 'TO EBERHART | FROM GINSBERG | [light gray (264)] AN HISTORIC DOCUMENT | [light gray] FROM THE BEAT ERA PUBLISHED | [light gray] NOW FOR THE FIRST TIME | [two photographs of Eberhart and Ginsberg] | Allen Ginsberg's remarkable 1956 letter | to Richard Eberhart and Eberhart's | "West Coast Rhythms" | with comments by both poets'. Down the spine in white on black: 'TO EBERHART FROM GINSBERG PENMAEN PRESS'. Across the back cover: '$5 | [2 rules 10.4 cm. long] | [15 lines] | [10.4 cm. rule] | Printed by letterpress with original prints, this book com- | bines an important text with an attractive format. A hard- | cover edition limited to 300 numbered copies signed by | each poet is also available. Bound in brushed denim, it can | be obtained for $15 through your book dealer or directly | from the Penmaen Press, *Lincoln, MA 01773.* | [2 rules 10.4 cm. long] | The Penmaen Press | *cover photographs by Gerard Malanga* ISBN 0-915778-08-4'. White wove paper unwatermarked. All edges trimmed.

$5.00. Published in early June 1976 in an impression of 989 copies, but of these 276 were rebound as the following:

a2.1b *First edition, first printing, paperbound rebound as hardbound*

[1-6]^4, pp. [1-6] 7-45 [46-48].

23.2 x 15.7 cm. Bound in moderate greenish blue (173) cloth or moderate bluish green (164) [see note below] covered boards. Up the front cover along the spine in silver: 'TO EBERHART FROM GINSBERG'. Down the spine in silver: 'TO EBERHART FROM GINSBERG PENMAEN PRESS'. White laid paper watermarked: 'WARREN'S | OLDE STYLE'. White endpapers. Issued in a clear plastic dust jacket.

$10.00. Issued over a period of a few months after August 1976 in an impression of 276 copies.

Note: The publisher states that 160 copies were bound in green Seta cloth (164) and that 116 copies were bound in blue English Seta cloth (173). Some copies were also shipped lacking the clear plastic dust jacket.

A35   **JOURNALS EARLY FIFTIES EARLY SIXTIES**   **1977**

a1.1 *First edition, first printing, hardbound*

JOURNALS | EARLY FIFTIES EARLY SIXTIES | *Allen Ginsberg* | EDITED BY GORDON BALL | *Grove Press, Inc., New York*

One hundred sixty-eight single leaves, pp. [i-vi] vii-xxx [1-2] 3-302 [303-306]. [i-ii]: blank. [iii]: half title page. [iv]: card page. [v]: title page. [vi]: 'Copyright © 1977 by Allen Ginsberg | [3 lines] | First Edition 1977 | First Printing 1977 | ISBN: 0-394-41349-0 | Grove Press ISBN: 0-8021-0134-8 | [4 lines] | GROVE PRESS, INC., 196 WEST HOUSTON STREET, NEW YORK, N.Y. 10014'. vii: appreciation. [viii]: blank. [ix]-xii: contents pages. xiii-xxx: introduction. [1]-302: text. [303-306]: blank.

24.2 x 16.3 cm. Bound in black cloth covered boards. Down the spine: '[in vivid purplish blue (194)] *Allen Ginsberg* [in 2 lines in silver] JOURNALS | EARLY FIFTIES EARLY SIXTIES [in 1 line in vivid purplish blue] *Grove Press*'. White wove paper unwatermarked. White endpapers. All edges trimmed. Issued in a white paper dust jacket printed in black, brownish orange and strong orange.

Contents: [introduction contains many quotes from AG] — Notes After An Evening With William Carlos Williams — And One Time Is All Time — The Wisdom Of Solomon (Carl) — A Novel — Up From My Books — Young Men In Their Prime Are — Green Valentine Blues — I Think In 1948 — A Motif A Theme — Serenade — Don't Tell Me The Truth — America — Already Time For Your Elegy, Dear Natalie? — Drinking My Tea — The Sparrow Shits — Mayan Head In A — Looking Over My Shoulder — I Didn't Know The Names — I Slapped The Mosquito — Reading Hiku — A Frog Floating — On The Porch — Another Year — The First Thing I Looked For — My Old Desk — My Early Journal — My Mother's Ghost — I Quit Shaving — The Madman — Cities Of Boys — Lying On My Side — On The Fifteenth Floor — A Hardon In New York — The Moon Over The Roof — My God! — Truth — I Beg You To Come Back And Be Cheerful — Beauty Kills — I Am The Flames [By Jack Kerouac And AG] — That Every Leaf Wave On The Tree — O Bullshit Artist Of Reality — America Is Covered With Lies — The Nameless Gives Names — Shot In The Back By A Fallen Leaf — Sunrise — Psalm IV — Man's Glory — When I Close My Eyes I Know, When I — Kerouac on Ayahuasca — The Eye Of Everything — We Will Widen Our Consciousness Till — Death Which Is The Mother Of The Universe, From Whose Black Lips The — "I Want To Be Wanted" Sings Marie — Politics On Opium — Subliminal — I Write This Type Poetry On Heroin — To Put A Microphone To The Sun — Hurrah For The American Revolution! — Poetry Is A Dynamo In The Void — Laugh Gas-12? — The Clown Of Subjective Being — Police — Otherwise Earth's Future Is An Upside-Down Candle — "I Saw The Sunflower Monkeys Of The Moon" — Lying In Bed — There's A Lot Of Nonsense In Those Snowballs — Policewomen Looking Up The Tragic Brown Ass Of Billie Holiday — Scrap Leaves — What's Left? Nothing But This Body With Reproductive Organs — The Great Snake From 0000 To 1961 Which Many Have Entered & Left — Artaud Expresses Himself — ...The Beasts! They Would Not Even — Agh! The Ants Work Hard — Aux Deux Magots I Did Not Destroy — Message From Subconscious--Which — ...At This Moment Tibet Which Possessed All — ...You Are Me, God — One Day — Bay Of Pigs — Death Is The Silence — To Have To Leave Life — Funeral Vomit — Mad Jump — Snicker Snoop — Take Them Out & Chop Their Hands Off — And There To Hear My Daughters Sing — All Nobility Leads To The

Tomb — The Din-Ringing Of Myriad Goatskin Water Sellers — The Sadness Of Goodbye Again--The Melancholy Sunset — Acropolis Like Any Golgotha — At Nite, Walking Around The Old Streets Under Acropolis — This Morning A Letter From A Poet — Sitting On The Third Large Grey Marble Stoop Leaning On A Mossy Column — Three Roads — The Names Of Cities Above, A Poem Of Peter — Quack Quack Quack Quack Quack — Old Meaning — Paris In Bronze — Face To Face With Those Beautys Too Awful For Logos — I Comb My Hair In The Mirror — Hymn To The Jukebox — Six Years I Eat — Israel — To Peter Orlovsky — A Little Bit Of Joy — Salt Slagheaps Move Down On Sodom — Between Island & Pallia — Floating Bodiless Above The World — What Was The War In Korea? — The Moon Of The Cuban — Rhythmic Paradigm — Lying Here On The Couch — There Was A Fair Young Maiden — On The Good Ship Lollipop — Jew Song — Peter Orlovsky, Ice Cream, Snot, Heroin, Movies — Hydro Hotel, Granite Floor — [photographs (see also D10)]

$10.00. Published Sept. 7, 1977 in an impression of 7,500 copies.

a2.1 *First printing, paperbound (1978)*

JOURNALS | EARLY FIFTIES EARLY SIXTIES | *Allen Ginsberg* | EDITED BY GORDON BALL | *Grove Press, Inc., New York*

One hundred seventy-six single leaves, pp. [i-vi] vii [viii-ix] x-xxx [1-2] 3-313 [314-322]. [i]: half title page. [ii]: blank. [iii]: card page. [iv]: blank. [v]: title page. [vi]: 'Copyright © 1977 by Allen Ginsberg | [3 lines] | Evergreen Edition 1978 | First Printing 1978 | ISBN: 0-394-17034-2 | Grove Press ISBN: 0-8021-4156-0 | [13 lines] | GROVE PRESS, INC., 196 WEST HOUSTON STREET, NEW YORK, N.Y. 10014'. vii: appreciation. [viii]: blank. [ix]-xii: contents pages. xiii-xxx: introduction. [1]-302: text. 303-313: index. [314]: blank. [315-318]: advertisement. [319-322]: blank.

23.4 x 15.5 cm. Perfect bound in stiff white paper wrappers. Across the front cover: '[all on a photograph of the author which also covers the spine] [publisher's device in white] | [in white] E-704 | [in white] $6.95 | [in 1 line] [in brownish orange (54)] Allen [in 5 lines all in white] "An utterly fascinating | revelation of one | of our most important poets, | it is a remarkable work." | —*Washington Post* | [brownish orange] Ginsberg | [brilliant blue (177)] Journals | [strong brown (55)] Early Fifties | [strong brown] Early Sixties | [white] Edited by Gordon Ball'. Across the spine: '[publisher's device in white] | [white] Grove | [white] Press | [down the spine] [brownish orange] Allen Ginsberg [brilliant blue] Journals [across the spine in white] E-704'. Across the back cover: '[all in white on brilliant blue] Allen Ginsberg [publisher's device] | Journals E-704 | Early Fifties — Early Sixties $6.95 | Edited by Gordon Ball | [2 columns of 42 and 39 lines]'. White wove paper unwatermarked. All edges trimmed.

Contents: As the first edition with the addition of a blurb by Allen Ginsberg on the back cover.

$6.95. Published ca. March 1978 in an impression of an unknown number of copies.

a2.2 *Second printing, paperbound (1992)*

JOURNALS | EARLY FIFTIES EARLY SIXTIES | *Allen Ginsberg* | EDITED BY GORDON BALL | [publisher's device] | *Grove Press* | *New York*

One hundred seventy-six single leaves, pp. [i-vi] vii [viii-ix] x-xxx [1-2] 3-313 [314-322]. [i-ii]: blank. [iii]: half title page. [iv]: blank. [v]: title page. [vi]: 'Copyright © 1977 by Allen Ginsberg | [4 lines] | Published by Grove Press | A division of Grove Press, Inc. | 841 Broadway | New York, NY 10003-4793 | [14 lines] | First Grove Press Edition 1977 | First Evergreen Edition 1978 | Second Evergreen Edition 1992 | 1 3 5 7 9 10 8 6 4 2'. vii: appreciation. [viii]: blank. [ix]-xii: contents pages. xiii-xxx: reader's guide. [1]-313: text. [314-322]: blank.

22.7 x 15.2 cm. Perfect bound in stiff white paper wrappers, printed all on light yellow green (119). Across the front cover: 'jou [in strong red (12)] r [in black] nals | [illustration of a figure with glasses on a very light greenish blue (171) irregular lozenge-shaped background] [up the left edge in 2 lines] ear [in red] l [in black] y sixti [in red] e [in black] s | Edited by Gordon Ball [down the right edge in 2 lines] [in red] al [in black] l [in red] e [in black] n [in red] g [in black] i [in red] n [in black] s [in red] be [in black] r [in red] g | With illustrations by the author | [across the bottom] ea [in red] r [in black] ly fif [in red] t [in black] ies'. Down the spine: '[in red] journals [in black] early fifties [in red] early sixties [in black] allen ginsberg [across the spine in red] [publisher's device] | [down the spine in red] Grove Press'. Across the back cover: '$11.95 | [23 lines about the book] | [publisher's device in red] | AN EVERGREEN BOOK | Published by Grove Press | [3 lines] [zebra bar code within white rectangle contains the following 3 sets of numbers] 90000> | 9 780802 133472 | ISBN 0-8021-3347-9'. White wove paper unwatermarked. All edges trimmed.

$11.95. Published Sept. 1992 in a quantity undisclosed by the publisher.

A36   **AS EVER**   **1977**

a1. *First edition, hardbound*

[ornamental type on sloping base line] As Ever | The | Collected | Correspondence of | Allen Ginsberg | & | Neal Cassady | Foreword by Carolyn Cassady | Edited with an Introduction by Barry Gifford | Afterword by Allen Ginsberg | [10.3 cm. rule] | Creative Arts Book Company | [publisher's device]

[1-15]^8, pp. [1-5] i-vi [vii] 1-227 [228]. [1]: half title page. [2]: blank. [3]: title page. [4]: 'AS EVER | [10.9 cm. rule] | Copyright © 1977 by Allen Ginsberg and Carolyn Cassady | Introduction copyright © 1977 by Barry Gifford | [18 lines] | ISBN 0-916870-08-1 (paper) | 0-916870-09-X (cloth) | Library of Congress Card Catalog Number 77-082182 | Published by Creative Arts Book Company | 833 Bancroft Way, Berkeley, California 94710 | [design of Buddha's footprint]'. [5]: contents page. i: reproduction of postcard from Neal Cassady. ii: reproduction of letter from Allen Ginsberg. iii: editor's note & acknowledgments. iv: foreword. v-vi: introduction. vii: blank. 1-218: text. 219: afterword. [220]: blank. 221-227: index. [228]: card page.

22.8 x 15.2 cm. Bound in moderate green (145) cloth covered boards. Across the front cover in gold: '[ornamental type on sloping base line] As Ever | [design of Buddha's footprint]'. Down the spine in gold: 'AS EVER Ginsberg/Cassady Edited by Barry Gifford Creative Arts'. White wove paper unwatermarked. White endpapers. All edges trimmed. Issued in frosted white glassine dust jacket.

Contents: [letters to Neal Cassady, Carolyn Cassady and Jack Kerouac throughout] — In Judgement — Bare Skin is My Wrinkled — Blind Visaged Worms of Time — An Interesting Couple — Put a Kiss and a Tear — I Came Home from the Movies with Nothing on my Mind — Sakamuni Coming Out from the Mountain — Fragment 1957 — Los Gatos — Afterword [prose]

$15.00. Published Dec. 1977 in an impression of 1,000 copies.

a2. *First edition, paperbound*

[ornamental type on sloping base line] As Ever | The | Collected | Correspondence of | Allen Ginsberg | & | Neal Cassady | Foreword by Carolyn Cassady | Edited with an Introduction by Barry Gifford | Afterword by Allen Ginsberg | [10.3 cm. rule] | Creative Arts Book Company | [publisher's device]

One hundred twenty single leaves, pp. [1-5] i-vi [vii] 1-227 [228]. As first issue.

21.3 x 14.5 cm. Perfect bound in stiff white paper wrappers. Across the front cover: '[16.2 x 12.0 cm. vivid reddish orange (34) panel framed by red and black borders, the panel becoming a darker orange at the bottom] [on this panel is the following] [extending beyond the borders of the panel at top, left and right edges in ornamental type outlined in white on a sloping base line] As Ever I The I Collected I Correspondence of I Allen Ginsberg I & I Neal Cassady I [below panel] [12.3 cm. rule] I Foreword by Carolyn Cassady I Edited with an Introduction by Barry Gifford I Afterword by Allen Ginsberg I [12.3 cm. rule]'. Down the spine: '[1.0 x 18.8 cm. vivid reddish orange panel framed by red and black borders, the panel becoming darker orange at the base of the spine] [all on the panel] AS EVER Ginsberg/Cassady Edited by Barry Gifford Creative Arts'. Across the back cover: '$5.95 I [18.9 x 11.9 cm. vivid reddish orange panel framed with red and black borders, the panel becoming darker at the bottom] [7.1 x 10.0 cm. black and white photograph of the authors framed by black and red borders] [up the right side of the photograph and outside of the borders] PHOTO 1963 BY CHARLES PLYMELL, COURTESY OF CITY LIGHTS. I [ornamental type outlined in white on a sloping base line] As Ever I [9.8 cm. rule] I [16 lines] I Creative Arts Book Company [publisher's device] I [9.8 cm. rule] [below panel] ISBN 0-916870-08-1'. White wove paper unwatermarked. All edges trimmed.

$5.95. Published Dec. 10, 1977 in an impression of ca. 12,500 copies.

A37 **MIND BREATHS** **1978**

a1. *First edition, hardbound*

MIND I BREATHS I Poems 1972-1977 I *ALLEN GINSBERG* I "Time after time for such a journey none but iron pens I Can write And adamantine leaves receive nor can the man who goes I The journey obstinate refuse to write time after time" I *—Wm. Blake* I [publisher's device] I CITY LIGHTS BOOKS I San Francisco

$[1-2]^{16} [3]^{4} [4-5]^{16}$, pp. [i-viii] 1-123 [124-128]. [i-ii]: blank. [iii]: title page. [iv]: '© 1977 by Allen Ginsberg I *Library of Congress Cataloging in Publication Data:* I [5 lines] I ISBN: 0-87286-092-2 I [3 lines]'. [v]: dedication page. [vi]: acknowledgments. [vii-viii]: contents page. 1-123: text. [124]: blank. [125-126]: bibliography. [127]: advertisement for 38 titles in 46 lines. [128]: advertisement for 39 titles in 45 lines.

16.6 x 12.7 cm. Bound in strong red (12) cloth covered boards. Across the front cover: 'MIND I BREATHS I *ALLEN GINSBERG*'. Down the spine: 'MIND BREATHS Allen Ginsberg City Lights'. White wove paper unwatermarked. White endpapers. All edges trimmed. Issued in a white paper dust jacket printed in black and white.

Contents: Ayers Rock Uluru Song — Xmas Gift — Thoughts Sitting Breathing [includes music notation] — "What Would You Do If You Lost It?" — Yes and It's Hopeless — Under the World There's a Lot of Ass, a Lot of Cunt — Returning to the Country for a Brief Visit — Night Gleam — What I'd Like To Do — On Neruda's Death — Mind Breaths — Flying Elegy — Teton Village — Sweet Boy, Gimme Yr Ass — Jaweh and Allah Battle — Manifesto — Sad Dust Glories — Ego Confession — Mugging — Who Runs America? — We Rise on Sun Beams and Fall in the Night — Written on Hotel Napkin: Chicago Futures — Hospital Window — Hadda Be Playing on the Jukebox — Sickness Blues [includes music notation] — Come All Ye Brave Boys — Cabin in the Rockies — Gospel Noble Truths — Rolling Thunder Stones — Two Dreams — Don't Grow Old [includes music notation for 'Father Death Blues' segment] — Land O' Lakes, Wisc. — "Drive All Blames into One" — Haunting Poe's Baltimore — Contest of Bards — The Rune [includes music notation] — I Lay Love on My Knee — Love Replied - [prose blurb on back cover of dust jacket]

$7.50. Published Jan. 1, 1978 in an impression of 300 copies.

Note: Although the publication date of 1977 is printed on the copyright page, the book was not actually published until Jan. 1, 1978 according to a letter from Lawrence Ferlinghetti (the publisher) to AG dated Jan. 6, 1978: "...we just sent it in to Pulitzer, with publication date of Jan. 1, 1978, since the review copies didn't get out until then anyway, and it will be reviewed as a 1978 book. (In each copy we sent Pulitzer we put a card stating that the publication date was/is Jan. 1, 1978). ((The pub deadline for 1977 was Nov. 1.))"

a2.1 *First edition, first printing, paperbound*

MIND I BREATHS I Poems 1972-1977 I *ALLEN GINSBERG* I "Time after time for such a journey none but iron pens I Can write And adamantine leaves receive nor can the man who goes I The journey obstinate refuse to write time after time" I *— Wm. Blake* I [publisher's device] I CITY LIGHTS BOOKS I San Francisco

Sixty-eight single leaves, pp. [i-viii] 1-123 [124-128]. As first issue.

15.9 x 12.3 cm. Perfect bound in stiff white paper wrappers with covers printed so that it appears that a white label has been wrapped around the front to the back covers. Across the front cover: '[above the panel in white] THE POCKET POETS SERIES I [on panel] MIND I [on panel] BREATHS I [on panel] POEMS 1972-1977 I [on panel] *ALLEN GINSBERG* I [below the panel in white] NUMBER THIRTY FIVE'. Down the spine: '[on panel] MIND BREATHS Allen Ginsberg City Lights'. Across the back cover: '[above the panel in white] $3.00 I [all on panel] MIND BREATHS: Australian songsticks measure oldest I [21 lines] I A.G. *September 23, 1977'*. White wove paper unwatermarked. All edges trimmed.

$3.00. Published January 1, 1978 in an impression of 10,000 copies.

a2.2 *First edition, second printing, paperbound (June 1978):* 10,000 copies.

Note: Second and subsequent printings are identified as such on the verso of the title page.

a2.3 *First edition, third printing, paperbound (Jan. 1985):* 3,000 copies.

a2.4 *First edition, fourth printing, paperbound (Aug. 1991):* 1,000 copies.

a2.5 *First edition, fifth printing, paperbound (Oct. 1992):* 1,500 copies.

| **A38** | **CARELESS LOVE** | **1978** |

[medium gray (265)] Allen Ginsberg I CARELESS LOVE I The Red Ozier Press, Madison

Single gathering of ten leaves, pp. [1-20]. [1-2]: blank. [3]: half title page. [4]: blank. [5]: title page. [6]: '[all in medium gray] These poems previously appeared in *Gay* I *Sunshine.* Copyright Nineteen hundred & I seventy-eight by Allen Ginsberg.' [7-8]: blank. [9-15]: text. [16]: blank. [17]: '[all in medium gray] *These poems were printed for the benefit of the Jack* I *Kerouac School of Disembodied Poetics at Boulder,* I *part of the Naropa Institute. This chapbook is the* I *joyous first piece to be printed at the old Washington* I *Hotel, Six thirty-six West Washington Avenue, Ma* I *dison, Wisconsin, new home of the Red Ozier Press.* I *Record-breaking ice, snow & cold helped by keeping* I *us inside & busy making books by hand. There are* I *two hundred & eighty copies in this edition, with ten* I *patron copies. Thanks to Mark Glass; April, 1978.* I [numbered in black ink]'. [18-20]: blank.

20.7 x 13.5 cm. Sewn into dark grayish blue (187) wrappers which are marbleized on one side, the wrapper is 20.7 x 67.2 cm. and folded 4 times so that only the marbleized surface shows. White laid paper unwatermarked. Top edges trimmed.

Contents: I Lay Love on My Knee — Love Replies

$20.00. Published April 1978 in an impression of 290 copies, 280 of which are numbered 1 to 280 and 10 additional copies which are signed but unnumbered.

A39   **MOSTLY SITTING HAIKU**   **1978**

MOSTLY SITTING HAIKU I Allen Ginsberg

Single gathering of fourteen leaves, pp. [i-iv] [1-2] 3-23 [24]. [i]: title page. [ii]: 'Copyright © 1978 Allen Ginsberg I First Edition I Some of the poems included here I first appeared in LOKA and in I MIND BREATHS (City Lights, I 1977), for which thanks. I FROM HERE PRESS I box 2702 XTRAS #6 I paterson Member COSMEP I nj 07509 ISBN 0-89120-010-X'. [iii]: contents page. [iv]: blank. [1]: half title page. [2]: blank. 3-23: text. [24]: blank.

21.6 x 13.8 cm. Stapled twice in stiff pale orange yellow (73) paper wrappers. Across the front cover: 'MOSTLY SITTING HAIKU I Allen Ginsberg'. Across the back cover: 'Allen Ginsberg $1.50 I MOSTLY SITTING HAIKU I [26 lines about the book] I XTRAS #6 ISBN 0-89120-010-X'. White wove paper unwatermarked. All edges trimmed.

Contents: Mostly Sitting Haiku — Chögyam Trungpa's Crazy Wisdom Lectures — Cabin in the Rockies — Park Avenue Paterson-2AM — The Withered Purple Roses Droop — Land O' Lakes, Wisc. Seminary — Sitting — For Creeley's Ear

$1.50. Published May 13, 1978 in an impression of 500 copies.

A40   **PLUTONIAN ODE**   **1978**

Plutonian Ode I by Allen Ginsberg

Four single sheets, ll. [1-4]. [1-4]: text.

27.9 x 21.6 cm. Inserted in stiff light orange yellow (70) paper wrappers on the front cover of which is the title page. Across the back cover: 'Copyright 1978 by Allen Ginsberg [wavy rule] All rights reserved'. Light orange yellow (70) wove paper unwatermarked. All edges trimmed.

Contents: Plutonian Ode

Distributed free. Published Aug. 3, 1978 in an impression of 400 copies, printed by the Renaissance Press, Boulder, CO, for the Rocky Flats Protest Benefit.

Note: The entire publication is a reproduction of calligraphy, not AG's.

A41   **POEMS ALL OVER THE PLACE**   **1978**

POEMS ALL OVER THE PLACE, I MOSTLY 'SEVENTIES I ALLEN GINSBERG I "Meeting, the two old friends laugh aloud; I In the grove, fallen leaves are many." I CHERRY VALLEY EDITIONS I 1978

Thirty-two single leaves, pp. [1-10] 11-61 [62-64]. [1]: title page. [2]: '(c) Copyright 1978 by Allen Ginsberg | All rights reserved | First edition. | [10 lines] | ISBN 0-916156-31-1 | ISBN 0-916156-32-X ltd. ed. | [2 lines]'. [3]: dedication page. [4]: blank. [5]: acknowledgments. [6]: blank. [7]: contents page. [8]: blank. [9]-61: text. [62-64]: advertisements.

21.4 x 13.6 cm. Perfect bound in stiff white paper wrappers. Across the front cover: '[all in facsimile holograph] POEMS | ALL [in 2 lines] OVER | THE [in 1 line] PLACE | [wavy squiggle] MOSTLY 'SEVENTIES [wavy squiggle] | Allen Ginsberg | Cherry Valley | Editions | 1978'. Down the spine: 'POEMS ALL OVER THE PLACE [bullet] ALLEN GINSBERG [bullet] C.V. Ed.' Across the back cover: 'ISBN 0-916156-31-1 $3.00 | [16.4 x 10.9 cm. photograph of the author] | MALANGA | CHERRY VALLEY EDITIONS'. White wove paper unwatermarked. All edges trimmed.

Contents: Introductory Comments [prose] — The Names — Fragment: The Names — Nov. 23, 1963: Alone — Silent Tingling [by Andre Vosnesensky, translated by AG and Vosnesensky] — These States-To Miami Convention — Who — On Illness — News Bulletin — Thoughts on a Breath — Reading French Poetry — C'mon Jack — Pussy Blues — Land O' Lakes, Wisconsin: Jajryana Seminary — For Creeley's Ear — "Junk Mail" — "You Might Get in Trouble" — T.S. Eliot Entered My Dreams — From Journals — Ballade of Poisons — Golden Court — After Basho — About the Author [autobiographical prose]

$3.00. Published Oct. 25, 1978 in an impression of 3959 copies and reprinted once. The second printing is not distinguishable from the first.

Note: Twenty-six copies of the above were signed by AG and lettered A to Z. These were sold for $25.00 each by the publisher.

A42   **OLD POND SONG**   **1979**

[all in strong red (12)] OLD POND SONG | by Allen Ginsberg | Introduction by Elsa Dorfman | Photographs by Rosalie Post | [publisher's device] | FIREFLY PRESS

$[1-2]^8$, pp. [1-32]. [1-2]: blank. [3]: title page. [4]: '[all in strong red] Music and text copyright © 1979 by Allen Ginsberg. | Photographs copyright © 1979 by Rosalie Post and Elsa Dorfman. | All rights reserved. | FIREFLY PRESS 49 PUTNAM AVENUE CAMBRIDGE MA 02139'. [5]: introduction. [6-25]: text. [26]: photograph of AG tipped in. [27]: '[all in strong red] This is number [number in black ink] of an edition of 50, each copy numbered and | signed by the poet. Designed and hand-printed by Carl Kay with | hand-set Bembo type of Mohawk Superfine paper on a Poco proof | press. Photographs by Rosalie Post. Photograph of Allen Ginsberg | by Elsa Dorfman. Handbound by Daniel Kelm and Peter Geraty in | quarter-cloth and Japanese paper over boards. Frog by Sengai (1750- | 1837). Many thanks to all friends of Firefly Press. Printed Spring, | 1979, while the kitten found the catnip and ate it all in one day. | [autographed in black ink]'. [28-29]: blank. [30]: design of a frog in dark greenish gray (156). [31-32]: blank.

16.2 x 20.9 cm. Quarter bound in moderate red (15) cloth with dark grayish yellow (91) paper covered boards. Across the front cover: '[in dark greenish gray] OLD POND SONG | [in dark greenish gray] Allen Ginsberg | [design of frog in moderate red] '. White wove paper unwatermarked. Moderate brown (58) endpapers.* All edges trimmed.

Contents: Old Pond Song [music notation included]

$35.00. Published Spring [ca. April 20] 1979 in an impression of 50 copies.

*Note: An unknown number of these copies were issued with greenish gray (155) endpapers.

A43   **COMPOSED ON THE TONGUE**   **1980**

a1.1 *First edition, first printing*

Allen Ginsberg I COMPOSED I ON THE TONGUE I Edited by Donald Allen I Grey Fox Press I Bolinas [bullet] California

Eighty-four single leaves, pp. [i-viii] 1-153 [154-160]. [i]: half title page. [ii]: blank. [iii]: title page. [iv]: 'Copyright © 1980, 1976, 1975, 1974, 1971, by Allen Ginsberg I [19 lines] I ISBN 0-912516-29-1 pbk.' [v]: contents page. [vi]: blank. [vii]: second half title page. [viii]: blank. 1-153: text. [154]: blank. [155]: 'GREY FOX BOOKS I [38 lines]'. [156-160]: blank.

21.5 x 14.0 cm. Perfect bound in stiff white paper wrappers printed all light gray (264). Across the front cover is a vivid red (11) panel with white border on which is printed the following in white: 'Allen Ginsberg I COMPOSED I ON THE TONGUE'. Down the spine in white: 'Allen Ginsberg [bullet] *Composed on the Tongue* Grey Fox'. Across the back cover in white: '$5.95 ISBN 0-912516-29-1 pbk.' White wove paper unwatermarked. All edges trimmed.

Contents: Encounters with Ezra Pound [prose journal entries] — Improvised Poetics [interview format] — The New Consciousness [interview format] — A Conversation [interview format] —First Thought, Best Thought [interview format] — An Exposition of William Carlos Williams' Poetic Practice [interview format] — Some Different Considerations in Mindful Arrangement of Open Verse Forms on the Page [prose]

$5.95. Published July 17, 1980 in an impression of 3,000 copies.

a1.2 *First edition, second printing (1983):* 2,000 copies.

Note: The second printing is identified as such on the verso of the title page. The price has been raised to $6.95 and the red panel on the cover has been replaced by purple, with purple lettering on the spine and back cover.

A44   **STRAIGHT HEARTS' DELIGHT**   **1980**

a1.1a *First edition, hardbound, unsigned copies*

ALLEN GINSBERG / PETER ORLOVSKY I STRAIGHT HEARTS' I DELIGHT I Love Poems and Selected Letters I 1947-1980 I Edited by Winston Leyland I *Sure, if that long-with-love acquainted eyes I Can judge of love, thou feel'st a lover's case...* I *—Sir Philip Sidney* I *from* Astrophel and Stella (1591) I Gay Sunshine Press I San Francisco

[1-6]^{16} [7]^8 [8]^{16}, pp. [1-5] 6-239 [240]. [1]: dedication page. [2]: '[photograph of the authors] I Peter Orlovsky (left) and Allen Ginsberg, NYC, 1963 I Photo by Richard Avedon'. [3]: title page. [4]: 'First Edition 1980 I Copyright © 1980 by Allen Ginsberg and Peter Orlovsky I [60 lines of acknowledgments]'. [5]-7: contents pages. 8: list of illustrations. 9-10: editor's note. 11-12: preface by Allen Ginsberg. 13-232: text. 233-236: biographical notes. 237-239: index. [240]: 'This edition is published in paper wrappers; there are 224 hardcover I trade copies, 50 hardcover copies numbered and

signed by the authors, I and 26 specially bound hardcover copies lettered and signed by the authors.'

23.5 x 15.6 cm. Bound in grayish purplish blue (204) cloth covered boards. Down the spine in gold: '[in 2 lines] GINSBERG I ORLOVSKY [in 1 line] STRAIGHT HEARTS' DELIGHT LEYLAND, ED. GAY SUNSHINE PRESS'. White wove paper unwatermarked. White endpapers. All edges trimmed. Issued in a white paper dust jacket printed all on black in vivid red (11), brilliant yellow (83) and white which includes the price on the back cover.

Contents: Preface [prose] — Chronology of Letters and Explanation of Texts [prose] — Psalm III [excerpt] — [letters with notes to Peter Orlovsky throughout] — A Further Proposal — In Society — Do We Understand Each Other? — A Western Ballad — Pull My Daisy — The Shrouded Stranger — I Made Love to Myself — The Green Automobile — Love Poem on Theme by Whitman — Song — Malest Cornifici Tuo Catullo — A Supermarket in California — The Names — Understand That This Is a Dream — Why Is God Love, Jack? — Morning — Message II — Kral Majales — Who Be Kind To — Chances "R" — City Midnight Junk Strains — Kiss Ass — Elegy for Neal Cassady — Please Master — On Neal's Ashes — Over Denver Again — Rain-wet Asphalt heat, Garbage Curbed Cans Overflowing — Graffiti 12th Cubicle Men's Room Syracuse Airport — After Thoughts — Over Laramie — Jimmy Berman Rag — Many Loves — Troost Street Blues — The House of the Rising Sun — Everybody Sing — Night Gleam — Sweet Boy, Gimme Yr Ass — 2 AM Dirty Jersey Blues — Hardon Blues — Come All Ye Brave Boys — Reading French Poetry — C'mon Jack, Turn Me on Your Knees — "Drive All Blames into One" — Punk Rock your My Big Crybaby — I Lay Love on My Knee — Love Replied — Lack Love — Love Returned — Love Forgiven — O Blake! Blake! Blake! — The Lion for Real — Vachel, the Stars Are Out — Since We Had Changed — It Stands Is Indifferent Like God--Blank Blind Eternal Red Silent — [autobiographical note] — [biographical note about Peter Orlovsky] — [photograph of Kerouac in Tangier taken by AG] — [facsimile of holograph letter]

$20.00. Published ca. Sept. 6, 1980 in an impression of 224 copies.

Note: Although proposed for Summer 1980 publication the book was not available until around Sept. 6, 1980.

a1.1b *First edition, hardbound, numbered copies*

ALLEN GINSBERG / PETER ORLOVSKY I STRAIGHT HEARTS' I DELIGHT I Love Poems and Selected Letters I 1947-1980 I Edited by Winston Leyland I *Sure, if that long-with-love acquainted eyes I Can judge of love, thou feel'st a lover's case... I —Sir Philip Sidney I from* Astrophel and Stella (1591) I Gay Sunshine Press I San Francisco

[1-6]^{16} [7]^8 [8]^{16}, pp. [1-5] 6-239 [240]. Numbered and initialed by the author on page [240].

Identical to the *First edition, hardbound, unsigned copies* except for the lack of the price on the back cover of the dust jacket and the autograph.

$30.00 and later raised to $50.00. Published after Sept. 13, 1980 in an impression of 50 copies numbered 1 to 50.

Note: Although proposed for Summer 1980 publication the book was not available until around Sept. 6, 1980.

a2.1 *First edition, paperbound*

ALLEN GINSBERG / PETER ORLOVSKY | STRAIGHT HEARTS' | DELIGHT | Love Poems and Selected Letters | 1947-1980 | Edited by Winston Leyland | *Sure, if that long-with-love acquainted eyes | Can judge of love, thou feel'st a lover's case... | —Sir Philip Sidney | from* Astrophel and Stella (1591) | Gay Sunshine Press | San Francisco

One hundred twenty single leaves, pp. [1-5] 6-239 [240]. As first issue above.

22.7 x 15.0 cm. Perfect bound in stiff white paper wrappers printed all on black. Across the front cover: '[design in vivid red (11), brilliant yellow (83) and white of a rope which divides the front cover into two panels in a figure 8 design, 2 knots shaped like hearts between the upper and lower panels] [the following in the upper panel in white] Allen Peter | Ginsberg Orlovsky | [in vivid red] STRAIGHT | [in vivid red] HEARTS' | [the following in the lower panel] [in vivid red] DELIGHT | [in white] LOVE POEMS AND | [in white] SELECTED LETTERS | [in white] Edited by Winston Leyland | [in white] Gay Sunshine Press'. Down the spine: '[in 2 lines in white] GINSBERG | ORLOVSKY [in 1 line in vivid red] STRAIGHT HEARTS' DELIGHT [in white] LEYLAND, ED. GAY SUNSHINE PRESS'. Across the back cover all in white: 'STRAIGHT HEARTS' DELIGHT is a crucial vol- | [16 lines] | $8.95 Gay Sunshine Press'. White wove paper unwatermarked. All edges trimmed.

$8.95. Published ca. Sept. 6, 1980 in an impression of 5,000 copies.

a3.1 *First edition, hardbound, lettered copies*

ALLEN GINSBERG / PETER ORLOVSKY | STRAIGHT HEARTS' | DELIGHT | Love Poems and Selected Letters | 1947-1980 | Edited by Winston Leyland | *Sure, if that long-with-love acquainted eyes | Can judge of love, thou feel'st a lover's case... | —Sir Philip Sidney | from* Astrophel and Stella (1591) | Gay Sunshine Press | San Francisco

$[1-6]^{16} [7]^8 [8]^{16}$, pp. [1-5] 6-239 [240]. Lettered and signed by the authors on page [240].

Quarter bound in deep blue (179) cloth with white and black stripes woven into the cloth with light grayish yellowish brown (79) paper covered boards. Across the front cover all in strong reddish orange (35)] Allen Peter | Ginsberg Orlovsky | STRAIGHT | HEARTS' | DELIGHT | Edited by Winston Leyland'. Down the spine: '[in strong reddish orange on a 1.3 x 13.3 cm. light grayish yellowish brown paper label in 2 line] GINSBERG | ORLOVSKY [in 1 line] STRAIGHT HEARTS' DELIGHT'. White wove paper unwatermarked. Black endpapers. All edges trimmed. Issued in a clear acetate dust jacket.

$50.00. Published after Sept. 13, 1980 in an impression of 26 copies lettered A to Z.

Note: The publisher sent the copies to AG to be signed on Sept. 13, 1980 and therefore they could not have been available before that date.

A45   **PLUTONIAN ODE: POEMS 1977-1980**   **1982**

a1. *First edition, hardcover*

PLUTONIAN ODE | Poems 1977-1980 | *ALLEN GINSBERG* | *"La science, la nouvelle noblesse! Le progrès. Le monde marche! | Pourquoi ne tournerait-il pas?"* —*Rimbaud* | The Pocket Poets Series: *Number Forty* | [publisher's device] | CITY LIGHT BOOKS | San Francisco

[1]^{16} [2]^8 [3-4]^{16}, pp. [1-10] 11-111 [112]. [1]: half title page. [2]: blank. [3]: title page. [4]: '© 1982 by Allen Ginsberg | First printing: January 1982 | [8 lines] | ISBN 0-87286-126-0 AACR2 | ISBN 0-87286-125-2 (pbk.) | CITY LIGHT BOOKS are edited by Lawrence Ferlinghetti | & Nancy J. Peters, and published at the City Lights | Bookstore, 261 Columbus Avenue, San Francisco, | California 94133'. [5]: dedication page. [6]: acknowledgments. [7-8]: contents pages. [9]: second half title page. [10] -107: text. 108-110: bibliography. 111: advertisement for 29 titles in 31 lines. [112]: blank.

16.5 x 12.8 cm. Bound in deep reddish orange (36) cloth covered boards. Down the spine in gold: 'GINSBERG PLUTONIAN ODE CITY LIGHTS'. White wove paper unwatermarked. Vivid orange yellow (66) endpapers. Issued in a white paper dust jacket printed in light gray, vivid orange yellow and black.

Contents: Plutonian Ode — Stool Pigeon Blues — Punk Rock Your My Big Crybaby — What's Dead? — Grim Skeleton — Lack Love — Father Guru — Manhattan May Day Midnight — Adapted from Neruda's "Que Dispierte El Lenador" — Nagasaki Days — Old Pond [music notation included] — Blame the Thought, Cling to the Bummer — "Don't Grow Old" — Love Returned — December 31, 1978 — Brooklyn College Brain — Garden State — Spring Fashions — Las Vegas: Verses Improvised for El Dorado H.S. Newspaper — To the Punks of Dawlish — Some Love — Maybe Love — Ruhr-Gebiet — Tubingen-Hamburg Schlafwagen — Love Forgiven — Verses Written for Student Antidraft Registration Rally 1980 — Homework — After Whitman & Reznikoff — Reflections at Lake Louise — "Tequakhuád Üslinw Üpideuhs Üjainomai" — Fourth Floor, Dawn, Up All Night Writing Letters — Ode to Failure — Birdbrain! — Eroica — "Defending the Faith!" — Capitol Air [music notation included] — [prose blurb on the back cover of the dust jacket]

$10.95. Published Jan. 1, 1982 in an impression of 1,200 copies.

Note: 150 copies of this edition were numbered 1 to 150 on Jan. 16, 1982 and signed by the author on the inside back fly leaf and sold for $35.00.

a2.1 *First edition, first printing, paperbound*

PLUTONIAN ODE | Poems 1977-1980 | *ALLEN GINSBERG* | *"La science, la nouvelle noblesse! Le progrès. Le monde marche! | Pourquoi ne tournerait-il pas?"* —*Rimbaud* | The Pocket Poets Series: *Number Forty* | [publisher's device] | CITY LIGHT BOOKS | San Francisco

Fifty-six single leaves, pp. [1-10] 11-111 [112]. As first issue above.

15.9 x 12.3 cm. Perfect bound in stiff white paper wrappers with covers printed so that it appears that a white label framed in black has been wrapped around the front to the back cover. Across the front cover: '[above the panel] THE POCKET POETS SERIES | [on panel in vivid reddish orange (34)] PLUTONIAN | [in vivid reddish orange] ODE | AND OTHER POEMS | 1977-1980 | [star] | *ALLEN GINSBERG* | [publisher's device below panel]'. Down the spine: '[on panel] GINSBERG PLUTONIAN ODE CITY LIGHTS'. Across the back cover: '[above the panel] 4.95 | [26 lines about the book by the author on the panel] | [publisher's device below the panel]'. White wove paper unwatermarked. All edges trimmed.

$4.95. Published Jan. 1, 1982 in an impression 5,000 copies.

Note: On Nov. 19, 1982 the Los Angeles Times rebound approximately 10 to 15 copies of this paperbound issue for presentation copies for the 1982 Book Prize winners. Bound in dark olive green (126) leather covered boards.

a2.2 *First edition, second printing, paperbound (Jan. 1983):* 5,000 copies

Note: Second and subsequent printings are identified as such on the verso of the title page.

a2.3 *First edition, third printing, paperbound (Jan. 1992):* 1,000 copies

a2.4 *First edition, fourth printing, paperbound (July 1993):* 2,000 copies

A46   **MANY LOVES**   **1984**

[left title page] [drawing of 3 male nude figures]
[right title page] [drawing of 1 of the male nude figures from the left title page extends onto this page plus another drawing of a male nude figure] MANY LOVES I by I Allen Ginsberg I Drawings by I Roberta L. Collier I Pequod Press

Single gathering of 10 leaves, pp. [i-vi] 1-9 [10-14]. [i-iii]: blank. [iv-v]: title pages. [vi]: '[drawing of a male nude figure] I © Allen Ginsberg, 1984.' 1- [10]: text. [11]: 'This book has been handset I in Goudy Old Style 12 point I by R'lene Howell Dahlberg I at the Pequod Press, I New York, N.Y. I March, 1984. I [design of a ship] I This is number [number in black ink] in an I edition limited to 500 copies.' [12-14]: blank.

22.6 x 14.4 cm. Stapled twice in stiff textured light gray (264) paper wrappers. Across the front cover: *'ManY I LoveS* I By Allen Ginsberg I Pequod Press'. Across the back cover: *'$6.00* I [drawing of a hand pointing upwards]'. White wove paper unwatermarked, first and last leaves are brownish pink (33) wove paper unwatermarked. All edges trimmed.

Contents: Many Loves

$6.00. Published March 1984 in an impression of 500 copies.

A47   **WHITE SHROUD**   **1984**

[all in facsimile of the author's holograph] White I Shroud I Allen Ginsberg I 1983

Sixteen single leaves, pp. [1-32]. [1]: original color painting of figure with circle for a head and a round red ball between the legs. [2-4]: blank. [5-6]: illustrations. [7]: title page. [8]: blank. [9-23]: text and illustrations. [24]: blank. [25]: '[circular design inside of which all the rest is written in facsimile of the author's holograph] [12 lines] I [2 Japanese name chop stamps in red]'. [26]: blank. [27]: *'This book was published on the occasion I of the exhibition of Francesco Clemente I at the Kunsthalle, Basel, May Thirteen to I June Twenty four, 1984. One thousand one hundred I and eleven numbered copies were printed and I handbound from hand woven cloth by I Kalakshetra Publications Press, Madras, India.* I "White Shroud" © Allen Ginsberg. I This Copy Number [number typeset]'. [28-32]: blank.

40.0 x 31.0 cm. Bound in white cloth covered boards*. Across the front cover all in gold in facsimile of the author's holograph: 'White I Shroud I Allen Ginsberg I 1983'. White coated paper, except leaves 1, 2, 15 and 16 which are white heavy watercolor paper. Strong greenish blue (169) textured endpapers. All edges trimmed. Issued with a clear plastic fitted dust jacket.

Note: The binding described above is only one example, the publisher states that "in fact every copy of 'White Shroud' is slightly different, because all are hand-coloured and hand-made." Besides the white cloth described other copies examined included the following bindings: deep yellowish pink (27), strong reddish orange (35), moderate reddish orange

(37), light brown (57), moderate brown (58), strong green (141), deep green (142), strong bluish green (160), moderate bluish green (164), strong greenish blue (169), deep blue (179), dark blue (183), and a leopardskin design in blackish red (21), dark reddish brown spots (44) on light orange yellow (70) background. These were randomly mixed with the following endpapers in addition to the strong greenish blue already cited: strong red (12), strong reddish orange (35), dark grayish reddish brown (47), brilliant orange yellow (67), moderate orange yellow (71), brilliant greenish blue (168), moderate blue (182), deep purplish pink (248).

Contents: White Shroud — [prose note on the writing of the poem]

50.-- Swiss francs. Published May 13, 1984 in an impression of 1111 copies.

A48   **COLLECTED POEMS**   **1985**

a1.1 *First edition, first printing, hardbound*

[in hollow type] ALLEN | [in hollow type] GINSBERG | [in hollow type] COLLECTED | [in hollow type] POEMS | [in hollow type] 1947-1980 | [design of 3 fish which share a common head] | *"Things are symbols of themselves."* | HARPER & ROW, PUBLISHERS, New York | *Cambridge, Philadelphia, San Francisco, London,* | *Mexico City, São Paulo, Singapore, Sydney*

$[1-27]^{16}$, pp. [1-2] [i-viii] ix-xxi [xxii] [1-2] 3-837 [838-840]. [1-2]: blank. [i]: half title page. [ii]: blank. [iii]: card page. [iv]: blank. [v]: title page. [vi]: 'Portions of this work have appeared in the following Allen Ginsberg books: | [26 lines] | FIRST EDITION | [1 line] | [11.9 cm. rule] | [6 lines] | ISBN 0-06-015341-5 | [11.9 cm. rule] | 84 85 86 87 88 10 9 8 7 6 5 4 3 2 1'. [vii]: dedication page. [viii]: blank. ix-xviii: contents pages. xix-xxi: author's preface. [xxii]: blank. [1] -817: text. [818]: blank. 819-837: index. [838-840]: blank.

24.2 x 16.0 cm. Bound in black cloth covered boards. Across the front cover in gold is a design of three fish which share a common head. Across the spine in gold: 'ALLEN | GINSBERG | [design of three fish which share a common head] | COLLECTED | POEMS | 1947-1980 | [4.3 cm. rule] | HARPER & ROW'. White wove paper unwatermarked. Moderate yellow (87) endpapers. All edges trimmed. Issued in a white paper dust jacket printed in black, gold and red.

Contents: Author's Preface, Reader's Manual [prose] — In Society — The Bricklayer's Lunch Hour — Two Sonnets — On Reading William Blake's "The Sick Rose" — The Eye Altering Alters All — A Very Dove — Vision 1948 — Do We Understand Each Other? — The Voice of Rock — Refrain — A Western Ballad [with music notation] — The Trembling of the Veil — A Meaningless Institution — A Mad Gleam — Complaint of the Skeleton to Time — Psalm I — An Eastern Ballad — Sweet Levinsky —Psalm II — Fie My Fum — Pull My Daisy [by AG, Jack Kerouac and Neal Cassady] — The Shrouded Stranger — Stanzas: Written at Night in Radio City — After All, What Else Is There to Say? — Sometime Jailhouse Blues — Please Open the Window and Let Me In — Tonite All is Well — Fyodor — Epigram on a Painting of Golgotha — I Attempted to Concentrate — Metaphysics — In Death, Cannot Reach What Is Most Near — This Is About Death — Hymn — Sunset — Ode to the Setting Sun — Paterson — Bop Lyrics — A Dream — Long Live the Spiderweb — The Shrouded Stranger — An Imaginary Rose in a Book — Crash — The Terms in Which I Think of Reality — The Night-Apple — Cezanne's Ports — The Blue Angel — Two Boys Went into a Dream Diner — A Desolation — In Memoriam: William Cannastra, 1922-1950 — Ode: My 24th Year — How Come He Got Canned at the Ribbon Factory — The Archetype Poem — A Typical Affair — A Poem on America — After Dead Souls — Marijuana Notation — Gregory Corso's Story — I Have Increased Power — Walking Home at Night — I Learned a World from Each — I Made Love to Myself — A Ghost May Come — I Feel as If I Am at a Dead — An Atypical Affair — I Came Home from the Movies with Nothing on My Mind — A Crazy Spiritual — Wild Orphan — The Green Automobile — An Asphodel — My Alba — Sakyamuni Coming Out from the Mountain — Havana 1953 — Green Valentine Blues [with music notation] — Siesta in Xbalba — Song ("The Weight of the World") — In Back of the Real — On Burroughs' Work — Love Poem on Theme by Whitman — Over Kansas — Malest Cornifici Tuo Catullo — Dream Record: June 8, 1955 — Blessed Be the Muses — Howl — Footnote to Howl — A Strange New Cottage in Berkeley — A Supermarket in California — Looking Over My Shoulder — Lying on My Side — I Didn't Know the Names — On the Porch — Sunflower Sutra — Transcription of Organ Music — Sather Gate Illumination — America — Fragment 1956 — Afternoon Seattle — Tears — Scribble — In the Baggage Room at Greyhound — Psalm III — Many Loves — Ready to Roll — Poem Rocket — Squeal — Wrote This Last Night — Death to Van Gogh's Ear! — Europe! Europe! — The Lion for Real — The Names — At Apollinaire's Grave — Message — To Lindsay — To Aunt Rose — American Change — 'Back on Times Square, Dreaming of Times Square' — Laughing Gas — Funny Death — My Sad Self — Ignu — Battleship Newsreel — Kaddish — Mescaline — Lysergic Acid — I Beg You Come Back & Be Cheerful — Psalm IV — To an Old Poet in Peru — Aether — Magic Psalm — The Reply — The End — Man's Glory — Fragment: The Names II — Who Will Take Over the Universe? — Journal Night Thoughts — Television Was a Baby Crawling Toward That Deathchamber — This Form of Life Needs Sex — Sunset S.S. Azemour — Seabattle of Salamis Took Place Off Perama — Galilee Shore — Stotras to Kali Destroyer of Illusions — To P.O. — Heat — Describe: The Rain on Dasaswamedh Ghat — Death News — Vulture Peak: Gridhakuta Hill — Patna-Benares Express — Last Night in Calcutta — Understand That This Is a Dream — Angkor Wat — The Change: Kyoto-Tokyo Express — Nov. 23, 1963: Alone — Why Is God Love, Jack? — Morning — Waking in New York — After Yeats — I Am a Victim of Telephone — Today — Message II — Big Beat — Café in Warsaw — The Moments Return — Kral Majales — Guru — Drowse Murmurs — Who Be Kind To — Studying the Signs — Portland Coliseum — Beginning of a Poem of These States — Carmel Valley — First Party at Ken Kesey's with Hell's Angels — Continuation of a Long Poem of These States — These States: Into L.A. — A Methedrine Vision in Hollywood — Hiway Poesy: L.A.--Albuquerque--Texas--Wichita — Chances "R" — Wichita Vortex Sutra — Auto Poesy: On the Lam from Bloomington — Kansas City to Saint Louis — Bayonne Entering NYC — Growing Old Again — Uptown — The Old Village Before I Die — Consulting I Ching Smoking Pot Listening to the Fugs Sing Blake — Wings Lifted Over the Black Pit — Cleveland, The Flats — To the Body — Iron Horse — City Midnight Junk Strains — A Vow — Autumn Gold: New England Fall — Done, Finished with the Biggest Cock — Holy Ghost on the Nod over the Body of Bliss — Bayonne Turnpike to Tuscarora — An Open Window on Chicago — Returning North of Vortex — Wales Visitation — Pentagon Exorcism — Elegy Che Guevara — War Profit Litany — Elegy for Neal Cassady — Chicago to Salt Lake by Air — Kiss Ass — Manhattan Thirties Flash — Please Master — A Prophecy — Bixby Canyon — Crossing Nation — Smoke Rolling Down Street — Pertussin — Swirls of Black Dust on Avenue D — Violence — Past Silver Durango over Mexic Sierra-Wrinkles — On Neal's Ashes — Going to Chicago — Grant Park: August 28, 1968 — Car Crash — Over Denver Again — Imaginary Universes — Rising Over Night-Blackened Detroit Streets — To Poe: Over the Planet, Air Albany--Baltimore — Easter Sunday — Falling Asleep in America — Northwest Passage — Sonora Desert-edge — Reflections in Sleepy Eye — Independence Day — In a Moonlit Hermit's Cabin — Rain-Wet Asphalt Heat, Garbage Curbed Cans Overflowing — Death on All Fronts — Memory Gardens — Flash Back — Graffiti 12th Cubicle Men's Room Syracuse Airport — After Thoughts — G.S. Reading Poesy at Princeton — Friday the Thirteenth — Anti-Vietnam War Peace Mobilization — Ecologue — Guru Om — "Have You Seen This Movie?" — Milarepa Taste — Over Laramie — Bixby Canyon Ocean Path Word Breeze — Hum Bom! — September on Jessore Road [with music notation] — Ayers Rock/Uluru Song — Voznesensky's "Silent Tingling" — These States: To Miami Presidential Convention — Xmas Gift — Thoughts Sitting Breathing [with music notation] — "What Would You Do If You Lost It?" — Who — Yes and It's Hopeless — Under the World There's a Lot of Ass, a Lot of Cunt — Returning to the Country for a Brief Visit — Night Gleam — What I'd Like to Do — On

Illness — News Bulletin — On Neruda's Death — Mind Breaths — Flying Elegy — Teton Village — Sweet Boy, Gimme Yr Ass — Jaweh and Allah Battle — Manifesto — Sad Dust Glories — Ego Confession — Mugging — Who Runs America? — Thoughts on a Breath — We Rise on Sun Beams and Fall in the Night — Written on Hotel Napkin: Chicago Futures — Hospital Window — Hadda Be Playing on the Jukebox — Come All Ye Brave Boys — Sickness Blues [with music notation] — Gospel Noble Truths [with music notation] — Rolling Thunder Stones [with music notation] — Cabin in the Rockies — Reading French Poetry — Two Dreams — C'mon Jack — Pussy Blues — Don't Grow Old [with music notation] — "Junk Mail" — "You Might Get in Trouble" — Land O' Lakes, Wisc. — "Drive All Blames into One" — Land O'Lakes, Wisconsin: Vajrayana Seminary — For Creeley's Ear — Haunting Poe's Baltimore — Contest of Bards [with music notation] — I Lay Love on My Knee — Stool Pigeon Blues — Punk Rock Your My Big Crybaby — Love Replied — What's Dead? — Grim Skeleton — Ballade of Poisons — Lack Love — Father Guru — Manhattan May Day Midnight — Adapted from Neruda's "Que Dispierte el Leñador" — Nagasaki Days — Plutonian Ode — Old Pond [with music notation] — Blame the Thought, Cling to the Bummer — "Don't Grow Old: Twenty Eight Years — Love Returned — December 31, 1978 — Brooklyn College Brain — Garden State — Spring Fashions — Las Vegas: Verses Improvised for El Dorado H.S. Newspaper — To the Punks of Dawlish — Some Love — Maybe Love — Ruhr-Gebiet — Tübingen-Hamburg Schlafwagen — Love Forgiven [with music notation] — Verses Written for Student Anitdraft Registration Rally 1980 — Homework — After Whitman & Reznikoff — Reflections at Lake Louise — Red Cheeked Boyfriends Tenderly Kiss Me Sweet Mouthed — Fourth Floor, Dawn, Up All Night Writing Letters — Ode to Failure — Birdbrain! — Eroica — "Defending the Faith" — Capitol Air [with music notation] — Notes [prose] — A Further Proposal — A Lover's Garden — Love Letter — Dakar Doldrums — Epigraphs from Original Editions [prose] — Dedications [prose] — Acknowledgments [prose] — Author's Cover Writ [prose] — [photographs (see also D25)]

$27.50. Published Dec. 31, 1984 in an impression of 17,500 copies.

Note: Although scheduled for 1984 release this book was not available until Jan. 2, 1985.

a1.2 *First edition, second printing, hardbound:, 1987* 1,500 copies printed.

Note: Second printing identified by the following line of figures at the bottom of page [vi]: '87 88 HC 10 9 8 7 6 5 4 3 2'.

a2.1 *First British issue, hardbound, 1985*

[in hollow type] ALLEN | [in hollow type] GINSBERG | [in hollow type] COLLECTED | [in hollow type] POEMS | [in hollow type] 1947-1980 | [design of 3 fish which share a common head] | *"Things are symbols of themselves."* | VIKING

$[1-27]^{16}$, pp. [1-2] [i-viii] ix-xxi [xxii] [1-2] 3-837 [838-840]. Identical to the American printing except for [vi]: 'Portions of this work have appeared in the following Allen Ginsberg books: | [20 lines] | VIKING | Penguin Books Ltd, Harmondsworth, Middlesex, England | [5 lines] | Published in Great Britain by Viking 1985 | [9 lines] | ISBN 0-670-80683-8 | [2 lines]'.

24.1 x 16.0 cm. Bound in black cloth covered boards. Across the front cover in gold is a design of three fish which share a common head. Across the spine in gold: 'ALLEN | GINSBERG | [design of three fish which share a common head] | COLLECTED | POEMS | 1947-1980 | [4.3 cm. rule] | VIKING'. White wove paper unwatermarked. Moderate yellow (87) endpapers. All edges trimmed. Issued in a white paper dust jacket printed in black, gold and red.

£16.95. Published Feb. 25, 1985 in an impression of 2,500 copies.

a3.1 *First British issue, paperbound, 1987*

[in hollow type] ALLEN | [in hollow type] GINSBERG | [in hollow type] COLLECTED | [in hollow type] POEMS | [in hollow type] 1947-1980 | PENGUIN BOOKS

Four hundred thirty-two single leaves, pp. [iii-viii] ix-xxi [xxii] [1-2] 3-837 [838-844]. [iii]: 'PENGUIN INTERNATIONAL POETS | ALLEN GINSBERG: COLLECTED POEMS 1947-1980 | [19 lines]'. [iv]: blank. [v]: title page. [vi]: 'Penguin Books Ltd, 27 Wrights Lane, London W8 5TZ (Publishing and Editorial) | *and* Harmondsworth, Middlesex, England (Distribution and Warehouse) | [6 lines] | Published in Penguin Books 1987 | [33 lines]'. [vii]: dedication page. [viii]: blank. ix-xviii: contents pages. xix-xxi: author's preface. [xxii]: blank. [1] -817: text. [818]: blank. 819-837: index. [838-844]: blank.

23.3 x 15.2 cm. Perfect bound in stiff white paper wrappers. Across the front cover: '[a photograph of the author in strong red (12) and white on the left side] [a vertical gold band dividing the two sides] [the rest on the right side in white on strong red unless noted] [in black on a light gray rectangular background within single rules on a white rectangular background within single rules] KING PENGUIN | ALLEN | GINSBERG | COLLECTED | POEMS | 1947-1980 | [design of three fish which share a common head in gold]'. Across the spine: '[publisher's device in gray and black] | [down the spine] ALLEN GINSBERG [bullet] COLLECTED POEMS 1947-1980 [design of three fish which share a common head in gold] [in 2 lines] ISBN 014 | 01.0289 2'. Across the back cover: ' [in black on a light gray rectangular background within single rules on a white rectangular background within single rules] KING PENGUIN | [a photograph of the author within single rule frame with 'ALLEN GINSBERG' underneath] [29 lines] | Poetry | [in 5 lines] U.K. £9.95 | AUST. $29.95 | (recommended) | N.Z. $32.00 | (incl. GST) [zebra bar code with 3 sets of numbers]'. White wove paper unwatermarked. All edges trimmed.

£9.95. Published Nov. 19, 1987 in an impression of 5,000 copies.

a4.1 *First American paperbound issue, first printing, 1988*

[in hollow type] ALLEN | [in hollow type] GINSBERG | [in hollow type] COLLECTED | [in hollow type] POEMS | [in hollow type] 1947-1980 | [design of 3 fish which share a common head] | *"Things are symbols of themselves."* | [publisher's device over which is printed one line] PERENNIAL LIBRARY | Harper & Row, Publishers, New York | *Cambridge, Philadelphia, San Francisco, Washington* | *London, Mexico City, São Paulo, Singapore, Sydney*

Four hundred thirty-two single leaves, pp. [1-2] [i-viii] ix-xxi [xxii] [1-2] 3-837 [838-840]. [1-2]: blank. [i]: half title page. [ii]: blank. [iii]: card page. [iv]: blank. [v]: title page. [vi]: 'Portions of this work have appeared in the following Allen Ginsberg books: | [26 lines] | First PERENNIAL LIBRARY edition published 1988. | [1 line] | [11.9 cm. rule] | [3 lines] | "Perennial Library." | [3 lines] | ISBN 0-06-091494-7 (pbk.) | [11.9 cm. rule] | 88 89 90 91 92 HC 10 9 8 7 6 5 4 3 2 1'. [vii]: dedication page. [viii]: blank. ix-xviii: contents pages. xix-xxi: author's preface. [xxii]: blank. [1] -817: text. [818]: blank. 819-837: index. [838]: blank. [839]: biographical note. [840]: blank.

23.2 x 15.3 cm. Perfect bound in stiff white paper wrappers printed all on vivid red (11) background. Across the front cover in black lettering outlined in gold unless noted: 'ALLEN | GINSBERG | [design of three fish which share a common head in black, white and gold] | COLLECTED | POEMS | 1947-1980 | [publisher's device in black]'. Across the spine: 'ALLEN | GINSBERG | [design of three fish which share a common head in black, white and gold] | COLLECTED | POEMS | 1947-1980 | [publisher's device] | PL 1494'. Across the back cover: 'POETRY | [3 lines] | [8.8 x

6.7 cm. black and white photograph of the author] [up the right side of the photo] © Robert Frank | [7 lines] | [publisher's device over which is printed one line] PERENNIAL LIBRARY | HARPER & ROW, PUBLISHERS [right in a white rectangle is a zebra bar code with 4 lines of numbers]'. White wove paper unwatermarked. All edges trimmed.

$15.95. Published May 18, 1988 in an impression of 13,500 copies.

a4.2 *First American paperbound issue, second printing*

Note: Second and subsequent printings identified on the verso of the title page.

a4.3 *First American paperbound issue, third printing*

a4.4 *First American papaerbound issue, fourth printing*

a4.5 *First American paperbound issue, fifth printing, 1992*

A49   **OLD LOVE STORY**   **1986**

[in deep purple (219) *Old Love Story* | ALLEN GINSBERG | illustrations by | Larry R. Collins | LOSPECCHIO PRESS | NEW YORK | 1986

Single gathering of eight leaves, pp. [1-16]. [1]: blank. [2]: frontispiece tipped in. [3]: title page. [4]: 'Copyright 1986 by Allen Ginsberg | Illustrations copyright 1986 by Larry R. Collins | All rights reserved | First Edition | [2 lines] | LOSPECCHIO PRESS | [2 lines]'. [5]: half title page. [6]: blank. [7]: illustration tipped in. [8-10]: text. [11]: illustration tipped in. [12]: blank. [13]: 'This first printing of Old Love Story is published | on June 3, 1986 and is limited to an edition of 150 | copies, signed and numbered by the author and | illustrator. | [signed and numbered in black and blue ink] | [4 lines]'. [14]: blank. [15]: 'BOOK DESIGN BY BILL MORGAN'. [16]: blank.

25.5 x 17.1 cm. Sewn into stiff tan laid paper wrappers watermarked 'INGRES-FABRIANO'. Across the front cover: '[2 vertical panels joined with single rule borders] [illustration tipped onto the upper panel] | [in the lower panel] *Old Love Story* | ALLEN GINSBERG'. White wove paper unwatermarked. Top edges trimmed.

Contents: Old Love Story

$45.00. Published June 3, 1986 in an impression of 150 copies numbered 1 to 150.

A50   **WHITE SHROUD POEMS**   **1986**

a1.1 *First edition, first printing, hardbound*

[in hollow type] ALLEN | [in hollow type] GINSBERG | [in hollow type] WHITE | [in hollow type] SHROUD | [in hollow type] POEMS | [in hollow type] 1980-1985 | [design of 3 fish which share a common head] | [4 lines] | HARPER & ROW, PUBLISHERS, New York | *Cambridge, Philadelphia, San Francisco, Washington | London, Mexico City, São Paulo, Singapore, Sydney*

Fifty-six single leaves, pp. [1-2] [i-viii] ix-xi [xii-xiv] 1-89 [90-96]. [1-2]: blank. [i]: half title page. [ii]: blank. [iii]: card page. [iv]: blank. [v]: title page. [vi]: '[9 lines] | WHITE SHROUD. Copyright © 1986 by Allen Ginsberg. All rights reserved. Printed in the | [5 lines] | FIRST EDITION | [1 line] | [11.9 cm. rule] | [6 lines] | ISBN 0-06-015714-3 86 87 88 89 90 HC 10 9 8 7 6 5 4 3 2 1 | ISBN 0-06-015715-1 (limited) | [11.9 cm. rule]'. [vii]: dedication page. [viii]: blank. ix-x: contents pages. xi:

acknowledgments. [xii]: blank. [xiii]: second half title page. [xiv]: blank. 1-85: text. [86]: blank. 87-89: index. [90-96]: blank.

24.0 x 15.8 cm. Bound in deep red (13) cloth covered boards. Across the front cover is a blind stamped design of three fish which share a common head. Down the spine in gold: 'ALLEN GINSBERG WHITE SHROUD HARPER & ROW'. White wove paper unwatermarked. Light yellowish brown (76) endpapers. All edges trimmed. Issued in a white paper dust jacket printed in black, white, red and gold.

Contents: Porch Scribbles — Industrial Waves — Those Two — Homage Vajracarya — Why I Meditate — Love Comes — Old Love Story — Airplane Blues — Do the Mediation Rock — The Little Fish Devours the Big Fish — Happening Now? — A Public Poetry — "What You Up To?" — Maturity — "Throw Out the Yellow Journalists of Bad Grammar & Terrible Manner" — Going to the World of the Dead — Irritable Vegetable — Thoughts Sitting Breathing II — What the Sea Throws Up at Vlissingen — I Am Not — I'm a Prisoner of Allen Ginsberg — 221 Syllables at Rocky Mountain Dharma Center — Fighting Phantoms Fighting Phantoms — Arguments — Sunday Prayer — Brown Rice Quatrains — They're All Phantoms of My Imagining — White Shroud — Empire Air — Surprise Mind — Student Love — The Question — In My Kitchen in New York — It's All So Brief — I Love Old Whitman So — Written in My Dream by W. C. Williams — One Morning I Took a Walk in China — Reading Bai Juyi — Black Shroud — World Karma — Prophecy — Memory Cousins — Moral Majority — The Guest — After Antipater — Jumping the Gun on the Sun — Cadillac Squawk — Things I Don't Know

$14.95. Published Nov. 19, 1986 in an impression of 10,000 copies.

a2.1 *First edition, signed copies*

[in hollow type] ALLEN | [in hollow type] GINSBERG | [in hollow type] WHITE | [in hollow type] SHROUD | [in hollow type] POEMS | [in hollow type] 1980-1985 | [design of 3 fish which share a common head] | [4 lines] | HARPER & ROW, PUBLISHERS, New York | *Cambridge, Philadelphia, San Francisco, Washington* | *London, Mexico City, São Paulo, Singapore, Sydney*

Fifty-six single leaves, pp. [1-2] [i-viii] ix-xi [xii-xiv] 1-89 [90-96]. [1]: *'Of the first edition of* | WHITE SHROUD | *two hundred copies* | *have been specially bound* | *and slipcased.* | *Each copy is signed* | *by the author* | *and numbered.* | *Number____* [numbered and autographed in black ink]'. [2]: blank. [i]: half title page. [ii]: blank. [iii]: card page. [iv]: blank. [v]: title page. [vi]: '[9 lines] | WHITE SHROUD. Copyright © 1986 by Allen Ginsberg. All rights reserved. Printed in the | [5 lines] | FIRST EDITION | [1 line] | [11.9 cm. rule] | [6 lines] | ISBN 0-06-015714-3 86 87 88 89 90 HC 10 9 8 7 6 5 4 3 2 1 | ISBN 0-06-015715-1 (limited) | [11.9 cm. rule]'. [vii]: dedication page. [viii]: blank. ix-x: contents pages. xi: acknowledgments. [xii]: blank. [xiii]: second half title page. [xiv]: blank. 1-85: text. [86]: blank. 87-89: index. [90-96]: blank.

24.2 x 15.8 cm. Bound in white cloth covered boards. Across the front cover in gold is a design of three fish which share a common head. Down the spine in metallic red: 'ALLEN GINSBERG WHITE SHROUD HARPER & ROW'. White wove paper unwatermarked. Strong red (12) endpapers. All edges trimmed. Issued in a strong red cloth covered slip in case.

$50.00. Published Nov. 12, 1986 in an impression of 200 copies, numbered 1 to 200.

a3.1 *First edition, first printing, paperbound (1987)*

[in hollow type] ALLEN I [in hollow type] GINSBERG I [in hollow type] WHITE I
[in hollow type] SHROUD I [in hollow type] POEMS I [in hollow type] 1980-1985 I
[design of 3 fish which share a common head] I [4 lines] I PERENNIAL LIBRARY I
Harper & Row, Publishers, New York I *Cambridge, Philadelphia, San Francisco,*
Washington I *London, Mexico City, São Paulo, Singapore, Sydney*

Fifty-six single leaves, pp. [1-2] [i-viii] ix-xi [xii-xiv] 1-89 [90-96]. [1-2]: blank. [i]:
half title page. [ii]: blank. [iii]: card page. [iv]: blank. [v]: title page. [vi]: '[9 lines] I
WHITE SHROUD. Copyright © 1986 by Allen Ginsberg. All rights reserved. Printed in
the United I [4 lines] I First PERENNIAL LIBRARY edition published 1987. I [1 line]
I [rule] I [7 lines] I ISBN 0-06-091429-7 (pbk.) I [rule] I 87 88 89 90 91 HC 10 9 8 7
6 5 4 3 2 1'. [vii]: dedication page. [viii]: blank. ix-x: contents pages. xi:
acknowledgments. [xii]: blank. [xiii]: second half title page. [xiv]: blank. 1-85: text.
[86]: blank. 87-89: index. [90-96]: blank.

23.4 x 15.4 cm. Perfect bound in stiff white paper wrappers. Across the front cover in
red lettering outlined in gold unless noted: 'ALLEN I GINSBERG I [design of three
fish which share a common head in black, white and gold] I WHITE I SHROUD I
POEMS I 1980-1985 I [publisher's device in black]'. Down the spine: '[in red] ALLEN
GINSBERG WHITE SHROUD [black] PL 1429 [publisher's device across the spine]'.
Across the back cover: 'POETRY I [8 lines] I [photograph of the author] I [publisher's
device over which is printed one line] PERENNIAL LIBRARY I ISBN 0-06-091429-7
I HARPER & ROW PUBLISHERS I [zebra bar code with 2 sets of numbers] I [2 lines]
I 1187 >> $8.95'. White wove paper unwatermarked. All edges trimmed.

$8.95. Published Nov. 11, 1987 in an impression of 15,500 copies and reprinted 6 times.

A51   **HOWL [ANNOTATED EDITION]**   **1986**

a1.1 *First edition, first printing, hardbound*

[in hollow type] ALLEN I [in hollow type] GINSBERG I [in hollow type] HOWL I
ORIGINAL DRAFT FACSIMILE, TRANSCRIPT I & VARIANT VERSIONS, FULLY
A N N O T A T E D   B Y   A U T H O R ,   I   W I T H   C O N T E M P O R A N E O U S
CORRESPONDENCE, ACCOUNT OF FIRST I PUBLIC READING, LEGAL
SKIRMISHES, PRECURSOR TEXTS I & BIBLIOGRAPHY I [design of three fish
which share a common head in brown] I *"For the nightly Visitor is at the window of the*
impenitent, I *while I sing a psalm of my own composing."* I *Edited by Barry Miles* I
HARPER & ROW, PUBLISHERS, New York I *Cambridge, Philadelphia, San*
Francisco, Washington I *London, Mexico City, São Paulo, Singapore, Sydney*

[1-5]^{16} [6]^8 [7]^{16}, pp. [i-vi] vii-xiv [1-2] 3-194. [i]: half title page. [ii]: card page.
[iii]: title page. [iv]: '*Copyright acknowledgments follow the Index.* I *Howl* was
originally published in 1956 I by City Lights Books, San Francisco, CA. I HOWL.
Copyright © 1986, 1956 by Allen Ginsberg. All rights reserved. I [6 lines] I FIRST
EDITION I [1 line] I [10.0 cm. rule] I [14 lines] I ISBN 0-06-015628-7 86 87 88 89
90 10 9 8 7 6 5 4 3 2 1 I ISBN 0-06-015651-1 (limited) I [10.0 cm. rule]'. [v]:
dedication page. [vi]: blank. vii-ix: contents pages. [x]: photographs. xi-[xii]: author's
preface. xiii-xiv: editor's preface. [1]-146: text. [147]-190: appendixes. 191:
acknowledgments page. 192-193: index. 194: copyright acknowledgments.

28.6 x 23.4 cm. Bound in moderate yellowish brown (77) cloth covered boards. A design
of three fish which share a common head is blind stamped across the front cover. Down
the spine in gold: 'ALLEN GINSBERG HOWL HARPER & ROW'. White wove paper
unwatermarked. Yellowish gray (93) endpapers with darker threads. All edges trimmed.
Issued in a white paper dust jacket printed in black, gold and blue.

Contents: [11 photographs (see also D42)] — Author's Preface: Reader's Guide [prose] — Howl [various states of the text] — Reintroduction to Carl Solomon [prose] — "O Carl!" A Dream [journal entry] — Annotations [prose] — [letters to Jack Kerouac, William Carlos Williams, Louis Ginsberg, Eugene Brooks, Richard Eberhart, Lionel Trilling, Ezra Pound, Lawrence Ferlinghetti, John Hollander] — [postcard advertisement for 6 Gallery] — First Reading at the Six Gallery, October 7, 1955 [prose by AG and Gregory Corso] — Model Texts [prose] — Acknowledgments [prose]

$22.50. Published Nov. 1986 in an impression of 10,000 copies.

a2.1 *First edition, signed copies*

[in hollow type] ALLEN I [in hollow type] GINSBERG I [in hollow type] HOWL I ORIGINAL DRAFT FACSIMILE, TRANSCRIPT I & VARIANT VERSIONS, FULLY ANNOTATED BY AUTHOR, I WITH CONTEMPORANEOUS CORRESPONDENCE, ACCOUNT OF FIRST I PUBLIC READING, LEGAL SKIRMISHES, PRECURSOR TEXTS I & BIBLIOGRAPHY I [design of three fish which share a common head in brown] I *"For the nightly Visitor is at the window of the impenitent,* I *while I sing a psalm of my own composing."* I *Edited by Barry Miles* I HARPER & ROW, PUBLISHERS, New York I *Cambridge, Philadelphia, San Francisco, Washington* I *London, Mexico City, São Paulo, Singapore, Sydney*

[1-5]^{16} [6]^8 [7]^{16}, pp. [i-vi] vii-xiv [1-2] 3-194. [i]: *'Of the first edition of* I HOWL I *two hundred and fifty copies* I *have been specially bound* I *and slipcased.* I *Each copy is signed* I *by the author* I *and numbered.* I [autographed in black ink] I *Number____* [numbered in black ink]'.

28.6 x 23.4 cm. Bound in very deep red (14) cloth covered boards. A design of three fish which share a common head in gold across the front cover. Down the spine in gold: 'ALLEN GINSBERG HOWL HARPER & ROW'. White wove paper unwatermarked. Pale yellow (89) endpapers. All edges trimmed. Issued in a very deep red cloth covered slip in case.

$75.00. Published Dec. 11, 1986 in an impression of 250 copies.

A52   FOTOGRAFIER 1947-87   1987

ALLEN GINSBERG I Fotografier 1947-87 I *Med et essay i 3 dele af Peter Laugesen* I KLIM

[1-7]^6, pp. [1-8] 9-84. [1]: half title page. [2]: '© Allen Ginsberg 1987 (fotos og billedtekst) I © Peter Laugesen 1987 (indledning) I © Forlaget Klim, Nørre Allé 59, 8000 Århus C. I [10 lines] I [printer's device]. [3]: title page. [4]: contents page. [5]: foreword. [6]: blank. [7] -84: text.

20.0 x 21.1 cm. Bound in stiff white paper wrappers. Across the front cover: 'ALLEN GINSBERG I Fotografier 1947-87 I *Med et essay i 3 dele af Peter Laugesen* I [12.2 x 18.1 cm. photograph] I [2 line legend in facsimile of author's holograph]'. Down the spine: 'ALLEN GINSBERG Fotografier 1947-87 KLIM'. Across the back cover: '[12.5 x 15.9 cm. photograph] I [in facsimile holograph] Steven Taylor Allen Ginsberg Peter Orlovsky'. White wove paper unwatermarked. All edges trimmed.

Contents: [47 photographs with legends (see also D54)]

169 D. Kr. Published Nov. 23, 1987 in an impression of 500 copies.

A53   **YOUR REASON & BLAKE'S SYSTEM**   **1988**

a1. *First edition, hardbound*

YOUR REASON & I BLAKE'S SYSTEM I by I Allen Ginsberg I HANUMAN
BOOKS I Madras & New York I 1988

$1-3^8$ [4]^2, pp. [1-7] 8-43 [44-52]. Color plates tipped onto pages 2, 8, 12, 19, 25 and 31.
[1]: half title page. [2]: blank. [3]: title page. [4]: '© 1988 Allen Ginsberg I © 1988
Hanuman Books I ISBN: 0-937815-23-3 I Cover photo: I George Holmes'. [5]:
second half title page. [6]: blank. [7]-41: text. [42]: blank. 43: acknowledgments.
[44]: blank. [45]: 'Designed & Printed by I C. T. Nachiappan of the I
KALAKSHETRA PRESS I Thiruvanmiyur, Madras-41, I INDIA. I HANUMAN
BOOKS I P. O. Box 1070 I Old Chelsea Station I New York, N.Y. 10113 I Hanuman
Books are I Published & Edited I by Raymond Foye & I Francesco Clemente'. [46-
48]: blank. [49-52]: advertisement.

10.3 x 7.0 cm. Bound in brilliant yellow green (16) cloth covered boards. White wove
paper unwatermarked. White endpapers. All edges trimmed. Issued in white paper dust
jacket printed in full color with gold lettering.

Contents: Your Reason & Blake's System [prose]

$10.95. Published Dec. 30, 1988 in an impression of 100 copies.

a2. *First edition, paperbound*

YOUR REASON & I BLAKE'S SYSTEM I by I Allen Ginsberg I HANUMAN
BOOKS I Madras & New York I 1988

$1-3^8$ [4]^2, pp. [1-7] 8-43 [44-52]. Color plates tipped onto pages 2, 8, 12, 19, 25 and 31.

10.3 x 7.0 cm. Bound in stiff brilliant yellow green (116)* paper wrappers. White wove
paper unwatermarked. White endpapers. All edges trimmed. Issued in white paper dust
jacket printed in full color with gold lettering.

$4.95. Published Dec. 30, 1988 in an impression of 1,500 copies.

Note: The publisher reports that other colors may have been used for the covers as the
printer used whatever paper was available. Other copies examined have strong orange
(50) paper.

A54   **REALITY SANDWICHES**   **1989**

a1. *First edition, hardbound*

ALLEN GINSBERG I *REALITY SANDWICHES* I Fotografien I Herausgegeben von
Michael Köhler I NiSHEN

Forty-eight single leaves, pp. [1-6] 7-95 [96]. [1]: half title page. [2]: blank. [3]: title
page. [4]: 'EDITORISCHE NOTIZ I [15 lines] I © 1989 für die Buchausgabe Verlag
Dirk Nishen GmbH & Co KG, I Am Tempelhofer Berg 6, D-1000 Berlin 61 I © 1989
Allen Ginsberg für die Fotografien I © 1989 Michael Köhler für die Texte I [10 lines] I
ISBN 3 88940 043 4'. [5]: contents page. [6]-16: introduction. [17]-95: text. [96]:
blank.

24.9 x 22.3 cm. Perfect bound in deep orange yellow (69) glossy paper covered boards.
Across the front cover: '*REALITY SANDWICHES* I [11.7 x 17.9 cm. photograph of

William Burroughs] I ALLEN GINSBERG I [in pale orange yellow (73)] NiSHEN'. Up the spine: '[in pale orange yellow] NiSHEN [in white] GINSBERG [bullet] [in black] *REALITY SANDWICHES*'. Across the back cover: '[13.5 x 17.0 cm. photograph of a group of men] I [12 lines about the book]'. White wove paper unwatermarked. White endpapers. All edges trimmed.

Contents: [72 photographs with legends (see also D69)]

DM 29,80 at museums, DM 36,00 in bookstores. Published May-June 1989 in an impression of 3,000 copies.

a2. *First edition, paperbound (1993)*

ALLEN GINSBERG I *REALITY SANDWICHES* I Fotografien I Herausgegeben von Michael Köhler I NiSHEN

Forty-eight single leaves, pp. [1-6] 7-95 [96]. [1]: half title page. [2]: blank. [3]: title page. [4]: 'EDITORISCHE NOTIZ I [15 lines] I © 1993 für die Buchausgabe Verlag Dirk Nishen GmbH & Co KG, I Am Tempelhofer Berg 6, D-1000 Berlin 61 I © 1993 Allen Ginsberg für die Fotografien I © 1993 Michael Köhler für die Texte I [10 lines] I ISBN 3 88940 077 9'. [5]: contents page. [6]-16: introduction. [17]-95: text. [96]: blank.

24.5 x 22.0 cm. Perfect bound in stiff white paper wrappers. Across the front cover is a black and white photo of Neal Cassady and Natalie Jackson standing under a theatre marquee on the left of which is a 15.9 x 6.2 cm. strong orange yellow (68) rectangle on which is printed all the following in deep red (13): 'ALLEN I GINSBERG I REALITY I SANDWICHES I FOTOGRAFIEN I NiSHEN'. Up the spine all on strong orange yellow: 'NiSHEN ALLEN GINSBERG [bullet] REALITY SANDWICHES'. Across the back cover is a black and white photograph of a group of men on a strong orange yellow background. White wove paper unwatermarked. All edges trimmed.

DM 19,80. Published Jan. 1993 in an impression of 2,500 copies.

b1. *First American edition (1993) [re-titled 'Snapshot Poetics']*

[left title page]   [2 vertical lines] I snapshot I poetics
[right title page] . a . photographic . memoir . of . the . beat . era. I . allen ginsberg . introduction by michael köhler . chronicle books . san francisco .

Forty-eight single leaves, pp. [1-5] 6-95 [96]. [1]: half title page. [2-3]: title pages. [4]: 'FIRST PUBLISHED IN THE UNITED STATES I IN 1993 BY CHRONICLE BOOKS I [6 lines] I [in lettering with gray shadow] con I [32 lines] I 10 9 8 7 6 5 4 3 2 1 I CHRONICLE BOOKS I 275 FIFTH STREET I SAN FRANCISCO, CALIFORNIA 94103'. [5]: contents page. 6-7: introduction. 8-16: preface. 17-80: text. 81: blank. 82-86: legends. 87-95: biographical sketches. [96]: 'the end. I [vertical rule] '.

24.2 x 21.9 cm. Perfect bound in stiff white paper wrappers. Across the front cover is a geometric pattern combining black, dark greenish blue (174) and pale yellow (89) rectangles with three black and white photographs from the book and with two examples of holograph legends over which is the printed the following: '[in vivid reddish orange (34)] snapshot I [in vivid reddish orange] poetics I [in pale yellow in facsimile holograph] Allen Ginsberg I a . photographic . memoir . I of . the . beat . era .' Down the spine in white on black unless otherwise noted: ' . SNAPSHOT POETICS . ALLEN GINSBERG . . CHRONICLE BOOKS . [across the spine on a pale yellow background in white is a solid square inside a diamond] I [in white on a dark greenish blue background] TM I [a white gunsight design on a black background] I [in white on a vivid reddish orange background] ® I [in black on a white background] W I [continuation of design of facsimile holograph from the front cover]'. Across the back cover is a continuation of the design of rectangles from the front cover and spine on which is printed three black and white photographs over one of which is printed 16 lines in white about the book] | [within a single rule frame is the following] ISBN 0-8118-0372-4 | [rule] | [zebra bar code with 2 sets of numbers] | [in white below the frame within a vivid reddish orange oval outlined in black] PHOTOGRAPHY'. Across the inside front flap all on a black background: '[on pale yellow triangle within an oval outlined in black] $12.95 | [6 lines in white] | [in pale yellow facsimile holograph] Allen Ginsberg | [19 lines in white about the book]'. Across the inside back flap is a continuation of the design from the back cover and a black rectangle with a notch above which is printed 4 lines beside a photograph of the author. White wove coated paper unwatermarked. All edges trimmed.

Contents: [As first edition photographs with the substitution of a photograph of William Burroughs for the one of Wolf Biermann, the final photograph in the book with accompanying legend] — Preface [prose] — Legends [prose] — Biographical Sketches [prose]

$12.95. Published July 1993 in an impression of an unknown number of copies.

A55 **ALLEN GINSBERG: PHOTOGRAPHS** **1991**

a1. *First edition, unsigned copies*

[left title page] [up the leading edge of the page] TWELVETREES PRESS 1990
[right title page] [up the right side of the page] ALLEN GINSBERG | [down the right side of the page] PHOTOGRAPHS

[1-15]^4, pp. [1-120]. [1]: frontispiece photograph of the author with his facsimile holograph legend underneath. [2-3]: title page. [4-5]: introduction. [6]: epigraphs. [7-119]: text. [120]: 'COLOPHON | This first edition of *Allen Ginsberg: Photographs* is | limited to five thousand casebound copies and one | hundred slipcased, autographed and numbered | copies. The photographs are copyright Allen | Ginsberg 1990. This edition copyright Twelvetrees | Press 1990. The photographs were selected by Allen | Ginsberg, Raymond Foye and Jack Woody. Book | design is by Jack Woody. Printing is by Toppan | Printing Company, Tokyo, Japan using sheet-fed | gravure and offset presses. Binding is by the Toppan | Printing Company. Published by Twelvetrees Press, | 2400 North Lake Avenue, Altadena, California 91001, | 818-798-5207, ISBN 0-942642-42-2'.

36.3 x 28.9 cm. Bound in dark bluish gray (192) cloth covered boards. Blind stamped on the front cover: '[up the right side] ALLEN GINSBERG | [down the right side] PHOTOGRAPHS'. Blind stamped down the spine: 'ALLEN GINSBERG PHOTOGRAPHS'. Blind stamped up the left side of the back cover: 'TWELVETREES PRESS 1990'. White wove paper unwatermarked. Black endpapers. All edges trimmed. Issued in a white paper dustwrapper printed black with white lettering. A 7.8 x 70.8 cm. white wrap around label printed black with white lettering is folded around the back cover.

Contents: [92 photographs with legends (see also D101)] — A Commentary on Sacramental Companions [prose] — Biographies [prose]

$55.00. Published March 28, 1991 in an impression of 5,000 copies.

a2. *First edition, signed copies*

[left title page] [up the leading edge of the page] TWELVETREES PRESS 1990
[right title page] [up the right side of the page] ALLEN GINSBERG | [down the right side of the page] PHOTOGRAPHS

Identical to the first edition unsigned except that they are numbered and autographed in black ink on page [120]. These copies were produced without a dust jacket and have a dark bluish gray cloth covered 28.8 x 36.8 x 2.4 cm. slip-in case. Blind stamped on the front cover of the case: '[up the left edge] ALLEN GINSBERG | [then down the left side] PHOTOGRAPHS'. Blind stamped down the spine of the case: 'ALLEN GINSBERG PHOTOGRAPHS'. Blind stamped up the right side of the back cover of the case: 'TWELVETREES PRESS 1990'.

$150.00. Although printed by March 28, 1991 in an impression of 100 copies they were not signed by AG until May 1991 and therefore available after that date.

A56   **HOWL [German Printing]**   **1991**

howl [solid bar] | for Carl Solomon [solid bar] | [solid bar] | Allen Ginsberg [solid bar]

Twenty single leaves, pp. [1-40]. [1]: title page. [2]: blank. [3]: '[all in white on black bands] Die amerikanische Orginalausgabe | erschien im Verlag City Lights Books, San Franzisko | Alle Rechte vorbehalten | © 1956, 1959 by Allen Ginsberg | Gestaltung: Peter Biler, Hochschule für Gestaltung Offenbach / Main | Fachrichtung: Buchtypografie, Prof. Friedrich Friedl | Druck: Bernhard Vatter | April 1991'. [4]: blank. [5-39]: text. [40]: blank.

28.0 x 18.1 cm. Perfect bound in stiff gray cardboard. White transparent paper unwatermarked. White transparent endpapers. All edges trimmed. Issued in a white transparent dust jacket printed in black and gray.

Contents: Howl

$150.00. Published May 1991 in an impression of 50 copies.

Note: This was produced as a printing trades class project with a few copies sold to cover expenses.

A57   **KISSINGER DREAM I & II**   **1991**

KISSINGER DREAM | [2 geometric forms in green] | ONE and TWO | *from the Journal of* Allen Ginsberg

Nine single leaves, pp. [1-18]. [1-2]: blank. [3]: title page. [4]: blank. [5-10]: text. [11]: design of 2 faces in green. [12]: blank. [13-15]: text. [16]: *'Hand set, printed, and bound,* | *using Baskerville & Spectrum typefaces* | *on Nideggen paper, in an edition of sixty,* | *of which this is number* [numbered in pencil] . | [autographed in black ink] | [design of lines representing 3 hills over the center hill is the following] WEST HILL | [over the right hill is the following] 1991'. [17-18]: blank.

12.8 x 12.8 cm. Sewn into stiff gray (264) paper covers with black thread which is visible to form a rectangular pattern of threads. Across the front cover: 'KISSINGER | DREAM | I [a geometric form in green] | II [a geometric form in green] | Allen Ginsberg'. Yellowish gray (92) laid paper unwatermarked. The entire publication is printed in dark gray ink unless noted. Yellowish gray laid endpapers have been glued to each of the front and back inside covers. All edges trimmed.

Contents: Back in N. Y. C. [prose] — Kissinger Dream I [prose] — Kissinger Dream II [prose]

Unknown price. Published Nov. 1991 in an impression of 60 copies.

A58   **LA NOUVELLE CHUTE DE L'AMERIQUE**   **1992**

ALLEN GINSBERG I LA NOUVELLE CHUTE I DE I L'AMÉRIQUE I dix gravures I de I ROY LICHTENSTEIN I ÉDITIONS DU SOLSTICE, PARIS 1992

Portfolio consisting of a combination of unsewn folded sheets and single sheet prints, pp. [i-ii] [1-7] 8-52 [53-54] [i-ii] 55-113 [114-117]. [i-ii]: blank. [1]: half title page. [2-4]: blank. [5]: title page. [6]: '© Éditions Flammarion à l'exception de I «America» © édition Christian Bourgois, et de I «Hüm Bom!» et «Denver to Montana» © Allen Ginsberg, 1992'. [7] - 113: text. [114]: blank. [115]: 'Pour les Éditions du Solstice, cette édition de I [16 lines] I De ce livre, signé chacun par l'auteur et l'illustrateur, il a été tiré: I 125 exemplaires dont 80 nominatifs numérotés de 1 à 80 pour les sociétaires I et 45 hors commerce numérotés de I à XLV réservés aux auteurs, I aux collaborateurs et au dépôt légal. I En outre, il a été tiré 42 suites des gravures sur Japon nacré I signées par l'artiste, numérotées de 1 à 42. I Achevé d'imprimer à Paris le 21 juin 1992. I Exemplaire NO I [numbered in pencil] I [autographs of author and artist in pencil]'. [116-118]: blank.

49.7 x 37.3 cm. Laid into portfolio. Vivid red (11) cloth covered boards printed across the spine all in white: 'ALLEN I GINSBERG [up the spine] LA NOUVELLE CHUTE DE L'AMÉRIQUE [across the spine] ROY I LICHTENSTEIN'. White wove paper unwatermarked. White endpapers are folded to make another portfolio containing the sheets by inserting the first and last leaves of the book in flaps. Top edges trimmed. Issued in a deep blue (179) cloth covered slip-in case.

Contents: Translation by Gerard-G. Lemaire and Anne-Christine Taylor: America II Amérique — Auto Poesy: On the Lam from Bloomington II Auto Poésie: En Cavale de Bloomington — Bayonne Entering NYC II Bayonne en Entrant Dans NYC — Autumn Gold: New England Fall II Or Autumnal: Arrière-Saison en Nouvelle Angleterre — An Open Window on Chicago II Une Fenêtre ouverte sur Chicago — Over Denver Again II De Nouveau au-Dessus de Denver — Northwest Passage II Passage du Nord-Ouest — Graffiti 12th Cubicle Men's Room Syracuse Airport — Graffiti 12e Cabine des Pissotières-Aéroport de Syracuse — Friday the Thirteenth II Vendredi Treize Translation, by Yves Le Pellec: Hum Bom! II Hüm Bom! — Denver to Montana II De Denver su Montana, Départ 27 Mai 1972

$1,200.00. Published June 21, 1992 in an impression of 125 copies, 80 copies numbered 1-80 and 45 copies numbered I-XLV.

Note: Barrier sheets are inserted between the prints and the facing pages. One additional print is inserted between pages 54 and 55, a print of Allen Ginsberg in a meditation position.

A59   **KADDISH FOR NAOMI GINSBERG**   **1992**

KADDISH I *for Naomi Ginsberg*, 1894-1956 I *by* I ALLEN GINSBERG I *with two other related poems* I WHITE SHROUD *and* BLACK SHROUD I *an introduction by* I HELEN VENDLER I *and lithograph portraits of the poet and his mother by* I R. B. KITAJ I *San Francisco* I THE ARION PRESS I 1992

[1-2]6 [3]8 [4-5]6 with 2 additional leaves tipped in between the 4th and 5th leaves of the second signature, pp. [i-ii] [1-6] 7-17 [18-23] 24-62 [63-66]. [i-ii]: blank. [1]: 'KADDISH *with* WHITE SHROUD *and* BLACK SHROUD I COPY [numbered and autographed in pencil] ALLEN GINSBERG'. [2]: blank. [3]: title page. [4]: acknowledgments. [5]: contents page. [6]: blank. 7-17: introduction. [18]: blank. [19]: '*Portraits of the poet and his mother, both at age thirty*. Lithograph by R. B. Kitaj.' [20-21]: lithographs signed in pencil on p. 21 by the artist. [22]: blank. [23]: half title page. 24-62: text. [63]: 'COLOPHON I This is the thirty-eighth publication of the

Arion Press. The edition is limited | to 226 copies, of which 200 numbered copies are for sale and 26 lettered copies | are hors de commerce. Each copy is signed by the author and the artist. The | types are Imprint, composed in Monotype by M & H Type, San Francisco, and | Weiss Titling, set by hand. The paper is T. H. Saunders mould-made, from | Inveresk, Wells, England. The lithographs were printed by Curwen Chilford | Prints Limited, Cambridge, England. The book was designed, printed, and | bound at the Arion Press under the direction of Andrew Hoyem, with the | assistance of Glenn Todd, Gerald Reddan, Lawrence Van Velzer, Peggy | Gotthold, and Leif Erlandsson. The project was completed in the fall of 1992.' [64-66]: blank.

32.1 x 26.4 cm. Bound in black cloth covered boards in a unique variation of quarterbinding with grayish green (150) cloth covers. The spine and part of each cover being black with triangular grayish green insets with a flap from the back cover that wraps around to the front cover and inserts into a recess in the front black cover by means of 2 tabs. Across the front cover on the flap thus folded: 'KADDISH'. White laid paper watermarked: '[hollow lettering] T H SAUNDERS | [crest] | [in ornamental type] *T H S*'. A barrier sheet is between the 2 lithographs. White laid endpapers watermarked as above. Top edges trimmed. *Note:* Also accompanying each book is a 10.8 x 14.0 cm. white paper label explaining how to open the book "A note on the binding".

Contents: Kaddish — White Shroud — Black Shroud

$600.00. Published Oct. 30, 1992 in an impression of 226 copies, 200 of which are numbered 1 to 200 and 26 of which are lettered A to Z.

Note: 20 copies of the book were available with an additional lithograph of the same image on larger paper each signed by the artist. The price for those 20 sets was $1,500.00. The 20 copies of the book were from the 200 numbered copies listed above.

A60   **VISITING FATHER & FRIENDS**   **1993**

Visiting | Father | & | Friends | Allen Ginsberg | Thinker Review International | [13.8 cm. rule] | Louisville, Kentucky | 1993

Single gathering of eight leaves, pp. [1-16]. [1-2]: blank. [3]: half title page. [4]: blank. [5]: title page. [6]: 'Copyright © 1993 by Allen Ginsberg | Published by: | Thinker Review International / Whitefield Press | Louisville, Kentucky'. [7]: second half title page. [8]: blank. [9-11]: text. [12]: blank. [13]: 'Limited Edition of Fifty Copies'. [14-16]: blank.

22.3 x 15.3 cm. Sewn into stiff pale yellow (89) paper wrappers with blue thread. Across the front cover all within a single rule frame: 'Allen Ginsberg | [4 lines inside a 6 rule frame] Visiting | Father | & | Friends | [below the six rule frame] a | Thinker Review | International | Chapbook'. Across the back cover all within a single rule frame: '[photograph of the author] | Thinker Review editors Kent Fielding and Ron Whitehead with | Allen Ginsberg at Twice Told Coffee House, Louisville, Kentucky.' Pale yellow wove paper unwatermarked. All edges trimmed.

Contents: Visiting Father & Friends

$5.00. Published April 1993 in an impression of 50 copies.

A61   **THIEVES STOLE THIS POEM**   **1993**

a1. First edition, paperbound

Thieves Stole | This Poem | Allen Ginsberg | Carnivorous Arpeggio (Press)! | Hull England

Single gathering of six leaves, pp. [1-12]. [1-2]: blank. [3]: title page. [4]: blank. [5]: *'Limited to fifty numbered copies | printed on Brightwater | laid paper | Copy No....* [numbered above the dots] | © 1993'. [6]: blank. [7-11]: text. [12]: blank.

21.1 x 12.6 cm. Stapled twice into stiff purplish gray (233) paper wrappers. Yellowish white (92) laid paper unwatermarked. All edges trimmed. Issued in a brownish pink paper dust jacket printed across the front cover: *'Thieves Stole | This Poem | Allen Ginsberg '.*

Contents: Research — Thieves Stole This Poem

£2.50. Published Sept. 20, 1993 in an impression of 50 copies, numbered 1 to 50.

a2. *First edition, hardbound, signed*

Thieves Stole | This Poem | Allen Ginsberg | Carnivorous Arpeggio (Press)! | Hull England

Single gathering of six leaves, pp. [1-12]. [1-2]: blank. [3]: title page. [4]: blank. [5]: *'This edition is hand-bound in boards | to a limit of 10 copies numbered | [numeral above a printed rule] to [numeral above a printed rule]. | Copy No....* [numeral above the dots] | © 1993'. [6]: blank. [7-11]: text. [12]: blank.

21.5 x 13.2 cm. Sewn into black cloth covered boards. Yellowish white (92) laid paper unwatermarked. Purplish gray (233) paste-down paper. Issued in a brownish pink paper dust jacket printed across the front cover: *'Thieves Stole | This Poem | Allen Ginsberg '.* This issued in a protective clear plastic dust jacket. All edges trimmed.

£10.00. Published Feb. 1994 in an impression of 10 copies, numbered I to X.

A62   **HONORABLE COURTSHIP**   **1993**

ALLEN GINSBERG | [in dark reddish purple (242) hollow type] Honorable Courtship | FROM THE AUTHOR'S JOURNALS, JANUARY 1-15, 1955 | WOOD ENGRAVINGS BY DEAN BORNSTEIN | EDITED BY GORDON BALL | [publisher's device in dark reddish purple] | ESPRESSO EDITION : COFFEE HOUSE PRESS : 1993

[1-5]^4, pp. [1-40]. [1-2]: blank. [3]: title page. [4]: 'Copyright © 1993 by Allen Ginsberg'. [5-6]: introduction. [7]: half title page. [8]: blank. [9-35]: text. [36]: blank. [37]: notes. [38]: 'The Goudy Modern type was set at the M&H typefoundry | in San Francisco. The entire edition has been printed on | handmade Fabriano Umbria paper and handbound by Jill | Jevne. This book was designed by Allan Kornblum, and | printed by Leslie Ross at Coffee House Press. Each book | comes with a separate suite of wood engravings. Of two | hundred copies signed by author and artist, you are holding | number [numbered in black ink] . | [autographed by artist and author in black ink]'. [39-40]: blank.

17.9 x 11.7 cm. Sewn into stiff purple, gold and black marbleized paper covered cardboard covers with black string. Inset in the front cover is a black framed deep red (13) paper label on which is printed: 'ALLEN GINSBERG | Honorable Courtship'.

White wove paper unwatermarked. Top edges trimmed. Laid into a dark purple (224) clamshell box. Inset in the front cover of the box is a black framed deep red paper label on which is printed: 'ALLEN GINSBERG | Honorable Courtship'. Also laid into the box is an additional set of the 5 prints which appear within the book.

Contents: Honorable Courtship [journal entries]

$500.00. Published Nov. 1, 1993 in an impression of 200 copies numbered 1 to 200.

A63   **COSMOPOLITAN GREETINGS**   **1994**

a1.1 *First edition, first printing, hardbound*

[in hollow type] ALLEN | [in hollow type] GINSBERG | [4.2 cm. rule] | [in hollow type] COSMOPOLITAN | [in hollow type] GREETINGS | [in hollow type] POEMS | [in hollow type] 1986-1992 | [design of 3 fish which share a common head] | [2 line epigraph] | [publisher's device] | HarperCollins*Publishers*

Seventy-two single leaves, pp. [1-2] [i-viii] ix-xi [xii] xiii-xv [xvi] xvii-xviii [xix-xx] 1-118 [119-122]. [1-2]: blank. [i]: half title page. [ii]: blank. [iii]: card page. [iv]: blank. [v]: title page. [vi]: '[24 lines] | COSMOPOLITAN GREETINGS: POEMS 1986-1992. Copyright © 1994 by Allen Ginsberg. All | [7 lines] | FIRST EDITION | [1 line] | [11.1 cm. rule] | [5 lines] | ISBN 0-06-016770-X | [3 lines] | [11.1 cm. rule] | 94 95 96 97 98 PS/RRD 10 9 8 7 6 5 4 3 2 1'. [vii]: dedication page. [viii]: blank. ix-x: contents pages. xi: acknowledgments. [xii]: blank. xiii-xv: preface. [xvi]: blank. xvii-xviii: prologue. [xix]: second half title page. [xx]: blank. 1-114: text. 115-118: index. [119-122]: blank.

24.1 x 15.8 cm. Quarter bound in black cloth spine with black paper covered boards. Across the front cover in gold is a design of three fish which share a common head. Down the spine in metallic purple: 'ALLEN GINSBERG [in 2 lines] COSMOPOLITAN | GREETINGS [across the spine] Harper | Collins'. White wove paper unwatermarked. White endpapers. Top and bottom edges trimmed. Issued in a white paper dust jacket printed in black, gold, strong orange yellow (68) and strong violet (207).

Contents: Improvisation in Beijing — Visiting Father & Friends — You Don't Know It — On the Conduct of the World Seeking Beauty Against Government — Hard Labor — Velocity of Money — Sphincter — Spot Anger — London Dream Doors — Cosmopolitan Greetings — Fifth Internationale [includes music notation] — Europe, Who Knows? [includes music notation] — Graphic Winces — Imitation of K. S. — I Went to the Movie of Life — When the Light Appears — On Cremation of Chögyam Trungpa, Vidyadhara — Nanao — Personals Ad — Proclamation — To Jacob Rabinowitz — Grandma Earth's Song — [drawing] — Salutations to Fernando Pessoa — [photograph taken from AG's kitchen window] — May Days 1988 — Numbers in U.S. File Cabinet (Death Waits to Be Executed) — Return of Kral Majales — Elephant in the Meditation Hall — Poem in the Form of a Snake That Bites Its Tail — Mistaken Introductions — CIA Dope Calypso [includes music notation] — N.S.A. Dope Calypso — Just Say Yes Calypso — Hum Bom! — Supplication for the Rebirth of the Vidyadhara Chögyam Trungpa, Rinpoche — After the Big Parade — Big Eats — Not Dead Yet — Yiddishe Kopf — John — A Thief Stole This Poem — Lunchtime — [drawing] — After Lalon — Get It? — Angelic Black Holes [by Andrei Voznesensky, translated by AG and Nina Bouis] — Research — Put Down Your Cigarette Rag (Dont Smoke) [includes music notation] — Violent Collaborations [includes music notation] — Calm Panic Campaign Promise — Now and Forever — Who Eats Who? — The Charnel Ground — Everyday — Fun House Antique Store — News Stays News — Autumn Leaves — In the Benjo — American Sentences — Notes [prose].

$20.00. Published May 18, 1994 in an impression of 10,000 copies and reprinted once in an impression of 5,000 copies.

Note: Second printing identified by the printing statement on the verso of the title page.

A64   **MIND WRITING SLOGANS**   **1994**

a1. First edition, regular copies

[5.0 x 5.0 cm. deep red (13) square on which the first 3 words are printed] Mind I Writing I Slogans I [below the square] Allen Ginsberg I *"First thought is best in art, second in other matters."* I — William Blake I [publisher's device] LIMBERLOST PRESS 1994

Single gathering of twelve leaves, pp. [1-24]. [1-2]: blank. [3]: half title page. [4]: blank. [5]: title page. [6]: 'ACKNOWLEDGEMENTS I [5 lines] I Copyright © 1994 by Allen Ginsberg I ISBN 0-936159-19-1 I 0-931659-20-5 (Signed Edition) I Limberlost Press I Rick & Rosemary Ardinger, Editors I HC 33, Box 1113 I Boise, Idaho 83706 I (208) 344-2120'. [7]: dedication page. [8]: blank. [9]: preface. [10]: [drawing by AG]. [11-19]: text. [20]: 'COLOPHON I MIND WRITING SLOGANS has been letterpressed I in a first edition of 800 copies, each page fed by I hand into the jaws of a Chandler & Price I platen press in June of 1994 for "The Beats and Other Rebel Angels" I conference honoring the poet at Naropa Institute. I The type is Pabst Old Style. The paper I is Mohawk Letterpress, sewn into Ingres Antique I endsheets and Magnani Pescia wrappers. I 100 copies I have been signed and numbered.' [21-24]: blank.

20.6 x 14.0 cm. Sewn into stiff yellowish white (92) paper wrappers. Across the front cover all on a design of a deep red (13) circle, a light greenish blue (172) star, a 5.0 x 5.0 cm. deep red square and a 5.0 x 5.0 cm. light greenish blue square is the following, the first three lines are on uneven base lines: 'MiNd I WRitiNg I SLOgaNs I ALLEN GINSBERG'. Across the back cover is a design of a black square, a light greenish blue triangle, a deep red diamond, a deep red circle and a light greenish blue square. The leading edge of the front cover is untrimmed. White wove paper unwatermarked, except the first and last leaves which are light yellowish brown (76) laid paper watermarked: 'INGRES-FABRIANO' (see note below). All edges trimmed.

Contents: Definitions, a Preface [prose] — [drawing of a seated Buddha-figure] — Mind Writing Slogans [collection of single phrases or sentences divided into the following sections] I. Ground; II. Path; III. Fruition

$12.00. Published July 2, 1994 in an impression of 700 copies.

Note: Several different color papers were used for the first and last leaves but all watermarked as above; light blue, yellow, brown and light green. Additional colors may have been used in unknown amounts according to the publisher.

a2. First edition, signed copies

[5.0 x 5.0 cm. deep red (13) square on which the first 3 words are printed] Mind I Writing I Slogans I [below the square] Allen Ginsberg I *"First thought is best in art, second in other matters."* I — William Blake I [publisher's device] LIMBERLOST PRESS 1994

Single gathering of twelve leaves, pp. [1-24]. [1-2]: blank. [3]: half title page. [4]: blank. [5]: title page. [6]: 'ACKNOWLEDGEMENTS I [5 lines] I Copyright © 1994 by Allen Ginsberg I ISBN 0-936159-19-1 I 0-931659-20-5 (Signed Edition) I Limberlost Press I Rick & Rosemary Ardinger, Editors I HC 33, Box 1113 I Boise, Idaho 83706 I (208) 344-2120'. [7]: dedication page. [8]: blank. [9]: preface. [10]:

[drawing by AG]. [11-19]: text. [20]: 'COLOPHON | MIND WRITING SLOGANS has been letterpressed | in a first edition of 800 copies, each page fed by | hand into the jaws of a Chandler & Price | platen press in June of 1994 for "The Beats and Other Rebel Angels" | conference honoring the poet at Naropa Institute. | The type is Pabst Old Style. The paper | is Mohawk Letterpress, sewn into Ingres Antique | endsheets and Magnani Pescia wrappers. | 100 copies | have been signed and numbered. | This copy is ʹ. [21-24]: blank.

20.6 x 14.0 cm. Sewn into stiff yellowish white (92) paper wrappers. Across the front cover all on a design of a deep red (13) circle, a light greenish blue (172) star, a 5.0 x 5.0 cm. deep red square and a 5.0 x 5.0 cm. light greenish blue square is the following, the first three lines are on uneven base lines: 'MiNd | WRitiNg | SLOgaNs | ALLEN GINSBERG'. Across the back cover is a design of a black square, a light greenish blue triangle, a deep red diamond, a deep red circle and a light greenish blue square. The leading edge of the front cover is untrimmed. White wove paper unwatermarked, except the first and last leaves which are light blue laid paper watermarked: 'INGRES-FABRIANO'. All edges trimmed.

Contents: As first issue.

$50.00. Published ca. Aug. 1994 in an impression of 100 copies, numbered 1-100 and signed by the author.

Note: All copies of this issue were bound with light blue first and last leaves.

A65   **POEM, INTERVIEW, PHOTOGRAPHS**   **1994**

Poem, Interview, Photographs | Allen Ginsberg | [7.6 x 11.0 cm. photograph of the author] | Allen Ginsberg | University of Louisville - October 1992 | *Charlie Coddington* | Published in Heaven Chapbook Series #28 | White Fields Press in support of the literary renaissance | Louisville, Kentucky | 1994

Single gathering of twelve leaves, pp. [1-24]. [1]: title page. [2]: blank. [3]: *'Poem, Interview, Photogrpahs* [sic] | Copyright © 1994 by Allen Ginsberg | published by: White Fields Press | p.o. box 3685 | louisville, kentucky | 40201-3685 | (502) 266-9471 | [6 lines]'. [4]: blank. [5]: half title page. [6]: blank. [7]: photograph of the author. [8]: blank. [9-21]: text. [22]: blank. [23]: *'Limited Edition of 250 Copies'*. [24]: advertisement.

21.5 x 13.7 cm. Stapled twice into stiff white paper wrappers. Across the front cover: '[all within single rule frame] Allen Ginsberg | [12.5 x 8.5 cm. photograph of the author] | *"Self-Portrait, 1947," Allen Ginsberg* | *Poem, Interview, Photographs* | Published | in | Heaven | Chapbook Series #28 | White Fields Press'. Across the back cover: '[9.9 x 12.5 cm. photograph of the author and editors] | Kent Fielding, Allen Ginsberg, Ron Whitehead | Standing in back room at Twice Told Coffeehouse | *Charlie Coddington'*. White wove paper unwatermarked. All edges trimmed.

Contents: Visiting Father and Friends — [an interview with Allen Ginsberg by Danny O'Bryan]

$15.00. Published ca. July 25, 1994 in an impression of 250 copies.

A66   **BEAT LEGACY, CONNECTIONS, INFLUENCES**   **1994**

Beat l Legacy, Connections, Influences: l Allen Ginsberg l Poems & Letters l by l Allen Ginsberg l Essay l by l Gordon Ball l Published l in l Heaven l Chapbook Series #40 l White Fields Press l in support of l the literary renaissance l Louisville, Kentucky l 1994

Single gathering of twelve leaves, pp. [1-24]. [1]: title page. [2]: blank. [3]: 'Beat l Legacy, Connections, Influences: l Allen Ginsberg l Copyright © 1994 by Allen Ginsberg (poems) l Copyright © by Gordon Ball (essay) l published by: White Fields Press l p.o. box 3685 l louisville, kentucky l 40201-3685 l [5 lines]'. [4-22]: text. [23]: 'Limited edition of 250 copies'. [24]: advertisement.

21.5 x 13.7 cm. Stapled twice into stiff white paper wrappers. Across the front cover: '[all within single rule frame] [the following within a triple rule frame] Beat l Legacy, Connections, Influences: l Allen Ginsberg l [below the triple rule frame] Published l in l Heaven l Chapbook Series #40 l White Fields Press'. Across the back cover: '[8.9 x 12.3 cm. photograph of the author] l Allen Ginsberg'. White wove paper unwatermarked. All edges trimmed.

Contents: [letter to Ron Whitehead] — Put Down Your Cigarette Rag — [letter to Ron Whitehead] — Cosmopolitan Greetings — [letter to Ron Whitehead] — [self-portrait photograph in bathroom mirror, not first appearance]

$15.00. Published ca. July 25, 1994 in an impression of 250 copies.

AA

Broadsides by Allen Ginsberg

AA1   **A STRANGE NEW COTTAGE IN BERKELEY**   **1963**

A Strange New Cottage in Berkeley I By Allen Ginsberg I [design of leaves surrounding a cottage] I All afternoon cutting bramble blackberries off a tottering I [13 lines] I [author's autograph in black ink] I 300 copies printed at the Grabhorn Press I San Francisco I Woodcut by Robert La Vigne I [artist's autograph in black ink]

Single 50.8 x 33. 8 cm. sheet printed on one side only. White laid paper watermarked: 'Hamilton Andorra'. Right edge untrimmed.

Contents: A Strange New Cottage in Berkeley

$12.50 for the portfolio, some portfolios were broken up and broadsides sold separately for $2.50 each. Published October 1963 in an impression of 300 copies, 250 copies were placed on sale, 25 copies were given to the author and 25 copies to the artist.

Note: Originally laid in a portfolio as 1 of 8 broadsides printed by various presses. Label on portfolio reads: 'SAN FRANCISCO ARTS FESTIVAL I A POETRY FOLIO I 1963' and another portfolio has been seen with the label as follows: 'San Francisco I Arts festival I A Poetry folio. 1963.' Priority or reason for the variant labeling is unclear.

AA2   **IN BED ON MY GREEN PURPLE RED PINK**   **ca. 1964**

[in two columns] [left column in facsimile holograph] From Journals I Jan New York 1961 [this is crossed out] I [in facsimile holograph] January N.Y. 1961 I [the rest typewritten with facsimile holograph corrections throughout] In bed on my green purple red pink I [55 lines]
[right column all in facsimile holograph] [number circled] 1   Sept 28 [with a caret under the date] 1964 I [scribble deletion] I E. 2 STREET I HIGH I [star] I w/Harry Smith I [star] I [2 lines] I [star] I [3 lines] I [star] I [1 line] I [star] I [2 lines] I [star] I [8 lines]

Single sheet folded once to form 4 pages, 24.1 x 19.7 cm. , pp. [1-4]. [1]: title page. [2-4]: text. Deep orange yellow (69) laid paper unwatermarked. All edges trimmed.

Contents: In Bed on My Green Purple Red Pink

Publication information is unknown, an educated guess is that it was printed ca. 1964-1965, probably shortly after the composition date of Sept. 28, 1964.

AA3   **KRAL MAJALES**   **1965**

KRAL MAJALES | [left 1/3 of sheet is an illustration of a nude AG in white silhouette within a penis-shaped frame] | [below the frame in facsimile autograph] Robert LaVigne [in the center 1/3 of sheet] [text in 79 lines] | *May 7, 1965* | [in facsimile autograph] Allen Ginsberg [right 1/3 of sheet is an illustration of a nude AG in black silhouette within a penis-shaped frame] | [below the frame] *oyez*

Single 51.3 x 37.6 cm. sheet printed on one side only. White wove paper unwatermarked. All edges trimmed.

Contents: Kral Majales

$7.50. Published 1965 in an impression of 350 copies.

AA4   **MESSAGE II**   **1965?**

Message II | Long since the years | [23 lines of text in which corrections are made in lines 15 and 17] | March 1965 [the M in March is set a little higher on the base line than the rest of the letters] | [all the rest in blue in AG's facsimile holograph] If you still want a poem to use on poster | here is one — if not OK. | AllenGinsberg

Single 76.1 x 58.3 cm. sheet printed on one side only. White wove paper unwatermarked. All edges trimmed.

Contents: Message II

Publication details are not known for this broadside, published ca. 1965.

Note: This is a blow-up of AG's typed and corrected manuscript.

AA5   **THIS FORM OF LIFE NEEDS SEX**   **1965**

[first 2 lines in facsimile holograph] This form of life needs | sex... [in type] : a poem by | ALLEN GINSBERG | I will have to accept women | [50 lines]

Single 27.9 x 21.6 cm. sheet printed on both sides, pp. [1]-2. [1]: title page. [2]: 'p. 2 | and buggered myself innumerably | [42 lines] | [line of asterisks] | Reprinted from Bugger (NYC: Fuckpress, Nov. 1964). Distributed | by the Sexual Freedom League of San Francisco as a contribution | to public dialogue on sexual matters. | [design of male and female symbols within Yin and Yang sign] SEXUAL FREEDOM LEAGUE | meetings 8pm Mondays at | THE BLUE UNICORN | 1927 Hayes, SF (at Ashbury)'. White wove paper unwatermarked. All edges trimmed.

Contents: This Form of Life Needs Sex

Distributed free on the streets of San Francisco. Published in the Spring 1965 in an impression of approximately 500 copies.

AA6   **CONSULTING I CHING SMOKING POT**   **1967**
              LISTENING TO THE FUGS SING BLAKE

[all printed around a woodcut design of a hookah and flowers] CONSULTING I CHING SMOKING POT LISTENING TO THE FUGS SING BLAKE | [16 lines of text] | Allen Ginsberg June '66 | Printed by Kriya Press of Sri Ram Ashrama, Pleasant Valley,

New York 1967 | Limited edition of one hundred copies of which this is number [numbered in black ink]

Single 45.6 x 32.9 cm. sheet printed on one side only. White wove paper unwatermarked. All edges trimmed.

Contents: Consulting I Ching Smoking Pot Listening to the Fugs Sing Blake

$3.00. Published 1967 in an impression of 100 copies.

AA7   **ENTERING KANSAS CITY HIGH**   **1967**

ENTERING KANSAS CITY HIGH | [42 lines of text] | [printed vertically up the page] ALLEN [across the page] [design of three fish which share a common head] GINSBERG | Formula Series #5, c/r A. Ginsberg, 1967: T. Williams, Publ.: 830 Missouri St., Lawrence, Kans.

Single 60.6 x 37.9 cm. sheet printed on one side only. Light brown (57) with darker flecks wove paper unwatermarked. All edges trimmed.

Contents: Entering Kansas City High

$1.00-$1.50. Published in 1967 in an unknown quantity.

AA8   **WHO BE KIND TO**   **1967**

a.1 *First edition, first printing*

[sheet is decorated with vivid red (11), vivid yellowish green (129) and deep violet (208) patterns, with a vivid yellowish green border and floral designs in each corner] [words circle the photograph of the author's head like a halo] [in light yellow (86)] WHO BE KIND TO [with two light yellow vertical strokes between each word] [the photograph of the author's hands appear to be holding a light yellow Ten Commandments-type tablet on which is the following in deep violet] [text in 2 columns of 69 lines each] | London June 10, 1965 | [publisher's device] A Cranium Broadside CRANIUM PRESS, 642 SHRADER, SAN FRANCISCO DESIGN: WES WILSON PHOTO: LARRY KEENAN, JR. | [below the tablet in deep violet within a lozenge-shaped frame in facsimile holograph] Allen Ginsberg

Single 77.5 x 40.5 cm. sheet printed on one side only. Light yellow (86) wove paper unwatermarked. All edges trimmed.

Contents: Who Be Kind To

$2.00. Published ca. May 1967 in an impression of 470 copies, possibly 26 of these were lettered and signed by AG, but AG does not remember this and no lettered copies have been found.

a.2 *First edition, second printing:* 3,000 copies.

As above but printed on white paper, many of which were discarded due to being off register according to the publisher.

AA9   **PRIMROSE HILL GURU**   **1967**

[all a facsimile of holograph manuscript] [in moderate yellowish green (136)] [small circle] [dash] Primrose Hill Guru [dash] [small circle] I [dark blue (183)] It is the moon that disappears I [3 lines in dark blue] [in moderate reddish purple (241)] [design of three fish which share a common head] I [dark blue] my invisible stockings I [dark blue] It is the call of a bell I [moderate yellowish green] May 1965 London Allen Ginsberg

Single 23.9 x 16.4 cm. sheet printed on one side only. White wove paper unwatermarked. Bottom edge untrimmed.

Contents: Primrose Hill Guru

$200.00 per portfolio, single sheets were hors commerce. Published ca. Dec. 7, 1967 in an impression of 225 copies, 115 of which are hors commerce and 110 of which are numbered 1 to 110 and collected in the following portfolio.

Portfolio: [all rubber stamped in green hollow letters unless noted] STAMPED I INDELIBLY I [design of chicken in red] I A COLLECTION OF RUBBERSTAMP PRINTS I EDITED BY WILLIAM KATZ

[1-3]^4 [4]^2, pp. [1-28]. [1]: title page. [2-3]: contents pages. [4-25]: text. [26]: blank. [27]: '[red] STAMPED INDELIBLY I [green] EXISTS IN AN EDITION OF 225 OF WHICH I [green] ONE HUNDRED AND TEN, NUMBERED 1 THROUGH I [green] 110, ARE FOR SALE THROUGH MULTIPLES, INC., I [green] 929 MADISON AVENUE, NYC. THE COLLECTION I [green] CONTAINS 14 RUBBERSTAMP PRINTS EACH SIGNED I [green] BY THE CREATOR AND PRINTED BY WILLIAM KATZ I [green] DURING MAY THOUGH DECEMBER OF 1967. EACH I [green] PORTFOLIO IS NUMBERED. THIS IS I [green] NO. ____ [numbered and signed by the printer in pencil] I [green chicken] I [red] © 1967 BY WILLIAM KATZ, 2 SPRING at the BOWERY, NYC. I [red] ANOTHER INDIANAKATZ PRODUCTION'. [28]: blank.

29.3 x 22.2 cm. Bound in light grayish yellowish brown (79) cloth covered boards. White wove paper unwatermarked. White endpapers. All edges untrimmed.

Note: Entire publication is produced by rubberstamps. Each of 14 different prints is stamped onto a sheet which is attached to the leaves bound into the book. Every page has a short stub at the binding which protects the thickness of the attached sheets. This portfolio was in production over a long period of time, at least one copy of AG's poem was inscribed by AG as early as July 10, 1965, but the entire book was not available until Dec. 7, 1967 at the earliest.

AA10   **MESSAGE 2**   **1968**

[multi color - gold, red, blue, black, orange, purple - illustration of the Statue of Liberty with sun and water over which is printed in red and blue] message 2 I [all the rest in black] Long since the years I [23 lines of text] I Alan [sic] Ginsberg March 1965 I an original poster by Michael English I poem by Alan [sic] Ginsberg March 1965 © I published by Ad Infinitum Ltd London 1968 © 102

Single 97.0 x 55.1 cm. sheet printed on one side only. White wove paper unwatermarked. All edges trimmed.

Contents: Message II

Ca. $3.50. Published in the first quarter of 1968 in an impression of 300 copies.

AA11   **GRANT PARK, AUG. 28, 1968**   **1968**

[all in light blue (181) on a photograph of the author with a vertical line on the right]
GRANT PARK AUGUST 28, 1968 | [20 LINES] | — ALLEN GINSBERG DAKOTA
BROADSIDES [bullet] BOX 782 [bullet] MONTREAL [bullet] DESIGN TERRY
MOSHER [bullet]

Single 35.5 x 21.5 cm. sheet printed on one side only. Light blue (181) card stock. All
edges trimmed.

Contents: Grant Park August 28, 1968

Published in late 1968 in an unknown number of copies.

AA12   **THE MAHARISHI AND ME**   **ca. 1968**

THE MAHARISHI AND ME | by Allen Ginsberg | San Francisco Express-Times |
LIBERATION News Service | I saw Maharishi speak here January 21st and then went
up to the Plaza Hotel | [43 lines of text] | (turn over page for more Allen meets
Maharishi...)

Single 27.9 x 21.6 cm. sheet printed on both sides, pp. [1-2]. [1]: title page. [2]:
'(Maharishi and Me continued) | In a sense his position is not far from Krishnamurti or
Leary (though Leary has | [17 lines of text] | --30-- | SOME GROOVIES ... | [21
lines] | --30--'.

Light green wove paper unwatermarked. All edges trimmed.

Contents: I Saw Maharishi Speak Here [prose]

Distributed free. Published ca. 1968 in an impression of an unknown number of copies.

AA13   **NO MONEY, NO WAR**   **1970**

[all in facsimile of a holograph manuscript unless noted] [in dark blue] No Money, No
War | [in dark blue] Government Anarchy prolongs illegal | [12 lines in dark blue] |
[design of three fish which share a common head in maroon] [in dark blue] Allen
Ginsberg | [in dark blue] Dec. 16, 1969 | [down the right edge in dark blue in facsimile
holograph] Mark Morris | [dark blue 41.1 cm. stripe] | [typeset in dark blue] *War Tax
Resistance* 339 LAFAYETTE STREET, NEW YORK, NEW YORK 10012 [design of a
flower which extends up through the stripe and on which is printed all the following]
Don't | Pay | War | Taxes

Single 55.7 x 43.1 cm. sheet printed on one side only. White wove paper unwatermarked.
All edges trimmed.

Contents: No Money, No War

25¢ and raised to 50¢ each within 2 weeks of publication. Published ca. Jan. 27, 1970 in
an unknown quantity.

AA14   **FOR THE SOUL OF THE PLANET IS WAKENING**   **1970**

[photograph of AG holding a mug] | [all in facsimile of holograph manuscript] For the
soul of the Planet is | [10 lines of text] Allen Ginsberg | (copyright 1970 DESERT
REVIEW PRESS — Santa Fe, N.M. — Photo: Doug Magneson — Text courtesy MGM
Records)

Single 56.3 x 34.2 cm. sheet printed on one side only. Glossy white wove paper unwatermarked. All edges trimmed.

Contents: For the Soul of the Planet is Wakening

Published in 1970 in an unknown quantity.

AA15   RAIN-WET ASPHALT HEAT, GARBAGE CURBED CANS   1970
OVERFLOWING

[all in dark brown (59)] Rain-wet Asphalt Heat, Garbage Curbed Cans Overflowing | [30 lines of text] | August 2, 1969 | ALLEN GINSBERG | *a free poem from* | THE ALTERNATIVE PRESS | *4339 Avery* | *Detroit, Michigan*

Single 30.3 x 20.3 cm. sheet printed on one side only. Dark orange yellow (72) wove paper unwatermarked. Bottom edge untrimmed.

Contents: Rain-wet Asphalt Heat, Garbage Curbed Cans Overflowing

Distributed free. Published May 1, 1970 in an impression of 400 copies.

AA16   SPRING ANTI-WAR GAMES   1971

[all in deep reddish purple (238)] [all within decorative border in calligraphy interspersed with drawings and designs initialed by "b.c." in the lower left corner of the border] SPRING ANTI-WAR GAMES | 1971 | [5 lines within design] | [11 lines below the design] | [2 columns of 25 and 23 lines] | [below the border in 1 line] MAY DAY [bullet] WASH. D.C. MAY 1-7 [bullet] MAY DAY TRIBE, [in 2 lines] 1029 VT. AVE. NW RM 906 | WASHINGTON, D.C. 20005

Single 43.2 x 27.8 cm. sheet printed on one side only. Very pale blue (184) wove paper unwatermarked. All edges trimmed.

Contents: Spring Anti-War Games

Distributed free. Published ca. May 1, 1971 in an impression of an unknown number of copies.

Note: Probably issued as a poster and no price, put up to promote the event.

AA17   HUM BOM!   1971

[left side of page is a drawing within a circle of two hands forming a sign] [right side of sheet in facsimile of holograph manuscript] HUM BOM! | [2 columns of 24 lines of text, and 16 lines of text followed in the second column by the following] U.S. Shiva Mantra | Bixby Canyon Sabdh | Allen Ginsberg May '71 | [drawing of a trident] | Om Namah Shivaye

Single 25.2 x 35.2 cm. sheet printed on one side only. White wove paper unwatermarked. All edges trimmed.

Contents: Hum Bom!

Published after May 1971 in an impression of an unknown number of copies.

AA18   **JAMES D. HART**   **1971**

[title in 2 lines printed over the artwork hand-colored in black, brown, yellow, blue and orange picturing James Hart walking through a stone archway, with a peddler in the background and AG in the foreground] JAMES D. HART | IN MODERN AMERICAN LITERATURE | [7 lines of text] | — ALLEN GINSBERG | "Sather Gate Illumination" | Berkeley 1956 | *Printed to annoy him on his sixtieth birthday, fifteen years later,* | *by Andrew Hoyem & Robert Grabhorn.*

Single 34.4 x 22.1 cm. sheet printed on one side only. White laid paper watermarked with a large round seal. Top edge only trimmed.

Contents: Sather Gate Illumination [excerpt]

Not for sale. Published June 1971 in an impression of possibly 5 to 10 copies as a gift for James Hart.

Note: This information according to the publishers.

AA19   **NOTED ON EDGE OF BOMBAY MAP**   **1971**

[illustration of a flower in moderate olive green (125)] Noted on edge of Bombay map | *Stop trying not to die* | [9 lines] | Allen Ginsberg

Single 20.2 x 13.7 cm. sheet printed on one side only. White laid paper unwatermarked. All edges trimmed.

Contents: Noted on Edge of Bombay Map

Not for sale. Published ca. 1971 in an impression of 15 to 20 copies.

Note: Publication information from letter by the publisher, Nelson Adams at Coach House Press, Toronto.

AA20   **THE OGRE THAT GOES WITH THE ROSE**   **1971**

ALLEN GINSBERG | *The Ogre that Goes with the Rose* | [32 lines of text]

Single 40.5 x 20.3 cm. sheet printed on one side only. White laid paper watermarked: 'TWEEDWEAVE'. All edges trimmed.

Contents: The Ogre That Goes with the Rose

Not for sale. Published ca. 1971 in an impression of 15 to 20 copies.

Note: Publication information from letter by the publisher, Nelson Adams at Coach House Press, Toronto.

AA21   **SEPTEMBER ON JESSORE ROAD**   **1972**

[left side of page has 152 lines of text] | Nov 14-16 1971
[right side of page] [down the edge] SEPTEMBER ON JESS [a deep reddish orange (36) circle overlaps the preceding and following letters RE ROAD [down the page in 7 lines each aligned at the base of the sheet] Designed by R. K. Joshi | Printed and published by | Ashok Shahane | at Mohan Mudranalaya, Acme Estate, Sewri East, Bombay 15 | PRICE — AS MUCH AS YOU CAN WILLINGLY PART WITH |

PROCEEDS TO GO TO REHABILITATION OF | BANGLA DESH REFUGEES [across the base] ALLEN GINSBERG

Single 87.1 x 27.6 cm. sheet folds 5 times to 14.6 x 27.6 cm. printed on one side only. Heavy textured light yellowish brown (76) wove paper unwatermarked. A variant of this paper has been seen with white wove paper unwatermarked.

Contents: September on Jessore Road

Distributed free by Bangla Desh Aid Committee. Published Jan. 21, 1972 in an unknown quantity.

Note: Priority between the two paper issues is undetermined as publisher could not be located.

AA22   **TEAR GAS RAG**   **1972**

[illustration in very deep red (14) of 2 nude figures] | Tear Gas Rag | (after Blind Blake) | [16 lines of text] | Allen Ginsberg | 10 May 1972 | Ft. Collins, Colo. | This poem is here printed for the first time, in an edition of 250 copies, of which this is No. [number in black ink]. Issued December 1972 by | The Pomegranate Press. Text Copyright 1972 by Allen Ginsberg. Illustration Copyright 1972 by The Pomegranate Press.

Single 50.6 x 25.3 cm. sheet printed on one side only. Printed on either buff French Rives paper or white wove paper unwatermarked. Right edge untrimmed.

Conttents: Tear Gas Rag

Those numbered 1 to 100 were sold for $10.00 on buff paper. Those numbered 101 to 250 were sold for $6.00 on white paper. Published Dec. 1972 in an impression of 250 copies.

Note: Some copies were available in a portfolio with 9 other broadsides for $85.00 and $50.00.

AA23   RETURNING TO THE COUNTRY FOR A BRIEF VISIT   1973

Returning To The Country For A Brief Visit | [26 lines of text] | Allen Ginsberg | *Printed for distribution at the National Poetry | Festival, Thomas Jefferson College | by the East Lansing Arts Workshop Press | copyright— '73 Allen Ginsberg*

Single 34.2 x 21.6 cm. sheet printed on one side only. Off-white laid paper watermarked '[papermaker's logo] | *Classic Laid*'. All edges trimmed.

Contents: Returning to the Country for a Brief Visit

Published June 17, 1973 in an unknown quantity.

AA24   **FIRST THOUGHT BEST THOUGHT**   **1974**

[entire broadside in facsimile of holograph manuscript] "First Thought Best Thought" | Before you think | [17 lines of text] | Allen Ginsberg | 4 PM 11 Aug. 1974

Single 27.9 x 21.6 cm. sheet printed on one side only. Pale yellow (89) wove paper unwatermarked. All edges trimmed.

Contents: First Thought Best Thought [prose]

Created as a fund raiser for Naropa Institute and sold for a contribution. Published mid-August 1974 in an unknown quantity.

Note: Issued in a portfolio of 8 broadsides all of the same size and paper. The 32.0 x 25.5 cm. portfolio is made from 2 sheets of stiff deep reddish orange (36) paper stitched together on the left, right and bottom and secured at the top of each side with a silver star-shaped fastener. The cover of this has the following cut out as in a stencil: '[stencil] 8 | [in holograph] from | [stencil] Naropa | [in holograph] 1974'. Other writers included are Diane di Prima, Anne Waldman, Grant Fisher, Sidney Goldfarb, George Quasha, Rose Arguelles, and Rick Fields.

AA25   **LAY DOWN YR MOUNTAIN**   **1977**

[facsimile of autograph manuscript unless noted] Lay Down Yr Mountain | To Bob Dylan | [14 lines of text] | om ah Hum Allen Ginsberg | (Oct. 31, 1975) | [all the rest in type] copyright 1977 Allen Ginsberg | March 7, 1977 | a | folger poetry broadside | series 1977

Single 35.4 x 20.3 cm. sheet printed on one side only. Pale blue (185) laid paper watermarked 'Kilmory | Executive'. All edges trimmed.

Contents: Lay Down Yr Mountain

Distributed free to audience at reading. Published March 7, 1977 in an impression of ca. 250 copies.

AA26   **MOLOCH**   **1978**

a1. First edition, signed copies

[design of cityscape with Moloch figure] | [autographed in black ink by the artist] | [vivid reddish orange (34)] MOLOCH | [29.3 cm. vivid reddish orange rule] | [33 lines of text] | [autographed in black ink by the author] 1956 | [29.3 cm. rule] | Six hundred broadsides were hand-printed at the Penmaen Press in Lincoln, Massachusetts during January 1978. Three hundred were printed on French Rives | paper, numbered 1-300 and signed by Allen Ginsberg and Lynd Ward. The text is Part II of *HOWL,* copyright 1956, 1959 by Allen Ginsberg. Reprinted | by permission of City Lights Books. Original wood engraving copyright 1978 by Lynd Ward. [numbered in black ink]

Single 63.9 x 48.1 cm. sheet printed on one side only. White wove paper watermarked: 'RIVES'. Left and right edges untrimmed.

Contents: Howl [excerpt]

$50.00. Published March 11, 1978 in an impression of 300 copies.

a2. First edition, unsigned copies

[design of cityscape with Moloch figure] | [deep reddish orange (36)] MOLOCH | [29.3 cm. deep reddish orange rule] | [33 lines of text] | 1956 | [29.3 cm. rule] | Six hundred broadsides were hand-printed at the Penmaen Press in Lincoln, Massachusetts during January 1978. Three hundred were printed on French Rives | paper, numbered 1-300 and signed by Allen Ginsberg and Lynd Ward. The text is Part II of *HOWL,* copyright 1956, 1959 by Allen Ginsberg. Reprinted | by permission of City Lights Books. The original wood engraving is copyright 1978 by Lynd Ward.

Single 63.2 x 45.5 cm. sheet printed on one side only. White wove paper unwatermarked. All edges trimmed.

$20.00. Published March 11, 1978 in an impression of 300 copies.

Note: The last line has additional words The and is which are not in the signed copies.

AA27   **THE RUNE**   **1977**

[facsimile of autograph manuscript unless noted] The RUNE [underlined once in black ink and once in red ink] | [music notation with chords printed above the lines in black and red] | Where the years have gone, where the clouds have flown, where the rainbow | [music notation with chord printed about the lines in black and red] | Shone, we vanish, and we make no moan (May 12, 1977 on | Ken Kesey's piano) | [text in 18 lines] [6 musical notes in red ink and a column of 9 drawings by AG in red ink on each side] From Contest of Bards, January 17-22, 1977 | A Punk Epic [underlining in red] Allen Ginsberg | [autograph by the author in pencil] | [blind stamped] ARCHER PRESS

Single 56.8 x 44.1 cm. sheet printed on one side only, with printer's numbering notation in pencil on the back. White wove paper watermarked: 'BFK RIVES | FRANCE'. Untrimmed.

Contents: The Rune

Price for the entire portfolio was $350.00, but some of the single broadsides were sold for $75.00 each. Published July 1978 in an impression of 75 copies. 50 copies of which are numbered 1 to 50 and sold to the public, 25 copies of which are numbered i to xxv as the poet's edition.

Note: Originally laid in a portfolio as 1 of 5 broadsides printed by Archer Press. Across the front of the white portfolio cover: '[facsimile of autograph manuscript unless noted] Gregory Corso | Allen Ginsberg | Michael McClure | Anne Waldman | Philip Whalen | [typeset] FIVE/I/'77 | five poems: | written out by the poets for | lithography, and hand printed | in two limited editions: | a public edition of 50, and | a poets' edition of 25. | This folio is number [numbered in pencil and underlined] . | Charles Gill and John Doane | were the printers, at | [typeset] Archer Press | Oakland, California | 1977'. Although the publication date is given as 1977, the portfolios were not actually ready until July 1978.

AA28   **PUNK ROCK YOUR MY BIG CRYBABY**   **1979**

[in ornamental type of safety pin design] PUNK ROCK YOUr | [in ornamental type of safety pin design] MY big CrybabY | [all the rest in blue] [14 lines of text] | Mabuhay Gardens, May 1977 | Allen Ginsberg | The Alternative Press Grindstone City

Single 27.8 x 20.0 cm. sheet printed on one side only. Light reddish purple (240) wove paper unwatermarked. All edges trimmed.

Contents: Punk Rock Your My Big Crybaby

Free to subscribers of the press, later sold at $1.00 each. Published Nov. 11, 1979 in an impression of 600 copies, 50 of which had a special glazed ink for the title.

Note: Issued as part of #9 and sent to subscribers in a manila envelope containing many broadsides and cards entitled "The Alternative Press Sampler".

AA29   **WHAT'S DEAD?**   **1980**

[ornamental type] What's Dead? I [32 lines of text] I October 16, 1977 I [autographed by the author] I This broadside was printed at The Toothpaste Press for Bookslinger on the occasion of I the author's reading at Coffman Union April 8, 1980, as part of Walker Art I Center's Reading Series. © 1980 by Allen Ginsberg. The edition I consists of 125 numbered & 26 lettered copies, all signed I by the author. This is [number in black ink] .

Single 32.4 x 24.8 cm. sheet printed on one side only. Pale orange yellow (73) wove paper unwatermarked. All edges trimmed.

Contents: What's Dead?

$200.00 for the entire portfolio, and $8.50 for individual copies. Published April 8, 1980 in an impression of 151 copies, 125 of which are numbered 1 to 125 and 26 of which are lettered A to Z.

Note: 54 sets were issued in a portfolio of 16 broadsides.

AA30   **FATHER DEATH BLUES**   **1983**

[all within a black border] [facsimile of autograph manuscript] Father Death Blues I [page divided roughly into 4 columns] [first column] FADER DØD I [9 lines of text in Danish] I FATHER DEATH BLUES I by Allen Ginsberg I translated (rather freely) I by Dan Turell I 11/I/1983, Aarhus I [autographed in black ink by Peter Orlovsky] I [second column] [9 lines of text in Danish] I [third column] [9 lines of text in Danish] I [music notation] [autographed in black ink by Steven Taylor] I [all the rest in this column within a line drawn border around the words] Music Notation: Steven Taylor I Graphics: Hans Krull I Lay-out: Jan Haugaard I Allen Ginsberg, Peter Orlovsky I & Steven Taylor: I North-European Tournée "War Against War" I Winter 1982-1983 I Aarhus, Denmark I GRAFISK VAERKSTED 17/1/'83 I [fourth column] [27 lines of text in English] I Allen Ginsberg I [autographed in black by Allen Ginsberg] I [number stamped in black ink] I [number written in black ink] I [across the bottom of the sheet is a drawing of the Four Horsemen of the Apocalypse] [up the right edge of the border] JH 83 HK 83

Single 44.2 x 60.2 cm. sheet printed on one side only. White wove paper unwatermarked. All edges trimmed.

Contents: Translation by Dan Turell: Fader Død I Father Death Blues [with music notation]

The price is unknown and it was published Jan. 17, 1983 in an impression of 100 copies.

AA31 THROW OUT THE YELLOW JOURNALISTS OF BAD GRAMMAR 1983

[facsimile of autograph manuscript unless noted] "Throw out the yellow journalists of bad grammar I and terrible manner [3 bullets] " Anne Waldman 1982 I Who report the Ten Commandments forgetting Thou Shalt I [23 lines of text] I JULY 10, 1982 ALLEN GINSBERG I [typeset] Folger Evening Poetry Series 1982-1983

Single 27.9 x 21.5 cm. sheet printed on one side only. Brilliant yellow (83) wove paper unwatermarked. All edges trimmed.

Contents: Throw Out the Yellow Journalists of Bad Grammar

Distributed free at the reading at the Folger Library in Washington, DC. Published Feb. 21, 1983 in an impression of 250 copies.

AA32   **ORWELL SERIES**   **1983**

a. ORWELL: OH, WELL — IT'S ONLY 1983

[all in white in facsimile of autograph manuscript on sloping base line] orwell | 'oh, well — | It's only | — 1983. | [numbered in white holograph and autographed in white by the author]

Single 76.2 x 56.6 cm. sheet printed on both sides, pp. [1-2]. [1]: title page. [2]: artwork by Nam June Paik and signed and numbered. Black wove paper unwatermarked. Right edge trimmed.

Contents: Oh, Well

$5,000 for the collection. Published Autumn 1983 in an impression of 250 copies.

Note: Originally issued in a collection of at least 3 sheets issued as part of *Goodmorning Mr. Orwell*, Nam June Paik's tribute to George Orwell on Jan. 1, 1984, a multi-media production televised internationally at that time. Other sheets include a Joseph Beuys print and a John Cage print on the same side of one sheet and another AG Orwell sheet filled with Haiku, see below.

b. ORWELL 1984

[all on a background of beige screen with pink stipple effect set at an angle on which all is printed in blue mirrored in yellow slightly off register so that much of the print appears to be a dark green and in other areas a light green] [facsimile of autograph manuscript] [the page consisting of 12 haiku by AG, 7 of which are signed and dated 8/18/83] [no other heading or identification is used except that one of the haiku is reproduced with background of Naropa Institute stationery letterhead] [4 columns of 3 haiku per column on the page]

Single 56.6 x 78.5 cm. sheet printed on one side only. White wove paper unwatermarked. Untrimmed.

Contents: Coke Machines Talk — At 4 A.M. — 1984 now — Orwell Oh, Well — George Orwell Had — Coke Machines Serve — Out the Window — In the Half-Light before Dawn — Tanks in Afghanistan

AA33   **"FOR C.S."**   **1985**

[all on an illustration in black, strong purplish pink (247), and brilliant purplish blue (195) of AG playing his harmonium] "for C.S." | (Colin Sanders) | Silvery morning waters clouds distant Isles | [5 lines] | Allen Ginsberg | May 5, 1985 | Cortes Island | Hollyhock Farm | *illustration by Lee Robinsong*

Single 28.0 x 21.6 cm. sheet printed on one side only. White wove paper unwatermarked. All edges trimmed.

Contents: "For C.S."

$5.00. Published May 28, 1985 in an impression of 500 copies.

Note: This is identical to the back cover of *Heartwood,* no. 12 (Summer [May 30] 1985) issue for which it was submitted.

AA34   **EUROPE, WHO KNOWS?**   **1987**

[all in very dark greenish blue (175) unless noted and all within single rule border] EUROPE, WHO KNOWS? I [with larger initial letter] All over Europe people are saying, "Who knows?" I [text of poem all over a very light screen of a design of three fish which share a common head] [3 lines all sharing the same large initial letter A as above mentioned] I [text in 12 lines on the left side and 8 lines on the right side] —*Allen Ginsberg* I [music notation and words in white on a moderate greenish blue (73) background made to resemble waves] I 9//12//86 Warsaw Airport, Allen Ginsberg & Steven Taylor

Single 45.8 x 30.5 cm. sheet printed on one side only. White wove paper unwatermarked. All edges trimmed.

Contents: Europe, Who Knows?

$50.00 for the unsigned portfolio. Published Sept. 7, 1987 in an impression of 250 copies.

Note: Originally laid in portfolio as 1 of 10 broadsides printed by Cottonwood Magazine & Press, the portfolio being a single sheet of pale blue (185) laid paper unwatermarked and folded twice to cover the broadsides. No label on this cover. Cover page of portfolio identifies it as *Cottonwood Commemorative: River City Portfolio 1987.* Sets are numbered 1 to 50 and signed by each contributor and hand stamped with the designer's mark. Sets numbered 51 to 250 are numbered only.

AA35   **CAPITOL AIR**   **1987**

[flag and star are blind stamped into the paper] [gray and pink design of building elements: roof, columns, frieze of figures within which all the following is printed] Allen [in dark grayish red (20] CAPITOL AIR [in black] Ginsberg I [below the frieze of people are 2 columns of text of 48 lines each, the last line in the right column being corrected by AG in black holograph to include the following word] FEED I [in gray] Frankfurt—New York, December 15, 1980 I [autograph in black ink by the author] I [in gray] Designed and printed at Red Ozier Press for Northouse & Northouse. Capitol Air was originally published in The Aquarian. I [in gray] Copies numbered 1-100 and lettered A-Z are published as a portion of the American Poetry Portfolio. I [in gray] Copies numbered i-xl are separately published in wrappers. I [in gray] Copyright © 1987 by Allen Ginsberg. I [in gray] This is copy [numbered in black ink]

Single 45.1 x 33.0 cm. sheet printed on one side only. Gray wove paper watermarked: 'BFK RIVES I FRANCE [infinity sign]'. Bottom untrimmed.

Contents: Capitol Air

$100. 00 per broadside and $450.00 per portfolio. Published Dec. 1987 in an impression of 166 copies; of which 100 copies are numbered 1 to 100, 26 copies are lettered A to Z and 40 copies are numbered with Roman numerals i-xl.

Note: Originally laid into a portfolio as 1 of 8 broadsides printed by 5 different presses. Cover sheet reads: '[in reddish brown] AMERICAN | Scott Davis [bullet] Allen Ginsberg [bullet] William Heyen [bullet] Heather McHugh | [in reddish brown] POETRY | Howard Nemerov [bullet] Linda Pastan [bullet] William Stafford [bullet] John Updike | [in reddish brown] PORTFOLIO | NORTHOUSE & NORTHOUSE | DALLAS [bullet] 1988'. This collection is issued in a heavy Plexiglas box suitable for use as a frame to display one of the broadsides, issued with everything including mounting screws.

Those with Roman numerals are laid into a white folded paper cover, untrimmed on top and bottom and unwatermarked, without the Plexiglas box.

AA36	**BIRDBRAIN**	**1989**

[all within panel framed by 2 rule frame in very deep red (14) on the outside with an interior 3 rule frame in very deep red between which are drawings which illustrate the characters in the poem; one of the characters on the top extends above the outside rules and one of the characters on the bottom extends through the outside rules; otherwise all figures are between the frame elements including the following artist's signature and ate which are in the lower right hand corner between the frame elements] [facsimile of autograph] Hechtlinger | © 1989 [all within all frame borders] *BIRDBRAIN* | [French rule] | Birdbrain runs the World! | [57 lines] | ALLEN GINSBERG | *Hotel Subrovka, Dubrovnik, October 14, 1980, 4:30* A.M. | [all the rest below all the frame elements] Copy No. [number in black ink] © ALLEN GINSBERG [in 3 lines] GRYPHON POETRY BROADSIDE NO. TWO | PRIVATELY PRINTED IN NEW HAVEN BY ROBERT REID AND TERRY BERGER | AT THE SIGN OF THE GRYPHON, SEPTEMBER, 1989 [publisher's device]

Single 61.1 x 42.1 cm. sheet printed on one side only. White laid paper unwatermarked. Top and left edges trimmed.

Contents: Birdbrain

Published Sept. 1989 in an unknown quantity.

AA37	**ALLEN IN VISION**	**1990**

[in gold] NAM JUNE PAIK ALLEN GINSBERG | [dark blue] ALLEN IN VISION | [3 oriental characters in gold] | [in dark blue] EDITIONS NICOLE FAUCHE

Single 110.6 x 76.1 cm. sheet which folds once to 55.3 x 76.1 cm. to form a portfolio, followed by eight loose leaves, pp. [1-20]. [1]: title page. [2]: blank. [3]: 'Cet album, Allen in Vision, comprenant un poème ed deux sérigraphies | d'Allen Ginsberg, ainsi que cinq sérigraphies de Nam June Paik, a été | tiré sur Velin Arches et Richard de Bas à cent exemplaires, plus vingt | épreuves d'artistes, trois hors commerce et un exemplaire réservé à la | Bibliothèque Nationale. | Toutes les sérigraphies sont signées. | Achevé d'imprimer à Paris pour le compte de Nicole Fauche, éditeur, le | 12 décembre 1990, sur les presses de l'Atelier. L'emboîtage a été réalisé | par Bernard Duval.' [4]: blank. [5]: 'Improvisation in Beijing | [2 columns of text of 45 lines and 41 lines] | [Allen Ginsberg]'. [6]: blank. [7]: [drawing by AG in dark blue and gold of the sun with the word 'AH' in the center, stars, moon and skull with flower in its teeth encircling a Buddha figure on which are the numbers '108' and the word 'AH'] | [AG's autograph in red]. [8]: blank. [9]: [drawing by AG in dark blue of a bald figure with 2 eyes, a mouth and 2 eyes with eyebrows on the breasts] | [AG's autograph in pencil]. [10]: blank. [11-20]: Nam June Paik's five video images of AG each in full color on one side of each sheet.

Laid into a vivid red (11) cloth covered portfolio with flaps, printed across the front: '[in gold] NAM JUNE PAIK ALLEN GINSBERG I [in dark blue] ALLEN IN VISION I [3 oriental characters in gold] I [in dark blue] EDITIONS NICOLE FAUCHE'. The first and second single leaves are white wove paper watermarked: 'ARCHES I FRANCE [infinity symbol] I [upside down U shape]', with the tope and left edges trimmed. The third single leaf is a special paper with leaves and flower petals embedded in it to make a very patterned background for the simple line drawing, watermarked: '[within lozenge] 1526 I [ornament]'.

Contents: Improvisation in Beijing — [2 drawings by AG]

$5,000.00. Published Dec. 12, 1990 in an impression of 123 copies, 100 of which are numbered 1 to 100, 20 of which are numbered as artist's copies, and 3 of which are unnumbered for the copyright office.

AA38 **PERSONALS AD** **1991**

[in deep red (16) Personals Ad I [in moderate bluish green (164)] "I will send a picture too I [in moderate bluish green] if you will send me one of you." I [in moderate bluish green] — R. Creeley I Poet professor in autumn years I [16 lines of text] I [in moderate bluish green] 10-8087 I [in deep red] Allen Ginsberg I Copyright 1991 by Allen Ginsberg & printed at Chax Press on the I occasion of the author's appearance for Tucson Poetry Festival IX, April 1991.

Single 43.1 x 27.9 cm. sheet printed on one side only. White laid paper unwatermarked. Left edge untrimmed, some copies are also untrimmed on the bottom edge.

Contents: Personals Ad

Published April 1991 in an unknown number of copies.

AA39 **CHERRY BLUES** **1992**

Cherry Blues I [18 lines of text] I © Allen Ginsberg 1/9/92 AM I [publisher's device] *Published by Bernard Stone and Raymond Danowski. The Turret bookshop, London August 1992.*

Single 29.7 x 21.0 cm. sheet printed on one side only. Vivid red (11) wove paper unwatermarked. All edges trimmed.

Contents: Cherry Blues

Distributed free. Published Aug. 1992 in an impression of 200 copies.

Note: An undisclosed number of copies were printed with the author's name misspelled as Allen Ginsburg, identical in every other way to the above. Not all of these were destroyed, but it is believed that fewer than 100 were distributed with the incorrect spelling.

AA40   POEM IN THE FORM OF A SNAKE THAT BITES ITS TAIL   1993

[in 4 lines] Poem in the Form | of a Snake that | Bites its Tail | By Allen Ginsberg, November 6, 1990 [right is a 4.2 x 11.0 cm. illustration of a bird standing by a river] | [text of poem in 3 columns of 83, 80 and 75 lines]

Single 43.2 x 28.0 cm. sheet printed on one side only. Yellowish white (92) wove paper unwatermarked. All edges trimmed.

Contents: Poem in the Form of a Snake That Bites Its Tail

Distributed free with *Friends of the Oleta Newsletter.* Published April 1993 in an impression of 1000 copies.

AA41   SUPPLICATION FOR THE REBIRTH OF THE VIDYADHARA   1993

Supplication for the Rebirth | of the Vidyadhara | CHÖGYAM TRUNGPA, | *Rinpoche* | [26 lines of text] | ALLEN GINSBERG | June 2, 1991 / 2:05 AM | Published by Big Bridge Press, Pacifica, California, Oct. 1992. Concept and drawing by Nancy Davis. The typography and printing | were done by the Arion Press, using Spectrum types and Rives paper. The scroll was executed by Arnold Martinez, using Japa- | nese patterned paper. The box was constructed by Tom Bass, using Alaskan yellow cedar. The edition is limited to 76 copies, | of which 26 copies, lettered A to Z, are hand colored and signed by the poet and the artist. Copyright © 1992 by Big Bridge Press. | [ornamental border of many baby sea turtles surrounds the text on left, right and bottom] | [author's autograph in black ink]

Single 46.9 x 65.4 cm. sheet printed on one side only. White wove paper watermarked: '[hollow type] RIVES [infinity symbol] | [upside down U shape]'. All edges trimmed. The broadside has been mounted on a scroll format as a Tibetan tanka designed to be hung. The broadside has been glued to a multi-colored, geometric background sheet which is rolled onto a black wooden rod at the bottom and secured at the top with a black wooden quarter-round piece. Attached to the top is a piece of black and gold cloth ribbon to use for hanging the scroll. When rolled up the scroll fits into a custom-made unpainted cedar box with a removable lid. On the lid is an engraved picture of a turtle which is colored a metallic blue.

Contents: Supplication for the Rebirth of the Vidyadhara

$500.00 for the lettered edition and $299.00 for the numbered edition. Published May 1993 in an impression of 76 copies, 26 copies of which are lettered A to Z and 50 copies or which are numbered 1 to 50.

Note: The lettered copies have one of the turtles hand colored by the artist and includes her autograph in black ink and her red chop mark on the lower right beside Allen Ginsberg's autograph, this protected by a small slip of white rice paper. Each copy was shipped in a white paper wrapping, the lettered copies tied with a gold string and the numbered copies tied with a silver string.

AA42   **COSMOPOLITAN GREETINGS**   **1994**

[all within a double rule frame] Allen Ginsberg | [photograph by AG of himself in the bathroom mirror] [up the right side of photo] *photo by Allen Ginsberg* | COSMOPOLITAN GREETINGS | To Struga Festival Golden Wreath Laureates | & International Bards 1986 | [35 lines] | Allen Ginsberg | Kral Majales | June 25, 1986 | Boulder, Colorado | "Cosmopolitan Greetings" © 1986 Allen Ginsberg. Permission to print granted by Allen Ginsberg. | [on curved base line] *Supporting a global literary community* | [ornamentation] | [in white on a black rectangle] *the literary renaissance* | [on curved base line] a non-profit corporation louisville, kentucky | *Published in Heaven Poster Series #8* | White Fields Press for the literary renaissance 1994 | editors Ron Whitehead and Kent Fielding | production Laura Loran, layout Ernest Sedgwick

Single 38.1 x 88.7 cm. sheet printed on one side only. White wove coated paper unwatermarked. All edges trimmed.

Contents: Cosmopolitan Greetings

$7.00. Published May 1994 in an impression of an undisclosed number of copies.

B

Contributions to Books by Allen Ginsberg

B1   **PATERSON, BOOK 4**   **1951**
by William Carlos Williams

PATERSON I (BOOK FOUR) I [4 lines within 5 single rule concentric frames] A NEW I DIREC- I TIONS I BOOK I [below frames] WILLIAM CARLOS I WILLIAMS

[1-8]⁴, pp. [1-64]. 23.9 x 16.0 cm. Bound in yellowish gray (93) cloth covered boards. A dark reddish orange (38) band across half the front cover, spine and half the back cover. Across the front cover, half above the band and half on the band in gold: 'PATERSON'. White laid paper watermarked: '[in black letter] Hamilton Victorian'. White laid endpapers watermarked as the paper. Top edges trimmed. Issued in a white paper dust jacket printed in dark red and white.

Contents: A.P. [anonymous letter to William Carlos Williams but written by AG], pp. [31-33] — [anonymous letter to William Carlos Williams but written by AG], p. [52].

$3.00. Published June 11, 1951 in an impression of 995 copies.

B2   **GASOLINE**   **1958**
by Gregory Corso

a1. *First edition, paperbound*

GASOLINE I *GREGORY CORSO* I INTRODUCTION BY I ALLEN GINSBERG I THE POCKET POETS SERIES: Number Eight I CITY LIGHTS BOOKS I San Francisco

Twenty-four single leaves, pp. [1-6] 7-48. 15.8 x 12.5 cm. Perfect bound in stiff white paper wrappers. Covers printed in strong red (12). White laid paper unwatermarked. All edges trimmed.

Contents: Introduction [prose], pp. 7-10.

95¢. Published Feb. 5, 1958 in an impression of 1,500 copies.

Note: Reprinted as follows: 2nd printing, July 1958; 3rd printing, April 1959; 4th printing, 1960; 5th printing, Dec. 1960, 3,000 copies; 6th printing, May 1964, 2,000 copies; 7th printing, Dec. 1965, 2,000 copies; 8th printing, Aug. 1966, 2,000 copies; 9th printing, April 1967, 3,000 copies; 10th printing, Nov. 1967, 5,000 copies; 11th printing,

Oct. 1968, 5,000 copies; 12th printing, June 1972, 3,000 copies. Second and subsequent printings are identified as such on the verso of the title page.

a2. *First edition, eleventh printing, re-issue, 1974*

THE I POCKET POETS I SERIES I Volume 2 I Numbers 8-14, Supplement I KRAUS REPRINT CO. I Millwood, New York I 1973

[1-15]^{16} [16]^4 [17]^{16}, pp. [1-520]. 22.3 x 14.4 cm. Bound in dark purplish red (259) cloth covered boards, lettered across the spine in gold: '[3 rules 3.8 cm. long] I THE I POCKET I POETS I SERIES I [3 rules 3.8 cm. long] I 2 I KRAUS I REPRINT'. White wove paper unwatermarked. White endpapers. All edges trimmed. Issued without a dust jacket.

Contents: As first edition, pp. [11-14].

$23.75 or sold as a four volume set at $95.00. Published Jan. 28, 1974 in an impression of 250 copies.

Note: Kraus Reprint Co. collected all the books comprising the Pocket Poets Series and re-issued them in a four volume set primarily for the library trade. No effort was made to reprint the first printings of many of the books in the series and here they have reprinted the 11th printing of the City Lights paperback.

a3. *Re-issue with The Vestal Lady on Brattle, first impression, 1976*

GASOLINE I GREGORY CORSO I THE I VESTAL LADY I ON BRATTLE I Pocket Poets Series Number 8 I CITY [publisher's device] LIGHTS

Fifty single leaves, pp. [1-6] 7-48 [49-54] 55-99 [100]. 15.8 x 12.3 cm. Perfect bound in stiff white paper wrappers. Covers printed in black. White wove paper unwatermarked. All edges trimmed.

$2.00. Published Feb. 5, 1976 in an impression of 3,000 copies.

Note: Reprinted as follows: 2nd printing, Dec. 1979, 3,000 copies; 3rd printing, Feb. 1986, 2,000 copies; 4th printing, June 1992, 2,500 copies. Second and subsequent printings are identified as such on the verso of the title page. The fourth printing has a new cover design.

B3   **PATERSON, BOOK FIVE**   **1958**
                    by William Carlos Williams

PATERSON I (BOOK FIVE) I [next four lines are within a frame of 5 single concentric rules] A NEW I DIREC- I TIONS I BOOKS I [below frame] WILLIAM CARLOS I WILLIAMS

[1-6]^4, pp. [1-48]. 24.0 x 16.5 cm. Bound in light grayish yellowish brown (79) cloth covered boards. A strong reddish orange (35) rectangle is printed on the front cover extending onto the spine and back cover. Across the front cover in gold: '[half on and half above the rectangle] PATERSON'. Down the spine in gold: 'PATERSON FIVE WILLIAM CARLOS WILLIAMS NEW DIRECTIONS'. White laid paper unwatermarked. White endpapers. Top and bottom edges trimmed. Issued with a white paper dust jacket printed in black and red.

Contents: A.G. [anonymous (pseud. of Allen Ginsberg) letter to William Carlos Williams], pp. 16-17.

$3.00. Published Sept. 17, 1958 in an impression of 2980 copies of which 1,500 were bound for the publication date and 1480 were bound in Dec. 1958.

Note: There appears to be no way to distinguish between the two binding stages as listed above.

B4   **WATERMELONS**   **1959**
                 by Ron Loewinsohn

WATERMELONS | RON | LOEWINSOHN | totem press | *NEW YORK*

Single gathering of sixteen leaves, pp. [i-ii] [1-2] 3-29 [30]. 21.3 x 14.1 cm. Stapled twice into stiff white paper wrappers. Covers printed in black and red. White wove paper unwatermarked. All edges trimmed.

Contents: Introduction [prose], p. [1].

$1.00. Published Spring 1959 in an impression of 1,000 copies.

Note: Some later copies were sold with an errata slip laid in.

B5   **A NEW FOLDER**   **1959**

a1. *First edition, numbered copies*

A NEW FOLDER | Edited by DAISY ALDAN | Americans: | Poems and Drawings | with a foreword by Wallace Fowlie | [publisher's device] FOLDER EDITIONS, NEW YORK

[1-8]^8, pp. [i-xii] 1-116. 26.0 x 18.3 cm. Bound in moderate reddish brown (43) cloth covered boards. Down the spine: '[in gold] A NEW FOLDER AMERICANS: POEMS AND DRAWINGS FOLDER EDITIONS'. White laid paper watermarked: '[in black letter] SULGRAVE TEXT'. White endpapers. All edges trimmed. Issued in a white paper dust jacket printed in black and vivid yellow (82).

Contents: Ignu, pp. 28-30.

$12.50. Published Christmas 1959 in an impression of 150 copies.

Note: These are numbered in black ink on p. 116.

a2. *First edition, trade copies, not numbered, 1959*

A NEW FOLDER | Edited by DAISY ALDAN | Americans: | Poems and Drawings | with a foreword by Wallace Fowlie | [publisher's device] FOLDER EDITIONS, NEW YORK

[1-8]^8, pp. [i-xii] 1-116. 26.0 x 18.3 cm. Bound in strong yellow (84) glossy paper covered boards. Across the front cover: 'A NEW FOLDER | AMERICANS: POEMS AND DRAWINGS | *Edited by* DAISY ALDAN | *with a foreword by* WALLACE FOWLIE | [reproduction of a painting of table and chairs across the bottom of the front, spine and back covers]'. Down the spine: 'A NEW FOLDER AMERICANS: POEMS AND DRAWINGS FOLDER EDITIONS'. Across the back cover: 'POETS DRAWINGS by | [5 columns of 15, 14, 14, 15 and 15 contributors]'. White laid paper watermarked: '[in black letter] SULGRAVE TEXT'. White endpapers. All edges trimmed.

$3.00. Published Christmas 1959 in an impression of 850 copies.

a3.   *First edition, paperbound, 1960*

A NEW FOLDER I Edited by DAISY ALDAN I Americans: I Poems and Drawings I with a foreword by Wallace Fowlie I [publisher's device] FOLDER EDITIONS, NEW YORK

[1-8]^8 [9]^6, pp. [i-x] 1-128 [129-130].   23.1 x 15.4 cm.   Bound in stiff white paper wrappers printed on strong reddish orange (35).   Across the front cover: '[a brush stroke design down the left side]   A NEW FOLDER I AMERICANS: POEMS AND DRAWINGS I *Edited by* DAISY ALDAN I *with a foreword by* WALLACE FOWLIE I *and photographs of contributors* I [list of 57 contributors inside single rule frame] I $1.75'.   Down the spine: 'A NEW FOLDER AMERICANS: POEMS AND DRAWINGS FOLDER EDITIONS'.   Across the back cover: '[2 columns of 12 and 11 lines] I *Jean Fanchette: Editor—Two Cities, Paris* I [design of horizontal brush stroke] I [reproduction of painting]'.   White wove paper unwatermarked.   All edges trimmed.

$1.75.   Published Dec. 1960 in an impression of 1,000 copies.

Note: This printing expanded to include the work of four additional writers and one painter and the work of one writer has been dropped.   Six pages of photos have been added.

B6   **THE PROPHET COFFEEHOUSE**   **ca. 1959**

[Islamic calligraphy] I *poetry of* I THE PROPHET COFFEEHOUSE I SEVEN O SEVEN MAIN ST. I *one dollar fifty cents*

Single gathering of thirty-four single leaves, pp. [1-68].   20.6 x 13.5 cm.   Stapled twice into stiff white paper wrappers.   Across the front cover all on a design in light gray of Islamic calligraphy: 'THE PROPHET I COFFEEHOUSE'.   Design of Islamic calligraphy continues across the back cover.   White wove paper unwatermarked.   All edges trimmed.

Contents: A Dream X August 28, 1958 [poem], pp. [23-24]

$1.50.   Published ca. 1959 in an impression of approximately 250 copies.

Note: The publication data is an estimate from Jack Micheline, one of the contributors, the publisher could not be located.

B7   **THE BEATS**   **1960**

The Beats I edited by Seymour Krim I [solid square] *A Gold Medal Anthology* I GOLD MEDAL BOOKS I FAWCETT PUBLICATIONS, INC., *Greenwich, Conn.*

One hundred twelve single leaves, pp. [1-7] 8-224.   17.8 x 10.8 cm.   Perfect bound in stiff white paper wrappers.   Covers printed in black, white, red, blue and brilliant yellow (83).   White wove paper unwatermarked.   All edges trimmed and stained yellow.

Contents: Death to Van Gogh's Ear, pp. 149-153.

35¢.   Published March 31, 1960 in an impression of 185,000 copies.

Note: Reprinted as follows: 2nd printing, July 30, 1963, 75,000 copies.   Second printing is identified as such by the new price of 50¢ on the front cover.

B8   **MINUTES TO GO**   **1960**
                  by Beilies, Burroughs, Corso and Gysin

a1. *First edition*

MINUTES TO GO I SINCLAIR BEILES I WILLIAM BURROUGHS I GREGORY
CORSO I BRION GYSIN I "Not knowing what is and is not knowing I *I knew not."* I
Hassan Sabbah's "Razor". I TWO CITIES EDITIONS

[1-4]^8, pp. [1-2] 3-63 [64]. 21.0 x 13.5 cm. Bound in stiff white paper wrappers.
Covers printed in strong greenish blue (169) and black. White wove paper unwatermarked.
All edges trimmed.

Contents: [letter by AG has been used as cut-up material by Corso], p. 34 — [poem by AG
has been used as cut-up material by Corso] p. 55.

7.20F. Published April 13, 1960 in an impression of 1,000 copies.

Note: Some copies were issued with a white wraparound band, 4.7 cm. wide, reading:
'Un reglement de comptes I avec la litterature'.

There was also a deluxe printing of 10 copies, numbered 1-10. Although a letter from the
publisher at the time of publication states that they are printed on "better paper," the
compiler has examined both the deluxe and regular papers and cannot discern between the
two, the papers appear identical. Each copy of the deluxe printing does include a note on
the back page written in black ink by the publisher: 'certified copy # I Jean Fanchette I
Publisher I 8/13/60 I [number stamped here in blue ink]'. Each copy has an envelope
containing 4 original letters, one from each author, plus 1 drawing by Brion Gysin, in an
envelope labeled: 'CUT THESE UP YOURSELVES I MINUTES TO GO'. Five copies
were for the authors and publisher and five copies were for sale at $25.00 each. Brown
University owns a copy which contains a letter from the publisher setting forth the price,
etc.

a2. *First American issue, 1968*

MINUTES TO GO I SINCLAIR BEILES I WILLIAM BURROUGHS I GREGORY
CORSO I BRION GYSIN I "Not knowing what is and is not knowing I *I knew not."* I
Hassan Sabbah's "Razor". I [publisher's device] I BEACH BOOKS, TEXTS &
DOCUMENTS I Distributed by I City Lights Books, 1562 Grant Avenue, San Francisco,
California 94133

Thirty-four single leaves, pp. [i-ii] [1-2] 3-63 [64-66]. 21.5 x 13.6 cm. Perfect bound in
stiff light brown (57) paper wrappers. Covers printed in black. White wove paper
watermarked: '[on a curved base line] WARREN'S I OLDE STYLE'. All edges trimmed.

$1.25. Published Sept./Oct. 1968 in an impression of ca. 1,000 copies.

Note: Information based on the publisher's estimate.

B9   **THE BEAT SCENE**   **1960**

The Beat Scene I PHOTOGRAPHS BY *Fred McDarrah* I EDITED AND I WITH AN
INTRODUCTION BY *Elias Wilentz* I   *Corinth Books,* NEW YORK, 1960 I
DISTRIBUTED BY *The Citadel Press*

[1-6]^{16}, pp. [1-7] 8-185 [186-192]. 20.3 x 13.5 cm. Bound in stiff white paper
wrappers. Across the front cover: '[on a 2.6 cm. strong red (12) band is printed in 3 lines]
$1.95 I Canada: $2.25 I CORINTH BOOK [in one line in white] THE BEAT SCENE I

PHOTOGRAPHS by FRED McDARRAH EDITED by ELIAS WILENTZ | [below band on a photograph of Jack Kerouac reading to an audience in 22 lines offset right in strong red are the contributors names]'. Down the spine all on a photograph in black and strong red: '[in white] THE BEAT SCENE'. Across the back cover: '[in 5 lines] $1.95 | Canada $2.25 | CORINTH BOOK | distributed by | THE CITADEL PRESS [7 lines] | [collage of photographs of some of the contributors each outlined in strong red and through the middle of which is a strong red transparent band with 3 lines about the book in white]'. White wove paper unwatermarked. All edges trimmed.

Contents: Corso, Gregory; Orlovsky, Peter and AG. [excerpt from a letter], pp. 13-14 — I Beg You Come Back and Be Cheerful, pp. 19-23.

$1.95. Published May 12, 1960 in an impression of 2,000-5,000 copies.

Note: Reprinted as follows: 2nd printing, April 1961, 1,000-3,000 copies; 3rd printing, 1,000-3,000 copies; 4th printing, 1,000-3,000 copies; 5th printing, 1968, 1,000-3,000 copies; 6th printing, 1973, 1,000-3,000 copies. Second, fifth and sixth printings are identified as such on the verso of the title page. Third and fourth printings lack the Canadian price of $2.25 on the cover.

Publication information according to conflicting reports by Ted Wilentz and Fred McDarrah as listed in Alexander Smith's *Frank O'Hara: a comprehensive bibliography* (New York: Garland, 1979).

B10   **THE NEW AMERICAN POETRY: 1945-1960**   **1960**

a1. *First edition, hardbound*

[a decorative pattern is repeated in 13 lines of 10 patterns] | *The New American* | *Poetry: 1945-1960* | EDITED BY DONALD M. ALLEN | [8.0 cm. rule] | GROVE PRESS, INC. [bullet] NEW YORK | EVERGREEN BOOKS LTD. [bullet] LONDON

[1-15]^{16}, pp. [i-iv] v-viii [ix-x] xi-xxiii [xxiv] [1] 2-454 [455-456]. 21.0 x 14.1 cm. Bound in black cloth covered boards. Across the front cover in gold: '*The New American* | *Poetry: 1945-1960*'. Down the spine in gold: '*The New American Poetry: 1945-1960* | EDITED BY DONALD M. ALLEN [across the spine] GROVE | PRESS'. White wove paper unwatermarked. Dark orange yellow (72) endpapers. All edges trimmed. Top edges stained black. Issued in a white paper dust jacket printed in black, red and gray.

Contents: The Shrouded Stranger, pp. 178-179 — Malest Cornifici Tuo Catullo, p. 179 — Sunflower Sutra, pp. 179-181 — A Supermarket in California, pp. 181-182 — Howl, pp. 182-190 — Sather Gate Illumination, pp. 190-194 — Message, p. 194 — Kaddish [excerpt], pp. 194-201 — Notes for *Howl* and Other Poems [prose], pp. 414-418.

$5.95. Published May 29, 1960 in an impression of 1,000 copies.

Note: A variant dust jacket has been reported printed only in black and gray but has not been seen by the compiler.

a2. *First edition, paperbound, 1960*

[a decorative pattern is repeated in 13 lines of 10 patterns] | *The New American* | *Poetry: 1945-1960* | EDITED BY DONALD M. ALLEN | [8.0 cm. rule] | GROVE PRESS, INC. [bullet] NEW YORK | EVERGREEN BOOKS LTD. [bullet] LONDON

Two hundred forty single leaves, pp. [i-iv] v-viii [ix-x] xi-xxiii [xxiv] [1] 2-454 [455-456]. 20.3 x 13.4 cm. Perfect bound in stiff white paper wrappers. Covers printed in deep blue (179), black, medium gray (265) and vivid reddish orange (34). White wove paper unwatermarked. All edges trimmed.

$1.95 or 14/6d. Published May 29, 1960 in an impression of approximately 8,000 copies.

Note: Issued with a green wraparound paper strip on which is printed all the following in white repeatedly: 'EVERGREEN | ORIGINAL [square] | FIRST PUBLICATION'. First printing identified as such on the verso of the title page.

Reprinted as follows: 2nd printing, Oct. 1960, 5,000 copies; 3rd printing, April 1961, 6,000 copies; 4th printing, June 1962, 5,000 copies; 5th printing, Nov. 1963, 5,000 copies; 6th printing, Aug. 1964, 5,000 copies; 7th printing, July 1965, 5,000 copies; 8th printing, Feb. 1966, 5,000 copies; 9th printing, May 1966, 7,500 copies; 10th printing, March 1967, 5,000 copies; 11th printing, Sept. 1967, 5,000 copies, 12th printing, Nov. 1967, 5,000 copies; 13th printing, Feb. 1968, 10,000 copies, 14th printing, Nov. 1968, 10,000 copies, 15th printing, March 1969, 10,000 copies, 16th printing, May 1970, 15, 000 copies; 17th-22nd printings, information unavailable.

Between 1963 and 1976, by arrangement with the publisher, Peter Smith of Gloucester offered copies of the paperback edition, bound in red cloth over boards and printed in black down and across the spine. Approximately 2,740 copies were bound between 1963 and 1976, in lots of 200 copies, sold at $5.00 (later $7.50). No copies have been so bound since Dec. 1976.

Publication information according to Alexander Smith's *Frank O'Hara: a comprehensive bibliography* (New York: Garland, 1979); Robert Wilson's *Bibliography of Denise Levertov* (New York: Phoenix, 1972); and David K. Kermani's *John Ashbery: a comprehensive bibliography* (New York: Garland, 1976).

B11   **BEATITUDE ANTHOLOGY**   **1960**

[ornamental type] BEATITUDE | [ornamental type] ANTHOLOGY | [publisher's device] | CITY LIGHTS BOOKS

Fifty-six single leaves, pp. [1-6] 7-111 [112]. 20.2 x 14.0 cm. Perfect bound in stiff white paper wrappers. Covers printed in black. White wove paper unwatermarked. All edges trimmed.

Contents: Hymn from *Kaddish*, p. 15 — Mescaline, pp. 15-18 — Sakyamuni Coming Out From the Mountain, pp. 18-19 — Afternoon Seattle, pp. 19-21 — Over Kansas, pp. 21-24 — On Visions, p. 25 — Poem [Scribble], p. 26 — [postscript to letter], p. 110 — [telegram to Lawrence Ferlinghetti], p. 111.

$1.50. Published Oct. 5, 1960 in an impression of 5,000 copies.

B12   **A CASEBOOK ON THE BEAT**   **1961**

a1. *First edition, paperbound*

A CASEBOOK ON THE BEAT | *Edited by* THOMAS PARKINSON | *University of California* | Thomas Y. Crowell Company | *New York, Established 1834*

[1-9]^{16} [10]^8 [11]^{16}, pp. [i-iv] v [vi] vii-ix [x] [1-2] 3-326. 21.3 x 14.3 cm. Bound in stiff white paper wrappers. Covers printed in strong purplish blue (196). White wove paper unwatermarked. All edges trimmed.

Contents: Howl, pp. 3-12 — America, pp. 13-15 — Sunflower Sutra, pp. 16-17 — Kaddish, pp. 18-24 — Poetry, Violence, and the Trembling Lambs [prose], pp. 24-27 — Notes Written on Finally Recording "Howl" [prose], pp. 27-30.

$3.00. Published Jan. 18, 1961 in an impression of an unknown number.

Note: Reprinted as follows: 2nd printing, July 1961; 3rd printing, March 1965. Second and third printings identified as such on the verso of the title pages.

a2.   First edition, hardbound, 1961

A CASEBOOK ON THE BEAT | *Edited by* THOMAS PARKINSON | *University of California* | Thomas Y. Crowell Company | *New York, Established 1834*

[1-9]^{16} [10]^8 [11]^{16}, pp. [i-iv] v [vi] vii-ix [x] [1-2] 3-326. 21.8 x 14.5 cm. Bound in blackish blue (188) cloth covered boards. Down the spine: '[in white] A CASEBOOK ON THE BEAT | [in strong purplish blue (196)] *Edited by* THOMAS PARKINSON *Crowell*'. White wove paper unwatermarked. White endpapers. All edges trimmed. Issued in a white paper dust jacket printed in vivid purplish blue (194).

$3.95. Published Feb. 27, 1961 in an impression of an unknown number.

B13   **THE REAL BOHEMIA**   **1961**
                by Francis J. Rigney and L. Douglas Smith

[left title page] A Sociological and Psychological | Study of the "Beats"

[right title page] THE REAL | BOHEMIA | FRANCIS J. RIGNEY | AND L. DOUGLAS SMITH | BASIC BOOKS, INC. NEW YORK

[1-7]^{16} [8]^8 [9]^{16}, pp. [i-vi] vii-xi [xii] xiii-xx [xxi-xxii] [1-2] 3-250. 21.5 x 14.4 cm. Bound in strong red (12) cloth covered boards. Down the spine in gold: 'THE REAL | BOHEMIA [across the spine] RIGNEY | [1.3 cm. rule] | SMITH | BASIC | BOOKS'. White wove paper unwatermarked. Black endpapers. All edges trimmed. Top edges stained black. Issued in a white paper dust jacket.

Contents: Mescaline, pp. 135-138 — [letter to the editor of the *San Francisco Chronicle*, May 1959] , pp. 152-153.

$5.00. Published May 15, 1961 in an impression of an unknown number of copies.

B14   **PULL MY DAISY**   **1961**
                by Jack Kerouac

a1.   First edition

PULL MY DAISY | Text ad-libbed by Jack Kerouac | for the film by Robert Frank | and Alfred Leslie | Introduction by Jerry Tallmer | Grove Press, Inc. New York | Evergreen Books Ltd. London

[1-2]^8 [3]^4 [4-5]^8, pp. [1-13] 14-38 [39-72]. 20.2 x 13.6 cm. Bound in stiff white paper wrappers. Across the front cover: '[in hollow letters the first 5 letters having yellow dots filling the hollow, the last 5 letters having red dots filling the hollow] PULL MY DAISY | [in hollow letters] TEXT BY JACK KEROUAC | [in hollow letters] FOR THE FILM | [in hollow letters] BY ROBERT FRANK | [in hollow letters] AND ALFRED LESLIE | [photograph of flag and man reading a book] [up the right edge in white] EVERGREEN ORIGINAL E-294 $1.45 (U.K. 10/6d.) [publisher's device]'. Down the spine: 'PULL MY DAISY [in yellow] BY [in red] KEROUAC, FRANK, & LESLIE [publisher's device in yellow] [in black] E-294 [in red] GROVE PRESS'. Across the back cover: '[in one line in red] EVERGREEN *ORIGINAL* [publisher's device] [in 2 lines in black] E-294 — $1.45 | U.K. — 10/6d | [all the rest on a 14.5 x 10.1 yellow panel] PULL MY DAISY | text by

Jack Kerouac for the film | by Robert Frank and Alfred Leslie | [24 lines]'. White wove paper unwatermarked. All edges trimmed.

Contents: Kerouac, Jack and AG. Pull My Daisy, pp. [11-13].

$1.45. Published June 15, 1961 in an impression of 3,200 copies.

Note: Information from the copyright office letter to the publisher.

a2. *Second printing unauthorized, 1984*

JACK | KEROUAC | PULL MY DAISY | [portrait of Jack Kerouac]

Single gathering of twenty-two leaves, pp. [i-xii] 1-18 [19-32]. 21.0 x 14.7 cm. Stapled twice into stiff yellowish gray (93) paper wrappers. Across the front cover is the title page. Across the back cover: '[hollow letters filled with dots] PULL MY DAISY | [all the rest hollow letters] TEXT BY JACK KEROUAC | FOR THE FILM | BY ROBERT FRANK | AND ALFRED LESLIE'. White wove paper unwatermarked. The first and last leaves are brilliant yellowish green (130) paper unwatermarked. All edges trimmed.

Contents: As first edition, pp. [ix-xi].

Note: Pirated between 1984 and 1990 in at least 4 variations, price and quantity printed are unknown. Probably published in England by Pacific Red Car Publications. Each has a different cover, but all reprinting the original Grove Press contents. The last variation published by Insight, Sept. 1990 in an impression of 50 copies.

B15   **BEAT COAST EAST**   **1961**

[left title page] [on sloping base line] *AN ANTHOLOGY OF REBELLION* | [on sloping base line in facsimile holograph] beat coast
[right title page] [on sloping base line] *EDITED BY STANLEY FISHER* | [on sloping base line in facsimile holograph] east | [on sloping base line] EXCELSIOR PRESS PUBLISHERS, NEW YORK

[1-3]^{16}, pp. [1-6] 7-9 [10] 11-96. 20.8 x 14.0 cm. Bound in stiff white paper wrappers. Covers printed in brilliant yellow (83) and black. White wove paper unwatermarked. All edges trimmed.

Contents: Epithalmium, p. 28.

95¢. Published Sept. 30, 1961 in an impression of 10,000 copies.

Note: Publication information from Bob Wilson's *Bibliography of Works by Gregory Corso.* [New York: Phoenix, 1966].

B16   **THE DRUG EXPERIENCE**   **1961**

a1. *First edition, hardbound*

THE DRUG | EXPERIENCE | *First-person accounts of addicts,* | *writers, scientists* | *and others* | EDITED, WITH INTRODUCTION | AND NOTES, BY | *David Ebin* | *The Orion Press* [bullet] *New York* | [publisher's device]

[1-11]^{16} [12]^{8} [13]^{16}, pp. [i-v] vi-xi [xii] [1] 2-385 [386-388]. 23.4 x 15.6 cm. Quarter bound in pale purplish blue (203) cloth covered boards with light greenish gray (154) spine cloth covered boards. Across the front cover: '[in dark blue (183)] THE [not on straight

base line] DRUG EXPERIENCE'. Down the spine '[in dark blue] THE DRUG EXPERIENCE EDITED BY DAVID EBIN [across the spine] ORION [publisher's device]'. White wove paper unwatermarked. White endpapers. All edges trimmed. Issued in a white paper dust jacket, printed in black and red (see note below).

Contents: [prose journal entry], pp. 301-307.

$5.95. Published Nov. 20, 1961 in an unknown quantity.

Note: Two states of the dust jacket are known. The earlier is identified by the publisher's name appearing inside a white rectangle at the base of the spine, the second state has no rectangle. Also the second paragraph of the blurb has been revised in the second. The first states: 'a Greenwich Village "pad," a Comanche tent on the Great Plains, a laboratory overlooking the Hudson River, a Paris night club for sensualists and a bandstand at a Chicago jazz session.' The second states: 'a Greenwich Village "pad," a Menomini tent in the Middle West, a laboratory overlooking the Hudson River, a private Parisian club for artists, and a bandstand at a Chicago jazz session.'

a2. *First edition, paperbound, 1965*

THE DRUG | EXPERIENCE | *First-person accounts of addicts,* | *writers, scientists, and others* | EDITED, WITH INTRODUCTION AND NOTES BY | *David Ebin* | *An Evergreen Black Cat* [publisher's device] *Book* | GROVE PRESS, INC. NEW YORK

Two hundred eight single leaves, [i-xx] [1] 2-385 [386-396]. 18.0 x 10.4 cm. Perfect bound in stiff white paper wrappers. Covers printed in black, red and purple. White wove paper unwatermarked. All edges trimmed and stained red.

95¢. Published April 1, 1965 and reprinted at least once in quantities unavailable from publisher.

Note: Later printings are identified as such on the verso of the title page.

B17　　　　THE VILLAGE VOICE READER　　　　1962

a1. *First edition, hardbound*

[left title page] *A Mixed Bag from the* | *Greenwich Village Newspaper* | Edited by | DANIEL WOLF | and | EDWIN FANCHER | With line drawings by | MURIEL JACOBS | HASSE NORDENSTROM | JULES FEIFFER | JEAN SHEPHERD | SHEL SILVERSTEIN | ALEK SMITT [continuation of drawing from the right title page] [right title page] THE VILLAGE | VOICE READER | *Doubleday & Company, Inc.* | *Garden City, New York* | 1962 | [reproduction of a drawing illustrating the Village Voice office building and a street in New York]

One hundred eighty single leaves, pp. [1-5] 6-349 [350-360]. 21.5 x 14.5 cm. Quarter bound in light yellowish green (135) cloth covered boards with a dark grayish yellow (91) cloth covered spine. Down the spine: '[the following 2 lines inside 2 single line frames] THE VILLAGE | VOICE READER [the following 2 lines inside 2 single line frames] Edited by DANIEL WOLF | and EDWIN FANCHER [across the spine inside 2 single line oval frames] DOUBLEDAY'. White wove paper unwatermarked. White endpapers. All edges trimmed. Issued in a white paper dust jacket, printed in black, purple, green, and orange.

Contents: [review of Jack Kerouac's *The Dharma Bums*], pp. 339-343.

$4.95. Published March 16, 1962 in a quantity undisclosed by the publisher.

a2. *First edition, paperbound, 1962*

[left title page] *A Mixed Bag from the* I *Greenwich Village Newspaper* I Edited by I DANIEL WOLF I and I EDWIN FANCHER I With line drawings by I MURIEL JACOBS I HASSE NORDENSTROM I JULES FEIFFER I JEAN SHEPHERD I SHEL SILVERSTEIN I ALEK SMITT [continuation of drawing from the right title page] [right title page] THE VILLAGE I VOICE READER I *Doubleday & Company, Inc.* I *Garden City, New York* I 1962 I [reproduction of a drawing illustrating the Village Voice office building and a street in New York]

One hundred eighty single leaves, pp. [1-5] 6-349 [350-360]. 20.6 x 13.7 cm. Perfect bound in stiff white paper wrappers. Covers printed in pink, black, orange, green and yellow. White wove paper unwatermarked. All edges trimmed.

$2.50. Published March 16, 1962 in a quantity undisclosed by the publisher.

a3. *First edition, paperbound, re-issue, 1963*

[left title page] Edited by I DANIEL WOLF I and I EDWIN FANCHER I With line drawings by I MURIEL JACOBS I HASSE NORDENSTROM I JULES FEIFFER I JEAN SHEPHERD I SHEL SILVERSTEIN I ALEK SMITT [continuation of drawing from the right title page]

[right title page] THE VILLAGE I VOICE READER I *A Black Cat* [publisher's device] *Book* I GROVE PRESS, INC. I NEW YORK I [line drawing illustrating the Village Voice office building and street in New York]

One hundred sixty single leaves, pp. [1-5] 6-320. 17.9 x 10.6 cm. Perfect bound in stiff white paper wrappers. Covers printed in pink, green, black, orange, blue and red. White wove paper unwatermarked. All edges trimmed and bottom edge stained black.

Contents: As first edition, pp. 311-315.

95¢. Published 1963 in a quantity undisclosed by the publisher.

B18   **THE PARTISAN REVIEW ANTHOLOGY**   **1962**

[left title page] The Partisan I [7.1 cm. rule]
[right title page] Review Anthology I [11.3 cm. rule] I Edited by William Phillips and Philip Rahv I HOLT, RINEHART AND WINSTON [bullet] NEW YORK

[1]^{14} [2-14]^{16} [15]^{12} [16]^{16}, pp. [i-vi] vii [viii-x] [1-2] 3-490. 23.9 x 15.9 cm. Quarter bound in dark gray (266) cloth with yellowish gray (93) cloth covered boards. Across the spine in gold: 'PHILLIPS/RAHV I [down the spine] The Partisan Review Anthology [across the spine] HOLT I RINEHART I WINSTON'. White wove paper unwatermarked. White endpapers with blue threads. All edges trimmed. Issued in a white paper dust jacket printed in dark brown, black and red.

Contents: Ready to Roll, p. 383.

$8.50. Published July 30, 1962 in a quantity undisclosed by the publisher.

B19   **POET'S CHOICE**   **1962**

a1. *First edition, hardbound*

POET'S | CHOICE | [4.6 cm. ornamental dash] | EDITED BY | Paul Engle and Joseph Langland | [publisher's device] | THE DIAL PRESS NEW YORK 1962

[1-8]^{16} [9]^4 [10-11]^{16}, pp. [1-2] [i-iii] iv-xvii [xviii-xx] 1-303 [304-306]. 23.7 x 15.8 cm. Bound in strong reddish brown (40) cloth, lettered down the spine in gold: '[ornamental bracket] POET'S CHOICE [ornamental bracket] [across the spine] EDITED BY | ENGLE | AND | LANGLAND [the G has an ornamental serif] | [publisher's device] | DIAL'. White wove paper unwatermarked. Moderate reddish orange (37) endpapers. Top edges trimmed. Issued in a pale orange yellow (73) dust jacket printed in black, gold and deep reddish orange (38).

Contents: Howl, pp. 234-235 — [prose note], pp. 235-236.

$6.00 until Dec. 31, 1962 and $6.95 thereafter. Published Oct. 9, 1962 in an impression of 10,000 copies.

Note: Publication data from B.C. Bloomfield and Edward Mendelson's *W.H. Auden, a bibliography.* 2nd ed. [Charlottesville, VA: University of Virginia, 1972]

a2. *First edition, paperbound, 1966*

POET'S | CHOICE | [ornamental dash] | EDITED BY | Paul Engle and Joseph Langland | [publisher's device] | A DELTA BOOK [bullet] 1966

One hundred sixty single leaves, pp. [i-iii] iv-vii [viii] ix-xi [xii] xiii-xvii [xviii] 1-302. 20.2 x 13.6 cm. Perfect bound in stiff white paper wrappers. Covers printed in medium gray (265), vivid green (139) and black. White wove paper unwatermarked. All edges trimmed.

$1.95. Published Jan. 1966 in a quantity undisclosed by the publisher.

Note: A second paperback edition of this title was published by Time Incorporated in 1966, but it did not include AG's contribution.

B20   **EROTIC POETRY**   **1963**

a1. *First edition*

[left title page] Erotic Poetry | [in blue] DECORATIONS BY WARREN CHAPPELL [right title page] [drawing in black & blue] *The Lyrics, Ballads, Idyls* | *and Epics of Love—* | *Classical to Contemporary* | *Edited by WILLIAM COLE* | Foreword by Stephen Spender | [publisher's device in blue] | [10.0 cm. rule in blue] | RANDOM HOUSE | [in blue] 1963

[1-13]^{16} [14]^8 [15-18]^{16}, pp. [1-2] [i-vi] vii-xxi [xxii-xxiii] xxiv-xxvii [xxviii-xxix] xxx-xlvii [xlviii] xlix-liv [1-4] 5-501 [502-504]. 24.4 x 16.3 cm. Bound in moderate bluish green (164) cloth covered boards. Across the front cover: '[in gold] EROTIC POETRY | [in red] [design]'. Across the spine: '[3 rules in red] | [design in red within single rules] | [in gold] Erotic | [in gold] Poetry | [bullet in gold] | [in gold] WILLIAM | [in gold] COLE | [design in red within single rules] | [publisher's device in gold] | [in gold] RANDOM HOUSE | [3 rules in red]'. White wove paper unwatermarked. Light grayish reddish brown (45) endpapers. Top edges trimmed and stained red. Bottom edges

trimmed. Issued in a white paper dust jacket printed in black, green, red, brown, blue and yellow.

Contents: Song: Fie My Fum, pp. 199-200.

$8.95. Published Sept. 15, 1963 in an impression of 8500 copies.

Note: First printing identified as such on the verso of the right title page. Both this book and *Neurotica* were published in 1963 and contain the identical version of the poem "Song: Fie My Fum". Although the exact date of Sept. 15, 1963 was assigned this edition by the publisher, no exact date of publication could be found for *Neurotica*. It was therefore impossible to determine which of the volumes actually appeared first and although this is assigned an earlier number it is only due to the fact that uncertainty exists concerning *Neurotica*.

a2. *First British issue, 1964*

Erotic Poetry | [9.1 cm. rule] | *The Lyrics, Ballads, Idyls* | *and Epics of Love —* | *Classical to Contemporary* | Edited by | WILLIAM COLE | Foreword by Stephen Spender | [9.1 cm. rule] | WEIDENFELD AND NICOLSON | 20 New Bond Street London W1

[A]^{16} B-F^{16} [G-H]^{16} [J-K]^{16} L-R^{16} [S]^8, pp. [i-vi] vii-xxi [xxii-xxiii] xxiv-xxvii [xxviii-xxix] xxx-xlvii [xlviii] xlix-liv [1-4] 5-501 [502-506]. 22.2 x 14.4 cm. Bound in black cloth covered boards. Across the spine: '[on a deep reddish orange (36) panel all in gold] [5 rules each 3.5 cm.] EROTIC | POETRY | [1.0 cm. rule] | Edited by | WILLIAM | COLE | [5 rules each 3.5 cm.] | [the rest in gold below panel] WEIDENFELD | & NICOLSON'. White wove paper unwatermarked. Strong reddish purple (237) endpapers. All edges trimmed. Issued in a white paper dust jacket printed in black, red and purple.

50s. Published June 1964 in a quantity undisclosed by the publisher.

B21   **NEUROTICA**   **1963**

[in white on an ink-blot design] NEUROTICA | *Editors:* | *Jay Irving Landesman* | *Gershon Legman* | *ST. LOUIS - NEW YORK* | *1948-51* | REPRINTED BY | HACKER ART BOOKS | NEW YORK | 1963

[1]^1 [2-18]^{18}, pp. [i-ii] [1] two [3] four-fifty four [1] two - fifty six [1-3] 4-61 [62] [1-2] 3-63 [64] [1-2] 3-63 [64] 1-3 [4] [1-2] 3-47 [48] [1-2] 3-47 [48] [1-2] 3-79 [80] [1-2] 3-64. 23.8 x 15.6 cm. Bound in strong orange (50) cloth covered boards printed down the spine in gold: '[all in ornamental type] THE [in 2 lines] COMP | LEAT [in 1 line] NEUROTICA [across the spine not in ornamental type] HACKER'. White wove paper unwatermarked. White endpapers. All edges trimmed. Issued in an orange paper dust jacket printed in black.

Contents: Song: Fie My Fum, p. [350].

$12.00. Published 1963 in an impression of 500 copies.

Note: Information from publisher, no date available, all nine issues of the periodical are reprinted here. See also the notes above for *Erotic Poetry*.

B22   **THE YAGE LETTERS**   **1963**

a1. *First edition*

THE | YAGE | LETTERS | William Burroughs | & | Allen Ginsberg | [publisher's device] | CITY LIGHTS BOOKS

[1]^{10} [2-4]^8, pp. [1-6] 7-68. 18.4 x 12.3 cm. Bound in stiff white paper wrappers. Covers printed in black. White wove paper unwatermarked. All edges trimmed.

Contents: [letter to William Burroughs], pp. 49-59 — Ether Notes, pp. 57-59 — [prose footnote to letter], p. 60 — [letter to whom it may concern], p. 65 — [anonymous prose blurb on the back cover is by AG]

$1.25. Published Nov. 31, 1963 in an impression of ca. 3,000 copies.

Note: Reprinted as follows: 2nd printing, Aug. 1965, 4,000 copies; 3rd printing, Nov. 1966, 5,000 copies; 4th printing, May 1968, 3,000 copies; 5th printing, Sept. 1969, 3,000 copies; 6th printing, Aug. 1971, 5,000 copies. Second and subsequent printings identified as such on the verso of the title page. Publication data from Joe Maynard and Barry Miles' *William S. Burroughs: a bibliography, 1953-73.* [Charlottesville, VA: University Press of Virginia, 1978].

a2. *First edition, enlarged re-issue, 1975*

THE | YAGE | LETTERS | William Burroughs | & | Allen Ginsberg | [publisher's device] | CITY LIGHTS BOOKS

Thirty-six single leaves, pp. [1-6] 7-72. 18.3 x 12.3 cm. Perfect bound in stiff white paper wrappers. Covers printed in black. White wove paper unwatermarked. All edges trimmed.

Contents: As first edition, pp. 53-64, 69.

$2.00. Published June 1975 in an impression of 3,000 copies.

Note: This includes an additional letter by William Burroughs and is identified as "Second Edition" on the verso of the title page, but the second printing of this issue is identified as the eighth printing and so on with reprints as follows: 8th printing, Feb. 1978, 3,000 copies; 9th printing, June 1981, 3,000 copies; 10th printing, Dec. 1985, 3,000 copies. Identified as such on the verso of the title page.

a3. *First edition, second enlarged re-issue, 1988*

THE | YAGE | LETTERS | William Burroughs | & | Allen Ginsberg | [publisher's device] | CITY LIGHTS BOOKS | San Francisco

Thirty-six single leaves, pp. [i-vi] [1]-66. 20.3 x 14.0 cm. Perfect bound in stiff white paper wrappers. Covers printed in light grayish yellowish brown (79) and black. White wove paper unwatermarked. All edges trimmed.

Contents: As first edition, pp. 49-59, 64.

$5.95. Published Feb. 1988 in an impression of 3,000 copies.

Note: This includes an additional routine by William Burroughs. This issue is identified as the 'Third edition' on the verso of the title page.

B23   **ROOSEVELT AFTER INAUGURATION**   **1964**

a1. *First edition*

[entire page in facsimile holograph] [design of a flag with 5 dollar signs instead of stars] |
ROOSEVELT [with crossed eyeballs and eyebrows added to the O's] | AFTER |
INAUGURATION | BY | "WILLY LEE" | ALIAS | WILLIAM S. BURROUGHS |
[design of the star of David with a skull in the center with a flower in its teeth]

Single gathering of fourteen leaves, pp. [1-28]. 14.1 x 10.7 cm. Stapled twice in self
cover. All edges trimmed.

Paper: Moderate pink (5) laid paper unwatermarked, pp. [1-6, 23-28]; white wove paper
unwatermarked, pp. [7-10, 19-22]; and very pale blue (184) wove paper unwatermarked,
pp. [11-18].

Contents: Cover designs by AG.

50¢ later raised to $1.00. Published Jan. 1964 in an impression of ca. 500 copies by the
Fuck You Press.

b1. *Second edition, 1979*

ROOSEVELT AFTER | INAUGURATION | and Other Atrocities | William S.
Burroughs | [publisher's device] | City Lights Books

Twenty-eight single leaves, pp. [1-6] 7-54 [55-56]. 17.7 x 12.7 cm. Perfect bound in stiff
white paper wrappers. Covers printed in black and purple. White wove paper
unwatermarked. All edges trimmed.

Contents: Cover design from the first edition reproduced on p. [11].

$2.50. Published Oct. 1979 in an impression of 3,000 copies.

Note: Reprinted once in Dec. 1980 in an impression of 3,000 copies. Second printing is
identified as such on the verso of the title page.

B24   **12 POETS & 1 PAINTER**   **1964**

WRITING 3 | [9.9 cm. rule] | 12 POETS & 1 PAINTER | [10.0 cm. rule] |
[ornamentation]

Single gathering of sixteen leaves, pp. [1-4] 5-32. 22.2 x 15.6 cm. Stapled twice in stiff
moderate yellow green (120) paper wrappers. Across the front cover: 'WRITING 3 |
[10.0 cm. rule] | 12 POETS & 1 PAINTER | [10.0 cm. rule] | [design of flowers]'.
Across the back cover: '*YERBA BUENA* drawing by JESS'. White wove paper
unwatermarked. Right edge of the front cover is untrimmed.

Contents: Last Night in Calcutta, pp. 27-28 — S.S. Azemour, p. 28.

$1.00. Published by Four Seasons Foundation, San Francisco, Sept. 4, 1964 in an
impression of 300 copies.

Note: Reprinted as follows: 2nd printing, Dec. 10, 1964, 483 copies; 3rd printing, Nov.
4, 1965, 750 copies; 4th printing, Jan. 26, 1967, 500 copies. Second and subsequent
printings identified as such on the verso of the title page.

B25   **BUGGER**   **1964**

[entire page in facsimile holograph] [design of eye, penis and sun rays] I BUGGER! I an Anthology of Buttockry I [6.4 x 13.9 cm. frame enclosing 11 lines] I published by I THE FUCK YOU/PRESS I [design of 2 penises and a cloud shape in which is the following line] fug-press [outside the cloud shape] ® I a name of distinction representing 3 years of quality printing I & aggressive innocence I in the pornography industry I YOU CAN BE SURE IF IT'S fug-press I "Some of my favorite poets I bugger each other all the time" I Ted Berrigan I editor of an evil *JOURNAL OF POETRY*

Twenty-two single leaves printed on rectos only, ll. [i-ii] 1-18 [iii] 19. 27.9 x 21.6 cm. Stapled 3 time on the left in 2 sheets of pale orange yellow (73) wove paper unwatermarked. Covers printed in black. Across the front cover: '[all in facsimile holograph] BUGGER I [design of Egyptian-style figures and boat within circle with radiating petals and buttocks] I an anthology'. Across the back cover: '[in facsimile holograph] BUGGER I [design] I [in facsimile holograph] fug-press 1964 I published in 5 editions: I 1) The Trade Edition of 400 copies I 2) The Rough Trade Edition of 15 numbered I & buggered copies I 3) The special "bugger fantasy" edition-- I an edition of 4 signed & numbered copies I for which additional pages have been added. I On these Al Fowler, Szabo, & Ed Sanders I have hand written, calligrammed, or I drawn, bugger fantasies; each signing his I work I 4) The Trembling Buttock edition: an edition I of 3 copies, numbered, each of which is I honored by the inclusion of a page I containing the hitherto legendary snapshot I of Harry Fainlight getting buggered by two I Greeks at a Times Square Hotel Dixie hustle scene. I 5) The Pygophile Edition: an edition of 2 copies, I numbered, with all poems signed by their authors I & containing a pygograph (buttock print) direct I from the Goddess of Buggery herself, Barbara Rubin, I on 6 ply Strathmore bond. I [within a cartouche] fug-press I peace perversion pussy'. Pale orange yellow (73) wove paper unwatermarked. All edges trimmed.

Contents: This Form of Life Needs Sex, pp. 2-3.

Published November 1964 in an impression of 400 copies and sold for an unknown price.

Note: Possibly other limited editions were issued as per the back cover descriptions (see above) but none have been found by the compiler.

B26   **OF POETRY AND POWER**   **1964**

[left title page] OF POETRY I POEMS OCCASIONED I AND BY THE DEATH I *Foreword by Arthur Schlesinger, Jr.*
[right title page] AND POWER I BY THE PRESIDENCY I OF JOHN F. KENNEDY I EDITED WITH AN INTRODUCTION I *by Erwin A. Glikes and Paul Schwaber* I BASIC BOOKS, INC. I PUBLISHERS/NEW YORK

[1-4]^{16} [5]^8 [6]^{16}, pp. [1-2] [i-iv] v-vii [viii-ix] x-xiv [xv-xvi] 1-155 [156-158]. 24.0 x 14.4 cm. Bound in black cloth covered boards. Down the spine: '[in blue] OF POETRY AND POWER I [in red] *Edited by Erwin A. Glikes and Paul Schwaber* [across the spine in red] BASIC I [in red] BOOKS'. White laid paper unwatermarked. White endpapers. All edges trimmed. Top edges stained light blue. Issued in a white paper dust jacket printed in black, red and blue with a full-color illustration.

Contents: Journals Nov. 22, '63 [poem], p. 26.

$5.95. Published Nov. 6, 1964 in a quantity undisclosed by the publisher.

B27   **BRIEFE AN EINEN VERLEGER**   **1965**

BRIEFE I AN EINEN VERLEGER I Max Niedermayer I zum 60. Geburtstag I LIMES VERLAG WIESBADEN

[1]^4 [2-24]^8 [25]^6, pp. [i-iv] v-viii, 1-379 [380]. 19.1 x 12.3 cm. Bound in light greenish gray (154) cloth covered boards. Across the spine in gold: 'BRIEFE I AN I EINEN I VERLEGER'. White wove paper unwatermarked. White laid endpapers. All edges trimmed. Issued in a white paper dust jacket, printed very light yellowish green (134), black, and vivid greenish yellow (97).

Contents: [letter to Max Niedermayer], p. 221 — [letter to Max Niedermayer], pp. 230-232.

Hors commerce. Published Jan. 1965 in an impression of 1,000 copies.

Note: This book was reprinted once but it is uncertain whether there is any way to distinguish the first from the second printing.

B28   **FESTSCHRIFT FOR MARIANNE MOORE'S**   **1965**
              SEVENTY SEVENTH BIRTHDAY

Festschrift I FOR I MARIANNE I MOORE'S I Seventy Seventh Birthday I *by various hands* I Edited by I TAMBIMUTTU I [publisher's device] I TAMBIMUTTU & MASS I *1964*

[1-5]^8 [6]^{10} [7-9]^8, pp. [1-10] 11-19 [20] 21-88 [i-iv] 89-137 [138-144]. 22.3 x 14.3 cm. Quarter bound in black cloth with grayish blue (186) paper covered boards with pink geometric design. In gold down the spine: 'Festschrift for Marianne Moore's Seventy Seventh Birthday Tambimuttu/Mass.' White laid paper watermarked: '*Ticonderoga* I *Text*'. White endpapers. All edges trimmed. Issued in a white paper dust jacket printed in black and strong purplish red (255).

Contents: Little Flower M. M., p. 100.

$4.95. Published ca. April 1965 in an impression of 1,000 copies.

Note: This issue was made by the publisher's use of old bindings from other books, being used over his sheets. Spine lettering has been blacked out and at least 7 different styles of covers have been seen. No order can be set for these. In addition, an early unissued edition was greatly revised and corrected for this issue, some copies may still exist, although none have been located by the compiler.

B29   **LAMI**   **1965**
          by Alden Van Buskirk

a1. *First edition, hardbound*

[2 red wavy rules] I [each of the following letters is separated by 5 red wavy rules between each one] LAMI I [2 red wavy rules] I by ALDEN VAN BUSKIRK I with an introductory note I by Allen Ginsberg I The Auerhahn Society I San Francisco I 1965

[12]^4, pp. [i-ii] [1-8] 9-91 [92-94]. 23.3 x 16.3 cm. Quarter bound in moderate reddish orange (37) with dark grayish yellow (91) paper covered boards with a series of wavy red vertical lines as pattern. Down the spine in gold: 'LAMI'. White wove paper watermarked: 'Saturn I Book'. White endpapers. All edges trimmed.

Contents: Introduction [prose], p. [3].

$10.00. Published Fall 1965 in an impression of ca. 250 copies.

a2. *First edition, paperbound, 1965*

[2 red wavy rules] I [each of the following letters is separated by 5 red wavy rules between each one] LAMI I [2 red wavy rules] I by ALDEN VAN BUSKIRK I with an introductory note I by Allen Ginsberg I The Auerhahn Society I San Francisco I 1965

[12]^4, pp. [i-ii] [1-8] 9-91 [92-94]. 23.4 x 16.0 cm. Bound in grayish yellow (90) paper wrappers. Covers printed in red and black. White wove paper watermarked: 'Saturn I Book'. All edges trimmed, the cover being slightly larger than the leaves.

$3.00. Published Fall 1965 in an impression of ca. 750 copies.

B30   WHOLLY COMMUNION   1965

a1. *First edition, first issue*

WHOLLY I COMMUNION I [publisher's device]

[A-D]^8 [E]^4, pp. [1] 2-72. 19.6 x 12.8 cm. Bound in stiff white paper wrappers. Across the front cover: '[all in white upon a black and white photograph of Lawrence Ferlinghetti reading on stage under the lights] WHOLLY I COMMUNION I [publisher's device]'. Across the back cover: '[14 lines] I LORRIMER FILMS Ltd., 18 Carlisle Street, London, W. 1.' White wove paper unwatermarked. All edges trimmed. Issued with a 5.1 cm. wide white paper wraparound label, all printed in black on vivid red (11).

Contents: Who Be Kind To, pp. 12-17 — The Change, pp. 18-24.

7s 6d. Published Dec. 1965 in an impression of 2,500 copies.

a2. *First edition, second issue, 1968*

WHOLLY I COMMUNION I the film by I Peter Whitehead I International Poetry Reading I at the Royal Albert Hall I London June 11th 1965 I [publisher's device]

[A]^4 [B-E]^8, pp. [1-11] 12-72. 20.0 x 13.5 cm. Bound in stiff white paper wrappers. Across the front cover: '[all in white upon a black and white photograph of Lawrence Ferlinghetti reading on stage under the lights] WHOLLY I COMMUNION I [publisher's device]'. Down the spine: 'WHOLLY COMMUNION LORRIMER'. Across the back cover: '[all inside a single rule border] [15 lines] I LORRIMER FILMS Ltd., 18 Carlisle Street, London, W. 1.' White wove coated paper unwatermarked. All edges trimmed.

Contents: As first edition, with the addition of 1 line of prose, p. [1].

8/6. Published April 1966 in an impression of 5,000 copies.

b1. *First American edition, 1968*

WHOLLY I COMMUNION I International Poetry Reading I at the Royal Albert Hall I London, June 11, 1965 I With stills from the film by I Peter Whitehead I GROVE PRESS, INC. [bullet] NEW YORK

[1]^{16} [2]^8 [3]^{16}, pp. [i-viii] [1-13] 14-71 [72]. Bound in stiff white paper wrappers. Covers printed in vivid reddish orange (34), black and vivid yellow green (115). White wove paper unwatermarked. All edges trimmed.

Contents: As first edition, pp. [13]-23.

$1.50. Published April 12, 1968 in a quantity undisclosed by the publisher.

Note: Second and third printings are identified as such on the verso of the title page. Although it was reprinted twice the dates and quantities are not available from the publisher.

B31   **HUNCKE'S JOURNAL**   **1965**
                           by Herbert Huncke

[ornamental type] HUNCKE'S I [ornamental type] JOURNAL I [ornamentation] I [ornamental type] HERBERT I [ornamental type] HUNCKE I [ornamentation] I Drawings by Erin Matson I [ornamentation] I *The Poets Press* I New York City: 1965

Single gathering of forty-four leaves, pp. [i-viii] 1-78 [79-80]. 23.3 x 18.4 cm. Stapled twice into stiff light blue (181) paper wrappers. Covers printed in black. White wove paper unwatermarked. All edges trimmed.

Contents: Introduction [prose], p. [v].

$2.00. Published 1965 in an impression of ca. 2,000 copies.

Note: This is the second edition of this book, although it is not identified as such. The introduction by AG does not appear in either the first edition or the first paperbound edition.

B32   **POEMS OF MADNESS**   **1965**
                           by Ray Bremser

a1. *First edition*

[all in red] RAY BREMSER I [up the left side] POEMS OF I [across the page in ornamental type] MAD I [ornamental type] NESS I 75¢ I INTRODUCTION BY ALLEN GINSBERG

Single gathering of eighteen leaves, pp. [i-ii] 1-31 [32-34]. 17.8 x 11.6 cm. Stapled twice into stiff pale violet (214) paper wrappers. Covers printed in red. White wove paper unwatermarked. All edges trimmed.

Contents: Introduction [prose], pp. [i-ii].

75¢. Published by Paper Book Gallery Editions in 1965 in an unknown quantity.

b1. *New edition, with Angel, paperbound, 1986*

poems of madness [one hollow triangle, one solid triangle] I & angel I [2 horizontal rows of 5 triangles each, 3 hollow, 2 solid] ray bremser I INTRODUCTION by ALLEN GINSBERG I ILLUSTRATIONS by AL DUFFY I [design of 4 solid squares] I WATER ROW PRESS [2 columns of 3 solid triangles] I SUDBURY

Forty-six single leaves, pp. [i-iv] 1-86 [87-88]. 27.4 x 21.3 cm. Perfect bound in stiff light gray (264) paper wrappers. Covers printed in black. White wove paper unwatermarked. All edges trimmed.

Contents: As first edition, pp. 1-2.

$8.95. Published Oct. 14, 1986 in an impression of 250 copies.

Note: Reprinted as follows: 2nd printing, 1987, 150 copies; 3rd printing, 1988, 150 copies. There are no variations between the printings, so that identification of printing is impossible.

b2. *New edition, with Angel, hardbound, 1986*

poems of madness [one hollow triangle, one solid triangle] I & angel I [2 horizontal rows of 5 triangles each, 3 hollow, 2 solid] ray bremser I INTRODUCTION by ALLEN GINSBERG I ILLUSTRATIONS by AL DUFFY I [design of 4 solid squares] [autographed in ink by the author] I WATER ROW PRESS [2 columns of 3 solid triangles] I SUDBURY I [a 2.4 x 10.2 cm. self-adhesive label has been attached here on which is typed all the following] TWENTY-SIX COPIES HAVE BEEN I SIGNED BY THE POET AND HANDBOUND I IN CLOTH AT TABULA RASA PRESS. I THIS IS COPY [letter typed here].

Forty-eight single leaves, pp. [i-vi] 1-86 [87-90]. 27.8 x 22.0 cm. Perfect bound in light gray (264) cloth covered boards. Across the front cover: '[in hollow letters] Poems of Madness & I [in hollow letters] Angel I [design] I Ray Bremser'. White wove paper unwatermarked, except for the first and last leaves which are stiff light gray paper (actually the cover for the paperbound issue). Light gray endpapers. All edges trimmed.

$30.00. Published Nov. 1, 1986 in an impression of 19 copies.

Note: Seven additional copies were bound in blue boards with an original hand-drawn colored portrait of Bremser by Tom Clark affixed to the covers.

B33   **APOCALYPSE ROSE**   **1966**
                             by Charles Plymell

APOCALYPSE ROSE I [ornament in grayish red (19)] I CHARLES PLYMELL I DAVE HASELWOOD I SAN FRANCISCO: 1966

Single gathering of twenty-six leaves, pp. [1-52]. 22.5 x 15.6 cm. Stapled twice in stiff white paper wrappers. Covers printed in grayish red, deep purplish blue (197) and black. White wove paper unwatermarked. All edges trimmed.

Contents: Plymell's Qualities [prose], pp. [5-6] plus the 9-line excerpt on the back cover.

$1.60. Published April 1966 in an impression of 1,000 copies.

B34   **THE DISTINCTIVE VOICE**   **1966**

[in facsimile holograph] *the distinctive voice* I TWENTIETH-CENTURY AMERICAN POETRY I WILLIAM J. MARTZ [bullet] RIPON COLLEGE I [9.2 cm. rule] I SCOTT, FORESMAN AND COMPANY

[1-11]^{16}, pp. [i-xviii] 1-334. 22.7 x 15.1 cm. Bound in stiff white paper wrappers. Covers printed in black and strong yellowish brown (74). White wove paper unwatermarked. All edges trimmed.

Contents: [prose], p. 260 — Howl, pp. 260-267 — A Supermarket in California, pp. 267-268 — The End, p. 268.

$3.50. Published May 20, 1966 in an impression of 9,910 copies.

Note: Reprinted as follows: 2nd printing, Feb. 1967, 10,274 copies; 3rd printing, April 1968, 8,500 copies; 4th printing, Feb. 1969, 13,000 copies; 5th printing, May 1971, 7,000 copies. Second and subsequent printings are identified as such at the base of p. 334.

B35   **BEAT LITERATURE**   **1966**
                      by Gregor Roy

MONARCH ® I *NOTES* [in 2 lines] *AND STUDY* I *GUIDES* I [10.6 cm. gray rule] I BEAT LITERATURE I [10.6 cm. gray rule] I by I Gregor Roy I [10.1 cm. gray rule] I EDITORIAL BOARD OF CONSULTANTS I STANLEY COOPERMAN, Ph.D., CHARLES LEAVITT, Ph.D., UNICIO J. VIOLI, Ph.D., I Dept. of English, Dept. of English, Dept. of English, I Simon Fraser Univ. Montclair State College Fairleigh Dickinson Univ. I [10.1 cm. gray rule] I Distributed by I MONARCH PRESS, INC. I 387 Park Avenue South I New York, N.Y. 10016

Single gathering of sixty-four leaves, pp. [1-4] 5-127 [128]. 21.3 x 13.4 cm. Stapled twice in stiff white paper wrappers. Covers printed in black and strong red (12). White wove paper unwatermarked. All edges trimmed.

Contents: [excerpt from a letter by Gregory Corso, Peter Orlovsky and AG], pp. 117-118.

$1.00. Published Aug. 19, 1966 in an unknown quantity.

B36   **THE MARIHUANA PAPERS**   **1966**

a1. *First edition, hardbound*

The I Marihuana Papers I Edited by David Solomon I Introduction by Alfred R. Lindesmith, PhD I *The Bobbs-Merrill Company, Inc.* I *A subsidiary of Howard W. Sams & Co., Inc., Publishers* I *Indianapolis* [bullet] *Kansas City* [bullet] *New York*

[1-14]^{16} [15]^{14}, pp. [i-vi] vii-xi [xii] xiii-xxi [xxii] xxiii-xxvi [1-2] 3-448 [449-450]. 23.5 x 15.5 cm. Moderate olive green (125) cloth covered boards. Printed across the spine in gold: 'Edited by I David Solomon I [down the spine] THE I MARIHUANA I PAPERS [across the spine] Bobbs-Merrill'. White wove paper unwatermarked. White endpapers. All edges trimmed. Issued in a white paper dust jacket printed in green, black, red, yellow, blue and orange.

Contents: First Manifesto to End the Bringdown [prose], pp. 183-200.

$10.00. Published Dec. 1966 in an impression of 5,000 copies, and reprinted once in March 1967, 2,500 copies.

Note: Publication information from Michael Horowitz, Karen Walls and Billy Smith's *An Annotated Bibliography of Timothy Leary* [Hamden, CT: Archon Books, 1988].

b1. *Second edition, paperbound, 1968*

THE I MARIHUANA I PAPERS I Edited by DAVID SOLOMON I Introduction by Alfred R. Lindesmith, PhD I [publisher's device] I A SIGNET BOOK I Published by The New American Library

Two hundred fifty-six single leaves, pp. [i-viii] ix-xi [xii] xiii-xxiii [xxiv] xxv-xxviii [29-30] 31-509 [510-512]. 17.7 x 10.6 cm. Perfect bound in stiff white paper wrappers. Covers printed in full color. White wove paper unwatermarked. All edges trimmed.

Contents: As first edition, pp. 230-248.

$1.50. Published April 1968 in an impression of 97,685 copies.

Note: Reprinted as follows: 2nd printing, April 1968, 5.295 copies; 3rd printing, Feb. 1969, 32,015 copies; 4th printing, March 1970, 51,420 copies; 5th printing, Feb. 1971, 48,770 copies. First printing identified as such on the verso of the title page.

c1. *First British edition, paperbound, 1969*

The Marijuana | Papers | *Edited by David Solomon* | *Introduction by* | *Alfred R. Lindesmith Ph.D.* | *Panther Modern Society*

Two hundred forty single leaves, pp. [1-7] 8-9 [10-13] 14-22 [23] 24-27 [28-31] 32-475 [476-480]. 17. 6 x 11.1 cm. Perfect bound in stiff white paper wrappers. Covers printed in full color. White wove paper unwatermarked. All edges trimmed.

Contents: As first edition, pp. 257-277.

12 S. Published 1969 in an unknown quantity.

Note: Reprinted once in 1970, quantity again unknown.

B37   **ASTRONAUTS OF INNER-SPACE**   **1966**

ASTRONAUTS | OF | INNER-SPACE | [design of fork, duck and airplane]

Thirty-six single leaves, pp. [i-iv] [1] 2-65 [66-68]. 20.9 x 17.3 cm. Perfect bound in stiff white paper wrappers. Covers printed in deep blue (179), black and strong red (12) Leaves, 1-2, 35-36 are light brown (57) wove paper unwatermarked; all other leaves are white wove paper unwatermarked. All edges trimmed.

Contents: Back to the Wall [prose], pp. 14-15.

$1.50. Edited by Jeff Berner and published in San Francisco by Stolen Paper Review Editions in 1966 in an unknown quantity.

B38   **THE NEW WRITING IN THE U.S.A.**   **1967**

THE | NEW WRITING | IN | THE USA | EDITED BY DONALD ALLEN AND | ROBERT CREELEY | PENGUIN BOOKS

One hundred sixty-eight single leaves, pp. [1-5] 6-7 [8-9] 10-11 [12-13] 14-15 [16-17] 18-24 [25] 26-331 [332-336]. 19.7 x 13.0 cm. Perfect bound in stiff white paper wrappers. Covers printed in deep blue (179), black, light greenish blue (172) and strong reddish orange (35). White wove paper unwatermarked. All edges trimmed.

Contents: The Change [poem with notes], pp. 89-96 — Kral Majales, pp. 97-99.

7s6d. Published Jan. 1967 in an impression of 25,000-30,000 copies.

Note: Penguin Books sold 24,178 copies of this book and destroyed the remainder. Publication data from Alexander Smith, Jr.'s *Frank O'Hara: a comprehensive bibliography.* [New York: Garland, 1979].

B39 **NOTHING MORE TO DECLARE** **1967**
by John Clellon Holmes

a1. *First edition*

NOTHING | MORE | TO DECLARE | *John Clellon Holmes* | E.P. Dutton & Co., Inc.
| New York [ornament] 1967

[1-8]^{16}, pp. [1-10] 11-13 [14-15] 16-253 [254-256]. 21.5 x 14.2 cm. Half bound in
moderate reddish orange (37) paper covered boards with white cloth spine. Down the spine
all in blue: 'NOTHING MORE | TO DECLARE *John Clellon Holmes* [across the
spine] DUTTON'. White wove paper unwatermarked. White endpapers. All edges
trimmed. Issued in a white paper dust jacket printed in black, orange and blue.

Contents: [letter to John Clellon Holmes], p. 64

$4.95. Published Feb. 16, 1967 in a quantity undisclosed by the publisher.

Note: A 5.1 x 8.9 cm. errata slip has been laid in. First printing identified as such on the
verso of the title page.

b1. *First British edition, 1968*

NOTHING | MORE | TO DECLARE | *John Clellon Holmes* | [publisher's device] |
ANDRE DEUTSCH

[A]-H^{16}, pp. [1-10] 11-13 [14-15] 16-253 [254-256]. 22.1 x 14.0 cm. Bound in strong
reddish orange (35) cloth covered boards. Across the spine all in gold: 'Nothing | More |
to | Declare | [ornament] | John | Clellon | Holmes | [publisher's device] | ANDRE |
DEUTSCH'. White wove paper unwatermarked. White endpapers. All edges trimmed.
Issued in a white paper dust jacket printed in purple, pink, yellow, orange, green, and blue.

30s. Published June 20,1968 in an unknown quantity.

B40 **HELL'S ANGELS** **1967**
by Hunter S. Thompson

a1. *First edition*

Hell's | *Angels* | *A Strange and Terrible Saga* | [9.6 cm. rule] | *by* Hunter S. Thompson
| RANDOM HOUSE [bullet] NEW YORK [publisher's device]

[1-9]^{16}, pp. [i-viii] [1-3] 4-278 [279-280]. 21.8 x 14.7 cm. Bound in black cloth covered
boards. Across the front cover is a design of a motorcycle and rider in silver. Down the
spine: '[in 2 lines in strong red (12)] *HELL'S ANGELS* | *A Strange and Terrible Saga*
[3.1 cm. silver rule across the spine] [in 2 lines down the spine] [in silver] *Hunter S.* | [in
silver] *Thompson* [across the spine] [in silver] [publisher's device] RANDOM | [in
silver] HOUSE'. White wove paper unwatermarked. White endpapers. Top edges
trimmed and stained black. Issued in a white paper dust jacket printed in black, strong
reddish orange (35) and deep reddish orange (36).

Contents: To the Angels, pp. 250-256.

$4.95. Published Feb. 17, 1967 in an impression of 35,700 copies.

Note: First printing is identified as such on the verso of the title page, later printings lack
this phrase. Reprinted at least 3 times.

b1. *Second edition, paperbound, 1967*

Hell's I Angels I A Strange and Terrible Saga I [8.8 cm. rule] I by Hunter S. Thompson I BALLANTINE BOOKS [bullet] NEW YORK

One hundred seventy-six single leaves, pp. [1-10] 11-349 [350-352]. 17.9 x 10.6 cm. Perfect bound in stiff white paper wrappers. Covers printed in deep blue (179), black, and strong reddish orange (35). White wove paper unwatermarked. All edges trimmed.

Contents: As first edition, pp. 316-322.

95¢. Published Nov. 1967 in an unknown quantity.

Note: Reprinted several times with a total count of 420,000 copies printed. First printing identified as such on the verso of the title page.

c1. *First British paperbound, 1967*

HUNTER S. THOMPSON I HELL'S ANGELS I [two 1.0 cm. rules] I [publishers' device] I PENGUIN BOOKS

One hundred forty-four single leaves, pp. [1-13] 14-282 [283] 284 [285-288]. 17.9 x 11.0 cm. Perfect bound in stiff white paper wrappers. Covers printed in full color. White wove paper unwatermarked. All edges trimmed.

Contents: As first edition, pp. 258-264.

5'-. Published 1967 in an unknown quantity.

B41   **WHERE IS VIETNAM?**   **1967**

AN ANTHOLOGY I OF CONTEMPORARY POEMS I [2.1 cm. rule] I WHERE IS VIETNAM? I American Poets Respond I *Edited by* I WALTER LOWENFELS I *with the assistance of Nan Braymer* I ANCHOR BOOKS I DOUBLEDAY & COMPANY, INC. I GARDEN CITY, NEW YORK I 1967

One hundred single leaves, pp. [i-vi] vii-viii [ix] x-xiii [xiv-xvii] xviii-xx [xxi-xxii] [1] 2-160 [161-178]. 18.1 x 10.5 cm. Perfect bound in stiff white paper wrappers. Covers printed in black, light gray (264), moderate purple (223) and deep yellowish pink (27). White wove paper unwatermarked. All edges trimmed.

Contents: Wichita Vortex Sutra [excerpt], pp. 43-47.

$1.25. Published March 17, 1967 in a quantity undisclosed by the publisher.

B42   **THE BOOK OF GRASS**   **1967**

a1. *First edition*

The Book of Grass I AN ANTHOLOGY ON INDIAN HEMP I *edited by* I GEORGE ANDREWS I *and* I Simon Vinkenoog I [publisher's device] I PETER OWEN [bullet] LONDON

[1]^1 [A]-C^{16} [2]^1 D^{16} [3]^1 E-H^{16}, pp. [1-2] [i-ii] iii-xiii [xiv] 1-82 [i-ii] 83-114 [i-ii] 115-242. 22.0 x 14.2 cm. Bound in light greenish gray (154) cloth covered boards. Printed across the spine in gold: 'The I Book I of I Grass I [ornament]   ANDREWS I [publisher's device] I PETER I OWEN'. White wove paper unwatermarked. White

endpapers. All edges trimmed. Issued in a white paper dust jacket printed in black and vivid green (139).

Contents: Night at the Burning Ghat [prose], pp. 129-130, 132.

37s6d. Published June 1967 in an impression of 2,000 copies.

Note: Leaves that are described above as [2] and [3] in the collation are actually wrapped around signature D.

a2. *First American issue, hardbound, 1967*

The Book of Grass | AN ANTHOLOGY ON INDIAN HEMP | *edited by* | GEORGE ANDREWS | *and* | *Simon Vinkenoog* | GROVE PRESS, INC. | NEW YORK

[1-8]^{16}, pp. [i-ii] iii-xiii [xiv] 1-242. 21.7 x 14.7 cm. Bound in deep blue (179) cloth covered boards. Across the spine in gold: 'The | Book | of | Grass | Andrews | & | Vinkenoog | Grove | Press'. White wove paper unwatermarked. White endpapers. All edges trimmed. Issued in white paper dust jacket printed in black, green and blue.

$5.00. Published Oct. 2, 1967 in a quantity undisclosed by the publisher.

a3. *First American issue, paperbound, 1968*

The Book of Grass | AN ANTHOLOGY ON INDIAN HEMP | *edited by* | GEORGE ANDREWS | *and* | *Simon Vinkenoog* | GROVE PRESS, INC. | NEW YORK

One hundred thirty single leaves, pp. [i-xiv] 1-114 [i-iv] 115-242. 17.8 x 10.7 cm. Perfect bound in stiff white paper wrappers. Covers printed in black, blue and green. White wove paper unwatermarked, the postcard and advertisements inserted between pages 114 and 115 are a stiff card stock. All edges trimmed and stained dark blue.

$1.25. Published 1968 in a quantity undisclosed by the publisher.

Note: Second and subsequent printings are identified as such on the verso of the title page. The book was reprinted four times, reprint dates and quantities unavailable from publisher.

a4. *First British issue, paperbound, 1972*

Edited by George Andrews | *and* Simon Vinkenoog | The Book of Grass | An Anthology of Indian Hemp | Penguin Books

One hundred ninety-two single leaves, pp. [1-5] 6-8 [9] 10-14 [15-16] 17-378 [379-384]. 18.0 x 11.0 cm. Perfect bound in stiff white paper wrappers. Covers printed in black, greenish white (153), green, yellow, pink, brown and orange. White wove paper unwatermarked. All edges trimmed.

Contents: As first edition, pp. 178-181.

Published 1972 in a quantity undisclosed by the publisher.

B43   **AUTHORS TAKE SIDES ON VIETNAM**   **1967**

a1. *First edition*

[1.9 cm. vertical rule] AUTHORS | TAKE SIDES ON VIETNAM | Two questions on the war in Vietnam | answered by the authors of several nations | EDITED BY | CECIL

WOOLF AND JOHN BAGGULEY | [publisher's device] | PETER OWEN [bullet] LONDON

[A]^{15} B-F^{16} G^8 H^{15}, pp. [1-2] [i-vi] vii-xii, 13-232 [233-234], see note below. 21.6 x 13.9 cm. Bound in black cloth covered boards. Down the spine in gold: 'authors take sides on Vietnam [across the spine] [publisher's device] | Peter Owen'. White wove paper unwatermarked. All edges trimmed. Issued in a white paper dust jacket printed in black and red.

Contents: [prose], pp. 140-142.

37s 6d, later raised to £2.00. Published Sept. 18, 1967 in an impression of 2,300 copies.

Note: The front and back leaves are pasted to the covers so that the first leaf of the first signature is glued to the cover.

b1. First American edition, paperbound, 1967

AUTHORS | TAKE | SIDES | ON VIETNAM | Two Questions | on the War in Vietnam | Answered by the Authors | of Several Nations | Edited by | CECIL WOOLF and | JOHN BAGGULEY | [publisher's device] SIMON AND SCHUSTER, NEW YORK

[1-3]^{16}, pp. [1-13] 14-15 [16] 17-92 [93-96]. 27.9 x 21.5 cm. Perfect bound in stiff white paper wrappers. Covers printed in black and red. White wove paper unwatermarked. All edges trimmed.

Contents: As first edition, p. 36.

$1.95. Published Oct. 31, 1967 in an impression of 10,000 copies.

Note: Reprinted once as follows: 2nd printing, April 1968, 3,500 copies. First printing is identified as such on the verso of the title page.

B44	**POEMS AND ANTIPOEMS**	**1967**
	by Nicanor Parra	

a1. First edition, hardbound

Nicanor Parra | POEMS AND ANTIPOEMS | *Edited by Miller Williams* | A New Directions Book

[1-5]^{16}, pp. [i-x] [1] 2-149 [150]. 20.8 x 14.1 cm. Quarter bound in grayish olive (110) cloth with strong red (12) paper covered boards. Down the spine in gold: 'Nicanor Parra Poems and Antipoems New Directions'. White wove paper unwatermarked. White endpapers. All edges trimmed. Issued in a white paper dust jacket printed in grayish olive and strong red.

Contents: The Individual Soliloquy, translated by Lawrence Ferlinghetti and AG, pp. 55, 57, 59, 61 — I Move the Meeting Be Adjourned, translated by AG, p. 79.

$5.50. Published Oct. 15, 1967 in an impression of 1,003 copies.

a2. First edition, paperbound, 1967

Nicanor Parra | POEMS AND ANTIPOEMS | *Edited by Miller Williams* | A New Directions Book

[1-5]^{16}, pp. [i-iv] v-ix [x] [1] 2-149 [150]. 20.2 x 13.7 cm. Bound in stiff white paper wrappers. Cover printed in black. White wove paper unwatermarked. All edges trimmed.

$1.95. Published Oct. 15, 1967 in an impression of 5,167 copies.

Note: Reprinted as follows: 2nd printing, March 20, 1972, 3,120 copies; 3rd printing, Aug. 7, 1978, 1,017 copies. Second and third printings identified as such on the verso of the title page and on the back cover.

b1. *First British edition, hardbound, 1968*

Poems & I *Antipoems* I *Nicanor* I *Parra* I A SELECTION I Edited by Miller Williams I Translated by Lawrence Ferlinghetti, I Allen Ginsberg, James Laughlin, Denise Levertov, I Thomas Merton, W. S. Merwin, Miller Williams I and William Carlos Williams I [7.9 cm. rule] I [publisher's device] I JONATHAN CAPE I THIRTY BEDFORD SQUARE I LONDON

Sixty-four single leaves, pp. [1-7] 8-125 [126-128]. 18.3 x 11.0 cm. Bound in black paper covered boards lettered up the spine in silver: '[publisher's device] Poems & Antipoems Nicanor Parra'. White wove paper unwatermarked. All edges trimmed. Issued in a white paper dust jacket printed in moderate greenish blue (173) and strong violet (207).

Contents: As first edition, pp. 53-59, 69.

21s. Published July 11, 1968 in an undisclosed number of copies.

Note: The publisher reports that this was out of print in 1975.

b2. *First British edition, paperbound, 1968*

Poems & I *Antipoems* I *Nicanor* I *Parra* I A SELECTION I Edited by Miller Williams I Translated by Lawrence Ferlinghetti, I Allen Ginsberg, James Laughlin, Denise Levertov, I Thomas Merton, W. S. Merwin, Miller Williams I and William Carlos Williams I [7.9 cm. rule] I [publisher's device] I JONATHAN CAPE I THIRTY BEDFORD SQUARE I LONDON

Sixty-four single leaves, pp. [1-7] 8-125 [126-128]. 17.6 x 10.7 cm. Perfect bound in stiff white paper wrappers. Covers printed in medium gray (265). White wove paper unwatermarked. All edges trimmed. Issued in a white paper dust jacket printed in moderate greenish blue (173) and strong violet (207).

7s 6d. Published July 11, 1968 in an undisclosed number of copies.

Note: The publisher reports that this was out of print in 1975.

B45   **WRITERS AT WORK**   **1967**

a1. *First edition*

[decorative horizontal border at top] I [single rule borders on left and right sides] *Writers at Work* I [ornamentation] I The *Paris Review* Interviews I THIRD SERIES I *Introduced by Alfred Kazin* I NEW YORK: THE VIKING PRESS I [2 lines of decorative horizontal border at the bottom divided by a single rule]

[1-12]^{16}, pp. [i-vi] vii-xv [xvi] [1-4] 5-368. 22.0 x 14.7 cm. Bound in black cloth covered boards. Across the front cover in strong blue (178) is a design of a bird with a helmet carrying a baton. Across the spine: '[decorative line in strong blue] I [in gold] *Writers* I [in gold] *at* I [in gold] *Work* I [in strong blue] The I [in strong blue] *Paris*

Review I [in strong blue] Interviews I [in gold] THIRD I [in gold] SERIES I [in gold] *Viking* I [2 decorative lines in strong blue]. White wove paper unwatermarked. White endpapers. All edges trimmed. Issued in a white paper dust jacket printed in black, light greenish blue (172) and gold.

Contents: Journal Night Thoughts [facsimile holograph], p. 280 — O ant, p. 295 — [prose note], p. 312.

$7.95. Published Nov. 20, 1967 in an undisclosed number of copies.

a2. *First British issue, 1968*

Writers at Work I [ornamentation] I The *Paris Review* Interviews I THIRD SERIES I *Introduced by Alfred Kazin* I LONDON [bullet] SECKER & WARBURG

[A-M]^{16}, pp. [i-vi] vii-xv [xvi] [1-4] 5-368. 22.3 x 14.2 cm. Bound in grayish reddish orange (39) cloth covered boards. Across the spine in gold: '[two 3.1 cm. rules] I WRITERS I AT I WORK I [two 3.1 cm. rules] I The I *Paris Review* I Interviews I VOLUME I THREE I SECKER & I WARBURG'. White wove paper unwatermarked. White endpapers. All edges trimmed. Issued in a white paper dust jacket printed in black, red and brown.

42s. Published 1968 in an undisclosed number of copies.

a3.* *First Viking Compass issue, 1968*

Note: The compiler has been unable to locate this issue which was reported to have been reprinted 5 times.

a4. *First Penguin issue, 1977*

[decorative horizontal border at top] I [single rule borders on left and right sides] *Writers at Work* I [ornamentation] I The *Paris Review* Interviews I THIRD SERIES I *Edited by George Plimpton* I *Introduced by Alred Kazin* I [publisher's device] I PENGUIN BOOKS I [2 lines of decorative horizontal border at the bottom divided by a single rule]

One hundred ninety-two single leaves, pp. [i-vi] vii-xv [xvi] [1-4] 5-368. 19.6 x 12.8 cm. Perfect bound in stiff white paper wrappers. Covers printed in orange, black, brown and red. White wove paper unwatermarked. All edges trimmed.

$7.95. Published 1977 in a quantity undisclosed by the publisher.

Note: Reprinted as follows: 2nd printing, 1979; 3rd printing, 1982; 4th printing, 1983. Second and subsequent printings identified as such on the verso of the title page.

B46   BACKGROUND PAPERS ON   1967
STUDENT DRUG INVOLVEMENT

BACKGROUND PAPERS I ON I STUDENT DRUG INVOLVEMENT I Edited by I Charles Hollander I The volume compiled under grants from I The van Ameringen Foundation I and I The Maurice Falk Medical Fund I Copyright, 1967 by the I UNITED STATES NATIONAL STUDENT ASSOCIATION I 2115 S. Street, N.W. I Washington, D.C.

Eighty-four single leaves, pp. [i-vi] 1-162. 21.5 x 13.9 cm. Stapled twice into stiff white paper wrappers. Across the front cover all in black letter: 'United States I National Student Association I Collection of I Background Papers I on I Student Drug I Involvement I Edited By I Charles Hollander I Introduction By I Philip Werdell'.

Across the back cover: 'OTHER USNSA PUBLICATIONS I [ad for 9 titles] I [2 lines] I PUBLICATIONS DEPARTMENT I USNSA, 2115 S Street I Washington, D.C. 20008'. White wove paper unwatermarked. All edges trimmed.

Contents: Fact Sheet: Small Anthology of Footnotes on Marijuana [prose, compiled by AG], pp. 9-13 — Seminar on Marihuana and LSD Controls Allen Ginsberg and James H. Fox [transcript], pp. 15-35.

Published 1967 in an impression of ca. 200 copies.

Note: Reprinted once in 1967 in an unknown quantity. The second printing is identified by the addition of the price of $3.00 to the front cover.

B47   A BIBLIOGRAPHY OF WORKS BY JACK KEROUAC   1967

a1. *First edition*

A BIBLIOGRAPHY OF WORKS BY I JACK KEROUAC I (Jean Louis Lebris De Kerouac) I 1939 — 1967 I compiled by I Ann Charters I The Phoenix Book Shop, Inc. I 18 Cornelia Street I New York, N.Y. 10014

Fifty-six single leaves, pp. [i-x] [1] 2-99 [100-102]. 21.6 x 13.9 cm. Perfect bound in stiff grayish yellow green (122) paper wrappers.   Covers printed in black. White wove paper unwatermarked. All edges trimmed.

Contents: [prose blurb from *Beetitood* magazine] p. 57.

Published 1967 in an unknown quantity.

b1. *First revised edition, 1975*

A BIBLIOGRAPHY OF WORKS BY I JACK KEROUAC I (Jean Louis Lebris De Kerouac) I 1939 — 1975 I [Revised Edition] I Compiled by I [vertical dash] Ann Charters [vertical dash] I [publisher's device] I THE PHOENIX BOOKSHOP I NEW YORK CITY I 1975

$[1-2]^{16}$ $[3]^4$ $[4-5]^{16}$, pp. [1-8] 9 [10] 11-12 [13-14] 15-136. 23.5 x 15.7 cm. Bound in grayish purplish blue (204) cloth covered boards. Across the front cover in gold: '[all within single dash rule frame] JACK KEROUAC I [dash rule] I A BIBLIOGRAPHY'. Down the spine in gold: 'JACK KEROUAC: A Bibliography [diamond] CHARTERS [diamond] PHOENIX'. White wove paper unwatermarked. Greenish gray (155) endpapers. All edges trimmed.

Contents: [prose] p. 84.

$10.00. Published 1975 in an unknown quantity.

B48   AMERICAN LITERARY ANTHOLOGY/1   1968

[left title page] the American Literary I Selected by John Hawkes, Walker Percy, William I Styron (fiction); John Ashbery, Robert Creeley, I James Dickey (poetry); and William Alfred, I Robert Burstein, Benjamin DeMott, F. W. Dupee, I Susan Sontag, John Thompson (essays and criticism)
[right title page] Anthology/1 I *The First Annual Collection of the* I *Best from the Literary Magazines* I [publisher's device] [in 3 lines] *Farrar,* I *Straus &* I *Giroux* I NEW YORK

[1-16]^{16}, pp. [i-v] vi-ix [x-xi] xii-xvi [1-3] 4-495 [496]. 21.5 x 14.3 cm. Bound in dark red (16) cloth covered boards. Down the spine: '[in white] the American Literary Anthology / 1 | [in gold] *Farrar, Straus & Giroux* [publisher's device]'. White wove paper unwatermarked. Strong yellow (84) endpapers. All edges trimmed. Top edges stained yellow. Issued in a white paper dust jacket, printed in black, deep yellow (85) and strong purplish red (255).

Contents: Kral Majales, pp. 86-88.

$2.95. Published in Jan. 1968 in an impression of 3,000 copies.

B49   **PARDON ME, SIR, BUT IS MY EYE**   **1968**
                 HURTING YOUR ELBOW?

[left title page] [all within a design of theater marquee and posters] PARDON ME, SIR, BUT | IS MY EYE HURTING | [the word YOUR is partially hidden by the design] ELBOW? | PRODUCED BY | Bob Booker | AND | George Foster | "THE MAN" | JACK GILFORD | PHOTOGRAPHY | BY | HORN/GRINER | CARTOONS | BY | [in facsimile holograph] MORT DRUCKER
[right title page] [all within a design of a theater marquee and a poster] PARDON ME, SIR, BUT | IS MY EYE HURTING | YOUR ELBOW? | Written by | GREGORY CORSO | BRUCE JAY FRIEDMAN | ALLEN GINSBERG | HERBERT GOLD | ARTHUR KOPIT | JACK RICHARDSON | PHILIP ROTH | ROBERT PAUL SMITH | TERRY SOUTHERN | ARNOLD WEINSTEIN | and | BOB BOOKER & | GEORGE FOSTER

[1-4]^{16} [5]^8 [6]^{16}, pp. [1-15] 16-170 [171-176]. 24.7 x 17.4 cm. Quarter bound in moderate blue cloth spine with white cloth covered boards. Across the front cover is a vertical row of white dots on moderate blue cloth and a design of a man on a ladder in gold on the white section. Down the spine in gold: '[in 2 lines] BOB BOOKER AND | GEORGE FOSTER [in 1 line] pardon me, sir, but is my eye hurting your elbow? [in 2 lines] BERNARD GEIS | ASSOCIATES'. White wove paper unwatermarked. Light greenish blue (172) endpapers. All edges trimmed. Issued in a white paper dust jacket printed in black, moderate greenish blue (173) and brilliant greenish yellow (98).

Contents: Don't Go Away Mad [prose screenplay], pp. 104-115.

$5.95. Published Jan. 30, 1968 in an unknown number of copies.

Note: One copy of an Author's edition was bound in black leather printed in gold with AG's name on the cover and spine is in Ginsberg's own collection, probably at least 1 for each of the 11 contributors exists.

B50   **A BIRTHDAY GARLAND FOR S. FOSTER DAMON**   **1968**

A BIRTHDAY GARLAND FOR S. FOSTER DAMON | Tributes Collected in Honor of | His Seventy-Fifth Birthday, | February 22, 1968 | Edited by Alvin Hirsch Rosenfeld and | Barton Levi St. Armand | Brown University | Providence, Rhode Island

Single gathering of twenty-two leaves, pp. [1-4] 5 [6] 7-44. 27.9 x 21.6 cm. Stapled twice into stiff dark greenish yellow (103) paper wrappers, the right edge of the front cover is untrimmed. Covers printed in black. White wove paper unwatermarked. All edges trimmed.

Contents: [prose], p. 40.

Published Feb. 19, 1968 in an impression of 200 copies.

B51   **HIGH PRIEST**   **1968**
                          by Timothy Leary

a1. *First edition*

[left title page] [photograph of the author which extends onto the right title page]
[right title page] HIGH I by [up the right side] PRIEST I Timothy Leary I [7.7 cm.
rule] I Original art by Allen Atwell I and Michael Green I AN NAL BOOK I The World
Publishing Company I New York Cleveland

[1-10]^{16} [11]^{12} [12]^{16}, pp. [i-xviii] [1] 2-353 [354-358]. 23.3 x 15.8 cm. Quarter bound
in black cloth and boards covered in gray paper with yellow and dark gray vertical stripes.
Down the spine in gold: 'HIGH PRIEST I [16.2 cm. rule] I Timothy Leary [across the
spine] [curved around the publisher's device] An NAL Book'. White wove paper
unwatermarked. Dark gray (266) endpapers. All edges trimmed. Issued in a white paper
dust jacket printed in black, gray, pink, orange and tan.

Contents: The Blueprint to Turn-On the World: Ecstatic Politics [prose notes], pp. 109-
133.

$7.95. Published March 25, 1968 in an impression of 10,000 copies.

a2. *First edition, paperbound, 1970*

[left title page] [photograph of the author which extends onto the right title page]
[right title page] HIGH I by [up the right side] PRIEST I Timothy Leary I [7.0 cm.
rule] I Original art by Allen Atwell I and Michael Green I COLLEGE I NOTES &
TEXTS, Inc. I NEW YORK, NEW YORK'.

One hundred eighty-four single leaves, pp. [i-xiv] [1] -347 [348] 349-353 [354]. 21.2 x
13.4 cm. Perfect bound in stiff white paper wrappers. Covers printed in gold, blue, black,
yellow, red, purple, green and orange. White wove paper unwatermarked. All edges
trimmed.

$2.95. Published Aug. 1970 in an impression of 25,000 copies combined for this and the
second printing [see next item].

a3. *First edition, paperbound, expanded issue, 1970*

[left title page] [photograph of the author which extends onto the right title page]
[right title page] HIGH I by [up the right side] PRIEST I Timothy Leary I [7.0 cm.
rule] I Original art by Allen Atwell I and Michael Green I COLLEGE I NOTES &
TEXTS, Inc. I NEW YORK, NEW YORK'.

Two hundred thirty-two single leaves, pp. [i-xiv] [1] -347 [348] 349-353 [354] [A-1] - A-
96. 21.2 x 13.4 cm. Perfect bound in stiff white paper wrappers. Covers printed in gold,
blue, black, yellow, red, purple, green and orange. White wove paper unwatermarked. All
edges trimmed.

$2.95. Published Nov. 1970 in an impression of 25,000 copies combined for this and the
first printing [see previous item].

Note: Identified as the second printing on the verso of the title page, but this is the first
printing to contain the 96 page publisher's appendix.

a4. *First Magus Studios issue, 1984*

High Priest | Timothy Leary | Magus Studios

Forty-four single leaves, pp. [1-88]. 27.7 x 21.5 cm. Bound in light gray paper wrappers with two plastic back-strips. Across the front cover on an illustration of a school of dolphins: 'High Priest | Timothy Leary | Magus Studios'. Across the back cover are illustrations of dolphins and the opening paragraphs of the book.

Published Nov. 1984 in an impression of 40 copies.

Note: This issue not seen by the compiler but is based on the description in Michael Horowitz; Karen Walls and Billy Smith's *An Annotated Bibliography of Timothy Leary*. [Hamden, CT: Archon Books, 1988].

B52   **WAR POEMS**   **1968**

WAR | POEMS | EDITED BY | DIANE DI PRIMA | THE POETS PRESS, INC. | NEW YORK CITY

Forty-eight single leaves, pp. [i-vi] [1] 2-86 [87-90]. 18.4 x 15.1 cm. Perfect bound in stiff white paper wrappers. Covers printed in black and strong reddish purple (237). White wove paper unwatermarked. All edges trimmed.

Contents: Wichita Vortex Sutra, pp. 16-34 — Pentagon Exorcism, pp. 35-36 — Genocide, pp. 37-38.

$2.00. Published April 1968 in an impression of 965 copies.

Note: A limited edition of 35 handbound copies was planned by Bob Wilson at the Phoenix Bookshop, but was never realized.

B53   **ORBS**   **1968**
                                    by John A. Wood

[deep brown (56)] ORBS | A Portfolio of Ten Poems by | John A. Wood | [7 ornaments in a line] | [deep brown] WOODCUTS | by | Harold Swayder | with an introduction by | Allen Ginsberg | [within a drawing of a figure with a background] THE APOLLYON PRESS | [15.4 cm. rule] | Copyright Harold Swayder and John Wood 1968

[1-11]^2, pp. [1-44]. 33.6 x 23.4 cm. Loose folded sheets laid into a portfolio made of one sheet of paper folded twice vertically. Enclosed within a 33.3 x 24.8 cm. portfolio made of moderate blue (182) cloth covered boards tied with blue yarn. The 10 poems each are a broadside folded once and laid in the portfolio. White wove paper unwatermarked. All edges trimmed.

Contents: Introduction [prose], p. [3].

Published May 27, 1968 in an impression of 50 copies.

B54   **THE ECSTATIC ADVENTURE**   **1968**

[left title page] *REPORTS OF CHEMICAL EXPLORATIONS OF | THE INNER WORLD BY PHILOSOPHERS* [bullet] *THEO- | LOGIANS* [bullet] *SCIENTISTS* [bullet] *ARCHITECTS* [bullet] *WRITERS* | [bullet] *ARTISTS* [bullet] *BUSINESSMEN* [bullet] *STUDENTS* [bullet] *HOUSE- | WIVES* [bullet] *MUSICIANS* [bullet]

MOTHERS [bullet]*CHILDREN* I *PATIENTS* [bullet] *CONVICTS* [bullet] *ADDICTS* [bullet] *SECRETARIES*
[right title page] *THE ECSTATIC* I *ADVENTURE* I *Edited, with an Introduction and Notes by* I RALPH METZNER I FOREWORD BY *ALAN WATTS* I THE MACMILLAN COMPANY, NEW YORK

[1-6]^{16} [7-8]^2 [9-12]^{16}, pp. [i-v] vi-ix [x-xi] xii-xiii [xiv] [1] 2-178 [i-viii] 179-306. 21.8 x 14.8 cm. Bound in black cloth covered boards. Across the spine: '[design of a flame in red] I [in gold] The I [in gold] Ecstatic I [in gold] Adventure I [two .7 cm. red rules] I [in gold] Metzner I [in gold] MACMILLAN'. Across the back cover: '[in gold] 58445'. White wove paper unwatermarked. Light yellow (86) endpapers. Top edges trimmed and stained red. Issued in a white paper dust jacket printed in black, orange and yellow.

Contents: A Glass of Ayahuasca, pp. 135-137.

$6.95. Published May 31, 1968 in an undisclosed number of copies and printings. First printing identified as such on the verso of the title page.

B55   **LIBERTY OR DEATH**   **1968**

[ornamental type] LIBERTY OR DEATH I edited by MARY BEACH [vertical rule] freaked out & zapped by CLAUDE PÉLIEU I DISTRIBUTED BY CITY LIGHTS BOOKS 1562 GRANT AVENUE, SAN FRANCISCO, CALIFORNIA U.S.A.

Single gathering of thirty-six leaves, pp. [1-72]. 27.1 x 21.7 cm. Stapled twice into stiff white paper wrappers. Covers printed in vivid purplish red (254) and black. White wove paper unwatermarked. All edges trimmed.

Contents: Allen Ginsberg's Answer to Claude Pelieu's Questionnaire [prose], pp. [47-50].

$1.95. Published ca. Sept. 1968 in an impression of 500-1,000 copies.

B56   **NOTES FROM THE NEW UNDERGROUND**   **1968**

a1. *First edition, hardbound*

Notes from the I New Underground I AN ANTHOLOGY I EDITED BY JESSE KORNBLUTH I NEW YORK / THE VIKING PRESS

[1-10]^{16}, pp. [i-vi] vii-ix [x] xi-xv [xvi] [1-3] 4-302 [303-304]. 24.3 x 17.2 cm. Bound in black cloth covered boards. Across the front cover is a design of random letters in brilliant violet (206). Down the spine in silver: 'Notes from [design of random letters in brilliant violet] [in silver] Edited by I the New Jesse Kornbluth I Underground Viking'. White wove paper unwatermarked. White endpapers. All edges trimmed. Top edges stained light gray. Issued in a white paper dust jacket printed in black and medium gray (265).

Contents: Renaissance or Die [prose], pp. 54-58 — Changes [transcript of panel discussion], pp. 121-183.

$7.50. Published Nov. 20, 1968 in an undisclosed number of copies.

a2. *First edition, paperbound, 1968*

Notes from the I New Underground I An Anthology I Edited by JESSE KORNBLUTH I AN ACE BOOK I Ace Publishing Corporation I 1120 Avenue of the Americas I New York, N. Y. 10036

One hundred and sixty single leaves, pp. [1-4] 5-6 [7-8] 9-320. 17.9 x 10.5 cm. Perfect bound in stiff white paper wrappers. Covers printed in purple, reddish orange and black. White wove paper unwatermarked. All edges trimmed and stained yellowish orange.

Contents: Public Solitude [appears as 'Renaissance or Die' in the first hardbound issue], pp. 67-75 — Changes, pp. 139-204.

$1.25. Published in 1968 in an undisclosed number of copies.

B57   **THE BHAGAVAD GITA AS IT IS**   **1968**

a1. *First edition, hardbound*

The Bhagavad Gita As It Is I With Introduction, Translation and Authorized Purport by I *A. C. BHAKTIVEDANTA SWAMI* I ACHARYA, INTERNATIONAL SOCIETY I FOR KRISHNA CONSCIOUSNESS I THE MACMILLAN COMPANY, NEW YORK I COLLIER - MACMILLAN LIMITED, LONDON

[1-10]^{16}, pp. [1-7] 8 [9] 10-12 [13] 14-15 [16] 17 [18] 19-22 [23] 24-41 [42-45] 46-318 [319-320]. 21.1 x 14.3 cm. Bound in grayish purplish blue (204) cloth covered boards. Across the spine: '[in ornamental type in gold] The I [in ornamental type in gold] Bhagavad I [in ornamental type in gold] Gita I [in gold] AS IT IS I [ornamentation in strong purplish blue (196)] I [in gold] *Bhaktivedanta* I [in gold] *MACMILLAN*'. Across the back cover: '[in gold] 51058'. White wove paper unwatermarked. White endpapers. All edges trimmed, top edges stained blue. Issued in a white paper dust jacket printed in pale violet (214) and black.

Contents: Swami Bhaktivedanta Chanting God's Song in America [prose], pp. [13]-15 — [blurb on dust jacket reprinted from the introduction]

$6.95. Published Nov. 25, 1968 in an undisclosed number of copies.

a2. *First edition, paperbound, 1968*

The Bhagavad Gita As It Is I With Introduction, Translation and Authorized Purport by I *A. C. BHAKTIVEDANTA SWAMI* I ACHARYA, INTERNATIONAL SOCIETY I FOR KRISHNA CONSCIOUSNESS I COLLIER BOOKS, NEW YORK I COLLIER - MACMILLAN LTD., LONDON

One hundred sixty single leaves, pp. [1-7] 8 [9] 10-12 [13] 14-15 [16] 17 [18] 19-22 [23] 24-41 [42-45] 46-318 [319-320]. 20.1 x 13.3 cm. Perfect bound in stiff white paper wrappers. Covers printed in light violet (210) and black. White wove paper unwatermarked. All edges trimmed.

$2.95. Published Nov. 25, 1968 in an undisclosed number of copies.

B58   **THE POEM IN ITS SKIN**   **1968**

a1. *First edition, hardbound*

[left title page] *A Big Table Book* [publisher's device] FOLLETT PUBLISHING COMPANY
[right title page] Paul Carroll I CHICAGO AND NEW YORK The Poem I In Its Skin

$[1-4]^{16}$ $[5]^8$ $[6-9]^{16}$, pp. [i-v] vi-ix [x] [1] 2-262. 21.9 x 14.4 cm. Bound in dark reddish orange (38) cloth covered boards. Across the spine in gold: 'The I Poem I In Its I Skin I [2.9 cm. rule] I Carroll I [2.9 cm. rule] I [publisher's device] I FOLLETT'. White wove paper unwatermarked. White endpapers. All edges trimmed. Issued in a white paper dust jacket printed in black and dark reddish orange.

Contents: Wichita Vortex Sutra, pp. 65-80 — [letter to Paul Carroll], p. 101.

$4.95. Published Dec. 19, 1968 in an undisclosed number of copies.

Note: First printing identified as such on the verso of the title page. Reprinted as follows: 2nd printing, Feb. 1969; 3rd printing, June 1970.

a2. *First edition, paperbound, 1968*

[left title page] A Big Table Book [publisher's device] FOLLETT
[right title page] Paul Carroll I CHICAGO AND NEW YORK The Poem I In Its Skin

$[1-4]^{16}$ $[5]^8$ $[6-9]^{16}$, pp. [i-v] vi-ix [x] [1] 2-262. 21.3 x 14.2 cm. Bound in stiff white paper wrappers. Covers printed in black and strong reddish brown (40). White wove paper unwatermarked. All edges trimmed.

$3.45. Published in Dec. 19, 1968 in an undisclosed number of copies.

Note: Second printing identified as such on the verso of the title page. Reprinted as follows:
  2nd printing, Feb. 1969.

B59   **THE EAST SIDE SCENE**   **1968**

a1. *First edition*

THE EAST SIDE SCENE I (an anthology of a time and a place) I Edited by Allen De Loach I University Press I State University of New York at Buffalo I Buffalo, New York

One hundred seventy-six single leaves, pp. [1-2] i-xxii [1] 2-326 [327-328]. 21.0 x 13.6 cm. Perfect bound in stiff pale yellow (89) paper wrappers. Covers printed in black. White wove paper unwatermarked. All edges trimmed.

Contents: Selections from Calcutta Journal [prose], pp. 76-80 — Whichita [sic] Vortex Sutra, pp. 80-91.

Published 1968 in an unknown quantity.

b1. *Second edition, 1972*

THE EAST SIDE SCENE I AMERICAN POETRY, 1960-1965 I EDITED WITH AN INTRODUCTION BY I ALLEN DE LOACH I ANCHOR BOOKS I DOUBLEDAY & COMPANY, INC. I GARDEN CITY, NEW YORK I 1972

One hundred eighty single leaves, pp. [i-xiv] xv-xx, 1-338 [339-340]. 17.9 x 10.5 cm. Perfect bound in stiff white paper wrappers. Covers printed in black. White wove paper unwatermarked. All edges trimmed.

Contents: As first edition, pp. 96-116.

$2.50. Published Feb. 4, 1972 in an undisclosed number of copies.

B60   **NAKED POETRY**   **1969**

a1. *First edition, hardbound*

[left title page] Naked | *And sketching open forms* | *with the arcs of the sailing regatta* | *space plays half awake—* | *a child who's not known the cradle.* | *—Osip Mandelstam* | The Bobbs-Merrill Company, Inc.
[right title page] Poetry | Recent American | poetry in | open forms | *edited by* | *Stephen Berg and Robert Mezey* | Indianapolis and New York

[1-13]^{16}, pp. [i-iv] v-ix [x] xi-xiii [xiv] xv-xxiv [1-3] 4-387 [388-392]. 23.4 x 15.7 cm. Bound in moderate purple (223) cloth covered boards. Down the spine all in gold: 'Naked Poetry EDITED BY STEPHEN BERG & ROBERT MEZEY [across spine] BOBBS-MERRILL'. White wove paper unwatermarked. White endpapers. All edges trimmed. Issued in white paper dust jacket printed in black and purple.

Contents: Howl, pt. 1, pp. 189-194 — In the Baggage Room at Greyhound, pp. 194-196 — A Supermarket in California, pp. 196-197 — Death to Van Gogh's Ear!, pp. 197-201 — Ignu, pp. 201-204 — America, pp. 204-206 — Love Poem on Theme by Whitman, p. 207 — Wichita Vortex Sutra, pt. 2, pp. 207-220 — Some Metamorphoses of Personal Prosody [prose], pp. 221-222.

$8.50. Published March 26, 1969 in an undisclosed number of copies. First printing identified as such on the verso of the title page.

a2. *First edition, paperbound, 1969*

[left title page] Naked | *And sketching open forms* | *with the arcs of the sailing regatta* | *space plays half awake—* | *a child who's not known the cradle.* | *—Osip Mandelstam* | The Bobbs-Merrill Company, Inc.
[right title page] Poetry | Recent American | poetry in | open forms | *edited by* | *Stephen Berg and Robert Mezey* | Indianapolis and New York

Two hundred and eight single leaves, pp. [i-iv] v-ix [x] xi-xiii [xiv] xv-xxiv [1-3] 4-387 [388-392]. 22.7 x 14.9 cm. Perfect bound in stiff white paper wrappers. Covers printed in dark purple (224) and black. White wove paper unwatermarked. All edges trimmed.

$2.95. Published March 26, 1969 in an undisclosed number of copies.

Note: First printing identified as such on the verso of the right title page. Reprinted at least 3 times.

B61   **ALLEN GINSBERG IN AMERICA**   **1969**
by Jane Kramer

a1. *First edition, hardbound*

[on sloping base line] ALLEN GINSBERG | in America | [French rule] | by Jane
Kramer | [publisher's device] | RANDOM HOUSE NEW YORK

[1-7]^{16}, pp. [i-xi] xii-xix [xx] [1-3] 4-202 [203-204]. 21.4 x 14.5 cm. Bound in
moderate red (15) cloth covered boards. Blind stamped across the front cover: '[on
sloping base line] ALLEN GINSBERG | IN AMERICA'. Down the spine in silver: '[on
sloping base line] ALLEN GINSBERG | [on sloping base line] IN AMERICA | [on
sloping base line] Kramer | [on sloping base line] Random House'. White wove paper
unwatermarked. All edges trimmed. Top edges stained red. Issued in a white dust jacket,
printed in black, red and blue.

Contents: [2 words from a postcard announcement], p. 48 — [letter to Robert McNamara],
pp. 87-90 — [prose excerpt from the charter of the Committee on Poetry], p. 100. — If
Money Made the Mind More Sane, p. 123 — The Change [excerpt], p. 131 — [letter to W.
C. Williams], p. 148 — [letter to John Hollander, by Nella Grebsnig (pseud. AG)], pp.
163-177 — [letter to *Time* magazine, by Gregory Corso, Peter Orlovsky and AG], p. 162
— [letter to *Partisan Review,* by Gregory Corso, Peter Orlovsky and AG], p. 163.

$4.95. Published April 25, 1969 in an impression of 5,631 copies.

Note: A review slip has been found laid in the book which gives the publication date as
May 20, 1969, the publisher in correspondence with the compiler has given the date of
publication as April 1969 and the paperbound issue indicates the publication date as April
25, 1969. This later date is the one considered most accurate.

a2. *First edition, British issue, 1970*

PATERFAMILIAS | ALLEN GINSBERG | in America | by | JANE KRAMER |
LONDON | VICTOR GOLLANCZ LTD | 1970

[A]^{16} B-G^{16}, pp. [i-xi] xii-xix [xx] [1-3] 4-202 [203-204]. 22.0 x 14.2 cm. Bound in
deep yellowish pink (27) cloth covered boards. Down the spine in gold:
'PATERFAMILIAS [across the spine] Allen | Ginsberg | in | America | JANE |
KRAMER | GOLLANCZ'. White wove paper unwatermarked. White endpapers. All
edges trimmed. Issued in a white paper dust jacket, printed in vivid yellowish pink (25)
and black.

42/- [£2.10 net]. Published Feb. 5, 1970 in an impression of 1,750 copies.

a3. *First edition, paperbound issue, 1970*

[on sloping base line] ALLEN GINSBERG | in America | [French rule] | by Jane
Kramer | [publisher's device] | VINTAGE BOOKS | A Division of Random House |
New York

One hundred twelve single leaves, pp. [iii-xi] xii-xix [xx] [1-3] 4-202 [203-206]. 18.3 x
11.0 cm. Perfect bound in stiff white paper wrappers. Covers printed in deep reddish
orange (36), deep blue (179) and black. White wove paper unwatermarked. All edges
trimmed.

$1.95. Published Feb. 15, 1970 in an impression of 13,615 copies.

B62   **ALLEN GINSBERG**   **1969**
                                  by Thomas F. Merrill

a1.   *First edition*

ALLEN GINSBERG | [10.1 cm. rule] | By THOMAS F. MERRILL | University of
Delaware | [within single rule oval frame] TUSAS [outside oval] 161 | Twayne
Publishers, Inc.::New York

[1-3]^{16} [4]^{12} [5-6]^{16}, pp. [1-14] 15-183 [184]. 21.0 x 14.1 cm. Bound in dark blue
(183) paper covered boards. Across the front cover in silver: 'ALLEN GINSBERG |
THOMAS F. MERRILL | [design of an eagle with a flag]'. Across the spine in silver:
'[2.3 cm. rule] | [down the spine] ALLEN GINSBERG | THOMAS F. MERRILL
[across the spine] Twayne | [2.3 cm. rule] | [within single rule oval frame] TUSAS |
161'. White wove paper unwatermarked. Vivid purplish blue (194) endpapers. All edges
trimmed. Issued in a white paper dust jacket printed in grayish reddish brown (46) and pale
green (149).

Contents: [excerpts from a letter to Thomas Merrill], pp. 8, 40, 127.

$3.95. Published Dec. 15, 1969 in an impression of 4,648 copies.

b1.   *First revised edition, 1988*

Allen Ginsberg | Revised Edition | By Thomas F. Merrill | University of Delaware |
Twayne Publishers | *A Division of G. K. Hall & Co.* [bullet] *Boston*

[1-3]^{16} [4]^{8} [5-6]^{16}, pp. [i-xiv] 1-161 [162]. 22.2 x 14.2 cm. Bound in deep blue (179)
cloth covered boards. All in gold across the spine: 'TUSAS | 161 | [down the spine in 2
lines] *Allen Ginsberg | Revised Edition* [in one line] Thomas F. Merrill [across the
spine] *Twayne'.* White wove paper unwatermarked. White endpapers. All edges
trimmed. Issued in a white paper dust jacket printed in black and red.

Contents: [condensation of the excerpts from the letter to Thomas Merrill printed in the first
issue above], p. 88.

$19.95. Published Feb. 1, 1988 in an impression of 1,500 copies.

B63   **COUNTER CULTURE**   **1969**

[ornamental type] COUNTER | [ornamental type] CULTURE | edited by | [ornamental
type] JOSEPH BERKE | designed by Paul Lawson | [publisher's device] | Peter Owen
Limited - London in association with Fire Books Limited

[A]-[N]^{16}, pp. [1-13] 14-405 [406-416]. 25.5 x 18.5 cm. Bound in deep yellowish pink
(27) cloth covered boards. Across the front cover in silver: '[design of a machine gunner
across with is written] BHUDDA BHUDDA'. Across the spine in silver: '[in ornamental
type] COUNTER | [ornamental type] CULTURE | [2.5 cm. rule] | Joseph Berke |
[publisher's device] | Peter Owen | [2.5 cm. rule] | Fire Books'. White wove paper
unwatermarked. White endpapers. All edges trimmed. Issued in a white paper dust jacket
printed in dark red (16) and deep blue (179).

Contents: Consciousness and Practical Action [prose], pp. 170-181.

90s, £4.50. Published 1969 in an undisclosed number of copies.

B64   **SOME OF IT**   **1969**

[design of a woman's head repeated in 7 columns over which are printed 2 white rectangles on which are all the following] [right rectangle] some of I [in white within a black circle] it I [left rectangle] *Edited by* I David Mairowitz I *with a special introduction by* I William S. Burroughs

Eighty-nine single leaves, pp. [1-4] 5-6 [7-8] 9 [10] 11 [12-14] 15-174 [175-178]. 28.0 x 22.2 cm. Perfect bound in stiff grayish red (19) paper wrappers, with a deep red (13) tape spine. Issued in a silver Melonex foil dust jacket which is attached to the wrappers. An oval paper label is pasted in the upper right corner of the front cover of the dust jacket which is printed with a pair of eyes in black and pale yellow (89). This is covered with a tissue outer dust jacket. White wove paper unwatermarked. All edges trimmed.

Contents: Ginsberg on Bunting [prose], p. 24 — Public Solitude [prose], pp. 62-65 — Maharishi and Me [prose], p. 107.

15s. Published in London by Knullar in 1969 in an unknown number of copies.

Note: The tissue outer dust jacket appeared only on a small number of the first edition, the remainder were issued without it. A second state was issued which did not contain the tissue or silver cover but had a paper wrapper with the repeated pattern of the woman as on the title page.

B65   **THE NEW LEFT**   **1970**

a1. *First edition, hardbound*

[ornamental type] THE I [ornamental type] NEW I [ornamental type] LEFT: I A DOCU- I MENTARY I HISTORY I Edited by I Massimo I Teodori I The Bobbs-Merrill Company I Indianapolis [bullet] New York

[1-15]^{16} [16]^{20}, pp. [i-vi] vii-xiv [1-2] 3-501 [502-506]. 23.3 x 15.5 cm. Bound in black cloth covered boards printed across the spine all in metallic red: 'THE I NEW I LEFT: I A DOCU- I MENTARY I HISTORY I Teodori I Bobbs I Merrill'. White wove paper unwatermarked. White endpapers. All edges trimmed. Issued in a white paper dust jacket printed in strong red (12) and black.

Contents: How To Make a March/Spectacle [prose], pp. 371-373.

$9.95. Published Jan. 16, 1970 in an unknown number of copies.

a2. *First edition, paperbound, 1970*

[ornamental type] THE I [ornamental type] NEW I [ornamental type] LEFT: I A DOCU- I MENTARY I HISTORY I Edited by I Massimo I Teodori I The Bobbs-Merrill Company I Indianapolis [bullet] New York

[1-15]^{16} [16]^{20}, pp. [i-vi] vii-xiv [1-2] 3-501 [502-506]. 23.3 x 15.5 cm. Bound in stiff white paper wrappers. Covers printed in strong red (12) and black. White wove paper unwatermarked. All edges trimmed.

Published Jan. 16, 1970 in an unknown number of copies.

B66   **SPEED**   **1970**
                        by William Burroughs, Jr.

a1.   *First edition*

Speed | WILLIAM BURROUGHS Jr. | THE OLYMPIA PRESS

Ninety-six single leaves, pp. [1-4] 5-6 [7-8] 9-191 [192]. 17.8 x 10.5 cm. Perfect bound in stiff white paper wrappers. Covers printed in full color. White wove paper unwatermarked. All edges trimmed.

Contents: Note on W.B. III's Speed [prose], p. 5.

$1.25. Published March 15, 1970 in a quantity undisclosed by the publisher.

a2.   *First edition, British issue, 1971*

Speed | WILLIAM BURROUGHS JR. | [publisher's device] | THE OLYMPIA PRESS

[A]^1 [1] ^{12} 2-8^{12}, pp. [i-ii] [1-8] 9-191 [192]. 18.5 x 11.3 cm. Bound in black cloth covered boards. Down the spine in silver: *'SPEED — William Burroughs Jr* [publisher's device across the spine]'. White wove paper unwatermarked. Strong red (12) endpapers. All edges trimmed. Issued in a white paper dust jacket printed in black and deep yellowish pink (27).

Contents: As first edition, pp. [i-ii].

£1.00. Published 1971 in a quantity undisclosed by the publisher.

B67   **EARTH WEEK '70**   **1970**

$1 | EARTH WEEK '70 | [design of a sunburst design above 2 wavy lines and ocean design in red, yellow, green and blue within a circle] | ALLEN GINSBERG: | The man and his poetry | EARTH WEEK: | Who, What, Why, When & Where | MUMFORD ON McHARG | RALPH NADER ON ECOTACTICS | HAIR! | PHILTHYDELPHIA | Official Publication of the Philadelphia Earth Week Committee

Single gathering of twenty-six leaves, pp. [i-ii] [1] 2-47 [48-50]. 30.4 x 30.4 cm. Stapled twice in stiff white paper wrappers. Covers printed in red, yellow, green, black and blue. Front cover forms the title page. White wove paper unwatermarked. All edges trimmed.

Contents: Swirls of Black Dust on Avenue D [poem in facsimile holograph with a small drawing of a flower], p. 18.

$1.00. Edited by John Zeh and published April 1970 in an unknown number of copies.

B68   **MOVING THROUGH HERE**   **1970**
                          by Don McNeill

a1.   *First edition, hardbound*

MOVING | THROUGH | HERE | by DON McNEILL | *Introduction by Allen Ginsberg* | *Epilogue by Paul Williams* | [publisher's device] *ALFRED A. KNOPF, New York* *1970*

[1-8]^{16}, pp. [1-2] [i-ix] x-xi [xii-xiii] xiv [1-3] 4-235 [236-240]. 21.9 x 14.6 cm. Bound in yellowish white (92) cloth covered boards. Across the front cover is a design of a head

within a single rule border. Down the spine: 'MOVING THROUGH HERE | DON McNEILL ALFRED A. KNOPF'. White wove paper unwatermarked. White endpapers. Top and bottom edges trimmed. Top edges stained blue. Issued in a white dust jacket printed in black and blue.

Contents: McNeill's Memory [prose], pp. [xiii]-xiv — [footnote], p. 35.

$5.95. Published April 14, 1970 in an impression of 5,000 copies.

Note: Publisher was unable to provide publication date. A review copy with slip laid in has been seen which gives the publication date of March 26, 1970 but that has been penciled out and April 14 is inserted, presumably by the publisher.

a2. *First edition, paperbound, 1970*

DON | McNEILL | MOVING | THROUGH | HERE | Introduction | by | ALLEN | GINSBERG | Epilogue | by | PAUL | WILLIAMS | LANCER BOOKS [publisher's device] NEW YORK

One hundred twelve single leaves, pp. [1-4] 5-8 [9-10] 11-219 [220] 221 [222-224]. 17.5 x 10.7 cm. Perfect bound in stiff white paper wrappers. Covers printed in dark reddish brown (44), deep reddish purple (238)] and black. White wove paper unwatermarked. All edges trimmed and stained grayish purple (228).

$.95. Published April 14, 1970 in an unknown number of copies.

b1. *First Citadel re-issue, 1990*

MOVING | THROUGH | HERE | by DON McNEILL | *Introductions by Todd Gitlin* | *and Allen Ginsberg* | *Epilogue by Paul Williams* | CITADEL UN [publisher's device] DERGROUND | CITADEL PRESS | A Division of Carol Publishing Group | New York

One hundred thirty-seven single leaves, pp. [1-8] [i-v] vi [vii] viii-xii [xiii] xiv [1-3] 4-127 [128-130] [i-viii] [131] 132-235 [236-244]. 20.9 x 13.6 cm. Perfect bound in stiff white paper wrappers. Covers printed in bright pink, gray, black and red. White wove paper unwatermarked. All edges trimmed.

Contents: As first edition, pp. [xiii]-xiv.

$9.95. Published June 18, 1990 in an impression of 5,100 copies.

B69   **MORNING IN SPRING AND OTHER POEMS**   **1970**
                            by Louis Ginsberg

a1. *First edition, hardbound*

MORNING IN SPRING | *And Other Poems* | [ornament] | *By Louis Ginsberg* | [publisher's device] | WILLIAM MORROW AND COMPANY, INC. | *New York 1970*

[1-4]^{16}, pp. [1-6] 7-125 [126-128]. 21.6 x 14.5 cm. Bound in moderate greenish blue (173) cloth covered boards. Down the spine: '[in 2 lines] LOUIS | GINSBERG [in 1 line] [ornament] [in 2 lines] MORNING IN SPRING | *And Other Poems* [across the spine] Morrow | [publisher's device]'. White laid paper unwatermarked. White endpapers with blue threads. All edges trimmed. Issued in a white paper dust jacket printed in brilliant greenish yellow (98), black, and brilliant greenish blue (168).

Contents: Confrontation with Louis Ginsberg's Poems [prose], pp. 11-20 — [excerpt from introduction on the back dust jacket cover].

$5.00. Published May 11, 1970 in an unknown number of copies.

a2.   *First edition, paperbound, 1970*

MORNING IN SPRING | *And Other Poems* | [ornament] | *By Louis Ginsberg* | [publisher's device] | WILLIAM MORROW AND COMPANY, INC. | *New York 1970*

Sixty-four single leaves, pp. [1-6] 7-125 [126-128]. 20.8 x 13.7 cm. Perfect bound in stiff white paper wrappers. Covers printed in brilliant greenish yellow (98), black, and brilliant greenish blue (168). White laid paper unwatermarked. All edges trimmed.

Contents: As first edition, but without the blurb on the back cover.

$1.95. Published May 11, 1970 in an unknown number of copies.

B70   **CONTEMPORARY POETS OF THE ENGLISH LANGUAGE   1970**

a1.   *First edition*

CONTEMPORARY POETS | OF THE | ENGLISH | LANGUAGE | WITH A PREFACE BY | C. DAY LEWIS | EDITOR | ROSALIE MURPHY | DEPUTY EDITOR | JAMES VINSON | ST JAMES PRESS | CHICAGO LONDON

$[A]^{10} B-Z^{16}$, A2-P2^{16}, Q2^{14}, pp. [i-iv] v [vi] vii-ix [x] xi [xii] xiii-xvii [xviii-xx] 1-1243 [1244]. 25.2 x 17.8 cm. Bound in blackish red (21) cloth covered boards printed all in gold. Across the front cover: 'Contemporary | Poets | of the | English | Language'. Across the spine: 'Contemporary | Poets | of the | English | Language | St. James Press'. White wove paper unwatermarked. White endpapers. All edges trimmed. Issued in a linen finish gray yellowish brown (80) paper dust jacket printed in gold.

Contents: [prose answers to questionnaire], pp. 419-421.

$25.00 or £8.50. Published August 1970 in an impression of 3,000 copies.

Note: Reprinted as follows: 2nd printing, June 1, 1973, 1000 copies; 3rd printing, March 15, 1974, in an unknown number of copies

b1.   *Second edition, 1975*

CONTEMPORARY | POETS | SECOND EDITION | WITH A PREFACE BY | C. DAY LEWIS | EDITOR | JAMES VINSON | ASSOCIATE EDITOR | D. L. KIRKPATRICK | ST. JAMES PRESS ST. MARTIN'S PRESS | LONDON NEW YORK

$[1-58]^{16} [59]^{8}$, pp. [i-iv] v [vi] vii-ix [x] xi [xii] xiii-xv [xvi] [1-10] 11-1849 [1850-1856]. 24.1 x 17.4 cm. Bound in black cloth covered boards. Across the front cover in gold: 'CONTEMPORARY | POETS'. Across the spine in gold: 'CONTEMPORARY | POETS | ST JAMES/ST MARTIN'S'. White wove paper unwatermarked. White endpapers. All edges trimmed. Issued in a white paper dust jacket printed in red.

Contents: [prose], pp. 549, 551.

Published in June 1975 in England and August 1975 in the United States in a total impression of 7000 copies.

c1. *Third edition, 1980*

CONTEMPORARY I POETS I THIRD EDITION I PREFACE TO THE FIRST EDITION I C. DAY LEWIS I PREFACE TO THE THIRD EDITION I MARJORIE PERLOFF I EDITOR I JAMES VINSON I ASSOCIATE EDITOR I D. L. KIRKPATRICK I ST. MARTIN'S PRESS I NEW YORK

$[1-57]^{16}$, pp. [i-vi] vii-xiv [xv-xvi] xvii-xix [xx] [1-2] 3-1804. 24.1 x 16.4 cm. Bound in black cloth covered boards. Across the spine in gold: 'CONTEMPORARY I POETS I Third Edition I ST MARTIN'S'. White wove paper unwatermarked. White endpapers. All edges trimmed. Issued in a white paper dust jacket printed in blue.

Contents: Abridged version from the second edition, pp. 555-556.

Published in 1980 in an undisclosed number of copies.

d1. *Fourth edition, 1985*

CONTEMPORARY I POETS I FOURTH EDITION I PREFACE TO THE FIRST EDITION I C. DAY LEWIS I PREFACE TO THE THIRD EDITION I MARJORIE PERLOFF I EDITORS I JAMES VINSON AND D. L. KIRKPATRICK I ST. MARTIN'S PRESS I NEW YORK

$[1-33]^{16}$ $[34]^{8}$ $[35]^{16}$, pp. [i-vi] vii-xiii [xiv-xvi] xvii-xviii [xix-xxviii] 1-1071 [1072-1076]. 25.4 x 19.5 cm. Bound in black cloth covered boards. Across the spine in gold: 'CONTEMPORARY I POETS I Fourth Edition I ST MARTIN'S'. White wove paper unwatermarked. White endpapers. All edges trimmed. Issued in a white paper dust jacket.

Contents: As third edition, pp. 303-304.

$85.00. Published in Nov. 1985 in an undisclosed number of copies.

e1. *Fifth edition, 1991*

CONTEMPORARY I POETS I FIFTH EDITION I PREFACE TO THE FIRST EDITION I C. DAY LEWIS I PREFACE TO THE FIFTH EDITION I DIANE WAKOSKI I EDITOR I TRACY CHEVALIER I [publisher's device] I ST. JAMES PRESS I CHICAGO AND LONDON

$[1-2]^{16}$ $[3]^{12}$ $[4-38]^{16}$, pp. [i-vi] vii-xi [xii] xiii-xv [xvi-xxiv] 1-1179 [1180-1184]. 28.7 x 22.2 cm. Bound in black cloth covered boards. Across the front cover in silver: '[11.6 cm. rule] I CONTEMPORARY I [11.6 cm. rule] I POETS I [11.5 cm. rule] I Fifth Edition'. Down the spine in silver: '[11.6 cm. rule] I CONTEMPORARY I [11.6 cm. rule] I POETS I [11.5 cm. rule] [across the spine] [publisher's device] I ST. JAMES'. Across the back cover in silver: 'ISBN 1-55862-035-4'. Across the inside back cover is a zebra bar code with the following three sets of numbers: 'ISBN 1-55862-035-4 I 90000 > I 9 781558 620353'. White wove paper unwatermarked. White endpapers. All edges trimmed.

Contents: As fourth edition, p. 343.

Published 1991 in an undisclosed number of copies.

B71   **SCENES ALONG THE ROAD**   **1970**

a1. *First edition, signed*

SCENES I ALONG I THE I ROAD I PHOTOGRAPHS OF THE I DESOLATION
ANGELS 1944-1960 I Compiled by Ann Charters I with three poems and comments by
Allen Ginsberg I *Portents/Gotham Book Mart*

[1]^4 [2-4]^8, pp. [1-10] 11-56. 26.1 x 18.5 cm. Bound in moderate brown (58) cloth
covered boards. Down the spine in gold: 'SCENES ALONG THE ROAD Charters'.
White wove paper unwatermarked. White endpapers. All edges trimmed.

Contents: [28 photographs with legends (see also D5)] — A Strange New Cottage in
Berkeley (excerpt), p. 27 — [journal entry], p. 30 — [letter to Louis Ginsberg], p. 40 —
[prose], p. 42 — Neal's Ashes, p. 47 — Memory Gardens, pp. 48-51 — In a Car, p. 52.

$30.00. Published ca. Sept. 15, 1970 in an impression of 50 copies.

Note: Colophon, autographed and numbered by Allen Ginsberg on page 55.

a2. *First edition, hardbound unsigned, 1970*

SCENES I ALONG I THE I ROAD I PHOTOGRAPHS OF THE I DESOLATION
ANGELS 1944-1960 I Compiled by Ann Charters I with three poems and comments by
Allen Ginsberg I *Portents/Gotham Book Mart*

[1]^4 [2-4]^8, pp. [1-10] 11-56. 26.1 x 18.5 cm. Bound in light brown (57) cloth covered
boards. Down the spine in gold: 'SCENES ALONG THE ROAD Charters'. White wove
paper unwatermarked. White endpapers. All edges trimmed. Issued in a white paper dust
jacket.

$7.50. Published ca. Sept. 15, 1970 in an impression of 200 copies.

a3. *First edition, paperbound, 1970*

SCENES I ALONG I THE I ROAD I PHOTOGRAPHS OF THE I DESOLATION
ANGELS 1944-1960 I Compiled by Ann Charters I with three poems and comments by
Allen Ginsberg I *Portents/Gotham Book Mart*

[1]^4 [2-4]^8, pp. [1-10] 11-56. 25.3 x 17.7 cm. Bound in stiff light yellowish brown (76)
paper wrappers. Covers printed in black. White wove paper unwatermarked. All edges
trimmed.

Contents: As first edition, signed, with an excerpt from the letter on p. 40 reprinted on the
back cover.

$3.00. Published ca. Sept. 15, 1970 in an impression of 1,750 copies.

Note: Reprinted at least 3 times.

a4. *First edition, City Lights re-issue, 1985*

Scenes I Along I the I Road I Photographs of the I Desolation Angels 1944-1960 I
Compiled by Ann Charters I with three poems and comments by Allen Ginsberg I
[publisher's device] I City Lights Books I San Francisco

Twenty-eight single leaves, pp. [1-10] 11-52 [53-55] 56. 25.5 x 17.8 cm. Perfect bound in stiff white paper wrappers. Covers printed in full-color. White wove paper unwatermarked. All edges trimmed.

$7.95. Published ca. June 1985 in an impression of 3,000 copies.

| B72 | **THIS IS MY BEST IN THE THIRD QUARTER OF THE CENTURY** | **1970** |

America's 85 Greatest Living Authors Present I THIS IS MY BEST I IN THE THIRD QUARTER OF THE CENTURY I [6.2 cm. rule] I Edited by Whit Burnett I 1970 I DOUBLEDAY & COMPANY, INC., GARDEN CITY, NEW YORK

Five hundred forty single leaves, pp. [i-iv] v-viii [ix] x-xii [xiii] xiv-xx [1-3] 4-1058 [1059] 1060. 21.4 x 14.2 cm. Perfect bound in light gray (264) cloth covered boards. Down the spine: THIS IS MY BEST I IN THE THIRD QUARTER OF THE CENTURY I [in gold] *Edited by Whit Burnett Doubleday* '. White wove paper unwatermarked. Grayish greenish yellow (105) endpapers. All edges trimmed. Issued in a white paper dust jacket, printed in black, blue and yellowish gray (93).

Contents: [letter to Whit Burnett], p. 498 — Wales Visitation, pp. 499-502.

$10.00. Published Sept. 18, 1970 in an impression of 3500 copies.

Note: The 2nd through 6th reprints were for book club editions; the price for the 7th printing was raised to $10.95. Reprinted as follows: 2nd printing, 300 copies; 3rd printing, 300 copies; 4th printing, 300 copies; 5th printing, 300 copies; 6th printing, 500 copies; 7th printing, 2500 copies. Second and subsequent printings are identified by the lack of the date on the title page and the Book Club imprint on the dust jacket.

| B73 | **MAY DAY SPEECH** **by Jean Genet** | **1970** |

JEAN GENET I MAY DAY I SPEECH I DESCRIPTION BY I ALLEN GINSBERG I [ornamental type] CITY [publisher's device] [ornamental type] LIGHTS

Single gathering of sixteen leaves, pp. [i-ii] 1-25 [26-30]. 20.0 x 13.8 cm. Stapled twice in stiff white paper wrappers. Covers printed in black. White wove paper unwatermarked. All edges trimmed.

Contents: Genet's Commencement Discourse [prose], pp. 1-6.

$1.00. Published Sept. 30, 1970 in an impression of 10,000 copies.

| B74 | **POT ART** | **1970** |

a1. *First edition*

[first 2 lines on black irregular background in black letter in white] POT I ART I First Edition I © 1970 Stone Mountain I [design of hands with scissors cutting marijuana]

Eighty single leaves, pp. [1-160]. 27.8 x 21.5 cm. Perfect bound in stiff white paper wrappers. Covers printed in deep yellowish pink (27) and vivid green (139). White wove paper unwatermarked. All edges trimmed.

Contents: The Great Marijuana Hoax [prose], pp. [76-82] — [prose blurb on back cover].

$2.98. Published ca. Oct. 1970 in an unknown quantity.

Note: First edition identified as such on the title page.

a2. *Second edition, 1972*

[first 2 lines on black irregular background] [left in white in black letter] POT | [right in white in black letter] ART | [right] © 1972 Apocrypha books | [design of hands with scissors cutting marijuana]

One hundred single leaves, pp. [1-200]. 27.8 x 21.4 cm. Perfect bound in stiff white paper wrappers. Covers printed in deep yellowish pink (27) vivid yellow green (115). White wove paper unwatermarked. All edges trimmed.

Contents: The Great Marijuana Hoax, pp. [86-92] — [prose blurb on back cover].

$3.95. Published 1972 in an unknown quantity.

B75   **JAIL NOTES**   **1970**
                                   by Timothy Leary

a1. *First edition, hardbound*

[page printed black with all lettering in white] TIMOTHY LEARY | JAIL NOTES | INTRODUCTION BY | ALLEN GINSBERG | A DOUGLAS BOOK | Distributed by The World Publishing Company

[1-5]^{16}, pp. [1-4] 5 [6] 7-154 [155-160]. 21.4 x 14.2 cm. Bound in silver paper covered boards. Down the spine: 'TIMOTHY LEARY / JAIL NOTES / DOUGLAS'. White wove paper unwatermarked. Strong reddish orange (35) endpapers. All edges trimmed. Issued in a white paper dust jacket printed in silver and black.

Contents: Introduction [prose], pp. 6-15.

$6.95. Published Nov. 1970 in an impression of ca. 2,500 copies.

a2. *First edition, paperbound, 1970*

[page printed black with all lettering in white] TIMOTHY LEARY | JAIL NOTES | INTRODUCTION BY | ALLEN GINSBERG | A DOUGLAS BOOK | Distributed by The World Publishing Company

Eighty single leaves, pp. [1-4] 5 [6] 7-154 [155-160]. 20.9 x 13.6 cm. Perfect bound in stiff white paper wrappers. Covers printed in silver, dark brown and black. White wove paper unwatermarked. All edges trimmed.

$2.95. Published Nov. 1970 in an impression of 10,000 copies.

a3. *First edition, Grove Press re-issue, 1972*

TIMOTHY LEARY | JAIL NOTES | INTRODUCTION BY | ALLEN GINSBERG | GROVE PRESS, INC., NEW YORK

Eighty single leaves, pp. [i-ii] [1-4] 5 [6] 7-154 [155-158]. 17.8 x 10.5 cm. Perfect bound in stiff white paper wrappers. Covers printed in red, black and gray. White wove paper unwatermarked. All edges trimmed.

$1.50. Published Feb. 1972 in an impression of 60,000 copies.

a4. *First edition, first British issue, 1972*

Timothy Leary I Jail Notes I INTRODUCTION BY I Allen Ginsberg I NEW ENGLISH LIBRARY I TIMES MIRROR

Eighty single leaves, pp. [1-6] 7-15 [16] 17-160. 17.8 x 10.8 cm. Perfect bound in stiff white paper wrappers. Covers printed in black, strong yellowish pink (26), brilliant greenish blue (168) and light yellow (86). White wove paper unwatermarked. All edges trimmed.

50p. Published Sept. 1972 in an unknown quantity.

B76   **FOR BILL BUTLER**   **1971**

For Bill Butler I Wallrich Books London I 1970

[A]^4 [B-H]^8 + one single sheet loosely inserted, pp. [1-7] 8-18 [i-ii] 19-48 [iii-iv] 49 [v-vi] 50-111 [112-114]. 25.2 x 18.4 cm. Bound in stiff white paper wrappers. Across the front cover: '[design of 4 rows of 4, 3, 4 and 4 solid quadrilaterals, in the second row instead of a quadrilateral is the title] FOR I BILL I BUTLER'. Down the spine on a .8 x 5.4 cm. paper label and attached to the spine: FOR BILL BUTLER [on spine] Wallrich Books'. Across the back cover: '[same design as on the front cover but the quadrilaterals are in outline only] FOR I BILL I BUTLER'. White wove paper unwatermarked. All edges trimmed.

Contents: Pentagon Exorcism [reproduction of manuscript with prose notes], pp. [v-vi].

2 guineas. Published early 1971 in an impression of 500 copies.

Note: The printer was billed for the binding of the book at the end of Oct. 1976 so his estimate for the date of publication was at first based on this; later he changed his mind to "early 1971", or even 1972.
  Sheet folded twice containing 1 poem included but not attached. Page [v] is a verso and page [vi] is a recto.

B77   **THE URBAN READER**   **1971**

a1. *First edition, hardbound*

[left title page] edited by SUSAN CAHILL and I MICHELE F. COOPER I Queens College of the City University of New York I *PRENTICE-HALL, INC.*, ENGLEWOOD CLIFFS, NEW JERSEY I [photo of city street scene]
[right title page]*THE URBAN* I *READER* I [continuation of the photo from the left title page]

[1-5]^{16} [6]^2 [7-12]^{16} [13]^2 [14]^{16} [15]^8 [16]^{16}, pp. [i-iv] v-vii [viii] ix-xv [xvi] [1-2] 3-143 [144] [i-iv] [145] 146-335 [336] [i-iv] 337-416. 23.4 x 16.4 cm. Bound in brilliant greenish yellow (98) cloth covered boards. Down the spine: '[in 2 lines] *THE URBAN* I *READER* [in 3 lines] CAHILL I [2.1 cm. rule] I COOPER [in 1 line] PRENTICE-HALL'. Across the back cover: '13-939058-8'. White wove paper unwatermarked. White endpapers. All edges trimmed. Issued in a white paper dust jacket.

Contents: By Air Albany-Baltimore, pp. 89-91.

$8.95. Published March 30, 1971 in an impression of 2,000 copies.

a2. *First edition, paperbound, 1971*

[left title page] edited by SUSAN CAHILL and | MICHELE F. COOPER | Queens College of the City University of New York | *PRENTICE-HALL, INC.*, ENGLEWOOD CLIFFS, NEW JERSEY | [photo of city street scene]
[right title page]*THE URBAN* | *READER* | [continuation of the photo from the left title page]

Two hundred twenty single leaves, pp. [i-iv] v-vii [viii] ix-xv [xvi] [1-2] 3-143 [144] [i-iv] [145] 146-335 [336] [i-iv] 337-416. Perfect bound in stiff white paper wrappers. White wove paper unwatermarked. All edges trimmed.

$4.95. Published March 30, 1971 in an impression of 20,000 copies.

B78   **MARK IN TIME**   **1971**

MARK IN TIME | PORTRAITS & POETRY/SAN FRANCISCO | PHOTOGRAPHER: CHRISTA FLEISCHMANN COORDINATOR: ROBERT E. JOHNSON | EDITOR: NICK HARVEY PUBLISHER: GLIDE PUBLICATIONS, SAN FRANCISCO

$[1-12]^8$, pp. [1-11] 12-189 [190-192]. 23.5 x 24.0 cm. Bound in brownish gray (64) cloth covered boards. Across the front cover in light greenish gray (154): 'MARK IN TIME | PORTRAITS & POETRY/SAN FRANCISCO'. Down the spine in light greenish gray: 'MARK IN TIME PORTRAITS & POETRY/SAN FRANCISCO'. White wove paper unwatermarked. Moderate purple (223) endpapers. All edges trimmed. Issued in a white paper dust jacket printed in black and strong reddish purple (237).

Contents: May Mobilization, p. 94.

$10.95. Published June 21, 1971 in an impression of 2,500 copies.

Note: Publication data from Jack W. C. Hagstrom and George Bixby's *Thom Gunn: A Bibliography 1940-1978.* [London: Bertram Rota, 1979].

B79   A BIBLIOGRAPHY OF WORKS BY ALLEN GINSBERG   1971
by George Dowden

A BIBLIOGRAPHY | of works by | ALLEN GINSBERG | October, 1943 to July 1, 1967 | [ornament] | Compiled by | GEORGE DOWDEN | with a chronology and index by | Laurence McGilvery | and a foreword by | Allen Ginsberg | [publisher's device] | CITY LIGHTS BOOKS

$[1-2]^{16}$ $[3]^{10}$ $[4-12]^{16}$, pp. [i-iv] v-x [xi-xii] xiii-xvi [xvii-xviii] 1-193 [194] [xix-xxiv] 195-293 [294] [xxv-xxviii] [295-296] 297-343 [344]. 23.4 x 15.6 cm. Bound in dark gray (266) cloth covered boards. Across the spine in silver: 'George | Dowden | [down the spine] ALLEN GINSBERG BIBLIOGRAPHY [across the spine] [publisher's device]'. White wove paper unwatermarked. White endpapers. All edges trimmed. Issued in a white paper dust jacket.

Contents: Foreword [prose], pp. v-vi — Autobiographical Statement [prose], inside front and back dust jacket flaps — [prose notes throughout]

$17.50. Published June 24, 1971 in an impression of 2,500 copies.

B80 **SCATTERED POEMS** **1971**
by Jack Kerouac

a1. *First edition*

Scattered Poems | Jack Kerouac | [publisher's device] | CITY LIGHTS BOOKS | THE
POCKET POETS SERIES NUMBER 28

Forty-two single leaves, pp. [i-vi] 1-76 [77-78]. 15.8 x 12.3 cm. Perfect bound in stiff
white paper wrappers. Covers printed in black. White wove paper unwatermarked. All
edges trimmed.

Contents: Kerouac, Jack. A translation from the French of Jean-Louis Incogniteau
[translation by Allen Ginsberg], p. 1 — Jack Kerouac & AG. Song, p. 2 — Jack Kerouac,
Neal Cassady and AG. Pull My Daisy, pp. 3-5 — Jack Kerouac, Neal Cassady and AG.
Pull My Daisy [another version], pp. 6-7.

$2.00. Published July 1971 in an impression of 3,000 copies.

Note: Reprinted as follows: 2nd printing, 3,000 copies; and an additional 4 printings that
total 29,000 copies. Second and subsequent printings are identified as such on the verso of
the title page.

a2. *First edition, Kraus re-issue, 1974*

THE | POCKET POETS | SERIES | Volume 4 | Numbers 22-28 | KRAUS REPRINT
CO. | Millwood, New York | 1973

$[1-14]^{16}$ $[15]^8$ $[16]^{16}$, pp. [1-496]. 22.3 x 14.4 cm. Bound in dark purplish red (259)
cloth covered boards, lettered across the spine in gold: '[3 rules 3.8 cm. long] | THE |
POCKET | POETS | SERIES | [3 rules 3.8 cm. long] | 4 | KRAUS | REPRINT'.
White wove paper unwatermarked. White endpapers. All edges trimmed.

Contents: As first edition, pp. [415-421].

$23.75 or sold as a four volume set at $95.00. Published Jan. 28, 1974 in an impression
of 250 copies.

B81 **JACK KEROUAC** **1971**
by Claude Pélieu

Burroughs—Kerouac | Pélieu | Jack Kerouac | L'Herne

$[1-6]^8$, pp. [1-8] 9-95 [96]. 21.0 x 13.6 cm. Bound in stiff black paper wrappers which
fold to make inside flaps. Covers printed in white and blue. White wove paper
unwatermarked. All edges trimmed.

Contents: Pull My Daisy, p. 10 — 'Jack Kerouac Est Mort Le 21 Octobre 1969 [prose],
pp. 93-95.

11 francs. Published July-Aug. 1971 in an impression of 1,200 copies.

B82   **CAMPFIRES OF THE RESISTANCE**   **1971**

a1. *First edition, hardbound*

Campfires I of the I Resistance I Poetry from the Movement I Edited by Todd Gitlin I
The Bobbs-Merrill Company, Inc. I Indianapolis New York

[1-9]^{16} [10]^4 [11]^{16}, pp. [i-iv] v-xix [xx] xxi-xxv [xxvi] xxvii-xxix [xxx-xxxii] 1-295
[296]. 23.5 x 15.6 cm. Bound in stiff black cloth covered boards. Down the spine in
yellow: '*CAMPFIRES OF THE RESISTANCE* Todd Gitlin [across the spine] Bobbs- I
Merrill'. White wove paper unwatermarked. White endpapers. All edges trimmed. Issued
in white paper dust jacket printed in vivid yellow (82), strong red (12) and black.

Contents: Returning North of Vortex, pp. 117-120 — Crossing Nation, pp. 120-121 —
Going to Chicago, pp. 121-122 — Grant Park, p. 122.

$7.50. Published Sept. 7, 1971 in an unknown quantity.

a2. *First edition, paperbound, 1971*

Campfires I of the I Resistance I Poetry from the Movement I Edited by Todd Gitlin I
The Bobbs-Merrill Company, Inc. I Indianapolis New York

One hundred sixty-four single leaves, pp. [i-iv] v-xix [xx] xxi-xxv [xxvi] xxvii-xxix [xxx-
xxxii] 1-295 [296]. 22.5 x 14.7 cm. Perfect bound in stiff white paper wrappers. Covers
printed in vivid yellow (82), strong red (12) and black. White wove paper unwatermarked.
All edges trimmed.

$3.95. Published Sept. 7, 1971 in an unknown quantity.

B83   **ANOTHER WORLD**   **1971**

a1. *First edition, hardbound*

ANOTHER I WORLD I *A Second Anthology of Works from the* I *St. Mark's Poetry
Project* I Edited by Anne Waldman I THE BOBBS-MERRILL COMPANY, INC. I
Indianapolis/New York

[1-13]^{16}, pp. [i-vi] vii-xix [xx-xxiv] 1-387 [388-392]. 21.5 x 14.5 cm. Bound in strong
red (12) cloth covered boards. Down the spine: 'Waldman ANOTHER WORLD [across
the spine] BOBBS I MERRILL'. White wove paper unwatermarked. White endpapers.
All edges trimmed. Issued in a white paper dust jacket printed in black and red.

Contents: Rain-wet Asphalt Heat, Garbage Curbed Cans Overflowing, p. 230.

$6.95. Published Sept. 8, 1971 in an impression of 15,000 copies.

Note: Publication data from Alexander Smith Jr.'s *Frank O'Hara: A Comprehensive
Bibliography.* [New York: Garland, 1979].

a2. *First edition, paperbound, 1971*

ANOTHER I WORLD I *A Second Anthology of Works from the* I *St. Mark's Poetry
Project* I Edited by Anne Waldman I THE BOBBS-MERRILL COMPANY, INC. I
Indianapolis/New York

Two hundred eight single leaves, pp. [i-vi] vii-xix [xx-xxiv] 1-387 [388-392]. 20.9 x 13.7 cm. Perfect bound in stiff white paper wrappers. Covers printed in black and red. White wove paper unwatermarked. All edges trimmed.

$2.95. Published Sept. 8, 1971 in an impression of 25,000 copies.

B84   **PRESCRIPTIONS FOR LIVING**   **1971**

a1. *First edition, hardbound*

PRESCRIPTIONS I for I LIVING I [prescription symbol] I [facsimile of autograph] Compiled by Jarvey Gilbert, M.D. I PRICE/STERN/SLOAN I *Publishers, Inc., Los Angeles*

$[1-5]^8$, pp. [1-80]. 14.6 x 22.0 cm. Bound in brilliant blue (177) paper covered boards. Across the front cover in gold: 'PRESCRIPTIONS I for I LIVING'. Down the spine in gold: 'PRESCRIPTIONS FOR LIVING GILBERT PRICE/STERN/SLOAN'. White wove paper unwatermarked. Pages are printed in grayish greenish yellow (105) and light grayish red (18) alternately. White endpapers. All edges trimmed. Issued in a white dust jacket printed in deep blue (179).

Contents: [prose in facsimile holograph], p. [33].

$3.95. Published Nov. 11, 1971 in an unknown quantity.

a2. *First edition, paperbound, 1971*

PRESCRIPTIONS I for I LIVING I [prescription symbol] I [facsimile of autograph] Compiled by Jarvey Gilbert, M.D. I PRICE/STERN/SLOAN I *Publishers, Inc., Los Angeles*

Forty single leaves, pp. [1-80]. Perfect bound in stiff white paper wrappers. Covers printed in deep blue (179). White wove paper unwatermarked. All edges trimmed.

$1.95. Published Nov. 11, 1971 in an unknown quantity.

B85   **ATTACKS OF TASTE**   **1971**

[all within a dark reddish orange (38) ornamental border inside single rules] [in dark reddish orange] ATTACKS I [in dark reddish orange] OF TASTE I [ornamentation] I *Compiled and Edited* I *by* I EVELYN B. BYRNE I & I OTTO M. PENZLER I [5 lines] I [below the frame] New York GOTHAM BOOK MART 1971

$[1-5]^8 [6]^1$, pp. [1-2] [i-vi] vii [viii-x] [1-2] xi-xii, 1-63 [64-66]. 24.1 x 16.2 cm. Bound in light grayish yellowish brown (79) cloth covered boards. On 10.4 x 9.3 cm. paper label attached to the front cover: '[all within dark reddish orange (38) ornamental border within single rules] [ornamentation] I [in dark reddish orange] ATTACKS OF TASTE I [ornamentation] I *Compiled and Edited* I *by* I EVELYN B. BYRNE I & I OTTO M. PENZLER'. Down the spine on a .8 x 12.0 cm. paper label attached to the spine: '[ornamentation in dark reddish orange] ATTACKS OF TASTE [ornamentation in dark reddish orange] Evelyn B. Byrne & Otto M. Penzler [ornamentation in dark reddish orange]'. White wove paper unwatermarked. Brownish orange (54) endpapers. All edges trimmed.

Contents: [prose response to questionnaire], p. 23.

$15.00. Published Dec. 25, 1971 in an impression of 500 copies.

Note: 400 copies were for sale and 100 copies were contributor's copies some of which were sold for $45.00. Publication information from Otto Penzler, one of the editors, who states that conflicting information found in other bibliographies is incorrect.

B86   ANTHOLOGY OF UNDERGROUND POETRY   1971

ANTHOLOGY OF UNDERGROUND POETRY | Section 9 | Edited by Herman Berlandt | <u>CONTRIBUTORS</u> | Allen Ginsberg | Herman Berlandt | Terence Clarke | Margaret A. Conway | Susan Efros | Anna Hartmann | Susan Higgins | Craig Lewis | Jim Marks | Sybil Morwood | Judith Stephens | John Yurechko | Cover by Elise Fraschina | *Copyright © 1971 Poets' Commune Publications, Berkeley*

Single gathering of sixteen leaves, pp. [1-32]. 21.4 x 17.6 cm. Stapled twice into stiff dark yellow (88) paper wrappers. Covers printed in black. White wove paper unwatermarked. All edges trimmed.

Contents: The Birth of a Poem [prose], pp. [3-6].

Published 1971 in an unknown quantity.

B87   C'MON EVERYBODY   1971

C'MON EVERYBODY | Poetry of the Dance | Edited with an introduction | by | PETE MORGAN | [publisher's device] | CORGI [in hollow type] BOOKS | TRANSWORLD PUBLISHERS LTD | A National General Company

Seventy-two single leaves, pp. [1-16] 17-143 [144]. 17.7 x 11.0 cm. Perfect bound in stiff white paper wrappers. Covers printed in full-color. White wove paper unwatermarked. All edges trimmed.

Contents: Liverpool Muse, p. 39 — Big Beat, p. 40 — Seabattle of Salamis Took Place Off Perama, p. 41.

30p. (6s.). Published 1971 in an unknown quantity.

B88   THE AGITATOR   1972

The Agitator | A Collection | of | Diverse Opinions | from America's | Not-so-Popular | Press | Edited by | Donald L. Rice | A [publisher's device] Schism Anthology | [8.8 cm. rule] | American | Library | Association | Chicago 1972

Two hundred and thirty-two single leaves, pp. [i-vi] vii-ix [x] xi-xxxi [xxxii] [1-2] 3-430 [431-432]. 20.2 x 13.4 cm. Perfect bound in stiff white paper wrappers. Covers printed in red and black. White wove paper unwatermarked. All edges trimmed.

Contents: Ginsberg Talks About Speed [prose], pp. 398-400.

$3.95. Published Jan. 1, 1972 in an impression of 5,000 copies.

B89   **AMERICA**   **1972**
by Victor Coleman

AMERICA | [facsimile of author's autograph] Victor Coleman | A GOVERNMENT
PUBLICATION

1-7⁶, pp. [1-84]. 20.5 x 20.4 cm. Bound in stiff white paper wrappers. The back cover
is 20.8 cm. longer than the front cover so that it will fold around the book to form an outer
wrapper. Covers printed in full-color. White wove paper unwatermarked. All edges
trimmed.

Contents: Coleman's *America,* inside back cover.

$4.95. Published Feb. 1972 in an impression of 1,000 copies.

Note: Inserted into the book is a 9.7 x 11.9 cm. negative of a photograph of a car in a
parking lot.

B90   **GINGER SNAPS**   **1972**

GINGER SNAPS | a collection of cut-ups / machine prose / word & image trips | Editor:
Michael Gibbs Co-editor: Hammond Guthrie | Published in an edition of 300 copies by
KONTEXTS Publications | March 1972 Copyright remains with the authors | [9 lines] |
Price: 30p./1 dollar/or equivalent | [1 line] | KONTEXTS Publications | 31 Pinhoe
Road | Exeter — Devon | England

Twenty-one single leaves, pp. [1-42]. 29.7 x 21.0 cm. Stapled three times on the left in
stiff white paper covers. Covers printed in black. White wove paper watermarked:
'ORBIT'. All edges trimmed.

Contents: Rain-wet Asphalt Heat, Garbage Curbed Cans Overflowing, p. [11] — [excerpt
from AG's Introduction to Charles Plymell's *Apocalypse Rose*].

30p. or $1.00. Published March 1972 in an impression of 300 copies.

B91   **UNDERGROUND READER**   **1972**

[left title page] THE | Assembled by Mel Howard
[right title page] UNDERGROUND | READER | and The Reverend Thomas King
Forçade | [publishers device] | A PLUME BOOK from | NEW AMERICAN LIBRARY
| TIMES MIRROR | New York, London, and Scarborough, Ontario

One hundred sixty-eight single leaves, pp. [i-iv] v-ix [x] 1-322 [323-326]. 20.3 x 13.7
cm. Perfect bound in stiff white paper wrappers. Covers printed in black and reddish
orange. White wove paper unwatermarked. All edges trimmed.

Contents: Declaration [prose], pp. 73-75.

$2.95. Published March 1972 in an unknown number of copies, and possibly reprinted.

Note: First printing identified as such on the verso of the title page.

B92   **JUKEBOXES**   **1972**
                              by Claude Pélieu

JUKEBOXES | (les micros hystériques) | *poèmes 1967-1970* | PAR | CLAUDE
PÉLIEU | introduction d'Allen Ginsberg | [publisher's device] | CHRISTIAN
BOURGOIS | DOMINIQUE DE ROUX

Ninety-six single leaves, pp. [1-5] 6 [7-11] 12-189 [190-192]. 17.6 x 10.7 cm. Perfect
bound in stiff white paper wrappers. Covers printed in vivid purplish red (254), brilliant
greenish yellow (98), black and vivid purplish blue (194). White wove paper
unwatermarked. All edges trimmed.

Contents: Notes on Claude Pelieu [prose], pp. [5]-6.

16,50 FF. Published Spring 1972 in an impression of 12,000 copies.

B93   **SPOOLS**   **1972**

[within single rule panel] spools | [ornamentation] | [all the rest within a single rule
panel] spools | an anthology of poems | by gay poets | for the Ohio Gay Pride Week |
May 15-21, 1972 | Copyrighted (c) by the Ohio Gay Pride Committee | 1739 North High
Street #3 | Columbus, Ohio 43210

Twenty single leaves, printed on rectos only, ll. [1-20]. 27.8 x 21.5 cm. White wove
paper unwatermarked. Single leaves, unbound.

Contents: Police State Blues, p. [4].

Published in 1972 in an unknown quantity.

B94   **VISIONS OF CODY**   **1973**
                              by Jack Kerouac

a1. *First edition*

[left title page] [in ornamental type] JACK | [in ornamental type] KEROUAC
[right title page] [in ornamental type] VISIONS | [in ornamental type] OF CODY |
Introduction by Allen Ginsberg | McGRAW-HILL BOOK COMPANY | New York
[bullet] St. Louis [bullet] San Francisco | Düsseldorf [bullet] Mexico [bullet] Toronto

[1-13]^{16}, pp. [i-vi] vii-xii [xiii-xiv] [1-2] 3-398 [399-402]. 23.3 x 16.0 cm. Bound in
dark red (16) cloth covered boards. Blind stamped across the front cover: '[within double
ruled panel with rounded corners in ornamental type] VISIONS OF CODY | [within
double ruled panel with rounded corners in ornamental type] JACK KEROUAC'. Across
the spine all in gold: 'JACK | KEROUAC | [down the spine within double ruled panel
with rounded corners in ornamental type] VISIONS OF CODY [across the spine]
McGRAW-HILL'. Across the back cover: '[in gold] 07-034201-6'. White wove paper
unwatermarked. Light yellowish brown (76) endpapers. All edges trimmed. Top edge
stained dark red. Issued with a light yellowish brown dust jacket, printed in multicolors.

Contents: The Great Rememberer [prose], pp. vii-xii.

$8.95. Published Jan. 8, 1973 in an undisclosed number of copies.

Note: Second and subsequent printings are identified as such by the numbering scheme on
the verso of the title page. Reprinted at least three times.

a2. *First edition, British issue, 1973*

[left title page] [in ornamental type] JACK I [in ornamental type] KEROUAC
[right title page] [in ornamental type] VISIONS I [in ornamental type] OF CODY I
Introduction by Allen Ginsberg I [publisher's device] I ANDRE DEUTSCH

[A-N]^{16}, pp. [i-vi] vii-xii [xiii-xiv] [1-2] 3-398 [399-402]. 23.9 x 15.8 cm. Bound in vivid purplish red (254) paper covered boards. Across the spine all in gold: 'JACK I KEROUAC I [2 rules] I VISIONS I OF CODY I [publisher's device] I André Deutsch'. White wove paper unwatermarked. All edges trimmed. Issued in a white paper dust jacket printed in black, red, blue, purple and pink.

£4.25. Published 1973 in an undisclosed number of copies.

a3. *First edition, paperbound issue, 1974*

[ornamentation] I [on 1 line] jack [on 2 lines] visions I of cody I kerouac I introduction by allen ginsberg I [publisher's device] I McGraw-Hill Book Company I New York [bullet] St. Louis [bullet] San Francisco [bullet] Düsseldorf I Mexico [bullet] Montreal [bullet] Panama [bullet] São Paulo [bullet] Toronto

Two hundred eight single leaves, pp. [i-vii] viii-xii [xiii-xiv] [1-2] 3-398 [399-402]. 20.1 x 13.2 cm. Perfect bound in stiff white paper wrappers. Covers printed in dark grayish yellowish brown (81), vivid reddish orange (34) and black. White wove paper unwatermarked. All edges trimmed.

$5.95. Published 1974 in a quantity undisclosed by the publisher.

Note: Second and subsequent printings are identified as such by the numbering scheme on the verso of the title page.

a4.* *First edition, British paperbound, June 1980*

Note: Published June 1980 by Wm. Collins/Granada.

B95   **THE GAY LIBERATION BOOK**   **1973**

a1. *First edition, hardbound*

[vertical rule] edited by I len richmond and gary noguera I [horizontal rule joining the vertical rule] I the I gay I liberation I book I *Ramparts Press* I san francisco

[1-6]^{16} [7]^8, pp. [1-10] 11-208. 20.8 x 20.9 cm. Bound in white coated cloth covered boards. Across the front cover: '[inside the center of a male eros symbol in rainbow colors is all the following] [on a curved base line] THE GAY LIBERATION I BOOK I *Edited By* I LEN RICHMOND & GARY NOGUERA I *With Special Contributions By* I *William Burroughs* I *Allen Ginsberg* I *Paul Goodman* I *Paul Jacobs* I *John Lennon* I *Huey Newton* I *Gore Vidal* I *Alan Watts* I [on a curved base line] *Writings & Photographs on Gay (Men's) Liberation*'. Down the spine: '[in purple] THE GAY LIBERATION BOOK [in orange] Richmond & Noguera [across the spine] *R* I *Ramparts* I *Press*'. Across the back cover: '[13 lines] I [6 lines by AG] I --Allen Ginsberg I [multicolored design of butterfly] I *Ramparts Press* I San Francisco 94101 I ISBN 0-87867-030-0 I *Cover by Dugald Stermer* I Trade distribution by I Monthly Review Press I New York I Order No. RC 0300 7.95'. White wove paper unwatermarked. White endpapers. All edges trimmed.

Contents: At the Conspiracy Trial [prose], pp. 200-202 — [prose blurb on back cover].

$7.95. Published Jan. 20, 1973 in an unknown quantity.

a2. *First edition, paperbound, 1973*

[vertical rule] edited by I len richmond and gary noguera I [horizontal rule joining the vertical rule] I the I gay I liberation I book I *R*amparts Press I san francisco

One hundred four single leaves, pp. [1-10] 11-208. 20.4 x 20.4 cm. Perfect bound in stiff white paper wrappers. Covers printed in yellow, orange, red, purple, blue, green and black. White wove paper unwatermarked. All edges trimmed.

$3.95. Published Jan. 20, 1973 in an unknown quantity.

B96   **HOMAGE TO GEORGE BARKER**   **1973**

a1. *First edition, paperbound*

HOMAGE TO I GEORGE BARKER I ON HIS SIXTIETH BIRTHDAY I *Edited by John Heath-Stubbs* I *and Martin Green* I MARTIN BRIAN I & O'KEEFFE I London

[A-F]^8 with a single leaf added between the first and second leaves of the first signature, pp. [i-ii] [1-4] 5 [6] 7 [8] 9-93 [94-96]. 21.6 x 13.8 cm. Bound in moderate orange yellow (71) stiff paper wrappers. Covers printed in dark brown (59) and black. White wove paper unwatermarked. All edges trimmed.

Contents: [letter to Martin Green], p. 25.

£1.00. Published Feb. 1973 in an impression of 250 copies.

a2. *First edition, hardbound, 1973*

HOMAGE TO I GEORGE BARKER I ON HIS SIXTIETH BIRTHDAY I *Edited by John Heath-Stubbs* I *and Martin Green* I MARTIN BRIAN I & O'KEEFFE I London

[A-F]^8 with a single leaf added between the first and second leaves of the first signature, pp. [i-ii] [1-4] 5 [6] 7 [8] 9-93 [94-96]. 22.1 x 14.2 cm. Bound in dark green (146) cloth covered boards. Down the spine in gold: 'Homage to GEORGE BARKER MB & O'K'. White laid paper watermarked: '[crown] I [black letter] A bbey Mills I [black letter] Greenfield'. White endpapers. All edges trimmed. Issued in a glassine dust jacket and also issued in a 23.0 x 14.6 x 1.7 cm. cardboard slip-in case covered with dark green cloth.

Hors commerce. Published Feb. 1973 in an impression of 25 copies.

B97   **RITES OF PASSAGE**   **1973**
                     by Eugene Brooks

RITES OF PASSAGE I By I EUGENE BROOKS I Introductions by I ALLEN GINSBERG and LOUIS GINSBERG

Sixty-seven single leaves, pp. [1-4] i-ix [x] [1] 2-119 [120]. 21.5 x 13.8 cm. Perfect bound in stiff white paper wrappers. Covers printed in black. White wove paper unwatermarked. All edges trimmed.

Contents: Brother Poet [prose], pp. v-viii.

$2.00. Published Feb. 10, 1973 in an impression of 500 copies.

B98   **FLOATING BEAR**   **1973**

a1. *First edition, hardbound*

THE FLOATING BEAR I a newsletter I Numbers 1-37, 1961-1969 I Edited by Diane di Prima & LeRoi Jones I *Introduction and Notes* I *Adapted from Interviews with* I *Diane di Prima* I Laurence McGilvery, La Jolla, California I 1973

Three hundred nine single leaves, pp. [1-4] [i-vi] vii-xviii [xix-xx] 1-156, 156a, 156b, 157-284, 284a [284b] 285-414, 414a [414b] [415-416] 417-503 [504] 504a [504b] 504c [504d] 504e [504f] 505-578 [579-582]. 28.6 x 22.1 cm. Bound in dark grayish blue (187) cloth covered boards. Across the spine in gold: 'THE I FLOATING I BEAR I a Newsletter I NOS. 1-37 I 1961-69'. White wove paper unwatermarked. White endpapers. All edges trimmed.

Contents: History of the Jewish Socialist Party in America [prose], pp. 163-164 — AG & Peter Orlovsky [letter to Charles Chaplin], p. 237 — Psalm IV [poem], p. 409.

$30.00. Published March 1, 1973 in an impression of ca. 300 copies.

Note: These copies were not all bound at the same time but as needed over the following 20 years.

a2. *First edition, paperbound, 1973*

THE FLOATING BEAR I a newsletter I Numbers 1-37, 1961-1969 I Edited by Diane di Prima & LeRoi Jones I *Introduction and Notes* I *Adapted from Interviews with* I *Diane di Prima* I Laurence McGilvery, La Jolla, California I 1973

Three hundred seven single leaves, pp. [1-2] [i-vi] vii-xviii [xix-xx] 1-156, 156a, 156b, 157-284, 284a [284b] 285-414, 414a [414b] [415-416] 417-503 [504] 504a [504b] 504c [504d] 504e [504f] 505-578 [579-580]. 27.7 x 21.0 cm. Perfect bound in stiff light grayish yellowish brown (79) paper wrappers. Covers printed in light olive brown (94). White wove paper unwatermarked. All edges trimmed.

$20.00. Published March 1, 1973 in an impression of 100-125 copies.

B99   **KEROUAC**   **1973**
                        by Ann Charters

a1. *First edition, hardbound*

[ornamental bracket] I [on curved base line] KEROUAC I [photograph of Kerouac within a single line cartouche frame] I *A Biography* I *by Ann Charters* I [ornamental bracket]

[1-2]^{16} [3]^8 [4-8]^{16} [9]^{20} [10-11]^{16} [12]^8 [13-14]^{16}, pp. [1-8] 9 [10] 11-18 [19-20] 21-419 [420-424]. 23.5 x 15.6 cm. Bound in yellowish white (92) cloth covered boards. Down the spine in light greenish blue (172): 'KEROUAC *A Biography by Ann Charters* [publisher's device across the spine]'. Light greenish blue endpapers. All edges trimmed. Issued in a pale orange yellow (73) dust jacket, printed in brown, red and blue.

Contents: Foreword [prose], p. 9 — [photographs see also D7] — [excerpt from foreword on the back dust jacket cover].

$7.95. Published March 1, 1973 in an impression of 10,000 copies.

Note: Published in San Francisco, CA by Straight Arrow Books. Reprinted at least twice. First printing identified as such on p. [5].

a2. *First edition, paperbound, 1974*

KEROUAC | *A Biography* | *by Ann Charters* | [on curved base line] A Straight Arrow Book | [publisher's device] | [publisher's device] | WARNER | PAPERBACK | LIBRARY | A Warner Communications Company

Two hundred eight single leaves, pp. [1-10] 11-18 [19] 20-416. 17.7 x 10.6 cm. Perfect bound in stiff white paper wrappers. Covers printed in brown, yellow, orange and black. White wove paper unwatermarked. All edges trimmed. All edges stained yellow.

$1.95. Published April 1974 and reprinted 4 times with a total printing of 175,500 copies.

Note: First printing identified as such on the verso of the title page.

b1. *First British edition, hardbound, 1974*

KEROUAC | *A biography by* | ANN CHARTERS | [publisher's device] ANDRE DEUTSCH

[A-N]^{16}, pp. [i-xii] 1-9 [10-12] 13-387 [388] 389-403 [404]. 22.1 x 14.2 cm. Bound in light green cloth covered boards with red cross-hatched threads. Across the spine in gold: 'ANN | CHARTERS | [down the spine] [in ornamental type] KEROUAC [publisher's device across the spine] | ANDRE | DEUTSCH'.   White wove paper unwatermarked. All edges trimmed. Issued in a white paper dust jacket printed in green, pink and black.

Contents: As first edition, p. [x] and reprinted on the back of the dust jacket.

£3.95. Published May 23, 1974 in an impression of 1500 copies.

b2. *First British edition, paperbound, 1974*

KEROUAC | *A biography by* | ANN CHARTERS | [publisher's device] ANDRE DEUTSCH

Two hundred and twelve single leaves, pp. [i-xii] 1-9 [10-12] 13-116 [xiii-xiv] 117-148 [xv-xvi] 149-276 [xvii-xviii] 277-308 [xix-xx] 309-387 [388] 389-403 [404]. 21.5 x 13.8 cm. Perfect bound in stiff white paper wrappers. Covers printed in strong yellowish green (131). White wove paper unwatermarked. All edges trimmed. Issued in a white paper dust jacket printed in strong yellowish green, light orange (52) and black.

Contents: As first British edition, hardbound.

£2.50. Published May 23, 1974 in an impression of 4,000 copies.

c1. *Second American edition, paperbound, 1987*

KEROUAC | A BIOGRAPHY | BY | ANN CHARTERS | St. Martin's Press | New York

Two hundred sixteen single leaves, pp. [i-x] [1-10] 11-416 [417-422]. 21.0 x 14.0 cm. Perfect bound in stiff white paper wrappers. Covers printed in light orange yellow (70), black, gray and red. White wove paper unwatermarked. All edges trimmed.

Contents: As first edition, p. [5] but without the reprinting on the cover.

$10.95. Published in 1987 in an undisclosed number of copies.

B100   **EPITAPHS FOR LORINE**   **1973**

EPITAPHS FOR LORINE I EDITED AND INTRODUCED I BY JONATHAN
WILLIAMS I THE JARGON SOCIETY I PENLAND NORTH CAROLINA I 1973

Twenty-four single leaves, pp. [1-48]. 16.5 x 10.0 cm. Perfect bound in stiff black paper
wrappers. Issued in a white paper dust jacket printed in black. White wove paper
unwatermarked. All edges trimmed.

Contents: For L.N., p. [23].

Distributed free. Published May 12, 1973 in an impression of 1,000 copies.

B101   **BEYOND STONEHENGE**   **1973**

a1. *First edition*

[left title page] [all on a photograph of Stonehenge] BEYOND
[right title page] [all on a continuation of the photograph of Stonehenge] GERALD S.
HAWKINS I STONEHENGE I [in white] HARPER & ROW, PUBLISHERS I [in
white] NEW YORK, EVANSTON, SAN FRANCISCO, LONDON

$[1-9]^{16} [10]^8 [11]^{16}$, pp. [i-viii] ix [x] xi [xii] xiii [xiv-xvi] 1-319 [320]. 24.1 x 18.6 cm.
Bound in black cloth covered boards. Across the front cover in dark gray is the publisher's
device. Down the spine in dark gray: 'BEYOND STONEHENGE HAWKINS [across the
spine] HARPER I & ROW'. White wove paper unwatermarked. Grayish green (150)
endpapers. All edges trimmed. Issued in a white paper dust jacket printed in black.

Contents: [drawing of three fish which share a common head], p. 263.

$10.00. Published May 30, 1973 in an impression of 30,447 copies.

Note: Reprinted at least 3 times. Second and subsequent printings identified as such by the
numbering code on the base of p. [320].

a2. *First British edition, hardbound, 1973*

[left title page] [all on a photograph of Stonehenge] BEYOND
[right title page] [all on a continuation of the photograph of Stonehenge] GERALD S.
HAWKINS I STONEHENGE I HUTCHINSON OF LONDON

$[A-J]^{16} [K]^8 [L]^{16}$, pp. [i-viii] ix [x] xi [xii] xiii [xiv-xvi] 1-319 [320]. 23.9 x 18.4 cm.
Bound in olive gray (113) cloth covered boards. Down the spine: 'BEYOND
STONEHENGE Gerald S. Hawkins [publisher's device across the spine] I
HUTCHINSON'. White wove paper unwatermarked. Light gray (264) endpapers. All
edges trimmed. Issued in a white paper dust jacket.

Published 1973 in an unknown quantity.

a3. *First British edition, paperbound, 1977*

[left title page] [all on a photograph of Stonehenge] BEYOND
[right title page] [all on a continuation of the photograph of Stonehenge] Gerald S.
Hawkins | STONEHENGE | Arrow Books

One hundred and sixty-eight single leaves, pp. [i-viii] ix [x] xi [xii] xiii [xiv-xvi] 1-309
[310] 311-317 [318] 319 [320]. 21.0 x 14.8 cm. Perfect bound in stiff white paper
wrappers. Covers printed in full color. White wove paper unwatermarked. All edges
trimmed.

£2.50. Published in 1977 in an unknown quantity. Second and subsequent printings
identified as such by the numbering code on the base of p. [320].

B102   **THE MALE MUSE**   **1973**

THE MALE MUSE | A Gay Anthology | [photograph of an ancient coin] | Edited by Ian
Young | The Crossing Press Trumansburg, New York

Sixty-four single leaves, pp. [1-4] 5-127 [128]. 20.8 x 13.4 cm. Perfect bound in stiff
white paper wrappers. Covers printed in black. White wove paper watermarked:
'LINWEAVE | TAROTEXT'. All edges trimmed.

Contents: Genocide, pp. 39-40 — After Thoughts, p. 40 — Flying Home, p. 41.

$3.95. Published June 30, 1973 in an unknown quantity.

Note: According to the verso of the title page, a hardcover issue was also produced of this
title. A thorough search by the compiler has failed to reveal the location of any copies of
this and the publisher can no longer be reached.

B103   **KEROUAC'S TOWN**   **1973**
                             by Barry Gifford

a1. *First edition, hardbound, signed*

Number Twelve — Yes! Capra Chapbook Series | [ornamental type] KEROUAC'S |
[ornamental type] TOWN [ornamentation] | *On the second anniversary of his death.* | *by
Barry Gifford* | *with photos by Marshall Clements* | 1973 | CAPRA PRESS | SANTA
BARBARA

[1]^8 [2-3]^4 [4]^2, pp. [1-6] 7-30 [31-36]. 18.5 x 13.3 cm. Bound in white paper covered
boards. Covers printed in yellowish gray (93) and black. White wove paper
unwatermarked. Strong red (12) endpapers. All edges trimmed.

Contents: [excerpt from letter to Barry Gifford], p. 10.

$10.00. Published July 1973 in an impression of 125 copies.

a2. *First edition, paperbound, 1973*

Number Twelve — Yes! Capra Chapbook Series | [ornamental type] KEROUAC'S |
[ornamental type] TOWN [ornamentation] | *On the second anniversary of his death.* | *by
Barry Gifford* | *with photos by Marshall Clements* | 1973 | CAPRA PRESS | SANTA
BARBARA

Twenty single leaves, pp. [i-ii] [1-6] 7-30 [31-38]. 17.6 x 12.7 cm. Perfect bound in stiff
white paper wrappers. Covers printed in yellowish gray (93) and black. White wove paper

unwatermarked, the first and last leaves being moderate reddish orange (37) wove unwatermarked. Strong red (12) endpapers. All edges trimmed.

$2.50. Published July 1973 in an unknown quantity.

b1. *Second edition, paperbound, 1977*

[photograph of Lowell, MA in four quarters] | KEROUAC'S | TOWN | *by* | *Barry Gifford* | *with Photographs by* | *Marshall Clements* | NUMBER TWO | MODERN AUTHORS MONOGRAPH SERIES | [publisher's device] | Creative Arts Book Company | Berkeley [bullet] 1977

Thirty-four single leaves, pp. [i-viii] 1-60. 17.8 x 10.4 cm. Perfect bound in staff white paper wrappers. Covers printed in deep blue (179) and medium gray (265). White wove paper unwatermarked. All edges trimmed.

Contents: As first edition, p. 6.

$2.50. Published in 1977 in an unknown quantity.

B104   **KESEY'S GARAGE SALE**   **1973**

a1. *First edition, hardbound*

[all ornamental type] [photograph of 2 men and one woman and a sign with the 3 word title on it] KESEY'S | GARAGE | SALE | [below the photograph] [publisher's device] A [publisher's device] | JOINT | PRODUCTION!

[1-8]^{16}, pp. [i-viii] ix-xi [xii] xiii-xviii [1] 2-238. 28.5 x 22.5 cm. Quarter bound in grayish blue (186) cloth with textured grayish blue cloth covered boards. Down the front and back cover spine cloth is a white dotted line. Across the front cover is a white illustration of a sign with the title of the book in three lines: 'KESEY'S | GARAGE | SALE'. Down the spine: '[all in light yellow green (119)] [in hollow type] Kesey [solid star] s [not in hollow type] GARAGE SALE VIKING'. White wove paper unwatermarked. Dark bluish gray (192) endpapers. All edges trimmed. Top edges stained brilliant yellow green (116). Issued in a white paper dust jacket printed in full color.

Contents: [letter to Ken Kesey], p. 212 — Troost Street Blues, p. 212 — First Party at Ken Kesey's with Hell's Angels, p. 213.

$8.95. Published in New York by Viking Press on Aug. 27, 1973 in an undisclosed number of copies.

a2. *First edition, paperbound, 1973*

[all ornamental type] [photograph of 2 men and one woman and a sign with the 3 word title on it] KESEY'S | GARAGE | SALE | [below the photograph] [publisher's device] A [publisher's device] | JOINT | PRODUCTION!

One hundred twenty-eight single leaves, pp. [i-viii] ix-xi [xii] xiii-xviii [1] 2-238. 27.7 x 21.5 cm. Perfect bound in stiff white paper wrappers. Covers printed in full color. White wove paper unwatermarked. All edges trimmed.

$3.95. Published in New York by Viking Press on Aug. 27, 1973 in a quantity undisclosed by the publisher.

B105   THE HARVARD LAMPOON CENTENNIAL CELEBRATION   1973

[all in vivid yellow (82) on a deep reddish purple (238) background] THE I HARVARD I LAMPOON I CENTENNIAL I CELEBRATION I 1876-1973 I EDITED BY MARTIN KAPLAN I WITH A FOREWORD BY JOHN UPDIKE I AN ATLANTIC MONTHLY PRESS BOOK I Little, Brown and Company — Boston — Toronto

[1-10]^{16}, pp. [i-x] [1-2] 3-310. 34.3 x 27.2 cm. Bound in moderate red (15) cloth covered boards. Down the spine in gold: 'THE HARVARD LAMPOON CENTENNIAL CELEBRATION 1876-1973 [across the spine] ATLANTIC I LITTLE, BROWN'. White wove paper unwatermarked. All edges trimmed. Photographic endpapers in moderate red (15) of a group of people.

Contents: [prose and a reproduction of a drawing of three fish which share a common head], p. 272.

$29.95. Published Nov. 15, 1973 in an impression of 14,000 copies.

B106   **PEACE AND PIECES**   **1973**

[design of a bird with an olive branch] Peace & Pieces: I An Anthology of Contemporary American Poetry I Editors: I Maurice Custodio I Grace Harwood I David Hoag I Todd S. J. Lawson I w/illustration and I photography by: I Ernesto Ferrera I L. A. (Happy) Hyder I Greg Irons I Lee Marrs I Efren Ramirez I William Samolis I Mal Warwick I [reproduction of a drawing of an early 20th century family]

One hundred and eight single leaves, pp. [1-4] i-viii [ix-x [sic]] x [xi] 1-197 [198-200]. 27.8 x 21.4 cm. Perfect bound in stiff white paper wrappers. Covers printed in full color. White wove paper unwatermarked. All edges trimmed.

Contents: NY Youth Call Annunciation [includes music notation], pp. 52-55 — Death on All Fronts, p. 56.

$5.00. Published Dec. 1973 in an impression of 1,000 copies.

Note: Published in San Francisco, CA by Peace & Pieces Press.

B107   **KALI-YUGA**   **1973**

KALI-YUGA I Poems I Wisconsin State University I [20 lines] I Edited by Chas. A. Grieder I Cover Design by Mike Winters I 2

Single gathering of 12 leaves, pp. [1] 2 [3] 4-24. 22.8 x 15.2 cm. Stapled twice in stiff moderate reddish orange (37) paper wrappers. Printed across the front cover: '[all on a design of circular graph paper, rocks and a man with a rock on his head] [in facsimile holograph] KALI-YUGA I [in facsimile holograph] POEMS I [within a hollow rectangle] WISCONSIN STATE UNIVERSITY'. Across the back cover: 'Harley Beal I [6 lines]'. Light yellow (86) wove paper unwatermarked. All edges trimmed.

Contents: The Ballad of Tommy the Traveller, pp. 15-16.

Distributed free. Published ca. 1973 in an unknown quantity.

Note: Publication date estimated by the date of cataloging of this book for the National Union Catalog by NBuU. It could possibly have been produced as early as 1969, but no later than 1973. Wisconsin State University could not locate any record of this student underground publication.

B108   **POETICS OF THE NEW AMERICAN POETRY**   **1973**

a1. *First edition, hardbound*

POETICS I OF THE NEW I AMERICAN POETRY I [10.2 cm. rule] I Edited by I Donald Allen & Warren Tallman I [10.2 cm. rule] I Grove Press, Inc., New York

[1-15]¹⁶, pp. [i-viii] ix-xv [xvi] [1-2] 3-463 [464]. 20.8 x 14.0 cm. Bound in moderate red (15) cloth covered boards. Down the spine all in gold: '[in 2 lines] POETICS OF THE I NEW AMERICAN POETRY [vertical rule] [in 3 lines] Edited by I Donald Allen & I Warren Tallman [vertical rule] [in 1 line] Grove Press'. White wove paper unwatermarked. White endpapers. All edges trimmed. Issued in a white paper dust jacket printed in black, vivid red (11) and deep blue (179).

Contents: Notes for *Howl and Other Poems* [prose from Fantasy liner notes], pp. 318-321 — Introduction to *Gasoline* [prose], pp. 322-324 — "When the Mode of the Music Changes the Walls of the City Shake" [prose], pp. 324-330 — Poetry, Violence and The Trembling Lambs [prose], pp. 331-333 — Prose Contribution to Cuban Revolution [prose], pp. 334-344 — How *Kaddish* Happened [prose], pp. 344-347 — Some Metamorphoses of Personal Prosody [prose], pp. 348-349 — On Improvised Poetics [prose], p. 350.

$10.00. Published in 1973 in an undisclosed number of copies.

Note: Reprinted once and identified as the second printing on the verso of the title page.

a2. *First edition, paperbound, 1973*

POETICS I OF THE NEW I AMERICAN POETRY I [10.1 cm. rule] I Edited by I Donald Allen & Warren Tallman I [10.1 cm. rule] I Grove Press, Inc., New York

Two hundred forty single leaves, pp. [i-viii] ix-xv [xvi] [1-2] 3-463 [464]. 20.2 x 13.2 cm. Perfect bound in stiff white paper wrappers. Covers printed in black, vivid red (11) and deep blue (179). White wove paper unwatermarked. All edges trimmed.

$3.95. Published in 1973 in an undisclosed number of copies.

Note: Reprinted several times. First printing identified as such on the verso of the title page.

B109   **CITY LIGHTS ANTHOLOGY**   **1974**

CITY LIGHTS I ANTHOLOGY I [publisher's device] I CITY LIGHTS BOOKS

One hundred twenty-eight single leaves, pp. [1-8] 9-250 [251-256]. 25.3 x 17.7 cm. Perfect bound in stiff white paper wrappers. Covers printed in black and gray. White wove paper unwatermarked. All edges trimmed.

Contents: Encounters with Ezra Pound [prose], pp. 9-21 — Jaweh and Allah Battle, pp. 140-141.

$5.95. Published Sept. 28, 1974 in an impression of 7,000 copies.

Note: The publisher reports the above quantity, the printer, Braun-Brumfield, reports that 8,000 copies were shipped to the publisher on Sept. 16, 1974.

B110   **MADEIRA & TOASTS FOR BASIL BUNTING'S**   **1975**
                              75TH BIRTHDAY

[2 title leaves fold out to form a drawing of the interior of a house the width of 4 pages and on the right quarter] MADEIRA & TOASTS I FOR BASIL BUNTING'S 75TH BIRTHDAY I *Edited by Jonathan Williams* I The Jargon Society I Dentdale I March 1, 1975

Sixty-three single leaves, pp. [1-126]. 22.7 x 15.1 cm. Perfect bound in stiff white paper wrappers. Covers printed in brown and black. White wove paper unwatermarked. All edges trimmed.

Contents: From "Ginsberg in Newcastle" [prose], p. [41].

Price unknown. Published March 1, 1975 in an impression of 1,250 copies.

Note: Leaf 24 also folds out to form a double-sized sheet as do leaves 1 and 2 (the title pages).

B111   **FOR NERUDA, FOR CHILE**   **1975**

a1. *First edition, hardbound*

For Neruda, For Chile I *An International Anthology* I *Edited by Walter Lowenfels* I Beacon Press [publisher's device] *Boston*

One hundred thirty-two single leaves, pp. [i-vi] vii [viii] ix [x] [1-2] 3-249 [250-254]. 21.0 x 14.0 cm. Perfect bound in strong red (12) cloth covered boards. Across the front cover in dark red (16) is the publisher's device. Down the spine in black: 'Lowenfels FOR NERUDA, FOR CHILE BEACON PRESS'. White wove paper unwatermarked. White endpapers. All edges trimmed. Issued in a white paper dust jacket printed in strong red, strong yellow (84) and brown.

Contents: To a Dead Poet, p. 34.

$9.95. Published March 6, 1975 in an impression of 3,000 copies.

a2. *First edition, paperback, 1975*

For Neruda, For Chile I *An International Anthology* I *Edited by Walter Lowenfels* I Beacon Press [publisher's device] *Boston*

One hundred thirty-two single leaves, pp. [i-vi] vii [viii] ix [x] [1-2] 3-249 [250-254]. 20.1 x 13.5 cm. Perfect bound in stiff white paper wrappers. Covers printed in brilliant orange yellow (67), strong red (12) and black. White wove paper unwatermarked. All edges trimmed.

$4.95. Published March 6, 1975 in an impression of 5,000 copies.

B112   **ANGELS OF THE LYRE**   **1975**

a1. *First edition, hardbound*

[ornamental type] ANGELS OF THE LYRE I A GAY POETRY ANTHOLOGY I *Edited by Winston Leyland* I Panjandrum Press [bullet] Gay Sunshine Press I San Francisco 1975

[1-2]^{16} [3]^{12} [4-8]^{16}, pp. [1-5] 6-248. 22.2 x 14.1 cm. Bound in strong purplish blue (196) cloth covered boards. Across the front cover in gold: 'Panjandrum Press [bullet] Gay Sunshine Press I ANGELS OF THE LYRE I A GAY POETRY ANTHOLOGY I *Edited by Winston Leyland* '. Down the spine in gold: '[in 2 lines] ANGELS OF THE LYRE I A GAY POETRY ANTHOLOGY [in 1 line] *Leyland* [in 2 lines] Panjandrum Press [bullet] I Gay Sunshine Press'. Across the back cover in gold: '$10.00 ISBN 0-915572-14-1'. White wove paper unwatermarked. White endpapers. All edges trimmed.

Contents: Night Gleam, p. 86 — Chances "R", p. 87 — Please Master, pp. 88-89 — On Neal's Ashes, p. 90 — Message, pp. 90-91 — Message II, p. 91 — City Midnight Junk Strains, pp. 92-94.

$10.00. Published June 1975 in an impression of 200 copies.

Note: A limited edition of 10 copies was produced, not for sale. They consisted of identical copies of the First edition with a sticker added to page [249]: "This edition is limited to 200 hard cover copies of which 10 are numbered and signed by the poet/editor. This is no. –".

a2. *First edition, paperbound, 1975*

[ornamental type] ANGELS OF THE LYRE I A GAY POETRY ANTHOLOGY I *Edited by Winston Leyland* I Panjandrum Press [bullet] Gay Sunshine Press I San Francisco 1975

One hundred twenty-four single leaves, pp. [1-5] 6-248. 21.5 x 13.6 cm. Perfect bound in stiff white paper wrappers. Covers printed in strong brown (55), black and light yellow (86). White wove paper unwatermarked. All edges trimmed.

$4.95. Published June 1975 in an impression of 3,000 copies.

Note: Second and subsequent printings identified as such on the verso of the title page and reprinted as follows:
Second printing, April 1976 and third printing, Aug. 1978.

B113   **LOKA**   **1975**

[all within single rules with ornamental corners] LOKA I A JOURNAL FROM NAROPA INSTITUTE I Edited by Rick Fields I Anchor Books Anchor Press/Doubleday Garden City, New York

Seventy-two single leaves, pp. [1-5] 6-142 [143-144]. 27.7 x 21.2 cm. Perfect bound in stiff white paper wrappers. Covers printed in black, vivid red (11) and brilliant orange yellow (67). White wove paper unwatermarked. All edges trimmed.

Contents: Chögyam Trungpa and AG. Lion Roars Sun Set Over Rockies' East Slope, pp. 72-75 — First Thought, Best Thought [prose], pp. 89-95.

$4.00. Published June 6, 1975 in a quantity undisclosed by the publisher.

B114   **JOHN KEATS'S PORRIDGE**   **1975**

[7.5 cm. rule] I JOHN KEATS'S I PORRIDGE I [7.5 cm. rule] I Favorite Recipes of I American Poets I [7.5 cm. rule] I *Victoria McCabe* I [7.5 cm. rule] I UNIVERSITY OF IOWA PRESS I [7.5 cm. rule]

Sixty single leaves, pp. [i-ii] [1-20] 21-115 [116-118]. 20.2 x 13.3 cm. Perfect bound in stiff white paper wrappers. Covers printed in dark blue (183), moderate yellow (87), strong reddish orange (35), strong purplish red (255), gold and black. White wove paper unwatermarked. All edges trimmed.

Contents: [prose recipe for borsht], p. 45.

$2.95. Published June 9, 1975 in an impression of 5,331 copies.

B115   **THE NEW NAKED POETRY**   **1976**

The New I Naked Poetry I Recent American poetry I in I open forms I edited by I Stephen Berg and Robert Mezey I The Bobbs-Merrill Company, Inc. I Indianapolis

Two hundred fifty-six single leaves, pp. [i-vi] vii-xix [xx] xxi-xxvii [xxviii-xxx] 1-478 [479-482]. 22.5 x 14.8 cm. Perfect bound in stiff white paper wrappers. Covers printed in solid deep blue (179), black, and vivid yellowish green (129). White wove paper unwatermarked. All edges trimmed.

Contents: This Form of Life Needs Sex, pp. 61-63 — Who Be Kind To, pp. 63-66 — Wales Visitation, pp. 66-69 — Bayonne Turnpike to Tuscarora, pp. 69-73 — Memory Gardens, pp. 74-77 — Friday the Thirteenth, pp. 77-80 — Thus Crosslegged on Round Pillow Sat in Space, pp. 80-83 — [letter to John Hollander], pp. 84-87.

$6.95. Published Jan. 2, 1976 in an unknown quantity. First printing identified as such on the verso of the title page.

B116   **THE DIARY OF ANAIS NIN**   **1976**

a1. *First edition, hardbound*

The I Diary I of I Anaïs Nin I [ornamental rule] I 1955-1966 I Edited and with a Preface by Gunther Stuhlmann I [publisher's device] I Harcourt Brace Jovanovich I New York and London I [publisher's device]

$[1-5]^{16} [6]^4 [7-10]^{16} [11]^4 [12-14]^{16} [15]^8 [16]^{16}$, pp. [i-viii] ix-xvi [xvii-xviii] [1-2] 3-142 [i-viii] 143-270 [i-viii] 271-414. 21.8 x 14.5 cm. Quarter bound in light gray (264) cloth covered boards with strong purplish blue (237) cloth spine. Across the front cover and blind stamped is the author's facsimile autograph. Across the spine in gold: 'The I Diary I of I Anaïs I Nin I [3.4 cm. ornamental rule] I 1955-1966 I [publisher's device] I Harcourt I Brace I Jovanovich'. Across the back cover in gold: '0-15-125594-6'. White wove paper unwatermarked. Pinkish gray (10) endpapers. All edges trimmed. Issued in a white paper dust jacket printed in black, purple and orange.

Contents: [letter to Anaïs Nin], pp. 63-64.

$12.95. Published May 31, 1976 in a quantity undisclosed by the publisher. First edition identified as such on the verso of the title page.

a2. *First edition, paperbound, 1977*

The I Diary I of I Anaïs Nin I [ornamental rule] I 1955-1966 I Edited and with a Preface by Gunther Stuhlmann I A Harvest/HBJ Book I [publisher's device] I Harcourt Brace Jovanovich I New York and London I [publisher's device]

Two hundred sixteen single leaves, pp. [i-viii] ix-xvi [1-2] 3-414 [415-416]. 20.0 x 13.3 cm. Perfect bound in stiff white paper wrappers. Covers printed in black, orange and red. White wove paper unwatermarked. All edges trimmed.

$3.95. Published 1977 in a quantity undisclosed by the publisher.

Note: First printing is identified on the verso of the title page by the line: 'ABCDEFGHIJ'. Reprinted several times.

B117   **LOKA 2**   **1976**

LOKA 2 [with large circle around the letter 'A' and number] ‖ A Journal From Naropa Institute ‖ edited by Rick Fields ‖ Anchor Books Anchor Press/Doubleday Garden City, New York 1976

Eighty-eight single leaves, pp. [1-6] 7-175 [176]. 27.7 x 21.0 cm. Perfect bound in stiff white paper wrappers. Covers printed in vivid greenish yellow (97), brilliant greenish blue (168, deep reddish orange (36) and black. White wove paper unwatermarked. All edges trimmed.

Contents: An Exposition of William Carlos Williams' Poetic Practice [prose], pp. 123-140 — Walking into King Sooper after Two-Week Retreat, p. 157 — Cabin in the Rockies, p. 157.

$4.95. Published July 2, 1976 in an undisclosed number of copies.

B118   **THE RETREAT DIARIES**   **1976**
                        by William S. Burroughs

The Retreat Diaries ‖ William S. Burroughs ‖ with The Dream of Tibet ‖ by Allen Ginsberg

Single gathering of twenty leaves, pp. [1-40]. 20.9 x 13.6 cm. Stapled twice in stiff white paper wrappers. Covers printed in black and red. White wove paper unwatermarked. All edges trimmed.

Contents: [footnotes], pp. [6, 8, 10] — The Dream of Tibet [prose], pp. [37-39].

$2.50. Published in New York by City Moon on Aug. 1, 1976 in an impression of 2,000 copies.

Note: Publication information from the publisher, James Grauerholz.

A copy has been seen on which the title page appears as follows: 'The Retreat Diaries ‖ William S. Burroughs ‖ [handstamped in red] THE RETREAT DIARIES ‖ [handstamped in red] William S. Burroughs ‖ with The Dream of Tibet ‖ by Allen Ginsberg'. It is unclear why this was produced or whether a significant number of copies were stamped as such.

The colophon states that a limited edition of 126 copies, 100 of which are numbered 1-100 and 26 of which are signed and lettered A-Z, was produced. The publisher states that this was produced but has never been released and is at this time (1993) still in storage. At least one copy of each has been seen but the publisher thinks these may be 'escaped' samples.

B119   **C'ERA UNA VOLTA UN BEAT**   **1976**

Fernanda Pivano ⏐ C'ERA UNA VOLTA ⏐ UN BEAT ⏐ 10 anni di ricerca alternativa ⏐ [10.2 x 10.6 cm. photograph of posters advertising the Fugs] ⏐ [page embossed with round seal] ⏐ ARCANA [publisher's device] EDITRICE

[1-8]8, pp. [1-6] 7-123 [124-128]. 27.5 x 20.6 cm. Bound in stiff white paper wrappers. Covers printed in moderate reddish brown (43), black and yellow. White wove paper unwatermarked. All edges trimmed.

Contents: [letter to Nanda Pivano dated April 30, 1961 in facsimile holograph, with an Italian translation], p. 33 — [letter to Nanda Pivano dated March 5, 1963 in facsimile holograph, with an Italian translation], p. 34 — [letter to Mr. Mondadori dated Aug. 18, 1965, with an Italian translation], pp. 58-59.

4.500 Lire. Published Oct. 1976 in an unknown quantity.

B120   **HEART BEAT**   **1976**
                        by Carolyn Cassady

a1. *First edition, hardbound, 1976*

HEART BEAT ⏐ My Life ⏐ with Jack & Neal ⏐ *by* ⏐ *Carolyn Cassady* ⏐ [publisher's device] ⏐ Creative Arts Book Company ⏐ Berkeley [bullet] 1976

Fifty-three single leaves, pp. [i-x] 1-93 [94-96]. 23.0 x 15.2 cm. Quarter bound in yellowish white (92) paper covered boards with grayish purplish red (262) cloth spine. Across the front cover all in metallic purplish red: 'HEART BEAT ⏐ My Life ⏐ with Jack & Neal ⏐ *by* ⏐ *Carolyn Cassady* '. Down the spine in metallic purplish red: '*Cassady* HEART BEAT *Creative Arts Book Company* '. White wove paper unwatermarked. White endpapers. All edges trimmed. Issued in a plain paper dust jacket.

Contents: [letter to Jack Kerouac and Neal Cassady], p. 37 — Put a Kiss and a Tear, pp. 37-39 — [letter to Kerouac], pp. 39-40 — [letter to Carolyn Cassady], pp. 40-41 — [letter to Carolyn Cassady], p. 41 — [letter to Carolyn Cassady], pp. 54-57 — [letter to Neal and Carolyn Cassady], p. 61 — [letter to Neal Cassady], pp. 61-63.

$15.00. Published Oct. 1976 in an impression of 150 copies.

a2. *First edition, paperbound*

HEART BEAT ⏐ My Life ⏐ with Jack & Neal ⏐ *by* ⏐ *Carolyn Cassady* ⏐ [publisher's device] ⏐ Creative Arts Book Company ⏐ Berkeley [bullet] 1976

Fifty-four single leaves, pp. [i-x] 1-93 [94-98]. 22.1 x 14.5 cm. Perfect bound in stiff white paper wrappers. Covers printed in vivid red (11) and black. White wove paper unwatermarked, the first and last leaves are strong red (12) wove paper unwatermarked. All edges trimmed.

$4.00. Published Oct. 1976 in an impression of 8,000 copies.

b1. *First Pocket Books edition, 1978*

HEART BEAT ⏐ My Life ⏐ with Jack & Neal ⏐ *by* ⏐ *Carolyn Cassady* ⏐ [publisher's device] ⏐ PUBLISHED BY POCKET BOOKS NEW YORK

Sixty-five single leaves, pp. [1-10] 11-64 [i-viii] 65-124 [125-128].   17.7 x 10.7 cm. Perfect bound in stiff white paper wrappers.   Covers printed in full color.   White wove paper unwatermarked.   All edges trimmed.

Contents: As first edition, pp. 56-62, 79-83 and 83-91.

$1.95.   Published Oct. 1978 in an impression of 60,000 .

Note: Reprinted once in an impression of 150,000 copies. First printing identified as such on the verso of the title page.

c1.   *First British edition, paperbound, 1980*

Carolyn Cassady l   Heart Beat l   My Life with Jack and Neal l   A PANTHER BOOK l   GRANADA l   London Toronto Sydney New York

Fifty-six single leaves, pp. [1-10] 11-108 [109-112].   17.5 x 11.0 cm.   Perfect bound in stiff white paper wrappers.   Covers printed in full color.   White wove paper unwatermarked.   All edges trimmed.

Contents: As first edition, pp. 50-55, 68-72 and 78-80.

95p.   Published 1980 in an undisclosed number of copies.

B121   **DEATH COLLEGE & OTHER POEMS**   **1976**
                              by Tom Veitch

DEATH COLLEGE l   And Other Poems l   (1964-1974) l   Tom Veitch l   Afterword by Allen Ginsberg l   Big Sky

Ninety-two single leaves, pp. [1-8] 9-183 [184].   22.8 x 15.1 cm.   Perfect bound in stiff white paper wrappers.   Covers printed in vivid red (11) and black.   White wove paper unwatermarked.   All edges trimmed.

Contents: Afterword [prose], pp. 175-183.

$4.50.   Published Nov. 27, 1976 in an impression of 1,500 copies, of which 26 copies are signed by the author and lettered A-Z.

B122   **SITTING FROG**   **1976**

SITTING FROG l   Poetry from Naropa Institute l   edited by Rachel Peters l   and l   Eero Ruuttila

[1-15]^4, pp. [1-120].   25.3 x 17.7 cm.   Bound in stiff white paper wrappers.   Covers printed in black.   White wove paper unwatermarked.   All edges trimmed.

Contents: Sickness Blues, p. [53] — [prose blurb], back cover.

$3.00.   Published in Brunswick, ME by Blackberry in 1976 in an unknown quantity.

B123   **STORIES & ILLUSTRATIONS**   **1976**
                              by Harley

[in brilliant yellow (83)] *Stories &* l   [in brilliant yellow] *Illustrations by* l   [in brilliant yellow] *Harley* l   [7.9 x 7.9 cm. color photograph of the author] l   [in brilliant yellow]

Introduced by | [in brilliant yellow] *Allen Ginsburg* [sic] | [in vivid red (11)] *Charlatan Press*

[1-4]⁴, pp. [1-30] [see note]. 20.3 x 14.4 cm. Bound in stiff strong red (12) cardboard covers with brilliant yellow tape covered spine. The front cover is the title page. Across the back cover: '[color reproduction of drawing by the author] [6 lines in brilliant yellow] | [6 lines in brilliant yellow] [color reproduction of drawing by the author] | [all the rest in vivid red] [publisher's device] [in 3 lines] *ISBN 87 87594 06 4* | © *Copyright 1976* | *by Charlatan Press'*. White wove paper unwatermarked. All edges trimmed.

Contents: Harley Flanagan lives in Denmark [poem], p. [2].

Price unknown. Published 1976 in an unknown quantity.

Note: The first and last leaves of the book are pasted down to the front and back covers.

B124   **ORGASMS OF LIGHT**   **1977**

a1. *First edition, hardbound*

ORGASMS OF LIGHT | THE GAY SUNSHINE | ANTHOLOGY | Poetry, Short Fiction, Graphics | *Edited by Winston Leyland* | Gay Sunshine Press | San Francisco | 1977

[1-2]¹⁶ [3]⁴ [4-9]¹⁶, pp. [1-6] 7-264. 23.4 x 15.3 cm. Bound in silver cloth covered boards. Across the front cover: 'ORGASMS | OF LIGHT | THE GAY SUNSHINE ANTHOLOGY | edited by Winston Leyland'. Down the spine: 'leyland ORGASMS OF LIGHT gay sunshine press'. White wove paper watermarked: '[on curved base line] WARREN'S | OLDE STYLE'. White endpapers. All edges trimmed.

Contents: A Dream, p. 85 — Sweet Boy, Gimme Yr Ass, p. 87 — Spring Anti-War Games 1971, p. 88 — Troost Street Blues, pp. 89-90 — Night Gleam, p. 90.

$20.00. Published Spring 1977 in an impression of 200 copies, 50 of which are signed and numbered by the editor and sold for $30.00.

Note: A special issue of 26 copies, lettered and signed by the editor and with a leaf inserted facing p. 264 on which is printed an original translation by Winston Leyland of two medieval Arab poems, one drawn from *A Thousand and One Nights* (the History of the Princess Zuleika), and the other from Jalal ad-Din Rumi (Sufi, Persian, 13th century) was produced. It sold for $50.00.

a2. *First edition, paperbound, 1977*

ORGASMS OF LIGHT | THE GAY SUNSHINE | ANTHOLOGY | Poetry, Short Fiction, Graphics | *Edited by Winston Leyland* | Gay Sunshine Press | San Francisco | 1977

One hundred thirty-two single leaves, pp. [1-6] 7-264. 22.5 x 14.7 cm. Perfect bound in stiff white paper wrappers. Covers printed deep blue (179), pink and green. White wove paper watermarked: '[on curved base line] WARREN'S | OLDE STYLE'. All edges trimmed.

$5.95. Published Spring 1977 in an impression of 3,000 copies.

B125   **JUNKY**   **1977**
             by William S. Burroughs

a1.1 *First edition, paperbound, first impression*

Junky | William S. Burroughs | With an Introduction by Allen Ginsberg | *The first complete and* | *unexpurgated edition,* | *originally published* | *as <u>Junkie</u> under the* | *pen name of William Lee* | [publisher's device] | PENGUIN BOOKS

Eighty-eight single leaves, pp. [i-iv] v-xvi [xvii-xviii] 1-158. 18.1 x 11.1 cm. Perfect bound in stiff white paper wrappers. Covers printed in black and vivid orange (48). White wove paper unwatermarked. All edges trimmed.

Contents: Introduction [prose], pp. v-x.

$1.95. Published March 31, 1977 in an undisclosed number of copies.

a1.2 *First edition, paperbound, second impression, 1979*

Junky | William S. Burroughs | With an Introduction by Allen Ginsberg | *The first complete and* | *unexpurgated edition,* | *originally published* | *as <u>Junkie</u> under the* | *pen name of William Lee* | [publisher's device] | PENGUIN BOOKS

18.0 x 10.6 cm. Covers printed in black and vivid orange (48).

Contents: Introduction [as the first impression but shortened by 5 paragraphs], pp. v-ix.

$2.50. Published 1979 in an undisclosed number of copies and reprinted 4 times.

a2. *Second edition, paperbound, 1984*

Junky | William S. Burroughs | With an Introduction by Allen Ginsberg | *The first complete and* | *unexpurgated edition,* | *originally published* | *as <u>Junkie</u> under the* | *pen name of William Lee* | [publisher's device] | PENGUIN BOOKS

Eighty-eight single leaves, pp. [i-iv] v-ix [x] xi-xvi [xvii-xviii] 1-158. 19.6 x 12.7 cm. Perfect bound in stiff white paper wrappers. Covers printed in full-color. White wove paper unwatermarked. All edges trimmed.

Contents: As *First edition, paperbound, second impression.*

$4.95. Published 1984 in an undisclosed number of copies with a new cover design beginning with the 20th printing.

B126   **TAKE CARE OF MY GHOST, GHOST**   **1977**

TAKE CARE OF MY GHOST, GHOST | * | Allen Ginsberg & Jack Kerouac | GHOST PRESS, 1977

Eighteen single leaves, ll. [1-18]. 27.8 x 21.5 cm. Stapled 3 times on the left edge into stiff paper sheets forming the front and back covers. Across the front cover is a photograph of the authors. Printed on the rectos only. White wove paper unwatermarked. All edges trimmed.

Contents: [7 letters to Jack Kerouac], ll. 3-6, 9 — Behold! The Swinging Swan, l. 3 — Thus on a Long Bus Ride, l. 7 — Leave the Bones Behind, l. 8.

Price unknown. Published ca. June 1977 in an impression of 200 copies.

Note: A note from a rare book catalogue states that this is "Pirated from the Humanities Research Center at the University of Texas". Publisher could not be located by the compiler.

B127   **LES ÉCRIVAINS BEATS ET LE VOYAGE**   **1977**
                         by Jacqueline Starer

Jacqueline Starer I LES I ÉCRIVAINS BEATS I ET LE I VOYAGE I *ÉTUDES ANGLAISES* I 68 I [publisher's device] Didier I 15, rue Cujas, 75005 Paris

[1-16]^8 [17]^{10}, pp. [1-9] 10-273 [274-276]. 23.8 x 15.4 cm. Bound in stiff white paper wrappers. Covers printed in red and black. White wove paper unwatermarked. All edges trimmed.

Contents: Flying Elegy, p. [224].

129 F. Published Oct. 1977 in an impression of 700 copies.

B128   **A BIBLIOGRAPHY OF THE AUERHAHN PRESS**   **1977**

A Bibliography of I the Auerhahn Press I *& its successor* I *Dave Haselwood Books* I *Compiled by a printer* I BERKELEY : A POLTROON PRESS PRODUCTION

[1-4]^8 [5]^4 [6]^{10}, pp. [i-ii] [1-4] 5-87 [88-90]. 24.1 x 16.6 cm. Bound in dark greenish blue (174) cloth covered boards silkscreened with a design of a bird within a circle. Down the spine on a 0.9 x 7.4 cm. white paper label is the following: 'AUERHAHN BIBLIOGRAPHY'. White wove paper watermarked: '[on curved line] WARREN'S I OLDE STYLE'. White endpapers printed with a design of a bird in gray. All edges trimmed. Issued without a dust jacket.

Contents: [blurb for *Dark Brown* by Michael McClure], p. 37 — [letter to *Poetry,* dated Oct. 14, 1963], p. 39 — [letter to Dave Haselwood, dated April 23, 1962], pp. 41-43 — [letter to Dave Haselwood, dated Oct. 12, 1962], pp. 43-44.

Published Dec. 1977 in an impression of "somewhat less than 500 copies".

Note: Although the date 1976 is given on the verso of the title page, Bob Wilson of the Phoenix Bookshop believes the true publication was delayed until Dec. 1977.
      There are 26 special copies with various pieces of ephemera included, and signed by various writers such as Michael McClure and Dave Haselwood. Not a special edition but 3 items inserted in each book as loose inserts at a higher price.

B129   **FIRST GLANCE**   **1978**

a1. *First edition, hardbound*

[photograph of a boy at left] I First I Glance I *Childhood Creations of the Famous* I Tuli Kupferberg and Sylvia Topp I HAMMOND INCORPORATED I MAPLEWOOD, NEW JERSEY I New York Chicago Los Angeles

Ninety-six single leaves, pp. [1-4] 5-192. 28.3 x 21.6 cm. Perfect bound in light yellowish brown (76) cloth covered boards. Across the front cover in gold: 'First I Glance I *Childhood Creations* I *of the Famous*'. Down the spine in gold: 'First Glance Kupferberg and Topp HAMMOND'. White wove paper unwatermarked. White endpapers. All edges trimmed. Issued in a white paper dust jacket printed in full-color.

Contents: A Night in the Village, p. 67.

$12.95. Published Spring 1978 simultaneously with the paperbound with a combined issue of 15,000 copies.

a2. *First edition, paperbound, 1978*

[photograph of a boy at left] I First I Glance I *Childhood Creations of the Famous* I Tuli Kupferberg and Sylvia Topp I HAMMOND INCORPORATED I MAPLEWOOD, NEW JERSEY I New York Chicago Los Angeles

Ninety-six single leaves, pp. [1-4] 5-192. 27.5 x 21.1 cm. Perfect bound in stiff white paper wrappers. Covers printed in full-color. White wove paper unwatermarked. All edges trimmed.

$7.95. Published Spring 1978 simultaneously with the hardbound with a combined issue of 15,000 copies.

**B130   WILLIAM S. BURROUGHS, A BIBLIOGRAPHY, 1953-73   1978
by Joe Maynard and Barry Miles**

William S. Burroughs I A Bibliography, 1953-73 I Compiled by Joe Maynard and Barry Miles I *Unlocking Inspector Lee's Word Hoard* I Published for the Bibliographical Society I of the University of Virginia I by the University Press of Virginia I Charlottesville

[1-5]^{16} [6]^8 [7-9]^{16}, pp. [i-ix] x-xii [xiii-xv] xvi-xix [xx-xxi] xxii-xxiii [xxiv-xxvi] [1] 2-242 [243-246]. 23.5 x 15.9 cm. Bound in black cloth covered boards. Blind stamped on the front cover is a design-collage of the titles of WSB's books: Junkie, Naked Lunch, Soft Machine, Dutch Schultz. Across the spine in gold: 'Maynard I and I Miles I [down the spine] William S. Burroughs I A Bibliography, 1953-73 [across the spine] Virginia'. White wove paper unwatermarked. White endpapers. All edges trimmed. Issued without a dust jacket.

Contents: Introduction [prose], p. [xiii] — [cover design for William Burroughs' *Roosevelt After Inauguration*]], p. 42.

$15.00. Published April 4, 1978 in an impression of 2,000 copies.

B131   GAY SUNSHINE INTERVIEWS, VOL. 1   1978

a1. *First edition, hardbound*

Gay I Sunshine I Interviews I Volume I I EDITED BY WINSTON LEYLAND I Gay Sunshine Press I San Francisco I 1978

[1-9]^{16} [10]^4 [11]^{16}, pp. [1-7] 8 [9] 10-325 [326-328]. 23.5 x 15.7 cm. Bound in moderate blue (182) cloth covered boards. Printed in gold down the spine: 'Leyland GAY SUNSHINE INTERVIEWS VOL. 1 Gay Sunshine Press'. White wove paper unwatermarked. White endpapers. All edges trimmed. Issued in a white paper dust jacket printed copper color, dark red and black.

Contents: Allen Ginsberg writes [prose], p. 126 — [prose blurb], on back dust jacket cover.

$15.00. Published June 1, 1978 in an impression of 500 copies; 26 of which being lettered A-Z and signed by the editor.

Note: All copies have a prospectus for *Gay Sunshine Press Interviews, vol. 2* laid in, on a blue card.

A special issue of five copies, bound in off-white sailcloth and printed in blue on the front cover were issued, not for sale. They are signed five of the interviewees: AG, Giorno, Harrison, Norse and Orlovsky.

a2. *First edition, paperbound, 1978*

Gay I Sunshine I Interviews I Volume I I EDITED BY WINSTON LEYLAND I Gay Sunshine Press I San Francisco I 1978

One hundred sixty-four single leaves, pp. [1-7] 8 [9] 10-325 [326-328]. 22.6 x 15.1 cm. Perfect bound in stiff white paper wrappers. Covers printed in copper, dark red (16) and black. White wove paper unwatermarked. All edges trimmed.

Contents: As first hardbound with the blurb on the back cover.

$7.95. Published June 1, 1978 in an impression of 5,000 copies.

Note: The second printing is identical to the first printing except that a new price sticker for $10.00 has been placed on the back cover and was issued in 1982. The third printing has a new cover design and was issued in 1984.

B132   JACK'S BOOK   1978
by Barry Gifford and Lawrence Lee

a1. *First edition, hardbound*

AN ORAL BIOGRAPHY OF JACK KEROUAC I JACK'S I BOOK I by Barry Gifford and Lawrence Lee I St. Martin's Press New York

[1-11]^{16}, pp. [i-xii] [1-2] 3-339 [340]. 23.9 x 16.5 cm. Quarter-bound in grayish yellowish brown (80) cloth with grayish yellow (90) paper covered boards lettered down the spine in gold: 'JACK'S BOOK [in 2 lines] by Barry Gifford I & Lawrence Lee [across the spine] St. Martin's'. White wove paper unwatermarked. White endpapers. Top and bottom edges trimmed. Issued in a white paper dust jacket printed in black, dark grayish yellowish brown (81) and yellowish gray (93).

Contents: [excerpt from a letter to Carolyn Cassady], p. 316.

$10.95. Published July 31, 1978 in an undisclosed number of copies.

a2. *First edition, first British paperbound, 1979*

AN ORAL BIOGRAPHY OF JACK KEROUAC I JACK'S I BOOK I by Barry Gifford and Lawrence Lee I [[publisher's device] I PENGUIN BOOKS

One hundred seventy-six single leaves, pp. [i-xii] [1-2] 3-339 [340]. 19.5 x 12.8 cm. Perfect bound in stiff white paper wrappers. Covers printed in black, yellow, orange and red. White wove paper unwatermarked. All edges trimmed.

$4.50. Published 1979 in an undisclosed number of copies.

a3. *First edition, first American paperbound, 1988*

AN ORAL BIOGRAPHY OF JACK KEROUAC I JACK'S I BOOK I by Barry Gifford
& Lawrence Lee I St. Martin's Press New York

One hundred and seventy-six single leaves, pp. [i-xii] [1-2] 3-339 [340]. 20.9 x 13.8 cm.
Perfect bound in stiff white paper wrappers. Covers printed in dark yellowish gray (91),
strong yellowish pink (26) and black. White wove paper unwatermarked. All edges
trimmed.

$9.95. Published 1988 in a quantity undisclosed by the publisher.

B133   THE VISIONARY POETICS OF ALLEN GINSBERG   1978
by Paul Portugés

a1. *First edition, hardbound*

THE VISIONARY POETICS I OF I ALLEN GINSBERG I BY I PAUL PORTUGÉS I
ROSS-ERIKSON, PUBLISHERS I *Santa Barbara* I 1978

[1-4]^{16} [5]^4 [6-7]^{16}, pp. [i-x] xi-xiv [1-2] 3-181 [82-186]. 22.1 x 14.1 cm. Bound in
black cloth covered boards. Down the spine in gold: 'The Visionary Poetics of Allen
Ginsberg Portugés Ross-Erikson'. White wove paper unwatermarked. White endpapers.
All edges trimmed.

Contents: As I Read William Blake, p. xi — [excerpt from letter to John Hollander], p. xii
— That Day I Heard Blake's Voice, p. 7 — Psalm IV, pp. 7-8 — [excerpt from letter to
Jack Kerouac], p. 10 — [prose], p. 14 — And I Heard a Physical Voice, p. 21 — The
Second Vision-The Worm Whose Love, p. 42 — [prose], p. 43 — Die, Die, the Spirit
Cried, p. 46 — On Reading Wm Blake's Poem, "The Sick Rose", p. 47 — [prose], p. 63
— Because I Believe In It As Miracles, p. 65 — [prose], p. 66 — [prose], p. 70 —
[excerpt from Howl], pp. 87-88 — It Spoke Aloud from Its Center, p. 100.

$11.95. Published Sept. 1978 in an impression of 500 copies.

a2. *First edition, paperbound, 1978*

THE VISIONARY POETICS I OF I ALLEN GINSBERG I BY I PAUL PORTUGÉS I
ROSS-ERIKSON, PUBLISHERS I *Santa Barbara* I 1978

One hundred single leaves, pp. [i-x] xi-xiv [1-2] 3-181 [82-186]. 21.4 x 13.9 cm. Perfect
bound in stiff white paper wrappers. Covers printed in black. White wove paper
unwatermarked. All edges trimmed.

$4.95 and later raised to $5.95. Published Sept. 1978 in an impression of 5,000 copies.

B134   THE PEOPLE'S ALMANAC #2   1978
by David Wallechinsky and Irving Wallace

a1. *First edition, hardbound*

[10.0 cm. rule] I THE I PEOPLE'S I ALMANAC ™ I #2 I [10.0 cm. rule] I by I
David Wallechinsky I and I Irving Wallace I *"The exact contrary of what is generally
believed is   I   often the truth."* I — Jean De La Bruyère (1645-1696) I WILLIAM
MORROW AND COMPANY, INC. I NEW YORK 1978

Seven hundred twenty single leaves, pp. [i-xviii] 1-1416 [1417-1422].   23.4 x 15.9 cm. Bound in black paper covered boards.   Down the spine in gold: '[in 2 lines] THE PEOPLE'S ALMANAC #2 I DAVID WALLECHINSKY AND IRVING WALLACE   [in 1 line] [solid square] I [across the spine] MORROW'.   White wove paper unwatermarked. White endpapers.   All edges trimmed.   Issued in a white paper dust jacket printed in red, orange and black.

Contents: [prose answers to a questionnaire], pp. 1349-1353.

$19.95.   Published Sept. 8, 1978 in a quantity undisclosed by the publisher.

Note: First printing identified by the TM symbol and the date on the title page, later printings substitute a © symbol.

a2.   *First edition, Book Club issue, 1978*

[10.0 cm. rule] I THE I PEOPLE'S I ALMANAC ® I #2 I [10.0 cm. rule] I by I David Wallechinsky I and I Irving Wallace I *"The exact contrary of what is generally believed is I often the truth."* I — Jean De La Bruyère (1645-1696) I WILLIAM MORROW AND COMPANY, INC. I NEW YORK

Seven hundred twenty single leaves, pp. [i-xviii] 1-1416 [1417-1422].   23.5 x 15.8 cm. Bound in black paper covered boards.   Down the spine in gold: 'THE PEOPLE'S ALMANAC #2 I DAVID WALLECHINSKY AND IRVING WALLACE   [across the spine] [solid square] I MORROW'.   White wove paper unwatermarked.   White endpapers.   All edges trimmed.   Issued in a white paper dust jacket printed in red, orange and black.

Book Club pricing.   Published 1978 in a quantity undisclosed by the publisher.

a3.   *First edition, paperbound, 1978*

[10.1 cm. rule] I THE I PEOPLE'S I ALMANAC ™ I #2 I [10.1 cm. rule] I by I David Wallechinsky I and I Irving Wallace I *"The exact contrary of what is generally believed is I often the truth."* I — Jean De La Bruyère (1645-1696) I [publisher's device]

Seven hundred twenty single leaves, pp. [i-xviii] 1-1416 [1417-1422].   22.8 x 15.2 cm. Perfect bound in stiff white paper wrappers.   Covers printed in brilliant orange yellow (67), red and black.   White wove paper unwatermarked.   All edges trimmed.

$9.95.   Published October 1978 in a quantity undisclosed by the publisher.

B135   **NOSTALGIA FOR THE PRESENT**   **1978**
                         by Andrei Voznesensky

a1.   *First edition, hardbound*

Andrei Voznesensky I NOSTALGIA I FOR THE I PRESENT I *Edited by* I *Vera Dunham and Max Hayward* I With Forewords by I Edward M. Kennedy and Arthur Miller I DOUBLEDAY & COMPANY, INC., GARDEN CITY, NEW YORK 1978

One hundred forty-four single leaves, pp. [i-ix] x-xi [xii-xiii] xiv-xvii [xviii-xx] [1] 2-268. 21.5 x 14.3 cm.   Perfect bound in quarter binding of dark grayish yellow (91) cloth with black paper covered boards.   Down the spine: '*Andrei Voznesensky* I NOSTALGIA FOR THE PRESENT [across the spine] *Doubleday*'.   White wove paper unwatermarked. White endpapers.   All edges trimmed.   Issued in a white paper dust jacket printed in black and very deep purple (220).

Contents: Silent Tingling, by Andrei Voznesensky, translated by Allen Ginsberg, pp. 143, 145.

$10.00. Published Oct. 20, 1978 in an undisclosed number of copies.

a2. *First edition, paperbound, 1978*

Andrei Voznesensky I NOSTALGIA I FOR THE I PRESENT I *Edited by* I *Vera Dunham and Max Hayward* I With Forewords by I Edward M. Kennedy and Arthur Miller I DOUBLEDAY & COMPANY, INC., GARDEN CITY, NEW YORK 1978

One hundred forty-four single leaves, pp. [i-ix] x-xi [xii-xiii] xiv-xvii [xviii-xx] [1] 2-268. 20.4 x 13.5 cm. Perfect bound in stiff white paper wrappers. Covers printed in very deep purple (220) and black. White wove paper unwatermarked. All edges trimmed.

$4.95. Published Oct. 20, 1978 in an undisclosed number of copies.

B136   **WOZU? A QUOI BON? WHY?**   **1978**

WOZU I *Dichter in dürftiger Zeit?* I A Quoi Bon I *des poëtes en un temps de manque?* I WHY I *poets in a hollow age?* I ouvrage collectif I [publisher's device] I *LE SOLEIL NOIR*

[1-20]⁸, pp. [1-6] 7-313 [314-320]. 23.8 x 16.3 cm. Bound in stiff white paper wrappers. Covers printed in brilliant green (140), vivid purplish red (254), brilliant green (140) and black. White wove paper unwatermarked. All edges trimmed.

Contents: [letter in facsimile holograph], p. 94 — The Rune, p. 95.

39,00 F. Published Oct. 20, 1978 in an impression of 10,000 copies.

B137   TALKING POETICS FROM NAROPA INSTITUTE, VOL. 1   1978

ANNALS OF THE I JACK KEROUAC SCHOOL I OF DISEMBODIED POETICS I Talking Poetics from I Naropa Institute I *Edited by Anne Waldman and Marilyn Webb* I *Introduction by Allen Ginsberg* I [publisher's device] I SHAMBHALA I *Boulder & London* I *1978*

One hundred twenty single leaves, pp. [1-2] [i-vii] viii-xiii [xiv] 1-220 [221-224]. 21.5 x 14.0 cm. Perfect bound in stiff white paper wrappers. Covers printed in strong bluish green (160), deep purplish red (256) and black. White wove paper unwatermarked. All edges trimmed.

Contents: Introduction [prose], pp. xi-xiii.

$6.95. Published Dec. 1978 in an impression of 7,500 copies.

B138   **REEFER MADNESS**   **1979**
by Larry Sloman

The I History of I Marijuana in I America I REEFER I MADNESS I Larry Sloman I THE BOBBS-MERRILL COMPANY, INC. I Indianapolis/New York

Two hundred twelve single leaves, pp. [i-ix] x [xi-xii] [1] 2-180 [xiii-xx] 181-404. 23.5 x 15.2 cm. Perfect bound in dark reddish orange (38) textured paper-covered boards. Down the spine in gold: 'Sloman REEFER MADNESS [across the spine] BOBBS- I

MERRILL'. White wove paper unwatermarked. White endpapers. All edges trimmed. Issued in a white paper dust jacket, printed in deep brown (56) and vivid yellow green (115).

Contents: [excerpts from a letter to Charles Joelson], pp. 222-224.

$12.95. Published Jan. 3, 1979 in an unknown quantity.

B139   TALKING POETICS FROM NAROPA INSTITUTE, VOL. 2   1979

ANNALS OF THE | JACK KEROUAC SCHOOL | OF DISEMBODIED POETICS | Talking Poetics from | Naropa Institute | VOLUME TWO | *Edited by Anne Waldman and Marilyn Webb* | *Introduction by Allen Ginsberg* | [publisher's device] | SHAMBHALA | *Boulder & London* | *1979*

One hundred and four single leaves, pp. [i-vii] viii [221-222] 223-428. 21.6 x 14.0 cm. Perfect bound in stiff white paper wrappers. Covers printed in strong purplish red (255), strong orange (50) and black. White wove paper unwatermarked. All edges trimmed.

Contents: AG with Anne Waldman and Michael Brownstein. General Practice of the Jack Kerouac School of Disembodied Poetics at Naropa Institute [prose], pp. 415-420.

$6.95. Published April 1979 in an impression of 7,500 copies.

B140   THE GREAT AMERICAN POETRY BAKE-OFF   1979
by Robert Peters

the | great american | poetry | bake-off | by | robert peters | 1979 | the scarecrow press, inc. [publisher's device] metuchen, n.j., & london

[1-6]^{16} [7]^4 [8-10]^{16}, pp. [1-2] [i-iv] v-xiii [xiv] [1-2] 3-274 [275-280]. 22.1 x 14.2 cm. Bound in grayish yellow (90) cloth covered boards. Across the front cover: '[an illustration of a head with a pile of food arranged as a hat under which is the signature all in very deep red (14)] m. peters'. Across the spine all in very deep red: 'peters | [down the spine] the great american poetry bake-off [across the spine] [publisher's device]'. White wove paper unwatermarked. White endpapers. All edges trimmed.

Contents: [prose response to questionnaire], pp. 9-10.

$13.50. Published Aug. 17, 1979 in an impression of 1,041 copies.

B141   LEAVE THE WORD ALONE   1979
by Edward Marshall

a1. *First edition, signed*

[vertical column of 4 design patterns] Leave the Word Alone | A POEM BY | Edward Marshall | Print by James Kearns | Introduction by Allen Ginsberg | PEQUOD PRESS | NEW YORK | 1979

Single gathering of ten leaves, pp. [1-4] i-iv, 1-9 [10-12]. 21.6 x 13.9 cm. Bound in stiff moderate orange yellow (71) paper wrappers. Covers printed in black. White wove paper unwatermarked. Colophon leaf is white laid paper watermarked 'CERTIFICATE | [ornamental type] Royale | 35% COTTON CONTENT'. All edges trimmed.

Contents: Introduction [prose], pp. i-iv.

$12.50. Published Nov. 1979 in an impression of 100 copies.

a2. *First edition, ordinary copies, 1979*

[vertical column of 4 design patterns] Leave the Word Alone I A POEM BY I Edward Marshall I Print by James Kearns I Introduction by Allen Ginsberg I PEQUOD PRESS I NEW YORK I 1979

Single gathering of ten leaves, pp. [1-4] i-iv, 1-9 [10-12]. 21.9 x 14.5 cm. Stapled in stiff white textured paper wrappers. Covers printed in black. White wove paper unwatermarked. All edges trimmed.

$3.50. Published Nov. 1979 in an impression of 250 copies.

B142 **CLEAN ENERGY VERSE** **1979**

[both left and right title pages are a photograph of a row of demonstrators standing on railroad tracks on which all the following is printed]
[left title page] [in hollow type] CLEAN ENERGY I Poetry from the Tracks I at Rocky Flats
[right title page] [in hollow type] VERSE

Single gathering of twenty leaves, pp. [1-10] 11-38 [39-40]. 21.0 x 13.6 cm. Stapled twice into stiff brownish pink (33) paper wrappers. Covers printed in black. White wove paper unwatermarked. All edges trimmed.

Contents: Nagasaki Day Peace Protests Arrests, p. 11 — Golden Court House, p. 11 — Visiting the Manager's Office, p. 11 — Plutonian Ode, pp. 12-16.

$3.00. Edited by Glenn Dorskind and Albert Santoli and published in Woodstock, NY by Safe Earth Press in 1979 in an unknown quantity.

B143 **THROAT** **1979**

Throat I — *A MEUSE ANTHOLOGY* I WHO'S GOT YOU BY THE THROAT???? I [8 lines] I COVER: Geoff Aldridge I THE EDITORS I [3 photographs cut in half and reassembled incorrectly] I GRANT CALDWELL I GEOFF ALDRIDGE I LES WICKS I [1 line]

Twenty-six single leaves, pp. [i-xviii] [34-1]. 26.0 x 20.6 cm. Bound in stiff white paper wrappers. Covers printed in vivid purplish blue (194), strong red (12) and black. White wove paper unwatermarked. All edges trimmed.

Contents: Manhattan: May Day Midnight, p. [iii] — Plutonian Ode, pp. [21-24].

Published ca. 1979 in an unknown quantity.

Note: The second pagination series are inverted pages, both covers are placed so that they are upside down. A 13.2 x 20.6 cm subscription form is attached before page 1.

B144 **A YEAR OF DISOBEDIENCE** **1979**

A YEAR OF I DISOBEDIENCE I PHOTOGRAPHS BY JOSEPH DANIEL I TEXT BY KEITH POPE I PREFACE BY DANIEL ELLSBERG I POETRY BY ALLEN GINSBERG I Dedicated to the people of Colorado.

Forty-eight single leaves, pp. [1-3] 4-95 [96]. 22.8 x 22.7 cm. Perfect bound in stiff white paper wrappers. Covers printed in black. White wove coated paper unwatermarked. All edges trimmed.

Contents: Visiting the Manager's Office, p. [3] — Blue Sky Cumulus Clouded, p. 63 — Golden Courthouse, p. 71 — Plutonian Ode, pp. 90-93.

Price unknown. Published 1979 in an unknown quantity.

Note: Although the verso of the title page calls for a simultaneous publication of a hardbound issue, none has been seen by the compiler. Published in Boulder, CO by Daniel Publications.

B145   **THE GREAT NAROPA POETRY WARS**   **1980**
                              by Tom Clark

a1. *First edition, hardbound*

Tom Clark I The I Great Naropa I Poetry Wars I [8.8 cm. rule] I *With a copious collection* I *of germane documents* I *assembled by* I *the author* I Cadmus Editions I Santa Barbara I 1980

[1-6]^8, pp. [1-6] 7-87 [88-96]. 22.4 x 14.7 cm. Quarter bound in dark reddish orange (38) cloth with yellowish white (92) paper covered boards. Across the front cover within a single rule frame of deep reddish orange (36) and an inner single rule frame of black: 'THE I GREAT I NAROPA I POETRY I WARS I [ornamental dash in deep reddish orange] I TOM I CLARK'. Down the spine on a 1.0 x 8.5 cm. yellowish white paper label attached to the upper spine: '[in brownish orange (54)] Tom Clark The Great Naropa Poetry Wars'. White wove paper unwatermarked. Brownish orange endpapers. All edges trimmed.

Contents: [letter to W.S. Merwin], pp. 67-70.

$20.00. Published Jan. 21, 1980 in an impression of 100 copies.

Note: Issued with a 20.2 x 12.7 cm. slip laid in containing a prose article by Kenneth Rexroth.

a2. *First edition, paperbound, 1980*

Tom Clark I The I Great Naropa I Poetry Wars I [8.8 cm. rule] I *With a copious collection* I *of germane documents* I *assembled by* I *the author* I Cadmus Editions I Santa Barbara I 1980

Forty-eight single leaves, pp. [1-6] 7-87 [88-96]. 21.5 x 13.7 cm. Perfect bound in stiff pale orange yellow (73) paper wrappers. Covers printed in strong reddish orange (35) and black. White wove paper unwatermarked. All edges trimmed.

$5.00. Published Jan. 21, 1980 in an impression of 3,900 copies.

B146   **SKINNY DYNAMITE**   **1980**
                       by Jack Micheline

SKINNY DYNAMITE I by I Jack Micheline I Second Coming Press

[1-3]^{16}, [i-vi] 1-88 [89-90]. 21.6 x 13.8 cm. Bound in stiff white paper wrappers. Covers printed in full color. White wove paper unwatermarked. All edges trimmed.

Contents: [letter to Stanley Flieschman], pp. 3-5 — [blurb] on back cover.

$4.95. Published July 1980 in an impression of 1,500 copies.

B147   **ALLEN GINSBERG:**   **1980**
          AN ANNOTATED BIBLIOGRAPHY, 1969-1977
                    by Michelle P. Kraus

ALLEN GINSBERG: | An Annotated Bibliography, | 1969-1977 | by | MICHELLE P. KRAUS | The Scarecrow Author Bibliographies, No. 46 | [publisher's device] | THE SCARECROW PRESS, INC. | METUCHEN, N.J., & LONDON | 1980

[1-2]^{16} [3]^8 [4-12]^{16}, pp. [1-2] [i-iv] v-xxi [xxii] xxiii-xxiv [xxv] xxvi-xvii [xvii] xxix-xxx [xxxi-xxxii] 1-328 [329-334]. 22.2 x 14.3 cm. Bound in dark red (16) cloth covered boards. Across the front cover in gold: 'ALLEN GINSBERG: | An Annotated Bibliography, | 1969-1977 | MICHELLE P. KRAUS'. Across the spine in gold: 'KRAUS | [down the spine] ALLEN GINSBERG [across the spine] [publisher's device]'. White wove paper unwatermarked. White endpapers. All edges trimmed.

Contents: Contemplation on Bibliography [prose], pp. ix-xii — Autobiographic Precis [prose], pp. xiii-xvii.

$17.50. Published Aug. 5, 1980 in an impression of 991 copies.

B148   **THE EVENING SUN TURNED CRIMSON**   **1980**
                    by Herbert Huncke

a1. *First edition, paperbound*

THE EVENING SUN TURNED CRIMSON | Herbert E. Huncke | Introduction | by | Allen Ginsberg | Cherry Valley Editions

One hundred twelve single leaves, pp. [1-6] 7-224. 21.3 x 14.0 cm. Perfect bound in stiff white paper wrappers. Cover printed in black, white and vivid red (11). White wove paper unwatermarked. All edges trimmed.

Contents: Introduction [prose], pp. 7-9.

$4.50. Published Aug. 15, 1980 in an impression of 1,000 copies.

Note: Fifty copies of this edition have been numbered 1-50 on the inside of the front cover and signed on the title page by the author and sold for $25.00. An additional 26 copies were lettered A-Z but the details of sale are unknown, possibly hors commerce copies.

a2. *First edition, hardbound, 1981*

THE EVENING SUN TURNED CRIMSON | Herbert E. Huncke | Introduction | by | Allen Ginsberg | Cherry Valley Editions

[1-7]^{16}, pp. [1-6] 7-224. 22.2 x 14.4 cm. Bound in strong red (12) cloth covered boards. Printed in gold down the spine: 'THE EVENING SUN TURNED CRIMSON [bullet] HERBERT HUNCKE [bullet] C.V.Ed.' White wove paper unwatermarked. White endpapers. All edges trimmed. Issued in a white paper dust jacket printed in vivid red (11) and black. On the back cover of the dust jacket is a small white label attached over the incorrect price of $5.00 on which is handwritten the correct price of $15.

Contents: Introduction [revised], pp. 7-10.

$15.00. Published 1981 in an impression of 500 copies.

Note: Some hors commerce copies were released without the additional price label. The verso of the title page incorrectly notes this as the "Second edition".

a3. *First edition, second issue, paperbound, 1981*

THE EVENING SUN TURNED CRIMSON | Herbert E. Huncke | Introduction | by | Allen Ginsberg | Cherry Valley Editions

One hundred and twelve single leaves, pp. [1-6] 7-224. 21.4 x 13.9 cm. Perfect bound in stiff white paper wrappers. Covers printed strong red (12), black and white. White wove paper unwatermarked. All edges trimmed.

Contents: As first edition hardbound.

$5.00. Published 1981 in an impression of 1,000 copies.

Note: This issue also identified as the "Second edition" on the verso of the title page.

B149 **RICHARD EBERHART: A CELEBRATION** **1980**

[left title page] *Richard Eberhart:* | edited by: Sydney Lea | Jay Parini | M. Robin Barone | designed by: Kate Emlen
[right title page] *A Celebration* | [7.9 x 12.0 cm. photograph of Richard Eberhart]

Thirty-eight single leaves, pp. [1-76]. 22.8 x 15.2 cm. Perfect bound in stiff grayish yellowish brown (80) paper wrappers. Covers printed in black. Pale yellow (89) wove paper unwatermarked. All edges trimmed.

Contents: And Always Will [prose], pp. [23-24].

$5.00. Published by Kenyon Hill Publications, Inc. on Oct. 10, 1980 in an impression of 500 copies.

B150 **WONDERS** **1980**

a1. *First edition, special copies*

[three 11.8 cm. rules] | *WONDERS* | *Writings and Drawings for* | *the Child in Us All* | [three 11.8 cm. rules broken in the center by a design of the man in the moon and 3 stars] | Edited By | JONATHAN COTT | & MARY GIMBEL | [three 11.8 cm. rules] | ROLLING STONE PRESS/SUMMIT BOOKS/NEW YORK | [11.8 cm. rule]

[1-20]^{16}, pp. [1-4] 5 [6] 7-15 [16] 17-636 [637-640]. 24.1 x 16.0 cm. Bound in very dark red (17) cloth covered boards. Across the front cover in gold are three 13.8 cm. rules broken in the center by a design of the man in the moon and 3 stars. Down the spine in gold: '[three 2.8 cm. vertical rules] WONDERS [2.6 cm. vertical rule] [across the spine] COTT & | GIMBEL | [three 2.6 cm. rules] | SUMMIT | BOOKS'. White wove paper unwatermarked. Moderate blue (182) endpapers. All edges trimmed. Issued in a glassine dust jacket.

Contents: Magic Spell [prose], pp. 226-227.

Prepared as a free gift for contributors. Published in Nov. 1980 in an impression of 175 copies.

Note: Page 1 has a special colophon which states the publication quantity for this issue, not reprinted in the first edition, ordinary copies.

a2. First edition, ordinary copies, 1980

[three 11.8 cm. rules] | WONDERS | *Writings and Drawings for* | *the Child in Us All* | [three 11.8 cm. rules broken in the center by a design of the man in the moon and 3 stars] | Edited By | JONATHAN COTT | & MARY GIMBEL | [three 11.8 cm. rules] | ROLLING STONE PRESS/SUMMIT BOOKS/NEW YORK | [11.8 cm. rule]

[1-20]^{16}, pp. [1-4] 5 [6] 7-15 [16] 17-636 [637-640]. 24.1 x 16.0 cm. Quarter bound in very dark red (17) cloth with grayish purplish red (262) paper covered boards. Across the front cover in gold are three 13.8 cm. rules broken in the center by a design of the man in the moon and 3 stars. Down the spine in gold: '[three 2.8 cm. vertical rules] WONDERS [2.6 cm. vertical rule] [across the spine] COTT & | GIMBEL | [three 2.6 cm. rules] | SUMMIT | BOOKS'. White wove paper unwatermarked. Moderate blue (182) endpapers. All edges trimmed. Issued in a white paper dust jacket printed in deep red (13), yellowish white (92) and black.

$17.95. Published in Nov. 1980 in an impression of 15,000 copies.

B151   HARPER ANTHOLOGY OF POETRY   1981

a1. First edition, paperbound

THE | HARPER | ANTHOLOGY | OF POETRY | JOHN FREDERICK NIMS | [publisher's device] | HARPER & ROW, PUBLISHERS, New York | Cambridge, Hagerstown, Philadelphia, San Francisco, | London, Mexico City, São Paulo, Sydney

Four hundred thirty-nine single leaves, pp. [i-iv] v-xxxiv [xxxv-xxxvi] 1-842. 23.3 x 15.1 cm. Perfect bound in stiff white paper wrappers. Covers printed in full color. White wove paper unwatermarked. All edges trimmed.

Contents: A Supermarket in California, p. 723 — Cafe in Warsaw, p. 724 — [prose notes to poems are printed here for the first time]

$10.95. Published Jan. 2, 1981 in an impression of 17,000 copies.

Note: The first printing is identified by the code on the bottom of page 842 which is: '80 81 82 83 84 9 8 7 6 5 4 3 2 1'.

a2. First edition, hardbound, 1981

THE | HARPER | ANTHOLOGY | OF POETRY | JOHN FREDERICK NIMS | [publisher's device] | HARPER & ROW, PUBLISHERS, New York | Cambridge, Hagerstown, Philadelphia, San Francisco, | London, Mexico City, São Paulo, Sydney

Four hundred thirty-nine single leaves, pp. [i-iv] v-xxxiv [xxxv-xxxvi] 1-842. 24.2 x 15.6 cm. Perfect bound in strong red (12) cloth covered boards. Down the spine in gold: 'THE HARPER ANTHOLOGY OF POETRY | NIMS [publisher's device across the spine] [down the spine] HARPER & ROW'. Across the back cover: '[in gold] ISBN 0-06-044847-4'. White wove paper unwatermarked. White endpapers. All edges trimmed. Issued in a white paper dust jacket printed in full color.

$15.00. Published Jan. 8, 1981 in an impression of 3,000 copies and reprinted at least 4 times.

Note: The first printing is identified by the code on the bottom of page 842 which is: '80 81 82 83 84 9 8 7 6 5 4 3 2 1'.

B152   JACK KEROUAC: AN ANNOTATED BIBLIOGRAPHY   1981

JACK KEROUAC: I An Annotated Bibliography I Of Secondary Sources, I 1944-1979 I by I ROBERT J. MILEWSKI I with the I assistance of I JOHN Z. GUZLOWSKI I and I LINDA CALENDRILLO I *The Scarecrow Author* I *Bibliographies, No. 52* I [publisher's device] I The Scarecrow Press, Inc. I Metuchen, N.J. & London I 1981

[1-3]^{16}, [4]^8, [5-8]^{16}, pp. [1-4] [i-iv] v-vii [viii] ix-x, 1-225 [226]. 22.1 x 14.2 cm. Bound in pale yellow (89) cloth covered boards, printed all in dark red (16). Across the front cover: 'JACK KEROUAC: I An Annotated Bibliography I Of Secondary Sources, I 1944-1979 I ROBERT J. MILEWSKI'. Across the spine: 'MILEWSKI I [down the spine] JACK KEROUAC [across the spine] [publisher's device]'. White wove paper unwatermarked. White endpapers. All edges trimmed.

Contents: [letter to whom it may concern], pp. 191-194 — [letter to Dennis McNally], pp. 199-203.

$12.50. Published Feb. 9, 1981 in an impression of 1,028 copies.

B153   KNOCK KNOCK   1981

[entire page within single rule frame] [3 rays emanating from the first and last letters of the first two words] KNOCK I KNOCK I A Funny Anthology I By Serious Writers I Edited by I Vicki Hudspith and Madeleine Keller I BENCH PRESS I 141 West 24th Street I New York, New York 10011 I [publisher's device]

One hundred fifteen single leaves, ll. [i] [1-3] 4-112 [113-114]. 27.0 x 21.2 cm. Stapled twice and then perfect bound in stiff white coated paper wrappers. Covers printed in black and white. White wove paper unwatermarked. All edges trimmed.

Contents: For School Kids in New Jersey, l. 51.

$5.95. Published June 1981 in an impression of 250 copies.

B154   THE CAMPAIGN AGAINST THE UNDERGROUND PRESS   1981

PEN AMERICAN CENTER REPORT I [12.6 cm. rule] I THE CAMPAIGN AGAINST I THE UNDERGROUND PRESS I Geoffrey Rips I *Coordinator: Freedom to Write Committee* I Foreword by Allen Ginsberg I [bullet] I with reports by I Aryeh Neier I Todd Gitlin I Angus Mackenzie I Edited by Anne Janowitz and Nancy J. Peters I [publisher's device] I CITY LIGHTS BOOKS I San Francisco

Eighty-eight single leaves, pp. [1-8] 9-176. 25.5 x 17.8 cm. Perfect bound in stiff white paper wrappers. Covers printed in strong blue (178) and vivid red (11). White wove paper unwatermarked. All edges trimmed.

Contents: Smoking Typewriters [prose], pp. 31-35.

$7.95. Published July 1981 in an impression of 5,000 copies.

Note: Cover title "Unamerican Activities".

B155   THE GREAT AMERICAN WRITERS' COOKBOOK   1981

The I Great I American I Writers' I Cookbook I Edited by I Dean Faulkner Wells I *Introduction by Craig Claiborne* I [publisher's device] I YOKNAPATAWPHA PRESS I Oxford, Mississippi

One hundred twenty-four single leaves, pp. [1-2] [i-v] vi-xvii [xviii] [1] 2-221 [222-228]. 22.8 x 15.1 cm. Spiral bound in a deep blue (179) plastic 16-hole spiral, with stiff white paper front and back covers. Covers printed in deep blue, white, vivid greenish yellow (9), vivid red (11) and brilliant blue (177). White wove paper unwatermarked. All edges trimmed.

Contents: Mushrooms & Steak Pork Fish Etc Broiled [prose recipe], p. 65.

$9.95. Published Sept. 1981 in an impression of 20,000 copies.

B156   WALT WHITMAN, THE MEASURE OF HIS SONG   1981

a1. *First edition, hardbound*

[all within single rule border] [ornamental type] WALT WHITMAN I THE MEASURE OF HIS SONG I *Edited by* JIM PERLMAN ED FOLSOM & DAN CAMPION I INTRODUCTION BY ED FOLSOM I [drawing of Whitman within single rule circle] I HOLY COW! PRESS / *Minneapolis* / *1981*

[1-2]^{16} [3]^4 [4-15]^{16}, pp. [i-iv] v-xviii [xix-xx] xxi-liii [liv-lvi] 1-394 [395-400]. 22.8 x 14.8 cm. Bound in deep red (13) cloth covered boards. Down the spine in gold: 'WALT WHITMAN I THE MEASURE OF HIS SONG [2.2 cm. vertical rule] PERLMAN [vertical dash] FOLSOM [vertical dash] CAMPION'. White wove paper unwatermarked. White endpapers. All edges trimmed. Issued in a white paper dust jacket printed in black and deep purplish red.

Contents: A Supermarket in California, pp. 123-124 — Allen Ginsberg on Walt Whitman: Composed on the Tongue [prose], pp. 231-254.

$20.00. Published December 25, 1981 in an impression of 1,000 copies.

Note: "Allen Ginsberg on Walt Whitman: Composed on the Tongue" by AG. AG read and discoursed on consecutive pages of the Modern Library Edition of Leaves of Grass in a sound studio in Boulder, Colorado (1980) for use by Centre Films as a spontaneous sketch of Whitman's works as a sound track for a film.

a2. *First edition, paperbound, 1981*

[all within single rule border] [ornamental type] WALT WHITMAN I THE MEASURE OF HIS SONG I *Edited by* JIM PERLMAN ED FOLSOM & DAN CAMPION I INTRODUCTION BY ED FOLSOM I [drawing of Whitman within single rule circle] I HOLY COW! PRESS / *Minneapolis* / *1981*

Two hundred twenty-eight single leaves, pp. [i-iv] v-xviii [xix-xx] xxi-liii [liv-lvi] 1-394 [395-400]. 22.1 x 14.5 cm. Perfect bound in stiff white paper wrappers. Covers printed in black and deep purplish red (256). White wove paper unwatermarked. All edges trimmed.

$10.00. Published December 31, 1981 in an impression of 2,000 copies.

B157   **THE POSTMODERNS**   **1982**

[hollow type] The Postmoderns: I THE NEW AMERICAN POETRY REVISED I Edited and With a New Preface by I Donald Allen & George F. Butterick I Grove Press, Inc./New York

Two hundred twenty four single leaves, pp. [i-xii] 1-436. 20.9 x 13.9 cm. Perfect bound in stiff white paper wrappers. Covers printed in blue and red. White wove paper unwatermarked. All edges trimmed.

Contents: Howl, pp. 175-182 — Supermarket in California, pp. 182-183 — America, pp. 183-185 — Kaddish [excerpts], pp. 186-189 — Kral Majales, pp. 189-191 — On Neal's Ashes, pp. 191 — [Autobiographic Precis, through 1979, prose] pp. 396-398.

$9.95. Published March 17, 1982 in a quantity undisclosed by the publisher.

B158   **SPARKS OF FIRE**   **1982**

a1.   *First edition, hardbound*

sparks of fire I Blake in a New Age I edited by I James Bogan & Fred Goss I North Atlantic Books I Richmond, California

Two hundred forty single leaves, pp. [i-xviii] [1]-458 [459-462]. 23.5 x 15.4 cm. Bound in moderate blue (182) cloth covered boards. Across the spine all in gold in ornamental type: 'BOGAN I & I GOSS I [down the spine] SPARKS OF FIRE: BLAKE [ornament of 6 solid squares and 1 solid circle]'. White wove paper unwatermarked. Strong blue (178) endpapers. All edges trimmed. Issued without a dust jacket.

Contents: Blake, William. Spring [with musical setting by AG], pp. [14-15] — To Young or Old Listeners [prose], pp. 17-23.

$35.00. Published May 1, 1982 in an impression of 100 copies.

a2.   *First edition, paperbound, 1982*

sparks of fire I Blake in a New Age I edited by I James Bogan & Fred Goss I North Atlantic Books I Richmond, California

Two hundred forty single leaves, pp. [i-xviii] [1]-458 [459-462]. 22.7 x 15.0 cm. Perfect bound in stiff white textured paper wrappers. Covers printed in light greenish yellow (101) and deep blue. White wove paper unwatermarked. All edges trimmed.

$35.00. Published May 1, 1982 in an impression of 2,500 copies.

B159   **LETTERS TO ALLEN GINSBERG 1953-1957**   **1982**
                        by William Burroughs

a1.   *First edition, hardbound*

[hollow type] LETTERS I [hollow type] TO I [hollow type] ALLEN I [hollow type] GINSBERG I [hollow type] 1953-1957 I [hollow type] William Burroughs I [hollow type] Full Court Press I NEW YORK

[1-3]^{16} [4]^8 [5]^{16} [6]^4 [7-8]^{16}, pp. [i-viii] 1-10 [ix-x] 11-203 [204-206]. 21.8 x 13.6 cm. Bound in dark gray (266) cloth covered boards. Printed down the spine in silver: 'LETTERS TO ALLEN GINSBERG William Burroughs Full Court Press [across the

spine] [within the outline of a basketball shirt] 9'. White wove paper unwatermarked. White endpapers. All edges trimmed. Issued in a white paper dust jacket printed in light yellowish brown (76) and deep red (13).

Contents: Recollections of Burroughs Letters [prose], pp. 5-10 — [prose footnotes throughout].

$17.95. Published May 15, 1982 in an impression of ca. 750-1,000 copies.

Note: The publisher has estimated the number of copies printed. Of this issue, 100 copies were numbered 1-100 and signed by the author and sold for $35.00; another 12 copies were lettered A-L and signed by the author as hors commerce copies.

a2. *First edition, paperbound, 1982*

[hollow type] LETTERS | [hollow type] TO | [hollow type] ALLEN | [hollow type] GINSBERG | [hollow type] 1953-1957 | [hollow type] William Burroughs | [hollow type] Full Court Press | NEW YORK

One hundred eight single leaves, pp. [i-viii] 1-10 [ix-x] 11-203 [204-206]. 21.0 x 13.4 cm. Perfect bound in stiff white paper wrappers. Covers printed in light yellowish brown (76) and deep red (13). White wove paper unwatermarked. All edges trimmed.

$7.95. Published May 15, 1982 in an impression of ca. 2,500 copies.

Note: Reprinted in an impression of 4,000 copies. Second printing identified as such on the verso of the title page and the spine and back cover lettering is in red.

B160   **WINDHORSE**   **1982**

W | I | N | D | H | O | R | S | E | Samurai Press | Boulder, Colorado

[1]^{16} [2]^{18} [3]^{16}, pp. [1-100]. 20.3 x 16.4 cm. Bound in stiff white paper wrappers covered with gold. Across the front cover is a design of calligraphy in black. White laid paper watermarked: 'STRATHMORE WRITING | 25% COTTON FIBER USA'. Brownish pink (33) endpapers. All edges trimmed.

Contents: Cats Scratching, p. [50].

Edited by John Castlebury and published in Boulder, CO by Samurai Press in July 1982 in an unknown quantity.

B161   **TAKE OVER**   **1982**
                          by Jeffrey C. Wright

JEFFREY C. WRIGHT: POEMS | [strong reddish orange (35)] TAKE OVER | [publisher's device in the form of the letter 'T'] HE TOOTHPASTE PRESS

Single gathering of fourteen leaves, pp. [1-28]. 21.7 x 12.7 cm. Sewn in stiff brownish pink (33) grained paper wrappers. Across the front cover: 'JEFFREY C. WRIGHT: POEMS | TAKE OVER'. Yellowish white (92) wove paper unwatermarked. All edges trimmed.

Contents: Foreword [prose], p. [7].

$6.00. Published June 1, 1983 in an impression of 500 copies.

B162   **QUIET LIVES**   **1983**
by David Cope

a1. *First edition, hardbound*

Quiet Lives | Poems by | David Cope | Humana Press [bullet] Clifton, New Jersey

[1-3]^{16}, pp. [i-iii] iv-v [vi] vii-viii [1] 2-88. 21.4 x 14.5 cm. Bound in moderate yellowish green (136) cloth covered boards, printed down the spine in gold: 'Cope Quiet Lives HUMANA PRESS'. White laid paper unwatermarked. Brownish pink (33) with darker flecks in the endpapers. All edges trimmed. Issued in a white paper dust jacket, printed in deep reddish brown (41) and strong green (141).

Contents: Foreword [prose], p. v — [prose blurb on inside front dust jacket flap].

$12.95. Published June 30, 1983 in an impression of 750 copies.

Note: The publisher states that the publication date was officially set as June 30, 1983 but that the editions were available from March 14, 1983.

a2. *First edition, paperbound, 1983*

Quiet Lives | Poems by | David Cope | Humana Press [bullet] Clifton, New Jersey

[1-3]^{16}, pp. [i-iii] iv-v [vi] vii-viii [1] 2-88. 20.8 x 13.7 cm. Bound in stiff white paper wrappers. Covers printed in deep reddish brown (41), strong green and white. White laid paper unwatermarked. All edges trimmed.

Contents: As first edition, hardbound, with the blurb on the back cover.

$4.95. Published June 30, 1983 in an impression of 1,398 copies.

a3. *First edition, special copies, 1983*

Quiet Lives | Poems by | David Cope | Humana Press [bullet] Clifton, New Jersey

[1-3]^{16}, pp. [i-iii] iv-v [vi] vii-viii [1] 2-88. 21.5 x 14.3 cm. Bound in dark reddish brown (44) leather covered boards. Down the spine in gold: '[ornament of rule, 8 diamonds, and rule] Quiet Lives DAVID COPE HUMANA [ornament of rule, 8 diamonds, and rule]'. White laid paper unwatermarked. All edges trimmed. Blackish red (21) ribbon attached at the top of the spine. Brownish pink (33) endpapers, with darker flecks.

Contents: As first edition, hardbound, without the blurb.

Hors commerce copies for the author, publisher and AG. Published June 30, 1983 in an impression of 3 copies.

B163   WILLIAM CARLOS WILLIAMS: MAN AND POET   1983

a1. *First edition, hardbound*

[left title page] WILLIAM CARLOS WILLIAMS | [publisher's device] [in 3 lines] NATIONAL | POETRY | FOUNDATION | UNIVERSITY OF MAINE AT ORONO [right title page] Man and Poet | Edited | with an introduction by | Carroll F. Terrell

[1-17]^{16} [18]^{1} [19]^{4} [20-21]^{16}, pp. [1-9] 10 [11-15] 16-29 [30-33] 34-617 [618]. 23.6 x 15.6 cm. Bound in dark green (146) cloth covered boards. Across the front cover in silver: 'WILLIAM CARLOS WILLIAMS: Man and Poet'. Across the spine in silver:

'WILLIAM I CARLOS I WILLIAMS I Man and I Poet I Terrell I [publisher's device]'. White wove paper unwatermarked. White endpapers. All edges trimmed. Issued in a white paper dust jacket.

Contents: Williams in a World of Objects [prose], pp. 33-39.

$28.50. Published Aug. 23, 1983 in an impression of 400 copies.

a2. *First edition, paperbound, 1983*

[left title page] WILLIAM CARLOS WILLIAMS I [publisher's device] NATIONAL I POETRY I FOUNDATION I UNIVERSITY OF MAINE AT ORONO
[right title page] Man and Poet I Edited I with an introduction by I Carroll F. Terrell

Three hundred and nine single leaves, pp. [1-9] 10 [11-15] 16-29 [30-33] 34-617 [618]. 22.7 x 15.0 cm. Perfect bound in stiff white paper wrappers. Covers printed in black and white. White wove paper unwatermarked. All edges trimmed.

$15.95. Published Aug. 23, 1983 in an impression of 1500 copies.

Note: One hundred copies of this issue have been numbered 1-100 and have a 12.7 x 10.7 cm. paper label with ornaments and borders attached to the inside front cover on which the following is printed: *'This book is one I of a special edition of I one hundred numbered I copies printed for I* William Carlos Williams Centennial Conference I *at I The University of Maine at Orono I August 23-26, 1983 I* Number [number in black ink]'. These were priced at $45.00 each.

B164   **ART CONTRE/AGAINST APARTHEID**   **1983**

[all in gray hollow type] ART I contre/against I APARTHEID

[1-9]^8, pp. [1-9] 10-137 [138-144]. 24.0 x 22.0 cm. Bound in stiff white paper wrappers. Covers printed in vivid reddish orange (34), moderate greenish yellow (102) and black. White wove coated paper unwatermarked. All edges trimmed.

Contents: Far Away, p. 36.

Edited by Antonio Saura and published in Paris by Artists of the World Against Apartheid in 1983 in an unknown quantity.

B165   **PEACE OR PERISH**   **1983**

PEACE OR PERISH I A Crisis Anthology I Edited by Herman Berlandt & Neeli Cherkovski I Graphics by Kenneth Patchen I Introduction by Miriam Patchen I POETS FOR PEACE

Sixty-six single leaves, pp. [i-vi] vii-x, 1-121 [122]. 21.2 x 13.6 cm. Perfect bound in stiff white paper wrappers. Covers printed in strong reddish brown (40) and black. White wove paper unwatermarked. All edges trimmed.

Contents: The Little Fish Devours the Big Fish, pp. 54-55.

$5.00. Published Dec. 5, 1983 in an impression of 1,000 copies.

B166   **THE WRITER AND HUMAN RIGHTS**   **1984**

a1. *First edition, hardbound*

THE WRITER I AND I HUMAN RIGHTS I Edited by the Toronto Arts Group I for Human Rights I ANCHOR PRESS/DOUBLEDAY I GARDEN CITY, NEW YORK I 1983

One hundred fifty-six single leaves, pp. [i-v] vi-vii [viii-ix] x-xiii [xiv-xv] xvi-xvii [xviii] [1-3] 4-294. 21.5 x 14.2 cm. Quarter bound in black paper covered boards with dark grayish yellow (91) cloth covered spine. Blind stamped across the front cover is the publisher's device. Down the spine in gold: 'THE WRITER AND HUMAN RIGHTS [across the spine] Anchor Press I Doubleday'. White wove paper unwatermarked. White endpapers. All edges trimmed. Issued in a white paper dust jacket printed in black, strong yellowish green (131), medium gray (265), strong orange yellow (68) and red.

Contents: Outline of Un-American Activities [prose], pp. 90-102.

$17.95. Published Jan. 1984 in an impression of 1,534 copies.

a2. *First edition, paperbound, 1984*

THE WRITER I AND I HUMAN RIGHTS I Edited by the Toronto Arts Group I for Human Rights I ANCHOR PRESS/DOUBLEDAY I GARDEN CITY, NEW YORK I 1983

One hundred fifty-six single leaves, pp. [i-v] vi-vii [viii-ix] x-xiii [xiv-xv] xvi-xvii [xviii] [1-3] 4-294. 20.5 x 13.5 cm. Perfect bound in stiff white paper wrappers. Covers printed all 1n black, strong yellowish green (131), medium gray (265), strong orange yellow (68) and red. White wove paper unwatermarked. All edges trimmed.

$10.95. Published Jan. 1984 in an impression of 1,666 copies.

B167   **FIRST THOUGHT, BEST THOUGHT**   **1984**
                          by Chögyam Trungpa

a1. *First edition, hardbound*

CHÖGYAM TRUNGPA I *First Thought* I *Best Thought* I *108 Poems* I [ornament] I Edited by David I. Rome I Introduction by Allen Ginsberg I [publisher's device] SHAMBHALA I *Boulder & London 1983*

[1-7]^{16}, pp. [i-x] xi-xxv [xxvi-xxviii] 1-195 [196]. 23.4 x 15.0 cm. Quarter bound in grayish greenish yellow (105) cloth with a design in strong yellowish brown (74) and dark blue decorations on boards with a black cloth spine. Down the spine in gold: 'CHÖGYAM TRUNGPA [in 2 lines] FIRST THOUGHT BEST THOUGHT I *108 Poems* [across the spine] [publisher's device] I [down the spine] SHAMBHALA'. White wove paper unwatermarked. Strong yellow (84) wove endpapers. All within an ornamental frame on the recto of the front free endpaper: '*Number __* [number in black ink] *of a limited* I *edition of 400 copies.*' White wove paper unwatermarked. All edges trimmed.

Contents: Introduction [prose], pp. xi-xviii.

$50.00. Published March 1984 in an impression of 400 copies.

Note: An additional 100 copies were signed and Roman numeraled I-C. Produced as above except for the colophon note on the front free endpaper which on these copies reads: '*Number __* [Roman numeral in black ink] *of a signed,* I *limited edition of 100 copies.*'

a2. *First edition, paperbound, 1984*

CHÖGYAM TRUNGPA | *First Thought* | *Best Thought* | *108 Poems* | [ornament] | Edited by David I. Rome | Introduction by Allen Ginsberg | [publisher's device] SHAMBHALA | *Boulder & London 1983*

One hundred twelve single leaves, pp. [i-x] xi-xxv [xxvi-xxviii] 1-195 [196]. 22.8 x 14.5 cm. Perfect bound in stiff white paper wrappers. Covers printed all on vivid violet (205) in brilliant yellow (83) and black. White wove paper unwatermarked. All edges trimmed.

$8.95. Published March 1984 in an impression of 9,000 copies.

B168   **THE DIARIES OF JUDITH MALINA**   **1984**

a1. *First edition, hardbound*

The Diaries of | JUDITH | MALINA | 1947 [bullet] 1957 | GROVE PRESS, INC./NEW YORK

Two hundred fifty-one single leaves, pp. [i-x] 1-485 [486-492]. 24.3 x 16.2 cm. Quarter bound in black paper covered boards with black cloth covered spine. Across the spine all in silver: '[publisher's device] | Grove | Press | [down the spine] THE DIARIES OF | JUDITH MALINA | 1947 [bullet] 1957 [across the spine] GP-867'. White wove paper unwatermarked. Dark orange yellow (72) endpapers. All edges trimmed. Issued in a white paper dust jacket printed in yellow, orange and black.

Contents: The Vision of the Shrouded Stranger of the Night [an early version of a poem, which was published in revised form in *The Gates of Wrath*], pp. 280-281.

$27.50. Published May 8, 1984 in an impression of unknown number of copies.

Note: The publisher stated that the publication date was March 1984 but a review slip was found giving the date of May 8, 1984 which seems more accurate.

a2. *First edition, paperbound, 1984*

The Diaries of | JUDITH | MALINA | 1947 [bullet] 1957 | GROVE PRESS, INC./NEW YORK

Two hundred fifty-one single leaves, pp. [i-x] 1-485 [486-492]. 23.4 x 15.6 cm. Perfect bound in stiff white paper wrappers. Covers printed all on black in yellow and orange. White wove paper unwatermarked. All edges trimmed.

$11.95. Published May 8, 1984 in an unknown number of copies.

B169   **FROM MODERN TO CONTEMPORARY**   **1984**
             by James E. B. Breslin

James E. B. Breslin | From Modern to Contemporary | American Poetry, 1945-1965 | The University of Chicago Press [bullet] Chicago and London

$[1-9]^{16}$, pp. [i-vi] vii [viii] ix-xvi, 1-272. 23.6 x 15.9 cm. Bound in black cloth covered boards. Printed down the spine in silver: 'James E. B. Breslin [1.7 cm. vertical rule] From Modern to Contemporary [1.7 cm. vertical rule] [across the spine] Chicago'. White wove paper unwatermarked. Light gray (264) endpapers. All edges trimmed. Issued in a white paper dust jacket printed in light gray, black and red.

Contents: To Live and Deal with Life as If It Were a Stone, p. 88 — [prose], pp. 89, 91 — I'll Sing of America and Time, p. 96.

$20.00. Published June 1984 in an impression of 3,700 copies.

Note: Reprinted twice.

B170   **ON THE POETRY OF ALLEN GINSBERG**   **1984**

a1. *First edition, hardbound*

On the Poetry of | Allen Ginsberg | Edited by Lewis Hyde | *Ann Arbor* | THE UNIVERSITY OF MICHIGAN PRESS

$[1-15]^{16}$, pp. [1-2] [i-v] vi-ix [x] [1] 2-461 [462-468].   21.0 x 13.7 cm.   Bound in yellowish gray (93) cloth covered boards. Down the spine: 'On the Poetry of Allen Ginsberg *HYDE* [across the spine is the publisher's device]'. White wove endpapers unwatermarked. White endpapers. All edges trimmed. Issued without dust jacket.

Contents: [prose poster], p. 4 — Notes Written on Finally Recording "Howl" [prose liner notes], pp. 80-83 — A Letter to Richard Helms [prose], pp. 252-253 — [excerpt from a letter to Lewis Hyde], p. 320.

$16.50. Published Nov. 14, 1984 in an impression of 503 copies.

Note: Reprinted once in an issue of 207 copies.

a2. *First edition, paperbound, 1984*

On the Poetry of | Allen Ginsberg | Edited by Lewis Hyde | *Ann Arbor* | THE UNIVERSITY OF MICHIGAN PRESS

Two hundred and forty single leaves, pp. [1-2] [i-v] vi-ix [x] [1] 2-461 [462-468].   20.4 x 13.4 cm.   Perfect bound in stiff white paper wrappers. Covers printed in light greenish gray (154) and black. White wove paper unwatermarked. All edges trimmed.

$8.95. Published Nov. 14, 1984 in an impression of 1,024 copies.

Note: Reprinted once in an issue of 811 copies.

B171   **SOMETHING TO SAY**   **1985**

[in facsimile holograph] Something to Say | William Carlos Williams | on Younger Poets | EDITED WITH AN INTRODUCTION | BY JAMES E. B. BRESLIN | The William Carlos Williams Archive Series: Volume I | General Editor: Emily Mitchell Wallace | A NEW DIRECTIONS BOOK

$[1-9]^{16}$, pp. [i-v] vi [vii-viii] 1-280. 21.1 x 14.0 cm. Bound in grayish purplish blue (204) cloth covered boards. Down the spine in gold: '[in facsimile holograph] Something to Say [typeset] William Carlos Williams on Younger Poets NEW DIRECTIONS'. White wove paper unwatermarked. White endpapers. All edges trimmed. Issued in white paper dust jacket printed in black and red.

Contents: [excerpt from letter to William Carlos Williams], pp. 18-19, 30 — [prose], p. 35 — [letter to Louis Ginsberg], pp. 26-27.

$23.95. Published Oct. 10, 1985 in an impression of 3,000 copies.

B172 ANTIPOEMS: NEW AND SELECTED **1985**
by Nicanor Parra

a1. *First edition, hardbound*

NICANOR PARRA | [8.7 cm. rule] | Antipoems: New and Selected | Edited by David
Unger, with an introduction by | Frank MacShane | Translated by Lawrence Ferlinghetti,
Allen Ginsberg, | Edith Grossman, James Laughlin, Patricio Lerzundi, | Thomas Merton,
W. S. Merwin, Paul Pines, George Quasha, | Sandra Reyes, Hardie St. Martin, William
Jay Smith, | Lynne Van Voorhis, Miller Williams, | William Carlos Williams, and the
editor | A New Directions Book

$[1-7]^{16}$, pp. [i-viii] ix-xiv [1] 2-208 [209-210]. 21.1 x 14.1 cm. Bound in vivid
yellowish pink (25) cloth covered boards. Printed down the spine in gold: 'NICANOR
PARRA Antipoems: New and Selected [across the spine] [publisher's device] | NEW |
DIRECTIONS'. White wove paper unwatermarked. White endpapers. All edges
trimmed. Issued in a white paper dust jacket printed in black.

Contents: The Individual's Soliloquy [revised form of poem published in B44], translated
by AG and Lawrence Ferlinghetti, pp. 31-37 — I Move the Meeting Be Adjourned,
translated by AG, p. 45.

$19.95. Published Oct. 24, 1985 in an impression of 1,000 copies.

a2. *First edition, paperbound, 1985*

NICANOR PARRA | [8.7 cm. rule] | Antipoems: New and Selected | Edited by David
Unger, with an introduction by | Frank MacShane | Translated by Lawrence Ferlinghetti,
Allen Ginsberg, | Edith Grossman, James Laughlin, Patricio Lerzundi, | Thomas Merton,
W. S. Merwin, Paul Pines, George Quasha, | Sandra Reyes, Hardie St. Martin, William
Jay Smith, | Lynne Van Voorhis, Miller Williams, | William Carlos Williams, and the
editor | A New Directions Book

One hundred twelve single leaves, pp. [i-viii] ix-xiv [1] 2-208 [209-210]. 20.1 x 13.0 cm.
Perfect bound in stiff white paper wrappers. Covers printed in black and white. White
wove paper unwatermarked. All edges trimmed.

$8.95. Published Oct. 24, 1985 in an impression of 4,000 copies.

B173 KAREL APPEL **1985**

[left title page] [full color photograph of Karel Appel carrying one of his artworks which
divides the following words] [all in facsimile holograph] STReeT ART, CeRAMICS, |
TAPeSTRIeS, MURALS,
[right title page] [in deep reddish orange (36) facsimile holograph] KaReL | [in deep
reddish orange facsimile holograph] aPPeL | [in facsimile holograph] SCULPTURe,
WOOD ReLIeFS, | [in facsimile holograph] VILLA eL SALVADOR | Texts by Pierre
Restany and Allen Ginsberg [bullet] Interview by Frédéric de Towarnicki | H.J.W.
BECHT — AMSTERDAM

$[1-16]^{8}$, pp. [1-6] 7-256. 39.0 x 30.2 cm. Bound in moderate blue (182) cloth covered
boards. Blind stamped across the front cover: '[in facsimile holograph] KaReL | [in
facsimile holograph] aPPeL'. Down the spine in silver: 'Karel Appel BECHT'. White
wove coated paper. Light gray (264) endpapers. All edges trimmed. Issued in a white
paper dust jacket printed in full color all on silver.

Contents: Playing with Appel [prose], pp. 247-248 — I Used to Live in Gay Sad Paris!, p. 249 — Lost in the Blue Mountains, p. 249 — Epigraphs on Appel's Square-nosed Canine, p. 249.

$95.00. Published Nov. 15, 1985 in an undisclosed number of copies.

B174   **NEW YORK TO NOVA SCOTIA**   **1986**
                         by Robert Frank

a1. *First edition, hardbound*

ROBERT I *New York to Nova Scotia* I FRANK I *Editor: Anne Wilkes Tucker* I *Associate Editor: Philip Brookman* I [8.5 cm. rule] I *A New York Graphic Society Book* I *Little, Brown and Company* [bullet] *Boston* I *The Museum of Fine Arts, Houston*

[1-7]^8, pp. [1-3] 4-112. 31.2 x 23.5 cm. Bound in dark blue (183) cloth covered boards. Down the spine in white: '[in 2 lines] Tucker/Brookman I The Museum of Fine Arts, Houston [in 1 line] ROBERT FRANK: *New York to Nova Scotia* [across the spine] NY I GS'. White wove coated paper unwatermarked. Light purplish blue (199) endpapers. All edges trimmed. Issued in white paper dust jacket printed in deep purplish blue (197), vivid red (11), strong orange yellow (68) and black.

Contents: Robert Frank to 1985 - A Man [prose], pp. 74-76 — [photograph (see also D36)] — [prose blurb], on back dust jacket cover.

$35.00. Published Feb. 14, 1986 in an undisclosed number of copies.

a2. *First edition, paperbound, 1986*

ROBERT I *New York to Nova Scotia* I FRANK I *Editor: Anne Wilkes Tucker* I *Associate Editor: Philip Brookman* I [8.5 cm. rule] I *The Museum of Fine Arts, Houston*

[1-7]^8, pp. [1-3] 4-111 [112]. 30.3 x 22.7 cm. Bound in stiff white paper wrappers. Covers printed in deep purplish blue (197), vivid red (11), strong orange yellow (68) and black. White wove coated paper unwatermarked. Dark gray (266) endpapers. All edges trimmed.

Contents: As first edition, hardbound, but without the blurb.

$19.95. Published Feb. 14, 1986 in an impression of 1,500 copies.

B175   **THE GOD LETTERS**   **1986**

[all within a double line frame with rounded single line corners] I The I [10.3 cm. rule] I God I [10.3 cm. rule] I Letters I [10.3 cm. rule] I Edited by I Paul Rifkin I [publisher's device] I WARNER BOOKS I A Warner Communications Company

One hundred twenty single leaves, pp. [i-iv] v [vi] vii-xiii [xiv] xv-xvi [xvii-xviii] 1-217 [218-222]. 20.3 x 13.3 cm. Perfect bound in stiff white paper wrappers. Covers printed all on moderate purplish pink (250) in strong greenish blue (169), black with a full color illustration. White wove paper unwatermarked. All edges trimmed.

Contents: [letter in response to a questionnaire], p. 93.

$5.95. Published April 1, 1986 in an impression of 21,000 copies.

B176   **SELECTED POEMS 1958-1984**   **1986**
                              by John Wieners

a1. *First edition, "limited" copies*

[strong yellowish brown (74) square] ∣ JOHN WIENERS ∣ [9.5 cm. deep red (13) rule] ∣ SELECTED POEMS ∣ 1958-1984 ∣ [in 2 lines] Edited by Raymond Foye ∣ Foreword by Allen Ginsberg [in 1 line] [strong yellowish brown square] ∣ [in 1 line] [strong yellowish brown square] [in 2 lines] BLACK SPARROW PRESS ∣ Santa Barbara — 1986

[1]^2 [2]^1 [3-12]^{16}, pp. [i-ii] [1-14] 15-317 [318-324]. 23.6 x 16.1 cm. Quarter bound in strong orange yellow (68) cloth with white paper covered boards. Across the front cover: '[strong yellowish brown (74) square] ∣ [in deep red (13)] JOHN WIENERS ∣ [design of 2 photographs in black and light pink (4) with strong yellowish brown colors connecting this with the bottom photograph] ∣ [in deep red] SELECTED POEMS ∣ [design of 1 photograph of the poet and a square containing 6 repetitions of the dates 1958-1984 in black on a light pink square except for the second 58 and the third 84 which are in strong yellowish brown] ∣ [5.7 cm. deep red rule]'. Down the spine on a 1.4 x 17.3 cm. white paper label: 'JOHN WIENERS [strong yellowish brown square] SELECTED POEMS'. White wove paper unwatermarked. Strong yellow (84) endpapers. All edges trimmed. Issued in a clear plastic dust jacket.

Contents: Foreword [prose], pp. 15-18.

$30.00. Published April 25, 1986 in an impression of 200 copies.

a2. *First edition, "deluxe limited" copies, 1986*

[strong yellowish brown (74) square] ∣ JOHN WIENERS ∣ [9.5 cm. deep red (13) rule] ∣ SELECTED POEMS ∣ 1958-1984 ∣ [in 2 lines] Edited by Raymond Foye ∣ Foreword by Allen Ginsberg [in 1 line] [strong yellowish brown square] ∣ [in 1 line] [strong yellowish brown square] [in 2 lines] BLACK SPARROW PRESS ∣ Santa Barbara — 1986

[1]^2 [2]^1 [3-12]^{16}, pp. [i-ii] [1-14] 15-317 [318-324]. 23.6 x 16.1 cm. Quarter bound in multi-colored (red, yellow and brown) cloth with white paper covered boards. Across the front cover: '[strong yellowish brown (74) square] ∣ [in deep red (13)] JOHN WIENERS ∣ [design of 2 photographs in black and light pink (4) with strong yellowish brown colors connecting this with the bottom photograph] ∣ [in deep red] SELECTED POEMS ∣ [design of 1 photograph of the poet and a square containing 6 repetitions of the dates 1958-1984 in black on a light pink square except for the second 58 and the third 84 which are in strong yellowish brown] ∣ [5.7 cm. deep red rule]'. Down the spine on a 1.4 x 17.3 cm. white paper label: 'JOHN WIENERS [strong yellowish brown square] SELECTED POEMS'. White wove paper unwatermarked. Strong yellow (84) endpapers. All edges trimmed. Issued in a clear plastic dust jacket.

$50.00. Published April 25, 1986 in an impression of 34 copies; 26 of which are lettered A-Z and 8 of which are hors commerce and labeled for author, editor, publisher and AG.

a3. *First edition, "trade" issue, 1986*

[strong yellowish brown (74) square] ∣ JOHN WIENERS ∣ [9.5 cm. deep red (13) rule] ∣ SELECTED POEMS ∣ 1958-1984 ∣ [in 2 lines] Edited by Raymond Foye ∣ Foreword by Allen Ginsberg [in 1 line] [strong yellowish brown square] ∣ [in 1 line] [strong yellowish brown square] [in 2 lines] BLACK SPARROW PRESS ∣ Santa Barbara — 1986

[1]^2 [2-11]^{16}, pp. [1-14] 15-317 [318-324]. 23.6 x 16.1 cm. Quarter bound in black cloth with white paper covered boards. Across the front cover: '[strong yellowish brown (74) square] ∣ [in deep red (13)] JOHN WIENERS ∣ [design of 2 photographs in black and light pink (4) with strong yellowish brown colors connecting this with the bottom

photograph] | [in deep red] SELECTED POEMS | [design of 1 photograph of the poet and a square containing 6 repetitions of the dates 1958-1984 in black on a light pink square except for the second 58 and the third 84 which are in strong yellowish brown] | [5.7 cm. deep red rule]'. Down the spine on a 1.4 x 17.3 cm. white paper label: 'JOHN WIENERS [strong yellowish brown square] SELECTED POEMS'. White wove paper unwatermarked. Strong yellow (84) endpapers. All edges trimmed. Issued in a clear plastic dust jacket.

$20.00. Published April 25, 1986 in an impression of 300 copies.

a4. *First edition, paperbound, 1986*

[strong yellowish brown (74) square] | JOHN WIENERS | [9.5 cm. deep red (13) rule] | SELECTED POEMS | 1958-1984 | [in 2 lines] Edited by Raymond Foye | Foreword by Allen Ginsberg [in 1 line] [strong yellowish brown square] | [left in 1 line] [strong yellowish brown square] [in 2 lines] BLACK SPARROW PRESS | Santa Barbara — 1986

One hundred sixty-three single leaves, pp. [i-ii] [1-14] 15-317 [318-324]. 22.8 x 14.9 cm. Perfect bound in stiff white paper wrappers. Covers printed in dark orange yellow (72), deep red (13), light pink (4) and black. White wove paper unwatermarked. The first & last leaves are strong yellow (84) wove paper unwatermarked. All edges trimmed.

$12.50. Published April 25, 1985 in an impression of 3,070 copies.

B177 **DOUBLY GIFTED** **1986**

a1. *First edition, hardbound*

DOUBLY GIFTED | *The* AUTHOR *as* VISUAL ARTIST | *Kathleen G. Hjerter* *Foreword by John Updike* | [illustration by Henry Miller] | HARRY N. ABRAMS, INC. [vertical rule] *Publishers* [vertical rule] *New York*

[1-10]^8 , pp. [1-6] 7-159 [160]. 29.8 x 23.7 cm. Bound in white cloth covered boards. Down the spine in gold: 'DOUBLY GIFTED: *The* AUTHOR *as* VISUAL ARTIST *Kathleen G. Hjerter* [vertical rule] *Abrams* '. White coated paper unwatermarked. White endpapers printed with an illustration by William Faulkner in grayish purplish red (262). All edges trimmed. White paper dust jacket printed in full color.

Contents: [drawing of three fish which share a common head], p. 142 — [drawing of 'The Hari Krishna Mantram'], p. 143.

$29.95. Published May 5, 1986 in an undisclosed number of copies.

a2. *First edition, paperbound, 1986*

DOUBLY GIFTED | *The* AUTHOR *as* VISUAL ARTIST | *Kathleen G. Hjerter* *Foreword by John Updike* | [illustration by Henry Miller] | HARRY N. ABRAMS, INC. [vertical rule] *Publishers* [vertical rule] *New York*

Eighty single leaves, pp. [1-6] 7-159 [160]. 29.2 x 22.8 cm. Perfect bound in stiff white paper wrappers. Covers printed in full color. White coated paper unwatermarked. All edges trimmed.

$19.95. Published May 5, 1986 in an undisclosed number of copies.

B178   **THE POET EXPOSED**   **1986**

a1. *First edition, hardbound*

[9.3 cm. rule] l THE l [9.3 cm. rule] l POET l [9.3 cm. rule] l EXPOSED l [9.3 cm. rule] l Portraits by Christopher Felver l Prologue by Gary Snyder l Foreword by Robert Creeley l Afterword by William E. Parker l [publisher's device] l ALFRED VAN DER MARCK EDITIONS [bullet] NEW YORK

[1-9]^8, pp. [1-6] 7-144. 31.1 x 23.5 cm. Bound in dark gray (266) cloth covered boards. Printed across the front cover in silver: '[11.6 cm. rule] l THE l [11.6 cm. rule] l POET l [11.6 cm. rule] l EXPOSED l [11.6 cm. rule]'. Down the spine in silver: 'THE POET EXPOSED [across the spine] [publisher's device]'. White wove coated paper unwatermarked. White endpapers. All edges trimmed. Issued in a white paper dust jacket printed in black and white.

Contents: R.M.D.C. [facsimile of holograph manuscript], pp. 44-45.

$26.95. Published June 1986 in an impression of 2,500 copies.

a2. *First edition, paperbound, 1986*

[9.3 cm. rule] l THE l [9.3 cm. rule] l POET l [9.3 cm. rule] l EXPOSED l [9.3 cm. rule] l Portraits by Christopher Felver l Prologue by Gary Snyder l Foreword by Robert Creeley l Afterword by William E. Parker l [publisher's device] l ALFRED VAN DER MARCK EDITIONS [bullet] NEW YORK

[1-9]^8, pp. [1-6] 7-144. 30.4 x 23.1 cm. Bound in stiff white paper wrappers. Covers printed in black and white. White wove paper unwatermarked. All edges trimmed.

$16.95. Published June 1986 in an impression of 5,000 copies.

B179   **BEST MINDS**   **1986**

a1. *First edition, signed copies*

BEST MINDS l A TRIBUTE TO l ALLEN GINSBERG l EDITED BY BILL MORGAN l & BOB ROSENTHAL l LOSPECCHIO PRESS l NEW YORK l 1986

[1-19]^8 [20]^4 [21]^8, pp. [i-iv] v [vi] vii-ix [x] xi [xii] xiii-xiv [xv-xvi] 1-311 [312]. 26.2 x 18.3 cm. Bound in black cloth covered boards. Across the front cover in gold: 'BEST MINDS l [10.3 cm. rule] l [a design of three fish which share a common head]'. Down the spine in gold: '[vertical rule] [in 2 lines] MORGAN AND l ROSENTHAL [in 1 line] BEST MINDS *A Tribute to Allen Ginsberg* [across the spine] Lospecchio l [rule]'. White wove paper unwatermarked. Strong red (12) endpapers. All edges trimmed.

Contents: [prose], p. xv — [drawing of Doctor Sax's grocery store man], p. 149 — If Money Made The Mind More Sane [poem], p. 172 — Pull My Daisy [poem], p. 173 — The Giant Phantom [poem], p. 173 — [letter to Elbert Lenrow], p. 173 — Black Meat Borne Upon a Bone, [poem & drawing], p. 174 — [letter to Ron Padgett], p. 213 — Morning Waking under Orange Sheets [poem & drawing], p. 295 — [drawing of three fish which share a common head], front cover.

$75.00 numbered edition and $125.00 lettered edition. Published June 3, 1986 in an impression of 226 copies; 200 of which are numbered 1-200; and 26 are lettered A-Z and contain a special signed self-portrait photograph of AG tipped in on page [312] see also D39.

a2. *First edition, unsigned copies, 1986*

BEST MINDS I A TRIBUTE TO I ALLEN GINSBERG I EDITED BY BILL MORGAN I & BOB ROSENTHAL I LOSPECCHIO PRESS I NEW YORK I 1986

[1-19]^8 [20]^4 [21]^8, pp. [i-iv] v [vi] vii-ix [x] xi [xii] xiii-xiv [xv-xvi] 1-311 [312]. 26.2 x 18.1 cm. Bound in deep red (13) cloth covered boards. Across the front cover in gold: 'BEST MINDS I [10.3 cm. rule] I [a design of three fish which share a common head]'. Down the spine in gold: '[vertical rule] [in 2 lines] MORGAN AND I ROSENTHAL [in 1 line] BEST MINDS *A Tribute to Allen Ginsberg* [across the spine] Lospecchio I [rule]'. White wove paper unwatermarked. White endpapers. All edges trimmed.

$25.00. Published June 3, 1986 in an impression of 505 copies, 250 of which are numbered and for sale, 250 of which are hors commerce for the contributors and 5 of which are review copies with slips laid in the front.

B180   **KANREKI**   **1986**

KANREKI I A TRIBUTE TO I ALLEN GINSBERG I pt. 2 I EDITED BY BILL MORGAN I LOSPECCHIO PRESS I NEW YORK I 1986

Forty-eight single leaves, pp. [i-vi] 1-90. 26.1 x 18.1 cm. Perfect bound in moderate blue (182) cloth covered boards. Across the front cover in gold: 'KANREKI I [7.7 cm. rule] I [drawing of three fish which share a common head] '. Down the spine in gold: '[vertical rule] MORGAN KANREKI *A Tribute to Allen Ginsberg* Lospecchio [vertical rule]'. White wove paper unwatermarked. White endpapers. All edges trimmed.

Contents: [drawing of three fish which share a common head], on front cover — [excerpt from letter to David Gascoyne], p. 48.

$30.00; lettered edition at $55.00. Published June 3, 1986 in an impression of 176 copies; 150 of which are numbered 1-150 and signed by the editor; 26 of which are lettered A-Z and signed by the editor and AG.

B181   **CHRISTIAN BOURGOIS 1966-1986**   **1986**

christian bourgois I [5.1 cm. rule] I 1966-1986

[1-11]^{16} [12]^8, pp. [1-4] 5 [6] 7-13 [14-16] 17-26 [i-ii] 27-36 [iii-iv] 37-46 [v-vi] 47-56 [vii-viii] 57-76 [77-78] 79-80 [1x-xii] 81-86 [xiii-xiv] 87-92 [xv-xvi] 93-98 [xvii-xviii] 99-106 [xix-xx] 107-112 [xxi-xxiv] 113-118 [xxv-xxvi] 119-128 [xxvii-xxviii] 129-132 [xxix-xxx] 133-140 [xxxi-xxxii] 141-146 [xxxiii-xxxiv] 147-152 [xxxv-xxxvi] 153-156 [xxxvii-xxxviii] 157-160 [xxxix-xl] 161-166 [xli-xlii] 167-172 [xliii-xlvi] 173-180 [xlvii-l] 181-192 [li-lii] 193-198 [liii-lvi] 199-207 [208-210] 211-230 [lvii-lviii] 231-238 [239-240] [lix-lx] 241-244 [lxi-lxii] 245-248 [lxiii-lxiv] 249-254 [lxv-lxvi] 255-260 [lxvii-lxviii] 261-262 [lxix-lxx] 263-266 [lxxi-lxxii] 267-270 [271-272] 273-295 [296]. 22.5 x 14.0 cm. Bound in stiff white paper wrappers. Covers printed in vivid red (11) and black. White wove paper unwatermarked. All edges trimmed.

Contents: [letter to Christian Bourgois], pp. 252-253.

Hors commerce. Published in Paris by Christian Bourgois in Sept. 1986 in an impression of 5,000 copies.

B182   **EZRU PAUNDO KENKYU**   **1986**

[title page in medium gray (265) and deep purplish red (256) entirely in Japanese characters]

One hundred fifty-four single leaves, pp. [1-4] [i] ii-iii [iv-vi] [1-3] 4-297 [298]. 15.4 x 21.5 cm. Perfect bound in light gray (264) paper covered boards. Covers printed in black in Japanese characters on spine. White wove paper unwatermarked except for the first two leaves. The first leaf is a thicker textured paper and the second leaf is a glossy coated paper. Yellowish white (92) endpapers. All edges trimmed. Issued in a white paper dust jacket, printed in black, red and gray.

Contents: [excerpt from notebook], pp. 273-278.

¥3,200. Published Oct. 10, 1986 in a quantity undisclosed by the publisher.

Note: [transliteration] Fukuda, Rikutaro and Yasukawa, Ryu (eds.). *Ezru Paundo Kenkyu.* Kyoto, Japan: Yamaguchi, 1986.

B183   **WRITERS OUTSIDE THE MARGIN**   **1986**

a1. *First edition, paperbound*

[21.4 cm. vertical rule that passes through the first letter of the second line of print] WRITERS OUTSIDE THE | MARGIN. | EDITED BY | JEFFREY H. WEINBERG | WATER ROW PRESS | SUDBURY | 1986

Fifty-nine single leaves, pp. [1-8] 9-116 [117-118]. 22.3 x 14.9 cm. Perfect bound in stiff white paper wrappers. Covers printed in black and white. White wove paper unwatermarked. All edges trimmed.

Contents: [letter to Vojo Sindolic], pp. 103-104.

$9.95. Published Nov. 1986 in an impression of 500 copies.

Note: Reprinted as follows: 2nd printing, March 1988, 250 copies; 3rd printing, February 1989, 150 copies; 4th printing, November 1992, 100 copies. Second printing identified as such by gray wrappers and acknowledgments page with Hunya Harland's first name crossed out and changed to nickname "Cisco". Third printing is identical to the second printing. Fourth printing identified by the slightly larger size of 23.0 x 15.2 cm. and pale orange yellow (73) wrappers. It also has the additional statement "THANKS AND A TIP OF THE BERET TO UNCLE ROD | R.I.P. THE MONTGOMERY BOYS" on page 5 of the acknowledgments making the total line count 27 for that page.

a2. *First edition, hardcover, 1986*

[21.4 cm. vertical rule that passes through the first letter of the second line of print] WRITERS OUTSIDE THE | MARGIN. | EDITED BY | JEFFREY H. WEINBERG | WATER ROW PRESS | SUDBURY | 1986

Fifty-nine single leaves, pp. [1-8] 9-116 [117-118]. 22.3 x 14.9 cm. Quarter bound in Cordovan leather printed in gold on the spine with marbleized boards. White wove paper unwatermarked. Tissue paper flyleaf. All edges trimmed.

Hors commerce for publisher's use. Published Nov. 1986 in an impression of 12 copies.

B184   **SELECTED POEMS**   **1986**
                           by Harry Fainlight

HARRY FAINLIGHT | SELECTED POEMS | Introduction by | *Ruth Fainlight* | a
memoir by | Allen Ginsberg | and | a poem by | Ted Hughes | TURRET [publisher's
device] BOOKS

[A]^{16} [B]^{10} [C]^{16}, pp. [i-iv] v [vi] 1-78. 25.1 x 17.5 cm. Bound in deep blue (179)
leather printed down the spine in black: 'SELECTED POEMS [facsimile autograph] Harry
Fainlight'. White wove paper unwatermarked. White endpapers. All edges trimmed.
Issued in a white paper dust jacket printed in black.

Contents: Harry Fainlight: In Memoriam [prose], p. 7.

£12.50. Published 1986 in an impression of 1,000 copies.

B185   **TEACHERS MAKE A DIFFERENCE**   **1987**

a1. *First edition*

[design of an apple with a heart shape cut into it] | TEACHERS MAKE | [rule with letter
'A' breaking it] | *Difference* | [7.9 cm. rule] | Compiled by | Sue Sheridan

Thirty single leaves, pp. [1-4] i-iv, 1-51 [52]. 21.6 x 14.0 cm. Spiral bound in black
plastic spiral on the left edge with stiff white paper covers. Covers printed in black and red.
White wove paper unwatermarked. All edges trimmed.

Contents: A Visionary Afternoon in High School [prose], p. 25.

$1.50. Published in Houston, TX by the Harris County Department of Education in Jan.
1987 in an impression of 2,000 copies.

b1. *Second edition, expanded, 1991*

[all within a double rule frame with ornamental corners] TEACHERS | MAKE A | [on a
sloping base line] Difference | [ornament] | Compiled by | Sue Sheridan

Eighty-two single leaves, pp. [1-6] i-vi, 1-151 [152]. 21.6 x 14.5 cm. Spiral bound in
black plastic spiral on the left edge with stiff white paper covers. Covers printed in blue
and purple. White wove paper unwatermarked. All edges trimmed.

$2.50. Published in Houston, TX by the Harris County Department of Education in May
1991 in an impression of 500 copies.

B186   **RIDING THE BIG EARTH**   **1987**
                           by Joseph Richey

RIDING THE BIG EARTH: | Poems 1980-86 | by | Joseph Richey | [publisher's
device] | THE NATIONAL POETRY FOUNDATION | University of Maine 1986

Single gathering of thirty-two leaves, pp. [1-16] 17-48 [49-56] 57-63 [64]. 22.8 x 17.6
cm. Stapled twice in stiff white paper wrappers. Covers printed all in white on black
background. White wove paper unwatermarked. All edges trimmed. *Note:* The fifth
through eighth and twenty-fifth through twenty-eighth leaves are not 22.8 cm. tall but 21.2
cm. tall and so the top edges may be found uncut on these leaves.

Contents: Introduction [prose], p. [9].

$5.95. Published Jan. 6, 1987 in an unknown number of copies.

Note: Although called for on the verso of the title page this book never appeared in cloth covers; the publisher also states that the publication date was Jan. 27 but a review slip has been found giving the date as Jan. 6.

B187   **THE BEAT VISION**   **1987**

a1. *First edition, hardbound*

[in white on black rectangular stripe] THE | [in white on black rectangular stripe] BEAT | [in white on black rectangular stripe] VISION | A PRIMARY SOURCEBOOK | *EDITED BY ARTHUR AND KIT KNIGHT* | [publisher's device] PARAGON HOUSE PUBLISHERS | NEW YORK | [10.6 cm. rule]

One hundred fifty-six single leaves, pp. [i-ix] x-xiii [xiv] [1] 2-292 [293-298]. 23.6 x 15.3 cm. Perfect bound in black cloth covered boards. Down the spine in gold: 'THE BEAT VISION [bullet] Arthur & Kit Knight [across the spine] [publisher's device] | PARAGON | HOUSE'. White wove paper unwatermarked. Pale yellowish pink (31) endpapers with darker threads. All edges trimmed. Issued in white paper dust jacket.

Contents: A Version of the Apocalypse [prose], pp. 185-191.

$18.95. Published Feb. 1, 1987 in an impression of 500 copies.

a2. *First edition, paperbound, 1987*

[in white on black rectangular stripe] THE | [in white on black rectangular stripe] BEAT | [in white on black rectangular stripe] VISION | A PRIMARY SOURCEBOOK | *EDITED BY ARTHUR AND KIT KNIGHT* | [publisher's device] PARAGON HOUSE PUBLISHERS | NEW YORK | [10.6 cm. rule]

One hundred fifty-six single leaves, pp. [i-ix] x-xiii [xiv] [1] 2-292 [293-298]. 22.9 x 15.0 cm. Perfect bound in stiff white paper wrappers. Covers printed in brilliant bluish green (159) and black. White wove paper unwatermarked. All edges trimmed.

$8.95. Published Feb. 1, 1987 in an impression of 2,000 copies.

Note: Reprinted once in 1988 in an impression of 2,000 copies.

B188   **INDIA**   **1987**
by Francesco Clemente

FRANCESCO | CLEMENTE | INDIA | TWELVETREES PRESS

Fifty-six single leaves, pp. [1-112]. 31.2 x 26.0 cm. Bound in deep reddish orange (36) cloth covered boards. Across the front cover is a design in silver and black of a serpent with Indian writing and designs. Down the spine in silver: 'FRANCESCO CLEMENTE'. White wove coated paper unwatermarked. Full color endpapers with reproductions of paintings. All edges trimmed. Issued with a white paper dust jacket printed in full color.

Contents: Maturity, p. 57.

$40.00. Published Sept. or Oct. 1987 in an impression of 3,000 copies.

Note: Also available in a signed edition of 50 numbered copies in a slip-in case, otherwise identical to the first edition.

B189   **AQUARIUS REVISITED**   **1987**
by Peter O. Whitmer

a1. *First edition, hardbound*

[angle pointing up] I AQUARIUS I REVISITED I [angle pointing down] I SEVEN
WHO CREATED THE SIXTIES I COUNTERCULTURE THAT CHANGED AMERICA
I William Burroughs Allen Ginsberg Ken Kesey I Timothy Leary Norman Mailer Tom
Robbins I Hunter S. Thompson I PETER O. WHITMER I WITH BRUCE
VANWYNGARDEN I MACMILLAN PUBLISHING COMPANY I New York

[1-2]^{16} [3]^4 [4-8]^{16} [9]^8 [10]^{16}, pp. [i-vi] vii-viii [ix-xii] 1-52 [xiii-xxviii] 53-260. 24.2
x 16.0 cm. Quarter bound in stiff light grayish yellowish brown (179) spotted paper
covered boards with light blue (181) cloth covered spine on which is printed all the
following. Down the spine in white: '[in 2 lines] AQUARIUS REVISITED I PETER O.
WHITMER WITH BRUCE VANWYNGARDEN [in 1 line] MACMILLAN'. Across the
back cover on the paper covered boards in light blue: 'ISBN 0-02-627670-4'. White wove
paper unwatermarked. White endpapers. All edges trimmed. Issued in a white paper dust
jacket printed in blue, yellow, orange and black.

Contents: [prose], p. 54 — [excerpt from letter to Peter O. Whitmer], p. 137 — [prose
note], p. 155 — To the Angels, p. 181.

$19.95. Published Sept. 15, 1987 in an undisclosed number of copies.

a2. *First edition, paperbound, 1991*

[angle pointing up] I AQUARIUS I REVISITED I [angle pointing down] I SEVEN
WHO CREATED THE SIXTIES I COUNTERCULTURE THAT CHANGED AMERICA
I William Burroughs Allen Ginsberg Ken Kesey I Timothy Leary Norman Mailer Tom
Robbins I Hunter S. Thompson I PETER O. WHITMER I WITH BRUCE
VANWYNGARDEN I CITADEL UN [publisher's device] DERGROUND I CITADEL
PRESS I *Published by Carol Publishing Group* I New York

One hundred and forty-one single leaves, pp. [1-2] [i-ii] iii-viii [ix-x] 1-132 [xi-xviii] 133-
260 [261-262]. 20.9 x 13.8 cm. Perfect bound in stiff white paper wrappers. Covers
printed in strong greenish blue (169), strong yellowish green (131), strong reddish purple
(237), vivid orange (48), vivid purplish red (254) and black. White wove paper
unwatermarked, the last leaf is stiff white card stock. All edges trimmed.

$10.95. Published April 15, 1991 in an impression of 4,100 copies.

B190   **FOR NELSON MANDELA**   **1987**

[all within a frame consisting of a rule and a line of triangular shapes at top and bottom and
2 vertical rules on each side] I [solid triangle] F [solid triangle] O [solid triangle] R [solid
triangle] I NELSON I MANDELA I [ornament of bar over two solid triangles] I
EDITED BY I JACQUES DERRIDA I MUSTAPHA TLILI I [publisher's device] I
SEAVER BOOKS I Henry Holt and Company [solid triangle] New York

[1-8]^{16} [9]^8, pp. [i-vi] vii-xv [xvi] [1-2] 3-256. 21.6 x 14.6 cm. Quarter bound in light
orange yellow (70) paper covered boards with pale yellow (89) cloth covered spine. Down
the spine in maroon: 'FOR I NELSON MANDELA [across the spine] [publisher's device]
I SEAVER I BOOKS I [solid triangle] I Henry I Holt'. White wove paper
unwatermarked. White endpapers. All edges trimmed. Issued in a white paper dust jacket
printed in very dark purplish red (260), pale green (149) and light orange yellow (70).

Contents: Far Away, p. 55 — "On the Conduct of the World Seeking Beauty Against Government", pp. 56-57.

$17.95. Published Oct. 11, 1987 in an undisclosed number of copies.

B191 **FLASHING ON THE SIXTIES** **1987**
by Lisa Law

Flashing on the Sixties | Photographs by Lisa Law | CHRONICLE BOOKS [bullet] SAN FRANCISCO

Seventy-two single leaves, pp. [1-4] 5-143 [144]. 24.4 x 25.5 cm. Perfect bound in stiff white paper wrappers with 10.9 cm. front and back flaps folded inside. Covers printed in full color. White wove coated paper unwatermarked. All edges trimmed.

Contents: [prose], p. 54.

$14.95. Published Oct. 15, 1987 in an impression of 20,000 copies.

Note: Reprinted at least once. Second printing identified as such on the verso of the title page.

B192 **BY SURPRISE** **1987**
by Henri Michaux

BY SURPRISE | HENRI MICHAUX | Translated by | Randolph Hough | HANUMAN BOOKS | Madras & New York | 1987

1^2, 1[sic]-2^8 [3-4]^8 5-6^8, 7^6, pp. [i-v] vi-xxvi [27-29] 30-110 [111-112]. 10.5 x 7.0 cm. Bound in stiff moderate yellow (87) paper wrappers printed in gold. Across the front cover: 'BY SURPRISE | *Henri Michaux*'. White wove paper unwatermarked. White endpapers. All edges trimmed. Issued in a white paper dust jacket printed in black, gold and pink.

Contents: Introduction [prose], pp. [v]-xxvi.

$4.00. Published Dec. 30, 1987 in an impression of 1,500 copies.

Note: Reprinted at least once. The second printing is identified by stiff white paper wrappers, otherwise identical to the first.

B193   AN ANNOTATED BIBLIOGRAPHY OF TIMOTHY LEARY   1988
by Michael Horowitz, Karen Walls and Billy Smith

An Annotated Bibliography of | TIMOTHY LEARY | *by* | Michael Horowitz | Karen Walls | *and* | Billy Smith | Foreword by Allen Ginsberg | Preface by Timothy Leary | Introduction by Frank Barron, Ph.D., Sc.D. | *Professor of Psychology,* | *University of California, Santa Cruz* | Archon Books | 1988

[1-8]^{16} [9]^{12} [10]^{16}, pp. [i-vi] 1-305 [306]. 23.5 x 16.1 cm. Bound in dark red (16) cloth covered boards. Across the front cover all in gold and within single rule frame: '*An Annotated Bibliography of* | TIMOTHY LEARY | Michael Horowitz | Karen Walls | *and* | Billy Smith'. Across the spine in gold: 'Horowitz | Walls | Smith | [down the spine] *An Annotated Bibliography of* | TIMOTHY LEARY [across the spine] Archon'. White wove paper unwatermarked. All edges trimmed. White endpapers.

Contents: Foreword [prose], pp. 1-4.

$37.50. Published May 1, 1988 in an impression of ca. 700 copies.

B194   **REPRESENTATIVE MEN**   **1988**
                              by John Clellon Holmes

a1. *First edition, hardbound*

Representative Men | The Biographical Essays | *Selected Essays by John Clellon Holmes*
| *Volume II* | The University of Arkansas Press | Fayetteville 1988 London

[1-2]^{16} [3]^{8} [4-10]^{16}, pp. [i-xii] xiii-xvii [xviii-xx] [1-2] 3-277 [278-284].   22.3 x 14.4
cm. Bound in grayish yellowish brown (80) cloth covered boards printed down the spine
in gold: 'Holmes Representative Men Arkansas'. White wove paper unwatermarked.
Yellowish gray (93) endpapers. All edges trimmed. Issued in stiff white paper dust jacket
printed in full color.

Contents: [letter to John Clellon Holmes], p. 98.

$22.95. Published June 28, 1988 in an impression of 700 copies.

a2. *First edition, paperbound, 1988*

Representative Men | The Biographical Essays | *Selected Essays by John Clellon Holmes*
| *Volume II* | The University of Arkansas Press | Fayetteville 1988 London

One hundred fifty-two single leaves, pp. [i-xii] xiii-xvii [xviii-xx] [1-2] 3-277 [278-284].
21.5 x 13.6 cm. Perfect bound in stiff white paper wrappers. Covers printed in full-color.
White wove paper unwatermarked. All edges trimmed.

$12.95. Published June 28, 1988 in an impression of 1,500 copies.

B195   **SPIRITUAL QUESTS**   **1988**

a1. *First edition, hardbound*

Spiritual Quests | [6.3 cm. rule] | THE ART AND CRAFT | OF RELIGIOUS WRITING |
MARY GORDON/DAVID BRADLEY | JAROSLAV PELIKAN/FREDERICK
BUECHNER | HUGH NISSENSON/ALLEN GINSBERG | *Edited by* WILLIAM
ZINSSER | [ornamentation] | [2.8 cm. rule] | HOUGHTON MIFFLIN COMPANY |
BOSTON

[1-6]^{16}, pp. [i-ii] [1-11] 12-189 [190].   21.5 x 14.9 cm. Quarter bound in grayish
purplish blue (204) cloth covered spine with moderate blue (182) paper covered boards.
Blind stamped with an ornament on the front cover. All in gold across the spine:
'WILLIAM | ZINSSER | *editor* | [down the spine] *Spiritual Quests* [across the spine]
Houghton | *Mifflin* | *Company*'. White wove paper unwatermarked. Top and bottom
edges trimmed. White endpapers. Issued in cream paper dust jacket printed in dark blue
and black.

Contents: Meditation and Poetics [prose], pp. 143-165.

$16.95. Published Oct. 6, 1988 in an undisclosed number of copies.

a2. *First edition, paperbound, 1988*

Spiritual Quests I [6.3 cm. rule] I THE ART AND CRAFT I OF RELIGIOUS WRITING I MARY GORDON/DAVID BRADLEY I JAROSLAV PELIKAN/FREDERICK BUECHNER I HUGH NISSENSON/ALLEN GINSBERG I *Edited by* WILLIAM ZINSSER I [ornamentation] I [2.8 cm. rule] I [publisher's device] I HOUGHTON MIFFLIN COMPANY I BOSTON

Ninety-six single leaves, pp. [i-ii] [1-11] 12-189 [190]. 20.2 x 12.7 cm. Perfect bound in stiff white paper wrappers. Covers printed in green, dark gray, purple, yellow, black and blue. White wove paper unwatermarked. All edges trimmed.

$8.95. Published Oct. 6, 1988 in an undisclosed number of copies.

B196   **LITERARY OUTLAW**   **1988**
                                  by Ted Morgan

a1. *First edition, hardbound*

TED MORGAN I [two 11.1 cm. rules] I Literary Outlaw I [11.1 cm. rule] I *The Life and Times of* I *William S. Burroughs* I [diamond] I *Henry Holt and Company* I NEW YORK

Three hundred and forty-eight single leaves, pp. [i-vii] viii [ix-xii] 1-116 [xiii-xx] 117-276 [xxi-xxviii] 277-436 [xxix-xxxvi] 437-659 [660]. 23.5 x 15.9 cm. Quarter bound in medium gray paper covered boards with black spine cloth. Down the spine in silver: 'TED MORGAN [in 3 lines] [10.9 cm. rule] I Literary Outlaw I [10.9 cm. rule] [across the spine] HENRY HOLT'. Across the back paper covered boards in silver: '[publisher's device] I 0-8050-0901-9'. White wove paper unwatermarked. White endpapers. All edges trimmed. Issued in a white paper dust jacket printed in black and grayish greenish yellow (105).

Contents: [prose], pp. 6, 8, 89, 102-104, 106, 144, 385 — All the doctors think I'm crazy [poem], p. 164 — [excerpt from letters to William S. Burroughs], pp. 114, 183, 310, 313, 420 — [letters to imaginary people], p. 205 — [excerpt from letter to Dwight Eisenhower], p. 226 — [excerpt from letter to Jack Kerouac], p. 250 — [excerpt from letters to Peter Orlovsky], pp. 285, 379.

$27.50. Published Oct. 31, 1988 in an impression of 15,000 copies.

a2. *First edition, paperbound, 1990*

LITERARY I OUTLAW I [10.2 cm. rule] I THE LIFE AND TIMES OF I WILLIAM S. BURROUGHS I [10.2 cm. rule] I TED MORGAN I AVON BOOKS [publisher's device] NEW YORK

Three hundred and forty-four single leaves, pp. [i-vii] viii [ix-xii] 1-340 [xiii-xxviii] 341-659 [660]. 20.3 x 13.3 cm. Perfect bound in stiff white paper wrappers. Covers printed in full color. White wove paper unwatermarked. All edges trimmed.

$12.95. Published April 1990 in an undisclosed number of copies.

a3. *First British hardbound, 1991*

TED MORGAN I [two 11.1 cm. rules] I Literary Outlaw I [11.1 cm. rule] I *The Life and Times of* I *William S. Burroughs* I [diamond] I [publisher's device] I THE BODLEY HEAD I LONDON

[A-D]^{16} [E]^4 [F-K]^{16} [L]^4 [M-Q]^{16} [R]^4 [S-Y]^{16}, pp. [i-vii] viii [ix-xii] 1-116 [xiii-xx] 117-276 [xxi-xxviii] 277-436 [xxix-xxxvi] 437-659 [660]. 24.0 x 16.0 cm. Bound in black cloth covered boards. Across the spine in gold: 'LITERARY I OUTLAW I THE LIFE AND I TIMES OF I WILLIAM S. I BURROUGHS I [4.3 cm. rule] I TED MORGAN I [publisher's device]'. White wove paper unwatermarked. White endpapers. All edges trimmed. Issued in a white paper dust jacket printed in black, gold and light green.

£20.00. Published 1991 in an unknown number of copies.

*a4. *First British paperbound, 1991*

Note: Published in London by the Pimlico Press. Not seen by the compiler as of press time.

B197   **THE STIFFEST OF THE CORPSE**   **1988**

An Exquisite Corpse Reader I THE STIFFEST OF THE CORPSE I edited by Andrei Codrescu I [publisher's device] I City Lights Books I San Francisco

One hundred thirty-two single leaves, pp. [i-iv] 1-255 [256-260]. 22.8 x 17.8 cm. Perfect bound in stiff white paper wrappers. Covers printed in pale yellow (89), grayish yellow (90), brilliant greenish blue (168), deep blue (179) and black. White wove paper unwatermarked. All edges trimmed.

Contents: You Don't Know It, pp. 211, 213.

$12.95. Published Nov. 1988 in an impression of 4,192 copies.

B198   **EMERGENCY MESSAGES**   **1988**
             by Carl Solomon

a1. *First edition, hardbound*

EMERGENCY I MESSAGES I An Autobiographical Miscellany I CARL SOLOMON I EDITED AND WITH A FOREWORD BY I JOHN TYTELL I [publisher's device] I PARAGON HOUSE I *New York*

[1-8]^{16}, pp. [i-x] xi-xvii [xviii] [1-2] 3-235 [236-238]. 21.5 x 14.3 cm. Bound in dark gray (266) cloth covered boards. Down the spine in silver: '[in 2 lines] CARL I SOLOMON [in 1 line] EMERGENCY MESSAGES [across the spine] [publisher's device] I PARAGON I HOUSE'. White wove paper unwatermarked. White endpapers. All edges trimmed. Issued in a white paper dust jacket printed dark gray (266), light gray (264), vivid purplish red (254), strong greenish blue (169) and black.

Contents: Solomon, Carl and AG. [letter to Chevalier de Chazal], pp. 177-178 — Solomon, Carl and AG. [letter to T.S. Eliot], pp. 178-181 — [prose blurb], on back dust jacket cover.

$18.95. Published Nov. 24, 1988 in an impression of 500 copies.

Note: Although the verso of the title page calls for 1989 as the copyright date, 1988 is the true publication date according to the publisher.

a2. *First edition, paperbound, 1988*

EMERGENCY | *MESSAGES* | An Autobiographical Miscellany | CARL SOLOMON | EDITED AND WITH A FOREWORD BY | JOHN TYTELL | [publisher's device] | PARAGON HOUSE | *New York*

One hundred twenty-eight single leaves, pp. [i-x] xi-xvii [xviii] [1-2] 3-235 [236-238]. 20.9 x 13.8 cm. Perfect bound in stiff white paper wrappers. Covers printed dark gray (266), light gray (264), vivid purplish red (254), strong greenish blue (169) and black. White wove paper unwatermarked. All edges trimmed.

Contents: As the first edition, hardbound, with the blurb here on the back cover.

$9.95. Published Nov. 24, 1988 in an impression of 2,000 copies.

B199   **ANDY WARHOL, A RETROSPECTIVE**   **1989**

a1. *First edition, hardbound*

ANDY WARHOL | *A RETROSPECTIVE* | *EDITED BY KYNASTON McSHINE* | *WITH ESSAYS BY* | *KYNASTON McSHINE* | *ROBERT ROSENBLUM* | *BENJAMIN H. D. BUCHLOH* | *MARCO LIVINGSTONE* | *THE MUSEUM OF MODERN ART, NEW YORK* | *DISTRIBUTED BY BULLFINCH PRESS/LITTLE, BROWN AND COMPANY, BOSTON*

[1-30]^8, pp. [1-6] 7-479 [480]. 28.6 x 24.8 cm. Bound in glossy paper covered boards printed in an abstract design in deep reddish orange (36), strong orange yellow (68), strong yellowish green (131), brilliant greenish blue (168) and black. Down the spine: '*ANDY WARHOL* | *A RETROSPECTIVE* [across the spine] *EDITED BY* | *KYNASTON* | *McSHINE* | *THE MUSEUM* | *OF MODERN ART* | *NEW YORK* '. White wove coated paper unwatermarked. Strong bluish green (160) endpapers. All edges trimmed. Issued in a clear acetate dust jacket printed in black.

Contents: [prose], p. 434.

$60.00. Published Feb. 1989 in an impression of an undisclosed number of copies.

a2. *First edition, paperbound, 1988*

EMERGENCY | *MESSAGES* | An Autobiographical Miscellany | CARL SOLOMON | EDITED AND WITH A FOREWORD BY | JOHN TYTELL | [publisher's device] | PARAGON HOUSE | *New York*

One hundred twenty-eight single leaves, pp. [i-x] xi-xvii [xviii] [1-2] 3-235 [236-238]. 20.9 x 13.8 cm. Perfect bound in stiff white paper wrappers. Covers printed dark gray (266), light gray (264), vivid purplish red (254), strong greenish blue (169) and black. White wove paper unwatermarked. All edges trimmed.

Contents: As the first edition, hardbound, with the blurb here on the back cover.

$9.95. Published Nov. 24, 1988 in an impression of 2,000 copies.

B199 **ANDY WARHOL, A RETROSPECTIVE** **1989**

a1. *First edition, hardbound*

ANDY WARHOL | A RETROSPECTIVE | EDITED BY KYNASTON McSHINE |
WITH ESSAYS BY | KYNASTON McSHINE | ROBERT ROSENBLUM |
BENJAMIN H. D. BUCHLOH | MARCO LIVINGSTONE | THE MUSEUM OF
MODERN ART, NEW YORK | DISTRIBUTED BY BULLFINCH PRESS/LITTLE,
BROWN AND COMPANY, BOSTON

[1-30]⁸, pp. [1-6] 7-479 [480]. 28.6 x 24.8 cm. Bound in glossy paper covered boards printed in an abstract design in deep reddish orange (36), strong orange yellow (68), strong yellowish green (131), brilliant greenish blue (168) and black. Down the spine: '*ANDY WARHOL | A RETROSPECTIVE* [across the spine] *EDITED BY | KYNASTON | McSHINE | THE MUSEUM | OF MODERN ART | NEW YORK* '. White wove coated paper unwatermarked. Strong bluish green (160) endpapers. All edges trimmed. Issued in a clear acetate dust jacket printed in black.

Contents: [prose], p. 434.

$60.00. Published Feb. 1989 in an impression of an undisclosed number of copies.

a2. *First edition, paperbound, 1989*

ANDY WARHOL | A RETROSPECTIVE | EDITED BY KNYASTON McSHINE |
WITH ESSAYS BY | KYNASTON McSHINE | ROBERT ROSENBLUM |
BENJAMIN H. D. BUCHLOH | MARCO LIVINGSTONE | THE MUSEUM OF
MODERN ART, NEW YORK

[1-30]⁸, pp. [1-6] 7-479 [480]. 27.9 x 24.1 cm. Bound in stiff moderate bluish green (164) paper wrappers. Covers printed in an abstract design in deep reddish orange (36), strong orange yellow (68), strong yellowish green (131), brilliant greenish blue (168) and black. White wove coated paper unwatermarked. All edges trimmed.

Published Feb. 1989 in an impression of an undisclosed number of copies.

Note: A British paperback is the same as the Museum of Modern Art's issue "with a special imprint for Hayward Gallery, South Bank Centre, London". This according to the publisher.

B200 **POETS FOR LIFE** **1989**

a1. *First edition, hardbound*

POETS FOR [8.4 cm. rule] | LIFE | SEVENTY-SIX | [wavy line] | POETS RESPOND | [wavy line] | TO AIDS | [wavy line] | Edited with an Introduction by Michael Klein | Essays by the Rt. Rev. Paul Moore, Jr., | Joseph Papp, and Carol Muske | Crown Publishers, Inc. | New York

[1-8]¹⁶, pp. [i-iv] v-xii, 1-244. 23.5 x 15.5 cm. Quarter bound in gray cloth covered boards with bluish gray cloth spine printed in metallic green across the spine: 'POETS | [wavy rule] | FOR | [wavy rule] | L | I | I | F | E | KLEIN | [rule] | CROWN'. Down the spine cloth on the back cover: 'ISBN 0-517-57242-7'. White wove paper unwatermarked. White endpapers. All edges trimmed. Issued in a white paper dust jacket printed in yellow, blue, green and orange and black.

Contents: Sphincter, p. 79.

$18.95. Published June 26, 1989 in an impression of 10,000 copies.

a2. *First edition, paperbound, 1992*

POETS | FOR LIFE | [13.1 cm. rule] | SEVENTY-SIX POETS | RESPOND TO AIDS | Edited with an Introduction by Michael Klein | Essays by the Rt. Rev. Paul Moore, Jr., | Joseph Papp, and Carol Muske | [publisher's device] | Persea Books | New York

One hundred and twenty-eight single leaves, pp. [i-iv] v-xii, 1-244. 22.9 x 15.2 cm. Perfect bound in stiff white paper wrappers. Covers printed in deep red (13), black and dark orange yellow (72). White wove paper unwatermarked. All edges trimmed.

$11.95. Published May 5, 1992 in an impression of 3,000 copies.

B201 **QUÉBEC KÉROUAC BLUES** **1989**

QUÉBEC KÉROUAC BLUES | ÉCRITS DES FORGES

Seventy-eight single leaves, pp. [1-6] 7-125 [126-156]. 17.7 x 12.6 cm. Perfect bound in stiff white paper wrappers. Covers printed in black and white. White wove paper unwatermarked. All edges trimmed.

Contents: A Western Ballad, p. 58 — Written in My Dream by W. C. Williams, pp. 59-61 — One Haiku [At four a.m.], p. 61 — Father Death Blues, pp. 62-63.

$10.00. Published in Trois-Rivières, Canada in July 1989 in an impression of 1,000 copies.

Note: Reprinted in 1990 in an additional impression of 500 copies. Second printing identified on the copyright page with the dates "1989, 1990" instead of only "1989" as on the first printing. Published in Trois-Rivières, Quebec by Écrits des Forges.

B202 **BROADWAY 2** **1988**

a1. *First edition, paperbound*

[in white on a black rectangle] BROADWAY 2 | A Poets and Painters Anthology | Edited by James Schuyler and Charles North | [design of a keyhole in white within a black rectangle] | [design of a brick wall] | Hanging Loose Press

Sixty-eight single leaves, pp. [1-10] 11-135 [136]. 27.8 x 21.7 cm. Perfect bound in stiff white paper wrappers. Covers printed in black and white. White wove paper unwatermarked. All edges trimmed.

Contents: May Days 1988, pp. 47-49.

$15.00. Published Aug. 23, 1989 in an impression of 1,000 copies.

a2. *First edition, hardbound, 1989*

[in white on a black rectangle] BROADWAY 2 | A Poets and Painters Anthology | Edited by James Schuyler and Charles North | [design of a keyhole in white within a black rectangle] | [design of a brick wall] | Hanging Loose Press

[1-4]^8 [5]^4 [6-9]^8, pp. [1-10] 11-135 [136].   28.6 x 22.0 cm.   Bound in stiff black cloth covered boards.   Across the front cover in white: 'BROADWAY 2'.   Down the spine in white: 'BROADWAY 2 Ed. James Schuyler and Charles North Hanging Loose Press'. White wove paper unwatermarked.   White endpapers.   All edges trimmed.

$25.00.   Published Sept. 25, 1989 in an impression of 100 copies.

B203   **GINSBERG, A BIOGRAPHY**   **1989**
                              by Barry Miles

a1.   *First edition, hardbound*

[in light gray (264)]   GINSBERG   [on top of the lettering in black]   A BIOGRAPHY   I BARRY   I MILES   I SIMON AND SCHUSTER [vertical rule] New York London Toronto Sydney Tokyo

Three hundred and eight single leaves, pp. [1-9] 10-352 [i-xvi] 353-512 [xvii-xxiv] 513-588 [589-592].   24.1 x 16.0 cm.   Quarter bound in black cloth spine with medium gray (265) paper covered boards.   Down the spine in silver: 'GINSBERG [in 2 lines] BARRY SIMON AND I MILES SCHUSTER'.   White wove paper unwatermarked.   Medium gray endpapers.   All edges trimmed.   Issued in a white paper dust jacket printed in grayish yellow green (122), vivid reddish orange (34) and black.

Contents: [excerpts from notebooks, poems and manuscripts throughout] — [photographs (see D72)] — [excerpts from letters to Eugene Brooks], pp. 53, 54, 56, 57, 66, 67, 205, 208, 225, 244-245 — [excerpts from letters to Jack Kerouac], pp. 67-68, 95, 105, 117, 119-121, 124-125, 128-129, 131, 144, 145, 149, 163, 168-170, 172-174, 177, 185, 191-192, 210-211, 226, 235-236, 252, 254, 262, 275, 296, 301, 305-306, 308-209, 333 — [excerpts from letters to William S. Burroughs], pp. 72, 123, 271 — [excerpts from letter to Hans Wassing], p. 77 — [excerpts from letters to Louis Ginsberg], pp. 92, 203, 228-231, 260-262 — [excerpts from letters to Neal Cassady], pp. 93, 97-98, 105, 132, 137, 141, 143, 145, 153-155, 162, 163, 165 — [excerpts from letter to Wilhelm Reich], p. 95 — [excepts from letters to William Carlos Williams], pp. 126-127, 145, 201 — [excerpts from letters to Lucien Carr], pp. 160, 224, 287 — [prose postcard announcing the Six Gallery Reading], p. 195 — [excerpts from letter to Robert LaVigne], p. 199 — [excerpts from letters to Lawrence Ferlinghetti], pp. 207, 209, 216, 253-255, 258, 260, 274, 291, 335, 388, 390, 392, 424, 434 — [excerpts from letters to Peter Orlovsky], pp. 238-240, 243, 267, 291-292, 321-323, 325, 327, 353-354, 359, 370-371, 396, 398-399, 408 — [excerpts from letters to Gregory Corso], pp. 275, 293, 306, 319, 385, 392, 464, 471, 473 — [excerpts from letter to Timothy Leary], p. 282 — [excerpts from letter to Gary Snyder], p. 291 — [excerpts from letters to Howard Schulman], pp. 294-296 — [excerpts from letters to Paul Bowles], pp. 308, 314 — [excerpts from letters to Charles Olson], pp. 338, 375 — [excerpts from letter to Nicanor Parra], p. 364 — [excerpts from letter to Herbert Huncke], p. 376 — [excerpts from letter to Carolyn Cassady], p. 428 — [excerpts from letter to W. S. Merwin], p. 481 — War is Black Magic, p. 330 — Two Brothers at Table on Their Birthday, p. 509.

$24.95.   Published Sept. 1989 in an undisclosed number of copies.

a2.   *First edition, paperbound, 1990*

GINSBERG: I A Biography   I BARRY   I MILES   I [publisher's device] HarperPerennial I *A Division of* HarperCollins *Publishers*

Two hundred ninety-two single leaves, pp. [5-9] 10-588.   20.3 x 13.6 cm.   Perfect bound in stiff white paper wrappers.   Covers printed on pale greenish yellow (104) in dark purplish gray (234), vivid reddish orange(34) and dark grayish yellowish brown (81).

White wove paper unwatermarked. All edges trimmed.

$12.95. Published Sept. 12, 1990 in an impression of 18,124 copies.

a3. *First edition, British paperbound, 1990*

GINSBERG | A Biography | [1.9 cm. rule] | BARRY MILES | [publisher's device] |
PENGUIN BOOKS

Three hundred twelve single leaves, pp. [1-9] 10-312 [i-xxiv] 313-588 [589-600]. 19.7 x
12.9 cm. Perfect bound in stiff white paper wrappers. Covers printed in vivid orange
(48), pale orange yellow (73) and black. White wove paper unwatermarked. All edges
trimmed.

£8.99. Published Dec. 6, 1990 in an undisclosed number of copies.

B204   **MINDFIELD**   **1989**
                              by Gregory Corso

a1. *First edition, hardbound*

GREGORY | CORSO | [each of the letters of the following word is separated by a square
bullet] M I N D F I E L D | With forewords by | WILLIAM S. BURROUGHS | &
ALLEN GINSBERG | and drawings by the Author

One hundred forty-four single leaves, pp. [i-vi] vii-xi [xii] xiii-xv [xvi] xvii-xix [xx] [1-2]
3-268. 22.3 x 14.5 cm. Quarter bound in black cloth spine with deep red (13) with black
thread paper covered boards. Down the spine in gold: 'MINDFIELD CORSO [publisher's
device across the spine]'. White wove paper unwatermarked. Deep red with black thread
endpapers. All edges trimmed. Issued in a white paper dust jacket printed in deep reddish
orange (36), vivid yellow (82) and black.

Contents: On Corso's Virtues [prose], pp. xiii-xv — blurb on back dust jacket cover
[excerpt from the introduction].

$24.95. Published by Black Sparrow Press on Oct. 31, 1989 in an impression of 1,500
copies.

a2. *First edition, paperbound, 1989*

GREGORY | CORSO | [each of the letters of the following word is separated by a square
bullet] M I N D F I E L D | With forewords by | WILLIAM S. BURROUGHS | &
ALLEN GINSBERG | and drawings by the Author

One hundred forty-four single leaves, pp. [i-vi] vii-xi [xii] xiii-xv [xvi] xvii-xix [xx] [1-2]
3-268. 21.6 x 13.8 cm. Perfect bound in stiff white paper wrappers. Covers printed in
deep reddish orange (36), vivid yellow (82) and black. White wove paper unwatermarked.
All edges trimmed.

Contents: As first impression, a1 but with the blurb on the back cover.

$12.95. Published October 31, 1989 in an impression of 5,000 copies.

a3. *First edition, hardbound, signed (alpha), 1989*

GREGORY | CORSO | [each of the letters of the following word is separated by a square
bullet] M I N D F I E L D | With forewords by | WILLIAM S. BURROUGHS | &
ALLEN GINSBERG | and drawings by the Author

One hundred forty-four single leaves, pp. [i-vi] vii-xi [xii] xiii-xv [xvi] xvii-xix [xx] [1-2] 3-268. 22.3 x 14.5 cm. Quarter bound in black cloth spine and deep red (13) with black thread paper covered boards. Down the spine in gold: 'MINDFIELD CORSO [publisher's device]'. White wove paper unwatermarked. Deep red with black thread endpapers. All edges trimmed. Issued in a deep red with black thread paper covered slip-in case.

Contents: As first impression, a1 but without the dust jacket blurb.

$300.00. Published Oct. 31, 1989 in an impression of 26 copies.

Note: Identified as the lettered issue by the colophon on page [ii].

a4. *First edition, hardbound, signed (numeric), 1989*

GREGORY | CORSO | [each of the letters of the following word is separated by a square bullet] M I N D F I E L D | With forewords by | WILLIAM S. BURROUGHS | & ALLEN GINSBERG | and drawings by the Author

One hundred forty-four single leaves, pp. [i-vi] vii-xi [xii] xiii-xv [xvi] xvii-xix [xx] [1-2] 3-268. 22.3 x 14.5 cm. Quarter bound in black cloth spine and deep red (13) with black thread paper covered boards. Down the spine in gold: 'MINDFIELD CORSO [publisher's device]'. White wove paper unwatermarked. Deep red with black thread endpapers. All edges trimmed. Issued in a deep red with black thread paper covered slip-in case.

Contents: As first impression, a1 but without the dust jacket blurb.

$50.00. Published Oct. 31, 1989 in an impression of 250 copies.

Note: Identified as the numbered issue by the colophon on page [ii].

B205   **SPACE AND OTHER POEMS**   **1990**
                          by Eliot Katz

SPACE | and Other Poems | for Love, Laughs, and | Social Transformation | *** | Eliot Katz | Northern Lights Publishing Company, Inc. | Orono, Maine

Eighty single leaves, pp. [1-2] 3-160. 21.5 x 14.0 cm. Perfect bound in stiff white paper wrappers. Covers printed in strong purplish red (255) and black. White wove paper unwatermarked. All edges trimmed.

Contents: [excerpt from Footnote to Howl], p. 4 — Introduction [prose], p. 8 — [prose blurb], on back cover.

$9.95. Published May 20, 1990 in an impression of 1,000 copies.

B206   **HIGH ON THE WALLS**   **1990**

HIGH ON | THE WALLS | AN ANTHOLOGY CELEBRATING | TWENTY-FIVE YEARS OF | POETRY READINGS AT | MORDEN TOWER | * | edited by | Gordon Brown | MORDEN TOWER | in association with | BLOODAXE BOOKS

[A-J]^8, pp. [1-5] 6-144. 21.4 x 13.8 cm. Bound in stiff white paper wrappers. Covers printed in green, purple, blue, gray, pink, orange and black. White wove paper unwatermarked. All edges trimmed.

Contents: [prose introduction], p. 59 — What the Sea Throws Up at Vlissengen, p. 60.

£5.95. Published May 31, 1990 in an impression of 2,000 copies.

B207   **UN HOMME GRAND**   **1990**

a1. *First edition, hardbound*

UN HOMME I Jack Kerouac at the Crossroads of Many Cultures I GRAND I Jack Kérouac à la confluence des cultures I [9.0 x 9.0 cm. photographic collage portrait of Kerouac] I EDITED BY PIERRE ANCTIL, LOUIS DUPONT, RÉMI FERLAND, ERIC WADDELL I Carleton University Press I Ottawa, Canada I 1990

One hundred thirty-six single leaves, pp. [i-vi] vii-xxxi [xxxii] 1-236 [237-240]. 22.2 x 14.3 cm. Bound in deep reddish orange (36) cloth covered boards. Down the spine: 'UN HOMME GRAND — JACK KEROUAC [across the spine] CARLETON I UNIVERSITY I PRESS'. White wove paper unwatermarked. White endpapers. All edges trimmed.

Contents: Kerouac's Ethic [prose], pp. 41-60.

$34.95. Published June 12, 1990 in an impression of 200 copies.

a2. *First edition, paperbound, 1990*

UN HOMME I Jack Kerouac at the Crossroads of Many Cultures I GRAND I Jack Kérouac à la confluence des cultures I [9.0 x 9.0 cm. photographic collage portrait of Kerouac] I EDITED BY PIERRE ANCTIL, LOUIS DUPONT, RÉMI FERLAND, ERIC WADDELL I Carleton University Press I Ottawa, Canada I 1990

One hundred thirty-six single leaves, pp. [i-vi] vii-xxxi [xxxii] 1-236 [237-240]. 21.6 x 13.8 cm. Perfect bound in stiff white paper wrappers. Covers printed in black, dark reddish orange (38), dark yellowish pink (30) and white. White wove paper unwatermarked. All edges trimmed.

$19.95. Published June 12, 1990 in an impression of 900 copies.

B208   **BAD DATES**   **1990**

BAD DATES I Celebrities I (and Other Talented Types) I Reveal Their Worst Nights Out I by Carole Markin I A Citadel Press Book I Published by Carol Publishing Group

One hundred thirty-six single leaves, pp. [i-vi] vii-xiv [1-2] 3-256 [257-258]. 21.0 x 14.0 cm. Perfect bound in stiff white paper wrappers. Covers printed in full color. White wove paper unwatermarked. All edges trimmed.

Contents: Ginsberg, Alan [sic]. [prose], pp. 98-99.

$9.95. Published Aug. 1, 1990 in an impression of 5,000 copies.

B209   **WITHOUT WARNING**   **1990**
                      by Patricia Donegan

[design of Trungpa's calligraphy] I *WITHOUT* I *WARNING* I by Patricia Donegan I Published by Parallax Press [bullet] Berkeley, California

Fifty-six single leaves, pp. [i-xii] 1-98 [99-100]. 20.3 x 13.3 cm. Perfect bound in stiff white paper wrappers. Covers printed in black and vivid reddish orange (34). White wove paper unwatermarked. All edges trimmed.

Contents: Donegan on the Line [prose], p. [ix] — [prose blurb], back cover.

$8.00. Published Aug. 1990 in an impression of 1,000 copies.

Note: On some copies a black rectangle with white lettering has been attached over the incorrect ISBN on the back cover giving the correct number: 'ISBN 0-938077-32-5'.

B210   FERLINGHETTI: THE ARTIST IN HIS TIME   1990
by Barry Silesky

a1. *First edition, hardbound*

Ferlinghetti: | the | Artist | in His Time | [11.6 cm. rule] | BARRY SILESKY | [publisher's device] | WARNER BOOKS | A Warner Communications Company

[1-5]^{16} [6]^8 [7-9]^{16} [10]^8 [11]^{16}, pp. [i-vi] vii-viii [ix-x] 1-150 [xi-xxvi] 151-294. 23.6 x 15.6 cm. Quarter bound in light gray (264) paper with darker rag threads covered boards with black cloth covered spine. Down the spine in metallic silver-blue: 'ferlinghetti the artist in his time barry silesky [across the spine] [publisher's device] | WARNER | BOOKS'. The publisher's device is blind stamped across the back cover on the cloth covering at the lower right corner. White wove paper unwatermarked. Light gray with darker rag threads endpapers. All edges trimmed. Issued in a white paper dust jacket printed in deep reddish orange (36), grayish greenish yellow (105), moderate greenish blue (173), dark gray (266) and black.

Contents: [prose postcard announcing the Six Gallery Reading], p. 64 — [excerpt from letter to Lawrence Ferlinghetti], p. 69.

$24.95. Published Aug. 8, 1990 in an impression of 8,500 copies.

a2. *First edition, paperbound, 1991*

ferlinghetti | the artist in his time | barry silesky | [publisher's device] | WARNER BOOKS | A Time Warner Company

One hundred fifty-two single leaves, pp. [i-vi] vii-viii [ix-x] 1-294. 20.3 x 13.3 cm. Perfect bound in stiff white paper wrappers. Covers printed in vivid red (11), strong greenish yellow (99), deep green (142), strong blue (178), light gray (264) and black. White wove paper unwatermarked. All edges trimmed.

$13.99. Published Aug. 1991 in an impression of 7,450 copies.

B211   COOKING BY THE BOOKS   1990

COOKING | by the | BOOKS | Favorite Recipes by | Favorite Authors | Compiled by the | Monroe County Library System | Monroe, Michigan

Ninety-two single leaves, pp. [i-iv] [1] 2-180. 21.5 x 15.0 cm. Spiral bound with blue plastic spirals. Stiff white paper front and back covers printed in strong blue (178), bluish white (189) and black. White wove paper unwatermarked. All edges trimmed.

Contents: Savory Oatmeal [prose recipe], pp. 86-87.

$9.95. Edited by Bernadine Smith and published Oct. 1990 in an impression of 800 copies.

B212   **A DAY IN THE LIFE**   **1990**

A DAY | [in white on a black rectangle] IN THE | LIFE | TALES FROM THE LOWER EAST | An Anthology of | Writings from the | Lower East Side, 1940-1990 | Edited by Alan Moore & Josh Gosciak | Evil Eye Books | New York City 1990 | [solid rectangle]

Ninety-eight single leaves, pp. [i-x] 1-168 [169-186]. 22.8 x 15.2 cm. Perfect bound in stiff white paper wrappers. Covers printed in dark purplish red (259), strong reddish orange (35), vivid yellow (82) and black. White wove paper unwatermarked. All edges trimmed.

Contents: [prose journal entries], pp. 129-135 — Up Late Sunday, Late Nite Reading Thru NY Times, pp. 132-133 — Will They Shoot Me?, p. 134.

$7.95. Published 1990 in an unknown quantity.

B213 THE SAN FRANCISCO POETRY RENAISSANCE, 1955-1960 1991

The San Francisco Poetry | *Renaissance, 1955-1960* | Warren French | *D.H.L., Ohio University* | Twayne Publishers | *A Division of G. K. Hall & Co.* • *Boston*

[1-2] ^{16} [3]^4 [4-5]^8 [6-7]^{16}, pp. [1-2] [i-vi] vii [viii] ix-xi [xii] xiii-xx, 1-143 [144-146]. 22.3 x 14.3 cm. Bound in moderate blue (182) cloth covered boards. Across the spine in gold: 'TUSAS | 575 | [down the spine] *The San Francisco Poetry Renaissance, 1955-1960* Warren French [across the spine] *Twayne* '. Across the back cover in gold: 'ISBN 0-8057-7621-4'. White wove paper unwatermarked. White endpapers. All edges trimmed. Issued in a white paper dust jacket printed in vivid red (11) and strong greenish blue (169).

Contents: [prose], pp. 44-45 — [excerpt from letter to Warren French], p. 111.

$24.95. Published Feb. 1, 1991 in an impression of 2,000 copies.

B214   **WITHOUT DOUBT**   **1991**
                                  by Andy Clausen

Without Doubt | *Andy Clausen* | Introduction by Allen Ginsberg | *Zeitgeist Press*

Forty-two single leaves, pp. [i-x] 1-70 [71-74]. 21.0 x 13.6 cm. Perfect bound in stiff white paper wrappers. Covers printed in black and white. White wove paper unwatermarked, except the first and last leaves which are black wove paper unwatermarked.

Contents: Introduction [prose], pp. [v-vii].

$6.96. Published March 27, 1991 in an impression of 500 copies.

B215   **NICE TO SEE YOU**   **1991**

a1. First edition, hardbound

NICE TO SEE YOU | [10.6 cm. rule] | Homage to Ted Berrigan | Edited and with an Introduction by | ANNE WALDMAN | [publisher's device] | COFFEE HOUSE PRESS :: MINNEAPOLIS :: 1991

[1-2]^{16} [3]^{10} [4-5]^{16} [6]^{18} [7-9]^{16}, pp. [1-16] i-x [1-2] 3-253 [254]. 26.0 x 18.3 cm. Quarter bound in light purplish blue (199) paper covered boards with a moderate blue (182) cloth covered spine. Across the front cover in gold is a portrait of Ted Berrigan. Across the spine in gold: 'EDITED BY | ANNE | WALDMAN | [down the spine] NICE TO SEE YOU | HOMAGE TO TED BERRIGAN'. White wove paper unwatermarked. White endpapers. All edges trimmed. Issued in a white paper dust jacket printed in black, light yellow (86) and brilliant blue (177).

Contents: Berrigan, Ted and AG. Pinsk after Dark, p. 116 — Berrigan, Ted and AG. Grace, p. 116 — Berrigan, Ted and AG. Reds, p. 118 — Berrigan, Ted and AG. Two Scenes, p. 118.

$24.95. Published April 1991 in an impression of 500 copies.

a2. *First edition, paperbound, 1991*

NICE TO SEE YOU | [10.6 cm. rule] | Homage to Ted Berrigan | Edited and with an Introduction by | ANNE WALDMAN | [publisher's device] | COFFEE HOUSE PRESS :: MINNEAPOLIS :: 1991

One hundred and forty single leaves, pp. [1-16] i-x [1-2] 3-253 [254]. 25.4 x 17.7 cm. Perfect bound in stiff white paper wrappers. Covers printed in light yellow (86), brilliant blue (177) and black. White wove paper unwatermarked. All edges trimmed.

$14.95. Published April 1991 in an impression of 2,500 copies.

B216   **THE SAN FRANCISCO ORACLE**   **1991**

a1. *First edition, limited issue*

[ornamental type] THE SAN FRANCISCO | [ornamental type] ORACLE | FACSIMILE EDITION | The Psychedelic Newspaper | of the Haight-Ashbury | 1966-1968 | EDITED BY | ALLEN COHEN | REGENT PRESS | BERKELEY, CA | 1991

Two hundred twenty-four single leaves, pp. [1-2] [i-iv] v-lvi [lvii-lviii] [1-2] 3-385 [386-388]. 36.2 x 28.5 cm. Bound in dark red (16) cloth covered boards. The front cover has been covered with moderate green (145) cloth on which is printed in gold: '[ornamental type] THE SAN FRANCISCO | [ornamental type] ORACLE | FACSIMILE EDITION'. The back cover has been covered with vivid red (11) cloth. White wove paper unwatermarked. Front endpapers are illustrated in rainbow colors. The back endpapers are a feathered multi-colored design. All edges trimmed. Issued in a dark red cloth covered slip-in case. This edition is accompanied by a separate portfolio of 13 cover reproductions from the Oracle within a gray paper portfolio with label printed in purple: '[ornamental type] THE SAN FRANCISCO | [ornamental type] ORACLE | FACSIMILE EDITION | COVERS'.

Contents: [letter to the editor], p. 21 — Renaissance or Die [prose], p. 100 [also on front endpapers] — Changes [interview format], pp. 150-151, 154-165, 177-182, 188-189.

$400.00 and later raised to $700.00. Published April 2, 1991 in an impression of 200 copies.

Note: Originally this edition was advertised to be 64 copies but was actually released in an edition of 200 copies.

a2. First edition, ordinary copies, 1991

[ornamental type] THE SAN FRANCISCO | [ornamental type] ORACLE | FACSIMILE EDITION | The Psychedelic Newspaper | of the Haight-Ashbury | 1966-1968 | EDITED BY | ALLEN COHEN | REGENT PRESS | BERKELEY, CA | 1991

Two hundred twenty-three single leaves, pp. [i-iv] v-lvi [lvii-lviii] [1-2] 3-385 [386-388]. 36.2 x 28.5 cm. Bound in dark red (16) cloth covered boards. Across the front cover in gold: '[ornamental type] THE SAN FRANCISCO | [ornamental type] ORACLE | FACSIMILE EDITION'. Across the spine in gold: 'ALLEN | COHEN | [down the spine] [ornamental type] THE SAN FRANCISCO | [ornamental type] ORACLE | FACSIMILE EDITION [across the spine] [publisher's device]'. White wove paper unwatermarked. Illustrated endpapers in rainbow colors. All edges trimmed.

$175.00. Published April 2, 1991 in an impression of 1,700 copies.

B217   **JOURNAL OF THE GULF WAR**   **1991**

JOURNAL OF THE GULF WAR | [9.1 cm. rule] | *Poetry from Home* | Editors | Michael Logue, John Penner, Meg Reed, Tina Rinaldi | POETS READING, INC. | FULLERTON 1991 CALIFORNIA

Thirty-six single leaves, pp. [i-vi] vii [viii] 1-62 [63-64]. 21.2 x 13.6 cm. Perfect bound in stiff white paper wrappers. Covers printed in full color. White wove paper unwatermarked. All edges trimmed.

Contents: Hum Bom!, pp. 52-55.

$9.00. Published April 20, 1991 in an impression of 1,000 copies.

B218   **GARY SNYDER: DIMENSIONS OF A LIFE**   **1991**

a1. First edition, hardbound

Gary Snyder: | DIMENSIONS OF A LIFE | EDITED BY JON HALPER | SIERRA CLUB BOOKS | SAN FRANCISCO

Two hundred thirty-two single leaves, pp. [i-viii] ix-xi [xii] [1-2] 3-451 [452]. 24.0 x 15.7 cm. Quarter bound in pale green (149) paper covered boards with moderate reddish orange (37) cloth covered spine. Across the spine: 'HALPER | [down the spine in 2 lines] *Gary Snyder:* | DIMENSIONS OF A LIFE [across the spine] SIERRA | CLUB | BOOKS'. White wove paper unwatermarked. White endpapers. All edges trimmed. Issued in a white paper dust jacket printed in black, deep orange (51) and brilliant greenish blue (168).

Contents: My Mythic Thumbnail Biography of Gary Snyder [prose], p. 203.

$30.00. Published May 31, 1991 in an impression of 2,500 copies.

a2. *First edition, paperbound, 1991*

Gary Snyder: I DIMENSIONS OF A LIFE I EDITED BY JON HALPER I SIERRA CLUB BOOKS I SAN FRANCISCO

Two hundred thirty-two single leaves, pp. [i-viii] ix-xi [xii] [1-2] 3-451 [452]. 23.4 x 15.3 cm. Perfect bound in stiff white paper wrappers. Covers printed in black, deep orange (51) and brilliant greenish blue (168). White wove paper unwatermarked. All edges trimmed.

$17.00. Published May 31, 1991 in an impression of 12,500 copies

B219   50 WAYS TO FIGHT CENSORSHIP   1991

50 Ways to Fight I Censorship I and Important Facts to Know I About the Censors I by Dave Marsh I and Friends I [in 3 lines] Thunder's I Mouth I Press [publisher's device] [in 2 lines] New I York

Seventy-two single leaves, pp. [i-viii] ix-xvi, 1-128. 21.5 x 13.6 cm. Perfect bound in stiff white paper wrappers. Covers printed in full color. White wove paper unwatermarked. All edges trimmed.

Contents: Statement on FCC Censorship [prose], pp. 79-81.

$5.95. Published June 1991 in an impression of 30,000 copies.

B220   THE DREAM AT THE END OF THE WORLD   1991
by Michelle Green

a1. *First edition, hardbound*

[within single rule frame] [thick rule] THE DREAM AT THE I END OF THE WORLD I [thick rule] I [below frame] *Paul Bowles and* I *the Literary Renegades* I *in Tangier* I *Michelle Green* I [publisher's device] I HarperCollins*Publishers*

$[1-7]^{16} [8]^8 [9-11]^{16} [12]^8 [13-14]^{16}$, pp. [i-vii] viii [ix-xi] xii-xvi [1] 2-208 [i-xvi] 209-381 [382-384]. 24.0 x 16.0 cm. Quarter bound in dark grayish reddish brown (47) paper covered boards with black cloth spine. Blind stamped with the publisher's logo on the front cover. Down the spine in gold: '[in 2 lines] THE DREAM AT THE I END OF THE WORLD [in 1 line] *Michelle Green* [across the spine] Harper I Collins'. White wove paper unwatermarked. Dark grayish reddish brown endpapers. All edges trimmed. Issued in a white paper dust jacket printed in full color.

Contents: [excerpts from letters to Lucien Carr], pp. 178, 180-182, 191-192 — [excerpts from letters to Jack Kerouac], pp. 192, 234-235, 242 — [excerpts from letters to Peter Orlovsky], pp. 200, 241 — [prose journal entry], p. 239 — [excerpt from letter to Barney Rossett], p. 241 — [photographs (see also D107)]

$22.95. Published Aug. 1, 1991 in an impression of 17,500 copies.

a2. *First edition, paperbound, 1992*

[within single rule frame] [thick rule] THE DREAM AT THE I END OF THE WORLD I [thick rule] I [below frame] *Paul Bowles and* I *the Literary Renegades* I *in Tangier* I *Michelle Green* I [publisher's device] I Harper Perennial I *A Division of* HarperCollins *Publishers*

Two hundred and eight single leaves, pp. [i-vii] viii [ix-xi] xii-xvi [1] 2-208 [i-xvi] 209-381 [382-384]. 20.2 x 13.5 cm. Perfect bound in stiff white paper wrappers. Covers printed in full color. White wove paper unwatermarked. All edges trimmed.

$12.00. Published July 1, 1992 in an impression of 10,500 copies.

B221 **FIRE READINGS** **1991**

[12.2 cm. rule] I FIRE READINGS I *A Collection of Contemporary Writing from* I *the Shakespeare & Company Fire Benefit Readings* I PARIS [bullet] LONDON [bullet] NEW YORK [bullet] BOSTON I *With Fireword by* I Lawrence Ferlinghetti I *Editorial Board* I David Applefield I Richard Hallward I T. Wignesan I In collaboration with Eric Mottram I *Associate Publisher,* Richard Hallward I Frank I [2 rules 1.8 cm. long] I BOOKS I [1.8 cm. rule] I B.P. 29 I F-94301 Vincennes, France I [12.2 cm. rule]

One hundred single leaves, pp. [1-3] 4-198 [199-200]. 21.0 x 14.7 cm. Perfect bound in stiff white paper wrappers. Covers printed in black, vivid red (11), deep brown (56) and strong yellow (84). White wove paper unwatermarked. All edges trimmed.

Contents: Homage to Paris at the Bottom of the Barrel, p. 133 — Europe! Europe!, p. 134 — At Apollinaire's Grave, pp. 135-137.

$12.95. Published Oct. 18, 1991 in an impression of 3,000 copies.

Note: An undisclosed number of copies of the first printing were altered to include an additional 3 lines of text on p. 9 to the bottom of Ferlinghetti's "Fireword". This was done by pasting a cut-out self-adhering photocopy of the missing 3 lines at the bottom of the page.

B222 **OUT OF THIS WORLD** **1991**

OUT OF THIS WORLD I An Anthology of the St. Mark's I Poetry Project I [solid square] 1966-1991 I Edited and I with an Introduction I by Anne Waldman I [solid square] I Foreword by Allen Ginsberg I [solid square] I Crown Publisher's, Inc. I New York

Three hundred sixty single leaves, pp. [i-iv] v-xxx, 1-690. 22.8 x 15.2 cm. Perfect bound in stiff white paper wrappers. Covers printed in yellowish gray (93), silver and black. White wove paper unwatermarked. All edges trimmed.

Contents: Foreword [prose], pp. xxiv-xxx — Bixby Canyon Ocean Path Word Breeze, p. 60 — Wyoming, p. 68 — Mugging, p. 68 — The Little Fish Devours the Big Fish, p. 71.

$22.00. Published Nov. 14, 1991 in an undisclosed number of copies.

B223 **TEACHERS & WRITERS GUIDE TO WALT WHITMAN** **1991**

The Teachers & Writers Guide I *to* I Walt Whitman I *Edited by Ron Padgett* I Teachers & Writers Collaborative I New York

One hundred twelve single leaves, pp. [i-v] vi-xiii [xiv] 1-208 [209-210]. 21.5 x 13.6 cm. Perfect bound in stiff white paper wrappers. Covers printed in vivid greenish yellow (97) and black. White wove paper unwatermarked. All edges trimmed.

Contents: Taking a Walk through *Leaves of Grass* [prose], pp. 1-35 — My High School English Teacher [prose], p. 125.

$13.95. Published Nov. 15, 1991 in an impression of 3,500 copies.

B224   **JOY! PRAISE!**   **1991**

JOY! I PRAISE! I a festschrift I for Jerome Rothenberg I on the occasion of I his sixtieth birthday I edited by Pierre Joris I [publisher's device] TA'WIL Books & Documents

Forty-four single leaves, pp. [i-ii] [1-4] 5-84 [85-86]. 22.8 x 15.1 cm. Perfect bound in stiff white paper wrappers. Covers printed in black and white. White wove paper unwatermarked. All edges trimmed.

Contents: [prose], p. 31.

$4.00. Published Dec. 1991 in an impression of 1,000 copies.

B225   **IN MY TAXI**   **1991**
                                by Ryan Weideman

IN MY TAXI I [8.0 x 11.4 cm. photograph of the author] I New York After Hours I [in facsimile holograph] Ryan Weideman I [publisher's device in 1 line] [in 2 lines] THUNDER'S MOUTH PRESS I NEW YORK

Forty-eight single leaves, pp. [i-iv] 1-12 [13-92]. 20.1 x 25.4 cm. Perfect bound in stiff white paper wrappers. Covers printed in black and gold. White wove coated paper unwatermarked. All edges trimmed.

Contents: [prose], p. [91].

$19.95. Published Dec. 2, 1991 in an impression of 3,000 copies.

B226   **SHAKESPEARE & COMPANY**   **1991**
                          by Sylvia Beach Whitman

SHAKESPEARE & COMPANY I *Biography of a Bookstore* I *in Pictures and Poems* I By I Sylvia Beach Whitman I [design of a postage stamp with a drawing of the bookstore on it] I [publisher's device of Shakespeare & Company] [publisher's device of City Lights] I *Shakespeare & Co. City Lights Books* I *Paris San Francisco*

Single gathering of eighteen leaves, pp. [1-36]. 21.0 x 14.9 cm. Stapled twice in stiff white paper wrappers. Covers printed in full color. All edges trimmed. White wove paper unwatermarked.

Contents: Cold January Ends Snowing on Sidewalks [prose], p. [32] — [drawing of a skull in a star with an autograph note], p. [34].

25 FF. Published ca. Winter 1991 in an impression of 10,000 copies.

B227   **WINDOW ON THE BLACK SEA**   **1992**

Window on the Black Sea I Bulgarian Poetry in Translation I Edited by Richard Harteis I
in collaboration with William Meredith I Carnegie Mellon University Press I Pittsburgh
1992

Ninety-two single leaves, pp. [1-14] 15-21 [22-24] 25-180 [181-182] 183 [184]. 23.4 x
13.9 cm. Perfect bound in stiff white paper wrappers. Covers printed in very dark
greenish blue (175), gold and black. White wove paper unwatermarked. All edges
trimmed.

Contents: Pavolov, Konstantin. Elegiac Optimism, translation by Allen Ginsberg, p. 80.

$14.95. Published Feb. 3, 1992 in an impression of 1,504 copies.

B228   **STOCKHAUSEN: A BIOGRAPHY**   **1992**
                         by Michael Kurtz

Stockhausen: A BIOGRAPHY I *Michael Kurtz* I TRANSLATED BY RICHARD TOOP I
[publisher's device] I *faber and faber* I LONDON [bullet] BOSTON

One hundred forty-four single leaves, pp. [i-vii] viii-xi [xii] xiii-xvii [xviii] 1-270. 24.1 x
15.6 cm. Perfect bound in dark grayish red (20) cloth covered boards. Across the spine all
in pale yellow (89): '[2.0 cm. rule] I [publisher's device] I [2.0 cm. rule] I [down the
spine] STOCKHAUSEN *A Biography* Michael Kurtz'. White wove paper
unwatermarked. White endpapers. All edges trimmed. Issued in a white paper dust jacket
printed in black and orange.

Contents: [prose], pp. 132-133.

£25.00. Published March 9, 1992 in an impression of 2,000 copies.

B229   **AFTER THE STORM**   **1992**

[all inside a single rule frame except for the title and subtitle which are wider than the frame
and the frame is broken at those points where the lettering extends beyond the frame] After
the Storm I Poems on the Persian Gulf War I Edited by I Jay Meek & F. D. Reeve I
MAISONNEUVE PRESS I Washington, D. C. 1992

Sixty-six single leaves, pp. [i-x] 1-121 [122]. 21.5 x 13.6 cm. Perfect bound in stiff
white paper wrappers. Covers printed in vivid yellowish pink (25), gray and vivid purplish
blue (194). White wove paper unwatermarked. All edges trimmed.

Contents: After the Big Parade, p. 36.

$10.95. Published April 17, 1992 in an impression of 1,557 copies.

B 230   **CULTURE WARS**   **1992**

CULTURE I WARS I Documents from I the Recent Controversies I in the Arts I
Edited by I RICHARD BOLTON I [publisher's device] I NEW PRESS I *New York*

One hundred ninety-two single leaves, pp. [i-xv] xvi-xviii [1-3] 4-363 [364-366]. 23.5 x
15.5 cm. Perfect bound in stiff white paper wrappers. Covers printed in purple, white,
rose and black. White wove paper unwatermarked. All edges trimmed.

Contents: [letter], p. 92.

$19.95. Published May, 1992 in an impression of 6,000 copies.

B231   **POMES ALL SIZES**   **1992**
                              by Jack Kerouac

JACK KEROUAC l POMES ALL SIZES l INTRODUCTION BY ALLEN GINSBERG
l THE POCKET POETS SERIES #48 l [publisher's device] l CITY LIGHTS BOOKS l
SAN FRANCISCO

Ninety-six single leaves, pp. [1-6] i-x, 1-175 [176]. 15.9 x 12.4 cm. Perfect bound in
stiff white paper wrappers. Covers printed in full color. White wove paper
unwatermarked. All edges trimmed.

Contents: Introduction [prose], pp. i-x.

$8.95. Published ca. May 1992 in an impression of 8,000 copies.

Note: Second printing in July 1992 in an impression of 5,000 copies. The publisher states
that the color was not correct on the cover of the first printing and that 5,000 additional
copies were printed with the corrected color. These are identified as the second printing by
the addition of the word 'KEROUAC' to the spine on the red panel at the top. No other
notice of printing is given.

B232   **HIGH ON THE BEATS**   **1992**

HiGH [illustration of an angel] l On l [illustration of an angel] the l BeAts l HeRscHEl
l SiLVERMan l iNTro l By l allen l GinsBERg l [illustration of an angel]

Single gathering of six leaves, pp. [1-12]. 10.8 x 28.0 cm. Stapled twice into stiff light
gray (264) paper wrappers. Covers printed in black. White wove paper unwatermarked.
All edges trimmed.

Contents: Homage to Hersch [prose], pp. [2-3].

Distributed free. Published in Brooklyn, NY by Pinched Nerves Press in Aug. 1992 in an
impression of 150 copies with another 50 identical copies printed in Sept. 1992; 25 of
which are signed by the author and sold for $5.00.

B233   **KEITH RICHARDS: THE BIOGRAPHY**   **1992**
                              by Victor Bockris
a1. *First edition, hardbound*

[11.0 cm. ornamental rule] l KEITH RICHARDS l [hollow type] THE BIOGRAPHY l
VICTOR BOCKRIS l [3 solid squares] l POSEIDON PRESS l NEW YORK LONDON
TORONTO SYDNEY TOKYO SINGAPORE l [11.0 cm. ornamental rule]

Two hundred and eight single leaves, pp. [i-ii] [1-4] 5-6 [7-15] 16-409 [410-414]. 24.2 x
16.1 cm. Perfect bound in quarterbinding in black paper covered boards with moderate
purple (223) cloth covered spine. Down the spine in copper: 'VICTOR BOCKRIS l
KEITH RICHARDS [across the spine] [publisher's device] l POSEIDON l PRESS'.
White wove paper unwatermarked. White endpapers. All edges trimmed. Issued in a
white paper dust jacket printed in full color.

Contents: [excerpt from letter to *The Times*], p. 136.

$24.00. Published Aug. 4, 1992 in an impression of 40,000 copies.

a2. First edition, paperbound, 1993

[10.9 cm. ornamental rule] I KEITH RICHARDS I [hollow type] THE BIOGRAPHY I
VICTOR BOCKRIS I [3 solid squares] I POSEIDON PRESS I NEW YORK LONDON
TORONTO SYDNEY TOKYO SINGAPORE I [10.9 cm. ornamental rule]

Two hundred and eight single leaves, pp. [1-6] 7-8 [9-15] 16-400 [401] 402-407 [408]
409-415 [416]. 23.2 x 15.4 cm. Perfect bound in stiff white paper wrappers. Covers
printed in full color. White wove paper unwatermarked. All edges trimmed.

$12.00. Published 1993 in an undisclosed number of copies.

B234   **A NEW GEOGRAPHY OF POETS**   **1992**

a1. First edition, paperbound

A I NEW I GEOGRAPHY I OF I POETS I COMPILED AND EDITED BY I
EDWARD FIELD I GERALD LOCKLIN I CHARLES STETLER I The University of
Arkansas Press / Fayetteville / 1992

One hundred eighty single leaves, pp. [i-vi] vii-xv [xvi] xvii-xxix [xxx-xxxii] [1-2] 3-324
[325-328]. 21.5 x 14.1 cm. Perfect bound in stiff white paper wrappers. Covers printed
in light brown (57), pale yellow (89) and deep green (142). White wove paper
unwatermarked. All edges trimmed.

Contents: Velocity of Money, pp. 109-110.

$14.95. Published Aug. 14, 1992 in an impression of 1,500 copies.

Note: Reprinted once in Jan. 1993 in an undisclosed number of copies. Second printing is
identified by the deletion of the number 1 and the date code 92 on the verso of the title page.

a2. First edition, hardbound, 1992

A I NEW I GEOGRAPHY I OF I POETS I COMPILED AND EDITED BY I
EDWARD FIELD I GERALD LOCKLIN I CHARLES STETLER I The University of
Arkansas Press / Fayetteville / 1992

[1-6]^{16} [7]^4 [8-12]^{16}, pp. [i-vi] vii-xv [xvi] xvii-xxix [xxx-xxxii] [1-2] 3-324 [325-328].
22.2 x 14.5 cm. Bound in yellowish gray (93) cloth covered boards. Blind stamped
across the front cover: 'A I NEW I GEOGRAPHY I OF I POETS'. Across the spine
all in copper color: 'FIELD I LOCKLIN I STETLER I [1.7 cm. rule] I [down the spine]
A NEW GEOGRAPHY OF POETS [across the spine] [1.7 cm. rule] I ARKANSAS I
[publisher's device]'. White wove paper unwatermarked. Strong green (141) endpapers.
All edges trimmed. Issued in a white paper dust jacket printed in light brown (57), pale
yellow (89) and deep green (142).

$30.00. Published Aug. 25, 1992 in an impression of 750 copies.

B235   **THE CONTINUAL PILGRIMAGE**   **1992**
                    by Christopher Sawyer-Laucanno

The | *Continual* | *Pilgrimage* | [ornament] | *American Writers in Paris,* | *1944-1960* |
CHRISTOPHER | SAWYER-LAUÇANNO | [publisher's device] | GROVE PRESS |
New York

One hundred eighty single leaves, pp. [i-vi] vii-viii [ix] x [xi-xii] [1-2] 3-345 [346-348].
24.2 x 16.0 cm. Perfect bound in quarterbinding with vivid purplish blue (194) paper
covered boards with a moderate yellow (87) imitation leather, paper covered spine. Down
the spine in gold: '[in 1 line] *The Continual Pilgrimage* [in 2 lines] CHRISTOPHER |
SAWYER-LAUÇANNO [across the spine] [publisher's device] | GROVE | PRESS'.
White wove paper unwatermarked. White endpapers. All edges trimmed. Issued in a
white paper dust jacket printed in full color.

Contents: [excerpt from letter to Jack Kerouac], p. 265 — [excerpt from early version of
Kaddish], p. 265.

$24.95. Published Sept. 1, 1992 in an undisclosed number of copies.

B236   TWO LECTURES ON THE WORK OF ALLEN GINSBERG   1992
                    by Barry Miles

TWO LECTURES | ON THE WORK OF | ALLEN GINSBERG | BY | BARRY
MILES | TURRET PAPERS | [publisher's device] | No. 1

Single gathering of eight leaves, pp. [1-16]. 24.8 x 16.2 cm. Sewn into stiff black paper
wrappers. A 7.0 x 6.7 cm. white paper label printed in dark reddish orange (38) has been
attached to the front cover, on which is the following all within a single rule frame: 'TWO
LECTURES | ON THE WORK OF | ALLEN GINSBERG | BY | BARRY MILES'.
White wove paper unwatermarked. All edges trimmed.

Contents: [excerpt from letters to Jack Kerouac], p. [12] — [prose], p. [13] — [excerpt
from letters to Lawrence Ferlinghetti], pp. [14-15].

Published September 7, 1992 in an impression of 500 copies.

B 237   WPFW 89.3 FM POETRY ANTHOLOGY   1992

WPFW 89.3 FM | Poetry Anthology | Edited by | Grace Cavalieri | *The Bunny and the
Crocodile Press* | *Washington, D.C.*

One hundred eighty-three single leaves, pp. [i-iv] v [vi] vii-ix [x] xi-xxiv [xxv-xxvi] [1-
2] 3-340. 22.6 x 15.0 cm. Perfect bound in stiff white paper wrappers. Cover printed in
black, light gray (264) and deep red (13). White wove paper unwatermarked. All edges
trimmed.

Contents: Spot Anger, p. 102.

$15.00. Published Sept. 21, 1992 in an impression of 600 copies.

B238   **DHARMA LION**   **1992**

a1. *First edition, hardbound*

DHARMA LION | *A Critical Biography of Allen Ginsberg* | MICHAEL
SCHUMACHER | ST. MARTIN'S PRES:3 | NEW YORK

Four hundred single leaves, pp. [i-vii] viii [ix] x-xi [xii] xiii [xiv] xv [xvi-xxii] [1-3] 4-245
[246-248] [i-iv] [249] 250-517 [518-520] [i-iv] [521] 522-769 [770]. 24.2 x 16.2 cm.
Perfect bound in quarterbinding of dark purplish red (259) paper covered boards and black
cloth covered spine. Down the spine in silver: 'DHARMA LION [across the spine]
SCHUMACHER | ST. MARTIN'S PRESS'. White wove paper unwatermarked. White
endpapers. Top and bottom edges trimmed. Issued in a white paper dust jacket printed in
black, dark grayish red (20), pale yellow (89), dark bluish green (165) and light gray
(264).

Contents: [excerpts from notebooks, poems and manuscripts throughout] — [photograph
(see also D120)]— [excerpt from letter to Gordon Canfield], pp. 21-22 — [excerpts from
letters to Eugene Brooks], pp. 48, 49, 57, 58, 232-234, 255-256, 265-266 — [excerpts
from letters to Jack Kerouac], pp. 57, 58, 87, 92, 119, 120, 126-127, 135, 140-143, 145,
147, 151, 159-162, 164-167, 173, 176-177, 181-183, 185-186, 190-191, 195-197, 199-
200, 203-205, 209, 240, 255, 268, 271-273, 275, 276, 285, 292, 296, 298, 314, 320,
224-335, 338, 340, 351, 357, 366, 369-370, 372-373, 375, 377-379, 381-383, 390, 402,
404, 407, 411 — [excerpts from letter to N. M. McKnight], p. 67 — [excerpts from letters
to Louis Ginsberg], pp. 85-86, 99, 178, 227-228, 264-265, 267-269, 273, 279, 309, 311,
313-314, 327, 329-330, 361-362, 364, 366, 367, 369, 373, 380, 383-384, 387, 391-393,
398, 423, 429-430, 446, 451, 456, 540, 572, 574, 575, 581, 584, 586-587, 605, 610,
694 — [excerpt from letter to Herbert Huncke], p. 87 — [excerpts from letters to Neal
Cassady], pp. 87, 91, 94, 99, 100, 107-109, 115, 117, 129-130, 133, 136-137, 139-142,
147, 152-154, 157-162, 164-167, 169, 348, 380 — [excerpt from letter to Wilhelm
Reich], p. 89 — [excerpts from letters to Lionel Trilling], pp. 92, 95 — [excerpts from
letters to William Carlos Williams], pp. 123, 224-225 — [excerpts from letters to Lucien
Carr], pp. 162, 164-165, 167, 252, 255, 270, 284, 322-325, 358, 385, 419, 461, 563-
564, 598 — [excerpts from letters to Richard Eberhart], pp. 206, 219 — [excerpts from
letters to Lawrence Ferlinghetti], pp. 233, 237, 242, 335, 359 — [excerpts from letters to
Mark Van Doren], pp. 238, 296 — [excerpts from letters to Peter Orlovsky], pp. 274-275,
278, 280-281, 283-284, 286, 322-323, 325, 327, 360, 391, 398-399, 423, 426, 440-442
— [excerpts from letters to William S. Burroughs], p. 328 — [excerpts from letters to
Howard Schulman], pp. 376, 444 — [excerpts from letter to Gregory Corso], p. 444 —
[excerpts from letters to Barry Miles], pp. 475, 523, 526, 557, 559 — [excerpts from
letters to Philip Whalen], pp. 522, 541, 575, 591, 624, 645-646 — [excerpts from letter to
Dave Haselwood], p. 527 — [excerpts from letter to W. S. Merwin], pp. 640-641 —
[excerpts from letter to Dana Naone], pp. 640-641.

$35.00. Published Oct. 1992 in a quantity undisclosed by the publisher.

a2. *First edition, paperbound, 1994*

DHARMA LION | *A Critical Biography of Allen Ginsberg* | MICHAEL
SCHUMACHER | ST. MARTIN'S PRESS | NEW YORK

Four hundred and two single leaves, pp. [1-2] [i-vii] viii [ix] x-xi [xii] xiii [xiv] xv [xvi-
xxii] [1-3] 4-245 [246-248] [i-iv] [249] 250-517 [518-520] [i-iv] [521] 522-769 [770-
772]. 22.7 x 14.5 cm. Perfect bound in stiff white paper wrappers. Covers printed in
black, dark grayish red (20), pale yellow (89), dark bluish green (165) and light gray
(264). White wove paper unwatermarked. All edges trimmed.

$18.95. Published in 1994 in an unknown number of copies.

B239   **THE VERDICT IS IN**   **1992**

[thick 10.8 cm. rule] | THE | [10.8 cm. rule] | VERDICT | [10.8 cm. rule] | IS IN | [thick 10.8 cm. rule] | EDITED BY | KATHI GEORGES | AND | JENNIFER JOSEPH | MANIC D PRESS | SAN FRANCISCO

Forty-eight single leaves, pp. [1-8] 9-94 [95-96]. 22.9 x 15.3 cm. Perfect bound in stiff white paper wrappers. Covers printed in blackish blue (188), black and brilliant blue (177). White wove paper unwatermarked. All edges trimmed.

Contents: Get It?, p. 9.

$9.95. Published Oct. 1992 in an impression of 3,000 copies.

B240   **A GATHERING OF POETS**   **1992**

a1. *First edition, hardbound*

A Gathering of Poets | *Edited by Maggie Anderson and Alex Gildzen* | *Raymond A. Craig, Associate Editor* | The Kent State University Press | Kent, Ohio, and London, England

[1-10]^{16}, pp. [i-v] vi-ix [x] 1-11 [12-14] 15-310. 23.5 x 15.5 cm. Bound in moderate bluish green (164) cloth covered boards. Across the front cover: 'A GATHERING OF | POETS | [within single rule frame] EDITED BY | MAGGIE ANDERSON & ALEX GILDZEN | [within single rule frame] ASSOCIATE EDITOR: | RAYMOND A. CRAIG'. Across the spine: 'ANDERSON | GILDZEN | CRAIG | [down the spine] A GATHERING OF POETS [across the spine] [publisher's device]'. Across the back cover: 'ISBN 0-87338-474-1'. White wove paper unwatermarked. Black endpapers. All edges trimmed.

Contents: Cosmopolitan Greetings, pp. 247-249.

$35.00. Published Oct. 26, 1992 in an impression of 750 copies.

a2. *First edition, paperbound, 1992*

A Gathering of Poets | *Edited by Maggie Anderson and Alex Gildzen* | *Raymond A. Craig, Associate Editor* | The Kent State University Press | Kent, Ohio, and London, England

One hundred sixty single leaves, pp. [i-v] vi-ix [x] 1-11 [12-14] 15-310. 22.8 x 15.3 cm. Perfect bound in stiff white paper wrappers. Covers printed in dark greenish blue (174), very light greenish blue (171), moderate red (15) and moderate pink (5). White wove paper unwatermarked. All edges trimmed.

$18.00. Published Oct. 26, 1992 in an impression of 1,000 copies.

B241   **TIKKUN**   **1992**

a1. *First edition, hardbound*

TIKKUN | [10.2 cm. rule composed of dots and dashes] | ...to heal, repair and transform the world | an anthology edited by | MICHAEL LERNER | TIKKUN BOOKS [bullet] [Hebrew characters] [bullet] Oakland, California [bullet] Jerusalem, Israel

[1-2]^{16} [3]^4 [4-19]^{16}, pp. [i-iv] v-ix [x] xi [xii] xiii-xxix [xxx-xxxii] 1-550 [551-552]. 26.1 x 18.1 cm. Bound in dark blue (183) cloth covered boards. Down the spine in silver: 'TIKKUN ANTHOLOGY [in 2 lines] Edited by I Michael Lerner [across the spine] TIKKUN BOOKS I [Hebrew characters]'. White wove paper unwatermarked. White endpapers. All edges trimmed. Issued in a white paper dust jacket printed in full color.

Contents: I Went to the Movie of Life, pp. 103-105.

$39.95. Published 1992 in an undisclosed number of copies.

a2. *First edition, paperbound, 1992*

TIKKUN I [10.2 cm. rule composed of dots and dashes] I ...to heal, repair and transform the world I an anthology edited by I MICHAEL LERNER I TIKKUN BOOKS [bullet] [Hebrew characters] [bullet] Oakland, California [bullet] Jerusalem, Israel

Two hundred ninety-two single leaves, pp. [i-iv] v-ix [x] xi [xii] xiii-xxix [xxx-xxxii] 1-550 [551-552]. 25.4 x 17.8 cm. Perfect bound in stiff white paper wrappers. Covers printed in full color. White wove paper unwatermarked. All edges trimmed.

$16.95. Published 1992 in an undisclosed number of copies.

B242   KEROUAC: VISIONS OF LOWELL   1993
by John J. Dorfner

Kerouac: I Visions of Lowell I John J Dorfner I Foreword by Allen Ginsberg I COOPER STREET PUBLICATIONS

Thirty-six single leaves, pp. [i-viii] [1] 2-60 [61-64]. 21.5 x 14.1 cm. Perfect bound in stiff white paper wrappers. Covers printed in black and white. White wove paper unwatermarked. All edges trimmed.

Contents: Foreword [prose], p. [vi] — [blurb on back cover from the foreword].

$11.95. Published May 1993 in an impression of 1,005 copies.

B243   MODERN MARRIAGE   1993
by Ali Zarrin

Modern Marriage I Poems by I Ali Zarrin I [publisher's device]

Single gathering of eighteen leaves, pp. [i-viii] 1 [2] 3-24 [25-28]. 21.6 x 13.8 cm. Stapled twice into stiff white coated paper wrappers. Covers printed in strong red (12) and black. White laid paper watermarked: '*Classic Text* '. All edges trimmed.

Contents: [letter to Ali Zarrin], p. 1.

$5.00. Published in Flint, MI by Alien Books in May 1993 in an impression of 500 copies.

B244 GAY ROOTS **1993**

a1. *First edition, hardbound*

GAY ROOTS | *An Anthology of Gay History,* | *Sex, Politics and Culture* | VOLUME 2 | EDITED BY WINSTON LEYLAND | GAY SUNSHINE PRESS | *San Francisco*

[1-10]^{16}, pp. [1-4] 5-8 [9-10] 11-319 [320]. 26.0 x 18.0 cm. Bound in moderate red (15) cloth covered boards printed in gold. Across the front cover: 'GAY ROOTS | Volume 2 | Edited by Winston Leyland'. Down the spine: '[in 1 line] GAY ROOTS Vol. 2 [in 2 lines] Edited by | Winston Leyland [in 1 line] Gay Sunshine Press'. White wove paper unwatermarked. White endpapers. All edges trimmed. Issued in a white paper dust jacket printed in black and vivid greenish yellow (97).

Contents: Many Loves [part 1 & 2], pp. 241-245 — Old Love Story, pp. 245-246.

$50.00. Published July 1993 in an impression of 200 copies.

a2. *First edition, paperbound, 1993*

GAY ROOTS | *An Anthology of Gay History,* | *Sex, Politics and Culture* | VOLUME 2 | EDITED BY WINSTON LEYLAND | GAY SUNSHINE PRESS | *San Francisco*

One hundred and sixty single leaves, pp. [1-4] 5-8 [9-10] 11-319 [320]. 25.4 x 17.7 cm. Perfect bound in stiff white paper wrappers. Covers printed in vivid greenish yellow (97) and black. White wove paper unwatermarked. All edges trimmed.

$19.95. Published July 1993 in an impression of 5,000 copies.

a3. *First edition, signed copied, 1993*

GAY ROOTS | *An Anthology of Gay History,* | *Sex, Politics and Culture* | VOLUME 2 | EDITED BY WINSTON LEYLAND | GAY SUNSHINE PRESS | *San Francisco*

[1-10]^{16}, pp. [1-4] 5-8 [9-10] 11-319 [320]. 26.2 x 17.6 cm. Half-bound in yellowish white (92) paper covered boards with grayish reddish purple cloth covered spine and corners. Across the spine all in gold: 'GAY | ROOTS | VOLUME 2 | Edited by | Winston | Leyland | GAY | SUNSHINE | PRESS'. White wove paper unwatermarked. Moderate violet (211) textured endpapers. All edges trimmed.

$200.00. Published Aug. 1993 in an impression of 26 copies, lettered A-Z.

B245 THE BOOK OF LISTS **1993**

[in white on a black stripe] THE PEOPLE'S ALMANAC ® | *Presents* | [2 lines with single rule frame with a solid triangle ornament in each corner] THE BOOK OF | *Lists* | [below the frame in white on a black stripe] THE '90S EDITION | DAVID WALLECHINSKY AND AMY WALLACE | [publisher's device] | LITTLE, BROWN AND COMPANY | Boston [bullet] New York [bullet] Toronto [bullet] London

Two hundred sixty-four single leaves, pp. [i-x] xi-xxvii [xxviii] xxix [xxx] xxxi-xxxii [1-2] 3-491 [492-496]. 24.0 x 13.7 cm. Quarter bound in light yellow (86) paper covered boards with strong purplish blue (196) paper spine. The publisher's device is blind stamped across the front cover. All in strong red (12): '[across the spine] *Wallechinsky* | *Wallace* | [down the spine] THE BOOK OF LISTS | THE '90S EDITION [across the spine] LITTLE, | BROWN'. White wove paper unwatermarked. White endpapers. All edges trimmed. Issued in a white paper dust jacket printed in yellow, orange, purple, blue, green and black.

Contents: Allen Ginsberg's 11 Greatest Blues Songs [list], p. 84.

$17.95. Published ca. Oct. 1993 in an impression of an undisclosed number of copies.

B246   **TO ELIZABETH & ELEANOR**   **1993**

TO ELIZABETH & ELEANOR | Great Queens Who Love Poetry | Lita Hornick & Poet Friends | GIORNO POETRY SYSTEMS

Thirty-eight single leaves, pp. [1-10] 11-74 [75-76]. 25.3 x 18.8 cm. Perfect bound in stiff white paper wrappers printed in black, moderate pink (5), strong red (12), strong greenish blue (169) and full color photograph on the back cover. White wove paper unwatermarked. All edges trimmed.

Contents: Cataract, by Lita Hornick, Allen Ginsberg and Peter Orlovsky, p. 16 — I Am So Happy, by Lita Hornick, Allen Ginsberg and Peter Orlovsky, p. 20 — [photograph (see also D133)].

$7.50. Published in Winter 1993 in an impression of 1,000 copies.

B247   **FRONTIER**   **1994**

[all on a green, blue, brown and black geological survey map] *Addie Anderson* | *Margo Burwell* | *James G. Davis* | *Electronic Cafe* | *Allen Ginsberg* | [on sloping base line] *First Edition FRONTIER* | *Alan Harrington* | *Fanny Howe* | *Timothy Leary* | *Karen Piovaty* | *Alfred Quiroz* | *Roy Walford* | *Joy Williams* | *Paula Wittner*

Twenty-eight single leaves, pp. [1-2] 3 [4-5] 6-54 [55-56]. 27.9 x 17.1 cm. Quarter bound in clear acetate covers with red leather spine. The clear acetate covers are printed in black, red and yellow and are backed by paper covers printed in full color design. Color and type of paper varies with each leaf. All edges trimmed. A clear acetate bookmark printed in black and a pair of 3-D glasses are included in each copy.

Contents: [drawing of a seated Buddha reproduced in gold foil], p. [5].

$100.00. Published Feb. 13, 1994 in an impression of 300 copies.

Note: Published in Oracle, AZ by Far Out West and edited by Margo Burwell.

B248   **THE WRITER'S DIGEST GUIDE TO GOOD WRITING**   **1994**

THE WRITER'S DIGEST | Guide TO | Good | Writing | *Edited by* | Thomas Clark | Bruce Woods | Peter Blocksom | Angela Terez | [publisher's device] | WRITER'S DIGEST BOOKS | Cincinnati, Ohio

One hundred seventy-six single leaves, pp. [i-xiv] [1] 2 [3-4] 5-338. 23.4 x 15.6 cm. Perfect bound in glossy paper covered boards. Covers printed in black, vivid red (11), moderate green (145) and deep blue (179). White wove paper unwatermarked. All edges trimmed.

Contents: What Way I Write! [prose], pp. 170-172.

$18.95. Published ca. March 14, 1994 in an undisclosed number of copies.

B249   **GAY PRIDE**   **1994**

GAY PRIDE | Photographs from Stonewall to Today | Fred W. McDarrah and Timothy S. McDarrah | Introductions by Allen Ginsberg and Jill Johnston | Historical essay by Robert Taylor | a cappella books

One hundred twelve single leaves, pp. [i] ii [iii-iv] v-vii [viii] ix-xi [xii] xiii-xxxiv [xxxv-xxxvi] 1-188. 25.3 x 20.2 cm. Perfect bound in stiff white paper wrappers. Covers printed in deep purplish pink (248) and black. White wove paper unwatermarked. All edges trimmed.

Contents: McDarrah's Parades [prose], pp. v-vii.

$20.00. Published ca. May 1994 in an undisclosed number of copies.

C

Contributions to Periodicals by Allen Ginsberg

All items are signed "Allen Ginsberg" unless otherwise indicated.

1941

C1 "Native Son" Makes Good! *Spectator,* vol. 16, no. 2 (Easter [April] 1941) p. 3.
[prose]
Note: This is the Central High School newspaper from Paterson, NJ.

C2 On Homework in General. *Spectator,* vol. 16, no. 2 (Easter [April] 1941) p. 13.
[prose]

C3 Central High Notes. *Paterson Evening News* (June 23, 1941) p. 24. [prose]

1943

C4 Class Poem. *Senior Mirror* ([June] 1943) p. [63].
Note: AG was also listed as literary editor of this, the senior yearbook of
Eastside High School from Paterson, NJ.

C5 Pass the Biscuits Pappy O'Daniel [and] Rep Gordon Canfield (Mine Own Dear
Congressman). *Columbia Jester,* vol. 43, no. 1 (Oct. 1943) p. 10.

Note: AG was listed in various editorial positions in issues of this college
humor magazine (hence some of the humorous position titles) between vol. 43,
no. 1 (Oct. 1943) and vol. 43, no. 14 (1945) as below:
 Editorial Staff — Alfonso Ginsberg [vol. 43, no. 1 (Oct. 1943)]
 Bereft Bard — Alabama Ginsberg [vol. 43, no. 2 (Nov. 1943)]
 Editorial Staff — Alfalfa Ginsberg [vol. 43, no. 3 (Dec. 1943)]
 Nubian — Angelo Ginsberg [vol. 43, no. 4 (Dec. 1943)]
 Micturitions Editor — Awynn Ginsberg [vol. 43, no. 5 (Feb. 1944)]
 Micturitions Editor — Awynn Ginsberg [vol. 43, no. 6 (May 1944)]
 Heeler — Angus Ginsberg [vol. 43, no. 7 (July 1944)]
 Editorial Board — Allan Ginsberg [vol. 43, no. 8 (July 1944)]
 Associate Editor — Allen Ginsberg [vol. 43, no. 9 (Oct. 1944)]
 Editorial Panel — Allen Ginsberg [vol. 43, no. 10 (Nov. 1944)]
 Editorial Panel — Allen Ginsberg [vol. 43, no. 11 (Christmas 1944)]
  [this issue incorrectly labeled as vol. VLIII, no. 3]
 Co-Editor — Allen Ginsberg [vol. 43, no. 12 (Jan. 1945)]
  [this issue incorrectly labeled as vol. VLIII, no. 4]

Co Editor — Allen Ginsberg [vol. 43, no. 13 (1945)]
[this issue incorreclty labeled as vol. VLIII, no. 5]
Editor Emeriti — Allen Ginsberg [vol. 43, no. 14 (1945)]
[this issue incorreclty labeled as vol. VLIII, no. 4]

C6 A Night in the Village. *Columbia Jester,* vol. 43, no. 6 (May 1944) p. 2.
Signed: Edgar Allen Ginsberg.

1944

C7 Epitaph for a Suicide [and] Epitaph for a Poet. *Columbia Jester,* vol. 43, no. 9 (Oct.
1944) p. 13.

C8 Song: The rose that scents [and] Mood [and] Ultimatum. *Columbia Jester,* vol. vliii,
no. 2 [vol. 43, no. 10] (Nov. 1944) pp. 3, 10.

C9 Pigskin is the Antichrist. *Columbia Jester,* vol. vliii, no. 3 [vol. 43, no. 11]
(Christmas 1944) p. 12. [prose]

C10 Flight. *Columbia Jester,* vol. vliii, no. 3 [vol. 43, no. 11] (Christmas 1944) p. 13.

1945

C11 [Kerouac, Jack]. A Translation from the French of Jean-Louis Incogniteau
[translated by AG]. *Columbia Jester,* vol. vliii, no. 4 [vol. 43, no. 12] (Jan.
1945) p. 4.

C12 Leda. *Columbia Jester,* vol. vliii, no. 4 [vol. 43, no. 12] (Jan. 1945) p. 12.

C13 Now, on this earth, by this seaside. *Columbia Review,* vol. 25, [no. 1] (April 1945)
p. 25.

C14 Do Not Despair, O Lonely Heart. *Columbia Review,* vol. 25 [no. 1] (April 1945) p.
28.

C15 [review of *V-Letter* by Karl Shapiro]. *Columbia Review,* vol. 25 [no. 1] (April
1945) pp. 30-31.

Note: AG was listed in various editorial positions in issues of this college
literary magazine between vol. 25, no. 1 (April 1945) and vol. 28, no. 3 (April
1948) as below:
Assistant Editor — Allen Ginsberg [vol. 27, no. 2 (Nov. 1946)]
Assistant Editor — Allen Ginsberg [vol. 27, no. 3 (Feb. 1947)]
Assistant Editor — Allen Ginsberg [vol. 27, no. 4 (May 1947)]
Associate Editor — Allen Ginsberg [vol. 28, no. 3 (April 1948)]
Associate Editor — Allen Ginsberg [vol. 28, no. 4 (May/June 1948)]

1946

C16 Pavel Tchelitchev's Cache-Cache: An Impression. *Columbia Review,* vol. 26, no.
3/4 (Jan.-March 1946) pp. 124-125. [prose]

C17 Boba's Birthday. *Columbia Review,* vol. 26, no. 5 (May 1946) pp. 138-140. [prose]

C18 [review of *For the Time Being* by W. H. Auden]. *Columbia Review,* vol. 26, no. 5
(May 1946) pp. 159-163. [prose]

C19 Spring Song [and] Spleen. *Columbia Review,* vol. 27, no. 1 (Sept. 1946) p. 19.

C20 [review of *Paterson, Book 1* by William Carlos Williams]. *Passaic Valley Examiner,* vol. 1, no. 49 (Sept. 14, 1946) p. 7.

C21 Hart Crane. *Columbia Review,* vol. 27, no. 2 (Nov. 1946) pp. 17-18.

1947

C22 A Paradox of Verbal Death. *Columbia Review,* vol. 27, no. 3 (Feb. 1947) p. 27.

C23 Song: Winds around the beaches blow. *Columbia Review,* vol. 27, no. 3 (Feb. 1947) p. 32.

C24 A Lover's Garden [and] The Proposal [and] Love Letter: Easter Sunday, 1947. *Columbia Review,* vol. 27, no. 4 (May 1947) pp. 15-16, 19-20.

1948

C25 From Denver Doldrums. *Columbia Review,* vol. 28, no. 2 (Feb. 1948) pp. 28-32.
Contents: Oedipus Eddie — Death Hath No Jurisdiction — Sweet and Sour Lyrics — Epithalamion for a Waste of Shame — Last Stanzas in Denver

C26 [review of *Death on the Installment Plan* by Céline]. *Halcyon,* vol. 1, no. 2 (Spring 1948) p. 51.

C27 Dakar Doldrums. *Columbia Review,* vol. 28, no. 4 (May/June 1948) pp. 3-9.
Note: This poem shared the Boar's Head Poetry First Prize with a poem by John Hollander.

1949

C28 I Cannot Sleep, I Cannot Sleep. *Columbia Review,* vol. 29, no. 2 (Feb. 1949) p. 26.

1950

C29 AG and Kerouac, Jack. Song: Fie My Fum. *Neurotica,* no. 6 (Spring 1950) p. 44.

C30 An Imaginary Rose in a Book [and] Crash. *Columbia Review,* vol. 31, no. 1 (Nov. 1950) p. 12.

1951

C31 [review of *Question on a Kite* by Nathaniel Burt]. *New York Herald Tribune* (Jan. 21, 1951) Book Review section, p. 11.
Unsigned.

C32 [review of *Toward Daybreak* by Collister Hutchinson]. *New York Herald Tribune* (Feb. 25, 1951) Book Review section, p. 19.

C33 [review of *The Emigrants* by Vilhelm Moberg and review of *The Dead Seagull* by George Barker]. *Newsweek,* vol. 38, no. 4 (July 23, 1951) p. 87.
Unsigned.

C34 [review of *The Iron Mistress* by Paul I. Wellman, (and possibly a review of *The Best American Short Stories 1951* edited by Martha Foley)]. *Newsweek,* vol. 38, no. 5 (July 30, 1951) pp. 69-70.
Unsigned.
Note: AG isn't certain if he wrote the review for *Short Stories* or not.

1953

C35 The Bricklayer's Lunch Hour. *New Directions in Prose and Poetry,* no. 14 (1953) p. 342.

C36 Psalm: This is the working. *New Directions in Prose and Poetry,* no. 14 (1953) pp. 373-374.

C37 I Dreamed. *New Directions in Prose and Poetry,* no. 14 (1953) pp. 385-386.

1954

C38 After All, What Else is There to Say? *Voices,* no. 154 (May/Aug. 1954) p. 9.

1955

C39 Last Stanzas in Denver. *Columbia Review,* vol. 35, no. 2 (Feb. 1955) p. 65.

C40 Sunset [and] Fragment of a Monument. *Variegation,* vol. 10, no. 39 (Summer 1955) pp. 50-51.

C41 Fragment of a Monument. *New York Herald Tribune* (Aug. 21, 1955) section 2, p. 4.

C42 Her Engagement. *Voices,* no. 158 (Sept.-Dec. 1955) p. 10.

C43 N.Y. '52. *Occident* (Fall 1955) p. 19.

C44 This Is about Death [and] A Sullen Interpolation. *Variegation,* vol. 11, no. 41 (Winter [Dec. 1955] 1956) pp. 12-13.

1956

C45 My Alba. *Needle,* vol. 1, no. 1 (April 1956) p. [7].

C46 Two Trees in Paterson-1952. *Variegation,* vol. 11, no. 43 (Summer 1956) pp. 52-53.

C47 A Dream Record: June 8, 1955. *i.e.; the Cambridge Review,* no. 6 (Dec. 1, 1956) pp. 116-117.

C48 The Trembling of the Veil: The flower. *Ark II Moby I* (1956/1957) pp. 20-22.

1957

C49 Shipyard No. 3 — Richmond. *Coastlines,* vol. 2, no. 3 [issue 7] (Spring/Summer 1957) pp. 26-27. [prose]

C50 Howl, part III. *Combustion,* no. 2 (April 1957) pp. 1-2.

C51 Howl. *Evergreen Review,* vol. 1, no. 2 ([May-June] 1957) pp. 137-147.

C52 Sunflower Sutra [and] Psalm III. *New Directions in Prose and Poetry,* no. 16 ([July 5] 1957) pp. 204-207.

C53 America. *Black Mountain Review,* no. 7 (Autumn 1957) pp. 25-29.

C54 Corso, Gregory [& AG]. The Literary Revolution in America. *Litterair Paspoort,* no. 110 (Nov. 1957) pp. 193-196. [prose]
Note: Although not credited, AG wrote much of this article.

C55 An Atypical Affair [and] A Typical Affair [and] How Come He Got Canned at the Ribbon Factory. *Ark III* (Winter 1957) pp. 19-21.

C56 Siesta in Xbalba and Return to the States. *Evergreen Review,* vol. 1, no. 4 (Winter 1957) pp. 29-47.

1958

C57 We Rode on a Lonely Bus [and] Hitch-hiking Key West [and] In a Red Bar [and] On Burrough's Work. *Yugen,* no. 1 ([March 13] 1958) pp. 22-23.

C58 Dawn [and] Malest Cornifici Tuo Catullo [and] The Nap. *Chicago Review,* vol. 12, no. 1 (Spring 1958) pp. 11-12.

C59 [2 letters to Paul Carroll]. *Chicago Review,* vol. 12, no. 3 (Autumn 1958) pp. 46-49.

C60 A New Cottage in Berkeley. *Yugen,* no. 3 ([Nov. 1] 1958) p. 14.

C61 Up Columbia [and] Going to Work [and] Sextillions of Infidels Staggering Home from Work [and] Wrote This Last Night [and] Squeal. *Isis,* no. 1330 (Nov. 5, 1958) pp. 20-21.

C62 [review of *Dharma Bums* by Jack Kerouac]. *Village Voice,* vol. 4, no. 3 (Nov. 12, 1958) Books section, pp. 3-5.

C63 Since We Had Changed. *Jargon,* no. 31 (Dec. 12-14, 1958) [issue called *14 Poets, 1 Artist*] 1 loose leaf sheet.

C64 [review of *Dances Before the Wall* performance with James Waring]. *Village Voice* (Dec. 17, 1958)

C65 [letter to Emmanuel A. Navaretta]. *It Is,* no. 3 (Winter [Dec. 22, 1958] / Spring 1959) pp. 73-75.

C66 Ready to Roll. *Partisan Review,* vol. 25, no. 1 (Winter 1958) p. 85.

C67 [prose blurb from Gregory Corso's *Gasoline*]. *Fortnightly,* no. 1 (ca. 1958) p. 4.

C68 A Dream X August 28, 1958. *Gaslight Poetry Review,* no. 1 (ca. 1958) pp. 21-22.

1959

C69 Mexican Suite. *Poetry Pilot* (Jan. 1, 1959) p. 2.

C70 Corso, Gregory and AG. [prose note]. *Chicago Sun-Times* (Jan. 30, 1959) p. 52.
Note: Printed in *Kup's Column* by Irv Kupcinet.

C71* To Lindsay. *Combustion,* no. 9 (Feb. 1959) p. 8.

C72 A Crazy Spiritual. *Yugen,* no. 4 ([Feb. 18] 1959) pp. 9-10.

C73 Orlovsky, Peter; Corso, Gregory and AG. [letter to the editor]. *Time,* vol. 73, no. 10 (March 9, 1959) p. 5.

C74 At Apollinaire's Grave. *Evergreen Review,* vol. 2, no. 8 (Spring 1959) pp. 59-62.

C75 The Shrouded Stranger. *Gemini,* vol. 2, no. 6 (Spring 1959) p. 52.

C76 Corso, Gregory; Orlovsky, Peter and AG. [letter to Mr. Maas's Children]. *Wagner Literary Magazine,* no. 1 (Spring 1959) pp. 30-31.

C77 Short Line Improvisation. *Grecourt Review,* vol. 2, no. 3 (April 1959) p. 191.
Note: A small number of these were produced as an offprint.

C78 Europe! Europe! [and] To Aunt Rose. *Liberation,* vol. 4, no. 2 (April 1959) pp. 9-10.

C79 Corso, Gregory; Orlovsky, Peter and AG. [letter to the editor with postscript signed by AG alone]. *Nation* (April 4, 1959) p. 2.

C80 Hymn from Kaddish. *Beatitude,* no. 1 ([May 9] 1959) unpaged.

C81 There's Nobody Here [and] Blessed Be the Muses. *Beatitude,* no. 2 (May 16, 1959) l. [5].

C82 Rexroth's Face Reflecting Human [and] Sex Perversion Destroys Reason. *Beatitude,* no. 3 (May 23, 1959) l. [8].

C83 [letter to the editor]. *San Francisco Chronicle* (May 27, 1959) p. 40.

C84 Letter from Paris. *Beatitude,* no. 4 (May 30, 1959) l. [3]. [poem]

C85 [short prose statement]. *Liberation,* vol. 4, no. 4 (June 1959) p. 10.

C86 The Green Automobile [and prose note]. *Mattachine Review,* vol. 5, no. 6 (June 1959) pp. 12-15.

C87 Mescaline. *Beatitude,* no. 6 (June [ca. 13] 1959) ll. 3-4.

C88 What's Buzzing. *Beatitude,* no. 6 (June [ca. 13] 1959) l. 17.

C89 Kaddish [pt. 1]. *Big Table,* vol. 1, no. 2 (Summer 1959) pp. 19-23. [see also D1]

C90 Mr. Ginsberg Replies to Mrs. Trilling. *Partisan Review,* vol. 26, no. 3 (Summer 1959). [prose]

C91 To Lindsay. *Playboy,* vol. 6, no. 7 (July 1959) p. 45.

C92 [prose note]. *Beetitood [Beatitude]* no. 7 (July 4, 1959) l. [4].

C93 Afternoon Seattle. *Beetitood [Beatitude]* no. 7 (July 4, 1959) l. [9].

C94 A Lion Met America. *Beetitood [Beatitude]* no. 7 (July 4, 1959) l. [16].

C95 Ginsberg 'Howls' Again — On the S.F. Poetry Controversy. *San Francisco [Sunday] Chronicle* (July 26, 1959) This World section, p. 27. [prose]
Note: Reprinted under the title of *Poetry, Violence, and the Trembling Lambs.*

C96 [telegram to Lawrence Ferlinghetti]. *Beatitude,* no. 8 (Aug. 15, 1959) l. [8].

C97 Sakyamuni Coming Out From the Mountain. *Beatitude,* no. 8 (Aug. 15, 1959) l. [12].

C98 From Kaddish. *Yugen,* no. 5 ([Aug. 20] 1959) pp. 2-4.

C99 Poetry, Violence, and the Trembling Lambs. *Village Voice,* vol. 4, no. 44 (Aug. 26, 1959) pp. 1, 8. [prose]

C100 That Golden Light. *Beatitude,* no. 9 (Sept. 18, 1959) l. [4].

C101 From the Notebook, Jan. 1959. *Nomad,* no. 4 (Fall 1959) pp. 6-7. [poem]

C102 Over Kansas. *Beatitude,* no. 10 (Oct. 1959) ll. [15-17].

C103* To Aunt Rose [and] To Lindsay [and] Kaddish (excerpt). *Jabberwock* ([Oct. 31] 1959) pp. 14-19.

C104 Kaddish (pts. II-IV). *Big Table,* vol. 1, no. 3 (Autumn [Nov./Dec.] -Winter 1959) pp. 7-10.

C105 [prose note]. *Big Table,* vol. 1, no. 3 (Autumn [Nov./Dec.] -Winter 1959) p. 118.

C106 Notes Written on Finally Recording Howl. *Evergreen Review,* vol. 3, no. 10 (Nov./Dec. 1959) pp. 132-135. [prose]

C107 On Visions. *Beatitude,* no. 11 (Nov. 2, 1959) l. [8].

C108 Death to Van Gogh's Ear. *Times Literary Supplement* (Nov. 6, 1959) p. 12.

C109 Message. *5 x 4* (1959) unpaged.

C110* Over Kansas. *Hearse,* no. 5 (1959) pp. 1-4.

C111 To Lindsay. *Semina,* no. 4 (1959) 1 loose leaf.

C112 Squeal. *Venture,* vol. 3, no. 1-2 (1959) p. 4.

C113* My Sad Self. *White Dove Review,* vol. 1, no. 3 (1959) pp. [2-3].

1960

C114 Sather Gate Illumination. *Evergreen Review,* vol. 4, no. 11 (Jan./Feb. 1960) pp. 96-99.

C115 Death to Van Gogh's Ear. *L.A.,* vol. 1, no. 10 (Jan. 1960) p. 19.

C116 [response to questionnaire]. *Mademoiselle,* vol. 50, no. 3 (Jan. 1960) pp. 34 & 17.

C117 Mandala [from Lysergic Acid]. *New Departures,* no. 2-3 (early 1960) p. 79.

C118 [letter to the editor]. *Shaw Society Newsletter,* vol. 3, no. 1 (Jan. 1960) p. 2.

C119 [prose autobiographical statement]. *WFMT Chicago Fine Arts Guide* (Jan. 1960) p. 18.

C120 [blurb for *Happy Birthday of Death* by Gregory Corso]. *Big Table,* vol. 1, no. 4 (Spring 1960) p. 6.

C121 Message. *Big Table,* vol. 1, no. 4 (Spring 1960) p. 95.

C122 Notes on Young Poets. *Big Table,* vol. 1, no. 4 (Spring 1960) pp. 124-126. [prose]

C123 Paterson. *Kulchur,* no. 1 (Spring 1960) pp. 36-37.

C124 [postscript to letter to John Kelly by Peter Orlovsky]. *Beatitude,* no. 14 (May 6, 1960) l. [27].

C125 On Visions. *Beatitude,* no. 15 (June 17, 1960) p. 21.

C126 [letter to Gregory Corso]. *Partisan Review,* vol. 27, no. 3 (Summer 1960) pp. 569-576.

C127 Poem Rocket. *Poetry London-New York,* vol. 1, no. 4 (Summer 1960) pp. 19-21.

C128 From LSD 25 [Mandala]. *Birth,* no. 3, book 1 (Autumn 1960) p. 64.

C129 From Journals, Sunday, April 19, 1952 [We're Flowers to Rocks]. *Birth,* no. 3, book 1 (Autumn 1960) pp. 71-78. [prose]

C130 [letter to the editor]. *Village Voice* (Sept. 29, 1960) p. 4.

C131 Laughing Gas, pt. 1. *Beatitude,* no. 17 (Oct.-Nov. 1960) ll. [4-6].

C132 Some Writing from a Journal (1959, NY). *Chelsea,* no. 8 (Oct. 1960) pp. 62-63. [poem]

C133 What Way I Write. *Writer's Digest,* vol. 40, no. 10 (Oct. 1960) pp. 35, 75-76. [prose]

C134 Aether. *Hasty Papers,* [no. 1] (ca. Dec. 1960) pp. 19-23.

C135 My Sad Self. *Folio,* vol. 25, no. 1 (Winter 1960) pp. 35-36.

C136 To an Old Poet in Peru. *Rhinozeros,* no. 2 (1960) pp. [6-7].

C137 Lysergic Acid. *Stand,* vol. 4, no. 4 (ca. 1960) pp. 23-25.

1961

C138 Love Poem on a Theme by Whitman. *Swank,* vol. 7, no. 6 (Jan. 1961) p. 13.

C139 [letter to the editor]. *Columbia Review,* vol. 41, no. 3 (Spring/Summer 1961) p. xxxviii.

C140 Five Gates of Wrath [and] Hearing Blake Read the Sick Rose [and] A Very Dove [and] A Vision 1948 [and] Do We Understand Each Other? *Columbia Review,* vol. 41, no. 3 (Spring/Summer 1961) pp. xxxix-xli.

C141 Kerouac, Jack; Cassady, Neal and AG. Pull My Daisy. *Metronome,* vol. 78, no. 4 (April 1961) p. 27.

C142 The End. *Yugen,* no. 7 ([April 25] 1961) p. 62.

C143 Lysergic Acid [and prose note]. *Evergreen Review,* vol. 5, no. 18 (May/June 1961) pp. 80-85.

C144 Corso, Gregory; Orlovsky, Peter and AG. [prose]. *Chicago Sun-Times* (May 17, 1961) section 2, p. 9.
Note: Printed in Art Buchwald's column.

C145 American Change. *Nomad,* no. 9 (Summer 1961) pp. 18-19.

C146 To an Old Poet in Peru. *Provincetown Review,* no. 4 (Summer 1961) pp. 31-32.

C147 When the Mode of the Music Changes the Walls of the City Shake [and note]. *Second Coming Magazine,* vol. 1, no. 2 (July 1961) pp. 2, 40-42.

C148 [letter to Miles Payne]. *Light Year* (Autumn 1961) unpaged.

C149 The End (To Kaddish). *Outsider,* vol. 1, no. 1 (Fall 1961) pp. 28-29.

C150 History of the Jewish Socialist Party in America. *Floating Bear,* no. 15 ([Nov.] 1961) pp. [7-8]. [prose]

C151 Galilee Shore. *Jerusalem Post* (Nov. 17, 1961) p. 6.

C152 The Lion for Real. *New Directions in Prose and Poetry,* no. 17 ([Nov. 30] 1961) pp. 147-149.

C153 Laughing Gas Fragments [and] The Real Distinguished Thing. *Damascus Road,* no. 1 (1961) pp. 45-46.

C154 Breughel—Triumph of Death. *Kulchur,* no. 3 (1961) pp. 33-34. [prose excerpt from a letter to Jack Kerouac]

C155* Mandala [from Lysergic Acid]. *Schriff-Taal,* no. 1 (1961) loose leaf page.
Note: In facsimile holograph on a folded paper leaf inserted and unnumbered in this collection of poems from various countries, each poem being in the individual poet's native language and holograph.

C156 Kaddish [excerpt]. *Sidewalk,* vol. 1, no. 1 (1961) pp. 61-62.

1962

C157 [prefatory note to *Ten Episodes from The Soft Machine* by William S. Burroughs]. *Olympia,* no. 1 (Jan. 1962) p. 4. [prose]
Note: Reprinted and expanded from the inside front jacket of *The Soft Machine.*

C158 Prose Contribution to Cuban Revolution. *Pa'Lante,* vol. 1, no. 1 (May 19, 1962) [issue also called *New Writing: Cuban Ivan USA*] pp. 61-73. [prose]

C159 [drawing entitled *The Vomiter*]. *Illustrated Weekly of India* (May 27, 1962) p. 45.

C160 Orlovsky, Peter and AG. [letter to Charlie Chaplin]. *Floating Bear,* no. 21 (Aug. 1962) p. [9].

C161 Havana 1953. *Between Worlds,* vol. 2, no. 1 [issue 3] (Fall/Winter 1962) pp. 6-9.

C162 Abstraction in Poetry. *Nomad,* no. 10/11 (Autumn 1962) pp. 50-51. [prose]

C163 [letter to the editor]. *Eros,* vol. 1, no. 4 (Winter 1962) p. 24.

1963

C164 Aether. *Quest,* no. 36 (Winter [Jan./March 1963] 1962-63) pp. 61-72.

C165 [letter to a young poet]. *Way Out* [formerly *Balanced Living*] vol. 19, no. 1 (Jan. 1963) pp. 17-18.

C166 [letters to Lawrence Ferlinghetti]. *City Lights Journal,* no. 1 ([June 1] 1963) pp. 7-14. [see also D3]

C167 [journal entry]. *Esquire,* vol. 60, no. 1 [issue 356] (July 1963) pp. 48, 115. [prose]
Note: Printed in *Back on the Open Road for Boys* by Alice Glaser.

C168 Tokyo Tower. *Ferret,* vol. 2, no. 6 (Oct. 16, 1963) p. 5.

C169 The Change. *Fuck You/A Magazine of the Arts,* no. 5, vol. 5 (Dec. 1963) pp. [3-6].
Note: This publisher reverses the roles of volume and issue numbers.

C170 [letter to Shakti Chatterjea]. *Chinha,* no. 1 (1963) pp. 41-43.

C171 [journal entries and] Jan. 9. 63 [poem]. *Krittibas,* no. 16 (1963) pp. 90-106.

C172 Black Magicians [and] I, Allen Ginsberg a Love Starved Eastern Jewish Hairy
Loss [excerpt of The Change]. *Now* (1963) pp. 17-18.

C173 To an Old Poet in Peru. *Outburst,* no. 2 (1963) pp. [24-26].

1964

C174 Owl. *Open Space,* no. 0 (Jan. 1964) [issue called *A Prospectus*] p. [22].

C175 [letter to the editor]. *Poetry,* vol. 103, no. 4 (Jan. 1964) p. 271.

C176 July 6, 1962 Calcutta 12 pm. *Poets at Le Metro,* vol. 11 (Feb. 1964) p. [5].

C177 [letter to the editor]. *Passaic Herald-News* (Feb. 26, 1964) p. 12.

C178 Who Will Take Over the Universe? *Wild Dog,* vol. 1, no. 6 (Feb. 29, 1964) p. 31.

C179* Heat. *Intrepid,* no. 1 (March 1964) p. [6].

C180 Seabattle of Salamis Took Place Off Perama. *Desert Review* (Spring 1964) p. 13.

C181 A Dream: Morn 9 AM Jan 5 1962. *Gnaoua,* no. 1 (Spring 1964) pp. 31-32.
[prose]

C182 A Writing (May 1963). *Gnaoua,* no. 1 (Spring 1964) p. 90.

C183 The Change. *Kulchur,* vol. 4, no. 13 (Spring 1964) pp. 44-48.

C184 Walt Whitman. *Fuck You, A Magazine of the Arts,* no. 5, vol. 6 (April 1964) l. [5].

C185 Who Will Take Over the Universe? [and drawing of three fish which share a
common head]. *Jester of Columbia* [also called *Columbia Jester*] vol. 67, no. 1
(April/May 1964) p. 11.

C186* [drawing entitled *The U.S. Federal Government is a Big Daisy*]. *Poets at Le
Metro,* vol. 13 (April 1964) p. [8].

C187 [letter to the editor]. *Wichita Beacon* (April 16, 1964) p. 8A.

C188 [letter to the editor]. *Fact,* vol. 1, no. 3 (May/June 1964) p. 27.

C189 Morning Dream [and] A Few Bengali Poets. *City Lights Journal,* no. 2
([June/Oct.] 1964) pp. 116-119.

C190 Carr, Lucien and AG. Some Thoughts about Elise Cowen. *City Lights Journal,*
no. 2 ([June/Oct.] 1964) p. 178. [prose]

C191 The Change. *C, a Journal of Poetry,* vol. 1, no. 9 (Summer 1964) pp. 50-53.
Note: This is the first version to include prose footnotes no. 1-12.

C192* In a Shaking Hand [and drawing with notes]. *Poets at Le Metro,* vol. 15 (July 1964) pp. 4-5.

C193 [letter to the editor]. *New York Post* (July 20, 1964) p. 16.
Note: Printed in *Rages and Outrages* column by Archer Winsten.

C194 May 22 Calcutta. *Nadada,* no. 1 ([Aug.] 1964) p. 5.

C195 Back to the Wall. *Times Literary Supplement,* no. 3258 (Aug. 6, 1964) pp. 678-679. [prose]

C196 Statement to *The Burning Bush. Burning Bush,* no. 2 (Sept. 1964) pp. 39-40. [prose]

C197 A Fuck You Position Paper. *Fuck You, A Magazine of the Arts,* no. 5, vol. 7 (Sept. 1964) ll. [2-5]. [prose]

C198 From Long Unfinished Poem [Television Was a Baby]. *Fuck You, A Magazine of the Arts,* no. 5, vol. 7 (Sept. 1964) ll. [17-18].

C199 [blurb for *Last Exit to Brooklyn* by Hubert Selby, Jr.]. *New York Times* (Oct. 27, 1964) p. 37.

C200 Why is God Love, Jack? *My Own Mag* (Nov. 1, 1964) p. [6].

C201 Journals Nov. 22, '63. *Poetry Newsletter,* no. 1 (Nov. 1964) p. [2]. [prose]

C202 Saraswati Stotra [mantra] [and] The Hari Krishna Great Mantra [mantra[[and notes]. *Poets at Le Metro,* vol. 18 (Nov. 1964) p. [4].

C203 An Indirect Encounter. *Illustrated Weekly of India,* vol. 85, no. 47 (Nov. 22, 1964) p. 39. [prose]

C204 [blurb for *Last Exit to Brooklyn* by Hubert Selby, Jr.]. *Evergreen Review,* vol. 8, no. 34 (Dec. 1964)

C205 [letter to the editor]. *Jewish Currents,* vol. 18, no. 11 (Dec. 1964) p. 45.

C206 The Classics and the Man of Letters. *Arion,* vol. 3, no. 4 (Winter 1964) pp. 54-56. [response to a questionnaire]

C207 The Change. *Poetmeat,* no. 7 (Dec. 25, 1964/1965) pp. [38-42].

C208 The Fall of America [Man's Glory]. *Pogamoggan,* no. 1 (1964) pp. 63-64.

1965

C209* Fragment from Boston Journals. *Poets at Le Metro,* vol. 20 (Jan. 1965) p. [4]. [poem]

C210* Mantra Commonly Sung India [mantra]. *Poets at Le Metro,* vol. 20 (Jan. 1965) p. [4].

C211 From Journals [Lying in Bed]. *Second Coming Magazine,* vol. 1, no. 6 (Jan. 1965) pp. 63-66.
Note: Includes: Nov. 5 62 — Nov. 14 — Dec. 13 — Dec. 14, 1962 — Jan. 9 63 [poem] — Jan. 13 [poem] — [prose introduction to *The Ivory Bastard* by Alden Van Buskirk]

C212 May Day. *Synapse,* no. 3 (Jan. 1965) p. 10.

C213 From Journals. *American Dialog,* vol. 2, no. 1 (Feb./March 1965) p. 10. [poem reprinted in *Journals, Early Fifties Early Sixties*]

C214 From Journals: '19 Dec. 1962 (Well, Where Now Me, What Next) [poem] [and] Dream: 21 Dec. 1962 [prose]. *Fuck You, A Magazine of the Arts* [Third Anniversary Mad Motherfucker Issue] (Feb. 1965) pp. [10-13].

C215 [blurb for *Last Exit to Brooklyn* by Hubert Selby, Jr.]. *Evergreen Review,* vol. 9, no. 35 (March 1965)

C216 From Calcutta Journal. *Intrepid,* no. 5 (March 1965) ll. 21-31. [prose]

C217 On the Roof from Journals 18 April 64 [prose] [and] Seabattle of Salamis Took Place Off Perama. *Residu,* vol. 1, no. 1 (Spring 1965) pp. 20-25.

C218 Today. *Yale Literary Magazine,* vol. 133, no. 5 (April 1965) pp. 55-58.

C219 [drawing and reproduction of notebook page]. *Mlada Fronta,* vol. 21, no. 117 (May 16, 1965) p. 5.

C220 Liverpool Muse. *Topolski's Chronicle,* vol. 13, no. 5-6 (Spring-Summer [ca. June] 1965) p. 5.

C221 [single line from journal]. *Paterson Morning Call* (June 2, 1965) pp. 1, 12.
Note: Printed in *Diary of Ex-Paterson Beat Poet Gives Czech Press Rare Excitement* by Jeff Endrst.

C222 [letter to the editor]. *Ladder,* vol. 10, no. 1 (Oct. 1965)

C223 Guru On Primrose Hill [and] After Yeats [and] To Robert Creeley. *Minnesota Review,* vol. 5, no. 4 (Oct./Dec. 1965) pp. 307, 309.

C224 Benares [reprinted as: Death News]. *Blitz,* no. 2 [ca. Nov/Dec. 1965] pp. [18-19].

C225 To the Angels. *Berkeley Barb,* vol. 1, no. 15 (Nov. 19, 1965) pp. 1-2.

C226 Ginsberg on March. *Berkeley Barb,* vol. 1, no. 15 (Nov. 19, 1965) pp. 1, 4. [prose]

C227 [drawing and reproduction of manuscript page]. *Film a Doba,* no. 11 (Nov. 20, 1965) p. 24.

C228 Studying the Signs [and] Guru. *Isis,* no. 1502 (Nov. 26, 1965) pp. 12-13.

C229 [letter to the editor] [and] Sakamuni [sic] Coming Out from the Mountain. *Esquire,* vol. 64, no. 6 (Dec. 1965) pp. 151, 276, 278, 280.

C230* I Am a Victim of Telephone. *Free Forum* [ca. Dec. 1965]

C231 Journals-1963 [Who Will Take Over the Universe?]. *Wild Dog,* no. 19/20 (Dec. 8, 1965) pp. 14-15.

C232 January NY 1961. *Brown Paper,* no. 1 (1965) insert.
Note: This is an unpaged insert of a reproduction of a manuscript with holograph notes in the margin.

C233 Liner Notes from *Howl and Other Poems. Everyday Theatre Bulletin* [no. 1] [1965] ll. 6-8. [prose]
Note: Date estimated based on an advertisement by the Gotham Book Mart.

C234 [letter to the editor]. *Intercourse,* no. 2 (1965) p. 26.

C235 [letter to the editor]. *Long Hair,* vol. 1, no. 1 (1965) inside front cover.

C236 Ankor Wat. *Long Hair,* vol. 1, no. 1 (1965) pp. 8-33.

C237 Back to the Wall. *Now Now* [*Now,* no. 2] (1965) pp. 31-32. [prose]

C238 November 23, 1963. *Now Now* [*Now,* no. 2] (1965) p. 44.

C239 Who Will Take Over the Universe? [and] Paterson. *Underdog,* no. 7 (1965) pp. 10,11.

1966

C240 New York to San Fran. *City Lights Journal,* no. 3 ([Jan. 1] 1966) pp. 108-128.

C241 I Am a Victim of Telephone. *East Side Review,* vol. 1, no. 1 (Jan./Feb. 1966) pp. 44-47.

C242 How to Make a March/Spectacle. *Liberation,* vol. 10, no. 10 (Jan. 1966) pp. 42-43. [prose]

C243 To the Hell's Angels. *Liberation,* vol. 10, no. 10 (Jan. 1966) pp. 43-47.

C244 Who Be Kind To. *Los Angeles Free Press,* vol. 3, no. 3 [issue 79] (Jan. 21, 1966) p. 7.

C245 Psalm IV. *Floating Bear,* no. 32 ([Feb.] 1966) p. [7].

C246 Auto Poesy to Nebraska. *Scrip* (Summer [after March 1 & before April 28] 1966) insert.

C247 Auto Poesy to Nebraska. *Do-It!,* vol. 1, no. 1 [Spring/Summer] 1966) ll. 3-6.

C248 From Calcutta Journal. *Intrepid,* no. 6 ([after March 18] 1966) ll. 3-5. [prose]

C249 Orlovsky, Peter and AG. [letter to Charlie Chaplin]. *Film Culture,* no. 40 (Spring 1966) p. 7.

C250 Gridhakuta Hill [and note]. *Hika,* vol. 28, no. 3 (Spring/Summer 1966) pp. 34-35.

C251 January N.Y. 1961 [and] Fragment 1957-The Names [and] O Ant. *Paris Review,* vol. 10, no. 37 (Spring 1966) pp. 56-61.

Related Item: [letter]. *Partisan Review,* vol. 33, no. 2 (Spring 1966) pp. [225-226].
Note: Although signed by AG and 119 others, he did not write this letter.

C252 Kral Majales. *Evergreen Review,* vol. 10, no. 40 (April 1966) pp. 22-23.

C253 Portland Aug. 27, 1965 [Portland Coliseum]. *Frice,* vol. 1, no. 1 [ca. April 1966] p. [5].

C254 [letter to the editor]. *Life* (April 15, 1966) p. 31.

C255 Wichita Vortex Sutra. *Village Voice,* vol. 11, no. 28 (April 28, 1966) pp. 17-19.

C256* Wichita Vortex Sutra. *Grist,* no. 8 ([after May 1] 1966) pp. 13-17, 20-24.

C257 Wales Visitation. *New Yorker,* vol. 44, no. 12 (May 11, 1966) pp. 44-45.

C258 Wichita Vortex Sutra. *Sunflower,* vol. 70, no. 83 (May 23, 1966) pp. 4-5, 7.

C259 Wichita Vortex Sutra. *Berkeley Barb,* vol. 2, no. 21 (May 27, 1966) pp. 1, 4-5, 7.

C260 [letter to Max Scherr]. *Berkeley Barb,* vol. 2, no. 21 (May 27, 1966) p. 1.

C261 Wichita Vortex Sutra [excerpt]. *Life,* vol. 60, no. 21 (May 27, 1966) p. 80.

C262 Wichita Vortex Sutra. *Peace News,* no. 1561 (May 27, 1966) pp. 5-8.

C263 [response to questionnaire]. *Win,* vol. 2, no. 9 (May 28, 1966) p. 19.

C264 Wichita Vortex Sutra. *Fifth Estate,* no. 9 (June 1966) pp. 4-5.

C265* Wichita Vortex Sutra. *Quixote,* vol. 1, no. 7 (June 1966) insert on blue paper.

C266 Wichita Vortex Sutra. *Los Angeles Free Press,* vol. 3, no. 22 (June 3, 1966) pp. 8-9, 11.

C267 [letter to Art Kunkin]. *Los Angeles Free Press,* vol. 3, no. 22 (June 3, 1966) p. 11.

C268 A Raw Place in New. *Library Journal,* vol. 91, no. 12 (June 15, 1966) pp. 3076-3077. [prose]

C269 Senate News. *San Francisco Chronicle* (June 15, 1966) p. 13.

C270 Senate News. *Washington Post* (June 15, 1966) pp. A1, A7.

C271 Selections from Journals. *Boss,* no. 1 (Summer 1966) pp. 3-15. [prose]

C272 [letter to the readers]. *Paris Review,* vol. 10, no. 38 (Summer 1966) p. 149.

C273 Senate News. *Village Voice,* vol. 11, no. 36 (June 23, 1966) p. 33.

C274 Fragments from a Diary [includes poems: Jan. 1, 1960 Sunrise — Shot in the Back by a Fallen Leaf — That Every Leaf Wave on the Tree — America is Covered with Lies]. *Evergreen Review,* vol. 10, no. 42 (Aug. 1966) pp. 28-29.

C275 [letter to the editor]. *Cleveland State University Cauldron* (Aug. 3, 1966)

C276 A National Hallucination. *Washington Bulletin,* vol. 19, no. 50 (Aug. 8, 1966) pp. 241-242. [prose]

C277 [open letter]. *San Francisco Oracle,* vol. 1, no. 1 (Sept. 20, 1966) p. 5.

C278 Drowse Murmurs. *Grist,* no. 9 ([Fall] 1966) p. 25.

C279 [letter to R. Peter Strauss]. *Village Voice* (Sept. 29, 1966) p. 9.
Note: Printed in *Pop Eye* by Richard Goldstein.

C280 [blurb for *Spare Parts* by Charles Henri Ford]. *East Village Other,* vol. 1, no. 22 (Oct. 15-Nov. 1, 1966) p. [20].

C281 Preface on Marijuana. *Spectrum,* vol. 17, no. 13 (Oct. 21, 1966) Marijuana section, pp. 1-2. [prose]

C282 The Great Marijuana Hoax. *Atlantic,* vol. 218, no. 5 (Nov. 1966) pp. 104, 107-112. [prose]

C283 [response to questionnaire]. *Fact:,* vol. 3, no. 6 (Nov./Dec. 1966) p. 14.

C284 Proem to Wichita Vortex Sutra. *Ramparts,* vol. 5, no. 5 (Nov. 1966) pp. 56-58.

C285 The Fugs. *Pro These,* no. 0/1 (Nov. 30, 1966) p. 34. [prose]

C286 Reflections on the Mantra. *Back to Godhead,* vol. 1, no. 3 (Dec. 1, 1966) ll. 5-9. [prose]

C287 To the Body. *Notes from the Garage Door,* vol. 3, no. 1 (Dec. 1966) pp. 8-9.

C288 Renaissance or Die. *East Village Other,* vol. 2, no. 2 (Dec. 15/Jan. [1966-1967]) pp. 6-7. [prose]

C289 Who Be Kind To. *Some/Thing,* vol. 2, no. 1 (Winter 1966) pp. 10-12.

C290 Renaissance or Die. *Los Angeles Free Press,* vol. 3, no. 51 (Dec. 23, 1966) pp. 3, 10. [prose]

C291 Understand That This Is a Dream. *Coyote's Journal,* no. 5-6 (1966) pp. 77-80.

C292 Entering Kansas City High. *Great Society,* no. 1 (1966) l. [10].

C293 Amsterdam Avenue Bar [reprinted as: Uptown]. *Ice,* vol. 1, no. 1 (1966) p. 2.

C294 A Glass of Ayahuasca. *Marrahwannah Quarterly,* vol. 2, no. 4 (1966) pp. 5, 7. [prose]

C295 Note Poem [reprinted as: First Party at Ken Kesey's with Hell's Angels]. *Underdog,* no. 8 (1966) p. 3.

C296 In Society. *Underdog,* no. 8 (1966) p. 19.

1967

C297 [letter to the editor]. *East Village Other,* vol. 2, no. 3 (Jan. 1-15, 1967) p. 2.

C298 May 26, 1960. *Marrahwannah Quarterly,* vol. 3, no. 1 (Jan. 1967) p. [14]. [poem]

C299 Who Be Kind To. *Playboy,* vol. 14, no. 1 (Jan. 1967) pp. 163, 252.

C300 Public Solitude. *Respond,* vol. 1, no. 1 (Jan. 1967) pp. 22-26. [prose]

C301 Wichita Vortex Sutra. *Respond,* vol. 1, no. 1 (Jan. 1967) pp. 27-35.

C302 Renaissance or Die. *San Francisco Oracle,* vol. 1, no. 5 (Jan. 1967) pp. 12-15, 17. [prose]

C303 [blurb for *Brigg Flatts* by Basil Bunting]. *International Times,* no. 6 (Jan. 16-29, 1967) p. 14.

C304 Public Solitude. *International Times,* no. 7 (Jan. 30-Feb. 12, 1967) pp. 4-5. [prose]

C305 [blurb for *Angel* by Ray Bremser]. *City of San Francisco Oracle,* vol. 1, no. 7 (Feb. 1967) p. 35.

C306 Public Solitude. *Renewal,* no. 7 (Feb. 1967) pp. 12-14. [prose]

C307 Reflections on the Mantra. *International Times,* no. 8 (Feb. 13-26, 1967) pp. 8-9. [prose]

C308 [letter to Dick Bakken]. *Salted Feathers,* vol. 4, no. 1-2 [issue 8/9] (March 1967) p. [19].

C309 Stotras to Kali Destroyer of Illusions. *Salted Feathers,* vol. 4, no. 1-2 [issue 8/9] (March 1967) p. [23].

C310 Nashville April 8. *Spectrum,* vol. 5, no. 3 (Spring 1967) pp. 24-25.

C311 [blurb for *The Beard* by Michael McClure]. *Berkeley Barb,* vol. 4, no. 13 (March 31, 1967) p. 10.

C312 Chances "R". *Evergreen Review,* vol. 11, no. 46 (April 1967) p. 57.

C313 Public Solitude. *Liberation,* vol. 12, no. 2 (April 1967) pp. 30-33. [prose]

C314 [blurb for *Angel* by Ray Bremser]. *Village Voice* (April 20, 1967) p. 6.

C315 [response to questionnaire]. *Writer's Forum,* vol. 3, no. 4 (Spring [April 24] 1967) p. 26.

C316 [drawing of three fish which share a common head and letter to the editor]. *Catholic Worker,* vol. 33, no. 7 (May 1967) p. 1.

C317 [blurb for *Krishna Consciousness* (recording)]. *San Francisco Oracle,* vol. 1, no. 8 ([May/June] 1967) p. 36.

C318 [letter to the editor]. *Oregonian* (June 4, 1967) Forum section, p. 2.

C319 [blurb for *Apocalypse Rose* by Charles Plymell]. *Last Times,* no. [1] [ca. Summer 1967] p. [10].

C320 Television Baby Crawling Toward That Death Chamber. *Last Times,* no. [1] [ca. Summer 1967] pp. [10-12].

C321 [letter to Leo Skir]. *Evergreen Review,* vol. 11, no. 48 (Aug. 1967) p. 70.
Note: Printed in *Elise Cowen : A Brief Memoir of the Fifties* by Leo Skir, pp. 70-72+.

C322 The Great Marijuana Hoax. *Philologistical Institute,* report 1, series 15 (Aug. 1967) pp. 7-23. [prose]

C323 Stotras to Kali Destroyer of Illusions. *Salted Feathers,* vol. 4, no. 3 [issue 10] (Aug. 1967) pp. [4-7]. [prose]

C324 [blurb for *Apocalypse Rose* by Charles Plymell]. *San Francisco Earthquake*, vol. 1, no. 1 (Fall [Aug. 7] 1967) p. 7.

C325 Artaud Expresses Himself Like a Can of Spy-Being, Exploded [and] One Day. *Interim Pad*, no. 1 (Sept. 1967) ll. 6-12.

C326 On Henri Michaux. *Interim Pad*, no. 1 (Sept. 1967) ll. 13-17. [prose]

C327 Journal Entry on Visit to Timothy Leary's House in Boston, Dec. 1960 [reprinted as: Police]. *Klacto [veedsedsteen]*, no. 23 (Sept. 1967) pp. [43-44]. [poem]

C328 [drawing of three fish which share a common head and] La Poesia è L'Anima [Poetry is the Soul]. *Il Lavoro* (Sept. 26, 1967) p. 3. [prose]

C329 Beginning of a Poem of "These States". *Evergreen Review*, vol. 11, no. 49 (Oct. 1967) pp. 46-49.

C330 Kansas City to Saint Louis. *Paris Magazine*, no. 1 (Oct. 1967) pp. 14-15.

C331 First Party at Ken Kesey's with Hell's Angels. *Paris Magazine*, no. 1 (Oct. 1967) p. 17.

C332 [blurb for *Portrait of Jason* by Shirley Clarke]. *Village Voice* (Nov. 16, 1967) p. 33.

C333 Reflections on the Mantra. *Fifth Estate*, vol. 2, no. 17 (Dec. 1-15, 1967) p. 10. [prose]

C334 Morning. *World*, no. 9 (Dec. 1967) l. [35].

C335 [blurb for *Apocalypse Rose* by Charles Plymell]. *Last Times*, no. [2-3] [ca. Winter 1967] p. [5].

C336 Black Magicians. *Love Street*, no. 2 [ca. 1967] p. 6.

C337 [prose]. *Marrahwannah Quarterly*, vol. 3, no. 3 (1967) l. [17].
Note: A short statement on censorship.

C338 [letter to the editor]. *Satori* (1967) pp. [5-6].

C339 Afternoon Light [reprinted as: Hiway Poesy LA-Albuquerque-Texas-Wichita]. *Sycamore*, vol. 1, no. 1 (1967) p. 2.

C340 Dreams Deferred in Bangkok and Saigon While India Burns Gandhi's Children. *Umbra* (1967/1968) pp. 64-66. [prose]

1968

C341 [letter]. *Village Voice* (Jan. 11, 1968) p. 12.
Note: Printed in *Bail Raised for Jones* by Don McNeill.

C342 [letter]. *Newark Evening News* (Jan. 14, 1968)
Note: Printed in *16 U.S. Poets Ask Jones Rally* by Bruce Bahrenburg.

C343 [letter to President Millar]. *Hilltop Press*, vol. 25, no. 12 (Jan. 19, 1968) p. 1.
Note: Printed in *Ginsberg Will Trip to Campus* by Alice Walsh.

C344 [letter]. *Los Angeles Free Press* (Jan. 20-26, 1968) p. 2.
Note: Printed in *LeRoi Jones Framed, Charge 16 Poets*.

C345 Paradigm of Latter Section of Long Poem "These States". *Liberation News Service,* no. 31 (Jan. 22, 1968) p. [14].

C346 [letter]. *Los Angeles Free Press* (Jan. 26, 1968) p. 4.
Note: Printed in *Radio Free America* by Lawrence Lipton.

C347 Paradigm of Latter Section of Long Poem "These States". *New York Free Press,* vol. 1, no. 6 (Feb. 1, 1968) p. 5.

C348 [letter]. *Peace News* (Feb. 9, 1968) p. 10.
Note: Printed in *LeRoi Jones (3 Years Jail).*

C349 Reflections on the Mantra. *Dime Bag,* vol. 1, no. 1 ([after Feb. 15] 1968) pp. 4, 6.
[prose]

C350 The Maharishi and Me. *International Times,* no. 26 (Feb. 16-29, 1968) p. 3.
[prose]

C351 Is This the Land That Started War on China? *Times Union* (Feb. 25, 1968) section G, p. 1.

C352 [letter to Lon Solomon]. *Nova Vanguard,* vol. 1, no. 1 (Feb. 28, 1968) p. 2.

C353 "Hey I'm Lucky My Body's Here to Keep Me Company--". *Poet,* vol. 9, no. 3 (March 1968) pp. 7-8.

C354 [letter to Mike Aldrich]. *Incense,* no. 16 (Jan./Feb. [March 5] 1968) p. 23.

C355 Reflections on the Mantra. *Incense,* no. 16 (Jan./Feb. [March 5] 1968) pp. 24-26.
[prose]

C356 [letter]. *Los Angeles Free Press* (March 15, 1968) p. 4.
Note: Printed in *Radio Free America* by Lawrence Lipton.

C357 Paradigm Latter Section of Long Poem "These States". *Washington Free Press* (March 19, 1968) p. 7.

C358 Reflections on the Mantra. *Buddhist Third Class Junkmail Oracle,* no. 12 ([Spring] 1968) p. 1. [prose]

C359 [journal entries and] May 22, Calcutta [poem]. *Intrepid,* no. 10 (Spring 1968) pp. [43-46].

C360 [prose]. *Bust,* no. 1 (Spring [ca. April 1] 1968) p. ii.
Note: Single line quoted "Why are you spending all this money?"

C361 Patna Berares [sic] Express [and] This Form of Life Needs Sex. *Bust,* no. 1 (Spring [ca. April 1] 1968) pp. 15-18.

C362 Drowse Murmurs. *Caterpillar,* no. 3/4 (April/July 1968) pp. 149-150.

C363 [letter to the editor]. *Evergreen Review,* vol. 12, no. 53 (April 1968) pp. 12-13, 88.

C364 The Maharishi and Me. *Los Angeles Free Press,* vol. 5, no. 16 (April 19, 1968) p. 6. [prose]

C365 Television was a Baby Crawling Toward That Death Chamber [and drawing of three fish which share a common head]. *Renaissance,* no. 1 (May [1-14], 1968) [Supplement to *Sunday Paper*] pp. 3-5.

C366 [prose]. *New York Times* (May 5, 1968) p. 118.
Note: Printed in *Federal Court to Hear Case Challenging the City Laws on Coffeehouses* by Edward Ranzal contains this excerpt from AG's affidavit to the court.

C367 Wales Visitation. *New Yorker,* vol. 44, no. 12 (May 11, 1968) pp. 44-45.

C368 We Leave the Youthful Pennants and the Books. *Paterson Morning Call* (May 14, 1968)

C369 The Maharishi and Me. *Georgia Straight,* vol. 2, no. 18 (May 17-30, 1968) p. 7. [prose]

C370 Lower East Side. *Chirimo,* no. 1 (June 1968) pp. 4-5.

C371 [letter to Bill Katz]. *Library Journal,* vol. 93, no. 11 (June 1, 1968) p. 2204.
Note: Printed in *Statistical Wailing Wall* by Bill Katz.

C372 A Methedrine Vision in Hollywood. *World,* no. 12 (June 1968) ll. 25-26.

C373 Pentagon Exorcism. *San Francisco Earthquake,* vol. 1, no. 4 (Summer/Fall 1968) p. 17.

C374 Pertussin. *Stone,* vol. 2, no. 1 (Summer [June 29] 1968) pp. 19-20.

C375 [letters to Timothy Leary]. *Esquire,* vol. 70, no. 1 [issue 416] (July 1968) pp. 86-87.
Note: Printed in *In the Beginning, Leary Turned on Ginsberg and Saw That It Was Good* by Timothy Leary.

C376 [letter to the editor]. *Pavan,* vol. 23, no. 2 [ca. July 1968] p. [1].

C377 Swirls of Black Dust on Avenue D. *Pavan,* vol. 23, no. 2 [ca. July 1968] pp. [1-2].

C378 [letter to John Wilcock]. *Other Scenes,* vol. 2, no. 5 (Aug. 1968) inside front cover and p. [2].

C379 [blurb for *Collected Poems* by Kenneth Patchen]. *New York Times Book Review* (Aug. 18, 1968) p. 39.

C380 Sanders, Ed and AG. Magic Password Bulletin. *Rat, Subterranean News,* vol. 1, no. 15 (Aug. 23/Sept. 5, 1968) p. 3. [prose]

C381 City Police Insist They'll Bust Anybody Sleeping in Lincoln Park. *Ramparts Wall Poster,* vol. 1, no. 2 (Aug. 25, 1968) p. 2. [prose]

C382 All Is Poetry. *New York Free Press,* vol. 1, no. 35 (Sept. 5-12, 1968) p. 13. [prose]

C383 All Is Poetry. *Rat, Subterranean News,* vol. 1, no. 16 (Sept. 6-19, 1968) p. 12. [prose]

C384 [letter to Elsa Dorfman]. *Boston Globe* (Sept. 15, 1968) Globe section, pp. 46, 48-52.
Note: Printed in *Ginsberg the Father (Ginsberg the Poet) Ginsberg the Son (Ginsberg the Poet)* by Elsa Dorfman.

C385 Carmel Valley. *Boston Globe* (Sept. 15, 1968) Globe section, p. 48.

C386 O Future Bards. *Concerning Poetry,* vol. 1, no. 2 (Fall 1968) p. 46.

C387 Stony Brook Poets' Prophesy — June 23, 1968. *Stony Brook,* no. 1/2 (Fall 1968) p. 255. [prose]

C388 Who Be Kind To. *Observation Post,* vol. 44, no. 9 (Nov. 15, 1968) p. 2.

C389 [response to questionnaire]. *Playboy,* vol. 15, no. 12 (Dec. 1968) p. 139.

C390 Crash! Thud-Nausea Hip to Heart. *Times Union* (Dec. 5, 1968) p. 3.

C391 Remarks on Leary's Politics of Ecstasy. *Village Voice,* vol. 14, no. 9 (Dec. 12, 1968) pp. 5-6, 8. [prose]

C392 [blurb for *Planet News* by AG]. *Village Voice,* vol. 14, no. 9 (Dec. 12, 1968) p. 7.

C393 Ankor Wat. *International Times, [IT],* no. 46 (Dec. 13-31, 1968) p. 2.

C394 I Met Kenneth Patchen. *Outsider,* vol. 2, no. 4/5 (Winter 1968-69) pp. [99-100]. [prose]

C395 City Midnight Junk Strains. *Paris Review,* vol. 11, no. 42 (Winter/Spring 1968) pp. 189-191.

C396 Pain in Albany. *Times Union* (Dec. 22, 1968) p. F-1.

C397 Reflections on the Mantra. *Anonym Quarterly,* no. 1 [1968] pp. 41-43. [prose]

C398 The Maharishi and Me. *Graffiti,* vol. 1, no. 8 (1968) p. 44. [prose]

C399 Carmel Valley. *Intransit* [The Andy Warhol-Gerard Malanga Monster issue] (1968) p. 19.

C400 [letter]. *Middle Earth,* vol. 1, no. 10 [1968] p. 17.

C401 Reflections on the Mantra. *Orpheus Magazine,* vol. 6, no. 3 (1968) pp. 6-7. [prose]

C402 Wales Visitation. *Second Aeon,* no. 6 (1968) pp. 14-15.

1969

C403 [blurb for *Planet News* by AG]. *El Corno Emplumado/Plumed Horn,* no. 29 (Jan. 1969) p. [37].

C404 Continuation of a Long Poem on These States [and] These States into L.A. *Pacific Nation,* no. 2 (Feb. 1969) pp. 11-18.

C405 Kral Majales. *Los Angeles Free Press* (Feb. 7, 1969) p. 26.

C406 [music notation for *Laughing Song* by William Blake]. *Intrepid,* no. 11/12 (March 1969) pp. 79-80.

C407 Kral Majales. *Georgia Straight,* vol. 3, no. 48 (March 7-13, 1969) p. 9.

C408 Imaginary Universes. *Plaintiff,* vol. 5, no. 3 (Spring/Summer 1969) p. 54.

C409 [captions to comic strips]. *Kingdom of Heaven is Within You Comix*, no. 1 (Spring 1969)
Note: Some of the captions are by AG but they are not identified.

C410 [music notation for *Tirzah* by William Blake]. *Georgia Straight*, vol. 3, no. 51 (March 28/April 3, 1969) p. 16.

C411 Albany Memorial Hospital [and journal entries]. *Caterpillar*, vol. 2, no. 2 [issue no. 7] (April 1969) pp. 18-19.

C412 Be Kind To Yourself. *Free A & A*, no. 1 (April 1969) p. 3.

C413 King of the May. *Good Times*, vol. 2, no. 17 (April 30, 1969) p. 2.

C414 [letter to Mike Aldrich]. *Marijuana Review*, vol. 1, no. 3 (June/Aug. 1969) p. 6.

C415 Comment [330 A.D.]. *Liberation*, vol. 14, no. 4 (July 1969) p. 38. [prose]

C416 July 4, 1969. *Fruitcup*, no. 0 ([after July] 1969) pp. [5-6].

C417 Chicago to Salt Lake by Air. *Win*, vol. 5, no. 14 (Aug. 1969) pp. 14-15.

C418 Chicago to Salt Lake by Air. *Northwest Passage*, vol. 1, no. 9 (Aug. 19, 1969) pp. 18-19.

C419 These States: Paradigm Latter Section of Long Poem "These States". *Dulocratic Review*, vol. 4, no. 3 [after Sept. 23, 1969] p. 1.

C420 Chicago to Salt Lake by Air. *Spectator*, vol. 9, no. 6 (Oct. 21, 1969) pp. 12-13.

C421 Quel Deluge. *Rat, Subterranean News* (Oct. 29/Nov. 12, 1969) p. 17.

C422 By Air Albany-Baltimore. *Look*, vol. 33, no. 22 (Nov. 4, 1969) p. 34.

C423 Quel Deluge. *Observation Post*, vol. 46, no. 8 (Nov. 7, 1969) pp. 6-7.

C424 Quel Deluge. *Georgia Straight*, vol. 3, no. 79 (Nov. 26/Dec. 3, 1969) p. 11.

C425 Grant Park. *Seed*, vol. 4, no. 10 ([Dec. 15] 1969) p. 4.

C426 No Money, No War. *Tax Talk* [ca. Dec. 29, 1989] p. [4].

C427 Holy Ghost on the Nod over the Body of Bliss. *Intransit* (1969) [The Gary Snyder issue] p. 54.

C428 Kansas City to Saint Louis. *Mikrokosmos*, no. 14 (1969) pp. 46-50.

C429 Violence. *Notes from Underground*, no. 3 (1969) p. 9.

C430* Public Solitude. *Paletten*, vol. 30, no. 4 (1969) pp. 5-10. [prose]

C431 The Moments Return. *Peri, Loseblattsammlung Zeitgenössischer Kunst und Dictung*, no. 3 (1969) pp. [1-2].

1970

C432 For Harry Hermon, M.D. *Marijuana Review*, vol. 1, no. 5 (Jan./June 1970) p. [21].

C433 Let's Issue a General Declaration. *Nickel Review,* vol. 4, no. 18 (Jan. 9, 1970) p. 5. [prose]

C434 My Free Bill of Rights. *Daily Planet,* vol. 1, no. 8 (Jan. 24, 1970) p. 4. [prose]

C435 Morning. *Daily Planet,* vol. 1, no. 8 (Jan. 24, 1970) p. 5.

C436 No Money, No War. *Tax Talk* (Jan. 27, 1970) p. [5].

C437 An Article by Allen Ginsberg [reprinted as: Confrontation with Louis Ginsberg's Poems]. *University Review* [no. 5] (Feb. 1970) pp. 17, 21-22. [prose]

C438 [letter to David Kennedy]. *Win,* vol. 6, no. 2 (Feb. 1, 1970) p. 33.

C439 Rain Wet Asphalt Heat, Garbage Curbed Cans Overflowing. *World,* no. 18 (Feb./March 1970) l. [28].

C440 Speed is a No-no. *Harry,* vol. 1, no. 7 (Feb. 5, 1970) p. 10. [prose]

C441 Pralim IV. *Los Angeles Free Press,* vol. 7, no. 6 [issue 290] (Feb. 6-12, 1970) p. 30.

C442* Speed is a No-no. *Spectator,* vol. 10, no. 2 (Feb. 11, 1970) p. 17. [prose]

C443 No Money, No War. *Win,* vol. 6, no. 3 (Feb. 15, 1970) back cover.

C444 Speed Kills. *Chinook,* vol. 2, no. 7 (Feb. 19, 1970) p. 4. [prose]

C445 Speed. *International Times,* no. 74 (Feb. 27/March 13, 1970) p. 8. [prose]

C446 [letter to Jeff Poland]. *Intercourse,* no. 6 (Spring [ca. March 1] 1970) p. 1.

C447 Continuation Long Poem "These States", Northwest Passage [reprinted as: Northwest Passage]. *Earth Read-Out,* no. 22 (March 8, 1970) pp. 3-5.

C448 [letter to Telford Taylor]. *Tax Talk* (March 10, 1970) pp. 1, 6.

C449 I Guess the Main Thing Is Money So. *Good Times,* vol. 3, no. 11 (March 13, 1970) p. 3. [prose]

C450 Ungaretti, Giuseppe. No More Yelling. [translated by AG]. *Agenda,* vol. 8, no. 2 (Spring 1970) p. 36.

C451 Neal's Ashes. *Madrugada,* no. 1 (Spring 1970) p. 26.

C452 [letter to Barry Gifford]. *Madrugada,* no. 1 (Spring 1970) pp. 27-28.

C453 Manhattan Thirties Flash. *New York Quarterly,* no. 2 (Spring 1970) p. 15.

C454 Crossing Nation. *East Village Other,* vol. 5, no. 16 (March 27, 1970) p. 10.

C455 [letter to David Kennedy]. *Chinook,* vol. 2, no. 11 (March 26, 1970) p. 6.

C456 Empty Skulled New. *Countdown,* no. 2 (April 1970) pp. 124-125.

C457 Flying Home. *Seven,* no. 1 ([April] 1970) p. [15].

C458* Police State Blues. *Helix,* vol. 11, no. 14 (April 2, 1970) p. 13.

C459 In New York State, According to the New York. *Good Times,* vol. 3, no. 16 (April 17, 1970) p. 11. [prose]

C460 Allen Ginsberg Comes Down on Speed. *Los Angeles Free Press,* vol. 7, no. 16 [issue 300] (April 17-23, 1970) p. 12. [prose]

C461 Ginsberg Talks About Speed. *Nola Express,* vol. 1, no. 53 (April 17-30, 1970) p. N6. [prose]

C462 Ginsberg Raps on Junkies' Fate. *Harry,* vol. 1, no. 13 (May 1, 1970) p. 6. [prose]

C463 Since I Hope to Breathe Together. *Win,* vol. 6, no. 8 (May 1, 1970) p. 28. [prose]

C464 May King's Prophecy. *Strike Newspaper* (May 2, 1970) p. [3].

C465 Left Should Organize Junk Liberation Front Against Mafia. *Georgia Straight,* vol. 4, no. 108 (May 6-13, 1970) p. 13. [prose]

C466 Allen Ginsberg on Mafia and Junk. *Los Angeles Free Press,* vol. 7, no. 21 (May 22-28, 1970) pp. 9, 11. [prose]

C467 [drawing and prose]. *Colby Library Quarterly,* vol. 9, no. 2 (June 1970) pp. 125-127.
Note: Reproduction of drawing of three fish which share a common head and inscriptions from books.

C468 Grant Park: Thurs Aug 29, 1968. *Countdown,* no. 3 (June 1970) p. 129.

C469 Friday the Thirteenth. *Rolling Stone,* no. 60 (June 11, 1970) pp. 28-29.

C470 [response to questionnaire]. *Win,* vol. 6, no. 11 (June 15, 1970) p. 25.

C471 Memory Gardens. *Evergreen Review,* vol. 14, no. 80 (July 1970) pp. 27-29.

C472 Police State Blues. *Organ,* vol. 1, no. 1 (July 1970) p. 7.

C473 Violence. *Sub 70,* no. 3 [ca. July 1970] p. 4.

C474 [response to questionnaire]. *New American Review,* no. 10 (Aug. 1970) pp. 212-213.

C475 [letter to Walter Harding]. *Thoreau Society Bulletin,* no. 112 (Summer [Sept.] 1970) p. 7.

C476 [2 drawings]. *Politiken* (Sept. 6, 1970) p. 40.
Note: Reproduction of drawing of three fish which share a common head and a self portrait.

C477 Ginsberg Talks about Speed. *Door to Liberation,* vol. 2, no. 8 (Sept. 10, 1970) p. 4. [prose]

C478 [letter to Tom Forcade & UPS]. *Free Ranger Intertribal News Service* (Sept. 14, 1970) p. 12.

C479 G. S. Reading Poesy at Princeton. *Antioch Review,* vol. 30, no. 3/4 (Fall/Winter 1970-71) p. 335.

C480 Ungaretti in Heaven. *Books Abroad,* vol. 44, no. 4 (Autumn 1970) p. 615.

C481 Friday the Thirteenth. *Schism,* vol. 1, no. 4 (Fall 1970) p. 32.

C482 [letter to the editor]. *Boulder Express,* no. 20 (Sept. 23, 1970) p. [6].

C483 Neal's Ashes. *Boulder Express,* no. 20 (Sept. 23, 1970) p. [6].

C484 Kral Majales. *Californian Librarian,* vol. 31, no. 4 (Oct. 1970) pp. 228-229.

C485 Bixby Canyon [and] Reflections in Sleepy Eye. *Caterpillar,* vol. 4, no. 1 [issue no. 13] (Oct. 1970) pp. 1-4.

C486* Police State Blues. *Harbinger* (Oct./Dec. 1970) pp. 10-11.

C487 The Character of the Happy Warrior. *Columbia Library Columns,* vol. 20, no. 1 (Nov. 1970) p. 15.

C488 [letter to Eugene Brooks]. *Columbia Library Columns,* vol. 20, no. 1 (Nov. 1970) pp. 10-17.
Note: Printed in *Allen Ginsberg and Jack Kerouac, Columbia Undergraduates* by Anne Charters.

C489 [letter to the editor]. *Columbia College Class of 1948 Newsletter,* vol. 22, no. 3 (Dec. 1970) p. 2.

C490 May King's Prophecy. *Black Swamp Review,* no. 2 (1970) p. 10.

C491 May King's Prophecy. *Brittania* (1970) p. [48].

C492 Falling Asleep in America. *Capella,* no. 5/6 [ca. 1970] p. 28.

C493 [3 poems and a letter]. *Clothesline,* no. 2 (1970) ll. 35-36.
Contents: The Bus Roars — The Mailman Slips — Taking a Pee — [letter includes poem "Frank O'Hara Darkly"]

C494 [prose]. *Helen Review,* vol. 1, no. 3 (1970) pp. 83-84.
Note: Printed in *The Poems of Jack Kerouac* by Lita Hornick, these quotes are taken from the margin notes in AG's copy of *Kerouac* by Ann Charters.

C495 Returning North of Vortex. *Partisan Review,* vol. 37, no. 2 (1970) pp. 180-183.

C496 Grey Cloud over Elmira. *Red Clay Reader,* no. 7 (1970) p. 21.

1971

C497 Blake Notes. *Caterpillar,* vol. 4, no. 2 [issue 14] (Jan. 1971) pp. 126-132. [prose]

C498 Air Opium. *Marijuana Review,* vol. 1, no. 6 (Jan./June 1971) pp. 14-15. [prose]

C499 Grant Park. *Seed,* vol. 6, no. 6 (Jan. 20, 1971) p. 34.

C500 Dylan, Bob and AG. Going to San Diego. *Door,* vol. 3, no. 16 (Jan. 13-27, 1971) pp. 12-13.

C501 Ballad of Tommy the Traveler. *Herald,* vol. 92, no. 15 (Feb. 8, 1971) p. 3.
Note: by Alan [sic] Ginsberg

C502 Documents on Police Bureaucracy's Conspiracy Against Human Rights of Opiate Addicts and Constitutional Rights of Medical Profession Causing Mass Breakdown of Urban Law and Order [prose]. *Realist,* no. 89 (March-April 1971) [issue called *The Last Supplement to the Whole Earth Catalog*], pp. 103-106.

C503 Hum! Hum! Hum! *Washington Post* (March 3, 1971) pp. C1, C6.
Note: Printed in *Mr. Bellow's 3d Award* by William McPherson.

C504* Anti-War Games. *Quicksilver Times,* vol. 3, no. 5 (March 17-30, 1971) p. 8.

C505 After Thoughts. *Sebastian Quill,* no. 2 (Spring [April] 1971) p. [3].

C506 [letter to the National Book Award judges]. *New York Times Book Review* (April 4, 1971) pp. 4-5, 14, 16, 18.

C507 [letter to the editor]. *Branding Iron,* vol. 78, no. 25 (April 23, 1971) p. 5.

C508 Anti-War Games. *Indications,* vol. 1, no. 1 (May 1971) p. 19.

C509 Anti-War Games. *Ramparts,* vol. 9, no. 10 (May 1971) pp. [40-42].

C510 Allen Ginsberg on the New Dylan. *Outlaw,* vol. 2, no. 2 (May 7-28, 1971) p. 12. [prose]

C511 Opium and...the CIA. *Quicksilver Times,* vol. 3, no. 9 (May 15-31, 1971) pp. 26-27. [prose]

C512 [review of *Speed* by William Burroughs Jr.]. *International Times [IT],* no. 104 (May 19/June 2, 1971) p. 21.

C513 Allen Ginsberg on the New Dylan. *Georgia Straight,* vol. 5, no. 170 (May 28/June 1, 1971) p. 11. [prose]

C514 [blurb for *Shards of God* by Ed Sanders]. *Evergreen Review,* vol. 15, no. 90 (June 1971) p. 35.

C515 Spring Anti War Games. *Gay Sunshine,* no. 7 (June/July 1971) p. 10.

C516 [letter to Jack Mooney]. *Alabama Journal* (June 14, 1971) p. 7.

C517 Who Am I? *Alabama Journal* (June 14, 1971) p. 7.

C518 [response to questionnaire]. *Avante-Garde,* no. 14 (Summer 1971) p. 23.

C519 Who Am I? [and] Hot Roach, Breath Smoke [and] Eyes Lid-Heavy. *Pathways,* vol. 5, no. 2 (Summer 1971) p. 10.

C520 Friday the Thirteenth. *Unspeakable Visions of the Individual,* vol. 1, no. 2 (July 1971) pp. 11-16.

C521 Declaration of Independence for Dr. Timothy Leary. *Los Angeles Free Press,* vol. 8, no. 29 [issue 365] (July 16-22, 1971) p. 3. [prose]

C522 Elegy Che Guevara. *Berkeley Tribe,* vol. 5, no. 25 [issue 105] (July 30-Aug. 6, 1971) p. 13.

C523 [prose]. *San Francisco Chronicle* (July 30, 1971) p. 42.
Note: Petition written by AG in support of the Living Theater.

C524 Declaration of Independence for Timothy Leary. *East Village Other,* vol. 6, no. 36 (Aug. 10, 1971) p. 2. [prose]

C525 Om Ah Hum! *Los Angeles Free Press,* vol. 8, no. 34 [issue 370] (Aug. 20-26, 1971) p. 6.
Note: Petition written by AG in support of the Living Theater.

C526 "Have You Seen This Movie?" *Alternative Features Service,* vol. 1, no. 13 (Sept. 10, 1971) loose leaf.

C527 "Have You Seen This Movie?" *Chinook,* vol. 3, no. 34 (Sept. 16, 1971) p. 7.

C528 "Have You Seen This Movie?" *Space City,* vol. 3, no. 16 (Sept. 21-27, 1971) p. 9.

C529 Emotion Recollected in Tranquillity. *Capella,* no. 8 [after Autumn 1971] p. 20.

C530 On a Hermit's Cabin. *Fits* [also called *If the Shoe Fits*] no. 2 ([Fall] 1971) pp. 18-19.

C531 Easter Sunday 1969. *Lampeter Muse,* vol. 6, no. 1 (Fall/Winter 1971) p. 18.

C532 Elegy Che Guevara. *East Village Other,* vol. 6, no. 39 (Sept. 22, 1971) p. 3.
Note: Includes AG's facsimile holograph corrections.

C533 Have You Seen This Movie? *Staff* (Sept. 24./Oct. 1, 1971) p. 5.

C534 [letter to the editor]. *Evergreen Review,* vol. 15, no. 93 (Oct. 1971) p. 73.

C535 Hum Bom! *Nola Express,* no. 91 (Oct. 7-20, 1971) p. 32.

C536 Bixby Canyon Ocean Path Word Breeze. *Berkeley Barb,* vol. 13, no. 14 [issue 322] (Oct. 15-21, 1971) p. 13.

C537 Get High Off the People — Smack the Enemy. *Berkeley Tribe,* vol. 6, no. 10 [issue 118] ([Oct. 15] 1971) pp. 10-11. [prose]

C538 Have You Seen This Movie? *Georgia Straight,* vol. 5, no. 213 (Oct. 26-29, 1971) pp. 12-13.

C539 Milarepa Taste. *KPFK Folio* (Nov. 1971) front cover.

C540 Wichita Vortex Sutra. *Common Sense,* vol. 1, no. 19 (Dec. 1971) p. 9.

C541 [letter to George Weaver]. *Common Sense,* vol. 1, no. 19 (Dec. 1971) p. 9.

C542 September on Jessore Road. *New York Times* (Dec. 17, 1971) p. 41.

C543 [letter to the editor]. *Blake Newsletter,* vol. 4, no. 3 [issue 15] (Winter 1971) p. 97.

C544 Commentary. *Blake Newsletter,* vol. 4, no. 3 [issue 15] (Winter 1971) pp. 98-103.
Note: Liner notes from *Songs of Innocence* written William Blake.

C545 September on Jessore Road. *East Village Other,* vol. 6, no. 44-45 (Dec. 23, 1971) pp. 11-13.
Note: Includes AG's facsimile holograph notes. [see also D6]

C546 Hum Bom! *Big Sky,* no. 1 (1971) p. [79].

C547 Raw Pine Walls, Ice-white Windows. *Buffalo Stamps,* no. 2 (1971) p. 59.

C548 [6 haiku]. *Coyote's Journal,* no. 9 (1971) back cover.
Contents: Hiss, Gaslamp — Hemp Smoke in Wood Hall — Yellow Light on Knotted Wall — Who Am I? — Hot Roach, Breath Smoke — Eye Lids Heavy.

C549 Two Interesting Dreams. *Io,* no. 8 (1971) pp. 80-81. [prose]

C550 Over Denver. *Mojo Navigator,* no. 3 (1971) p. [21].

C551 Rain-wet Asphalt Heat, Garbage Curbed Cans Overflowing. *Montagna Rossa* (1971) pp. 39-40.

C552 A Vow [and] Sonora Desert-edge. *New American Review,* no. 11 (1971) pp. 9-12.

C553 Neal's Ashes. *Rain,* no. 1/2 (1971) p. 79.

1972

C554 Elegy for Neal Cassidy [sic]. *Paris Review,* vol. 14, no. 53 (Winter [Jan.] 1972) pp. 76-79.

C555 September on Jessore Road. *Sing Out!,* vol. 21, no. 1 (Jan./Feb. 1972) pp. 1-2.
Note: Includes music notation in periodical as well as a plastic flexible recording containing a short excerpt from the poem read by AG, item F35.

C556 Bixby Canyon Ocean Path Word Breeze. *World,* no. 24 (Winter [Jan.] 1972) ll. [46-55].

C557 We're in Science Fiction Now. *Good Times,* vol. 5, no. 3 (Jan. 28/Feb. 10, 1972) pp. 14-15. [prose]

C558 September on Jessore Road. *Times Weekly,* vol. 2, no. 25 (Jan. 30, 1972) p. 9.

C559 [letter to Claude Pelieu and Mary Beach]. *Unmuzzled Ox,* vol. 1, no. 2 (Feb. 1972) pp. 19-20.

C560 Hiway Poesy-LA-Albuquerque-Texas-Wichita. *Sunday Paper,* no. 1 (Winter [Feb. 3-9] 1972) Renaissance 8 supplement, pp. [21-24].

C561 Jimmy Berman Newsboy Gay Lib Rag. *Gay,* vol. 3, no. 70 (Feb. 21, 1972) p. 5.

C562 [letter to Ken]. *Symposium News,* vol. 1, no. 1 (Feb. 21, 1972) p. 9.

C563 Troost Street Blues. *Symposium News,* vol. 1, no. 1 (Feb. 21, 1972) p. 9.

C564 September on Jessore Road. *Westport Trucker,* vol. 2, no. 20 [issue 44] (Feb. 21-28, 1972) p. 4.

C565 [letter]. *Westport Trucker,* vol. 2, no. 21 [issue 45] (Feb. 29/March 7, 1972) p. 5.

C566 No Fuss Is Necessary [and] Troost Street Blues. *Westport Trucker,* vol. 2, no. 21 [issue 45] (Feb. 29/March 7, 1972) p. 5.

C567 Slack Key Guitar [and] Reef Mantra [and reproduction of holograph note to Jack Collum]. *The,* no. 13 [ca. late March 1972] ll. 22-23.

C568 New England in the Fall: Autumn Gold. *Adventures in Poetry,* no. 9 (Spring 1972) pp. [41-48].

C569 From Iron Horse. *Bastard Angel,* no. 1 (Spring 1972) pp. 4-6.

C570 On the Lam from Bloomington. *Fervent Valley*, no. 1 (Spring 1972) p. [11].

C571 The Car Crash Poem III. *Seventies*, vol. 3, no. 1 (Spring 1972) pp. 83-84.

C572 [letter to the editor]. *Art Direction*, vol. 23, no. 11 (April 1972) p. 59.
Note: Title page incorrectly gives Feb. 1972 as the issue date, cover date of April 1972 appears correct.

C573 Mind Consciousness Be In [and] Going to San Diego. *Win*, vol. 8, no. 6 (April 1, 1972) pp. 14-15 and back cover.

C574 Mind Consciousness Be In. *Los Angeles Free Press*, vol. 9, no. 15 [issue 404] (April 14-20, 1972) part 2, p. 2.

C575 Caribou Blues. *Polar Star*, vol. 29, no. 24 (April 14, 1972) p. 8.

C576 Mind Consciousness Be In. *Western Courier*, vol. 70, no. 33 (April 18, 1972) p. 20.

C577 Police State Blues. *Sixpack*, no. 1 (May 1972) p. [3].

C578 Madison Vietnam Blues [and] The Wisconsin Alliance Blues. *Wisconsin Patriot*, vol. 2, no. 4 (May 1972) pp. 1, 9.

C579 An Open Window on Chicago. *Paris Review*, vol. 14, no. 54 (Summer 1972) pp. 27-29.

C580 Ah, Wake Up! *Newsday* (Aug. 27, 1972) Ideas supplement, pp. 1, 12-14. [prose]

C581 Police State Blues. *Toothpick, Lisbon & the Orcas Islands*, vol. 2, no. 1-2 (Fall 1972) pp. 55-59.

C582 Christmas Blues. *Unmuzzled Ox*, vol. 1, no. 4 (Autumn 1972) pp. [51-52].

C583 It Is with Great Pleasure That We Wish to Add P.E.N. *Berkeley Barb*, vol. 15, no. 12 [issue 373] (Oct. 6-12, 1972) p. 2. [prose]

C584 Bayonne Tuscarora. *American Poetry Review*, vol. 1, no. 1 (Nov./Dec. 1972) pp. 30-31.

C585 The Great Rememberer. *University Review*, no. 25 (Nov. 1972) pp. 20-22, 36. [prose]

C586 It Is with Great Pleasure That We Wish to Add P.E.N. *International Times [IT]*, no. 141 (Nov. 2-16, 1972) p. 8. [prose]

C587 [letter to Peter Orlovsky]. *Gar*, vol. 2, no. 4 (Nov. 3] 1972) p. 2.

C588 [prose]. *Broadside*, vol. 3, no. 3 (Nov. 6, 1972) p. 1.
Note: Statement in support of McGovern campaign with notes and corrections in AG's facsimile holograph.

C589 It Is with Great Pleasure That We Wish to Add P.E.N. *Rock* (Nov. 6, 1972)

C590 [prose]. *L.A. Star* (Nov. 9, 1972)
Note: Statement in support of John Lennon and Yoko Ono.

C591 Please Master. *Gay Sunshine*, no. 16 ([Dec. 1972] Jan./Feb. 1973) p. 9.

C592 Apocatastasis. *Matchbook,* no. E (Dec. 1972) unpaged.
Note: This is a one-word poem.

C593 The Great Rememberer. *Saturday Review, The Arts,* vol. 55, no. 49 (Dec. 1972) pp. 60-63. [prose]

C594 It Is with Great Pleasure That We Wish to Add P.E.N. *New Yorker,* vol. 48 (Dec. 9, 1972) pp. 138+.
Note: Printed in *A Reporter at Large* by Hendrik Hertzberg.

C595 Graffiti in the 12th Cubicle Men's Room Syracuse Airport. *Big Sky,* no. 2 (1972) pp. [3-4].

C596 Iron Horse. *Buffalo Stamps,* no. 3/4 (1972) pp. 43-48.

C597 On the New Cultural Radicalism: January 1972. *Partisan Review,* vol. 39, no. 3 (1972) pp. 423-424. [prose]

C598 Done, Finished with the Biggest Cock. *Stonecloud,* no. 1 (1972) p. 45.

1973

C599 [letter to the Advertising Trade Pubs.]. *Art Direction,* vol. 26, no. 10 (Jan. 1973) p. 39.

C600 Empty Skulled New. *Starscrewer,* no. 1 (Jan. 1973).

Related Item: Ford's Better Idea. *New York Review of Books,* vol. 19, no. 11-12 (Jan. 25, 1973) pp. 45-46.
Note: AG is one of 73 signers to this statement but he did not write it.

C601 Ecologue. *American Review,* no. 16 (Feb. [1] 1973) pp. 124-144.

C602 [blurb for *Pressure* by Anne Waldman]. *Contact,* no. 5 (Feb. 1, 1973) back cover.

C603 [letter to Philip Mahony]. *Images,* vol. 6 (Spring 1973) pp. 15-17.

C604 Ginsberg in Newcastle. *Iron,* no. 1 (Spring 1973) pp. 2-3. [prose]

C605 Masturbation is the Massage. *Suck,* no. 31 [ca. Spring 1973]

C606 Please Master. *Berkeley Barb,* vol. 17, no. 16 [issue 401] (April 20-26, 1973) p. 17.

C607 [letter to the editor]. *Playboy,* vol. 20, no. 5 (May 1973) p. 14.

C608 Masturbation is the Massage. *Starscrewer,* no. 3 (May 1973)

C609 [letter to the editor]. *University Review,* no. 29 (May 1973) p. 2.

C610 You Live Apart on the River and Seas. *Villager,* vol. 41, no. 5 (May 10, 1973) p. 5.

C611 Troust [sic] Street Blues [and] House of the Rising Sun [and] What Would You Do If You Lost It? *Berkeley Barb,* vol. 17, no. 19 [issue 404] (May 11-17, 1973) p. 13.

C612 House of the Rising Sun [and] Troust [sic] Street Blues [and] What Would You Do If You Lost It? *Georgia Straight,* vol. 7, no. 294 (May 24-31, 1973) pp. 12-13.

C613 [announcement for Timothy Leary benefit reading]. *Berkeley Barb,* vol. 17, no. 21 [issue 406] (May 25-31, 1973) p. 15. [prose]

C614 Everybody Sing. *Berkeley Barb,* vol. 17, no. 21 [issue 406] (May 25-31, 1973) p. 18.

C615 Schoenfeld, Eugene and AG. [letter to the editor of the *San Francisco Examiner*]. *Berkeley Barb* (June 1-7, 1973) p. 9.

C616 Snyder, Gary and AG. Totem Protectors. *Place,* vol. 3, no. 1 (June 1973) inside front and back covers.

C617 Thoughts Sitting Breathing. *Georgia Straight,* vol. 7, no. 296 (June 7-14, 1973) p. 12.

C618 [response to questionnaire]. *Christian Century,* vol. 90, no. 26 (July 4-11, 1973) p. 731.

C619 Everybody Sing [and] Troost Street Blues [and] The House of the Rising Sun. *Gay News,* no. 28 (July 26/Aug. 8, 1973) p. 8.

C620 [2 letters]. *Nelly Heathen* ([Aug. 15] 1973) pp. 13, 15.

C621 Artists on Watergate. *Changes,* no. 84 (Sept./Oct. 1973) pp. 23-24. [prose]

C622 [letter to Gerald Lefcourt]. *Liberation,* vol. 18, no. 2 (Sept./Oct. 1973) pp. 7, 43.

C623 New York Blues [and] NY Youth Call Annunciation [and] Tear Gas Rag. *Scottish International,* vol. 6, no. 7 (Sept. 1973) pp. 20-21, 23.

C624 [letter to Gerald Lefcourt]. *Georgia Straight,* vol. 7, no. 311 (Sept. 20-27, 1973) pp. 4-5, 21.

C625 To a Dead Poet. *American PEN,* vol. 5, no. 4 (Fall 1973) p. 8.

C626 Please Master. *Manroot,* no. 9 (Fall 1973) pp. 7-8.

C627 Returning to the Country for a Brief Visit [and] Thoughts Sitting Breathing [and] What Would You Do If You Lost It? *Chicago,* no. 1 [European edition] (Oct. 1973) ll. 12-16, 57-58.

C628 [letter to Gerald Lefcourt]. *Hi: Young People's Newsletter,* vol. 5, no. 23 (Oct. 4, 1973) pp. 1, 7, 12.

C629 [letter to Gerald Lefcourt]. *Berkeley Barb,* vol. 18, no. 13 [issue 425] (Oct. 5-11, 1973) pp. 4-5, 14.

C630 [letter to Gerald Lefcourt]. *College Press Service,* no. 5 (Oct. 6, 1973) pp. 4-5.

C631 [letter to Gerald Lefcourt]. *Magic Ink* (Oct. [14] 1973) pp. 62-65.

C632 [response to questionnaire]. *New York,* vol. 6, no. 43 (Oct. 22, 1973) pp. 36-37.

C633 [letter to Gerald Lefcourt]. *Westport Trucker,* vol. 3, no. 22 [issue 71] (Oct. 22, 1973) pp. 44-45.

C634 [letter to Gerald Lefcourt]. *City,* vol. 3, no. 22 (Oct. 24-30, 1973) pp. 21-23.

C635 These States-To Miami Convention. *Athanor,* no. 5 (Winter 1973) pp. 12-19.

C636 Put Down Yr Cigarette Rag. *Sixpack,* no. 6 (Winter 1973/74) pp. 25-27.

C637 The Visions of the Great Rememberer. *Mulch,* vol. 2, no. 2 [issue 4] (Winter 1973-74) pp. 55-97.

C638 Car Crash, Pt. I-II. *Buffalo Stamps,* no. 6 (1973) pp. 20-22.

C639 [letter to the editor]. *Camels Coming Newsletter,* no. 3 (1973) p. 1.

C640 After Wales Visitacione. *La Huerta,* vol. 1, no. 3 (1973) pp. [57-60].

C641 On Huncke's Book. *Unspeakable Visions of the Individual,* vol. 3, no. 1-2 (1973) pp. 20-23. [prose]

1974

C642 Mountain Snow Fields. *Poetry Project Newsletter,* no. 11 (Jan. 1, 1974) p. [1].

C643 Wyoming. *Poetry Project Newsletter,* no. 11 (Jan. 1, 1974) p. [6].

C644 Lennon/Ono & Poetic Tradition. *Changes,* no. 86 ([ca. Feb.] 1974) p. 13. [prose and note]

C645 [self-portrait drawing and prose note]. *Drummer,* no. 282 (Feb. 12, 1974) p. 3.

C646 [drawing]. *Catholic Worker,* vol. 40, no. 3 (March/April 1974) p. 1.
   Note: Drawing of three fish which share a common head.

C647 What Would You Do If You Lost It? [and] In Later Days, Remembering This I Shall Certainly Go Mad. *North Country,* vol. 1, no. 2 (March 1974) pp. 4-6.

C648 Thoughts and Recurrent Musings on Israeli Arguments. *Liberation,* vol. 18, no. 6 (Feb. [March 11] 1974) p. 14. [prose]

C649 Exemplary Buddhist Shocker [and] To Mike [and] Xmas Gift. *Bastard Angel,* no. 2 (Spring 1974) p. 13.

C650 [letter to John Currier]. *Gone Soft,* vol. 1, no. 3 (Spring 1974) p. 19.

C651 Bird Slammed into Window. *Kumanitu,* no. 1 (Spring 1974) p. 54.

C652 To a Dead Poet. *Review,* no. 11 (Spring 1974) p. 29.

C653 Paul Blackburn. *Sixpack,* no. 7/8 (Spring/Summer 1974) p. 147.

C654 Jaweh and Allah Battle. *Win,* vol. 10, no. 11 (March 28, 1974) pp. 12-13.

C655 [prose]. *New York Times Magazine* (March 31, 1974) pp. 69-71.
   Note: Inscription from a guest book is printed in *Ode to a 'Y'* by Veronica Geng.

C656 [letter to Gerald Lefcourt]. *PENewsletter* (April 1974)

C657 [prose footnote]. *World,* no. 29 (April 1974) p. 7.

C658 [blurb for *Ah* recording by Bhagavan Das]. *Michigan Daily* (April 11, 1974)

C659 Jaweh and Allah Battle. *Los Angeles Times* (April 17, 1974) part 2, p. 7.

C660 [autobiographical statement]. *Library of Congress Information Bulletin,* vol. 33, no. 16 (April 19, 1974) pp. 128-129. [prose]

C661 [prose]. *Washington Post* (April 28, 1974) Book World section, pp. 3-4.
Note: Printed in *The Book Awards* by Carol Eron, excerpt from AG's acceptance prose for the National Book Award.

C662 Acceptance Speech for the National Book Award. *Poetry Project Newsletter,* no. 15 (May 1, 1974) pp. [7-8]. [prose]

C663 [prose]. *Georgia Straight,* vol. 8, no. 342 (May 2-9, 1974) p. 12.
Note: Prose disclaimer about the transcription from the tape which forms the accompanying interview.

C664 [response to questionnaire]. *Win,* vol. 10, no. 16 (May 2, 1974) p. 13.

C665 I Love Abbie Hoffman, a Brother. *Win,* vol. 10, no. 16 (May 2, 1974) p. 19.

C666 D. C. Mobilization [and prose acceptance speech for the National Book Award]. *Lanthorn,* vol. 6, no. 20 (May 9, 1974) Special Arts supplement, p. [2].

C667 [letter to the editor]. *Rolling Stone* (May 9, 1974) p. 7.

C668 A Vow. *Ann Arbor Sun,* vol. 2, no. 10 (May 17-31, 1974) p. 15.

C669 [prose]. *Berkeley Barb* (May 17-23, 1974) p. 12.
Note: Prose disclaimer about the transcription from the tape which forms the accompanying interview.

C670 Thus Crosslegged on Round Pillow Set in Teton Space [and prose note]. *Rolling Stone,* no. 161 (May 23, 1974) pp. 46-47.

C671 [letter to the Internal Revenue Service]. *Win,* vol. 10, no. 18 (May 23, 1974) P. 17.

C672 [prose]. *Changes,* no. 88 (June 1974) p. 18.
Note: AG's acceptance prose for the National Book Award.

C673 Advice to Youth. *Changes,* no. 88 (June 1974) pp. 18-20.

C674 Troost Street Blues. *Fag Rag,* no. 9 [and] *Gay Sunshine,* no. 22 [combined issue] (Summer 1974) p. 18.

C675 Night Gleam. *Fag Rag,* no. 9 [and] *Gay Sunshine,* no. 22 [combined issue] (Summer 1974) p. 24.

C676 2 AM Dirty Jersey Blues. *Fervent Valley,* no. 4 (Summer 1974) p. [37].

C677 A Vow. *Georgia Straight,* vol. 8, no. 353 (July 18-25, 1974) p. 20.

C678 Snyder, Gary and AG. Totem Protectorates [part 1]. *Not Man Apart,* vol. 4, no. 10 (Aug. 1974) p. 3.

C679 Snyder, Gary and AG. Totem Protectorates [part 2]. *Not Man Apart,* vol. 4, no. 12 (mid-Sept. 1974) p. 3.

C680 Om Ah Hum: 44 Temporary Questions for Dr. Leary. *Berkeley Barb,* vol. 20, no. 10 [issue 475] (Sept. 20-26, 1974) p. 1. [prose]

C681 For Sale For Sale. *Bastard Angel,* no. 3 (Fall 1974) pp. 28-29.

C682 Don't Know Who I Am [and drawing]. *Fag Rag,* no. 10 (Fall 1974) cover.

C683 The Wind Charges a Propeller. *Wild Onion* (Fall/Winter 1974-1975) back cover.

C684 44 Temporary Questions on Dr. Leary. *City,* vol. 7, no. 49 (Oct. 2-15, 1974) pp. 48-49. [prose]

C685 Om Ah Hum: 44 Temporary Questions on Dr. Leary. *Georgia Straight,* vol. 8, no. 364 (Oct. 3-10, 1974) p. 13. [prose]

C686 Exorcism. *Seven Days* (Oct. 5, 1974) p. 7.

C687 Om Ah Hum: 44 Temporary Questions on Dr. Leary. *San Francisco Phoenix,* vol. 2, no. 26 [issue 53] (Oct. 11, 1974) p. 2. [prose]

C688 [autobiographical prose]. *Gazette,* vol. 1, no. 3 (Nov. 5, 1974) p. 4.

C689 Om Ah Hum: Temporary Questions on Dr. Leary. *Soho Weekly News,* vol. 2, no. 5 (Nov. 7, 1974) p. 10. [prose]

C690 Om Ah Hum: 44 Temporary Questions on Tim Leary. *Win,* vol. 10, no. 39 (Nov. 21, 1974) pp. 10-11. [prose]

C691 Stay Away [from the White House]. *Om* (Dec. 1974) pp. 58-59.

C692 Mugging. *Poetry Project Newsletter,* no. 20 (Dec. 1, 1974) pp. [7-8].

C693 Jaweh and Allah Battle. *Holy Beggar's Gazette* (Winter [Dec. 22, 1974]/Spring 1975) pp. 26-27.

C694 What Would You Do If You Lost It? *Bountiful Lord's Delivery Service,* no. 5 (1974) pp. 24-26.

C695 Prayer Blues. *Bountiful Lord's Delivery Service,* no. 5 (1974) pp. 37-38.

C696 N.Y.C. Blues. *Choice,* no. 9 (1974) p. 64.

C697 I Guess the Main Thing is Money. *Panderma,* no. 12 (1974) p. 3. [prose]

C698 [letter to Peter Orlovsky]. *Unspeakable Visions of the Individual,* vol. 4 [issue also called *The Beat Book*] (1974) pp. 34-36. [see also D9]

C699 [letter to Howard Schulman]. *Unspeakable Visions of the Individual,* vol. 4 [issue also called *The Beat Book*] (1974) pp. 74-80.

C700 [letter to Mark Van Doren]. *Unspeakable Visions of the Individual,* vol. 4 [issue also called *The Beat Book*] (1974) pp. 127-129.

1975

C701 Stop the Bomb Stop the Bomb. *Illinois Entertainer* (Jan./Feb. 1975) p. 2.

C702 Mugging. *New York Times Magazine* (Jan. 5, 1975) p. 71.

C703 Exorcism. *Ann Arbor Sun,* vol. 3, no. 1 (Jan. 6, 1975) p. 12.

C704 [open letter]. *Liberation,* vol. 19, no. 2 (Feb. 1975) p. 25.

C705   Power [and] NY Youth Call Annunciation. *New Age Journal,* vol. 1, no. 2 (Feb. 1975) pp. 25-27.

C706   [letter to S. Dillon Ripley]. *Poetry Project Newsletter,* no. 22 (Feb. 1, 1975)

C707*   Thoughts Sitting Breathing. *Georgia Straight,* vol. 7, no. 296 (June 7-14, 1975) pp. 12-13.

C708   Ego Confession. *Chicago Review,* vol. 27, no. 1 (Summer 1975) pp. 36-37.

C709   4 AM Blues. *Cross Country,* no. 2 (Summer 1975) p. 25.

C710   News Bulletin. *Milk Quarterly,* no. 8 (Summer 1975) pp. 47-49.

C711   Neglected Books of the Twentieth Century, part 2. *Antaeus,* no. 19 (Autumn 1975) p. 137. [prose list]

C712   Returning to the Country for a Brief Visit. *Stone Press Weekly,* no. 65 (Oct. 20, 1975) postcard format periodical.

C713   Night Gleam. *Transatlantic Review,* no. 52 (Autumn [Nov. 5] 1975) p. 17.

C714   Sweet Boy, Gimme Yr Ass. *Gay Sunshine,* no. 26/27 (Winter 1975/76) back cover.

C715   Thoughts on a Breath. *Southwest Review,* vol. 60, no. 1 (Winter 1975) pp. 37-40.

C716   Snyder, Gary and AG. Eyes Full of Pitchpine Smoke [and] Pitchpine Smoke [and] Bookkeeping in the Moonlight. *End,* no. 9 (1975) p. [24].

C717   Old One the Dog Stretches Stiff-Legged [poem] [and] Om Ah Hum: 43 Temporary Questions on Dr. Leary [prose]. *Grosseteste Review,* vol. 8, no. 2 [issue also called *An Alleghany Star Route Anthology*] (1975) pp. 14-18.

C718   Mr. Sharpe the Carpenter from Susanville [and] Energy Vampire. *Kuksu,* no. 4 (1975) pp. 54-56.

C719   [blurb about Michael Horovitz]. *New Departures,* no. 7/8, 10/11 (1975) p. xvii.

C720   Yes and It's Hopeless [and] Under the World There's a Lot of Ass, a Lot of Cunt [and] Returning to the Country for a Brief Visit. *New Departures,* no. 7/8, 10/11 (1975) pp. 66-69.

C721   Old One the Dog Stretches Stiff Legged. *West Coast Paria,* no. 2 (1975) p. 21.

1976

C722   Come All Ye Brave Boys. *Toy Sun,* no. 1 (Jan. 1, 1976) p. 5.
  Note: Includes music notation.

C723   Rolling Thunder Stones. *Rolling Stone,* no. 204 (Jan. 15, 1976) p. 39.
  Contents: A Crystal Ball's on the Piano — Lay Down Lay Down Yr Mountain — Rolling Thunder Sunrise Ceremony Nov. 5, 1975 — Heroic Ecstasy! — Snow Blues — My Own Voice Rose to Heaven in Elation — Local Noise — To the Six Nations at Tuscarora Reservation — Snow Falls

C724   [letter to Michael Rumaker]. *Westchester Dish,* no. 2 (March 1976) pp. 1, 6-8.
  Note: Printed in *On Allen Ginsberg* by Michael Rumaker.

C725 [letter to Pam and Charlie Plymell]. *Coldspring Journal,* no. 10 (April 1976) p. 80.

C726 Gospel Noble Truths. *New Age Journal,* vol. 1, no. 12 (April 1976) p. 26.

C727 Hadda Be Playing on the Jukebox. *Seven Days,* no. 7 (April 19, 1976) p. 14.

C728 To Louis Ginsberg. *Rutgers Daily Targum* (May 5, 1976) p. 18.

C729 Spring Night Four A.M. *Villager,* vol. 44, no. 20 (May 13, 1976) p. 2.

C730 A Dream [and] C'mon Jack. *Gay Sunshine,* no. 29/30 (Summer/Fall 1976) p. 36.

C731 Don't Grow Old. *Berkeley Barb,* vol. 24, no. 8 [issue 577] (Sept. 3-9, 1976) p. 11.

C732 Hospital Window. *Painted Bride Quarterly,* vol. 3, no. 3 (Fall 1976) pp. 9-10.

C733 [music notation for *Songs of Experience* by William Blake]. *Quarterly West,* no. 1 (Fall 1976) p. 48.
Note: Score by AG.

C734 [prose]. *Proceedings of the American Academy of Arts & Letters and the National Institute of Arts and Letters,* second series, no. 26 ([Oct. 19] 1976) p. 13.
Note: Unsigned citation in support of William S. Burroughs.

C735 To Dulles Airport. *Bombay Gin* [no. 1] (Winter 1976/Spring 1977) ll. 6-10.

C736 Though the Conception "America". *Creative Living,* vol. 5, no. 1 (Winter 1976) p. 25. [prose]

C737 Don't Grow Old. *River Styx,* no. 2 (Winter [Dec. 22, 1976] 1977) p. [133].

C738 The Dream of Tibet [and] Dream: Mycenae. *Attaboy,* no. 1 (1976) pp. 68-74. [prose]

C739 Mabillon Noctambules. *Big Sky,* no. 10 (1976) pp. [130-131].

C740 Prayer Blues [and] Broken Bone Blues. *Intrepid,* no. 25/35 [issue also called *Intrepid Anthology: A Decade and Then Some*] (1976) pp. 121-125.

C741 [blurb for *The Trashing of America* by Charles Plymell]. *Northeast Rising Sun,* vol. 1, no. 4/5 (1976) p. 25.

C742 Don't Grow Old. *A Shout in the Street,* vol. 1, no. 1 (1976) p. 49.

C743 Hearing. *Unmuzzled Ox,* vol. 4, no. 1 [issue 13] (1976) pp. 101-104.

1977

C744 [response to questionnaire]. *Oui,* vol. 6, no. 2 (Feb. 1977) pp. 116-117.

C745 'Junky' Restored. *New York Times Book Review* (Feb. 6, 1977) p. 35. [prose]

C746 [prose]. *Newsletter on the State of the Culture* (Feb. 6, 1977) pp. 1-2.
Note: Statement in support of Abbie Hoffman.

C747 [letter to Louis Ginsberg]. *Iowa Review,* vol. 8, no. 2 (Spring 1977) pp. 82-108.
Note: Printed in *Allen Ginsberg: The Origins of "Howl" and "Kaddish"* by James Breslin.

C748 Uptown. *Tufts Observer,* vol. 2, no. 19 (March 25, 1977) p. 7.

C749 [response to questionnaire]. *Extra,* vol. 1, no. 1 (April 1977) p. 11.
Note: Printed in *VIP Q & A* by Susan Epstein.

C750 [prose]. *Fight to Save WBAI,* no. 1 (April 1977) p. 1.
Note: Statement in support of WBAI

C751 "I Want To Be Wanted" Sings Marie [and] Politics on Opium [and] Subliminal.
Christopher Street, vol. 1, no. 11 (May 1977) pp. 18-23.

C752 [response to questionnaire]. *Win,* vol. 13, no. 19 (June 2, 1977) p. 14.

C753 Dateless Dream Song [and] Stool Pigeon Blues. *Bombay Gin,* no. 4 (Summer/Fall 1977) pp. [95-98].
Note: Although the contents page calls for 3 songs there are only 2.

C754 I Lay Love On My Knee. *Gay Sunshine,* no. 33/34 (Summer/Fall 1977) back cover.

C755 [7 poems and prose]. *Daily [Sunday] Camera* (July 17, 1977) Focus section, pp. 24-25.
Contents: Hearing 'Lenore' Read Aloud at 203 Amity Street — War Profit Litany — Near the Scrap Yard My Father'll Be Buried — What's To Be Done About Death? — Easter Sunday — Describe: The Rain on Dasaswamedh — Galilee Shore — From Indian Journals [prose]

C756 Gospel Noble Truths. *Stupa,* vol. 3, no. 9 [ca. Aug. 1977] p. 5. [includes music notation]

C757 Flying Elegy. *Skyway Peninsula,* no. 1 ([ca. Fall] 1977) p. 1.

C758 Flying Elegy. *Colorado-North Review,* vol. 14, no. 1 (Fall 1977) p. 26.

C759 Contest of Bards: III Epilogue. *Roof,* vol. 1, no. 4 (Fall 1977) p. 15.

C760 You Might Get in Trouble. *Waves,* vol. 6, no. 1 (Autumn 1977) p. 21.

C761 Ginsberg on Lowell. *Poetry Project Newsletter,* no. 48 (Oct. 1, 1977) p. [7]. [prose]

C762 Hearing "Lenore" Read Aloud at 203 Amity Street [and] Poe in Dust. *Hundred Posters,* no. 23 (Nov. 1977) pp. 1-2.

C763 [response to questionnaire]. *TWA Ambassador,* vol. 10, no. 11 (Nov. 1977) p. 23.

C764 [prose]. *Proceedings of the American Academy and Institute of Arts and Letters,* second series, no. 27 ([Nov. 18] 1977) p. 17.
Note: Unsigned citation in support of Louis Zukofsky.

C765 Sickness Blues. *After-Image,* no. 1 ([Dec. 1977] 1978) p. 22.

C766 Father Guru Unforlorn. *Bombay Gin,* [no. 5] (Winter [1977]/Spring 1978) p. 16.

C767 [prose]. *Gay Sunshine,* no. 35 (Winter [Dec. 1977] 1978) p. 29.
Note: Introductory statement about Gavin Arthur.

C768 Haiku Objective Images Written Down. *Third Coast Archives,* no. 10/11 (Winter 1977/1978) p. [7]. [prose]

C769 [letter to Gerard Malanga]. *Travelers Digest,* vol. 1, no. 2 (Winter 1977) p. 10.

C770 Ginsberg Sez. *Search and Destroy,* no. 1 (1977) p. 13. [prose]

C771 Independence Day Meditation. *Unspeakable Visions of the Individual,* vol. 5 [issue called *The Beat Diary*] (1977) p. [1]. [prose]

C772 Returning to the Country for a Brief Visit. *Unspeakable Visions of the Individual,* vol. 5 [issue called *The Beat Diary*] (1977) p. 79.

C773 The Journal of Allen Ginsberg. *Unspeakable Visions of the Individual,* vol. 5 [issue called *The Beat Diary*] (1977) pp. 162-166.

1978

C774 The Names. *Folio,* vol. 15, no. 1 (Fall/Winter [Jan. 1, 1978] 1977/1978) pp. 50-51.

C775 Punk Rock Your My Big Crybaby. *Saturday Morning,* vol. 2, no. 1/2 (Summer [March] 1978) p. [19].

C776 Orlovsky, Peter and AG. [letter to Charlie Chaplin]. *Saturday Morning,* vol. 2, no. 1/2 (Summer [March] 1978) p. [44].

C777 On Creeley's Ear Mind [prose] [and] Lines for Creeley's Ear. *Boundary 2,* vol. 6, no.. 3 & vol. 7, no. 1 (Spring/Fall 1978) pp. 443-445.

C778 News Bulletin [and] Reading French Poetry. *UBU,* no. 1 (Spring 1978) pp. 10-12.

C779 Don't Grow Old. *New Directions in Prose and Poetry,* no. 36 ([April] 1978) pp. 1-4.

C780 Haunting Poe's Baltimore [and prose note]. *Washington Post* (April 2, 1978) Magazine section, pp. 4-5.

C781 T. S. Eliot Entered My Dreams. *City Lights Journal,* no. 4 ([April 15] 1978) pp. 61-65. [prose]

C782 Some Different Considerations in Mindful Arrangement of Open Verse Forms on the Page. *City Lights Journal,* no. 4 ([April 15] 1978) p. 137. [prose]

C783 Ferlinghetti, Lawrence and AG. [prose note]. *City Lights Journal,* no. 4 ([April 15] 1978) p. 138.

C784 Waldman, Anne; Brownstein, Michael and AG. General Practice of Kerouac School of Disembodied Poetics at Naropa Institute. *City Lights Journal,* no. 4 ([April 15] 1978) pp. 241-248. [prose]

C785 [response to questionnaire]. *Win,* vol. 14, no. 16 (May 4, 1978) p. 10.

C786 [drawing and inscription]. *Bergen Record* (May 5, 1978) p. B19.
Note: Drawing and inscription from the title page of a copy of *Howl* is reproduced here.

C787 I Dare Your Reality! [excerpt from: Plutonian Ode] *Rocky Mountain News* (June 16, 1978)

C788 Manhattan May Day Midnight [and] A Pleasant Afternoon. *Bombay Gin,* no. 6 (Summer 1978/Spring 1979) pp. 61-62.

C789 [letter to Dennis McNally]. *Moody Street Irregulars,* vol. 1, no. 2 (Summer 1978) p. 12.

C790 A Note on McNally's Kerouac Biography. *Moody Street Irregulars,* vol. 1, no. 2 (Summer 1978) p. 14. [prose]

C791 Plutonian Ode. *Ins and Outs,* vol. 1, no. 3 (Aug./Sept. 1978) pp. 22-23.

C792 [footnotes to interview]. *Some,* no. 9 (Aug. 23, 1978) p. 57.

C793 Plutonian Ode [with prose note]. *Greenpeace Chronicles,* no. 8 (Sept. 1978) p. 8.

C794 Smith, Sutton and AG. Nuts to Plutonium! *CoEvolution Quarterly/Journal for the Protection of All Beings,* no. 19 (Fall [Sept. 22] 1978) pp. 13-19.

C795 Plutonian Ode. *CoEvolution Quarterly/Journal for the Protection of All Beings,* no. 19 (Fall [Sept. 22] 1978) pp. 21-23.

C796 Versus Included in Howl Reading Boston City Hall April 20, 1978. *Fag Rag,* no. 23/24 (Fall 1978) p. 1.

C797 Manifesto. *So & So* (Fall 1978) p. [29].

C798 Editor's Choice. *New Directions in Prose and Poetry,* no. 37 ([Oct.] 1978) pp. 38-39. [prose]
Note: AG is also the editor for this section of poetry, pp. 38-60.

C799 Golden Courthouse. *Poetry Project Newsletter,* no. 58 (Oct. 1978) p. [3].

C800 Plutonian Ode, pts. I-III. *Boulder Monthly* (Nov. 1978) p. 56.

C801 Plutonian Ode. *Take Over,* vol. 8, no. 9 (Nov. 1978) p. 19.

C802 Plutonian Ode. *Pearl,* no. 6 (Fall/Winter [Nov. 19] 1978) pp. 37-42.

C803 [letter to the editor]. *Village Voice* (Nov. 27, 1978) p. 4.

C804 Plutonian Ode. *Weekly What Is To Be Done?,* vol. 3, no. 10 (Dec. 7, 1978) pp. 8-9.

C805 Punk Rock Your My Big Crybaby. *Village Voice,* vol. 23, no. 50 (Dec. 11, 1978) p. 34.

C806 [response to questionnaire]. *Sentinel,* vol. 5, no. 25 (Dec. 15, 1978) p. 9.

C807 Plutonian Ode [and notes]. *Grapevine,* vol. 10, no. 18 (Dec. 20, 1978) p. 13.

C808 Plutonian Ode. *Win,* vol. 14, no. 43 (Dec. 28, 1978) pp. 6-7.

C809 Punk Rock. *Birthstone,* no. 4 (1978) p. 4.

C810 Punk Rock You're My Big Crybaby. *Juice,* no. 2 (1978) l. [30].

C811 From Journals, Oct. 16, 1977. *Mag City,* no. 5 (1978) p. 52. [prose]

C812 What's Dead. *Mag City,* no. 5 (1978) pp. 52-53.

C813 Kidneystone Opium Traum [and] "You Might Get in Trouble". *Portage* (1978) pp. 36-37.

C814 What Would You Do If You Lost It? *River Styx,* no. 3 (1978) pp. 71-72.

1979

C815 Plutonian Ode. *Village Voice* (Jan. 29, 1979) p. 30.

C816 Punk Rock Your My Big Crybaby. *Little Caesar,* no. 8 (Feb. 1979) p. 6.

C817 Plutonian Ode. *Read Street,* vol. 1, no. 2 (March 1979) pp. 10-11.

C818 [response to questionnaire]. *CoEvolution Quarterly,* no. 21 (March 21, 1979) pp. 83-86.

C819 Dombey, Oliver C. [Jonathan Robbins] and AG. Contest of Bards. *Hudson Review,* vol. 32, no. 1 (Spring 1979) pp. 36-40.

C820 Through Rockies [and note]. *Plainspeak,* vol. 1, no. 2 (Spring 1979) pp. 27-33.

C821 Fake Saint [and] Old Pond. *Zero,* vol. 2 ([April] 1979) pp. [41-43].

C822 [8 poems]. *American Poetry Review,* vol. 8, no. 3 (May/June 1979) pp. 21-26.
Contents: All the Things I've Got To Do — Everybody's Fantasy — Grim Skeleton — Lack Love — Love Returned — No Way Back to the Past — Numbers — What's Dead

C823 [response to questionnaire]. *Instructor,* vol. 88, no. 10 (May 1979) p. 25.

C824* Punk Rock Your My Big Crybaby. *Starscrewer,* no. 12 (May 1979)

C825 [letter to the editor]. *Berkeley Barb,* vol. 28, no. 16 [issue 701] (May 10-23, 1979) p. 4.

C826 Plutonian Ode. *Rolling Stone,* no. 291 (May 17, 1979) pp. 56-57.

C827 [response to questionnaire]. *Win,* vol. 15, no. 18 (May 24, 1979) p. 17.

C828 Koch, Kenneth and AG. Snowmen perpetuate. *New Yorker,* vol. 55 (May 28, 1979) pp. 29-31.

C829 [review of *Gleanings* by Marie Syrkin]. *Poetry Project Newsletter,* no. 66 (June 1979) p. [3].

C830 Returning to the Country for a Brief Visit [and] The Rune [includes music notation]. *Contact II,* vol. 3, no. 13 (Summer 1979) pp. 5-6.
Note: Printed in *Please Were Me: The Poetry Postcard as Art* by Rochelle Ratner, pp. 4-8.

C831 [open letter]. *Canal,* no. 29/31 (July/Sept. 1979) p. 21.

C832 Plutonian Ode. *Poetry Toronto,* no. 43/44 (July/Aug. 1979) pp. 24-26.

C833 Corso, Gregory and AG. Imagination. *Beatitude,* no. 29 ([Aug.] 1979) p. 50.

C834 Lack Love. *Beatitude,* no. 29 ([Aug.] 1979) p. 51.

C835 An Appreciation of the Flood. *Flood* (Sept. 21, 1979) p. 1. [prose]

C836 Brooklyn College Assignment. *Riverrun,* no. 11 (Fall 1979) p. 29.

C837 Plutonian Ode. *West Hills Review,* vol. 1, no. 1 (Fall 1979) pp. 38-42.

C838 Old Pond [and] What's Dead [and] Fake Saint [and] A Pleasant Afternoon [and] Manhattan May Day Midnight. *Poetry London/Apple Magazine,* vol. 1, no. 1 (Autumn [Oct. 31] 1979) pp. 75-78.
Note: Includes Plutonium Ode (recording) see item F73.

C839 Aztec Sandstone Waterholes. *Advocate* (Dec. 1979)

C840 [response to questionnaire]. *Moneysworth* (Dec. 1979) pp. 1, 12-13.

C841 Congress and American People. *Other Voices* (Dec. 1979) pp. 8-9.

C842 [prose]. *De Sentenaar* (Dec. 1, 1979)
Note: Printed in *Blitzbezoek van Allen Ginsberg* by W.C., is this inscription.

C843 [blurb for *Factory* by Antler]. *CoEvolution Quarterly,* no. 24 (Winter [Dec. 22] 1979/80) p. 5.

C844 Pasolini, Pier Paulo. [letter translated by AG and Annette Galvano]. *Lumen Avenue A,* vol. 1, no. 1 (1979) pp. 22-24.

C845 A Brief Praise of Anne's Affairs. *Possible Flash* [no. 1?] (1979) pp. [17-18].

C846 Plutonian Ode. *River Styx,* no. 5 (1979) pp. 61-66.

C847 Junk Mail. *Unmuzzled Ox* [issue also called *The Poets' Encyclopedia*] (1979) pp. 154-157.

C848 A Collage of Haiku, Kerouac's Spontaneous Writ. *Zero,* vol. 3 (1979) pp. 158-170. [prose]

1980

C849 Tune. *Rocky Ledge,* no. 4 (Feb./March 1980) p. 63.

C850 On Appearance of Waldman and Dylan on Poetic Film. *Filmkritik,* vol. 24, no. 3 [issue 279] (March 1980) p. 98.

C851 Clattering of Dishes in the Ivy Room. *Archive,* vol. 92, no. 2 (Spring 1980) p. 7.

C852 Plutonian Ode. *Contact II,* vol. 3, no. 16/17 (Spring 1980) Nuke Chronicles supplement, pp. [3-8].

C853 Notebook Cherry Valley 1970. *United Artists,* no. 10 (April 1980) pp. [14-21]. [prose]

C854 Warrior. *Los Angeles Times* (April 20, 1980) part 4, p. 2.

C855 Garden State. *Ahnoi,* no. 3 (Spring [May] 1980) pp. 4-5.

C856 Pink Sky Streaked with Clouds. *Wit and Whimsy, John Hill School Art and Literary Magazine,* vol. 2 ([June 19] 1980) p. [3].

C857 The Master [and] I Don't Know the Names. *Contemporary Literature,* vol. 21, no. 3 (Summer 1980) p. 447.
Note: Printed in *Allen Ginsberg's Paul Cezanne and the Pater Omnipotens Aeterna Deus* by Paul Portugés, pp. 435-449.

C858 Jennie Skerl's "A Beat Chronology" Revised and Continued. *Moody Street Irregulars,* no. 8 (Summer/Fall 1980) p. 20. [prose]

C859 Andrei Voznesensky and Allen Ginsberg: A Conversation. *Paris Review,* vol. 22, no. 78 (Summer 1980) pp. 149-150. [contains a prose introductory note by AG]

C860 What's Dead? *Passaic Review,* no. 2 (Summer 1980) pp. 84-85.

C861 [letter to Michael A. Rockland]. *New Jersey Monthly,* vol. 4, no. 9 (July 1980) p. 57.

C862 Ode to Failure. *Rocky Ledge,* no. 5 (July/Aug. 1980) p. 39.

C863 [prose]. *Vajradhatu Sun,* vol. 2, no. 6 (Aug./Sept. 1980) p. 18.
Note: One sentence only: "I'd like to create an order that would be poetic."

C864 Trungpa, Chögyam. Trans World Air. [translated by AG]. *Vajradhatu Sun,* vol. 2, no. 6 (Aug./Sept. 1980) Ten Years in North America supplement, p. [12].

C865 Berrigan, Ted and AG. First Spontaneous Collaboration into the Air, Circa 23 May 1980 [and] Second Spontaneous Collaboration into the Air, Circa 23 May 1980 (Sonnet). *United Artists,* no. 11 (Sept. 1980) pp. [27-28].

C866 [letter to the editor]. *Gay Sunshine,* no. 44/45 (Autumn/Winter 1980) p. 3.

C867 Everybody Loves the First Glimpse of Naked Love. *Gay Sunshine,* no. 44/45 (Autumn/Winter 1980) p. 21.

C868 Woke Me Up Naked. *Gay Sunshine,* no. 44/45 (Autumn/Winter 1980) p. 24.

C869 Fellow Meditators, Fellow Students, Friends, Parents. *Vajradhatu Sun,* vol. 3, no. 1 (Oct./Nov. 1980) p. 14. [prose]

C870 Verses Written for Student Anti Draft Rally 1980. *Stonechat,* no. 1 (Nov. 1980) p. 7.

C871 Punk Rock You're My Big Crybaby. *Zdravo!,* no. 118 (Nov. 10, 1980) p. 50.

C872 [blurb for *Idols* by Dennis Cooper]. *Little Caesar,* no. 11 (Dec. 1980) p. 239.

C873 To the Punks of Dawlish. *City Paper,* vol. 4, no. 84 (Dec. 12-25, 1980) p. 1.

C874 Some Different Considerations in Mindful Arrangement of Open Verse Forms on the Page. *Epoch,* vol. 29, no. 2 (Winter 1980) p. 189. [prose]

C875 Verses Written for Student Anti Draft Registration Rally 1980. *Harpoon,* vol. 2, no. 3 (Winter 1980/1981) p. 28.

C876 Amnesiac Thirst for Fame. *Rolling Stone,* no. 335 (Jan. 22 [Dec. 24, 1980] 1981) p. 70.

C877 Kerouac, Jack; Corso, Gregory and AG. Nixon. *Bombay Gin,* no. 7 (Summer/Fall [1980] 1979) p. [1].
Note: Includes a prose note on the poem by Gregory Corso and AG.

C878 On Farm. *Bombay Gin,* no. 7 (Summer/Fall [1980] 1979) p. 82.

C879 Ungaretti in Heaven. *Bombay Gin,* no. 7 (Summer/Fall [1980] 1979) p. 83.

C880 Kalyanapongs, Angkarn. I Lost You. [translated by AG]. *International Portland Review*, no. 26 (1980) p. 400.

C881 Don't Grow Old. *Intrepid*, no. 39/41 [issue also called *Bill Williams and Flossie's Special*] (1980)

C882 [letter]. *Little River Message Project*, no. 2 (1980) pp. 45, 47.

C883 Meditation and Poetics. *New Wilderness Letter*, no. 9 (1980) p. 1.

C884 [letter to John Clellon Holmes]. *Unspeakable Visions of the Individual*, vol. 10 (1980) pp. 103-121.

C885 [blurb for *Zero*]. *Zero*, vol. 4 (1980) p. [1].

1981

C886 Journals 1978. *United Artists*, no. 12 (Jan. 1981) pp. [100-109].
Contents: Go, Go Little Rose — Bebbe Put Me on Your Lap — [2 drawings] — [prose journal entries edited by Lewis Warsh]

C887 Amnesiac Thirst For Fame. *Rolling Stone* (Jan. 22, 1981) p. 70.

C888 [letter to Eileen Leeds]. *Open Door* ([Feb.] 1981) p. 10.

C889 Plutonian Ode. *Open Door* ([Feb.] 1981) pp. 29-33.

C890 Power and Weakness of Poetry. *Poetry Project Newsletter*, no. 80 (Feb. 1981) pp. [8-9]. [prose]

C891 Good Steambaths Make Clean Minds. *Toronto Sun* (Feb. 22, 1981) p. 20.
Note: Printed in '*Expect Protests for Raid*' by John Paton, this single line only from a poem.

C892 My Neighborhood. *New Blood* ([March] 1981) p. 44.

C893 [Kerouac, Jack]. A Translation from the French of Jean-Louis Incogniteau [translated by AG]. *Columbia College Today*, vol. 8, no. 2 (Spring/Summer 1981) p. 41.

C894 Epitaph for a poet. *Columbia College Today*, vol. 8, no. 2 (Spring/Summer 1981) p. 41.

C895 Verses Written for Student Anti Draft Registration Rally 1980. *Purchase Poetry Review*, vol. 5 (Spring 1981) unpaged.

C896 Ode to Failure. *River Styx*, no. 8 (April 1981) p. 83.

C897 Reflections at Lake Louise. *Vajradhatu Sun*, vol. 3, no. 4 (April/May 1981) p. 23.

C898 [letter to Ms. Soloff]. *Daily News* (April 6, 1981) Manhattan Magazine section, p. M2.

C899 [response to questionnaire]. *Win*, vol. 17, no. 7 (April 15, 1981) p. 14.

C900 Homework. *New Blood*, no. 3 ([May] 1981) p. 95.

C901 Capitol Air. *Aquarian Weekly*, no. 372 (June 17-24, 1981) p. 11.

C902 Verses Written for Student Anti Draft Registration Rally 1980. *Harpoon* (Summer/Fall 1981) p. 12.

C903 Birdbrain! *Outskirts,* no. 1 ([ca. July] 1981) pp. 6-7.

C904 [blurb for *Factory* by Antler]. *Poetry Flash,* no. 100 (July 1981)

C905 Eörsi, István. Ominous Prognosis [and] Snafu. [translated by AG]. *Szivárvány,* no. 4 (July 1981) p. 29.

C906 Neruda, Pablo. Let the Woodcutter Awake! [translated by Sidney Goldfarb and AG]. *Pearl,* no. 8 (Summer [Aug.] 1981) pp. 42-44.

C907 Power & Weakness of Poetry. *Amanda Blue,* vol. 2, no. 1 (Sept./Oct. 1981) pp. 15-16. [prose]

C908 Why I Meditate. *Naropa Institute Bulletin* (Fall 1981/Winter 1982) p. 6.

C909 Verses Written for Student Anti Draft Registration Rally. *Echo Park Press,* no. 1 (Oct. 1981) pp. 24-25.

C910 Capitol Airlines. *Nation,* vol. 233, no. 10 (Oct. 3, 1981) pp. 296-297.

C911 Wherein Lies the Power of the Poet. *Relations,* no. 1 [new series] (Oct. [5] 1981) pp. 38-29. [prose]

C912 Garden State. *New Jersey Monthly,* vol. 6, no. 1 (Nov. 1981) p. 62.

C913 To Kerouac in the Hospital. *Unspeakable Visions of the Individual,* vol. 12 [issue also called *Beat Angels*] ([Nov. 1981] 1982) p. 175. [see also D15]

C914 [letter to Jack Kerouac]. *Unspeakable Visions of the Individual,* vol. 12 [issue also called *Beat Angels*] ([Nov. 1981] 1982) pp. 176-179.

C915 Berrigan, Ted; Rosenthal, Bob and AG. [list of stolen books]. *AB Bookman's Weekly,* vol. 68, no. 20 (Nov. 16, 1981) p. 3596.

C916 Eörsi, István. Tunnel Through Mist [and] Four Movements [and] Allen Ginsberg, Sworn Enemy of T.V. [and] The Warsaw Pact Liberates Warsaw from Itself. [translated by AG]. *New Blood,* no. 5 (Dec. 1981) pp. 22-24.

C917 The Warrior. *Lomi School Bulletin* (Winter 1981) p. 18.

C918 Nagasaki Days IV. *Uranus,* no. 3 (Autumn [Dec. 29] 1981) p. 5.

C919 Porch Haikus. *Bombay Gin,* no. 8 (Summer/Fall [1981] 1980) p. 6.
Contents: It's a Whale — It's Midsummer — Sitting on the Porch — Everyone Loves the Rain — Did Will Unicorn Chop
Note: This issue is also edited in part by AG.

C920 Dear Laura Boss Here's a Poem. *Lips,* no. 2 (1981) p. 1.

C921 From Journals. *Mag City,* no. 12 (1981) pp. 7-15.
Contents: January 19, 1968 — December 19, 1974 — Capitol Air — Trungpa Lectures — [prose journal entries]

C922 Padgett, Ron and AG. Thundering Undies. *Mag City,* no. 12 (1981) p. 16.

C923 Verses Written for Student Anti Draft Registration Rally 1980. *Scumbag,* no. 3 (1981) p. 3.

1982

C924 [response to questionnaire]. *American Book Review,* vol. 4, no. 2 (Jan./Feb. 1982) p. 9.

C925 No Hope Communism No Hope. *American Book Review,* vol. 4, no. 2 (Jan./Feb. 1982) p. 9.

C926 blurb for *Factory* by Antler]. *American Book Review,* vol. 4, no. 2 (Jan./Feb. 1982) p. 13.

C927 Introduction to the Poems of David Cope. *Ferro Botanica,* no. 2 (Jan. 1982) p. 4. [prose]

C928 Woke Me Up Naked [and] Maybe Love. *Gay Sunshine Journal,* no. 47 [issue also called *Gay Fiction Anthology*] ([Jan.] 1982) pp. 161-164.

C929 [blurb for *Factory* by Antler]. *Poetry Flash,* no. 106 (Jan. 1982) p. 8.

C930 A Knock, Look in the Mirror. *Shearsman,* no. 7 ([First quarter] 1982) p. 31.

C931 Yevtushenko, Yevgeny; Cardenale [sic], Ernesto and AG. Declaration of Three. *Soho News* (Feb. 16, 1982) p. 11. [prose]

C932 Evtuchenko, Eugenio; Cardenal, Ernesto and AG. Declaration of Three. *Nation,* vol. 234, no. 7 (Feb. 20, 1982) p. 194. [prose]

C933 Evtuchenko, Eugenio; Cardenal, Ernesto and AG. Declaration of Three. *Washington Tribune,* vol. 6, no. 4 (Feb. 26/March 11, 1982) p. 2. [prose]

C934 Evtuchenko, Eugenio; Cardenal, Ernesto and AG. Declaration of Three. *Poetry Project Newsletter,* no. 89 (March 1982) p. [16]. [prose]
Note: Includes introductory note by AG.

C935 Plutonian Ode. *Link,* vol. 3, no. 3 (March 8-28, 1982) p. 14.

C936 Yevtushenko, Yevgeny; Cardenal, Ernesto and AG. The Declaration of Three. *L. A. Weekly,* vol. 4, no. 15 (March 12-18, 1982) p. 9. [prose]

C937 Poets of the Revolution. *New Haven Advocate,* vol. 7, no. 31 (March 17, 1982) pp. 6-7. [prose journal entry]

C938 Yevtuchenko, Eugenio; Cardenal, Ernesto and AG. The Declaration of Three Poets. *New Haven Advocate,* vol. 7, no. 31 (March 17, 1982) p. 10. [prose]

C939 Why I Meditate. *Here Now,* no. 2 (Spring 1982) p. 4.

C940 Yevtuchenko, Yevgeny; Cardenal, Ernesto and AG. From the "Declaration of Three". *El Salto Leap* (Spring 1982) p. [8]. [prose]

C941 Poets of the Revolution. *Valley Advocate,* vol. 9, no. 33 (March 31, 1982) p. 6A. [prose journal entry]
Note: Printed in *A Breakthrough of Bohemian Culture* by Larry Estridge.

C942 Evtuchenko, Eugenio; Cardenal, Ernesto and AG. Declaration of Three. *New Blood,* no. 6 (April 1982) pp. 30-31.
Note: Includes introductory note by AG.

C943 Rosenthal, Bob and AG. [blurb for *First Blues (recording)* by AG]. *NYC Poetry Calendar* (April 1982) p. [2].

C944 Berrigan, Ted and AG. Two Scenes. *Poetry Project Newsletter,* no. 90 (April 1982)

C945 Henry Miller 1891-1980. *Proceedings of the American Academy and Institute of Arts and Letters,* second series, no. 32 ([April 22] 1982) pp. 76-78. [prose]

C946 Birdbrain. *High Times,* no. 81 (May 1982) p. 106.

C947 Evtuchenko, Eugenio; Cardenal, Ernesto and AG. Declaration of Three. *Poetry Flash,* no. 110 (May 1982) p. 9.

C948 Evtuchenko, Eugenio; Cardenal, Ernesto and AG. Declaration of Three. *San Francisco Review of Books,* vol. 6, no. 12 (May 1982) p. 2.
Note: Includes introductory note by AG.

C949 Things I've Got to Do. *Long Shot,* vol. 1, no. 1 (June 1982) p. 62.

C950 Porch Scribbles [and] Those Two on Marine Street. *Bombay Gin,* [no. 9] (Summer 1982) pp. 51-53.

C951 Eroica. *River Styx,* no. 11 ([Summer] 1982) pp. 41-43.

C952 The Little Fish Devours the Big Fish. *New Blood,* no. 7 (July 1982) pp. 38-39.

C953 It's Happening Now. *Gay Community News,* vol. 10, no. 6 (Aug. 21, 1982) p. [9].

C954 Dharma Poetics: Bare Attention and Mindfulness Slogans. *Naropa Institute Bulletin* (Fall 1982/Winter 1983) pp. 22, 28. [prose]

C955 [review of *Historical Document* by Nichola Manning]. *Poetry Project Newsletter,* no. 92 (Oct. 1982) p. [4].

C956 Dream of Naomi. *Moment,* vol. 7, no. 10 (Nov. 1982) Forthcoming section [vol. 1, no. 1] p. F26. [prose]

C957 When Young I Drank Beer. *New Blood,* no. 8 (Nov. 1982) p. 45.

C958 [response to questionnaire]. *Flipside,* no. 36 ([Dec.] 1982) p. [20].

C959 Harry Fainlight: In Memoriam. *Poetry Project Newsletter,* no. 94 (Dec. 1982) p. 6. [prose]

C960 The Little Fish Devours the Big Fish. *L. A. Weekly* (Dec. 24-30, 1982) p. 7.

C961 [drawing]. *Mediums* (1982) p. 7.
Note: Reproduction of drawing of Mary Help of Christians Church.

C962 New Year's Eve Poem [and] To the Punks of Dawlish. *New Departures,* no. 14 (1982) pp. 51-56.

C963 Plutonian Ode. *Open Door,* vol. 1 (1982) pp. 24-27.

C964 Things I've Got To Do. *Windmill* (1982) pp. 49-50.

1983

C965 A Definition of the Beat Generation. *Friction,* vol. 1, no. 2/3 (Winter [Feb. 27, 1983] 1982) pp. 50-52. [prose]

C966 As the Rain Drops from the Gutter on to the Bushes. *Friction,* vol. 1, no. 2/3 (Winter [Feb. 27, 1983] 1982) p. 82.

C967 Having Bowed Down My Forehead on the Pavement [and] Although the Rain Has Stopped. *Friction,* vol. 1, no. 2/3 (Winter [Feb. 27, 1983] 1982) p. 84.

C968 Act III. *Friction,* vol. 1, no. 2/3 (Winter [Feb. 27, 1983] 1982) pp. 97-98. [prose]

C969 [letter to the editor]. *NAMBLA Bulletin,* vol. 4, no. 3 (April 1983) p. 6.

C970 I Approached the Talk Show. *Channels of Communication,* vol. 3 (May/June 1983) pp. 45-47. [prose]

C971 [blurb for *Beat Hotel* by Harold Norse]. *Poetry Flash,* no. 122 (May 1983) p. 2.

C972 Kenneth Rexroth. *Proceedings of the American Academy and Institute of Arts and Letters,* second series, no. 34 ([May 15] 1983) pp. 98-100. [prose]

C973 To John Allen Cassady. *Seattle Times* (May 29, 1983) Pacific section, pp. 8-14. [prose]
Note: Printed in *Searching for Jack & Neal* by Darrell Bob Houston.

C974 Nov. 23, 1963 [and] From Wichita Vortex Sutra I [and] Kral Majales [and] Pentagon Exorcism [and] On Neal's Ashes. *High Times,* no. 94 (June 1983) pp. 62-65.
Note: Introductory notes included for each poem.

C975 The Pot Calls the Kettle Black! *NAMBLA Bulletin,* vol. 4, no. 5 (June 1983) p. 5. [prose]

C976 Why I Meditate. *New Age,* vol. 8, no. 11 (June 1983) p. 38.

C977 [blurb for *Beat Hotel* by Harold Norse]. *Poetry Flash,* no. 124 (July 1983) p. 2.

C978 Grey Clouds Hang Over. *Daily Camera* (Nov. 20, 1983) Sunday Camera Magazine section, p. [1].

C979 204 Syllables at Rocky Mountain Dharma Center. *Vajradhatu Sun,* vol. 6, no. 2 (Dec. 1983/Jan. 1984) p. 24.

C980 [letter to Herschel Silverman]. *New York Times,* New Jersey edition (Dec. 18, 1983) section 11, pp. 1, 24.
Note: Printed in *The 2¢ Plain Papers: A Tale of 2 Poets* by Pamela Margoshes.

C981 Airplane Blues. *Poesi,* no. 1 (1983) pp. 155-156.

C982 [letter]. *Rolling Stock,* no. 6 (1983) p. 2.

1984

C983 A Note on Obscure Genius. *Friction,* no. 5/6 [issue also called *Obscure Genius*] (Winter [Jan.] 1984) p. 9. [prose] [see also D20]

C984 Notes on Contributors. *Friction,* no. 5/6 [issue also called *Obscure Genius*] (Winter [Jan.] 1984) pp. 99-101. [prose]

C985 [response to questionnaire]. *Rolling Stone,* no. 415 (Feb. 16, 1984) p. 22.

C986 U.S. "Secretary of War" Got. *Alternative Media,* vol. 14, no. 4 (Spring 1984) pp. 23-24. [prose]

C987 Awakened at Dawn Trying to Run Away. *Notebook,* no. 3 (April 1984) p. [4].

C988 [prose note]. *Tribu,* no. 6 ([April/June] 1984) p. 34.

C989 Crawling on All Fours. *Tribu,* no. 6 ([April/June] 1984) pp. 36-37.

C990 Empire Air. *Action,* no. 2 (June 1984) pp. 11-13.

C991 From Lake Louise Notebook [and] Those Two. *Long Shot,* no. 3 ([June] 1984) pp. 61-62.

C992 [blurb for *From the Dark* by Len Roberts]. *New York Times Book Review* (June 3, 1984) p. 24.

C993 Rejection Letters to Famous People. *CoEvolution Quarterly,* no. 42 (Summer [June 22] 1984) pp. 118-122. [prose]

C994 Ginsberg's Rejection Letters to the Famous. *San Francisco Chronicle* (June 27, 1984) [prose]

C995 [letter to Shig Murao]. *Shig's Review,* no. 7 (June 25, 1984) ll. [3-4].

C996 [prose]. *Horizon,* vol. 27, no. 9 (Nov. 1984) p. 4.
Note: Printed in *Hearing a Poetic Voice* by Dana Tripoli, this is a blurb in support of Alice Notley.

C997 White Shroud. *New York Times Magazine* (Nov. 11, 1984) p. 70.

C998 In My Kitchen in New York. *Full Circle,* vol. 1, no. 1 (Dec. 1984) p. 14.

C999 The Little Fish Devours the Big Fish. *Contact II,* vol. 6, no. 34/35 (Winter/Spring 1984-85) pp. 58-59.

C1000 Some Writings from a Journal. *Chelsea,* no. 42/43 (1984) pp. 70-71. [prose]

C1001 Listening to Susan Sontag. *City,* vol. 1, no. 9 (1984) pp. 61-62.

C1002 Surviving Death. *Unmuzzled Ox,* vol. 6, no. 3/vol. 12, no. 1 [issue 23] (1984) p. 17.

C1003 A Version of the Apocalypse. *Unspeakable Visions of the Individual,* vol. 14 [issue also called *The Beat Road*] (1984) pp. 37-43. [prose]

1985

C1004 Happening Now? [and] Sunday Prayer. *Vanity Fair,* vol. 48, no. 1 (Jan. 1985) pp. 58-65.
Note: Printed in *The Beats Go On* by John Tytell. [see also D24]

C1005 What Thoughts I Have Of [and] Detroit Has Built a Million Automobiles Of [and] This Is My Rocket. *Ann Arbor News* (Feb. 10, 1985) pp. G1.

C1006 November 11, 1984 Sunday Afternoon. *Big Scream,* no. 20 ([Feb. 15] 1985) p. 4.
Note: This is a letter to David Cope printed in the form of a poem.

C1007 Allen Ginsberg on China Today. *Boston Globe* (Feb. 20, 1985) p. 2. [prose]

C1008 China Through Poet's Eyes. *San Jose Mercury News* (Feb. 20, 1985) pp. 1D, 4D.
Contents: I Went Through China [prose] — Traveler in a Strange Country — China Bronchitis

C1009 Allen Ginsberg Takes a Poetic Look at China. *San Francisco Examiner* (Feb. 26, 1985) pp. B7, B9.
Contents: Traveler in a Strange Country — China Bronchitis — One Morning I Took a Walk in China — I Went Through China Asking Everybody I Met [prose]

C1010 I Went Through China Asking Everybody I Met. *Gazette-Mail* (March 3, 1985) p. 4A. [prose]

C1011 Reading Bai Chu Yi [and] I Lay My Cheek on the Pillow to Nap [and] China Bronchitis. *Vajradhatu Sun,* vol. 6, no. 4 (April/May 1985) p. 13.

C1012 Far Away. *Guardian* (April 10, 1985) p. 20.

C1013 [letter to Wenjin Zhang]. *PEN Freedom-to-Write Bulletin* (April 24, 1985) p. 2.

C1014 For C.S. *Heartwood,* no. 12 (Summer [May 30] 1985) back cover.

C1015 In My Kitchen in New York. *Portable Lower East Side,* vol. 2, no. 1 (Summer [June] 1985) pp. 29-30.

C1016 [letter to Edouard Roditi]. *Frank,* no. 4 (Summer/Fall 1985) p. 83.
Note: Includes a reproduction of a drawing.

C1017 Improvisation in Beijing. *Inquiring Mind,* vol. 2, no. 1 (Summer 1985) p. 20.

C1018 [letter to Shig Murao]. *Shig's Review,* no. 16 [ca. Summer 1985] l. 1. [see also D31]

C1019 Far Away. *Spao Spassiba,* no. 1 ([June 29] 1985) p. 6.

C1020 Living Theater & Its U.S. Critics. *Third Rail,* no. 7 ([Aug. 28] 1985/86) pp. 32-33. [prose] [see also D32]

C1021 Transcription of Notebook Jan Feb '56. *Credences,* vol. 3, no. 3 (Fall 1985) pp. 77-80. [prose]

C1022 Sacramental Portraits. *Vajradhatu Sun,* vol. 7, no. 1 (Oct./Nov. 1985) p. 13. [prose] [see also D33]

C1023 The Moral Majority. *National Lampoon,* vol. 2, no. 88 (Nov. [Oct. 22] 1985) p. 57.

C1024 Twelve Poems. *American Poetry Review,* vol. 14, no. 6 (Nov./Dec. 1985) pp. 16-18.
Contents: The Black Man — Homage Vajracarya — Those Two — Maturity — "Throw Out the Yellow Journalists of Bad Grammar & Terrible Manner" — Far Away — What the Sea Throws Up At Vlissengen — I Am Not — I'm a Prisoner of Allen Ginsberg — Arguments — They Are All Phantoms of My Imagining — Empire Air

C1025 Going to the World of the Dead. *Beatitude,* no. 33 (1985) pp. 70-71.
Note: Includes music notation.

1986

C1026 My High School English Teacher. *Teachers and Writers,* vol. 17, no. 3 (Jan./Feb. 1986) p. 5. [prose]

C1027 The Black Man. *Zonë,* vol. 1 (Winter [Jan. 1986] 1986) p. 53.

C1028 204 Syllables at Rocky Mountain Dharma Center. *Long Shot,* vol. 4 ([Feb.] 1986) p. 26.

C1029 Face to Face. *Poetry Project Newsletter,* no. 119 (Feb. 1986) p. 7.

Related Item: [letter]. *New York Review of Books,* vol. 33, no. 2 (Feb. 13, 1986) p. 44.
Note: AG is one of the signers but he did not write this.

C1030 [open letter]. *Poetry Project Newsletter,* no. 120 (March 1986) p. 2.

C1031 Homage to Paris at the Bottom of the Barrel. *Frank,* no. 5 (Spring 1986) p. [18].

C1032 It's All So Brief [and] No Longer. *Big Scream,* no. 22 (April 1986) p. [13].

C1033 [review of *Selected Poems* by John Wieners]. *Christopher Street,* vol. 9, no. 3 [issue 99] (April 1986) pp. 45-46.
Note: This issue has been mislabeled as 1985.

C1034 Hard Labor. *National Poetry Magazine of the Lower East Side,* vol. 1, no. 4 (April 1986) pp. [31-32].

C1035 Love Comes. *Christopher Street,* vol. 9, no. 4 [issue 100] (May 1986) p. 45.
Note: This issue has been mislabeled as 1985.

C1036 Student Love. *NAMBLA Journal,* no. 7 ([May 17] 1986) p. 26.

C1037 Corso, Gregory and AG. Ten Angry Men. *Esquire,* vol. 105, no. 6 (June 1986) pp. 260-262. [prose] [see also D38]

C1038 [8 poems]. *Minnesota Daily,* vol. 87, no. 153 (June 9-13, 1986) pp. 7-15.
Contents: Irratable Vegatable [sic] — Going to the World of the Dead — Old Love Story — Industrial Waves — The Guest — "What You Up To?" — Surprised Mind — Student Love

C1039 [response to questionnaire]. *Guardian Book Review Supplement,* no. 4 [issued also called *What's Left To Read?*] (Summer 1986) pp. 1, 16.

C1040 World Karma. *Open Magazine,* no. 2 ([ca. Summer] 1986) p. 9.

C1041 I Love Old Whitman So. *Atlantic,* vol. 258, no. 1 (July 1986) p. 66.

C1042 The Blue Rug in the Motel. *Dandelion Review,* vol. 2, no. 4 (July 1986) p. 9.

C1043 Written in My Dream by W. C. Williams. *Poetry,* vol. 148, no. 5 (Aug. [July 22] 1986) pp. 256-257.

C1044 [letter to Claude Pelieu and Mary Beach]. *Devil-Paradis,* no. 18 (Aug. 1986) pp. [38, 42]

C1045 [prose and 4 poems]. *Struga,* no. 5 (Aug. 1986) pp. 1, 5-6.
Contents: I Am Honored by the Golden Wreath Prize [prose] — The Eye Altering Alters All — Song — A Supermarket in California — Things I Don't Know

Related Item: [letter]. *New York Review of Books,* vol. 33, no. 13 (Aug. 14, 1986).
Note: AG is one of the signers but he did not write this.

C1046 You Don't Know It [and] Velocity of Money. *Exquisite Corpse,* vol. 4, no. 9/10 (Sept./Oct. 1986) pp. 10-11.

C1047 World Karma [and] Russia. *Gandhabba,* no. 4 ([Sept.] 1986) pp. 1-4.

C1048 Cadillac Squawk. *Big Scream,* no. 23 (Fall 1986) p. 11.

C1049 [prose course description]. *English Majors' Newsletter,* vol. 5, no. 1 (Fall 1986) p. 23.
Note: Description of 71 GJK *Seminar in American Literature: Literary History of the Beat Generation 1950's.*

C1050 World Karma. *Poetry Project [Newsletter],* no. 123 (Oct./Nov. 1986) p. 1.

C1051 Reading Bai Juyi [and] Black Shroud [and] Things I Don't Know. *Sulfur,* vol. 6, no. 2 [issue 17] ([Oct. 1] 1986) pp. 17-25.

C1052 [letter to Julian Beck and Judith Malina]. *Exquisite Corpse,* vol. 4, no. 11/12 (Nov./Dec. 1986) p. 12.

C1053 [letter to Herschel Silverman]. *Kerouac Connection,* no. 12 (Nov. 1986) pp. 5-7.
Note: Printed in *High and Nostalgic on the Beats* by Herschel Silverman.

C1054 [music notation for *Nurses Song* by William Blake]. *We,* vol. 1, no. 1 (Nov. 1986) back cover.

C1055 Quatrains. *Paris Review,* vol. 28, no. 100 (Summer/Fall [Nov. 8] 1986) p. 163.

C1056 "On the Conduct of the World Seeking Beauty Against Government" [and] Fifth Internationale [includes music notation]. *Brooklyn Review,* no. 3 (1986) pp. 79-80.

C1057 Surviving Death. *Unmuzzled Ox,* vol. 12, no. 2 [issue 24] (1986) pp. 17-18.
Note: Identified here as Canto 125.

1987

C1058 [blurb for *On the Bridge* by David Cope]. *And,* vol. 1, no. 2 (Jan./Feb. 1987) p. 20.

C1059 Notes from a Chinese Journal. *Equivalencias,* no. 14 (Jan. 1987) pp. 64-78.

C1060 Velocity of Money. *Harper's,* vol. 274, no. 1640 (Jan. 1987) p. 38.

C1061 [drawing]. *Infolio,* no. 58 (Jan. 30, 1987) front cover.
Note: Reproduction of drawing of an insect and caption.

C1062 Berrigan, Ted and AG. Kenneth Rexroth 1905-1982. *Third Rail,* no. 8 ([Feb.] 1987) pp. 9-10. [prose]

C1063 [drawing]. *We Magazine,* no. 3 ([early March] 1987) inside front cover.
Note: Reproduction of drawing of cityscape with flower, snake and skeleton.

C1064 Poetry or Fiction? *Margin,* no. 2 (Spring 1987) pp. 20-23. [prose]

C1065 CIA Dope Calypso. *Underground Forest,* vol. 4, no. 2 (Spring [April 19] 1987) p. 28.

C1066 Europe, Who Knows? *Reality Sandwich,* no. 2 (May 1987) p. 2.

C1067 [drawing]. *Mainichi Shinubun* (May 21, 1987)
Note: Reproduction of drawing of a bearded nude self portrait.

C1068 Velocity of Money. *Core,* no. 1 (June 1987) p. 12.

C1069 Visiting Father & Friends. *Mill Street Forward,* vol. 1, no. 1 (June 1987) p. 8.

C1070 [letter to the editor]. *We Magazine,* no. 5 ([June] 1987) p. 2.

Related Item: [letter]. *New York Review of Books,* vol. 34, no. 10 (June 11, 1987) p. 53.
Note: AG is one of the signers but he did not write this.

C1071 Cosmopolitan Greetings [and] Velocity of Money. *Gown Literary Supplement,* vol. 32, no. 6 ([June 20] 1987) pp. 3, 7.

C1072 [letter to Pierre Lagayette]. *Revue Francaise d'Etudes Américaines,* vol. 12, no. 33 (July 1987) pp. 436-446.
Note: Printed in *Robinson Jeffers: La Redécouverte* by Pierre Lagayette.

C1073 I Noticed the Sea. *Vajradhatu Sun,* vol. 8, no. 6 (Aug./Sept. 1987) p. 17.

C1074 Waldman, Anne and AG. Fifth Internationale. *Underground Forest,* vol. 4, no. 3 (Summer [Aug. 14] 1987) p. 22.

C1075 I Noticed the Sea. *Talus,* no. 2 (Autumn 1987) pp. 4-5.

C1076 Taylor, Steven and AG. Europe, Who Knows? *Cover,* vol. 1, no. 8 (Oct. [1] 1987) pp. 20-21.

C1077 On the Conduct of the World Seeking Beauty Against Government. *Long Shot,* vol. 6, no. 1 ([Oct. 12] 1987) p. 115.

C1078 [drawing]. *We Magazine,* no. 7 (Nov. 1987) p. 7.
Note: Reproduction of drawing of a snake, flower and skeleton.

C1079 Sphincter. *Gandhabba,* no. 5 (Dec. 1987) p. 21.

C1080 Fifth Internationale. *Bombay Gin* [new series] vol. 1, no. 2 (Winter 1987) p. 53.
Note: Includes music notation.

C1081 Personals Ad. *Moorish Science Monitor,* vol. 2, no. 8 (Winter 1987/1988) p. [23].

C1082 I Noticed the Sea. *New Letters,* vol. 54, no. 1 (Fall [Dec. 30] 1987) p. 77.

C1083 Texas Power Apocalypse. *City Lights Review,* no. 1 (1987) pp. 172-173. [prose]

C1084 Cosmopolitan Greetings. *City Lights Review,* no. 1 (1987) pp. 175-176.

C1085 Spot Anger. *Nightmares of Reason,* no. 3 (1987) p. [6].

C1086 The Guest. *Semiotexte,* vol. 13 (1987) p. 84.

C1087 Improvisation in Beijing. *Semiotexte,* vol. 13 (1987) pp. 193-194.

1988

C1088 [letter to Leanne Miller]. *We Magazine,* no. 8 ([Jan.] 1988) p. 10.

C1089 I Heard Robert Duncan Read. *Poetry Flash,* no. 180 (March 1988) p. 3. [prose]

C1090 Julian Was a Monster of Aesthetics. *Downtown,* no. 96 (May 11, 1988) p. 1. [prose] [see also D59]

C1091 On Cremation of Chögyam Trungpa, Vidyandara. *Venue,* no. 1 (Summer [May 31] 1988) pp. 22-24.

C1092 Do the Meditation Rock. *Inquiring Mind,* vol. 5, no. 1 (Summer 1988) p. 12.
Note: Includes music notation.

C1093 [letter to PEN Center]. *New York Times* (June 25, 1988)

C1094 Visiting Father & Friends. *Bombay Gin,* new series, vol. 1, no. 3 (Summer [July] 1988) pp. 46-47.

C1095 [drawing]. *First Line,* no. 5 ([July 15] 1988) p. 39.
Note: Reproduction of a drawing of a seated Buddha with stars and skull.

C1096 Taylor, Steven and AG. Europe, Who Knows? *First Line,* no. 5 ([July 15] 1988) p. 83.

C1097 [drawing]. *First Line,* no. 5 ([July 15] 1988) p. 121.
Note: Reproduction of a drawing of a snake and flower design.

C1098 Snow in Big Skull. *Big Fish* [no. 7] (Oct. 1988) p. 27.

C1099 To Carlos Edmundo De Ory in the Gas Station. *Columbia: A Magazine of Poetry & Prose,* no. 13 ([Oct.] 1988) p. 61.

C1100 I Went to the Movie of Life. *Tikkun,* vol. 3, no. 6 (Nov./Dec. 1988) pp. 66-68.

C1101 M.F.A. Classes and Friends and AG. Graphic Winces. *Brooklyn Review,* no. 5 (1988) pp. 57-59.

C1102 Do the Meditation Reggae Rag. *Unmuzzled Ox,* vol. 12, no. 4 [issue 26] (1988) p. 54.

1989

C1103 [letter to Jack Kerouac]. *Chicago History,* vol. 17, no. 1/2 (Spring/Summer [Jan. 1989] 1988) p. 5.
Note: Printed in *Big Table* by Gerald Brennan, pp. 4-23.

C1104 Put on My Shirt and Took It Off [and] At 2 a.m. the Two Middle-Aged Men. *Alternative Orange*, vol. 1, no. 5 (March 2-23, 1989) p. 6.

C1105 Introduction. *Shits and Giggles, Beast Quarterly*, no. 1 ([April-June] 1989) p. 1. [prose]

C1106 Graphic Winces. *Harper's*, vol. 278, no. 1667 (April 1989) p. 38.

C1107 [blurb for *Mindfield* by Gregory Corso]. *News from Thunder's Mouth Press*, vol. 1, no. 1 (June 1989) p. 3.

C1108 [letter to the editor]. *LunchBox*, no. 1 (June 1989) p. [20].

C1109 DeOry, Carlos Edmundo. Eveningvisit to Allen Ginsberg. [translated by AG]. *Portable Lower East Side*, vol. 6, no. 1 ([June] 1989) pp. 76-79.

C1110 Proclamation. *Moment*, no. 10 (Spring [June 8] 1989) p. 4.

C1111 Birdbrain. *Voice* (June 27, 1989) p. 8.

C1112 CIA Dope Calypso. *Voice* (June 27, 1989) p. 10.

C1113 Salutations to Fernando Pessoa. *Bombay Gin* [new series], vol. 1, no. 4 (Summer [July] 1989) pp. 94-95.

C1114 We Haven't Landed on Earth Yet. *San Diego Union* (July 16, 1989) p. D3.

C1115 A Draft of an Introduction to *Renaldo & Clara. Telegraph*, no. 33 (Summer [Aug.] 1989) pp. 7-8. [prose]

C1116 [open letter]. *Bad Newz*, no. 13 ([Aug. 14] 1989) p. 54.

C1117 [open letter]. *Freedom-to-Write Bulletin* (Sept. 1989) p. 1.

C1118 Spincter [sic] [and] Graphic Winces [and] Cosmopolitan Greetings. *Grand Rapids College Review*, vol. 2, no. 1 (Fall 1989) pp. 4-5.

C1119 [open letter]. *Poetry Project Newsletter*, no. 134 (Oct./Nov. 1989) p. 29.

C1120 December 2, 1988 [and] August 8, 1989 — N.Y. *We Magazine*, no. 12 [Nov. 1989] pp. [47-48]. [prose]

C1121 Poetry for the Next Society. *Poetry Project Newsletter*, no. 135 (Dec./Jan. 1989/1990) pp. [2-4]. [prose]

C1122 Improvisation in Beijing [and] Cosmopolitan Greetings. *Alpha Beat Soup*, no. 6 (Winter 1989/1990) pp. 33-37.

C1123 [letter to editor]. *MLA Newsletter* (Winter 1989) p. 5.

C1124 Tompkins Park. *This Is Important*, no. 16 ([ca. Dec. 25] 1989) p. 1.

C1125 I Went to the Movie of Life. *Big Scream*, no. 27 (1989) pp. 13-15.

C1126 [open letter]. *White Punkturist Crash*, no. 1 (ca. 1989) p. [3].

1990

C1127 Personals Ad. *Long Shot,* vol. 9 ([Jan. 4] 1990) p. 40.

C1128 [open letter]. *Out Week,* no. 29 (Jan. 14, 1990) pp. 60-61.
Note: Printed in *Howling for the Masses?* by Ira Silverberg.

C1129 [response to questionnaire]. *Haggis/Baggis,* no. 27 (Spring 1990) p. 64.

C1130 CIA Dope Calypso. *Organica,* vol. 9, no. 31 (Spring 1990) p. 5.

C1131 Censorship Howl. *Nation,* vol. 250, no. 14 (April 9, 1990) p. 477. [prose]

C1132 CIA Dope Calypso. *Exit Zero,* no. 1 ([after April 9] 1990) pp. 96-99.

C1133 Statement of Allen Ginsberg. *Exit Zero,* no. 1 ([after April 9] 1990) pp. 100-101.

C1134 Personals Ad. *Harper's,* vol. 280, no. 1681 (June 1990) p. 32.

C1135 [open letter]. *Turkish Daily News* (June 18, 1990) p. 12.

C1136 CIA Dope Calypso. *Vagabond,* vol. 2, no. 5 (Aug. 1990) p. 12.

C1137 Richey, Joseph and AG. The Right to Depict Children in the Nude. *Aperture,* no. 121 (Fall 1990) pp. 42-45. [prose]

C1138 A Definition of Beat Generation. *Dirty Goat,* [vol. 1] no. 4 [Fall 1990] pp. 1-3. [prose]

C1139 Full Moon. *Moment,* no. 13 (Fall 1990) p. 5.

C1140 Facing the FCC. *OutWeek,* no. 70 (Oct. 31, 1990) pp. 61-62, 73. [prose]

C1141 A Spiritual War. *Bill of Rights Journal,* vol. 23 (Dec. 1990) pp. 8-9. [prose]

C1142 Velocity of Money. *Holunderground,* vol. 1, no. 1 (1990) p. [2].

1991

C1143 Grandma Earth's Song. *Napalm Health Spa* ([Feb.] 1991) pp. 22-23.

C1144 Hum Bomb. *New Censorship,* vol. 1, no. 11/12 (Feb./March 1991) pp. 16-17.

C1145 Return of Kral Majales. *Boulevard,* vol. 5, no. 3/vol. 6, no. 1 (Spring 1991) p. 96.

C1146 Hum Bom! *English Majors Newsletter,* vol. 9, no. 2 (Spring 1991) pp. 29-30.

C1147 What I'd Like To Do Is. *Border Crossings,* vol. 10, no. 2 (April 1991) pp. 23-24. [prose] [see also D102]

C1148 Return of Kral Majales. *Brooklyn Review,* no. 8 ([April] 1991) p. 10.

C1149 Voznesensky, Andrei; Bouis, Antonina and AG. Angelic Black Holes. *New York Times* (May 12, 1991) pp. A15, A23.

C1150 Hard Labor. *New Observations,* no. 82 (Feb. 15/May 14 [May 14] 1991) p. 16.

C1151 Just Say Yes Calypso. *Nation,* vol. 252, no. 19 (May 20, 1991) p. 652.

C1152 Ferlinghetti, Lawrence and AG. Under the Bodhi Tree. *Bombay Gin,* vol. 2, no. 2 (Summer 1991) p. 19.

C1153 Just Say Yes Calypso. *Pearl,* no. 12 (Summer/Fall 1991) pp. 20-21.

C1154 Visiting the Pythian Oracle in Didyma at the End of the 2nd Millenium. *Howling Mantra,* no. 4 ([Aug.] 1991) p. [46].

C1155 Supplication for the Rebirth of the Vidyadhara Chogyam Trungpa, Rinpoche. *Naropa Institute Summer Writing Program* [issue also called *A Fleshlike Rubbery Semi-Solid Mass*] (July 1991) p. 72.

C1156 [blurb for *Mindfield* by Gregory Corso]. *Vanity Fair,* vol. 54, no. 7 (July 1991) p. 70.

C1157 Hum Bum. *City,* vol. 2, no. 7 (Aug. 1991) pp. 24-25.

Spurious Work: Do Self. *Mesechabe,* no. 9/10 (Winter 1991) p. 21.
Note: This poem has been incorrectly attributed to AG, but AG states that it is not his work.

C1158 [drawing]. *City of Dis,* vol. 1, no. 1 (1991) p. 33.
Note: Reproduction of drawing entitled "The Spirit of American Oil Conservation."

C1159 American Haikus. *Ergo,* vol. 6 (1991) p. 81.
Contents: Standing on the Porch — Mad at Oryoki — Put on My Shirt — A Dandelion Seed — At 4:00 AM the Two Middleaged Men — In the Half-light of Dawn — Caught Shoplifting Ran Out the Department — Tompkins Square — On Hearing the Muezzin Cry Allah Akbar — The Weary Ambassador — Approaching Seoul by Bus — To Be Sucking Your Thumb in Rome — Bearded Robots Drink

C1160 Just Say Yes Calypso [and] Graphic Winces. *Long Shot,* vol. 12 (1991) pp. 5-9.

C1161 Return of Kral Majales. *Lovely Jobly,* vol. 2, no. 1 (1991) p. 16.

1992

C1162 Just Say Yes Calypso. *Napalm Health Spa* ([Jan.] 1992) p. 11.

C1163 American Haikus. *World,* no. 42 (Jan. 1992) pp. 34-35.
Contents: Standing on the Porch — Mad at Oryoki — Put on My Shirt — A Dandelion Seed — At 4:00 AM the Two Middle-aged Men — In the Half-light of Dawn — Caught Shoplifting — Four Skin Heads — At Sunset Apollos's Columns Echo — The Weary Ambassador — Get Used to Your Body — To Be Sucking Your Thumb — Bearded Robots Drink

C1164 Bearded Robots Drink [and] Put on a Tie in My Taxi. *Washington Square News,* vol. 19, no. 82 (Feb. 24, 1992) pp. 1, 5.

C1165 Shambhala Kingdom. *Riverrun* (Spring 1992) p. 6.

C1166 Improvisation in Beijing. *Peckerwood,* no. 1 ([March 23] 1992) pp. 28-30.

C1167 After the Big Parade [and] Just Say Yes Calypso. *City Lights Review,* no. 5 ([April 15] 1992) pp. 119-121.

C1168 Last Night I Went with Bill Burroughs. *Observer Magazine* (April 26, 1992) pp. 26-27, 29-30. [prose] [see also D114]

C1169 I Went to the Movie of Life. *Off the Wall,* vol. 1, no. 3 ([June 6] 1992) p. 12.

C1170 Mind Writing Slogans. *Astarte,* vol. 1, no. 1 (Summer 1992) pp. 69-71.
Note: Numbered 1-46 in 3 sections.

C1171 Hornick, Lita; Orlovsky, Peter and AG. I Am So Happy. *Cover,* vol. 6, no. 5 (Summer 1992) p. 34.

C1172 Last Night I Went with Bill Burroughs. *San Francisco Review of Books,* vol. 17, no. 1 (Summer 1992) p. 32. [prose]

C1173 Remembering Chaim Gross. *Provincetown Arts,* vol. 8 ([July 1] 1992) pp. 121-122. [prose] [see also D116]

C1174 Chaim Gross, 1904-1991. *Proceedings of the American Academy and Institute of Arts and Letters,* second series, no. 42 ([Aug. 1992] 1991) pp. 63-66. [prose]

C1175 Birds Chirping in the Brick Backyard. *Flower Thief,* no. 1 ([Aug. 19] 1992) p. 23.

C1176 Parra, Nicanor. Gallant Conversation. [translated by Mario Trejo; Esteban Moore and AG]. *La Carta de Oliver,* vol. 3, no. 6 (Winter/Spring [Sept.] 1992) p. 21.

C1177 American Sentence. *Man Alive!,* no. 1 (Fall [Sept. 20] 1992) front cover.

C1178 Whitman's Influence. *Sulfur,* no. 31 (Fall 1992) pp. 229-230. [prose]

C1179 Negative Capability: Kerouac's Buddhist Ethic. *Tricycle: The Buddhist Review,* vol. 2, no. 1 (Fall 1992) pp. 8-13. [prose]

C1180 Confession Is Dream for the Soul. *Cover,* vol. 6, no. 7 (Oct. 1992) p. 21.

C1181 [poem with inscription and drawing]. *Culturas,* vol. 16, no. 364 (Oct. 3, 1992) p. 2.
Note: Reproduction of title page of *Collected Poems* inscribed with text of "To Carlos Edmundo de Ory in the Gas Station" and a drawing all in holograph.

C1182 Autumn Leaves. *New York Times* (Nov. 5, 1992) p. A33.

C1183 [response to questionnaire]. *Rumor* (Thanksgiving Special [Nov. 3, 1992]) p. 19.

C1184 Deadline Dragon Comix. *Ruh-Roh!,* no. 1 (Dec. 1992) p. 29.
Note: Reproduction of drawing with comic strip captions.

C1185 Retro Axioms for New White House. *Washington Post* (Dec. 13, 1992) p. F4.

C1186 CIA Dope Calypso. *Portable Lower East Side,* vol. 9, no. 1 [issued also called *Chemical City*] (1992) pp. 12-16.

1993

C1187 Course Description, W337. *Shambhala Sun,* vol. 1, no. 5 (Jan./Feb. 1993) p. 56. [prose]

C1188 Maturity [and] Must Be Diabetes [and] The Moon in the Dewdrop Is the Real Moon. *Shambhala Sun,* vol. 1, no. 5 (Jan./Feb. 1993) p. 57.

C1189 New Democracy Wish List. *New York Newsday* (Jan. 20, 1993) pp. 44, 78.

C1190 New Democracy Wish List. *New York Planet,* vol. 1, no. 6 (Feb. 24, 1993) p. 7.

C1191 Big Eats. *Esquire,* vol. 119, no. 3 (March 1993) p. 190.

C1192 [drawing]. *Wood River Journal* (March 17, 1993) section B, p. 1.
Note: Reproduction of drawing of Buddha and thunderbolt and calligraphy.

C1193 Retro Axioms. *Bombay Gin* ([Spring] 1993) pp. 56-57.

C1194 Fighting Society [and] Poem in the Form of a Snake That Bites Its Tail. *Sulfur,* no. 32 (Spring 1993) pp. 113-127.

C1195 Dream [and] I Visited Vidyadara Chogyam Trungpa in His Big New House He'd Moved [and] Mind Writing Slogans. *Sulfur,* no. 32 (Spring 1993) pp. 113-127. [prose]

C1196 Last Conversation with Carl. *Poetry Project Newsletter,* vol. 149 (April/May 1993) pp. 6-7.

C1197 Images from Mind and Space New York City. *Cover,* vol. 7, no. 4 (May 1993) p. 21.

C1198 Sphincter [and] Spot Anger [and] Visiting Father and Friends [and] New Democracy Wish List. *Gown Literary Supplement,* new series, no. 2 (June 1993) pp. 12-14.

C1199 Meditation Exercise Poem. *Work,* no. [1] (Summer [July] 1993) p. [118].
Note: Anonymous poem assembled by AG from classroom contributors.

C1200 New Years Greeting [and] Christmas Eve Bassett Hospital. *Northern Centinel,* vol. 205, no. 4 (Fall 1993) p. 8.

C1201 Noticing What Is Vivid. *Northern Centinel,* vol. 205, no. 4 (Fall 1993) pp. 8-9. [prose]

C1202 San Jose Area Diary 1954. *San Jose Studies,* vol. 19, no. 3 (Fall 1993) pp. 7-21. [journal entries and drawings]

C1203 Paris Review Soirée. *Trembling Ladder,* no. 1 (Fall 1993) p. 71.

C1204 In Memoriam, Carl Solomon. *PEN American Center Newsletter,* no. 82 (Oct. 1993) p. 8.

C1205 Autumn Leaves. *New Age Journal,* vol. 10, no. 6 (Nov./Dec. 1993) p. 8.

C1206 As I Sit Writing Here. *Süddeutsche Zeitung* (Nov. 5, 1993).

C1207 [drawing]. *Zurnal UP,* no. 3 (ca. Nov. 24, 1993) p. 8.

C1208 Peace in Bosnia-Herzegovina. *Prognosis,* vol. 3, no. 25 (Dec. 10-23, 1993) p. 1B.

C1208X [drawing]. *Technes Grammata* (Dec. 21, 1993)

C1209 CIA Dope Calypso. *Covert Action Quarterly,* no. 47 (Winter 1993/1994) p. 37.

C1210 Elegy for Mama. *New Press,* vol. 10, no. 1 (Winter 1993/1994) pp. 6-7.

C1211 American Sentences [and] In the Benjo. *Big Scream,* no. 32 (1993) pp. 12-13.

C1212 A Definition of the Beat Generation. *Square 1,* no. 3 (1993) pp. 2-3. [prose]

1994

C1213 Elephant in the Meditation Hall. *Shambhala Sun,* vol. 2, no. 3 (Jan. 1994) p. 43.

C1214 [drawing] *Tucson Citizen* (Jan. 18, 1994) Features section.

C1215 [letter] *Daily Camera* (March 1, 1994) p. 1A.

C1216 [response to questionnaire]. *Vanity Fair,* vol. 57, no. 3 (March 1994) p. 186.

C1217 [2 drawings] [and] Four Skinheads. *Broadshirt Poetry Magazine,* no. 1 (Spring 1994) [issue also called "The Beats"].
Note: This magazine is printed on a t-shirt.

C1218 It's True I Got Caught In [and] I Sat at the Foot of a [and] It's 2AM and I Got To [and] Sleepless I Stay up & [and] 4AM [and] I Had My Chance and Lost It. *Michigan Quarterly Review,* vol. 33, no. 2 (Spring 1994) pp. 354-358.

C1219 Salutations to Fernando Pessoa. *Threepenny Review,* vol. 15, no. 1 (Spring 1994) p. 5.

C1220 Peace in Bosnia-Herzegovina. *Nation,* vol. 258, no. 14 (April 11, 1994) p. 498.

C1221 Now and Forever. *Nation,* vol. 258, no. 16 (April 25, 1994) p. 572.

C1222 [7 poems]. *American Poetry Review,* vol. 23, no. 3 (May/June 1994) pp. 3-5.
Contents: Imitation of K.S. — When the Light Appears — Fun House Antique Store — Who Eats Who? — Not Dead Yet — Yiddishe Kopf — A Thief Stole This Poem.

C1223 [4 poems]. *Chaos: The Crestone Literary Review,* vol. 2, no. 2 [issue 4] ([May] 1994) pp. 2-4.
Contents: Images from Mind and Space New York City — Kerouac's Haiku Conception Is: — Autumn Leaves — Christmas Eve Bassett Hospital.

C1224 Busted. *High Times,* no. 225 (May 1994) p. 36.

C1225 Get It? *New York Newsday* (May 18, 1994) p. B5.

C1226 [photograph legend]. *New Censorship,* vol. 5, no. 4 (July 1994) front cover.
Note: Although the legend is written in AG's holograph the photo was not taken by him.

C1227 The Vomit of a Mad Tyger. *Shambhala Sun,* vol. 2, no. 6 (July 1994) pp. 14-23, 54-59. [prose] [see also D137]

C1228 Hermaphrodite Market. *Ma!,* no. 7 [ca. 1994], front cover.

D

Photographs by Allen Ginsberg

D1 *Big Table,* vol. 1, no. 2 (Summer 1959)
Contents:
i: William S. Burroughs, Fall 1953, New York City, looking over books, without legend, p. 35.
ii: William S. Burroughs, Fall 1953, New York City, posing as prize fighter, without legend, p. 36.

D2 Bowles, Paul. *A Hundred Camels in the Courtyard.* San Francisco, CA: City Lights, [Sept. 1] 1962.
Contents:
i: Paul Bowles, July 20, 1961, Tangier, sitting on floor, without legend, back cover.

D3 *City Lights Journal,* no. 1 ([June 1] 1963)
Contents:
i: Peter Orlovsky, 1962, India, standing on Howrah Bridge carrying guitar case, without legend, p. 11.

D4 AG. *Indian Journals.* San Francisco, CA: City Lights Books, [May] 1970.
Contents: [all the following in photo section between pp. 44-45]
i: Oct. 16, 1962, India, under Howrah Bridge, without legend.
ii: Oct. 16, 1962, India, on Howrah Bridge, without legend.
iii: July 1962, Calcutta, India, transvestite singing at Hotel Amjadia corner, without legend.
iv: 1962, Calcutta, India, Baul Saint on street corner, without legend.
v: July 1962, Calcutta, India, rickshaw boys outside Amjadia Hotel, without legend.
vi: 1962, India, Bidi shop proprietor, without legend.
vii: 1962, Calcutta, India, starving beggar with bowl on chest, without legend.
viii: 1962, Calcutta, India, standing and seated beggars with bowl, without legend.
ix: Dec. 1962, Calcutta, India, a woman rolling spices into red paste on the sidewalk, without legend.
x: 1962, Calcutta, India, children and cattle searching in garbage near Chinatown, without legend.
xi: Oct. 1962, India, woman with food sitting under umbrella on ground, without legend.
xii: 1962, Bengal, papier-maché Kali statue, without legend.
Note: [all the following in photo section between pp. 100-101]
xiii: Dec. 1962, Benares, India, beggars along the cobblestone street, without legend.
xiv: Peter Orlovsky, Dec. 1962, Benares, India, lying dressed in pants with book on mattress, without legend.
xv: Dec. 1962, Benares, India, street scene with lame dog, without legend.
xvi: Dec. 1962, Benares, India, street scene from balcony, without legend.

xvii: Dec. 1962, Benares, India, Kali Ma woman crouching in street, without legend.

xviii: Dec. 1962, Benares, India, Kali Ma with arm raised, without legend.

xix: Dec. 1962, Benares, India, Kali Ma with both arms raised, without legend.

xx: Dec. 1962, Benares, India, group of Sadhus, without legend.

xxi: Dec. 1962, Benares, India, group of Sadhus, without legend.

xxii-xxiv: Shambu Bharti Baba, Dec. 1962, Benares, India, in various states of undress, without legend.

Note: [all the following in photo section between pp. 140-141]

xxv: Dec. 1962, Benares, India, street scene of people seated in long line begging, without legend.

xxvi: Dec. 1962, Benares, India, street scene from above, without legend.

xxvii: Dec. 1962, Dasawamedh Ghat, Benares, India, people seated on wide steps, without legend.

xxviii: Dec. 1962, Benares, India, boy squatting with pail, without legend.

xxix: Dec. 1962, Dasawamedh Ghat, Benares, India, beggars & lepers, without legend.

xxx: Dec. 1962, Dasawamedh Ghat, Benares, India, beggar with bowl, without legend.

xxxi: Peter Orlovsky, Christmas 1962, Taj Mahal, India, Peter standing in front of the structure, without legend.

Note: [the following on front cover]

xxxii: Shambu Bharti Baba, Dec. 1962, Benares, India, standing with trident, without legend.

D5　　Charters, Ann (ed.). *Scenes Along the Road.* New York, NY: Portents/Gotham Book Mart, [Sept. 15] 1970.

Contents:

i: Jack Kerouac and Lucien Carr, Summer 1944, Columbia fountain, with legend, p. 13.

ii: Herbert Huncke, Summer 1947, Texas, with straw hat and without shirt, with legend, p. 14.

iii: William S. Burroughs, 1953, New York City, without shirt or glasses, with legend, p. 16.

iv: William S. Burroughs, 1953, New York City, seated at table with typewriter without shirt, with legend, p. 17.

v: William S. Burroughs and Jack Kerouac, 1953, New York City, both seated on sofa with Kerouac slouching, without legend, p. 17.

vi: Jack Kerouac, 1953, New York City, on fire escape, with legend, p. 20.

vii: Neal Cassady, 1956, San Francisco, CA, Cassady with salesman in car lot, with legend, p. 22.

viii: Neal Cassady, driving car with torn ceiling, with legend, p. 26.

ix: Peter Orlovsky, 1956, Berkeley, CA, walking down garden path, without legend, p. 27.

x: 1955, Montgomery St. room with Bach record, with legend, p. 28.

xi: Peter Orlovsky, 1955, Hotel Wentley, San Francisco, profile in chair, with legend, p. 28.

xii: Gary Snyder, 1956, Berkeley, sitting crosslegged cupping tea in hands, without legend, p. 30.

xiii: Gary Snyder, 1956, Berkeley, shaving, with legend, p. 30.

xiv: Gary Snyder, 1956, Berkeley, in garden in robe, with legend, p. 31.

xv: Philip Whalen, Mohammed Hassan and Tom Jackrell, July 1963, Portland, OR, in front of store, without legend, p. 32.

xvi: Peter Orlovsky and Jack Kerouac, 1957, Tangier, Peter standing on Jack's shoulders at beach, without legend, p. 35.

xvii: Jack Kerouac, Peter Orlovsky and William Burroughs, 1957, Tangier, William clothed sleeping on beach, with legend, p. 36.

xviii: Peter Orlovsky and Jack Kerouac, 1957, Tangier, wrestling on beach, without legend, p. 36.

xix: William Burroughs, 1957, Tangier, portrait on beach with casual hat taken by Kerouac, with legend, p. 37.

xx: Gregory Corso and Alan Ansen, 1957, without legend, p. 41.

xxi: Gregory Corso, Athens, sitting in front of temple, without legend, p. 42.

xxii: Orlovsky, Burroughs, AG, Ansen, Bowles, Corso, Sommerville, Tangier, group portrait, with legend, p. 43.
xxiii: Jack Kerouac, 1957, Tangier, with hat in garden taken by Burroughs, with legend, p. 44.

D6 *East Village Other,* vol. 6, no. 44-45 (Dec. 23, 1971)
Contents:
i: Nov. 1971, India, refugees and tents on Jessore Road, without legend, p. 11.
ii: Nov. 1971, India, refugees, tents, cattle and pools of mud on Jessore Road, without legend, p. 11.
iii: Nov. 1971, India, refugee tents and Jessore Road, without legend, p. 12.
iv: Nov. 1971, India, water filled road and cattle cart, without legend, p. 12.
v: Nov. 1971, India, family preparing meal and kneeling, without legend, p. 12.
vi: Nov. 1971, India, family preparing meal and standing, without legend, p. 12.
vii: Nov. 1971, India, crowds of refugees, without legend, p. 13.
viii: Nov. 1971, India, crowds of refugees, without legend, p. 13.
ix: Nov. 1971, India, crowds of refugees, without legend, p. 13.
x: Nov. 1971, India, family seated writing letters, without legend, p. 13.
xi: Nov. 1971, India, tents and families under trees on Jessore Road, without legend, p. 13.

D7 Charters, Ann. *Kerouac: A Biography.* San Francisco, CA: Straight Arrow Books, [March 1] 1973.
Contents:
i: Lucien Carr and William Burroughs, 1944, New York City, outdoors on Morningside Heights, without legend, p. 64A.
ii: William Burroughs and Jack Kerouac, 1945, New York City, playing a scene from Dashiell Hammett, without legend, p. 64C.
iii: Peter Orlovsky, 1955, Yosemite, CA, without shirt overlooking the valley, without legend, p. 64K.
iv: Natalie Jackson and Neal Cassady, 1956, San Francisco, standing in parking lot, without legend, p. 64O.

D8a AG. *Visions of the Great Rememberer.* Amherst, MA: Mulch Press, [July] 1974.
Contents:
i: Jack Kerouac, Fall 1953, New York City, Jack looking out over books on East 7th St., without legend, p. ix.
ii: Ginsberg, Tangier?, self-portrait without shirt, without legend, p. 46.
iii: Neal Cassady, 1955-56, with can of beer and the top of Natalie Jackson's head, without legend, p. 54.
D8b [2nd edition contains a different set of photos]
i: Jack Kerouac, New York City, Jack looking out over books on East 7th St., without legend, p. ix.
ii: Ginsberg, self-portrait with double image, without legend, p. 46.
iii: Ginsberg, 1947, close-up self-portrait without glasses on board ship in undershirt, without legend, p. 52.
iv: Ginsberg, 1947, close-up self-portrait with glasses, without legend, p. 52A.
v: Neal Cassady, 1955-56, with can of beer and the top of Natalie Jackson's head, without legend, p. 54.

D9 *Unspeakable Visions of the Individual* [issue also called *The Beat Book*] vol. 4 (1974)
Contents:
i: Anne Murphy and Neal Cassady, 1963, Bolinas, CA, Murphy standing, Neal seated in chair reading, without legend, p. 87.

D10   AG. *Journals: Early Fifties Early Sixties.* New York, NY: Grove Press, [Sept. 7] 1977.
Contents:
i: Jan. 1, 1954, Mérida, Mexico, cathedral and plaza, without legend, p. 30.
ii: Jan. 1, 1954, Chicén Itzá, Mexico, view of skull design on wall, without legend, p. 32.
iii: Jan. 1, 1954, Chicén Itzá, Mexico, view of the great pyramid, without legend, p. 32.
iv: Jan. 1, 1954, Chicén Itzá, Mexico, view of temple doorway, without legend, p. 32.
v: Jan. 1954, Mexico, train stopped along tracks with many people waiting, without legend, p. 36.
vi: Jan. 1954, Valladolid, Mexico, candlelight procession, without legend, p. 36.
vii: Jan. 12, 1954, Uxmal, Mexico, view of great pyramid in the distance, without legend, p. 39.
viii: Jan. 1954, Palenque, Mexico, view of the ancient city in the jungle, without legend, p. 43.
ix: March 1954, Finca Tacalapan, Mexico, a thatch-roof shelter in the forest, without legend, p. 45.
x: Peter Orlovsky, Gregory Corso and William Burroughs, July 1961, Tangier, standing for photo in front of covered door, without legend, p. 213.
xi: Peter Orlovsky, Jan. 27, 1962, Mombasa, standing in front of the Hydro Hotel, without legend, p. 299.

D11   *Unspeakable Visions of the Individual* [issue called *The Beat Journey*]   vol. 8 (1978)
Contents:
i: William Burroughs and Alene Lee, Winter 1953, New York City, looking into each other's eyes on the fire escape with laundry in background, without legend, p. 172.

D12   McNally, Dennis. *Desolate Angel: Jack Kerouac, the Beat Generation and America.* New York, NY: McGraw Hill, [Aug. 1] 1979.
Contents: [photo section between pp. 146-147]
i: Hal Chase and Jack Kerouac, 1945, Morningside Heights, NY, Chase with scarf, Kerouac with derby hat in a discussion, without legend.
ii: Hal Chase, John Kingsland and Jack Kerouac, 1945, Morningside Heights, NY, all standing in sun with topcoats, no hats, without legend.
iii: Lucien Carr, ca. 1950, seat in chair with mustache and disheveled hair, without legend.
iv: Neal Cassady and Natalie Jackson, 1956, San Francisco, Natalie lighting cigarette with Model T car in background, without legend.
v: Jack Kerouac, 1957, Tangiers, portrait on beach with disheveled hair, no shirt, without legend.
vi: Peter Orlovsky, Jack Kerouac, Gregory Corso and William Burroughs, 1957, Tangiers, on beach Corso and Burroughs laying on sand, Orlovsky squinting, Burroughs with head down, without legend.
[photo section between pp. 306-307]
vii: Al Sublette, 1954, San Francisco, sitting on floor in front of phonograph, without legend.

D13   *Esquire,* vol. 92, no. 4 (Oct. 1979)
Contents:
i: 1964, Millbrook, NY, view of Kesey's bus 'Further' parked on a tree lined street with a dark car facing it hood to hood, without legend, p. 46.
ii: Neal Cassady and Natalie Jackson [incorrectly identified as Carolyn Cassady], 1956, San Francisco, CA, Neal looking serious and Jackson laughing while looking at Cassady, in front of Model T, without legend, p. 50.
iii: Timothy Leary and Neal Cassady, 1964, Millbrook, NY, both on Kesey's bus laughing, without legend, p. 53.
iv: Neal Cassady, ca. 1964, driving while wearing headphones, dark glasses and a Captain America style striped shirt, without legend, p. 54.

D14   *After Dark*, vol. 12, no. 10 (Feb. 1980)
Contents:
i: Neal Cassady and Natalie Jackson [incorrectly identified here as Carolyn Cassady], 1956, San Francisco, CA, both standing in parking lot looking off to the right, p. 54.

D15   *Unspeakable Visions of the Individual* [issue called *Beat Angels*] vol. 12 ([Nov. 1981] 1982)
Contents:
i: Jack Kerouac and Hal Chase, 1945-46?, Morningside Heights, New York, both sitting on park bench and staring upwards, without legend [incorrectly attributed to John Kingsland], p. 66.
ii: Jack Kerouac, 1953, Sheepshead Bay, NY, Jack at dock looking into sunlight, without legend [incorrectly placed at Coney Island and incorrectly attributed to John Kingsland], p. 67.
iii: Neal Cassady, ca. 1963, Bolinas, CA, Neal in white t-shirt sitting in driver's seat of car with cigarette in mouth and staring into back seat, without legend, p. 90.

D16   Bockris, Victor. *With William Burroughs; a Report from the Bunker*. New York, NY: Seaver Books, 1981.
Contents:
i: William Burroughs, 1957, Tangier, close-up of Burroughs with dress hat and jacket in the garden of the Villa Mouneria, without legend, p. 23.

D17   Kyger, Joanne. *Japan and Indian Journals 1960-1964*. Bolinas, CA: Tombouctou Books, 1981.
Contents:
i: Gary Snyder and Joanne Kyger, June 1963, on train in Japan, coming home from the Japan Sea both looking out of the train car window, without legend, p. 137.

D18   *Radio Times* (Feb. 23, 1983)
Contents:
i: William Burroughs and Jack Kerouac, 1953, New York City, fighting with a knife, without legend, p. 47.

D19   Snyder, Gary. *Passage through India*. San Francisco, CA: Grey Fox Press, 1983.
Contents:
i: Joanne Kyger and Gary Snyder, India, sitting on wall in front of Himalayas, without legend, on front cover.

D20   *Friction*, no. 5/6 (Winter [Jan.] 1984) [issue called *Obscure Genius*]
Contents:
i: Group photo of Clausen, Antler, Cope, Ruggia and others, 1983, New York, NY, AG's kitchen, without legend, front cover.
Note: issued in an edition of 50 signed and numbered copies, and 350 unsigned and unnumbered copies.

D21   Clark, Tom. *Jack Kerouac*. San Francisco, CA: Harcourt Brace Jovanovich, [May 31] 1984.
Contents:
i: Jack Kerouac, Aug. 12, 1944, New York City, Kerouac posing fully erect staring into camera in front of Columbia fountain, without legend, p. 66.

D22   *Shig's Review*, no. 15 (Nov. 1984)
Contents:
i: Mark Green, Oct. 20, 1984, Cafe Trieste, San Francisco, CA, with holograph legend, p. 6.

D23   [exhibition flyer]   *Allen Ginsberg: Memory Gardens: Jan. 4—26, 1985.*   New York, NY: Holly Solomon Gallery [Dec. 20, 1984].   Single sheet, 12.7 x 17.8 cm.
Contents:
i: William Burroughs, 1953, New York City, looking over books, with holograph legend.
[photo published earlier with variation of this legend]
Note: Published Dec. 20, 1984 in an impression of 4,000 copies.

D24   *Vanity Fair,* vol. 48, no. 1 (Jan. 1985)
Contents:
i: Jack Kerouac, 1964, New York, NY, Jack high on last visit to AG's apartment, with hat on and hand to head, without legend, p. 58.
ii: Neal Cassady, 1955, San Francisco, CA, Neal in used car lot in North Beach, with partial legend, p. 58.
iii: William S. Burroughs, 1953, New York, NY, Burroughs laying on floor reading book entitled "Winds", without legend, p. 59.
iv: William S. Burroughs, 1953, New York, NY, Burroughs on roof of Allen's apartment, shading eyes from the sun, without legend, p. 63.
v: Group photo of Burroughs, AG, Ansen, Corso, Bowles in garden at Tangier, 1961, with partial holograph legend, p. 63.
vi: AG and Peter Orlovsky, 1956, San Francisco, CA, without shirts seated on chairs in kitchen, with partial holograph legend, p. 63.
vii: 1955, 1010 Montgomery Street apartment with Bach record, with holograph legend, p. 64.
viii: Peter Orlovsky, Jack Kerouac, Gregory Corso and William S. Burroughs, 1957, Tangier beach scene with Corso and Burroughs laying on beach, with holograph legend, p. 64.

D25   AG.   *Collected Poems.*   New York, NY: Harper and Row,   [Dec. 31] 1984.
Contents:
i: William S. Burroughs, 1953, New York, NY, Burroughs posing as a prize fighter, with legend, p. 757.
[photo published earlier without legend]
ii: Jack Kerouac, 1953, New York, NY, Kerouac on Avenue A in profile looking to the right, with legend, p. 759.
iii: Herbert Huncke, 1983, New York, NY, portrait, without legend, p. 760.

D26   *Washington Post* (Jan. 8, 1985)
Contents:
i: Neal Cassady and Natalie Jackson, 1955, San Francisco, CA, standing under theater marquee, without legend, p. C7.

D27   [series of 12 postcards]   Fotofolio, New York, NY, [Feb.] 1985.   10.8 x 15.3 cm.
Contents:
i: Group photo of Orlovsky, Burroughs, AG, Ansen, Corso, Bowles, and Sommerville, 1961, Tangier, in garden, with holograph legend.
[photo published earlier with variation of this legend]
ii: Neal Cassady, 1955, San Francisco, CA, looking at cars, with holograph legend.
[photo published earlier with variation of this legend]
iii: AG and Peter Orlovsky, 1956, San Francisco, CA, sitting in kitchen without shirts, with holograph legend.
[photo published earlier with variation of this legend]
iv: William S. Burroughs, 1961, Tangier, Burroughs portrait in his garden with hat, with holograph legend.
[photo published earlier with variation of this legend]
v: AG, 1953, New York, NY, on roof of apartment with St. Brigid's church steeples, with holograph legend.
vi: Gary Snyder, 1965, Glacier Peak, Snyder sitting beside lake, with holograph legend.

vii: Jack Kerouac, 1953, New York, NY, fire escape portrait, with holograph legend.
      [photo published earlier with variation of this legend]
viii: Robert Creeley, July 1984, Boulder, CO, Creeley at table with dish in foreground,
      with holograph legend.
ix: Paul Bowles, 1961, Tangier, sitting on floor with dish and spoon, with holograph
     legend.
     [photo published earlier with variation of this legend]
x: Peter Orlovsky, Jack Kerouac, Gregory Corso and William Burroughs, March-April
    1957, Tangier, on beach, with holograph legend.
    [photo published earlier with variation of this legend]
xi: Jack Kerouac, 1957, Tangier, portrait on beach, with holograph legend.
     [photo published earlier with variation of this legend]
xii: AG and Gregory Corso, 1961, Tangier, nude in shower, with holograph legend.
      [photo published earlier with variation of this legend]

D28 [exhibition catalog] *New Acquisitions: Photographs/Prints: Feb. 1-May 17, 1985.*
New York, NY: New York Public Library, Feb. 1, 1985. 23.0 x 89.6 cm. sheet, folds 6
times to 23.0 x 12.8 cm.
Contents:
i: Robert Frank, March 7, 1984, New York, NY, portrait in the Kiev restaurant, with
    holograph legend.

D29 *Washington International Arts Letter,* vol. 24, no. 3 (March 1985)
Contents:
i: Ira Lowe, p. 1.

D30 *Daily News Magazine* (May 19, 1985)
Contents:
i: William Burroughs, 1953, sitting at kitchen table in underwear with toaster plugged in,
    scratching head, without legend, p. 8.

D31 *Shig's Review,* no. 16 [ca. Summer 1985]
Contents:
i-vi: photographs of AG's cabin in the Sierra Nevadas, Bed Rock Mortar, with holograph
       legends.

D32 *Third Rail,* no. 7 ([Aug. 28] 1985/86)
Contents:
i: Judith Malina, Julian Beck, and Hanon, Oct. 1984, New York City, Beck in hospital
    bed with tray of liquids in front, with legend, p. 34.

D33 *Vajradhatu Sun,* vol. 7, no. 1 (Oct.-Nov. 1985)
Contents:
i: Nicanor Parra, Fall 1984, New York City, riding on the subway, without legend, p.
    13.
ii: Robert Frank, Fall 1984, New York City, portrait in Kiev restaurant, with legend, p.
     13.
     [photo published earlier with variation of this legend]
iii: March 1985, New York City, skyline of the city from David Rome's office, with
      legend, p. 13.
iv: Robert Duncan, Oct. 12, 1984, San Francisco, CA, sitting in his home with glasses in
     hand, with legend, p. 13.
v: Anne Waldman and William Burroughs, July 1984, Boulder, CO, snuggling in corner
    of restaurant booth, with legend, p. 13.
vi: Philip Whalen, March 1984, New York City, in bathrobe reading in AG's apartment,
     with legend, p. 13.

D34   Burroughs, William S. *Queer.* New York, NY: Viking, [Nov. 18] 1985.
Contents:
   i: William S. Burroughs, 1953, New York, NY, Burroughs sitting on sofa in AG's apartment with shadows across his face, staring directly at the camera, with holograph legend, p. [2].

D35   *Aperture,* no. 101 (Winter 1985)
Contents:
   i: Jack Kerouac, Fall 1953, New York City, on fire escape, with holograph legend, p. 8.
      [photo published earlier with variation of this legend]
   ii: Neal Cassady and Natalie Jackson, 1955, San Francisco, CA, in front of theater marquee, with holograph legend, p. 9.
      [photo published earlier with variation of this legend]
   iii: Robert Frank, March 7, 1984, New York City, portrait in Kiev restaurant, with holograph legend, p. 10.
      [photo published earlier with variation of this legend]
   iv: Richard Avedon, Sept. 1984, New York City, posing beside camera on tripod, with holograph legend, p. 11.
   v: Julius Orlovsky, Labor Day 1984, Barnet, VT, posing in woods, with holograph legend, p. 12.
   vi: Group photo of Corso, Bowles, Sommerville, Burroughs, Portman, 1961, Tangier, Bowles and Burroughs with cameras, Sommerville and Portman kneeling, with holograph legend, p. 13.
      [photo published earlier with variation of this legend]
   vii: Francesco Clemente and Nachiappan, his Indian printer, Oct. 1984, New York City, Clemente posing with hands on head in the Kiev restaurant, with holograph legend, p. 15.

D36   Frank, Robert. *New York to Nova Scotia.* Boston, MA: Little, Brown and Co., [Feb. 14] 1986.
Contents:
   i: AG and Robert Frank, 1984, New York City, Frank taking AG's photo for *Collected Poems* [photo taken by Peter Orlovsky] with holograph legend by AG, p. 75.

D37   *Fag Rag,* no. 42/43 (ca. April 1986)
Contents:
   i: Herbert Huncke, early 1984, New York, NY, at AG's kitchen table, with holograph legend, front cover.

D38   *Esquire,* vol. 105, no. 6 (June 1986)
Contents:
   i: Willem de Kooning, New York, sitting in wooden chair, hands on arm rests, without legend, p. 260.
   ii: William Burroughs, sitting at desk with papers and fingers to head, without legend, p. 260.
   iii: Julian Beck, 1984, New York City, laying in hospital bed, tape on arms, without legend, p. 261.

D39   Morgan, Bill & Rosenthal, Bob (eds.). *Best Minds.* New York, NY: Lospecchio Press, [June 3] 1986. [ltd. ed. of 26 copies only, photo does not appear in other editions]
Contents:
   i: Allen Ginsberg, 1985, self-portrait, with holograph legend

D40   Ansen, Alan. *William Burroughs: An Essay.* Sudbury, MA: Water Row Press, [Aug.] 1986.
Contents:
   i: William S. Burroughs and Alan Ansen, 1957, Tangier, re-enactment of the hanging scene, without legend, p. [ii].

D41 *Vogue,* vol. 176, no. 9 [issue 3254] (Sept. 1986)
Contents:
i: Gary Snyder, 1985, China, standing beside stone horses at the Ming Tombs, without legend, p. 476.
ii: Francine du Plessix Gray, 1985, China, in Hangzhou Gardens, without legend, p. 476.

D42 AG. *Howl [Facsimile Edition]* New York, NY: Harper & Row, [Nov.] 1986.
Contents:
i: 1955, San Francisco, CA, 1010 Montgomery Street room with Bach record, with legend, p. x.
[photo published earlier with variation of this legend]
ii: 1955, San Francisco, CA, 1010 Montgomery Street room with LaVigne's picture of Orlovsky, with legend, p. x.
iii: Carl Solomon, 1953, New York, NY, seated on bed smoking cigarette, with legend, p. 110.
iv: Carl Solomon, 1983, City Island, New York, NY, in boat making fist, with legend, p. 110.
v: Herbert E. Huncke, Fall 1953, New York, NY, sitting with elbow resting on sink in hotel room, with legend, p. 133.
vi: Peter Du Peru, 1955, San Francisco, CA, crossing street with long coat, with legend, p. 135.
vii: Donlin, Cassady, Orlovsky, LaVigne, Ferlinghetti, 1955, San Francisco, CA, standing in front of City Lights, LaVigne with foot up on bookrack, with legend, p. 148.

D43 *Miami Herald* (Feb. 1, 1987)
Contents:
i: William S. Burroughs, sitting at a table wearing a headset, without legend (in) Buschsbaum, Herbert. The Beat Family Album Comes To Life.

D44 *Cover,* vol. 1, no. 3 (March 1987)
Contents:
i: Robert Creeley, July 1984, Boulder, CO, sitting at table with dish, with holograph legend, p. 35.
[photo published earlier with variation of this legend]

D45 [flyer] *Poems, Plays, Stories.* Brooklyn, NY: Brooklyn College, ca. April 27, 1987. Single sheet, 40.6 x 21.6 cm.
Contents:
i: Brooklyn Bridge, New York, NY, close-up of walkway and pier with 3 pedestrians at right.

D46 [exhibition catalog] *A Tribute to John Cage.* Cincinnati, OH: Carl Solway Gallery, May 7, 1987.
Contents:
i: Aug. 18, 1984, New York, NY, view from AG's kitchen window, with holograph legend, p. 24a.
ii: Dec. 20, 1985, New York, NY, view from AG's kitchen window, with holograph legend, p. 24b.
iii: April 26, 1986, New York, NY, view from AG's kitchen window, with holograph legend, p. 24c.
iv: Nov. 26, 1986, New York, NY, view from AG's kitchen window, with holograph legend, p. 24d.

D47   [postcard] *Allen Ginsberg & Robert Frank.* Tokyo, Japan: Galerie Watari, May 20, 1987. Single sheet, 15.0 x 10.5 cm.
Contents:
  i: AG and Robert Frank, Jan. 1984, New York City, [photo taken by Peter Orlovsky] with holograph legend by AG.
      [photo published earlier with variation of this legend]

D48   [exhibition catalog] *Allen Ginsberg & Robert Frank.* Tokyo, Japan: Galerie Watari, May 20, 1987.
Contents:
  i: AG & Robert Frank, Jan. 1984, New York, NY. [photo taken by Peter Orlovsky], with holograph legend by AG, front cover.
      [identical to photo with holograph published on postcard for this exhibition]
  ii: AG, Sept. 24, 1985, New York, NY, self-portrait in mirror of sushi bar bathroom, with holograph legend, p. 1.
  iii: William S. Burroughs, Fall 1953, New York, NY, Burroughs looking out over books, variation of photo published earlier, this one more out-of-focus, with holograph legend, p. 1.
  iv: AG, Oct. 10, 1947, New York harbor, AG on board ship smoking cigarette in undershirt, [photo not taken by AG] with holograph legend by AG, p. 2.
  v: AG, Feb. 1962, Kauseni, India, AG with mountains in the background [photo not taken by AG] with holograph legend by AG, p. 2.
  vi: AG, Nov. 18, 1985, Moscow, USSR, self-portrait with pajamas in oval bathroom mirror, with extreme close-up at left, with holograph legend, p. 2.
  vii: AG, March 24, 1972, Ayer's Rock, Australia, self-portrait at arm's length, without glasses, with holograph legend, p. 3.
  viii: Group photo, Orlovsky, Burroughs, AG, Ansen, Corso, Bowles, Sommerville, 1961, Tangier, [photo not taken by AG] with holograph legend by AG, p. 3.
      [photo published earlier with variation of this legend]
  ix: AG & R.F., Aug. 1986, Boulder, CO, self-portrait, nude in bathroom mirror, with holograph legend, p. 3.
  x: AG, Aug. 1, 1985, Boulder, CO, self-portrait, nude with socket below bathroom mirror, with holograph legend, p. 4.
  xi: John Giorno, James Grauerholz, William S. Burroughs, March 26, 1985, New York, NY, stage-lit black backdrop, with holograph legend, p. 5.
  xii: Aug. 18, 1984, New York, NY, view from AG's kitchen window with tacked up curtain, with holograph legend, p. 6.
      [photo published earlier with variation of this legend]
  xiii: Robert Frank, June 1984, New Smyrna Beach, FL, leaning on back bumper of his car, with holograph legend, p. 6.
  xiv: Group photo of Garrick Beck, Issha, Malina, Karlbach, Sept. 19, 1985, New Jersey, Living Theater friends leaving the cemetery after Julian Beck's funeral, with holograph legend, p. 6.
  xv: Neal Cassady and Natalie Jackson, 1955, San Francisco, CA, under theatre marquee, with holograph legend, back cover.
      [photo published earlier with variation of this legend]

D49   *Asahi Kamera*, no. 699 (June 1, 1987)
Contents:
  i: AG nude in lotus position, in bathroom mirror, without legend, p. 80.
  ii: Pablo and Robert Frank, Oct. 1984, with holograph legend, p. 81.

D50   Clemente, Francesco. *India.* Pasadena, CA: Twelvetrees Press, [Sept.-Oct.] 1987.
Contents:
  i: Francesco Clemente and Julius Orlovsky, Fall 1984, with holograph legend, p. 12.
  Note: Book was published in 1987 according to the publisher, not 1985 as stated in the copyright notice.

D51 *Whole Earth Review,* no. 56 (Fall [Sept. 1] 1987)
Contents:
   i: AG, Nov. 18, 1985, Moscow, USSR, self-portrait with pajamas in bathroom mirror, with holograph legend, p. 20.
   ii: Gregory Corso, March 17, 1986, Lowell, MA, visiting Kerouac's Grotto below crucifix, with holograph legend, p. 22.
   iii: Aug. 18, 1984, New York, NY, view from AG's kitchen window, with holograph legend, p. 24.
   [photo published earlier with variation of this legend]

D52 *Camera Austria,* no. 24 ([ca. Oct.] 1987)
Contents:
   i: Jack Kerouac, 1953, Sheepshead Bay, New York, Kerouac squinting into sunlight, with holograph legend, p. 28.
   [photo published earlier with variation of this legend]
   ii: William Burroughs, 1953, New York City, sitting at kitchen table with toaster in underwear, with holograph legend, p. 29.
   [photo published earlier with variation of this legend]
   iii: Gregory Corso, 1957, Paris, France, standing in an attic room with cape and stick, with holograph legend, p. 30.
   iv: William Burroughs, 1974, New York City, Burroughs sitting cross-legged in coat and tie with cigarette in hand, with holograph legend, p. 31.
   v: Eugene and Connie Brooks, Aug. 1984, Plainview, New York, sitting at restaurant table, with holograph legend, p. 32.
   vi: Julian Beck, May 1984, New York City, Beck in hospital bed with tape and nose tube, with holograph legend, p. 33.
   [photo published earlier with variation of this legend]
   vii: Lou Reed, Sept. 14, 1984, New York City, seated backstage of Public Theater, with holograph legend, p. 33.
   viii: Harry Smith, Jan. 1985, New York City, pouring milk, with holograph legend, p. 34.
   ix: Jack Micheline, Jan. 1985, San Francisco, CA, writing in book at cafe table with cigarette in mouth, with holograph legend, p. 35.
   x: Kathy Acker, Feb. 14, 1985, Detroit, MI, sitting backstage of the Detroit Institute of the Arts, with holograph legend, p. 36.
   [all legends translated into German on p. 37]

D53 [exhibition poster] *Allen Ginsberg; Fotografier 1947-87.* Aarhus, Denmark: Aarhus Kunstmuseum, 1987. Single sheet, 62.0 x 45.0 cm.
Contents:
   i: Lou Reed, Sept. 14, 1984, New York, NY, Reed in the makeup room, with holograph legend.
   [photo published earlier with variation of this legend]

D54 AG. *Fotografier 1947-87.* Århus, Denmark: KLIM, [Nov. 23] 1987.
Contents:
   i: AG and Gregory Corso, 1961, Tangier, portrait of both as Siamese twins, [photo taken by Peter Orlovsky] with holograph legend by AG, front cover.
   ii: AG, Oct. 20, 1947, New York Harbor, on board ship with cigarette, [photo taken by Peter Orlovsky] with holograph legend by AG, p. 35.
   [photo published earlier with variation of this legend]
   iii: William Burroughs, Fall 1953, New York City, typing at AG's kitchen table, with scotch tape in foreground, with holograph legend, p. 36.
   iv: William Burroughs, Fall 1953, New York City, looking over books, with holograph legend, p. 37.
   [photo published earlier with variation of this legend]
   v: Jack Kerouac, Fall 1953, New York City, on fire escape, with holograph legend, p. 38.
   [photo published earlier with variation of this legend]

vi: William Burroughs, Fall 1953, New York City, standing beside sphinx at Metropolitan Museum of Art, with holograph legend, p. 39.

vii: AG, Dec. 1953, Jacksonville, FL, standing on wet street in front of hotel awning, with holograph legend, p. 40.

viii: Neal Cassady and Natalie Jackson, 1955, standing under theater marquee, with holograph legend, p. 41.

[photo published earlier with variation of this legend]

ix: Peter Orlovsky, 1955, San Francisco, CA, standing on hill beside car at Hodges Street, with holograph legend, p. 42.

x: Neal Cassady, 1956, San Francisco, CA, standing beside car, eyes downcast, with holograph legend, p. 43.

Note: also published by Image of Aarhus as a postcard.

xi: Gregory Corso, 1957, Paris, France, standing in attic with cape and stick, with holograph legend, p. 44.

[photo published earlier with variation of this legend]

xii: Gregory Corso, 1957, Paris, France, looking out skylight of attic room, with holograph legend, p. 45.

xiii: William Burroughs and Alan Ansen, 1961, Tangier, re-enacting the hanging scene, with holograph legend, p. 46.

[photo published earlier without legend]

xiv: AG and Gregory Corso, Summer 1961, both nude in shower [photo taken by Peter Orlovsky] with holograph legend by AG, p. 47.

[photo published earlier without legend]

Note: also published by Image of Aarhus as a postcard.

xv: Group photo of Orlovsky, Burroughs, AG, Ansen, Corso, Sommerville with Bowles seated on ground, 1961, Tangier, in Burroughs' garden, with holograph legend, p. 48.

[photo published earlier with variation of this legend]

xvi: Paul Bowles, 1961, Tangier, seated on floor with spoon and teapots, with holograph legend, p. 49.

[photo published earlier with variation of this legend]

xvii: AG, 1963, Benares, India, feeding the monkey on the balcony, [photo taken by Peter Orlovsky] with holograph legend by AG, p. 50.

xviii: Gary Snyder, Peter Orlovsky and AG, 1962, India, all three with blankets, sitting on wall with mountains in the background, [photo taken by Joanne Kyger] with holograph legend by AG, p. 51.

xix: Timothy Leary and Neal Cassady, 1964, Millbrook, NY, Leary leaning back and Neal laughing, with holograph legend, p. 52.

[photo published earlier with variation of this legend]

xx: AG and Gary Snyder, Summer 1965, Glacier Peak Wilderness, Allen with hand on Snyder's head, [photo not taken by AG] with holograph legend by AG, p. 53.

xxi: Robert Frank, March 1984, New York City, Frank with camera and light focusing on AG, with holograph legend, p. 54.

xxii: AG and Robert Frank, Jan. 1984, New York City, [photo taken by Peter Orlovsky in Frank's studio] with holograph legend by AG, p. 55.

[photo published earlier with variation of this legend]

xxiii: Philip Whalen, March 1984, New York City, Whalen in bathrobe reading book in AG's apartment, with holograph legend, p. 56.

[photo published earlier with variation of this legend]

xxiv: Robert Creeley, July 1984, Boulder, CO, Creeley sitting at dining table with dish, with holograph legend, p. 57.

[photo published earlier with variation of this legend]

xxv: Aug. 18, 1984, New York City, view from AG's kitchen window, focusing on the raindrops on the clothesline, with holograph legend, p. 58.

xxvi: Simon Pettet and Rosebud Felieu wedding party, Aug. 1984, New York City, in courthouse waiting room, with holograph legend, p. 59.

xxvii: Richard Avedon, Sept. 1984, New York City, Avedon standing beside his camera and tripod, with holograph legend, p. 60.

[photo published earlier with variation of this legend]

xxviii: Lou Reed, Sept. 1984, New York City, Reed sitting in the dressing room of the Public Theater, with holograph legend, p. 61.
[photo published earlier with same legend on poster for the exhibition]
xxix: Judith Malina, Julian Beck, and Hanon, Oct. 1984, New York City, Beck in hospital bed with jars on counter, with holograph legend, p. 62.
[photo published earlier with variation of this legend]
xxx: Francesco Clemente and Nachiappan, Oct. 1984, New York City, Clemente posing with hands on head in Kiev restaurant, with holograph legend, p. 63.
[photo published earlier with variation of this legend]
xxxi: Group photo of Neeli Cherkovski and boyfriend, Gregory Corso, Nile Corso, Kaye McDonough, March 17, 1985, San Francisco, CA, street scene with outdoor painter, with holograph legend, p. 64.
xxxii: AG, March 22, 1985, New York City, nude portrait reclining on bed [photo not taken by AG] with holograph legend by AG, p. 65.
xxxiii: AG, Aug. 1, 1985, Boulder, CO, nude self-portrait in bathroom mirror with socket below mirror, with holograph legend, p. 66.
[photo published earlier with variation of this legend]
xxxiv: William Burroughs, March 26, 1985, New York City, in Bunker in front of black background with stun gun, with holograph legend, p. 67.
xxxv: Amiri Baraka, Aug. 5, 1985, Boulder, CO, portrait outdoors at picnic, with holograph legend, p. 68.
xxxvi: AG, Aug. 1, 1985, Boulder, CO, nude self-portrait sitting on bathroom counter in lotus position with camera, with holograph legend, p. 69.
xxxvii: Anne Waldman, Aug. 15, 1985, Boulder, CO, in robe at table with books, cup, salt and peppers, etc., with holograph legend, p. 70.
xxxviii: Group photo at Julian Beck's funeral, Aug. 19, 1985, New Jersey, Garrick Beck putting shovel of dirt on grave, with holograph legend, p. 71.
xxxix: Sept. 29, 1985, New York City, view of Mary Help of Christians Church through window of AG's apartment, with holograph legend, p. 72.
xl: Group photo of Julian Beck's funeral, Sept. 19, 1985, Malina distraught being led from the gravesite, with holograph legend, p. 73.
[photo published earlier with variation of this legend]
xli: AG, Nov. 18, 1985, Vilnius, Lithuania, self-portrait in pajamas in hotel bathroom oval mirror, with extreme close-up at left, with holograph legend, p. 74.
[photo published earlier with variation of this legend]
xlii: AG, Sept. 24, 1985, New York City, self-portrait in bathroom mirror of sushi bar, with holograph legend, p. 75.
[photo published earlier with variation of this legend]
xliii: Group photo, 1985, Minsk, USSR, tour guide for the Museum of the Great Patriotic War, with holograph legend, p. 76.
xliv: Louis Auchincloss, Nov. 30, 1985, Leningrad, USSR, standing behind Dostoyevski's desk, with holograph legend, p. 77.
xlv: Group photo of Ilga Koutick and friends, Dec. 16, 1985, Moscow, USSR, seated around table, with holograph legend, p. 78.
xlvi: Street scene, Jan. 29, 1986, Nicaragua, unloading sides of beef from truck, with holograph legend, p. 79.
xlvii: Aunt Clara Lehman and Morris Jacobs, Jan. 26, 1987, West Orange, NJ, in retirement home, with holograph legend, p. 80.
xlviii: AG and R.F., Aug. 1986, Boulder, CO, nude portraits in mirror of bathroom, with holograph legend, p. 81.
[photo published earlier with variation of this legend]

D55 *Shiny,* no. 3 ([Dec.] 1987)
Contents:
i: Cityscape, March 27, 1985, New York City, view from David Rome's office, with holograph legend, p. 20.
ii: Peter Orlovsky, 1955, Yosemite, CA, bare-chested standing on Half-Dome, with holograph legend, p. 21.
[photo published earlier without legend]

iii: John Wieners, Oct. 3, 1985, New York City, portrait in Christine's restaurant, with holograph legend, p. 22.
iv: Nov. 12, 1984, Yangtze River, China, view of locks from boat deck, with holograph legend, p. 23.
v: Mary de Rachewiltz and Olga Rudge, June 20, 1985, Orono, ME, posing on pavement, with holograph legend, p. 24.
vi: Jack Shuai, Dec. 24, 1987, Kunming, China, portrait sitting outdoors, with holograph legend, p. 25.
vii: Tommy and Bruce Parker, 1953, New York City, Helen Parker's young sons, with holograph legend, p. 26.
viii: Kiki and William Burroughs, 1953, Tangier, sitting at outdoor cafe [photo not taken by AG] but with holograph legend by AG, p. 27.

D56   [publisher's catalog] *Twin Palms/Twelvetrees: 1987—1988.* Altadena, CA: Twin Palms Publishers, ca. 1987.
Contents:
i: Jack Kerouac, 1964, New York City, last visit to AG's apartment, with mouth closed, with holograph legend, p. 14.

D57   *Open Magazine* ([ca. Feb. 3] 1988)
Contents:
i: Kate, Peter and Marie Orlovsky, ca. 1960, happy around the kitchen table, with holograph legend, p. 44-45.

D58   [flyer] *Living Poetry: Spring 1988 Readings.* Brooklyn, NY: Brooklyn College, The Humanities Institute, ca. Feb. 17, 1988. Single sheet, 27.9 x 21.6 cm.
Contents:
i: Group photo, Antler, Clausen, Jackson, Zivancevic, Cope, Ruggia, Kraut, Rosenthal, and others, Spring 1983, in AG's kitchen with children, with holograph legend.

D59   *Downtown,* no. 96 (May 11, 1988)
Contents:
i: Julian Beck, May 1984, New York City, in hospital bed with bandages and nose tube, with holograph legend, p. 11.
[photo published earlier with variation of this legend]

D60   *Kansas City Magazine & The Town Squire,* vol. 13, no. 6 (June 1988)
Contents:
i: Keith Haring, drawing a picture of AG with camera on sidewalk, without legend, p. 28.

D61a   [flyer] *Summer Exhibits.* Lowell, MA: Whistler House Museum of Art, [June] 1988. Single sheet, 21.6 x 9.1 cm.
Contents:
i: Jack Kerouac, Fall 1953, New York City, Kerouac on fire escape, with holograph legend.
[photo published earlier with a variation of this legend]
D61b   [poster] *Visions: Reflections of Jack Kerouac.* Lowell, MA: Whistler House Museum of Art, [June] 1988. Single sheet, 35.5 x 27.9 cm.
Contents: [as above photo and legend]
Note: Published simultaneously with the flyer for the same exhibition.

D62   *Shig's Review,* no. 85 (Fall [Sept. 21] 1988)
Contents:
i: AG and Shig Murao, June 3, 1988, San Francisco, CA, self-portrait in mirror at window table of Trieste cafe, with holograph legend, p. 4.

D63 *Bay Windows,* vol. 6, no. 40 (Oct. 6-12, 1988)
Contents:
  i: Peter Orlovsky, Jack Kerouac, Gregory Corso and William Burroughs, 1957, Tangier, Corso and Burroughs clothed and laying on the beach, with holograph legend, p. 22.
    [photo published earlier with variation of this legend]

D64 [exhibition catalog] *Literary Vision.* New York, NY: Jack Tilton Gallery, Nov. 1988.
Contents:
  i: Judith Malina, Julian Beck, and Hanon, Oct. 1984, New York City, Beck in hospital bed with tray of liquids in front, with holograph legend, p. 29.
    [photo published earlier with variation of this legend]

D65 [exhibition brochure] *150 Years of Pop Photographica.* East Islip, NY: Islip Art Museum, Dec. 11, 1988—Jan. 22, 1989. Single sheet folds 7 times to 15.3 x 11.5 cm.
Contents:
  i: Gregory Corso, Paul Bowles, Ian Sommerville, William S. Burroughs, and Michael Portman, 1961, Tangier, group photo in Burroughs' garden, Bowles and Burroughs with camera, Corso with cigarette and two other boys crouching, with legend.
    [photo published earlier with variation of this legend]

D66 [publisher's catalog] *Twin Palms Publishers/Twelvetrees Press, Fine Art Books: 1988-1989.* Altadena, CA: Twin Palms/Twelvetrees, ca. 1988.
Contents:
  i: Jack Kerouac, Fall 1953, New York City, Kerouac on fire escape, with holograph legend, p. 4.
    [photo published earlier with variation of this legend]
  ii: Neal Cassady and Natalie Jackson, 1955, San Francisco, CA, standing beneath theater marquee, with holograph legend, p. 5.
    [photo published earlier with variation of this legend]

D67 *New York City Tribune* (Jan. 17, 1989)
Contents:
  i: photo of a cluttered desk top without legend, (in) Stern, Gary. It's Not the Best Of Times For Producing Experimental Films.

D68 Burroughs, William S. *Interzone.* New York, NY: Viking, [Feb. 28] 1989.
Contents:
  i: William Burroughs, 1957, Tangier, profile looking to the right in the Arab quarter walking in crowd, without legend, back cover of dustjacket.

D69a AG. *Reality Sandwiches: Fotografien.* Berlin, Germany: Nishen, [May] 1989.
Contents:
  i: Berenice Abbot, 1985, New York City, posing at AG's photo exhibition, without legend, p. 13.
  ii: Robert Frank, 1984, New York City, portrait in the Kiev restaurant, with hand on cheek [first appearance of this pose, variation of earlier published photo] without legend, p. 14.
  iii: AG, 1953, New York City, on roof of East 7th Street apartment with skyline in the background, [photo taken by William Burroughs] with holograph legend by AG, p. 19.
    [identical to photo and legend in Fotofolio postcard series, Feb. 1985]
  iv: Jack Kerouac, Fall 1953, New York City, Kerouac on fire escape, with holograph legend, p. 20.
    [identical to photo and legend in *Fotografier 1947-87*]
  v: William Burroughs and Jack Kerouac, Fall 1953, New York City, sitting on sofa in AG's apartment with Jack slouching, with holograph legend, p. 21.
    [photo published earlier without legend]

vi: William Burroughs, Fall 1953, New York City, Burroughs on roof shielding eyes from the sun, with holograph legend, p. 22.
[photo published earlier with variation of this legend]
vii: William Burroughs, Fall 1953, New York City, Burroughs looking over books, with holograph legend, p. 23.
[photo published earlier with variation of this legend]
viii: Spring 1955, San Francisco, CA, Montgomery Street apartment room with LaVigne portrait on wall, with holograph legend, p. 25.
[photo published earlier with variation of this legend]
ix: Donlin, Cassady, AG, LaVigne, and Ferlinghetti, 1955, San Francisco, CA, Group outside City Lights Bookshop with Ferlinghetti leaning on parking meter, with holograph legend, p. 26.
[photo published earlier with variation of this legend]
x: Used car salesman and Neal Cassady, 1955, San Francisco, CA, looking over cars in lot, with holograph legend, p. 27.
xi: Neal Cassady, 1955, San Francisco, CA, looking over used car in lot, AG has combined 2 photos here with one holograph legend, p. 28.
Note: the first photo published earlier with variation of this legend and the second photo published here for the first time.
xii: Neal Cassady and Natalie Jackson, 1955, San Francisco, CA, standing under theatre marquee, with holograph legend, p. 29.
[photo published earlier with variation of this legend]
xiii: Peter Orlovsky, 1955, San Francisco, CA, Peter in bed with head on pillow, staring directly at camera, with holograph legend, p. 30.
xiv: Lafcadio and Peter Orlovsky, Fall 1956, San Francisco, CA, both standing in doorway of apartment with Peter's arm on Lafcadio's shoulder, with holograph legend, p. 31.
xv: Jack Kerouac, 1957, Tangier, portrait with hat in Burroughs' garden, with holograph legend, p. 32.
[photo published earlier with variation of this legend]
xvi: Peter Orlovsky, Jack Kerouac, Gregory Corso, William Burroughs, April 1957, Tangier, on the beach with Corso and Burroughs laying down clothed, with holograph legend, p. 34.
[photo published earlier with variation of this legend]
xvii: Orlovsky, Burroughs, AG, Ansen, Corso, Sommerville and seated Bowles, 1961, Tangier, group portrait in garden, with holograph legend, p. 35.
[photo published earlier with variation of this legend]
xviii: Gregory Corso, Paul Bowles, and William Burroughs, with Sommerville and Portman kneeling, 1961, Tangier, Bowles and Burroughs with cameras, with holograph legend, p. 36.
[photo published earlier with variation of this legend]
xix: AG, William Burroughs and Gregory Corso, 1961, Tangier, all in doorway to Burroughs' garden, Ginsberg and Burroughs putting on sun glasses, with holograph legend, p. 36.
xx: William Burroughs, 1961, Tangier, portrait in Burroughs' garden, slightly zonked looking with hat and black shirt, with holograph legend, p. 37.
[photo published earlier with variation of this legend]
xxi: William Burroughs, 1961, Tangier, close-up portrait of Burroughs in suit with cigarette, with holograph legend, p. 38.
xxii: Gregory Corso, 1957, Paris, France, portrait in Corso's attic room holding and eating grapes, with holograph legend, p. 39.
xxiii: AG and Gregory Corso, 1961, Tangier, both nude in shower, [photo taken by Peter Orlovsky] with holograph legend by AG, p. 40.
[photo published earlier with variation of this legend]
xxiv: AG and Gregory Corso, 1961, Tangier, Siamese twin portrait, [photo by Peter Orlovsky] with holograph legend by AG, p. 41.
[photo published earlier with variation of this legend]

xxv: AG, 1963, Benares, India, AG feeding monkey on the balcony, [photo by Peter Orlovsky] with holograph legend by AG, p. 42.

[identical to photo and legend in *Fotografier 1947-87*]

xxvi: Gary Snyder, June 1963, Kyoto, Japan, Snyder sitting at booth in cafe with head on hand, with holograph legend, p. 43.

xxvii: AG, July 1963, Sea of Japan, nude photo of AG with spear at edge of sea, [photo not taken by AG] with holograph legend by AG, p. 44.

xxviii: Jerry Heiserman, AG, Bobbie Louise Hawkins, Warren Tallman, Robert Creeley, Charles Olson, Thomas Jackrell, Philip Whalen, Don Allen, and another unidentified poet, July 1963, Vancouver, Canada, all sitting on car in street, [photo not taken by AG] with holograph legend by AG, p. 45.

xxix: Philip Whalen, Jerry Heiserman and Thomas Jackrell, July 1963, Portland, OR, sitting in front of store on pavement, with holograph legend, p. 46.

[photo published earlier with variation of this legend]

xxx: Timothy Leary and Neal Cassady, 1964, Millbrook, NY, on Kesey's Prankster bus, AG has combined 2 photos here with one holograph legend, p. 47.

Note: The first photo published earlier with variation of this legend and the second photo published here for the first time.

xxxi: Neal Cassady and girlfriend, Fall 1964, Millbrook, NY, Cassady sleeping flat on back in bed under gable window with girlfriend sitting up smoking, with holograph legend, p. 48.

xxxii: Jack Kerouac, Fall 1964, New York City, last visit to AG's apartment, high with hand to head, with holograph legend, p. 49.

[photo published earlier with variation of this legend]

xxxiii: Aug. 18, 1984, New York City, view from the kitchen window of AG's apartment with curtain pinned back, with holograph legend, p. 51.

[photo published earlier with variation of this legend]

xxxiv: Herbert Huncke, 1984, New York City, portrait sitting in AG's kitchen, with holograph legend, p. 52.

[photo published earlier with variation of this legend]

xxxv: Robert Creeley, July 1984, Boulder, CO, portrait sitting at table with bowl, with holograph legend, p. 53.

[identical to photo and legend in *Fotografier 1947-87*]

xxxvi: William Burroughs, July 1984, Boulder, CO, Burroughs with headset sitting at table, with holograph legend, p. 54.

[photo published earlier without legend]

xxxvii: Richard Avedon, Sept. 1984, New York City, Avedon holding earlier photo of AG and Orlovsky nude, with holograph legend, p. 55.

xxxviii: Lou Reed, Sept. 1984, New York City, Reed sitting in backstage at Public Theater, with holograph legend, p. 56.

[identical to photo and legend in *Fotografier 1947-87*]

xxxix: Pablo and Robert Frank, Oct. 1984, New York City, Robert sitting and Pablo leaning against AG's sink, with holograph legend, p. 57.

[photo published earlier with variation of this legend]

xl: Francesco Clemente and Nachiappan, Oct. 1984, New York City, Clemente with his hands on head in Kiev restaurant, with holograph legend, p. 58.

[identical to photo and legend in *Fotografier 1947-87*]

xli: Kaye McDonough, Nile and Gregory Corso, Oct. 1984, San Francisco, CA, McDonough breast feeding baby, with holograph legend, p. 59.

xlii: Lawrence Ferlinghetti, Oct. 1984, San Francisco, CA, standing with his dog in office of City Lights Bookshop, with holograph legend, p. 60.

xliii: Stewart Meyer, Ira Silverberg, John Giorno, Andrew Wylie, James Grauerholz, William Burroughs, Jan. 19, 1985, New York City, standing group photo, Burroughs in topcoat and cane, with holograph legend, p. 61.

xliv: Raymond Foye and Holly Solomon, Jan. 1985, New York City, sitting in living room talking, with holograph legend, p. 62.

xlv: Kathy Acker, Feb. 1985, Detroit, MI, sitting on table in Detroit Institute of Arts, with holograph legend, p. 63.

[photo published earlier with variation of this legend]

xlvi: Dick McBride, Shig Murao, Jack Micheline, March 16, 1985, San Francisco, CA, sitting at table in Cafe Trieste window, with holograph legend, p. 64.

xlvii: Neeli Cherkovski and friend, Gregory Corso and Nile, Kaye McDonough, March 16, 1985, San Francisco, CA, street scene with outdoor painter, with holograph legend, p. 65.
[photo published earlier with variation of this legend]

xlviii: John Giorno, Henry Geldzahler, AG, Francesco Clemente, William Burroughs, Alan Ansen, Ira Silverberg, James Grauerholz, March 30, 1985, New York City, group photo in garden, [photo not taken by AG] with holograph legend by AG, p. 66.

xlix: Sandro Chia, April 1985, New York City, posing seated with shotgun on lap and Schnabel painting in background, with holograph legend by AG, p. 67.

l: Ed Sanders, June 30, 1985, Woodstock, NY, Sanders in the yard of his home leaning on hood of car, with holograph legend, p. 68.

li: Amiri Baraka, Aug. 1985, Boulder, CO, posing outside at picnic, with holograph legend, p. 69.
[photo published earlier with variation of this legend]

lii: Anne Waldman, Aug. 15, 1985, Boulder, CO, at table with cup, salt and pepper, books, etc., with holograph legend, p. 70.
[photo published earlier with variation of this legend]

liii: Norman Mailer and William Burroughs, Summer 1985, Boulder, CO, in driveway with cars, with holograph legend, p. 71.

liv: Willem de Kooning, Sept. 13, 1985, Long Island, NY, sitting in chair with hands on arm rests with plant at left, with holograph legend, p. 72.

lv: Yevgeny Yevtuchenko, Dec. 1985, Moscow, USSR, with 2 other guests at the dinner table, with holograph legend, p. 73.

lvi: Gregory Corso, March 17, 1986, Lowell, MA, Corso looking up at crucifix, with holograph legend, p. 74.
[photo published earlier with variation of this legend]

lvii: Peter Hale and Peter Orlovsky, Dec. 2, 1986, New York City, sitting at AG's kitchen table with coffee cups, with holograph legend, p. 75.

lviii: Philip Whalen, Mach 16, 1987, New York City, Whalen in underwear sitting on bed in AG's apartment, with holograph legend, p. 76.
[photo published earlier with variation of this legend]

lix: James Grauerholz and William Burroughs, Dec. 21, 1986, New York City, Burroughs, seated, being interviewed before camera and lights with Grauerholz looking on seated at left, with holograph legend, p. 77.

lx: Peter, Lafcadio, Kate and Marie Orlovsky, July 26, 1987, Long Island, NY, all sitting sad on bed with slippers, robes, etc., with holograph legend, p. 78.

lxi: Gary and Masa Snyder, May 30, 1988, Kitkitdizze, CA, sitting in kitchen, Masa looking at papers, with holograph legend, p. 79.

lxii: Wolf Biermann, June 12, 1988, Hamburg, Germany, playing guitar in backyard, with holograph legend, p. 80.

D69b AG. *Snapshot Poetics.* San Francisco, CA: Chronicle Books, 1993.
Contents: [identical to *Reality Sandwiches* except for a few differences in pagination and the following photograph substituted for the one of Wolf Biermann]

lxii: William Burroughs, May 28, 1991, Lawrence, KS, Burroughs leaning back on rock in his backyard, with holograph legend, p. 80.
[photo published earlier without legend]

D70 *New City* (June 25, 1989)
Contents:

i: Jack Kerouac, Fall 1964, New York City, last visit by Kerouac to AG's apartment, high with hand on head, mouth closed, with holograph legend, (in) Hanson, Joyce. New City Juxtaposes [review of Annie Leibovitz/Allen Ginsberg exhibition at Catherine Edelman Gallery].
[photo published earlier with variation of this legend]

D71   *Männer Vogue,* no. 9 (Sept. 1989)
Contents:
i: AG, Oct. 10, 1985, Charlottesville, VA, self-portrait in underwear holding camera chest-high, with holograph legend, p. 169.
ii: Kathy Acker, Feb. 1985, Detroit, MI, drinking a cup of coffee, without legend, p. 169.

D72   Miles, Barry. *Ginsberg: A Biography.* New York, NY: Simon and Schuster, [Sept.] 1989.
Contents:
i: Peter Orlovsky, Spring 1955, San Francisco, CA, seated before large LaVigne portrait of Orlovsky with Mass in B Minor record sitting beside him on ledge, without legend, between pp. 352-353.
ii: Peter Orlovsky, 1962, India, standing beside Indian fabric with hand on cloth, without legend, between pp. 352-353.

D73   [exhibition post card] *Allen Ginsberg: Photographs: Oct. 26—Nov. 25, 1989.* Los Angeles, CA: Fahey/Klein Gallery, Oct. 26, 1989. Single sheet, 17.8 x 12.7 cm.
Contents:
i: Jack Kerouac, Fall 1953, New York, NY, Kerouac on fire escape, with holograph legend.
[photo published earlier with variation of this legend]

D74   *Interview,* vol. 19, no. 12 (Dec. 1989)
Contents:
i: Jack Kerouac, 1957, Tangier, Kerouac with jacket and cap holding cat in arms in Burroughs' garden, without legend, p. 67.
ii: AG, 1961, Tangier, self-portrait bare chested sitting upright in bed, without legend, p. 67.

D75   Corso, Gregory. *Mind Fields.* New York, NY: Hanuman Books, [Dec. 30] 1989.
Contents:
i: Gregory Corso holding a feather, colorized, without legend, on front cover.

D76   Clemente, Francesco. *Twelve Gold Paintings.* Zurich, Switzerland: Bruno Bischofberger, [March 22] 1990.
Contents:
i: Francesco Clemente, ca. 1985, New York City, portrait standing beside a print in gallery, without legend, unpaged.
ii: Gregory Corso, ca. 1985, New York City, portrait with dog tags around neck, without legend, unpaged.

D77   *Poetry Flash,* no. 204 (March 1990)
Contents:
i: John Wieners and Raymond Foye, without legend, p. 7.

D78   *New York Press,* vol. 3, no. 19 (May 9-15, 1990)
Contents:
i: René Ricard, New York City, portrait of Ricard, without legend, p. 9.

D79   Huncke, Herbert. *Guilty of Everything.* New York, NY: Paragon House, [May 30] 1990.
Contents:
i: William Burroughs, 1946, New York City, Burroughs with hat sitting on subway platform, without legend, between pages 108 and 109.

D80   *Du,* no. 6 [issue 592] (June 1990)
Contents:
   i: Orlovsky, Burroughs, AG, Ansen, Corso, Sommerville and Bowles, 1961, Tangier, group photo in garden with Bowles sitting on the ground, with holograph legend, p. 49.
       [photo published earlier with variation of this legend]
   ii: Peter Orlovsky, Jack Kerouac, Gregory Corso, and William Burroughs, 1957, Tangier, Orlovsky squinting and standing beside Kerouac on the beach with Corso and Burroughs laying down clothed, with holograph legend, p. 52.
       [photo published earlier with variation of this legend]

D81   *New Mexican* (July 18, 1990) Pasa Tiempo section
Contents:
   i: William Burroughs, 1961, Tangier, portrait in garden of Burroughs' villa with dark shirt and hat, with holograph legend, p. 2.

D82   Percy, Ann and Foye, Raymond. *Francesco Clemente Three Worlds.* Philadelphia, PA: Philadelphia Museum of Art, [Oct. 20] 1990.
Contents:
   i: Francesco Clemente, 1984, New York City, in Clemente's Great Jones Street loft, with holograph legend, p. 112.
   ii: Francesco and Alba Clemente, 1988, without legend, p. 115.
   iii: Gregory Corso, 1988, New York City, Corso at AG's kitchen table, without legend, p. 122.
   iv: René Ricard, without legend, p. 123

D83   Kesey, Ken. *The Further Inquiry.* New York, NY: Penguin Viking, [Oct. 25] 1990.
Contents:
   i: ca. 1964, New York state, photo of Kesey's bus 'Further' from the side, without legend, pp. 86-87.

D84   [flyer] *Galerie FNAC: Oct. 30—Dec. 29, 1990.* Paris, France: Galerie FNAC, Oct. 30, 1990. Single sheet folds once to 42.0 x 29.8 cm.
Contents:
   i: William S. Burroughs, Fall 1953, New York, NY, Burroughs sitting on AG's sofa with shadow falling across his face, with holograph legend.
       [photo published earlier with variation of this legend]

D85   [exhibition calendar] *L'Agenda, Des Activites Culturelles de la FNAC.* Paris, France: FNAC Galerie, Nov. 1990. Single gathering of 10 leaves, 29.7 x 20.9 cm.
Contents:
   i: Jack Kerouac, Sept. 1953, New York City, Kerouac on fire escape, with holograph legend, back cover.
       [photo published earlier with variation of this legend]

D86   [exhibit catalog] *Mois de la Photo a Paris: Catalogue General.* Paris, France: Mairie de Paris/Paris Audiovisuel, Nov. 1990.
Contents:
   i: Jack Kerouac, Sept. 1953, New York City, on fire escape, with holograph legend, p. 137.
       [identical to photo and legend published in *L'Agenda* (Nov. 1990)]

D87   *Photomagazine,* no. 117 (Nov. 1990)
Contents:
   i: Jack Kerouac, Sept. 1953, New York City, on fire escape, with holograph legend, p. 51.
       [identical to photo and legend in *L'Agenda* (Nov. 1990)]

ii: Robert Frank, June 1984, New Smyrna Beach, FL, Frank with foot up on bumper of car, with holograph legend, p. 51.
[photo published earlier with variation of this legend]
iii: Corso, Bowles, Burroughs, with kneeling Sommerville and Portman, 1961, Tangier, Bowles and Burroughs with cameras in garden of Burroughs' villa, with holograph legend, p. 51.
[photo published earlier with variation of this legend]

D88 *Zoom,* no. 160 (Nov. 1990)
Contents:
i: Willem de Kooning, Sept. 13, 1985, Long Island, NY, de Kooning sitting in chair with his hands on the arm rests, with holograph legend, p. 59.
[photo published earlier without legend]
ii: Lafcadio and Peter Orlovsky, 1956, San Francisco, CA, both sitting bare chested in kitchen of apartment, with holograph legend, p. 62.
[photo published earlier with variation of this legend]
iii: Robert Frank, June 1984, New Smyrna Beach, FL, Frank with leg up on car bumper, with holograph legend, p. 63.
[identical to photo and legend in *Photomagazine* (Nov. 1990)]

D89 Perry, Paul and Babbs, Ken. *On the Bus.* New York, NY: Thunder's Mouth Press, [Nov. 1] 1990.
Contents:
i: Neal Cassady, Ken Babbs and Merry Pranksters, 1964, New York state, view of the interior front of the bus from the back, without legend, p. 40.
ii: Ken Babbs and Neal Cassady, 1964, New York state, Cassady driving with headphones and dark glasses, Babbs on passenger side of bus, without legend, p. 53.
iii: Neal Cassady, 1964, New York state, Cassady having a cup of coffee, without legend, p. 55.
iv: 1964, Poughkeepsie, NY, Kesey's bus 'Further' stopped for gas, with dark car pulled up to the hood, without legend, p. 61.
[this a reverse angle from the other published of similar shot]
v: Neal Cassady, 1964, New York state, Cassady sitting behind wheel talking, without legend, p. 92.
vi: Ron Bevirt, 1964, New York state, Bevirt sitting in the back of the bus, with film crew at left, without legend, p. 95.
vii: Timothy Leary and Neal Cassady, 1964, Millbrook, NY, sitting on the bus without smiles, without legend, p. 96.
viii: Ron Bevirt, Susan Metzner, Ken Babbs, Ken Kesey, George Walker and Sandy Lehmann-Haupt, 1964, Millbrook, NY, sitting on porch railing, without legend, pp. 98-99.
ix: Neal Cassady and Susan Metzner, 1964, Millbrook, NY, Metzner giving Cassady a shot of DMT, without legend, p. 103.
x: Susan Metzner and Neal Cassady, 1964, Millbrook, NY, after the DMT shot, Metzner sitting on edge of bed and Cassady propped on elbow on side in bed, without legend, p. 104.

D90 *Revolution* (Nov. 16, 1990)
Contents:
i: Neal Cassady and Natalie Jackson, 1955, San Francisco, CA, standing under theater marquee, with holograph legend.
[photo published earlier with variation of this legend]

D91 [exhibition catalog] *Larry Rivers, Public and Private: educational guide.* Youngstown, OH: Butler Institute of American Art, Dec. 16, 1990.
Contents:
i: Larry Rivers, July 7, 1985, Southhampton, NY, portrait with painting of John Ashbery, with holograph legend, p. 2.

D92 *Kyoto Journal,* no. 16 (Winter [Dec. 22, 1990] 1991)
Contents:
i: Nanao Sakaki, Daitoku-ji Roshi, Fukumura

D93 Creeley, Robert. *Autobiography.* New York, NY: Hanuman Books, [Dec. 30] 1990.
Contents:
i: Robert Creeley, 1985, Boulder, CO, portrait at table with dish, with holograph legend, front cover.
[photo published earlier with variation of this legend]

D94 *Taos Review,* no. 2 (1990)
Contents:
i: Jan. 23, 1987, New York City, view from kitchen window in the snow, with legend, p. 84.
[photo published earlier with variation of this legend]
ii: Harry Smith, June 17, 1985, New York City, Smith sitting at AG's kitchen table with head in hand, food on table, with legend, p. 85.
iii: Francesco Clemente, Oct. 1984, New York City, Clemente sitting at table looking at AG's book, with legend, p. 86.
iv: Louise Nevelson, Nov. 9, 1986, New York City, Nevelson sitting with a large fur coat, with legend, p. 87.
v: Sandro Chia, April 1985, New York City, Chia sitting on the sofa with a shotgun and Schnabel portrait in the background, with legend, p. 88.
[photo published earlier with variation of this legend]
vi: Paul Bowles, July 1961, Tangier, Bowles sitting on floor with teapot and spoon, with legend, p. 89.
[photo published earlier with variation of this legend]
vii: Julian Beck, May 1984, New York City, Beck in hospital bed with tape and tube in nose, with legend, p. 90.
[photo published earlier with variation of this legend]
viii: Aug. 18, 1984, New York City, view from AG's kitchen window with curtain tacked back, with legend, p. 91.
[photo published earlier with variation of this legend]

D95 Crone, Rainer and Marsh, Georgia. *Francesco Clemente.* Köln, Germany: Verlag Kiepenheuer & Witsch, 1990.
Contents:
i: Francesco Clemente, 1984, Clemente looking at AG poem book, with legend, p. 8.
[photo published earlier with variation of this legend]

D96 [publisher's catalog] *Twin Palms Publishers / Twelvetrees Press, Fine Art Books 1990−1991.* Altadena, CA: Twin Palms/Twelvetrees, 1990.
Contents:
i: Jack Kerouac, Fall 1953, New York City, on fire escape, with holograph legend, p. 4.
[photo published earlier with variation of this legend]
ii: Sandro Chia, April 1985, New York City, sitting on sofa with shotgun and Schnabel painting in background, with holograph legend, p. 5.
[photo published earlier with variation of this legend]
iii: Aug. 18, 1984, New York City, view from AG's kitchen window with the curtain tacked back, with holograph legend, back cover.
[photo published earlier with variation of this legend]

D97   [flyer]   *Allen Ginsberg: Strange Familiar Snapshots: March 20—April 13, 1991.*
New York, NY: Brent Sikkema Fine Art, March 1, 1991.   Single sheet, 20.3 x 25.4 cm.
in envelope.
Contents:
i: Eugene & Connie Brooks, Aug. 1984, Plainview, NY, at a luncheonette table, with
holograph legend.
[photo published earlier with variation of this legend]

D98   *Maandblad 'O',* vol. 2, no. 5 (March 1991)
Contents:
i: AG and Gregory Corso, 1961, Tangier, Siamese twin portrait [photo taken by Peter
Orlovsky] with holograph legend by AG, pp. 14-15.
[photo published earlier with variation of this legend]
ii: AG, 1953, New York City, portrait on roof top with skyline of city in background
[photo taken by William Burroughs] with holograph legend by AG, p. 17.
[photo published earlier with variation of this legend]
iii: Neal Cassady and Natalie Jackson, 1955, San Francisco, CA, standing under theatre
marquee, with holograph legend, p. 20.
[photo published earlier with variation of this legend]
iv: William Burroughs, 1961, Tangier, close-up portrait of Burroughs with cigarette in
hand, suit and tie, with holograph legend, p. 21.
[photo published earlier with variation of this legend]
v: Timothy Leary and Neal Cassady, Fall 1964, Millbrook, NY, both sitting and talking
on bus, two photos with a single holograph legend, p. 23.
[photo published earlier with variation of this legend]
vi: Kaye McDonough, Nile and Gregory Corso, Oct. 12, 1984, San Francisco, CA,
McDonough breast feeding baby, with holograph legend, p. 25.
[photo published earlier with variation of this legend]

D99   *Rolling Stone,* issue 600 (March 21, 1991)
Contents:
i: AG, Oct. 30, 1947, New York Harbor, AG standing at rail with cigarette [photo taken
by radio-man] with holograph legend by AG, p. 43.
[photo published earlier with variation of this legend]
ii: Paul Bowles, July 20, 1961, Tangier, Bowles sitting on the floor with teapot and
spoon, with holograph legend, p. 44.
[photo published earlier with variation of this legend]
iii: William Burroughs, Fall 1953, New York City, Burroughs posing as prize fighter,
with holograph legend, p. 44.
[photo published earlier with variation of this legend]
iv: Ken Kesey, Dec. 14, 1989, New York City, posing in dramatic lighting with top hat,
with holograph legend, p. 44.
[photo published earlier with variation of this legend]
v: Timothy Leary and Neal Cassady, Fall 1964, Millbrook, NY, sitting on the bus
talking, 2 photos joined with a single holograph legend, p. 45.
[photo published earlier with variation of this legend]
vi: Jack Kerouac, Sept. 1953, New York City, on the fire escape, with holograph
legend, p. 45.
[photo published earlier with variation of this legend]
vii: Jack Kerouac, Fall 1964, New York City, last visit to AG's apartment with hand on
head and mouth closed, with holograph legend, p. 46.
[photo published earlier with variation of this legend]
viii: Orlovsky, Burroughs, AG, Ansen, Corso, Sommerville, Bowles, July 1961,
Tangier, group photo in Burroughs' garden with Bowles sitting on ground, with
holograph legend, p. 46.
[photo published earlier with variation of this legend]

D100 *Contact II,* vol. 10, no. 59-61 (Spring 1991)
Contents:
i: Gregory Corso, July 29, 1985, Boulder, CO, portrait of Corso seated and looking to his left at camera, without legend, p. 74.

D101 AG. *Allen Ginsberg: Photographs.* Altadena, CA: Twelvetrees Press, [March 28] 1991.
Contents:
i: AG, Oct. 30, 1947, New York Harbor, AG posing at rail with cigarette in hand [photo taken by the radio man] with holograph legend by AG, p. 1.
[identical to photo and legend in *Rolling Stone* (March 21, 1991)]
ii: Jack Kerouac, Sept. 1953, New York City, on fire escape, with holograph legend, p. 7.
[identical to photo and legend in *Rolling Stone* (March 21, 1991)]
iii: Jack Kerouac, Fall 1953, New York City, walking on 7th Street with statue of Samuel Cox in the background, with holograph legend, p. 8.
[photo published earlier with variation of this legend]
iv: William Burroughs, 1961, Tangier, Burroughs portrait in his garden with black shirt and dress hat, with holograph legend, p. 9.
[photo published earlier with variation of this legend]
v: 1955, San Francisco, CA, Montgomery Street apartment with LaVigne's drawing on wall, Mass in B Minor record on stand, with holograph legend, p. 10.
[photo published earlier with variation of this legend]
vi: Neal Cassady and Natalie Jackson, 1955, San Francisco, CA, standing under theater marquee, with holograph legend, p. 11.
[photo published earlier with variation of this legend]
vii: Peter Orlovsky, Spring 1955, San Francisco, CA, seated before large LaVigne portrait of Orlovsky, with holograph legend, p. 12.
[photo published earlier without legend]
viii: William Burroughs, Fall 1953, New York City, posing as a prize fighter, with holograph legend, p. 13.
[identical to photo and legend in *Rolling Stone* (March 21, 1991)]
ix: William Burroughs, 1953, New York City, intently typing in AG's apartment, with holograph legend, p. 14.
[photo published earlier with variation of this legend]
x: Neal Cassady, 1955, San Francisco, CA, standing in front of black car in used car lot, with holograph legend, p. 15.
[photo published earlier with variation of this legend]
xi: William Burroughs, Fall 1953, New York City, sitting in window looking out over books, with holograph legend, p. 16.
[photo published earlier with variation of this legend]
xii: Jack Kerouac, Fall 1953, New York City, sitting in window looking out over books, with holograph legend, p. 17.
[photo published earlier with variation of this legend]
xiii: William Burroughs and Jack Kerouac, Fall 1953, New York City, sitting on sofa with Burroughs explaining and Kerouac slouching, with holograph legend, p. 18.
[photo published earlier with variation of this legend]
xiv: William Burroughs and Jack Kerouac, Fall 1953, New York City, staging a knife fight, with holograph legend, p. 19.
[photo published earlier with variation of this legend]
xv: Jack Kerouac, 1957, Tangier, portrait in Burroughs' garden with flat soft hat and jacket over plaid shirt, with holograph legend, p. 20.
[photo published earlier with variation of this legend]
xvi: Bob Donlin, Neal Cassady, AG, Robert LaVigne, Lawrence Ferlinghetti, 1955, San Francisco, CA, group photo taken in front of City Lights Book Shop, [photo taken by Peter Orlovsky] with holograph legend by AG, p. 21.
[photo published earlier with variation of this legend]
xvii: Michael Portman, 1961, Tangier, portrait sitting in chair with arm resting on chair back, with holograph legend, p. 22.

xviii: Lafcadio and Peter Orlovsky, 1956, San Francisco, CA, standing in front of door with Peter's head on Lafcadio's shoulder, with holograph legend, p. 23.
[photo published earlier with variation of this legend]
xix: William Burroughs, Fall 1953, New York City, sitting on couch in AG's apartment with shadow falling across his face, with holograph legend, p. 24.
[photo published earlier with variation of this legend]
xx: Lafcadio and Peter Orlovsky, 1956, San Francisco, CA, both sitting at table in kitchen bare-chested, Peter's hand on Lafcadio's shoulder, with holograph legend, p. 25.
[photo published earlier with variation of this legend]
xxi: William Burroughs, 1953, New York City, Burroughs on floor reading book entitled "Winds", with holograph legend, p. 26.
[photo published earlier without legend]
xxii: AG and Gregory Corso, 1961, Tangier, Siamese twin photograph [photo taken by Peter Orlovsky] with holograph legend, p. 27.
[photo published earlier with variation of this legend]
xxiii: Jack Kerouac, Fall 1953, New York City, squinting into sun at the Staten Island Ferry dock, with holograph legend, p. 28.
[photo published earlier with variation of this legend]
xxiv: Peter Orlovsky, Summer 1955, San Francisco, CA, Orlovsky standing next to black car in street, with holograph legend, p. 29.
[photo published earlier with variation of this legend]
xxv: Gregory Corso, 1957, Paris, France, Corso sitting in attic with pole, glaring sideways at camera, with holograph legend, p. 30.
xxvi: Gregory Corso, 1957, Paris, France, Corso eating grapes and looking up to the right, with holograph legend, p. 31.
[photo published earlier with variation of this legend]
xxvii: AG, 1963, Benares, India, AG feeding a monkey on the balcony, with holograph legend, p. 32.
[photo published earlier with variation of this legend]
xxviii: Peter Orlovsky, Nov. 1962, Konarak, India, Orlovsky smoking beside a fallen sculpture in temple, with holograph legend, p. 33.
xxix: Paul Bowles, July 1961, Tangier, sitting on floor with spoon and teapot, with holograph legend, p. 34.
[identical to photo and legend in *Rolling Stone* (March 21, 1991)]
xxx: Orlovsky, Burroughs, AG, Ansen, Corso, Sommerville and Bowles, July 1961, group photo with Bowles sitting on ground in garden [photo taken by Michael Portman] with holograph legend, p. 35.
[identical to photo and legend in *Rolling Stone* (March 21, 1991)]
xxxi: Peter Orlovsky, Jack Kerouac, Gregory Corso and William Burroughs, 1957, Tangier, Corso and Burroughs laying on the beach fully clothed, with holograph legend, p. 36.
[photo published earlier with variation of this legend]
xxxii: William Burroughs, Summer 1961, Tangier, Burroughs standing examining photos on desk with a magnifying glass, with holograph legend, p. 37.
xxxiii: Jack Kerouac, 1957, Tangier, Kerouac in Burroughs' garden holding cat in arms and wearing hat and jacket, with holograph legend, p. 38.
[photo published earlier with variation of this legend]
xxxiv: AG and Gregory Corso, July 1961, Paris, France, both nude in shower [photo taken by Peter Orlovsky] with holograph legend by AG, p. 39.
[photo published earlier with variation of this legend]
xxxv: William Burroughs, Fall 1953, New York City, Burroughs standing beside sphinx in the Metropolitan Museum of Art, with holograph legend, p. 40.
[photo published earlier with variation of this legend]
xxxvi: AG, July 1963, Sea of Japan, AG standing nude with long stick in front of ocean [photo taken by Gary Snyder] with holograph legend, p. 41.
[photo published earlier with variation of this legend]

xxxvii: Gary Snyder, Summer 1963, Kyoto, Japan, Snyder sitting in cafe booth with head on hand, with holograph legend, p. 42.
[photo published earlier with variation of this legend]

xxxviii: Susan Metzner and Neal Cassady, Fall 1964, Millbrook, NY, Metzner sitting up in bed smoking, Cassady asleep, with holograph legend, p. 43.
[photo published earlier with variation of this legend]

xxxix: Herbert Huncke, Fall 1953, New York City, Huncke sitting in hotel room with elbow on sink, with holograph legend, p. 44.
[photo published earlier with variation of this legend]

xl: Alan Ansen, 1957, Venice, Italy, Ansen profile looking out on canal to the right, with holograph legend, p. 45.

xli: Jack Kerouac, Fall 1964, New York City, last visit to AG's apartment, with hand to forehead and mouth closed, with holograph legend, p. 46.
[identical to photo and legend in *Rolling Stone* (March 21, 1991)]

xlii: Timothy Leary and Neal Cassady, Fall 1964, Millbrook, NY, talking on Ken Kesey's bus, 2 photographs with a single holograph legend, p. 47.
[identical to photo and legend in *Rolling Stone* (March 21, 1991)]

xliii: Lou Reed, Sept. 1984, New York City, Reed seated in makeup room of Public Theater, with holograph legend, p. 48.
[photo published earlier with variation of this legend]

xliv: Anne Waldman, Sept. 14, 1984, New York City, Waldman having makeup applied backstage at the Public Theater, with holograph legend, p. 49.

xlv: Rudy di Prima and William Burroughs, July 1984, Boulder, CO, Burroughs pointing pistol at camera, with holograph legend, p. 50.

xlvi: Jello Biafra, Oct. 6, 1987, New York City, sitting at AG's kitchen table with newspaper, with holograph legend, p. 51.

xlvii: Julius Orlovsky, April 4, 1987, Kirkwood, NY, portrait with hands folded, with holograph legend, p. 52.

xlviii: Peter, Lafcadio, Katherine and Marie Orlovsky, July 26, 1987, all sitting on the edge of a bed, with holograph legend, p. 53.
[photo published earlier with variation of this legend]

xlix: Rob MacKercher, Jan. 3, 1986, New York City, asleep on floor with sheets and pillow, with holograph legend, p. 54.

l: Abe Ginsberg, April 13, 1986, West Orange, NJ, in hospital bed with raised hand, with holograph legend, p. 55.

li: Wavy Gravy, Nov. 26, 1988, New York City, in costume at the Cathedral of Saint John the Divine, with holograph legend, p. 56.

lii: AG and Robert Frank, Summer 1984, New York City, Frank taking AG's photo for book cover, with holograph legend, p. 57.
[photo published earlier with variation of this legend]

liii: Philip Whalen, March 1984, New York City, reading book in bathrobe in AG's apartment, with holograph legend, p. 58.
[photo published earlier with variation of this legend]

liv: Julian Beck, May 1984, New York City, laying in hospital bed with tape on arms and nose tube, with holograph legend, p. 59.
[photo published earlier with variation of this legend]

lv: Harry Smith, Jan. 12, 1985, New York City, Smith pouring milk, with holograph legend, p. 60.
[photo published earlier with variation of this legend]

lvi: Yevgeny Yevtuchenko, Feb. 18, 1986, New York City, sitting at AG's kitchen table with his head on hand, with holograph legend, p. 61.

lvii: Louis Auchincloss, Nov. 20, 1985, Leningrad, USSR, standing beside Dostoyevsky's desk, with holograph legend, p. 62.
[photo published earlier with variation of this legend]

lviii: Gregory Corso, March 17, 1986, Lowell, MA, standing beneath crucifix, with holograph legend, p. 63.
[photo published earlier with variation of this legend]

lix: Francesco Clemente, Oct. 1984, New York City, sitting at table looking at AG's book, with holograph legend, p. 64.
[photo published earlier with variation of this legend]
lx: Basil Bunting, Summer 1973, England, standing in field at fence, with holograph legend, p. 65.
lxi: Louise Nevelson, Nov. 9, 1986, New York City, sitting with heavy coat, with holograph legend, p. 66.
[photo published earlier with variation of this legend]
lxii: Julius Orlovsky, Sept. 3, 1984, St. Johnsbury, VT, standing in forest, with holograph legend, p. 67.
[photo published earlier with variation of this legend]
lxiii: René Ricard, July 29, 1986, New York City, sitting behind flowers at AG's kitchen table, with holograph legend, p. 68.
[photo published earlier with variation of this legend]
lxiv: Small Free Inn Band and Jimmy Gutierrez, May 23, 1988, San Francisco, CA, group standing in soup kitchen with costumes and instruments, with holograph legend, p. 69.
lxv: John Wieners, Feb. 1, 1985, Boston, MA, writing in book at table in hotel room, with holograph legend, p. 70.
lxvi: Francesco Clemente and Julius Orlovsky, Fall 1984, New York City, both standing in ashram, with holograph legend, p. 71.
[photo published earlier with variation of this legend]
lxvii: Ray Bremser, March 14, 1987, New York City, sitting at AG's kitchen table with a can of Budweiser beer, with holograph legend, p. 72.
lxviii: Sandro Chia, April 1985, New York City, sitting on sofa with shotgun and Schnabel portrait on wall, with holograph legend, p. 73.
[photo published earlier with variation of this legend]
lxix: Philip Whalen and Lloyd Reynolds, July 1963, Portland, OR, both sitting on sofa talking, 2 photos joined with a single holograph legend, p. 74.
lxx: Sept. 29, 1985, New York City, view of window and Mary Help of Christians church outside, with holograph legend, p. 75.
[photo published earlier with variation of this legend]
lxxi: Pablo Frank and Robert Frank, Oct. 1984, New York City, Pablo leaning against sink and Robert sitting in AG's apartment, with holograph legend, p. 76.
[photo published earlier with variation of this legend]
lxxii: Juanita Lieberman, March 3, 1985, New York City, portrait at table with holograph legend, p. 77.
[photo published earlier with variation of this legend]
lxxiii: Peter Orlovsky, Dec. 1980, Zurich, Switzerland, standing beside James Joyce's grave in snow, with holograph legend, p. 78.
lxxiv: Lucien Carr, Dec. 2, 1986, New York City, sitting at table filled with newspapers and magazines, with holograph legend, p. 79.
lxxv: Harry Smith, June 17, 1985, New York City, Smith sitting at AG's kitchen table with food and head in hands, with holograph legend, p. 80.
[photo published earlier with variation of this legend]
lxxvi: Larry Rivers, July 7, 1985, Southhampton, NY, standing in front of his portrait of John Ashbery, with holograph legend, p. 81.
[photo published earlier with variation of this legend]
lxxvii: Herbert Huncke, March 1984, New York City, portrait in AG's kitchen, with holograph legend, p. 82.
[photo published earlier with variation of this legend]
lxxviii: Dorothy Norman, July 7, 1985, Easthampton, NY, sitting on sofa with leg up, with holograph legend, p. 83.
lxxix: Nicanor Parra, Sept. 5, 1984, New York City, sitting on subway, with holograph legend, p. 84.
[photo published earlier without legend]
lxxx: Lois Snyder Hennessy and Gary Snyder, April 2, 1986, Grass Valley, CA, Gary in the background carrying birthday cake, with holograph legend, p. 85.

lxxxi: William Burroughs, July 1984, Boulder, CO, Burroughs at table with headset, with holograph legend, p. 86.
[photo published earlier with variation of this legend]
lxxxii: Robert Frank, Nov. 8, 1988, New York City, sitting at his kitchen table, with holograph legend, p. 87.
lxxxiii: 2 young boys, Jan. 11, 1985, New York City, portrait on chairs in AG's kitchen, with holograph legend, p. 88.
lxxxiv: Ken Kesey, Dec. 14, 1989, New York City, dramatically lit photo with top hat, with holograph legend, p. 89.
[identical to photo and legend in *Rolling Stone* (March 21, 1991)]
lxxxv: Patrick Warner, Feb. 2, 1985, Cambridge, MA, nude portrait laying in bed, with holograph legend, p. 90.
lxxxvi: John Giorno, James Grauerholz and William Burroughs, March 26, 1985, dramatically lit group photo with Burroughs using blackjack, with holograph legend, p. 91.
[photo published earlier with variation of this legend]
lxxxvii: Robert Frank, June 1984, New Smyrna Beach, FL, Frank with foot up on bumper of car, with holograph legend, p. 92.
[photo published earlier with variation of this legend]
lxxxviii: Olga Rudge, June 20, 1985, Orono, ME, sitting in chair with cane, with holograph legend, p. 93.
lxxxix: Aug. 18, 1984, New York City, view from AG's kitchen window, with curtain tacked back, with holograph legend, p. 94.
[photo published earlier with variation of this legend]
xc: Jan. 23, 1987, New York City, view from AG's kitchen window, with snow falling heavily, with holograph legend, p. 95.
[photo published earlier with variation of this legend]
xci: AG, Nov. 18, 1985, Moscow, USSR, self-portrait in oval bathroom mirror with close-up at left side, with holograph legend, p. 96.
[photo published earlier with variation of this legend]

D102 *Border Crossings,* vol. 10, no. 2 (April 1991)
Contents:
i: July 1986, Boulder, CO, sleeping nude man, without legend, p. 23.

D103 *City Magazine International,* no. 70 (May 1991)
Contents:
i: Peter Orlovsky, Jack Kerouac, Gregory Corso and William Burroughs, 1957, Tangier, Corso and Burroughs fully clothed laying on the beach, with holograph legend, pp. 44-45.
[photo published earlier with variation of this legend]

D104 Halper, Jon (ed.). *Gary Snyder: Dimensions of a Life.* San Francisco, CA: Sierra Club Books, [May 31] 1991.
Contents:
i: Gary Snyder, Jan. 1962, Almora or Kausani, India, Snyder with mountains in background, without legend, p. 184.
ii: Joanne Kyger, Gary Snyder, Peter Orlovsky, March 1962, Jaipur, India, standing in geometrical stone observatory, without legend, p. 185.
iii: Gary Snyder, July 1963, Japan, Snyder sleeping with walking stick and sandals, without legend, p. 186.
iv: Gary Snyder, May 30, 1989, Kitkitdizze, CA, Snyder on porch looking at report on table, without legend, p. 198.

D105 *Poetry Flash,* no. 219 (June 1991)
Contents:
i: Nicanor Parra, Fall 1984, New York City, riding on subway car, with holograph legend, p. 5.
[photo published earlier with variation of this legend]

ii: Judith Malina, Julian Beck and Hanon, Fall 1984, New York City, Beck in hospital
bed with tray of liquids in front, with holograph legend, p. 5.
[photo published earlier with variation of this legend]

D106 *Photo Metro,* vol. 9, no. 91 (Aug. 1991)
Contents:
i: Neal Cassady and Natalie Jackson, 1955, San Francisco, CA, standing under theater
marquee, with holograph legend, p. 5.
[photo published earlier with variation of this legend]
ii: Neal Cassady, 1955, San Francisco, CA, standing beside black car lot, with
holograph legend, p. 5.
[photo published earlier with variation of this legend]
iii: William Burroughs, 1961, Tangier, portrait in garden with dark shirt and dress hat,
with holograph legend, p. 7.
[photo published earlier with variation of this legend]
iv: Gary Snyder, ca. 1965, Glacier Peak Wilderness area, Snyder standing on hillside
slope, urinating, with holograph legend, p. 9.
Note: Contained in a portfolio of 17 photos, the other 13 being reprints identical to earlier
publications.

D107 Green, Michelle. *The Dream at the End of the World.* New York, NY: Harper
Collins, [Aug. 1] 1991.
Contents:
i: Peter Orlovsky and Gregory Corso, 1961, Tangier, on balcony overlooking the city,
without legend, between pp. 208-209.
ii: Peter Orlovsky and William Burroughs, 1957, Tangier, seated in outdoor park,
Orlovsky with glasses, without legend, between pp. 208-209.

D108 [advertising flyer] *Allen Ginsberg: Photographs: Aug. 8—Sept. 14, 1991.* San
Francisco, CA: Robert Koch Gallery, Aug. 8, 1991. Single sheet, 12.7 x 17.8 cm.
Contents:
i: Neal Cassady and Natalie Jackson, 1955, San Francisco, CA, standing under theater
marquee, with holograph legend.
[identical to photo and legend in *Photo Metro* (Aug. 1991)]

D109 Snyder, Gary. *Turtle Island.* Kyoto, Japan: Yamaguchi, 1991.
Contents:
i: Nanao Sakaki and Gary Snyder, May 28, 1988, Bedrock Mortar, CA, both sitting at
desks and working on telephones, with holograph legend, on back cover.

D110 [cassette] *Gutterboy.* New York, NY: Mercury/Polygram, [March 17] 1992.
Cassette 314-510917-4.
Contents:
i: Barb Morrison, Danny Hulsizer, Dito Monteil, Johnny Koncy, Erick Hulsizer, Sept.
12, 1991, group photo on AG's apartment roof, with holograph legend, on cassette
liner notes.
[photo with variation of this legend appears on the compact disc]

D111 [compact disc] *Gutterboy.* New York, NY: Mercury/Polygram, [March 17] 1992.
CD 314 510 917-2.
Contents:
i: Barb Morrison, Danny Hulsizer, Dito Monteil, Johnny Koncy, Erick Hulsizer, Sept.
12, 1991, group photo, with holograph legend, on CD cover.
[photo with variation of this legend appears on the cassette]

D112 [compact disc] Gutterboy. *Every Other Night*. New York, NY: Mercury/Polygram, [March 17] 1992. CDP 643.
Contents:
  i: Barb Morrison, Danny Hulsizer, Dito Monteil, Johnny Koncy, Erick Hulsizer, Sept. 12, 1991, group photo at AG's kitchen table, with holograph legend, on inside CD cover.

D113a [exhibit brochure] *Allen Ginsbergs Photographien / Robert Rauschenbergs: April 4, — May 9, 1992*. Cologne, Germany: Alfred Kren, April 4, 1992. Single sheet folds once to 25.0 x 17.4 cm.
Contents:
  i: William Burroughs, Fall 1953, New York City, Burroughs posing as a prize fighter, with holograph legend.
  [photo published earlier with variation of this legend]
D113b [photo also appears on poster for the same exhibit] 61.1 x 42.9 cm.

D114 *Observer Magazine* (April 26, 1992)
Contents:
  i: William Burroughs, 1991, Lawrence, KS, with denim jacket and jeans laying on rock looking skyward, without legend, pp. 26-27.
  ii: William Burroughs, 1991, Lawrence, KS, without glasses looking at one of his own paintings, without legend, p. 29.
  iii: William Burroughs, 1991, Lawrence, KS, a frail looking Burroughs on telephone, without legend, p. 30.

D115 [program] *Cosmopolitan Greetings: Jazz Opera, by George Gruntz and Allen Ginsberg*. Cologne, Germany: WDR, May 26, 1992.
Contents:
  i: George Gruntz, Jan. 23, 1987, New York City, standing with overcoat in AG's kitchen, with holograph legend, p. 2.

D116 *Provincetown Arts*, vol. 8 ([July 1] 1992)
Contents:
  i: AG and Peter Money, with holograph legend

D117 Jezer, Marty. *Abbie Hoffman: American Rebel*. New Brunswick, NJ: Rutgers University Press, [Aug. 26] 1992.
Contents:
  i: Abbie Hoffman and son, 1986, Boulder, CO, without legend, between pp. 142-143.
  ii: Abbie Hoffman, 1987, Washington, DC, wearing Oliver North button, between pp. 142-143.

D118 *Aperture*, no. 129 (Fall 1992)
Contents:
  i: William Burroughs, May 28, 1991, Lawrence, KS, laying on couch in yard, with holograph legend, p. 5.

D119 *Zone*, no. 7 (Oct. 1992 — Feb. 1993)
Contents:
  i: William Burroughs, 1991, Lawrence, KS, sitting outside on sofa with cane, without legend, p. 13.

D120 Schumacher, Michael. *Dharma Lion: A Biography of Allen Ginsberg*. New York, NY: St. Martin's Press, [Oct.] 1992.
Contents:
  i: Louis Ginsberg, 1976, Paterson, NJ, Louis asleep in an easy chair in his living room, without legend, between pp. 520-521.

D121 Burroughs, William S. *Painting and Guns.* New York, NY: Hanuman, [Dec.] 1992.
Contents:
i: William Burroughs, 1984, standing in front of a painting with a gun, without legend, on front cover.

D122 Clemente, Francesco. *Evening Raga & Paradiso.* New York, NY: Rizzoli, 1992.
Content:
i: Francesco Clemente, New York City, portrait, without legend, p. [2].

D123 Friend, David and the Editors of Life. *More Reflections on the Meaning of Life.* Boston, MA: Little, Brown & Co., 1992.
Contents:
i: Aug. 18, 1984, view from AG's kitchen window with curtain tacked back, with holograph legend, p. 133.
[photo published earlier with variation of this legend]

D124 Kerouac, Jack. *Big Sur.* New York, NY: Penguin Books, 1992.
Contents:
i: ca. 1965, fragment of contact sheet printed as the front and back covers contains views of the mountains, some with Gary Snyder, and views of the city and restaurant signs, without legend.

D125 Kerouac, Jack. *Dharmovi Tulaci.* Prague, Czechoslovakia: Winston Smith, 1992.
Contents:
i: Gary Snyder, 1955, Berkeley, CA, sitting in robe with round light globe, without legend, p. 293.
[very similar photo the one with the pine cone but not the same]

D126 Kerouac, Jack. *Tristessa.* New York, NY: Penguin Books, 1992.
Contents:
i. ca. 1955, fragment of contact sheet printed as front and back covers, contains views of buildings in Mexico, without legend.

D127 [advertising prospectus] *Blind Spot.* New York, NY, Spring 1993. Single sheet folds three times to 26.8 x 22.9 cm.
Contents:
i: Harry Smith, June 17, 1985, New York, NY, Smith at AG's kitchen table with food and plates, head on hand, with holograph legend.
[photo published earlier with variation of this legend]

D128 *Blind Spot,* vol. 1, no. 1 (Spring-Summer 1993)
Contents:
i: Harry Smith, Jan. 12, 1985, New York, NY, writing on book packages, with holograph legend, p. 34.
ii: Harry Smith, Aug. 30, 1986, New York, NY, smelling flowers at AG's kitchen table, with holograph legend, p. 36.
iii: Harry Smith, April 19, 1987, Mississippi, riding in a car, 2 photos grouped together with a single holograph legend, p. 37.
iv: Harry Smith, AG, Edith Ginsberg, April 18, 1987, Mississippi, Edith on the telephone while AG takes group photo in mirror, with holograph legend, p. 38.
v: Harry Smith, June 17, 1985, New York, NY, Smith at AG's kitchen table head on hand, with holograph legend, p. 39.

D129 [liner notes] *Howls, Raps & Roars.* Berkeley, CA: Fantasy Records, [June] 1993. 4 compact disc set, #4 FCD-4410-2.
Contents:
i: Gregory Corso, 1957, Paris, France, Corso sitting in attic with pole, staring head-on at camera, without legend, p. 20.

D130 [legend] *Vogue Italia,* vol. 3, no. 70 (Aug. 1993)
Contents:
   i: George & Anna Condo and AG [photo not taken by AG], with holograph legend by
       AG, p. 106.

D131 *Outside,* vol. 18, no. 11 (Nov. 1993)
Contents:
   i: Gary Snyder, 1965, Glacier Peak area, sitting on rock near lake, with holograph
       legend, p. 61.
       [photo published earlier with variation of this legend]
   ii: Lois Snyder Hennessy and Gary Snyder, April 2, 1986, Grass Valley, CA, Gary in
       the background carrying birthday cake, with holograph legend, p. 64.
       [photo published earlier with variation of this legend]

D132 *Paris Review,* vol. 35, no. 129 (Winter 1993)
Contents:
   i: James Baldwin, March 22, 1986, Amherst, MA, portrait with holograph legend, p.
        192.
   ii: Jim Carroll, Sept. 1984, New York, NY, sitting at table with paper coffee cup, with
        holograph legend, p. 193.
   iii: Barney Rossett, June 20, 1991, New York, NY, sitting at table at censorship
        symposium, with holograph legend, p. 194.
   iv: Andrei Voznesenski, March 29, 1987, New York, NY, sitting at table in Christine's
        restaurant, with holograph legend, p. 195.
   v: Czeslaw Miloscz, April 28, 1984, Philadelphia, PA, standing on street, with
        holograph legend, p. 196.
   vi: Sandro Chia and William S. Burroughs, March 30, 1985, New York, NY, standing at
        art opening, with holograph legend, p. 197.
   vii: James Schuyler, Nov. 7, 1987, New York, NY, sitting at restaurant table, with
        holograph legend, p. 198.
   viii: Ken Kesey, Dec. 14, 1989, New York, NY, sitting on sofa in hotel room with
        unshaded light bulb, with holograph legend, p. 199.
   ix: Evgeny Yevtuchenko, April 1986, New York, NY, sitting at AG's kitchen table, with
        holograph legend, p. 200.

D133 Clark, Tom. *Robert Creeley and the Genius of the American Common Place.* New
York, NY: New Directions, 1993.
Contents:
   i: Francesco Clemente and Robert Creeley, 1989, sitting in Clemente's studio in New
       York City, without legend, p. 118.
   ii: Robert Creeley, July 1984, Boulder, CO, sitting at table with dish, with holograph
       legend, p. 118.
       [not first appearance]

D134 Hornick, Lita. To Elizabeth and Eleanor: Great Queens Who Love Poetry. New
York, NY: Giorno Poetry Systems, 1993.
Contents:
   i. Lita Hornick, May 1, 1992, New York, NY, sitting in her apartment, with holograph
   legend, p. [2].

D135 Kerouac, Jack. *On the Road.* New York, NY: Penguin Books, 1976, 1993. [19th
printing, the first printing to include these cover photographs]
Contents:
   i: Neal Cassady and Natalie Jackson, 1956, San Francisco, CA, standing on a street
       beside a motorcycle with a church spire in the distant background, without legend, on
       front cover.
   ii: Neal Cassady, 1956, close up and out of focus portrait, without legend, on front
       cover.

D136 Kerouac, Jack. *Tangier Poem.* Louisville, KY: White Fields Press, 1993. [broadside]
Contents:
   i: Peter Orlovsky, Jack Kerouac, Gregory Corso, William Burroughs, April 1957, Tangier, on the beach with Corso and Burroughs laying down clothed, with holograph legend.
   [photo published earlier with variation of this legend]

D137 Kerouac, Jack. *Visions of Cody.* New York, NY: Penguin Books, 1993.
Contents:
   i: Neal Cassady and Natalie Jackson, 1956, San Francisco, CA, standing beside a convertible in a parking lot, without legend, on front cover.
   ii: Neal Cassady, 1956, San Francisco, CA, Neal standing beside a car in a parking lot with cigarette in hand and hand in pocket, without legend, on front cover.
   iii: Neal Cassady and Al Hinckle?, ca. 1956, sitting in living room playing a game, without legend, on front cover.

D138 *Shambhala Sun,* vol. 2, no. 6 (July 1994).
Contents:
   i: Chögyam Trungpa, April 12, 1985, Boulder, CO, standing outside house wearing epilets, with holograph legend, p. 56.

D139 Köhler, Michael (ed.). *Burroughs: Eine Bild-Biographie.* Berlin, Germany: Nishen, 1994.
Contents:
   i: Hal Chase and William S. Burroughs, 1944-45, Morningside Heights, NY, sitting on bench overlooking Harlem, without legend, p. 35.
   ii: Joan Adams, ca. 1945, Columbia University, New York, with a winter coat, without legend, p. 36.

E
Miscellaneous Publications Containing Work by Allen Ginsberg

1958

E1a [exhibition flyer] *Robert LaVigne: An Exhibition of Selected Works.* San Francisco, CA: The Lion Bookstore, July 11, 1958. Single sheet folded 3 times to 8.4 x 21.6 cm.
Contents: AG prose.
Note: Published ca. July 11, 1958 in an impression of 250-300 copies.

E1b [exhibition flyer] *Gotham Book Mart and Gallery.* New York, NY: Gotham Book Mart, ca. Sept. 29 — Oct. 11, 1969. Single sheet, 27.9 x 21.6 cm.
Contents: AG prose as above.

1959

E2 [flyer] *Poetics: Mind is Shapely, Art is Shapely.* San Francisco, CA: Poetry Center, April 27, 1959. Single sheet, 27.9 x 21.6 cm.
Contents: AG prose.
Note: Published April 27, 1959 in an impression of ca. 250 copies. This estimate is based on the seating capacity of the auditorium.

E3 [exhibition catalog] *10th Street.* Houston, TX: Contemporary Arts Association of Houston, Oct. 15-Nov. 8, 1959. 8 pages.
Contents: AG letter to Adrian Rosenberg, p. [3].

1961

E4 [cover blurb] Burroughs, William S. *The Soft Machine.* Paris, France: Olympia Press, 1961. [paperbound issue]
Contents: AG prose blurb.
Note: Published June 1961 in an impression of 5,000 copies.

E5a [advertising card] *Dark Brown by Michael McClure.* San Francisco, CA: Auerhahn Press, 1961. Single sheet, 8.0 x 15.3 cm.
Contents: AG prose blurb.

E5b [prose blurb] McClure, Michael. *Dark Brown.* San Francisco, CA: Dave Haselwood Books, 1967.
Contents: As above advertising card.

1964

E6   [petition] *Lenny Bruce Arrest.* New York, NY: Committee for Free Speech, May 22, 1964. Single sheet, 27.9 x 21.6 cm.
Contents: AG prose.
Note: Published May 22, 1964 in an impression of ca. 25-50 copies.

E7   [rare book catalog] *Ed Sanders' Catalogue,* no. 1 (June/July 1964). Subtitled: *Catalogue of Manuscripts, Holographs, Literary Relics ... tractata, ejaculata, drek & other effluvia of the literary divinity.* New York, NY: Peace Eye Bookstore, 1964.
Contents: AG prose description of one item.
Note: Published June 1964 in an impression of ca. 200 copies, estimate according to Ed Sanders.
Reprinted in *Ed Sanders' Catalogue,* no. 2 (Oct./Nov. 1964).

E8   [press release] *Arts, Educational Leaders Protest Use of New York Obscenity Law in Harassment of Controversial Social Satirist Lenny Bruce.* New York, NY: C.O.P. [Committee on Poetry], June 13, 1964. 4 sheets, 28.0 x 21.7 cm.
Contents: AG has written most of the prose for this press release.
Note: Published June 13, 1964 in an impression of ca. 500 copies, according to *Ed Sander's Catalogue,* no. 2.

E9   [rare book catalog] *Ed Sanders' Catalogue,* no. 2 (Oct./Nov. 1964). New York, NY: Peace Eye Bookstore, 1964.
Contents: AG prose description of item #75 as above and an additional poem "Down with Death" as item #82.
Note: Published Oct. 1964 in an impression of ca. 200 copies, estimate according to Ed Sanders.

E10a [exhibition flyer] *Ahmed Yacoubi.* New York, NY: Amici Gallery, Nov. 1964. Single sheet folded twice to form 6 pages, 26.9 x 21.4 cm.
Contents: AG prose blurb, p. [4].
E10b [exhibition flyer] *Recent Paintings: Ahmed Yacoubi.* New York, NY: Bodley Gallery, Jan. 20-Feb. 5, 1966.
Contents: AG prose blurb as above.

E11   [program] *Hippolytus by Euripides.* Bennington College Theatre, Bennington, VT, Dec. 15-17, 1964.
Contents: Song [The Weight of the World].
Note: Published Dec. 15, 1964 in an impression of ca. 200 copies.

1965

E12   [exhibition flyer] *Wynn Chamberlain.* New York, NY: Fischbach Gallery, Feb. 2-19, 1965. Single brilliant green (140) sheet folds twice to 10.1 x 25.9 cm.
Contents: Chamberlain's Nakeds [prose].
Note: Published shortly before Feb. 2, 1965 in an unknown quantity.

E13   [poster] *International Poetry at the Royal Albert Hall London.* London, England, June 11, 1965.
Contents: Liverpool Muse.

E14   [program] *International Poetry Incarnation.* London, England: Royal Albert Hall, June 11, 1965. Single sheet folded once to 27.9 x 10.3 cm.
Contents: England! Awake! Awake! Awake! [unsigned poem on front cover is by AG].
Note: Published June 11, 1965 in an impression of ca. 500 copies and passed out at the reading.

E15a [flyer, first state] *Demonstration of Spectacle as Example, as Communication.*
Berkeley, CA: Nov. 20, 1965. Single sheet, 27.9 x 21.6 cm. printed on both
sides.
Contents: Demonstration of Spectacle as Example, as Communication [prose].
Note: Published shortly before Nov. 20, 1965 in an impression of ca. 150 copies.
This estimate is from Dowden's bibliography. This first state has 63 line
statement on the verso of the flyer, the second state has 66 lines.

E15b [flyer, second state] *Demonstration of Spectacle as Example, as Communication.*
Berkeley, CA: Nov. 20, 1965. Single sheet, 27.9 x 21.6 cm. printed on both
sides.
Contents: As first state but with additional lines.
Note: The following note is handwritten by George Dowden on his own copy of
this item now at the University of Texas, Austin: "This item in biblio as 'Ginsberg
on March: Demonstration as Spectacle' wrong title and in fact there are 2 slightly
different flyers here, so something of a muddle of very rare items."

E16 [advertising flyer] *About the "Four New Poets" Long-Play Recording.* Anderson,
IN: Satori Records, ca. 1965. Single sheet, 27.9 x 21.6 cm.
Contents: AG prose blurb.

E17a [playscript] *Kaddish: A Dramatic Mass, by Allen Ginsberg.* Playscript created by
Jerry Benjamin, New York, NY, 1965. 60 mimeographed sheets in a folder.
Contents: Kaddish.

E17b [filmscript] *Kaddish [with Robert Frank].* New York, NY: September 20
Productions, 1964.
Contents: Kaddish.
Note: This was created as the script for a film being made by Robert Frank, with
expected production in 1966 never produced. Photocopied in an edition of about
15 working-copy scriptbooks.

E17c [playscript] *Kaddish.* New York, NY: Jerome Benjamin and A New Kinda
Theatre, 1965.
Contents: Kaddish.
Note: This is a revised version of the filmscript. This version was created by Jerry
Benjamin for play production, expected in 1966 or 1967 and never produced.
Mimeographed and stapled in an edition of from 14-18 working copies.

1966

E18a [flyer] *The Beard: by Michael McClure.* San Francisco, CA: Wharf Theatre, March
31, 1966. Single moderate yellowish pink (29) sheet, 28.1 x 19.7 cm.
Contents: AG prose blurb.

E18b [cover blurb] McClure, Michael. *The Beard.* San Francisco, CA: Coyote, 1967.
Contents: AG prose blurb as above on back cover.
Note: Published March 1967 in an impression of 4960 copies and reprinted at least
once; an additional 40 copies were specially bound and signed but did not include
AG's blurb.

E18c [cover blurb] McClure, Michael. *The Beard.* New York, NY: Grove Press,
1967.
Contents: AG prose blurb as above on back cover.

Related item: [flyer] *The Responsible Community is Shocked at the Harsh Sentencing
of Psychologist Dr. Timothy Leary.* New York, NY: Timothy Leary Defense
Fund, April 3, 1966. Single sheet, 37.9 x 34.1 cm.
Contents: AG is one of 52 signers but he did not write the statement.

Related item: [flyer] *Timothy Leary Defense Fund.* New York, NY: April 9, 1966.
27.8 x 21.5 cm.
Contents: AG is one of 2 signers, but he did not write the statement.

E19   [transcript of speech before Congress] *Statement of Allen Ginsberg June 14, 1966.* Washington, DC: June 14, 1966. 35.6 x 21.7 cm. 12 sheets stapled in the upper left corner.
Contents: AG prose statement.
Note: Published June 14, 1966 in an impression of ca. 25 copies for distribution as a press release.

E20   [press release]   *Chelsea Girls by Andy Warhol.* New York, NY: Film-Makers' Cinematheque, Nov. 3, 1966. Single sheet, 35.5 x 21.7 cm.
Contents: AG prose blurb.

E21a   [exhibition catalog]   *Takis: Magnetic Sculpture and the White Signals.* London, England: Indica Gallery, Nov. 25-Dec. 1966.
Contents: AG prose statement, p. [8].
Note: Published Nov. 21, 1966 in an unknown number of copies.
E21b   [exhibition catalog]   *Takis: Magnetic Sculpture.* New York: Howard Wise Gallery, April 7-29, 1967.
Contents: AG prose as above, here on p. 10.

E22   [transcript]   *Seminar on Marihuana and LSD Controls.* [Washington, DC]: National Student Association, ca. Dec. 20, 1966. 18 single sheets, 28.0 x 21.7 cm.
Contents: Transcript of a taped debate between AG and James H. Fox, from a seminar given before the National Student Association Convention at the Univ. of Illinois, Aug. 24, 1966.
a.   First Printing: Identified by the title page beginning in hollow type "UNITED STATES NATIONAL STUDENT ASSOCIATION".
b.   Second Printing: Identified by the title page beginning "SEMINAR ON MARIHUANA AND LSD CONTROLS*".

E23   [liner notes]   *The Fugs.* ESP, ESP-DISK 1028, New York, NY, 1966. 33 1/3 rpm, 12" Lp mono.
Contents: AG prose liner notes.

1967

Related item: [press release] *More Than 400 Say "No Tax for War".* Cincinnati, OH: No Tax for War Committee, April 14, 1967. 4 single sheets, 35.5 x 21.6 cm.
Contents: AG is one of 400 signers, but he did not write the statement.

E24   [liner notes]   *Krishna Consciousness: A. C. Bhaktivedanta Swami.* Happening Records, Inc., New York, NY, ca. May 1967. 33 1/3 rpm, 12" Lp.
Contents: AG blurb on back cover.

E25a   [cover blurb] Lamantia, Philip.   *Selected Poems 1943-1966.* San Francisco, CA: City Lights Books, 1967.
Contents: AG prose blurb on back cover.
Note: Published May 1967 in an impression of 5,000 copies and reprinted as follows: 2nd printing, July 1968, 3,000 copies [indistinguishable from the first printing]; 3rd printing, June 1969, 5,000 copies [copyright page erroneously reports this as "Second Printing"].
E25b   [cover blurb]   *The Pocket Poets Series,* vol. 3, nos. 15-21. Millwood, NY: Kraus Reprint Co., 1974.
Contents: As above, here on p. [485].
Note: Published Jan. 28, 1974 in an impression of 250 copies.

E26   [cover blurb] Bremser, Ray. *Angel*. New York, NY: Tompkins Square Press, 1967. [paper ed.]
Contents: AG prose blurb.
Note: Published May 5, 1967 in an impression of 5,000 copies, the blurb is not included on the clothbound edition.

E27   [cover blurb] Patten, Brian. *Little Johnny's Confession.*
Contents: AG prose blurb.
a. London, England: George Allen and Unwin, Ltd., 1967. [hardbound]
Note: Published June 8, 1967.
b. London, England: George Allen and Unwin, Ltd., 1987. [paperbound]
Note: Published June 8, 1967 and reprinted in 1979 in an impression of 5,000 copies.
c. New York, NY: Hill and Wang, 1968. [hardbound]
Contents: AG blurb is abbreviated for the American editions.
Note: Published April 12, 1968 in an impression of 500 copies.
d. New York, NY: Hill and Wang, 1968. [paperbound]
Note: Published April 12, 1968 in an impression of 2,000 copies.

E28   [cover blurb] Lucie-Smith, Edward (ed.). *The Liverpool Scene.*
Contents: AG prose blurb.
a. London, England: Donald Carroll, 1967.
b. Garden City, NY: Doubleday & Co., 1968.
c. Magnolia, MA: Peter Smith, 1968.

E29   [liner notes] *Malachi: Holy Music.* Verve, V-5024, New York, NY, 1967. 33 1/3 rpm, 12" Lp.
Contents: AG prose blurb on inside jacket cover.

E30   [poster] *Apocalypse Rose by Charles Plymell.* San Francisco, CA: 1967. 56.2 x 44.5 cm.
Contents: AG prose blurb and drawings.

1968

E31a   [flyer] *[C.O.P. Statement about LeRoi Jones Arrest].* New York, NY: Committee on Poetry, Jan. 6, 1968. Single sheet, 27.9 x 21.6 cm.
Contents: AG open letter.
E31b   [press release] *For Release 8 P.M. Saturday, January 31, 1968.* New York, NY: Committee on Poetry, Jan. 13, 1968. 27.9 x 21.6 cm.
Contents: AG open letter as above flyer.

E32   [classroom handouts] *Experimental College Course in Mantra Chants.* Buffalo, NY: SUNY at Buffalo, Feb. 1968. Each printed on a single sheet, 27.9 x 21.6 cm.
Contents: Texts and Translations of Hindu, Tibetan and Muslim Chants, compiled by AG.
Note: At least 3 different mimeograph printings of 75-100 copies each were made as follows:
a. First printing: EXPERIMENTAL COLLEGE COURSE IN MANTRA CHANTS--taught by I *ALLEN GINSBERG* I HINDU I [16 lines] I TIBETAN I [11 lines] I MUSLIM:
b. Second printing: EXPERIMENTAL COLLEGE COURSE IN MANTRA CHANTS--taught by I *ALLEN GINSBERG* I HINDU I [16 lines] I TIBETAN I [11 lines] I MUSLIM: I [3 lines up the right edge]
c. Third printing: EXPERIMENTAL COLLEGE COURSE in MANTRA CHANTS taught by ALLEN GINSBERG I HINDU I [18 lines] I TIBETAN I [11 lines] I MUSLIM: [2 lines]

E33   *Mantras as Taught by Allen Ginsberg*. Buffalo, NY: Incense Press, SUNYAB
LEMAR, March 8, 1968. Single sheet, 28.0 x 21.6 cm.
Contents: Texts and translations of 11 chants compiled by AG.

E34   [advertising flyer] Mead, Taylor. *On Amphetamine and in Europe, Vol. 3*. New
York, NY: Boss Books, ca. Summer 1968. Single sheet folded once to form 4
pages, 21.4 x 13.7 cm.
Contents: AG prose blurb, p. [3].
Note: At least 2 states of the flyer were printed, the first state gives the publisher's
address as Boss Books, Box 231, Village Station; the second state gives the
publisher's address as Box 370, Madison Square Station.

E35   [flyer] *Stony Brook Poets' Prophesy*. Stony Brook, NY: June 23, 1968. Single
sheet, 27.9 x 21.6 cm.
Contents: AG is one of 23 signers and is directly quoted.

Related item: [flyer] *Dear Friend,.* New York, NY: War Resisters League, July 9,
1968. Single sheet, 35.5 x 21.6 cm.
Contents: AG is one of 8 signers but he did not write the statement.

E36   [press release] *Regarding Conduct of Police*. Chicago, IL: Aug. 27, 1968. 2
single sheets, stapled once in upper left corner, 27.9 x 21.4 cm.
Contents: All is Poetry [prose]
Note: AG has noted that this was "Mimeo'd by John Berendt (or Richard Seaver?)
for use in Chicago 1968 convention."

E37   [flyer] *Youth International Party!* Chicago, IL: Lemar International Press, Aug.
27, 1968. Single sheet, very pale green (148), 27.8 x 21.5 cm.
Contents: 7 Mantras and Chants compiled by AG.

E38   [cover blurb] Crumb, Robert. *Head Comix*. New York, NY: Viking Press, 1968.
Contents: AG prose blurb.
Note: Published Oct. 7, 1968 in an impression of 1,000 hardbound copies and
9,000 paperbound copies.

E39   [press release] *Planet News*. San Francisco, CA: City Lights Books, Nov. 11,
1968. 2 single sheets, 27.9 x 21.6 cm.
Contents: Reproduction of AG manuscript prose, p. [2].
Note: Published Nov. 11, 1968 in an impression of 150 copies.

E40   [advertising flyer] *The Bhagavad Gita As It Is*. New York, NY: ISKCON, ca.
Nov. 25, 1968. Single sheet, 27.9 x 21.6 cm.
Contents: AG prose blurb.

E41   [publisher's catalog] *Festival of Two Worlds Spoleto, Italy*. New York, NY:
Spoleto Festival Recordings, ca. 1968. Single sheet, folds twice to 15.2 x 20.2
cm.
Contents: AG prose blurb.

E42   [cover blurb] Pickard, Tom. *High on the Walls*. London, England: Fulcrum
Press, 1968. [2nd edition]
Contents: AG prose blurb.
Note: The first edition of this book does not contain this blurb.

E43   [cover blurb] Solomon, Carl. *More Mishaps*. San Francisco, CA: Beach Books,
Texts & Documents/City Lights Books, 1968.
Contents: AG prose blurb.

E44 [press release] *Statement to: The National Commission on Marijuana and Drug Abuse, by Michael R. Aldrich.* Mill Valley, CA: Amorphia, ca. 1968. 8 single sheets.
Contents: AG prose, p. [12].

E45 [dress] *Uptown N.Y.* London, England: Poster Dress, ca. 1968. 90.0 x 63.5 cm.
Contents: Uptown N.Y. [poem]
Note: This was designed as a dress made of paper, rayon and nylon, probably available in small, medium and large sizes. The dimensions given above are for the medium size which is the only size the compiler has seen. Poster Dresses Ltd., were made in the United States by Nodine Products Corp. Issued in a plastic bag with advertising flyer and washing directions on flap.

1969

E46 [cover blurb] Cruz, Victor Hernandez. *Snaps.* New York, NY: Vintage Books, 1969.
Contents: Poesy News from Space Anxiety [blurb in the form of a poem]
Note: Published Feb. 1969 in an impression of 6,500 copies paperbound and an unknown number hardbound.

E47 [flyer] *Some Mantras.* New York, NY: New School, Feb. 20, 1969. Single sheet, 35.5 x 21.6 cm.
Contents: 8 Mantras and Chants compiled and translated by AG.
Note: Some copies are stapled in the upper left corner to 3 additional sheets of the same size containing the Great Prajna Paramita Sutra, this not produced by AG.

Related item: [flyer] *Dear WIN Reader,.* New York, NY: WIN, July 11, 1969. Single sheet, 27.9 x 21.6 cm.
Contents: AG is one of 4 signers but he did not write the statement.

E48 [press release] *Dear Mr. [David] Kennedy.* New York, NY: July 16, 1969. 2 single sheets, stapled in upper left corner, 27.9 x 21.6 cm.
Contents: AG letter to David Kennedy concerning Vietnam War Tax Resistance.
Note: These copies were made by AG and sent out for publication and information purposes. Some copies have another single page letter attached from Spencer Smith to Michael Tigar.

E49a [flyer] *[Autobiographic Precis].* New York, NY: Edmiston-Rothschild Mgt., Inc., ca. Sept. 1969. 2 single sheets, stapled in upper left corner, 27.9 x 21.6 cm.
Contents: AG prose.
E49b [flyer] *The Poetry Center.* New York, NY: Poetry Center of the 92nd Street YM-YWHA, Nov. 24, 1969. Single sheet, 27.9 x 21.5 cm.
Contents: Autobiographic Precis [prose] as above.

E50 [poster] *Allen Ginsberg Reading for the John Sinclair Defense Fund.* Detroit, MI: Wayne State Univ., Oct. 14, 1969. Single sheet, pale orange yellow (73), 43.1 x 27.9 cm.
Contents: Howl (excerpt).

E51 [flyer] *Release! Release! Release! Release! Release!* New York, NY: Poetry Project, Nov. 1969. Single sheet, 27.8 x 21.6 cm.
Contents: 8 Mantras and Chants compiled and translated by AG.

1970

E52   [college yearbook] Forshay, Ann (ed.). *Skidmore 1970.* Saratoga Springs, NY: Skidmore College, 1970.
Contents: [AG letter to Barbara D'Andrea], p. 128 — By Air: Albany-Baltimore, pp. 130-131.
Note: Published June 1970 in an impression of 1,900 copies.

E53   [college yearbook] Heitzman, Tim (ed.). *Klipsun 1970.* Bellingham, WA: Western Washington State College, ca. June 1970.
Contents: Friday the Thirteenth by Allan [sic] Ginsberg, pp. 140-142.

E54   [publisher's catalog] *Big Table Books.* Chicago, IL: Big Table Books, ca. Summer 1970. One gathering of 8 leaves, stapled twice on the left edge, 21.6 x 13.9 cm.
Contents: AG prose blurb on p. [3].

E55   [booklet] *Poets & Writers.* New York, NY: Poets and Writers, Sept. 1, 1970. Galen Williams, Director.
Contents: Kaddish [reproduction of a page of the manuscript on the front cover]
Note: This was an application form and description of the Poets & Writers program.

E56   [cover blurb] Lamantia, Philip. *The Blood of the Air.* San Francisco, CA: Four Seasons Foundation, 1970. [paperbound]
Contents: AG prose blurb.
Note: Published Sept. 15, 1970 in an impression of 2,997 copies. Fifty copies of the book were specially bound by the Schuberth Bookbindery but did not include AG's blurb.

E57   [flyer] *Second Annual LEMAR Communal Mantra Chant OM Orgy.* Buffalo, NY: LEMAR, Nov. 19, 1970. Single sheet, 27.8 x 21.6 cm.
Contents: 6 Mantras and Chants compiled by AG.

E58   [booklet] *Documents on Police Bureaucracy's Conspiracy against Human Rights of Opiate Addicts & Constitutional Rights of Medical Profession Causing Mass Breakdown of Urban Law & Order.* Compiled by Allen Ginsberg. 20 single sheets, stapled once in the upper left corner, 27.9 x 21.6 cm.
Contents: Bibliography assembled by AG.
Note: Published ca. Dec. 1970 in an impression of 300 copies and re-xeroxed at least once in an impression of several dozen copies by Gotham Book Mart in Jan. 1971. These sold for $1.50 each. The second printing has the additional facsimile holograph note on the front cover after AG's autograph "Xmas 1970 N.Y.C. 325 Copies", with additional notes on pp. 10-11, 14-15, 18.

E59   [cover blurb] Pritchard, N. H. *The Matrix Poems 1960-1970.* Garden City, NY: Doubleday & Co., 1970.
Contents: AG prose blurb.

E60a   [publisher's catalog] *Grove Press: Books and Films.* New York, NY: Grove Press, ca. 1970.
Contents: AG prose blurb p. 34.
E60b   [cover blurb] Sanders, Ed. *Shards of God.* New York, NY: Grove Press, 1970.
Contents: AG prose blurb as above but here on cover.

1971

E61 [open letter] *Dear Marijuana Research Association.* Mill Valley, CA: Amorphia, May 19, 1971. 2 single sheets, stapled once in upper left corner, 27.8 x 21.6 cm.
Contents: Grass Haiku [poem]
Note: This is Marijuana Research Association mailings #6 and 7 combined.

E62a [flyer] *Declaration of Independence for Dr. Timothy Leary, July 4, 1971.* San Francisco, CA: privately printed, July 4, 1971. Nine single sheets printed on one side only, stapled once in upper left corner, 27.9 x 21.6 cm.
Contents: Declaration of Independence for Dr. Timothy Leary [prose]
Note: Facsimile signature of AG at the end of the statement indicating his complete authorship, followed by list of 7 people giving approval.

E62b [press release] *Declaration of Independence for Dr. Timothy Leary, July 4, 1971.* San Francisco, CA: San Francisco Bay Area Prose Poets' Phalanx, July 14, 1971. Nine single sheets printed on one side only, stapled once in upper left corner, 27.9 x 21.6 cm.
Contents: As above.
Note: 30 signers are listed here at the end of the prose.

E62c [pamphlet] *Declaration of Independence for Dr. Timothy Leary, July 4, 1971.* San Francisco, CA: San Francisco Bay Area Prose Poets' Phalanx, July 1971. Single gathering of 4 leaves, pp. [1-8], 22.0 x 14.6 cm.
Contents: As above.
Note: Copies seen in 2 different colors: greenish white (153) and grayish purplish pink (253). Published late July [after July 14] 1971 in an impression of 200-250 copies. Photocopies of this were made on white paper ca. April 4, 1973 and attached to Leary appeal material.

E63 [postcard] *Milarepa Taste.* Detroit, MI: Alternative Press, 1971. Single sheet, 16.3 x 10.0 cm. Moderate orange yellow (71) wove paper unwatermarked.
Contents: Milarepa Taste.
Note: Published July 1971 in an impression of 500 copies.

E64a [petition and press release]. *The Living Theatre.* San Francisco, CA: Committee on Poetry, July 23, 1971. 27.9 x 21.6 cm. 3 single sheets printed on one side only, ll. [1] 1-2, stapled once in the upper left corner.
Contents: Undersigned Fellow Artist statement, p. [i] — On Living Theater Mass [prose], pp. [1-2].
Note: Some of the petition page of the above were issued without the press release attached.

E64b [petition] *The Living Theatre.* New York, NY: Paradise Defense Fund, July 23, 1971. Single sheet printed on one side only, brilliant orange yellow (67), 27.9 x 21.7 cm.
Contents: Undersigned Fellow Artist statement, slightly revised from the first petition above.
Note: Issued shortly after July 23, 1971.

E64c [petition] *The Living Theatre.* Mill Valley, CA: Amorphia, July 23, 1971. Single sheet printed on one side only, 35.5 x 21.6 cm.
Contents: As above petition, b.

E64d [petition] *The Living Theatre.*
Note: As item c above, but here printed on 27.9 x 21.6 cm. paper.

E64e [press release] *On Living Theater Mass Imprisonment in Brazil.* New York, NY: July 23, 1971. 27.9 x 21.6 cm. Two single sheets printed on one side only, ll. 1-2, stapled once in upper left corner.
Contents: On Living Theater Mass [prose as above section a]

E64f [open letter] *Dear Mr.* San Francisco, CA: Bay Area Poets' Phalanx, July 30, 1971. 27.9 x 21.6 cm. Two sheets printed on one side only, ll [1]-2, stapled once in upper left corner.
Contents: Prose note by AG.

E64g [press release] *On Living Theatre Mass-Imprisonment in Brazil.* San Francisco, CA: Bay Area Poet's Phalanx, July 30, 1971. 27.9 x 21.6 cm. Two sheets printed on one side only, pp. [1-2], stapled once in upper left corner.
Contents: Revised form of "On Living Theater Mass".
Note: Also printed as 2 sides of single sheet flyer with additional marginal note "Om Ah Hum!" by AG on p. 1.

E64h [press release] *The Living Theatre.* Mill Valley, CA: Amorphia, after July 30, 1971. 35.5 x 21.6 cm. Single sheet printed on one side only.
Contents: As item b above.

E64i [open letter] *Dear Democratic Theater Lovers.* New York, NY: Paradise Defense Fund, Aug. 2, 1971. 27.9 x 21.6 cm. Single sheet printed on both sides, pp. [1-2]. *Note:* Page 2 is a photocopy of an article from the *San Francisco Chronicle* (July 30, 1971) which reprints a poem by AG.
Contents: Letter to Democratic Theater Lovers.

E64j [petition] *The Living Theatre.* Mill Valley, CA: Amorphia, July 23, 1971. 27.9 x 21.6 cm. Single page printed on both sides, pp. [1-2].
Contents: As item i above with 5 corrections made in facsimile holograph.

E64k [flyer] *Statement by Julian Beck Judith Malina.* New York, NY: Aug. 5, 1971. 21.7 x 35.6 cm. Single sheet printed on one side only.
Contents: Prose notes and drawing by AG.

E64l [flyer] *Bulletin.* New York, NY: Paradise Defense Fund, Aug. 17, 1971. 28.0 x 21.6 cm. Single sheet printed on one side only.
Contents: Living Theatre to be Charged [prose] and drawings by AG.

E65 [advertising flyer] *Howl.* San Francisco, CA: Grabhorn-Hoyem, 1971. Single sheet folded once to form 4 pages, 28.4 x 22.3 cm.
Contents: Note: 1971 Printing Howl & The Names [prose], p. [3]
Note: Published Aug. 1971 in an unknown number of copies.

E66 [press release] *Minzey Marijuana Sacrament Trial.* Berkeley, CA: Committee on Religious Cannabis, ca. Aug. 1971. 21 single sheets, stapled once in upper left corner, 27.9 x 21.6 cm.
Contents: [letter from AG to the Court]

E67 [film catalog] *Film-Makers' Cooperative Catalogue, no. 5.* New York, NY: Film-Makers' Cooperative, 1971.
Contents: AG prose blurb, p. 25.
Note: Reprinted in catalogue, no. 6 (1975), p. 19.

E68 [cover blurb] Holst, Spencer. *The Language of Cats.*
Contents: AG prose blurb.
a. New York, NY: McCall Pub., 1971. [hardbound]
b. New York, NY: Avon, 1973. [paperbound]

E69 [cover blurb] McClure, Michael. *The Adept.* New York, NY: Delacorte Press, 1971.
Contents: AG prose blurb.

1972

E70 [high school yearbook] Rothe, Laurie and Trauberman, Jeffrey (eds.). *Embers.* Wayne, NJ: Wayne Valley Senior High School, 1972.
Contents: The World's an Illusion [poem], p. 134.
Note: Published June 1972 in an impression of 800 copies.

E71 [musical setting] Feliciano, Richard. *Two Hymns to Howl by, for equal voices.* Boston, MA: E. C. Schirmer Music Co., 1972. [E.C.S. Choral Music No. 2806]
Contents: Sunflower Sutra [excerpts]

E72   [cover blurb] Harris, Marguerite. *A Reconciling of Rivers.* New York, NY: El Corno Emplumado, 1972.
Contents: AG prose blurb.

E73   [cover blurb] Holst, Spencer. *Spencer Holst Stories.* New York, NY: Horizon Press, 1972.
Contents: AG prose blurb.

E74   [cover blurb] Mottram, Eric. *Allen Ginsberg in the Sixties.* Brighton, England/Seattle, WA: Unicorn Bookshop, 1972.
Contents: AG prose blurb.

1973

E75   [musical setting] Living Music (group). *To Allen Ginsberg.* RCA, Lp No. DPSL 10574, Rome, Italy, March 1973. Produced by Roberto Marsala. 33 1/3 rpm, 12" stereo.
Contents: Howl — Song — Lysergic Acid
Note: Accompanied by a 12 page booklet which includes the above poems and their Italian translations by F. Pivano.

E76a   [book distributor's catalog] *Book People.* Berkeley, CA: Book People, Spring 1973.
Contents: AG prose blurbs, pp. 54, 56, and 76.
E76b   [book distributor's catalog] *Book People's Complete Catalogue.* Berkeley, CA: Book People, Spring 1973.
Contents: AG prose blurb from p. 76 above, here printed on page 130.

E77   [poster] *Allen Ginsberg.* Hanover, NH: Dartmouth College, March 29, 1973. Single sheet, 45.7 x 60.9 cm.
Contents: On Burrough's Work.

E78   [flyer] *Appeal Against Further Trial & Persecution of Dr. Timothy Leary.* New York, NY: April 4, 1973. Single sheet, 27.9 x 21.6 cm.
Contents: Appeal Against Further Trial & Persecution of Dr. Timothy Leary [prose].

Related item: [flyer] *An Appeal for Dr. Timothy Leary's Liberty.* Cayucos, CA: Leary House, April 7, 1973.
Note: AG is one of 5 signers but he did not write the statement.

E79   [flyer] *Mock-Sestina.* New York, NY: Rallying Point Magazine, ca. May 16, 1973. Single sheet, 27.9 x 21.6 cm.
Contents: Mock-Sestina [poem]

E80   [concert handout] *AH.* London, England: Shaw Theatre, July 22, 1973. 20.3 x 20.3 cm. 5 sheets printed on both sides, distributed in a 20.7 x 20.7 cm. white envelope with a window cut in it so that AG's hand shows through.
Contents: Since Visiting London in 1967 [prose], p. [3] — AH, Some Mantras [5 mantras], p. [5] — On Neal Cassidy's [sic] Ashes, p. [7] — Washington D.C. Indochina Peace Mobilization, p. [7] — Returning to the Country for a Brief Visit — CIA Dope Calypso, p. [9].

E81   [open letter] *To Whom It May Concern. On Behalf of Political Poet Abbie Hoffman Reported Arrested With.* New York, NY: Aug. 29, 1973. 4 single pages, 27.9 x 21.6 cm.
Contents: AG open letter.

E82   [program] *The Writer's Forum.* Brockport, NY: SUNY at Brockport, Oct. 19, 1973. Single moderate purple (223) sheet folded once to form 4 pages, 25.4 x 19.0 cm.
Contents: Love Poem on Theme by Whitman, p. [3].
Note: Published Oct. 19, 1973 in an impression of 200-300 copies.

E83   [cover blurb] Cruz, Victor Hernandez. *Mainland.* New York, NY: Random House, 1973.
Contents: AG prose blurb.

E84   [playscript] *Kaddish by Allen Ginsberg.* New York, NY: Charles R. Rothschild Productions Inc., 1973. 78 single leaves, 29.3 x 23.0 cm. Issued in a black simulated leather folder with 2 brass screws on the left side and across the front cover is the title, etc. in gold.
Contents: Kaddish.

E85   [cover blurb] Kerouac, Jack. *Lonesome Traveler.* New York, NY: Ballantine Books, 1973.
Contents: AG prose blurb reprinted here from the dedication page to *Howl and other poems.*

1974

E86   [flyer] *David Gitin.* Madison, WI: ca. Jan. 1974. Single cream sheet folded once to 21.5 x 10.1 cm. to form 4 pages.
Contents: AG prose blurb, p. [3].

E87   [open letter] *Dear Friend.* New York, NY: Feb. 25, 1974. 2 single sheets, 27.9 x 21.6 cm.
Contents: AG open letter.

E88   [publicity flyer] *Michael Horovitz.* Hampden Highlands, ME: Tom Bailey, 1974. Single sheet, 21.7 x 35.6 cm.
Contents: AG prose blurb.
Note: Published ca. March 1974.

E89   [cover blurb] Norse, Harold. *Hotel Nirvana.* San Francisco, CA: City Lights, 1974.
Contents: AG prose blurb.
Note: Published March 1974 in an impression of 3,000 copies.

E90   [press release] *Dan Berrigan Defended on Charges of Anti-Semitism.* New York, NY: Liberation, March 11, 1974. 3 single leaves, 27.9 x 21.6 cm. stapled once in upper left corner.
Contents: AG prose.

E91   [reproduced manuscript] *Om Ah Hum: 44 Temporary Questions on Dr. Leary.* March 18, 1974. 3 single sheets, stapled once in upper left corner, 27.9 x 21.6 cm.
Contents: Om Ah Hum: 44 Temporary Questions of Dr. Leary.
Note: Published ca. March 18, 1974 and reprinted at least once in Aug. 1974. Some copies were re-photocopied from other copies and these are identified by the faint and washed out look of the heavily crossed out word in the title on p. 1, and the date on page 3 of 18 March 1974 has been crossed out in the photocopy and the new date Aug added.

E92a [poster] *In Concert: Bhagavan Das.* Kansas City, MO: Univ. of Missouri at Kansas City, March 25, 1974. Single light yellow green (119) sheet, 27.8 x 43.1 cm.
Contents: AG prose blurb.

E92b [poster] *In Concert.* Portland, OR: Center for Truth, [Spring] 1974. Single sheet, 25.3 x 37.9 cm.
Contents: AG prose blurb as above and his Autobiographic Precis.
Note: The same artwork for this poster was used in a series of concerts given during this period by AG & Bhagavan Das.

E93 [press release] *Renowned Poet to Speak at Massasoit.* Brockton, MA: Massasoit Community College, March 27, 1974. 4 single sheets, stapled once in upper left corner, 27.9 x 21.7 cm.
Contents: America, pp. [3-4].

E94a [press release] *Acceptance Speech for the National Book Award.* New York, NY: April 17, 1974. 2 single sheets, 27.9 x 21.6 cm.
Contents: Poem book *Fall of America* is time capsule [prose].
Note: A note in Peter Orlovsky's handwriting has been found which states that 16 copies of this packet containing a press release, photo of the 6 NBA recipients and another text of speech were issued.

E94b [acceptance speech] *"The Fall of America" Wins a Prize.* April 18, 1974. Single sheet, 35.6 x 21.6 cm.
Contents: As above.
Note: Probably passed out at the National Book Awards Presentations which AG was unable to attend.

E95 [flyer] *A 19-Year Old Girl and Poet Allen Ginsberg Talk About 'Speed'.* Phoenix, AZ: Do It Now Foundation, ca. June 28, 1974. Single very light greenish blue (171) sheet which folds twice to 9.4 x 21.6 cm.
Contents: Let's Issue a General Declaration [prose].

E96 [reading handout] *Sunflower Sutra / From Kaddish / A Vow.* San Francisco, CA: Lone Mountain College, Nov. 1974. Three sections of 7, 4 & 2 sheets, mimeographed on one side only, each section individually stapled once in upper left corner, 27.8 x 21.6 cm.
Contents: Sunflower Sutra — America — Howl (excerpt) — Kaddish (excerpt) — Scribble — Dream Record: June 8, 1955 — A Vow — Imaginary Universes — Ecologue.

E97 [publisher's catalog] *The Coldspring Journal; Letters... : Press, etc.* Cherry Valley, NY: Cherry Valley Editions, ca. Nov. 4, 1974.
Contents: AG prose blurb, p. [2, 8].

E98 [reading handout] *Howl for Carl Solomon, I Allen Ginsberg.* Dallas, TX: Southern Methodist Univ., Dec. 4, 1974. 3 single sheets, stapled once in upper left corner, 35.6 x 21.6 cm.
Contents: Howl — A Supermarket in California — Sunflower Sutra — America — In the Baggage Room at Greyhound.

E99 [post card] *New York Blues by Allen Ginsberg.* Austin, TX: Cold Mountain Press, 1974. Single light bluish gray (190) sheet, 12.6 x 16.4 cm.
Contents: New York Blues.
Note: Available singley or in a portfolio of 10 different postcards.

E100 [musical setting] Schäffer, Boguslaw. *Howl.* Warsaw, Poland: Polskie Wydawnictwo Muzyczne, 1974.
Contents: Howl [excerpts].

1975

E101 [legal brief] *Affidavit of Allen Ginsberg.* New York, NY: Jan. 1975. 8 single
sheets, stapled once in the upper left corner, 28.0 x 21.6 cm.
Contents: [prose statement in defense of Timothy Leary written by a lawyer with
AG's assistance]

E102 [chronology] *Rough Chronology Timothy Leary.* New York, NY: ca. Jan. 8,
1975. 10 single leaves, stapled once in the upper left corner, 27.9 x 21.6 cm.
Contents: Detailed chronology of Leary case, compiled by AG.
Note: Possibly this was meant to go with the 'Affidavit of Allen Ginsberg' from the
same time, possibly these were only in-house notes and never reproduced in
quantity.

E103 [college catalog] *Naropa Institute: Degree & Certificate Programs, [Winter/Spring
1976].* Boulder, CO: Naropa Institute, ca. Sept. 1975.
Contents: Prose course descriptions written by AG: W311, pp. 30-31; W312, p.
31.

E104 [liner notes] *Hard Times in the Country: Happy and Artie Traum.* Rounder
Records, No. 3007, Somerville, MA: 1975. 33 1/3 rpm, 12" Lp.
Contents: Footstomping Smokestacks [prose]

E105 [cover blurb] Micheline, Jack. *Yellow Horn.* San Francisco, CA: Golden
Mountain Press, 1975.
Contents: AG prose blurb.

E106 [cover blurb] Sackheim, Eric (ed.). *The Blues Line.* New York, NY: Schirmer
Books, 1975. [paperbound]
Contents: AG prose blurb.
Note: The hardbound edition does not have a blurb by AG.

E107 [book] Whittemore, Reed. *William Carlos Williams, Poet from Jersey.* Boston,
MA: Houghton Mifflin Co., 1975.
Contents: Short excerpts from letters to William Carlos Williams (included here
instead of B section because there are no complete sentences, only phrases), pp.
180, 322, 325.

1976

E108a [liner notes] *Desire: Bob Dylan.* CBS Records, CBS 86003, New York, NY,
released Jan. 16, 1976. 33 1/3 rpm, 12" Lp stereo.
Contents: AG prose.
E108b [songbook] Dylan, Bob. *Desire.* New York, NY: Ram's Horn Music, sold by
Warner Brothers Pub., 1976.
Contents: As above liner notes.

E109 [rare book catalog] *Phoenix Bookshop, catalog no. 129.* New York, NY: Feb.-
March 1976.
Contents: AG prose, item #162.

E110 [flyer] *Spencer Holst.* New York, NY: Carnegie Recital Hall, March 1976. Single
sheet, 27.9 x 21.7 cm.
Contents: AG prose blurb.

E111 [program] *Poetry Readings.* Brooklyn, NY: Brooklyn Museum and the Brooklyn
Arts & Culture Association, April 14, 1976. Single sheet, folded once to 21.6 x
17.8 cm.
Contents: Gospel Noble Truths.

E112 [publisher's flyer] *New From Penmaen Press.* Lincoln, MA: Penmaen Press, May 1976. Single sheet, 46.6 x 30.4 cm.
Contents: Reproduction of AG's drawing and prose description of the poem "Howl".

E113 [press release] *Marijuana Minister Serving Thirteen Years.* San Diego, CA: Committee on Religious Cannabis, ca. June 20, 1976. 11 single leaves, stapled once in the upper left corner, 27.9 x 21.7 cm.
Contents: AG letter to the Court, ll. [8-9].

E114 [college catalog] *Naropa Institute. Summer 1976.* Boulder, CO: Naropa Institute, ca. June 22 1976.
Contents: Prose course descriptions written by AG: W311a, W312a, p. 8.

E115 [post card] *Returning to the Country for a Brief Visit.* California, PA: Unspeakable Visions of the Individual, 1976. Single sheet, 8.0 x 13.8 cm.
Contents: Returning to the Country for a Brief Visit.
Note: Published July or early Aug. 1976 in an impression of 1,000 copies and sold for 10¢ each.

E116 [departmental ballot] *American Academy & Institute of Arts and Letters, Department of Literature.* New York, NY: 1977 ballot mailed Oct. 11, 1976, approx. 120 copies.
Contents: AG prose citation for the nomination of W. S. Burroughs.

E117 [cover blurb] Micheline, Jack. *North of Manhattan.* South San Francisco, CA: Manroot, 1976. [paperbound]
Contents: AG prose blurb.
Note: Published Nov. 12, 1976 in an impression of 1,000 copies. Also available in a limited edition of 200 copies which do not contain the blurb by AG.

1977

E118 [flyer] *Dear Friends.* Bearsville, NY: Culhane-McGivern Defense League, ca. March 18, 1977. Single sheet, 32.5 x 21.6 cm.
Contents: AG prose.

E119 [flyer] *On Mindfulness.* Washington, DC: Washington Dharmadattu, ca. April 21, 1977. Single sheet, 27.9 x 21.6 cm.
Contents: Cabin in the Rockies — Doing Nothing's a Sober Way — Five Minutes Silent Practice — This Practice is Called.

E120 [auction catalog] *Fine Modern First Editions, Part 2.* New York, NY: Sotheby Parke Bernet Inc., 1977. [The collection of Jonathan Goodwin] Sale 4035 (auction Oct. 25, 1977). *Note:* The regular issue was bound in wrappers and a specially bound edition of 35 copies was also published.
Contents: Inscriptions, pp. [25-26].

E121 [publisher's catalog] *New Titles Spring-Summer 1978.* Santa Barbara, CA: Black Sparrow Press, Dec. 1977.
Contents: AG prose blurb on the back cover.
Note: Published ca. Dec. 1977-Jan. 1978 in an impression of 3,000-4,000 copies.

E122 [publisher's catalog] *Pomegranate Press.* North Cambridge, MA: Pomegranate Press, ca. Dec. 1977.
Contents: Tear Gas Rag, p. [2].

E123 [poster] *Poetry Project Saint Marks Church.* New York, NY: Dec. 21, 1977. Single sheet, 27.9 x 21.6 cm.
Contents: Text of poster by Peter Orlovsky and AG [for reading by Peter Orlovsky and Herbert Huncke].

E124 [college catalog] *Naropa Institute: Winter-Spring 1978.* Boulder, CO: Naropa Institute, Dec. 22, 1977.
Contents: Prose course descriptions written by AG: W248, p. 55.

E125a [publisher's catalog] *And/Or Press, Publishing Ideas in Transition, 1977 Catalog.* Berkeley, CA: And/Or Press, 1977.
Contents: AG prose blurb, p. [16].
E125b [cover blurb] Stafford, Peter. *Psychedelics Encyclopedia.* Berkeley, CA: And/Or Press, 1977.
Contents: AG prose blurb as above, but here on back cover.

E126 [rare book catalog] *The Beat Generation and Other Avant-Garde Writers: Anacapa Books catalog 3.* Santa Barbara, CA: Anacapa Books, 1977.
Contents: AG prose and inscriptions in items #496, 501, 504, 514, 534, 540, 553.

E127 [publisher's catalog] *Creative Arts Book Co. Catalogue 1977-78.* Berkeley, CA: Creative Arts, 1977. 22.8 x 10.2 cm.
Contents: [letter to Neal Cassady], p. 9.

E128 [cover blurb] Plymell, Charles. *Rod McKuen Reads in Memory of My Father.* Cherry Valley, NY: Cherry Valley Editions, 1977.
Contents: AG prose blurb, p. [14].

E129a [post card] *The Rune.* New York, NY: Hard Press, 1977. Single pale orange yellow (73) sheet, 14.7 x 11.2 cm.
Contents: The Rune.
Note: A variation reproduces the first line of the poem twice, probably an early mistake corrected by the printer, otherwise identical in format but on a smaller 14.0 x 10.7 cm. piece of card stock.
E129b New York, NY: Hardly Press, 1978. 13.9 x 10.6 cm. White card stock.
E129c New York, NY: Hard Press, 1978. 13.9 x 10.6 cm. [typeset poem] White card stock.
E129d New York, NY: Hard Press, 1978. 13.9 x 10.6 cm. [holograph reproduction] White card stock.

1978

E130 [rare book catalog] *Phoenix Book Shop, catalog 145, Modern Firsts.* New York, NY: Phoenix Book Shop, Jan. 1978.
Contents: AG inscription in item #398.

E131 [advertising post card] *The Visionary Poetics of Allen Ginsberg.* Santa Barbara, CA: Ross-Erikson Publishers, ca. Jan. 12, 1978. Single sheet, 15.2 x 10.1 cm.
Contents: AG prose.

E132 [flyer] *P.A.C.E. Advisory Board Meeting.* New York, NY: Prisoners' Accelerated Creative Exposure, ca. Jan. 17, 1978. Single sheet, 27.9 x 21.6 cm.
Contents: AG prose included in their letterhead.

E133 [flyer] *Dear:* New York, NY: Feb. 11, 1978. Single sheet, 27.9 x 21.6 cm.
Contents: [open letter].
Note: Attached to a 2 page letter from Basil Bunting and sent out soliciting funds for him.

E134a [advertising flyer] *Allen Ginsberg & Lynd Ward.* Lincoln, MA: Penmaen Press, ca. March 1978. Single yellowish white (92) sheet, folds once to 25.4 x 17.8 cm.
Contents: Reproduction of "Moloch" broadsides.
Note: Published Spring 1978 in an impression of ca. 900-1,000 copies.

E134b [advertising flyer] *What is Penmaen Press?* Lincoln, MA: Penmaen Press, Spring 1979.
Contents: As above.
Note: Published ca. March 1979 in an impression of 3,000-4,000 copies.

E135 [auction catalog] *Fine Modern First Editions, Part 3.* New York, NY: Sotheby Parke Bernet Inc., 1978. [The collection of Jonathan Goodwin] Sale 4109B (auction April 12, 1978). *Note:* The regular issue was bound in wrappers and a specially bound edition of 35 copies was also published.
Contents: Inscriptions, items #678, 679, 755.

E136 [open letter] *Dear Dharma Brothers & Sisters.* New York, NY: May 14, 1978. Single sheet, 27.9 x 21.6 cm.
Contents: [open letter from AG].

E137 [pamphlet] *Visual Dharma Seminar.* Boulder, CO: Naropa Institute, July 9-14, 1978. 48 pages, 27.9 x 21.5 cm.
Contents: Transcript of seminar gives AG comments, pp. 143-144.

E138a [cover blurb] Orlovsky, Peter. *Clean Asshole Poems and Smiling Vegetable Songs.* San Francisco, CA: City Lights Books, 1978.
Contents: AG prose blurb.
Note: Published Nov. 1978 in an impression of 3,200 copies of which 3,000 are paperbound and 200 are hardbound. The paperbound was reprinted in May 1980 in an impression of 3,000 additional copies.

E138b [cover blurb] Orlovsky, Peter. *Clean Asshole Poems and Smiling Vegetable Songs.* Orono, ME: Northern Lights, 1993.
Contents: AG prose blurb as above.

E139 [departmental ballot] *American Academy & Institute of Arts and Letters, Department of Literature.* New York, NY: 1979 ballot mailed Nov. 13, 1978, approx. 120 copies.
Contents: AG prose citation for the nomination of W. S. Burroughs as in the 1977 ballot, and prose citation for the nomination of Gary Snyder.

E140 [book distributor's catalog] *Best of the Independent Presses, Fall 1978.* Nashville, TN: Ingram Book Co., Nov. 20, 1978.
Contents: AG prose blurbs, pp. 16, 69.

E141 [college catalog] *Naropa Institute: Winter-Spring 1979.* Boulder, CO: Naropa Institute, Dec. 1978.
Contents: Prose course descriptions written by AG: W329, p. 22; W350, p. 23.

E142 [cover blurb] Bunting, Basil. *Collected Poems.* Oxford, England: Oxford University Press, 1978.
Contents: AG prose blurb.

Related item: [cover blurb] Resnick, Marcia. *Re-Visions.* Toronto, Canada: Coach House Press, 1978.
Contents: AG prose blurb [actually this is a spoof and not really by AG]

1979

E143 [cover blurb] Pélieu-Washburn, Claude. *Trains de Nuit.* Paris, France: Le
Cherche Midi Editeur, 1979.
Contents: AG prose blurb.
Note: Published April 1979.

E144 [publisher's catalog] *Cherry Valley Editions Catalog.* Cherry Valley, NY: Cherry
Valley Editions, ca. 1979.
Contents: AG prose blurb, p. 19.
Note: Published ca. May 22, 1979, printed with at least two different cover colors,
cream and gray.

E145 [cover blurb] Rumaker, Michael. *A Day and a Night at the Baths.* Bolinas, CA:
Grey Fox Press, 1979.
Contents: AG prose blurb.
Note: Published Oct. 1979 in a regular edition and a limited signed edition; a copy
has been examined which was signed and dated by the author on Aug. 29, 1979,
however a publisher's catalogue estimates the publication date as Oct. 1979.

E146 [departmental ballot] *American Academy & Institute of Arts and Letters,
Department of Literature.* New York, NY: 1980 ballot mailed Oct. 10, 1979,
approx. 120 copies.
Contents: AG prose citation for the nomination of W. S. Burroughs as in the 1977
ballot, and prose citation for the nomination of Gary Snyder on pp. 5, 22.

E147 [college catalog] *Naropa Institute: Winter-Spring 1980.* Boulder, CO: Naropa
Institute, Dec. 1979.
Contents: Prose course descriptions written by AG: W343, p. 27; W350, p. 28;
W334b, p. 29.

E148 [calendar] *Cody's Calendar of Contemporary Poets.* Soldofsky, Alan (ed.).
Berkeley, CA: Cody's Books, Inc., 1979.
Contents: Nagasaki Day Peace Protest [poem], printed opposite the August
calendar.

E149 [flyer] *Fried Shoes Cooked Diamonds.* Santhià, Italy: Carmina Cinematografica
S.R.L., ca. 1979. Single sheet folded twice to 16.5 x 22.5 cm.
Contents: Reproduction of holograph letter and Italian translation.

E150 [cover blurb] Horovitz, Michael. *Growing Up.* London, England: Allison &
Busby, 1979.
Contents: AG prose blurb.
Note: Of the first edition, 50 are signed and numbered and have an extra original
hand-drawn picture-poem by the author.

E151 [cover blurb] Pickard, Tom. *Hero Dust.* London, England: Allison and Busby,
1979.
Contents: AG prose blurb.

E152 [publisher's catalog] *Second Coming Press Catalog.* San Francisco, CA: 1979.
Contents: AG prose blurb, p. 15.

1980

E153 [flyer] *Verses Written for Student Anti Draft Rally 1980.* Boulder, CO: Boulder
Street Poets, ca. March 15, 1980. Single sheet, 27.8 x 21.6 cm.
Contents: Verses Written for Student Anti Draft Rally 1980.

E154 [auction catalog] *20th Century Literature.* New York, NY: Swann Galleries, 1980. Sale 1175 (auction March 20, 1980).
Contents: Inscription, item #156, p. 14.

E155 [publisher's catalog] *Cherry Valley Editions Catalog.* Cherry Valley, NY: Cherry Valley Editions, ca. April 1980.
Contents: AG prose blurbs, pp. 1, 5.
Note: Published ca. April 1980 in an impression of 500 copies.

E156 [flyer] *Allen Ginsberg, Lecture Abstract.* Minneapolis, MN: Walker Art Center, April 7, 1980. 8 single sheets, stapled once in the upper left corner, 27.9 x 21.6 cm.
Contents: Mediation and Poetics [poem], p. i — Autobiographic Precis [prose], pp. 1-3 — Mind Breaths, pp. [7] 2-4.
Note: Published April 7, 1980 in an impression of 350 copies.

E157 [college catalog] *Naropa Institute: Summer 1980; Winter-Spring 1981.* Boulder, CO: Naropa Institute, 1980.
Contents: Prose course description written by AG: W350, p. 19.

E158 [brochure] *Ten Years in North America.* [Boulder, CO: Naropa Institute] July 1, 1980. 24 pages, 39.2 x 28.6 cm.
Contents: Trans World Air [by Chögyam Trungpa and translated by AG], p. 12.
Note: Commemorative publication for the 10th anniversary of Trungpa's coming to America.

E159 [departmental ballot] *American Academy & Institute of Arts and Letters, Department of Literature.* New York, NY: 1981 ballot mailed Oct. 15, 1980, approx. 120 copies.
Contents: AG prose citation for the nomination of W. S. Burroughs, p. 7.

E160 [program] *Poets & Writers Inc., Tenth Birthday Party, Roseland, October 22, 1980.* New York, NY: Poets & Writers, Inc., 1980.
Contents: Composed for Poets & Writers: Fourth Floor, Dawn, Up All Night Writing Letters [poem], p. 19.
Note: Published Oct. 22, 1980 in an impression of 3,000 copies.

E161 [cover blurb] Antler. *Factory.* San Francisco, CA: City Lights Books, 1980.
Contents: AG prose blurb.
Note: Published Dec. 1980 in an impression of 2,790 paperbound copies and 210 hardbound copies.

E162 [flyer] *Dear.* New York, NY: Committee on Poetry, Inc., Dec. 25, 1980. Single sheet, 27.9 x 21.6 cm.
Contents: Open letter asking for help for Basil Bunting.

E163a [rare book catalog] *Bulletin,* no. 1002. Berkeley, CA: Anacapa Books, ca. late Dec. 1980.
Contents: Inscription, item #399.
Note: Published lated Dec. 1980 in an impression of 1,000 copies.
E163b [rare book catalog] *Anacapa Books, Modern Literature,* no. 14. Berkeley, CA: Anacapa Books, ca. mid-June 1981.
Contents: As above, here item #303.
Note: Published mid-June 1981 in an impression of 1,000 copies.

E164 [liner notes] *Fried Shoes, Cooked Diamonds.* Mystic Fire Video, VHS-B109, New York, NY, 1980. Produced by Carmina Cinematografica S.R.L. Cassette.
Contents: AG prose blurb on back cover of the cassette case.

E165 [flyer] *I'll Be Singing.* New York, NY: The Other End Club, ca. 1980. Single sheet, 28.0 x 21.6 cm.
Contents: Flyer completely in AG's facsimile holograph.

E166 [publication flyers and catalogs] *Zero Magazine.* Los Angeles, CA: Zero Press, ca. 1980.
Contents: AG prose blurb.
a. 28.0 x 21.6 cm. *Zero.* White flyer, folded once to this size, in black, gray and red. AG quoted on top of pp. 2-3.
b. 9.0 x 16.0 cm. *Zero.* White envelope printed in black and red, the inside flap contains the AG quote.
c. 20.5 x 15.0 cm. *Zero.* White flyer, folded twice to this size, printed in black and gray. AG quoted on back flap.
d. 19.7 x 16.3 cm. *Unity Press, Spring/Summer 1980, Complete Catalog.* 32 p. printed in black and red. AG quote on p. 12.
e. 20.3 x 15.0 cm. *Zero.* White flyer, folded twice to this size, printed in black. AG quote on back flap.

1981

E167 [school newspaper pamphlet] *Naropa Institute Update,* [ca. Jan. 1, 1981] Winter 1981.
Contents: Allen Ginsberg Addresses Graduates [prose], pp. 3-4.

E168 [cover blurb] *Meat.* San Francisco, CA: Gay Sunshine Press, 1981.
Contents: Everybody Loves the First Glimpse of Naked Love [poem].
Note: Published Jan. 2, 1981 in an impression of 10,000 copies and reprinted in July 1981 and again in Sept. 1983 and identified as such.

E169a [flyer/open letter] *To Whom It May Concern.* New York, NY: ca. Jan. 13, 1981. Single sheet, 27.9 x 21.6 cm.
Contents: [AG letter in support of Amiri Baraka]
E169b [press release] *Amiri Baraka's Jail Sentence.* New York, NY: People's Defense Committee, ca. April 22, 1981. 11 single sheets, stapled once in upper left corner, 27.9 x 21.6 cm.
Contents: Letter to whom it may concern in support of Amiri Baraka, p. [2]; and letter 'Dear Judge Bernard Fried' pp. [6-7] as mentioned later.

E170 [classroom handout] *Bericht über das Erste Hamburger Haiku-Treffen am 20. Januar 1981.* Hamburg, W. Germany: Sabine Sommerkamp, 1981. 10 pages.
Contents: Good God I Got High Bloodpressure Answering [poem], p. 7.

E171 [flyer/open letter] *Dear.* New York, NY: Jan. 27, 1981. Single sheet, 27.9 x 21.6 cm.
Contents: letter from AG and Peter Orlovsky concerning David Gascoyne.

E172 [flyer/open letter] *Dear Mr. Freund.* New York, NY: Feb. 16, 1981. 2 single sheets, stapled once in the upper left corner, 27.9 x 21.6 cm.
Contents: letter to Mr. Freund in support of Amiri Baraka.

Related item a: [flyer/open letter] *Dear Judge Bernard Fried.* New York, NY: Poetry Project, Feb. 25, 1981. 2 single sheets, stapled once in the upper left corner, 27.9 x 21.6 cm.
Contents: AG is one of 5 signers but he did not write the statement.
Related item b: [press release] *Amiri Baraka's Jail Sentence.* New York, NY: People's Defense Committee, ca. April 22, 1981. 11 single sheets, stapled once in upper left corner, 27.9 x 21.6 cm.
Contents: Letter to whom it may concern in support of Amiri Baraka, p. [2]; and letter 'Dear Judge Bernard Fried' pp. [6-7] as mentioned earlier.

E173 [prose blurb] Washington, Jerome. *A Bright Spot in the Yard.* Trumansburg, NY: The Crossing Press, 1981. [paperbound]
Contents: AG prose blurb.
Note: Published ca. March 1981 in an impression of 2,500 copies. AG's blurb does not appear on the hardbound issue.

E174 [publisher's catalog] *City Lights Books, Four Seasons Foundation, Grey Fox Press: Spring-Summer 1981.* Eugene, OR: Subterranean Co., 1981.
Contents: AG prose blurb, p. [7].

E175 [publisher's catalog] *Loose Blätter Presse, Spring 1981.* Hamburg, W. Germany: Loose Blätter Presse, 1981. Single light gray (264) sheet, folds twice to 21.5 x 10.0 cm.
Contents: AG drawing on the front cover.

E176 [press release packet] *Tom Pickard.* New York, NY: Spring 1981. 7 single sheets, stapled once in the upper left corner, 27.9 x 21.6 cm.
Contents: Tom Pickard [prose] and blurb reprinted from *Hero Dust,* pp. [2, 3].
Note: Published ca. April 21, 1981.

E177 [college catalog] *Naropa Institute: Summer 1981.* Boulder, CO: Naropa Institute, 1981.
Contents: Prose course description written by AG: W346, pp. 11-12.

E178 [unpublished dissertation] Warmbier, Dieter. *Allen Ginsberg, A Study in Literary Development.* Bochum, W. Germany: Wissenschaftlichen Prüfungsamt Bochum, Aug. 1981.
Contents: Excerpts from the then-unpublished manuscript of *Plutonian Ode and other poems* on pages 90-93, 96.

E179 [college catalog] *Naropa Institute: Fall 1981.* Boulder, CO: Naropa Institute, 1981.
Contents: Prose course descriptions written by AG: W343, p. 2; W350, p. 3.

Related item: [autograph catalog] *Lion Heart Autographs, Catalogue No. 5.* New York, NY: Lion Heart Autographs, Inc., Sept. 18, 1981.
Contents: Inscription by AG as item #27, but in reality this is a forgery.

E180 [college catalog] *Naropa Institute: Fall 1981-Spring 1983.* Boulder, CO: Naropa Institute, 1981.
Contents: Poetic [anonymous but actually by AG], pp. 44-45 — Prose course descriptions written by AG: W320, 324, p. 47; W343, W344, W350, W355, W356, p. 49.

E181 [departmental ballot] *American Academy & Institute of Arts and Letters, Department of Literature.* New York, NY: 1982 ballot mailed Oct. 9, 1981, approx. 120 copies.
Contents: AG prose citation for the nomination of W. S. Burroughs, p. 3 — prose citation for the nomination of Gary Snyder, p. 22.

E182 [musical setting] *Emil Mangelsdorff Quartett and Sebastian Norden.* Das Geheul u. Amerika. Trion Sound Production Gmbh., No. 5101/2, Frankfurt am Main, W. Germany, Nov. 1981. 33 1/3 rpm, 2-12" Lps.
Contents: Carl Weissner's translation of *Howl* as set to music, not read by AG.

E183 [course catalog] *Ojai Foundation: Spring 1982 Retreats.* Ojai, CA: Ojai Foundation, ca. Nov. 1981.
Contents: Prose course description written by AG, p. 3.
Note: Published ca. Nov. 1981 in an impression of 6,000-7,000 copies.

E184 [flyer/open letter] *To Whom It May Concern.* New York, NY: Nov. 27, 1981. Single sheet, 27.9 x 21.6 cm.
Contents: [letter to the New York State Supreme Court]
Note: Text re-written from the letter dated Jan. 13, 1981.

E185 [flyer] *Naropa Institute: The Jack Kerouac Poetics School.* Boulder, CO: Naropa Institute, ca. Dec. 8, 1981. Single sheet, 27.9 x 21.6 cm.
Contents: The Jack Kerouac Poetics School [anonymous prose, but written mostly by AG].

E186 [cover blurb] Camus, Renaud. *Tricks, 25 Encounters.* New York, NY: St. Martin's Press, 1981.
Contents: AG prose blurb.

E187 [pamphlet] Norris, John. *Psych Swive.* Cambridge, MA: privately printed, ca. 1981-82.
Contents: AG prose reproduced in AG's facsimile holograph, p. [8].

1982

E188 [rare book catalog] *Anacapa Books, Bulletin 1009: A Selection from Our Stock.* Berkeley, CA: Anacapa Books, Jan. 1982.
Contents: In Spite of the Apocalypse [poem], item #141, p. 7.

E189 [publisher's catalog] *The Other Publishers Catalogue; Station Hill, Treacle Press, Printed Editions: Winter 1981-82.* Barrytown, NY: Other Publishers, 1982.
Contents: AG prose blurb, p. [30].
Note: Published Jan. 1982 in an impression of 18,000 copies.

E190 [flyer/open letter] *PEN American Center.* New York, NY: PEN American Center, Jan. 7, 1982. Single sheet, 27.9 x 21.6 cm.
Contents: [letter to members of PEN]

E191 [flyer] Evtushenko, Eugenio; Ginsberg, Allen and Cardenal, Ernesto. *Declaración de los tres.* Managua, Nicaragua: Ministry of Culture, Jan. 28, 1982. 2 single pages, stapled once in the upper left corner, 27.6 x 21.4 cm.
Contents: Declaration of Three [prose].
Note: Published Jan. 28, 1982 in an impression of 50 copies. Reprinted a few days later in an unknown quantity to distribute to the media for publication. The reprinted version is also photocopied but identified from the first printing by the lack of the "Declaración de los tres" heading on page 2.

E192 [advertising flyer] *Factory: by Antler.* San Francisco, CA: City Lights, ca. Feb. 3, 1982. Single sheet, 21.6 x 27.9 cm.
Contents: AG prose blurb.
Note: Although advertising a City Lights book, this flyer appears to have been produced by the author and therefore not a City Lights publication itself.

E193a [press release] Evtushenko, Eugenio; Ginsberg, Allen and Cardenal, Ernesto. *"Declaration of Three" to World's Writers.* New York, NY: Feb. 4, 1982. 3 single sheets, stapled once in the upper left corner, 27.9 x 21.6 cm.
Contents: Declaration of Three [prose] — [prose introduction].
Note: Published Feb. 4, 1982 in an impression of 50 copies, reprinted at least once in the following few days. Reprints are generally lighter in shade than the first copies of these sheets. On p. [3] is a line in the upper right corner which does not appear on the original 50 copies; also each of the pages of the reprint has a small dot in the left margin approximately 18 cm. from the top of the sheet caused by dirt on the photocopy machine. Prepared by AG for distribution to publishers, he sent out many of these to interested periodicals, editors, etc.

E193b [press release] *"Declaration of Three" to World's Writers.* Long Beach, CA: ca. Feb. 4, 1982. Single sheet, 27.9 x 21.6 cm.
Contents: [prose introduction] — Declaration of Three [prose]

E194 [flyer/open letter] *To Whom It May Concern,.* New York, NY: March 1982. Single sheet, 27.9 x 21.6 cm.
Contents: AG and Bob Rosenthal. [letter about missing notebooks].

E195 [flyer] *University of Wisconsin, Milwaukee Ballroom Reading.* Milwaukee, WI: March 11, 1982. Single pink sheet, 27.8 x 21.5 cm.
Contents: Evtuchenko, Evgeny; AG and Cardenal, Ernesto. "Declaration of Three" to World's Writers.

E196 [advertising flyer] Cooper, Dennis. *The Tenderness of the Wolves.* Trumansburg, NY: Crossing Press, 1982. Single sheet, 27.7 x 21.4 cm.
Contents: AG prose blurb.
Note: Published April 1982 in an impression of 200 copies.

E197 [course flyer] *'82 Summer Programs at Dai Bosatsu Zendo Kongo-Ji.* Livingston Manor, NY: Dai Bosatsu Zendo, April 30, 1982. Single yellowish white (92) sheet, folded 3 times to 21.5 x 16.1 cm.
Contents: AG prose course description.

Related item: [letter] *Dear Friends and Inquirers.* Boulder, CO: Naropa Institute, May 7, 1982. Single sheet, 27.9 x 21.6 cm.
Contents: [letter signed by AG but not written by him].

E198 [college catalog] *Naropa Institute: Summer 1982.* Boulder, CO: Naropa Institute, June 1982.
Contents: AG prose course description, W320, p. 4 — Walking into King Sooper after Two-Week Retreat [poem], p. 4.

E199 [rare book catalog] *Bradford Morrow Bookseller Ltd. Catalogue 10.* Santa Barbara, CA: Bradford Morrow Bookseler, Ltd., June 12, 1982.
Contents: AG inscription, item 356.

E200 [conference flyer] *On the Road: The Jack Kerouac Conference.* Boulder, CO: Naropa Institute, July 23-Aug. 1, 1982. Single sheet of newsprint, folded once to form 4 pages, 43.0 x 57.7 cm.
Contents: AG prose course description, W310, p. 3.

E201 [exhibition catalog] *Kerouaciana.* Boulder, CO: Boulder Center for the Visual Arts, July 24-Aug. 22, 1982.
Contents: Marx, Carlo [pseud.] prose introduction, p. 3 — Goldbook, Alvah [pseud.] prose commentary on the exhibit, pp. 4-7.
Note: Published in an impression of 450 copies; 100 of which are signed and contain an original photo of Jack Kerouac by AG.

E202 [pamphlet] *The Jack Kerouac School of Poetics: Fall 1982-Spring 1983.* Boulder, CO: Naropa Institute, Sept. 1982.
Contents: Slogans for Poets [prose], pp. 3-7.

E203 [college catalog] *Poetics: Naropa Institute, Fall 1982-Spring 1983.* Boulder, CO: Naropa Institute, Sept. 1982.
Contents: AG prose course descriptions for W321, W343, W350.

E204a [departmental ballot] *American Academy & Institute of Arts and Letters, Department of Literature.* New York, NY: 1983 ballot mailed Oct. 8, 1982, approx. 120 copies.
Contents: AG prose citation for the nominations of W. S. Burroughs, p. 3.

E204b [final ballot] *American Academy & Institute of Arts and Letters.* New York, NY: [1983 ballot mailed Nov. 17, 1982, approx. 250 copies.
Contents: AG prose as above, p. 10.

E205 [cover blurb] DeGrazia, Edward and Newman, Robert K. *Banned Films.* New York, NY: Bowker, 1982.
Contents: AG prose blurb.
Note: Published Oct. 29, 1982 in an undisclosed number of copies.

E206 [poster] *The Untold Tradition.* Hidden Knowledge/Public Insight; A Naropa Institute Free Lecture Series: Boulder Public Library, Boulder, CO. Nov. 10, 1982. Single brilliant orange yellow (67) sheet, 27.8 x 42.9 cm.
Contents: AG prose lecture description.

E207 [cover blurb] Creeley, Robert. *The Collected Poems.* Berkeley, CA: University of California Press, 1982.
Contents: AG prose blurb.

E208 [publisher's catalog] *Gay Sunshine Press.* San Francisco, CA: Gay Sunshine Press, 1982.
Contents: Everybody Loves the First Glimpse of Naked Love [poem], p. [10] — [prose blurb for *Gay Sunshine Journal*, p. [20]].

E209 [classroom handout] *Suggestions for Readings in William Carlos Williams by Allen Ginsberg According to Hardness, Objectivity, Vividness (or Suggestive Formulation of Theory).* Boulder, CO: 1982. 4 single sheets, 27.9 x 21.5 cm.
Contents: Syllabus selected by AG.

1983

E210 [press release] *The Bard Returns.* New York, NY: Poetry Project, March 2, 1983. Single sheet, 27.9 x 21.6 cm.
Contents: AG prose blurbs about the Poetry Project and for *Factory* by Antler.

E211 [poster] *Dharma and Poetics.* Barnet, VT: Karme-Choling, ca. March 27, 1983. Single sheet, 41.3 x 30.5 cm.
Contents: AG prose workshop description.

E212 [press release] *The Humana Press Inc. Press Release.* Clifton, NJ: Humana Press, ca. June 1983. Single sheet, 27.9 x 21.6 cm.
Contents: AG prose blurb.

E213 [rare book catalog] *Fine First Editions and Literary Autographs, no. 9.* Santa Barbara, CA: Maurice F. Neville, ca. July 1983.
Contents: AG inscription in item #143, p. [19].

E214 [auction catalog] *English Literature.* London, England: Sotheby Parke Bernet & Co., 1983. (auction July 21-22, 1983).
Contents: Inscription, items #342, 343, p. 128.

Related item: [flyer] *A Few Words Concerning Senator Cohen.* Orono, ME: Aug. 23-26, 1983. Single sheet, 35.4 x 21.6 cm.
Contents: Prose signed by AG and 6 others but he did not write the statement.

Related item: [press release] *Report on the Death of Michael Smith.* New York, NY: PEN American Center, Aug. 26, 1983. 5 single sheets, 27.9 x 21.6 cm. *Contents:* Letter signed by AG and others but he did not write the statement.

E215 [college catalog] *Naropa Institute: Fall 1983/Spring 1985.* Boulder, CO: Naropa Institute, Sept. 1983. *Contents:* AG course descriptions, W400, W361, W382 on pp. 44-45.

E216 [advertising flyer] *The Toothpaste Press: Fall 1983.* West Branch, IA: Toothpaste Press, Sept. 1983. Single sheet folded once. *Contents:* AG prose blurb, p. [1].

E217 [rare book catalog] *Words Etcetera, no. 42.* London, England: Words Etcetera, Sept. 1983. *Contents:* [excerpt from letter to Robert DeMaria], item #312, p. [18].

E218 [rare book catalog] *Special List of "Beat" Items.* New York, NY: Daniel Stokes, Nov. 1983. *Contents:* AG inscriptions in items #13-28, pp. 3-4

E219 [program] *Visions of Kerouac, Film Northampton at the Arts Centre.* Northampton, England: Arts Centre, Nov. 19, 1983. *Contents:* Pull My Daisy [3 versions], pp. 7-8.

E220 [advertising flyer] *Allen Ginsberg on Tour Feb. 16, 1983 with Peter Orlovsky & Steven Taylor.* Wuppertal, W. Germany: Lichtblick Video Production, 1983. Single sheet folded once to 21.0 x 15.0 cm. *Contents:* AG quotes from the film, p. [2].

E221 [booklet] Ortmanns, Joachim & Mohrhenn, Wolfgang (eds.). *Allen Ginsberg on Tour Feb. 16, 1983.* Wuppertal, W. Germany: Lichtblick Video, 1983. [booklet accompanies video cassette from S-Press] *Contents:* Back to Wuppertal [in facsimile holograph], p. 8 — Gospel Noble Truths, pp. 9-10 — America, pp. 11-14 — Homework, p. 19 — Punk Rock Your My Big Crybaby, p. 20 — Warrior, p. 21 — Dope Fiend Blues, pp. 24-25 — Everybody Sing, pp. 25-26 — Ruhr-Gebiet, pp. 31-33 — Lower East Side, p. 34 — Don't Grow Old, pp. 41-43 — Father Death Blues, pp. 44-46 — Interview with Allen Ginsberg, pp. 51-63 — Interview mit Allen Ginsberg [German translation of interview], pp. 67-80.

E222 [liner notes] *Back to Wuppertal.* Wuppertal, W. Germany: S Press Video, 1983. Accompanies videocassette. *Contents:* Back to Wuppertal [poem] — They Hurt Me To [prose].

E223 [cover blurb] McLaren, Ken. *Yes with Variations.* New York, NY: The Smith, 1983. *Contents:* AG prose blurb.

E224 [cover blurb] Shinder, Jason (ed.). *Divided Light: Father and Son Poems.* New York, NY: Sheep Meadow Press, 1983. *Contents:* AG prose blurb.

E225 [film catalog] *World Wide Video Festival, 1983.* The Hague, The Netherlands: Kijkhuis, 1983. *Contents:* Am I a Spy from the Moon? [poem], p. 108.

1984

E226 [college catalog] *New School Bulletin: Spring 1984.* New York, NY: New School, Jan. 1984.
Contents: AG prose course description, A0040.

E227 [cover blurb] Waldman, Anne. *Makeup on Empty Space.* West Branch, IA: Toothpaste Press, 1984. [paperbound]
Contents: AG prose blurb.
Note: Published Jan. 1984 in an impression of 1,400 copies. 100 hardbound copies were printed but they do not include the blurb by AG.

E228 [rare book catalog] *David Schulson Autographs, no. 18.* New York, NY: David Schulson Autographs, Jan. 27, 1984.
Contents: [letter to Ted Berrigan], item #41, p. 9.

E229 [exhibition catalog] *John Cage; Merce Cunningham; Nam June Paik.* Seoul, South Korea: Won Gallery, Feb. 1-10, 1984.
Contents: Orwell, Oh Well, p. iii — The Rune, p. 9.

E230 [course catalog] *Omega Institute, Summer 1984.* Rhinebeck, NY: Omega Institute, Feb. 1984.
Contents: AG course description, #0820, p. 44.
Note: Published Feb. 1984 in an impression of 100,000 copies.

E231 [exhibition flyer] *Yu Suwa.* Tokyo, Japan: March 1984. Single sheet, 22.1 x 22.0 cm.
Contents: [letter to Yu Suwa], p. [2].

E232 [rare book catalog] *Autograph Letters, No. 7.* Philadelphia, PA: David J. Holmes Autographs, May 1984.
Contents: [letter to Larry Dingman], item #119, p. 20.

E233 [booklet] *Camp Kerouac Summer '84.* Boulder, CO: Jack Kerouac School of Disembodied Poetics Summer Writing Program/Naropa Institute, July 1984. 44 pages.
Contents: Rose is Gone [poem], l. [40].

E234 [rare book catalog] *Wm. Reese Co., Catalogue 26, Literature.* New Haven, CT: Wm. Reese Co., July 1984.
Contents: AG inscription, item #398, p. [41].

E235a [rare book catalog] *Black Sun Books, Recent Acquisitions no. 8.* New York, NY: Black Sun Books, Sept. 1984.
Contents: AG inscriptions, items #25-28, p. [4].
E235b [rare book catalog] *Black Sun Books, Rare Books and First Editions, Catalogue no. 65.* New York, NY: Black Sun Books, ca. Aug. 1985.
Contents: [letter], item #50, p. 7.

E236a [classroom handout] *A Supermarket in California.* Baoding, Hebei, China: Baoding, Hebei University, Nov. 1984. 6 single sheets, stapled twice on the left edge, 27.1 x 19.5 cm.
Contents: A Supermarket in California — Howl, pt. II — Kaddish, pt. iv & v — Returning to the County for a Brief Visit — Don't Grow Old — Gospel Noble Truths — Spring Fashions.
Note: Distinguished from the class handout issued at Fudan University in Dec. 1984 by the page numbers appearing at the bottom of each page. About 100 copies printed for AG's classes here.

E236b [classroom handout] *A Supermarket in California*. Fudan, China: Fudan University, Dec. 1984. 6 single sheets, 27.0 x 19.5 cm.
Contents: As above.
Note: The page numbers are at the top of each page and it is re-typed here. About 100 copies printed for AG's classes here.

E237a [classroom handout] *W. C. Williams*. Baoding, Hebei, China: Baoding, Hebei University, Nov. 1984. 10 single sheets, stapled twice on the top edge, 39.0 x 27.0 cm.
Contents: American poetry anthology edited by AG.
Note: About 100 copies printed for AG's classes here.
E237b [classroom handout] *W. C. Williams*. Fudan, China: Fudan University, Dec. 1984. 10 single sheets, stapled twice on the top edge, 38.8 x 26.8 cm.
Contents: As above.
Note: About 100 copies printed for AG's classes here.

E238 [rare book catalog] *Pharos Books, November Short List G-H*. New Haven, CT: Pharos Books, Nov. 7, 1984.
Contents: AG inscription, item #38, p. 2.

E239 [classroom handout] *September on Jessore Road*. Suchow, China: Suchow University, Dec. 19, 1984. 8 single sheets, stapled once on the left edge, 26.0 x 35.8 cm.
Contents: September of Jessore Road — A Supermarket in California — Howl, pt. II — Kaddish, pt. iv & v — Returning to the County for a Brief Visit — Don't Grow Old — Gospel Noble Truths — Spring Fashions.
Note: About 100 copies printed for AG's classes here.

E240 [advertising flyer] *Friction: issue #5/6*. Boulder, CO: Friction Magazine, Naropa Institute, Winter [Dec. 22] 1984. Single sheet, 27.9 x 21.7 cm.
Contents: AG prose blurb.

E241 [cover blurb] Borawski, Walta. *Sexually Dangerous Poet*. Boston, MA: Good Gay Poets, 1984.
Contents: AG prose blurb.

E242 [cover blurb] Chapman, Harold. *The Beat Hotel*. Montpellier, France: Gris Banal, 1984.
Contents: AG prose blurb.

E243 [photograph legend] Green, Jonathan. *American Photography*. New York, NY: Harry Abrams, 1984.
Contents: [legend underneath a photograph of Neal Cassady and Jack Kerouac, the photo not taken by AG], p. 86.

1985

E244 [rare book catalog] *Post-Holiday Specials!* New York, NY: The Rare Book Room, Feb. 13, 1985.
Contents: AG inscription, p. [2].

E245 [course catalog] *Hollyhock Farm, Summer Program 1985*. Cortes Island, Canada: Hollyhock Farm, ca. Feb. 18, 1985.
Contents: AG prose course description, p. 4.

E246 [poster] *Allen Ginsberg.* Los Angeles, CA: UCLA Campus Events, Cultural and Recreational Affairs and UCLA Public Lectures, March 12, 1985. Single cream colored sheet, 27.9 x 21.6 cm.
Contents: Autobiographic Precis [prose]
Note: Published late Feb. 1985 in an impression of 2,500 copies.

E247 [publication flyer] *Forever Wider, by Charles Plymell.* Metuchen, NJ: Scarecrow Press, 1985. Single sheet, 22.3 x 9.7 cm.
Contents: AG prose blurb.
Note: Published ca. March 1, 1985.

E248 [exhibition catalog] *Gomariz: Recent Paintings.* New York, NY: Galeria Bonino, Ltd., March 2-30, 1985.
Contents: Alberti, Rafael. Osvaldo Gomariz, Today [poem translated by AG and in his holograph], p. [3].

E249 [rare book catalog] *Words Etcetera: Catalogue Fifty-One, Summer 1985.* London, England: Words Etcetera, June 1985.
Contents: [letter to Robert DeMaria], item #362, p. 23.

E250 [postcard] *McGivern Appeal.* New York: Nov. 1985. Single sheet, 10.2 x 15.3 cm.
Contents: [letter to Mario Cuomo]
Note: Published ca. Oct. 15, 1985.

E251 [auction catalog] *Auction Catalog.* Detroit, MI: Friends of the Detroit Public Library, Nov. 21, 1985.
Contents: AG legend from a photograph, item #38, p. 6 [the photo is not reproduced].

E252 [cover blurb] Burroughs, William S. *Queer.* New York, NY: Viking, 1985.
Contents: AG prose blurb.

E253 [cover blurb] Lee, Martin A. and Shlain, Bruce. *Acid Dreams.* New York, NY: Grove Press, 1985.
Contents: AG prose blurb.

E254 [pamphlet] Shiraishi, Kazuko. *Little Planet: The Goanna God.* Japan: Shoshi-Yamada, 1985.
Contents: Shiraishi, Kazuko. Little Planet [translated by AG], p. [2].

1986

E255 [talking book] *Collected Poems 1947-1980, by Allen Ginsberg.* Read by George Guidell. Washington, DC: National Library Service for the Blind and Physically Handicapped, Library of Congress Talking Book Program, recorded Feb. 1986.

E256 [program] *1986 Readings by Poets and Writers.* New York, NY: Arts Apprenticeship Program, Feb. 1-15, 1986.
Contents: AG prose blurb, p. 8.

E257 [cover blurb] Antler. *Last Words.* New York, NY: Ballantine Books, March 1986.
Contents: AG prose blurb.

E258 [program] *Ceremonial Program.* New York, NY: American Academy and Institute of Arts and Letters, May 21, 1986. 16 page booklet, stapled twice, 27.9 x 21.5 cm.
Contents: Prose biography of Gregory Corso [anonymous but by AG], p. [7].

E259 [rare book catalog] *David Schulson Autographs, no. 37.* New York, NY: David Schulson Autographs, Nov. 1986.
Contents: [letter to Advertising Trade Publication], item #88, p. 21.

E260 [flyer] *Giorno Poetry Systems.* New York, NY: Giorno Poetry Systems Institute, Nov. 1986. Single sheet, 34.1 x 21.5 cm.
Contents: AG prose blurb.
Note: Published Nov. 1986 in an impression of 5,500 copies.

E261 [cover blurb] Cope, David. *On the Bridge.* Clifton, NJ: Humana Press, 1986.
Contents: AG prose blurb.

1987

E262 [flyer] *Spiritual Quests.* New York, NY: New York Public Library, Feb. 11, 1987. Single light bluish gray (190) sheet, folded 4 times to 10.3 x 21.6 cm.
Contents: AG prose blurb.

E263 [flyer] *Literary History of the Beat Generation.* Brooklyn, NY: Brooklyn College, Feb. 23, 1987. Single sheet, 40.6 x 21.6 cm.
Contents: AG prose blurbs.

E264 [rare book catalog] *Literature 51.* New Haven, CT: Wm. Reese Co., March 27, 1987.
Contents: AG inscriptions, items #471-472.

E265 [flyer] *Poems, Plays, Stories.* Brooklyn, NY: Brooklyn College, ca. April 27, 1987. Single sheet, 40.6 x 21.6 cm.
Contents: AG prose blurbs.

E266 [exhibition catalog] *Allen Ginsberg & Robert Frank.* Tokyo, Japan: Galerie Watari, May 20, 1987. 29.6 x 21.0 cm.
Contents: AG letter to Mrs. Watari, inside front cover — [reproduction of 2 manuscript pages], p. 7.

E267 [musical setting] Gruntz, George; Ginsberg, Allen; Libermann, Rolf and Wilson, Robert. *Cosmopolitan Greetings, Jazz Opera.* Euromusic, 1987. Premiered June 11, 1987.
Contents: Happening Now? — Those Two — Maturity — Bop Lyrics — Funny Death — An Eastern Ballad — Song — Prophecy.

E268 [11 postcards] *Allen Ginsberg.* Tokyo, Japan: Galerie Watari, Summer 1987. 15.0 x 10.5 cm. each.
Contents: 11 different AG drawings reproduced from early notebooks.

E269 [bookmark] *Rocky Mountain Dharma Center.* Grindstone City, MI: Alternative Press, ca. Summer 1987. Single beige sheet, 4.8 x 17.5 cm.
Contents: Rocky Mountain Dharma Center [poem]

E270 [flyer] *A Benefit for the Homeless.* New York, NY: Zen Community of New York, Oct. 26, 1987. Single sheet, 35.5 x 21.6 cm.
Contents: [open letter by AG]

E271 [clothing catalog] *Be Released in Los Angeles.* Tokyo, Japan: Be Released, ca. Nov. 1987.
Contents: Proclamation "Be Released" [poem], p. [2].

E272 [program] Claiborne, Sybil (ed.). *Climbing Fences.* New York, NY: War Resisters League, Dec. 14, 1987. *Note:* Village Gate ceremonies in honor of Grace Paley's 65th Birthday.
Contents: Peace Protest Syllables [Four skinheads stand], p. 30.

E273 [cover blurb] Foster, Barbara M. and Foster, Michael. *Forbidden Journey.* San Francisco, CA: Harper and Row, 1987.
Contents: AG prose blurb.

E274 [cover blurb] Sakaki, Nanao. *Break the Mirror.* CA: North Point, 1987.
Contents: Brain Washed by Numerous Mountain Streams [poem]

E275 [advertising brochure] *What Happened to Kerouac?* Los Angeles, CA: Overseas Filmgroup, 1987. 4 page description of film.
Contents: AG prose blurb, p. 2.

1988

E276 [rare book catalog] *Rare Books, List 88-A.* Great Barrington, MA: George Robert Minkoff Inc., Jan. 4, 1988.
Contents: [letter to Gregory Corso], item #59.
Note: Published Jan. 4, 1988 in an impression of 1,600 copies.

E277 [flyer] *Living Poetry.* Brooklyn, NY: Brooklyn College, ca. Feb. 17, 1988. Single sheet folded once to 27.9 x 21.6 cm.
Contents: AG prose descriptions of readings.

E278 [rare book catalog] *New Arrivals, List G-1.* Sudbury, MA: Water Row Books, Inc., April 1988.
Contents: AG inscription, p. 4.

E279 [program] *Ceremonial.* New York, NY: American Academy and Institute of Arts and Letters, May 18, 1988.
Contents: AG prose citations for David Cope and John Clellon Holmes, p. [5].

E280 [advertising flyer] *An Annotated Bibliography of Timothy Leary.* Hamden, CT: Archon Books, ca. June 1988. Single yellow sheet, 21.6 x 14.0 cm.
Contents: AG prose blurb.

E281 [flyer] *Save the World's Oldest Blue Coral Reef!* San Francisco, CA: Friends of the Blue Coral Reef, ca. June 1988. Single sheet, folds twice to form 6 pages, 21.6 x 35.5 cm.
Contents: AG, Gary Snyder, Michael McClure, Joanne Kyger and Nanao Sakaki. Message to Friends in Japan [prose].

E282 [musical setting] Amram, David. *Pull My Daisy.* RCA, Empress Music ASCAP, SPS-45-298 ARKS-3898, New York, NY, June 24, 1988. Produced by Max Wilcox. 45 rpm, 7" stereo. Matrix side 1: ARKS-3898.
Contents: AG and Jack Kerouac. Pull My Daisy.

E283 [postcard] *Haiku.* Boise, ID: Limberlost Press, 1988. 10.8 x 14.6 cm. Published in various colors: Brownish orange (54); pale yellow (89); light greenish gray (154) and bluish white (189) card stock.
Contents: Haiku [Four Skinheads Stand].
Note: Published July 27, 1988 in an impression of 650 copies. Also issued in a portfolio of 20 postcards entitled *A Collection of Poetry Postcards from Limberlost Press,* and sold for $9.95.

E284 [pamphlet] *Howl: Forest, Water and People, by Allen Ginsberg.* Kyoto, Japan: Kyoto University, Nov. 3, 1988.
Contents: AG inscription and drawing, p. [xi].

E285 [cover blurb] Selby, Hubert, Jr. *Last Exit to Brooklyn.* New York, NY: Grove Press, Evergreen Edition, 1988.
Contents: AG prose blurb.

1989

E286 [rare book catalog] *Skyline Books, no. 2.* Forest Knolls, CA: Skyline Books, March 15, 1989.
Contents: AG inscriptions, items #119, 129; pp. 12-13.
Note: Published March 15, 1989 in an impression of 1,400 copies.

E287 [program] *The Poetry Center of the 92nd Street Y: Amiri Baraka and Allen Ginsberg.* New York, NY: Poetry Center, March 29, 1989. 27.9 x 21.8 cm. Three single light gray (264) sheets printed on both sides.
Contents: White Shroud [manuscript page in facsimile holograph].

E288 [rare book catalog] *Maurice F. Neville, Rare Books, no. 18.* Santa Barbara, CA: Maurice F. Neville, July 14, 1989.
Contents: [letters to Carolyn Cassady], pp. [24-25].
Note: Published July 14, 1989 in an impression of ca. 1,400 copies.

E289 [cover blurb] Ansen, Alan. *Contact Highs, Selected Poems 1957-1987.* Elmwood Park, IL: Dalkey Archive Press, 1989.
Contents: AG prose blurb.
Note: Published Nov. 2, 1989 in an impression of 800 copies; 300 of which are hardbound and 500 of which are paperbound.

E290 [program] *Fetus of Nature: Koichi Tamano and Harupin-Ha, World Survival Tour.* Berkeley, CA: 1989.
Contents: AG prose blurb, p. 1.

E291 [cover blurb] Kerouac, Jack. *Lonesome Traveler.* New York, NY: Grove Press, Evergreen Edition, 1989. [New Evergreen Edition]
Contents: AG prose blurb.

E292 [musical setting] Little, David. *Reality Sandwiches.* Amsterdam, The Netherlands: Donemus, 1989.
Contents: On Burroughs' Work — Funny Death — Battleship Newsreel — Sakyamuni Coming Out From the Mountain.

E292X [drawing]. Watari, Shizuko. *Ai Rabu Ato.* Tokyo, Japan: Nihon/Japan Broadcast Publishing, 1989, plate 22.
Contents: AG drawing of "Fighting Cocks Of Pucalpa"

1990

E293 [flyer] *The Wolfe Institute, Rainbow Body Poetry, Spring 1990.* Brooklyn, NY: Brooklyn College, Feb. 5, 1991. Single sheet, folded 3 times to 10.0 x 21.4 cm.
Contents: AG drawing of rainbow.

E294 [cover blurb] Cope, David. *Fragments from the Stars.* Clifton, NJ: Humana Press, 1990.
Contents: AG prose blurb.
Note: Published Feb. 15, 1990 in an impression of 650 hardbound copies. Paperbound issue was published Feb. 22, 1990 in an impression of 800 copies.

E295 [rare book catalog] *Skyline Books, no. 4.* Forest Knolls, CA: Skyline Books, April 27, 1990.
Contents: [letter to Gregory Corso], item #148 — [inscription], item #150.

E296 [libretto] *Hydrogen Jukebox.* Music by Philip Glass. Commissioned by Spoleto Festival USA and American music Theater Festival. New York, NY: Dunvagen Music Publishers, Inc., 1990. Premiered in May 1990.
Contents: Iron Horse [excerpt] — Jaweh and Allah Battle [excerpt] — Consulting I Ching Smoking Pot Listening to the Fugs Sing Blake — Marijuana Notation — To P.O. — Patna-Benares Express — Last Night in Calcutta [excerpt] — Crossing Nation [excerpt] — Over Denver Again — Going to Chicago [excerpt] — To Poe: Over the Planet, Air Albany-Baltimore [excerpt] — Friday the Thirteenth — Wichita Vortex Sutra [excerpt] — Howl [excerpt] — Manhattan Thirties Flash — Nagasaki Days [excerpt] — Cabin in the Rockies — To Aunt Rose — Ayers Rock/Uluru Song — The Green Automobile [excerpt] — Violence — CIA Dope Calypso [excerpt] — Ayers Rock/Uluru Song — Throw Out the Yellow Journalism of Bad Grammar & Terrible Manner [excerpt] — Don't Grow Old [excerpt] — Numbers in U.S. File Cabinet.
Note: Also distributed free at performances at the Brooklyn Academy of Music, May 7-12, 1991, Brooklyn, NY.

E297 [cover blurb] Huncke, Herbert. *Guilty of Everything.* New York, NY: Paragon House, 1990.
Contents: AG prose blurb.
Note: Published May 30, 1990 in an impression of 2,500 copies.

E298a [blurb] Williams, Paul. *Performing Artist: The Music of Bob Dylan, vol. 1.* Novato, CA: Underwood-Miller, 1990.
Contents: AG prose blurb, p. [3].
Note: Published June 15, 1990 in an impression of 1,800 copies; 800 of which are hardbound and 1,000 of which are paperbound.

E298b [blurb]. Williams, Paul. *Bob Dylan: Performing Artist, the Middle Years: 1974-1986.* Novato, CA: Underwood-Miller, 1992, p. i.
Contents: AG prose blurb as above.

E299 [advertising flyer] *The Jack Kerouac Collection.* Santa Monica, CA: Rhino Records, ca. June 18, 1990.
Contents: AG prose blurb, p. 4.

E300 [liner notes/booklet] *The Jack Kerouac Collection.* Rhino Records, R14H 70939, Santa Monica, CA, June 18, 1990. 3 compact disc boxed set.
Contents: AG prose, p. [8].
Note: Booklet also accompanies 4 cassette boxed set, R44R 70939 and 4 phonorecording boxed set, R23K 70939.

E301 [publisher's catalog] *City Lights Books, Fall/Winter 1990.* San Francisco, CA: City Lights Books, 1990.
Contents: AG prose blurb, p. 5.

E302 [rare book catalog] *Skyline Books, no. 5.* Forest Knolls, CA: Skyline Books, Oct. 5, 1990.
Contents: [letters to Basil King], items #203, 208, p. 19.

E303 [press release] *Without Warning by Pat Donegan.* Berkeley, CA: Parallax Press, Dec. 1, 1990. Single sheet, 27.9 x 21.6 cm.
Contents: AG prose blurb.
Note: Published Dec. 1, 1990 in an impression of 100 copies.

E304 [program] *A Garden of Earthly Desserts.* New York, NY: Poets and Writers, Dec. 6, 1990.
Contents: Cosmopolitan Greetings, p. 25.

E305 [cover blurb] DiPrima, Diane. *Pieces of a Song.* San Francisco, CA: City Lights Books, 1990.
Contents: AG prose blurb.

E306 [cover blurb] Griffin, Michael. *Nationwide Butterpump.* Los Angeles, CA: Disciple 'n' Anarchy Press, 1990.
Contents: AG prose blurb.

E307 [cover blurb] Kerouac, Jack. *Mexico City Blues.* New York, NY: Grove Weidenfeld, 1990.
Contents: AG prose blurb.

E308 [exhibition catalog] *Lyrical Vision: The 6 Gallery.* Davis, CA: Natsoulas/Novelozo Gallery, 1990.
Contents: Howl, pp. 27-31 — [advertising postcard for the 6 Gallery reading in 1955 is reproduced], p. 31.

E309 [cover blurb] Mezzrow, Milton and Wolfe, Bernard. *Really the Blues.* New York, NY: Citadel Press Book, 1990.
Contents: AG prose blurb.

E310 [cover blurb] Sanders, Ed. *Tales of Beatnik Glory, vol. 1 and 2.* New York, NY: Citadel Press, 1990.
Contents: AG prose blurb.

E311 [rare book catalog] *This Is Catalogue #50.* Sudbury, MA: Water Row Books, ca. 1990.
Contents: [excerpt of letter], item #193, p. 28.

E312 [rare book catalog] *Waiting for Godot Books: Literary First Editions (& Miscellany), no. 12.* Cambridge, MA: Waiting for Godot Books, 1990.
Contents: AG inscription, item #442, p. 47.

E313 [rare book catalog] *Water Row Books, no. 46.* Sudbury, MA: Water Row Books, 1990.
Contents: AG inscription, item #112, p. [13].

1991

E314 [cover blurb] Money, Peter. *These Are My Shoes.* New York, NY: Boz, 1991.
Contents: AG prose blurb.
Note: Published Jan. 21, 1991 in an impression of 560 copies.

E315 [flyer] *The Wolfe Institute, Rainbow Body Poetry, Spring 1991.* Brooklyn, NY: Brooklyn College, Feb. 4, 1991. Single sheet, folded 3 times to 10.0 x 21.7 cm.
Contents: AG prose descriptions of readings.

E316 [cover blurb] Bartlett, Jeffrey. *One Vast Page.* Berkeley, CA: Provine Press, 1991.
Contents: AG prose blurb.
Note: Published June 1, 1991 in an impression of 500 copies.

E317 [rare book catalog] *Pepper & Stern: Rare Books, Inc., List P2.* Santa Barbara, CA: Pepper & Stern, ca. June 1991.
Contents: AG inscriptions, items #33, 369, 372-3, 375, 377-8, 380.

E318 [rare book catalog] *Pepper & Stern: Rare Books, Inc., List Q2.* Santa Barbara, CA: Pepper & Stern, ca. June 1991.
Contents: AG inscriptions, items #335, 340, 343, 351.

E319 [rare book catalog] *Pepper & Stern: Rare Books, Inc., List R2.* Santa Barbara, CA: Pepper & Stern, ca. Aug. 1991.
Contents: AG inscriptions, items #104, 363-5, 369-372, 374.

E320 [exhibition catalog] *Nam June Paik: Video Time — Video Space.* Basel, Switzerland: Kunsthalle/Zurich, Switzerland: Kunsthaus/Düsseldorf, W. Germany: Stadtische Kunsthalle/Wien, Austria: Museum Moderner Kunst Stiftung Ludwig Museum des 20. Jahrhunderts. Aug. 15, 1991-April 12, 1992.
Contents: AG drawing of Nam June Paik, p. 117.

E321 [rare book catalog] *Pepper & Stern: Rare Books, Inc., List S2.* Santa Barbara, CA: Pepper & Stern, Sept. 1991.
Contents: AG inscriptions, items #282, 284-86, 288, 299, 300.

E322 [rare book catalog] *Water Row Books, Inc., no. 54.* Sudbury, MA: Water Row Books, Sept. 1991.
Contents: AG inscription, item #109.

E323 [program] *Hydrogen Jukebox: 1991-1992 Concert Hall Series, issue no. 2.* Fairfax, VA: Institute of the Arts, George Mason University, Oct. 26-27, 1991.
Contents: Iron Horse [excerpt] — Jaweh and Allah Battle [excerpt] — Consulting I Ching Smoking Pot Listening to the Fugs Sing Blake — Marijuana Notation — Patna-Benares Express — Last Night in Calcutta [excerpt] — To P.O. — Crossing Nation [excerpt] — Over Denver Again — Going to Chicago [excerpt] — To Poe: Over the Planet, Air Albany-Baltimore [excerpt] — Friday the Thirteenth — Wichita Vortex Sutra [excerpt] — Howl [excerpt] — Manhattan Thirties Flash — Cabin in the Rockies — Nagasaki Days [excerpt] — Ayers Rock/Uluru Song — Throw Out the Yellow Journalism of Bad Grammar & Terrible Manner [excerpt] — Don't Grow Old [excerpt] — Numbers in the File Cabinet.

E324 [cover blurb] Catullus, Gaius Valerius. *Complete Poetic Works.* Dallas, TX: Spring Publications, 1991.
Contents: AG prose blurb.

E325 [musical setting] Kitzke, Jerome P. *Mad Coyote Madly Sings.* New York, NY: American Composers Alliance, 1991.
Contents: Text by AG, the Tewa Indians and the Lakota Indians.

E326 [rare book catalog] *Literary First Editions, no. 14.* Huntington, NY: Polyanthos, Park Avenue Books, 1991.
Contents: AG inscriptions in items #613, 614, 616, 627, 629.

E327 [pamphlet] *A Little Help from Our Friends.* Cambridge, MA: Public Eye, 1991. 23.3 x 10.2 cm.
Contents: AG prose blurb, p. [2].

E328 [program] Shapiro, Leonardo (ed.). *Collateral Damage:.* New York, NY: Shaliko Co., 1991.
Contents: Hum Bomb, pp. 10-12.

E329 [rare book catalog] *Water Row Books, no. 55.* Sudbury, MA: Water Row Books, 1991.
Contents: AG inscriptions, items #42, 174.

1992

E330 [rare book catalog] *Pepper & Stern: Rare Books, Inc., List U2.* Santa Barbara, CA: Pepper & Stern, Jan. 1992.
Contents: AG inscriptions, items #376, 379-381, 383-386, 390.

E331 [publisher's catalog] *Peace Press (Haight-Ashbury).* San Francisco, CA: ca. March 1992.
Contents: AG letter, p. [6].

E332 [publisher's catalog] *Spring Publications, Inc., Complete Catalog, Spring/Summer 1992.* Dallas, TX: Spring Publications, March 1992.
Contents: AG prose blurb, p. 11.

E333 [rare book catalog] *Pepper & Stern: Rare Books, Inc., List V2.* Santa Barbara, CA: Pepper & Stern, March 15, 1992.
Contents: AG inscriptions, items #346, 348-354.

E334 [program] *Schule für Dichtung in Wien.* Vienna, Austria: Schule für Dichtung in Wien, April 7-11, 1992.
Contents: AG letter, p. 26.

E335 [program] *Cosmopolitan Greetings: Jazz Opera by George Gruntz and Allen Ginsberg.* Cologne, Germany: WDR, May 26, 1992.
Contents: Jumping the Gun on the Sun — Happening Now? — Those Two — Maturity — Bop Lyrics — 7th Avenue Express — Funny Death — An Eastern Ballad — Song — Prophecy.

E336 [rare book catalog] *Alphabet Bookshop, Beat Literature, 50's & 60's, Juvies.* Port Colborne, Canada: Alphabet Bookshop, June 1992.
Contents: AG inscriptions, items #221, 225.

E337 [rare book catalog] *Ken Lopez, Bookseller: Modern Literature, catalog 59.* Hadley, MA: Ken Lopez, June 1, 1992.
Contents: AG inscriptions, items #145, 146, 155, 156.

E338 [cover blurb] Trocchi, Alexander. *Cain's Book.* New York, NY: Grove Press, 1992.
Contents: AG prose blurb.
Note: Published Sept. 1992 in an impression of 5,000 copies.

E339 [flyer] *Thinker Review Presents an Evening with Allen Ginsberg.* Louisville, KY: University of Louisville Student Center, Oct. 1, 1992. Single sheet folded twice to 21.6 x 27.9 cm.
Contents: Some Biographical Notes on Allen Ginsberg [prose from Autobiographical Precis].

E340 [exhibition catalog] *Karl Appel: Recent Work.* New York, NY: Andre Emmerich Gallery, Nov. 14-Dec. 31, 1992.
Contents: Get Used to Your Body [poem], p. 19.

E341 [cover blurb] Beck, Julian. *Living in Volkswagen Buses.* Seattle, WA: Broken Moon Press, 1992.
Contents: AG prose blurb.

E342a [cover blurb] Charters, Ann (ed.). *The Portable Beat Reader.* New York, NY: Viking, 1992.
Contents: AG prose blurb.

E342b [cover blurb] Charters, Ann (ed.). *The Penguin Book of the Beats*. London, England: Penguin Books, 1993.
Contents: As above [this is the British title for *The Portable Beat Reader*].

E343 [cover blurb] Gant, Glenn Edwards. *King Death and Other Poems*. Boulder, CO: Selva Editions, 1992.
Contents: AG prose blurb.

E344 [postcard] *In the Benjo*. Ann Arbor, MI: Alternative Press, 1992. 16.4 x 10.0 cm. White wove paper unwatermarked.
Contents: In the Benjo.

E345 [cover blurb] Jezer, Marty. *Abbie Hofman: American Rebel*. New Brunswick, NJ: Rutgers University Press, 1992.
Contents: AG prose blurb.

E346 [cover blurb] Kerouac, Jack. *Big Sur*. New York, NY: Penguin Books, 1992.
Contents: AG prose blurb.

E347 [cover blurb] Kerouac, Jack. *Tristessa*. New York, NY: Penguin Books, 1992.
Contents: AG prose blurb.

E348 [cover blurb] Woll, Alfred. *Lighting the Lamp*. Wheaton, IL: Quest Books, 1992.
Contents: AG prose blurb.

1993

E349 [advertising flyer] *Bite the Night by Terrell Hunter*. Orono, ME: Northern Lights, ca. Jan. 4, 1993. Single sheet.
Contents: AG prose blurb.

E350 [rare book catalog] *Literary First Editions, no. 17*. Huntington, NY: Polyanthos/Park Avenue Books, Feb. 1993.
Contents: [letter to Carl Solomon], item #441 — [letter to Herbert Huncke], item #443 — AG inscription, item #452.

E351 [flyer] *The Wolfe Institute, Rainbow Body Poetry, Spring 1993*. Brooklyn, NY: Brooklyn College, Feb. 3, 1993. Single sheet, 40.6 x 21.6 cm.
Contents: AG drawing.

E352 [rare book catalog] *Signed Literary First Editions (& Miscellany), no. 30*. Hadley, MA: Waiting for Godot Books, ca. April 15, 1993.
Contents: AG inscription, item #348, p. 45.

E353 [exhibition catalog] Brown, James. *The Moroccan*. New York, NY: Lococo-Mulder, ca. June-July 1993.
Contents: AG journal entry, pp. [52-53].

E354 [cover blurb] Bezner, Kevin. *About Water*. Lemon Cove, CA: Dry Crik Press, 1993.
Contents: AG prose blurb.

E355 [cover blurb] Brinkley, Douglas. *The Magic Bus*. New York, NY: Harcourt Brace & Co., 1993.
Contents: AG prose blurb.

E356 [cover blurb] Cardenal, Ernesto. *Cosmic Canticle*. Willimantic, CT: Curbstone Press, 1993.
Contents: AG prose blurb.

E357 [libretto] *Cosmopolitan Greetings: Jazz Opera by George Gruntz and Allen Ginsberg.* Zurich, Switzerland: MGB; Migros-Genossenschafts-Bund, 1993. CD-9203, 2 compact disks. 20 page booklet contains the following: *Contents:* Jumping the Gun on the Sun — Happening Now? — Those Two — Maturity — Bop Lyrics — 7th Avenue Express — Funny Death — An Eastern Ballad — Song — Prophecy.

E358 [rare book catalog] *The Hippie Papers.* Sudbury, MA: Water Row Books, 1993. *Note:* Issued in the form of a perfect bound book edited by Cisco Harland. *Contents:* Do You Smoke Pot? [prose], item #43.

E359 [advertising flyer] *Honorable Courtship, by Allen Ginsberg.* Minneapolis, MN: Coffee House Press, 1993. Single sheet folds once to 17.6 x 10.6 cm. *Contents:* AG journal entry, p. [2].

E360 [cover blurb] Kerouac, Jack. *Visions of Cody.* New York, NY: Penguin Books, 1993. *Contents:* AG prose blurb.

E361 [cover blurb] Krassner, Paul. *Confessions of a Raving, Unconfined Nut.* New York, NY: Simon & Schuster, 1993. *Contents:* AG prose blurb.

E362 [cover blurb] Waldman, Anne. *Iovis.* Minneapolis, MN: Coffee House Press, 1993. *Contents:* AG prose blurb.

1994

E363 [proceedings] *Proceedings: American Photography Institute. National Graduate Seminar: June 6-19, 1993.* New York, NY: New York University, Tisch School of the Arts, Photography Department, ca. Feb. 1994. *Contents:* Bodhisattva Art: Awareness Turn-on [prose], pp. 16-23.

E364 [program] *Robert Creeley/Allen Ginsberg.* New York, NY: DIA Center for the Arts, Feb. 8, 1994. 27.6 x 12.2 cm. *Contents:* Now and Forever.

E365 [rare book catalog] *Modern Literature, no. 99.* Berkeley, CA: Anacapa Books, April 4, 1994. *Contents:* [letter to David Ossman], item #128.

E366 [exhibition catalog] *Allen Ginsberg In and Out of Town.* Boulder, CO: Boulder Public Library, July 1994. *Contents:* [short prose description of a photograph], p. 4.

E367 [exhibition catalog] *Beats and Other Rebel Angels.* Boulder, CO: University of Colorado at Boulder Libraries, Special Collection Department, July 1, 1994. *Contents:* [reproduction of inscription with drawing on title page of *Howl*]

E368 [flyer] *Beats and Other Rebels Angels: A Tribute to Allen Ginsberg, Free Public Exhibits.* Boulder, CO: Naropa Institute, July 1994. Single sheet folds once to 21.5 x 13.8 cm. *Contents:* AG prose blurbs, pp. [3-4].

E369 [program] *Crossing Border Magazine.* The Hague, The Netherlands: Sept. 9-11, 1994. *Contents:* Approaching Seoul by Bus in Heavy Rain [American Sentences].

F

Recordings of Allen Ginsberg and His Work

F1a *San Francisco Poets.* Evergreen Records, Lp No. EVR-1, New York, NY, 1958. 33 1/3 rpm, 12" mono. Matrix side 2: XTV 26577-1A.
Contents: AG reads "Howl, part 1".
Note: Included is a booklet with texts of the poems read and photographs of the poets, identical to *Evergreen Review,* vol. 1, no. 2 (1957).

F1b *San Francisco Poets.* Hanover Records, Lp. No. M-5001, New York, NY, 1959. 33 1/3 rpm, 12" mono. Matrix side B: HMG 117. *Note:* Reissue of Evergreen Records, Lp No. EVR-1 without the booklet.

F2a *Allen Ginsberg Reads Howl and Other Poems.* Fantasy Records, No. 7006, San Francisco, CA, 1959. 33 1/3 rpm, 12" mono. Matrix side 1: V-5998-1854-X, matrix side 2: V-5998-1855.
Contents: AG reads "Howl — The Sunflower Sutra — Footnote to Howl — A Supermarket in California — Transcription of Organ Music — America — In the [sic] Back of the Real — Strange New Cottage in Berkeley — Europe! Europe! — Kaddish"
Note: Notes for *Howl and Other Poems* [prose], on back cover. The first pressing of this is made on a transparent red vinyl, later issues with the more common black vinyl.

F2b *Howl.* Fantasy Records, Lp. No. 7013, Berkeley, CA, 1959. 33 1/3 rpm, 12" mono. Matrix side 1: V-5998-1854-X, matrix side 2: V-5998-1855 D 12883-X.
Note: Reissue of Fantasy Records, Lp No. 7006.

F2c *Howl.* Fantasy Records, Lp. No. 7013, Berkeley, CA, 1959. 33 1/3 rpm, 12" mono. Matrix side 1: F-1854, matrix side 2: F-1855.
Note: The cover was changed during the last quarter of 1968 to include a large photographic design on the front cover.

F3 *Junge Amerikanische Lyrik.* Carl Hanser Verlag, Munich, West Germany, 1961. 45 rpm, 7" mono. Matrix side A: 006 404 A.
Contents: AG reads "Sunflower Sutra".

F4 *Allen Ginsberg, Lawrence Ferlinghetti, Gregory Corso, Andrei Voznesensky.* Lovebooks Ltd., Lp No. LB-0001, London, England, 1965. 33 1/3 rpm, 12" mono. Matrix side A: LLP 161721, matrix side 2: LLP 161731.
Contents: AG reads "Ignu — Message II — Big Beat — [closing comments]".
Note: Printed in a limited edition of 100 copies.

F5 *Allen Ginsberg Reading at Better Books.* Better Books, London, England, 1965. 33 1/3 rpm, 12" mono. Matrix side 1: 16156-1, matrix side 2: 16156-2.
Contents: AG reads "Who Will Take Over the Universe? — From Journals [Journal Night Thoughts] — Women [Now I Am Brooding on a Pillow] — From Journals [although listed on the liner notes this is not on the record] — Vulture

Peak — Poem around the Greek Jukeboxes [Seabattle of Salamis Took Place Off Perama] — The Olympics [Big Beat] — [mantra] — Music of the Spheres [Any Town Will Do] — Morning [although listed on the liner notes this is not on the record] — Why Is God Love, Jack? — The Moments Return — The Spectres [Cafe in Warsaw] — King of May [Kral Majales]".
Note: Blurb by AG on liner. Printed in a limited edition of 100 copies.

F6 *Spoken Anthology of American Literature, vol. 2: The Twentieth Century.* University of Arizona Press Series, Tucson, AZ, 1965. 33 1/3 rpm, set of four 12" mono. Matrix side 7: REC 2-7 vol II.
Contents: AG reads from "Paterson" by William Carlos Williams.

F7 *Allen Ginsberg Reads Kaddish, A Twentieth Century Ecstatic Narrative Poem.* Atlantic Recording Corp., Atlantic 4001, New York, NY, June 1966. Verbum Series. 33 1/3 rpm, 12" mono. Matrix side 1A: A-12239-A, side 2A: A-12240-A.
Contents: AG reads "Kaddish".
Note: Back cover contains 10 lines of AG's handwritten manuscript of Kaddish. Inside fold out contains a 2 page statement by AG entitled "How Kaddish Happened" [prose].

F8 *The East Village Other: Electric Newspaper.* ESP Records, Lp No. 1034, New York, NY, 1966. 33 1/3 rpm, 12" mono. Matrix side 1: ESPS 1034-A.
Contents: AG and Peter Orlovsky chant the mantra "Hari Om Namo Shivaye".

F9 *LSD: Documentary Report on the Current Psychedelic Drug Controversy!* Capitol Records, Lp No. 2574, Hollywood, CA, 1966. Produced by Alan W. Livingston and Lawrence Schiller. 33 1/3 rpm, 12" stereo. Matrix side 2: TAO 2 2574 F5.
Contents: AG chants a mantra and includes short interview statement.

F10a *Poems for Peace.* Portents Records, Inc., Lp No. PTS 2001, New York, NY. Recorded and edited by Ann Charters. Produced by Samuel Charters. 33 1/3 rpm, 12". Matrix side 1: PTS 2001 A.
Contents: AG reads "Auto Poesy to Nebraska [Wichita Vortex Sutra]"
F10b *Poems for Peace.* Broadside Records, Lp No. BR 465, Highland Park, MI, 1967. 33 1/3 rpm, 12". *Note:* Reissue of Portents Records, Lp No. PTS 2001.

F11 *Shivaye Mantra / Padma-Sambhava Mantra.* Averica Enterprise, Lp No. ASR 132, ca. 1966. 45 rpm, 7" stereo. Matrix side 1: ASR 132-B, matrix side 2: ASR 132-A.
Contents: AG chants mantras "Shivaye Mantra — Padma-Sambhava Mantra.

F12 *The ESP Sampler.* ESP Records, Lp No. 1051, New York, NY, Summer 1967. 33 1/3 rpm, 12". Matrix side B: ESPS (c) 1051 B.
Contents: AG and Peter Orlovsky chant the mantra "Hari Om Namo Shivaye" [from *East Village Other: Electric Newspaper* ESP 1034 (1966].

F13 *The Ginsbergs at the I.C.A.* Saga Psyche, PSY 30002, London, England, 1967. 33 1/3 rpm. 12". Matrix side 1: PSY 30002A, matrix side 2: PSY 30002B.
Contents: AG reads "Invocation to Saraswati, Goddess of Learning, Poetry & Music — Iron Horse [excerepts] — Wales Visitation — Introduction".
Note: Prose blurb on back cover by AG.

F14 *The New Religion.* Big Sur Recordings, no. M2390, Carmel, CA, 1967. 2 cassettes, 2 hrs. [also issued on reel-to-reel records, 3 3/4 or 7 1/2 ips, mono or stereo, 5" or 7"].
Contents: AG included in panel discussion of the question: "What is Christianity's answer to the present dropout generation?"

F15 [*Dialectics of Liberation.*] *International Dialectics of Liberation Congress London, July 1967. Public Meeting and Discussion: Includes Stokely Carmichael, David Cooper, Allen Ginsberg, and Ronald Laing.* Institute of Phenomenological Studies, Lp. No. DL 13, London, England, 1968. 33 1/3 rpm, 12". Matrix side 2: DL 13B.
Contents: AG chants mantra "Highest Perfect Wisdom" and is a participant in the panel discussion.
Note: from a 23 record set of the Congress all of which have the same record jacket design.

F16 [*Dialectics of Liberation.*] *International Dialectics of Liberation Congress London, July 1967. Public Meeting and Discussion: Includes Stokely Carmichael, David Cooper, Allen Ginsberg, and Ronald Laing.* Institute of Phenomenological Studies, Lp. No. DL 14, London, England, 1968. 33 1/3 rpm, 12". Matrix side 1: DL+14+A+2US, matrix side 2: DL+14+B+1US.
Contents: AG is a participant in the panel discussion.
Note: from a 23 record set of the Congress all of which have the same record jacket design.

F17 [*Dialectics of Liberation.*] *International Dialectics of Liberation Congress London, July 1967. Consciousness & Practical Action.* Institute of Phenomenological Studies, Lp. No. DL 16, London, England, 1968. 33 1/3 rpm, 12". Matrix side 1: DL+16+A2+US, matrix side 2: DL+16+B2+US.
Contents: AG reads from *Nova Express* by William S. Burroughs, and lectures.
Note: from a 23 record set of the Congress all of which have the same record jacket design.

F18 [*Dialectics of Liberation.*] *International Dialectics of Liberation Congress London, July 1967. 'Challenge Seminar: Ecological Destruction by Technology', A Discussion Led by Gregory Bateson and Including: Roy Battersby, Allen Ginsberg, Francis Huxley, Ronald Laing, and Joseph Rosenstein.* Institute of Phenomenological Studies, Lp. No. DL 23, London, England, 1968. 33 1/3 rpm, 12". Matrix side 1: DL+23+B+2US.
Contents: AG is a participant in the panel discussion.
Note: from a 23 record set of the Congress all of which have the same record jacket design.

F19 *Mother,* no. 9. Mother, Lp No. DM 41968, Buffalo, NY, Spring 1968. Edited by Duncan McNaughton and Lewis MacAdams, Jr. 33 1/3 rpm, 12". Matrix side 2: DM 41968 B.
Contents: AG reads "City Night Junk Strains [City Midnight Junk Strains]".

F20 *Poetry of Madness.* Big Sur Recordings, no. M1031-1032, Carmel, CA, 1968. 2 cassettes, 2 hrs. [also issued on 2 reel-to-reel, 3 3/4 or 7 1/2 ips, mono or stereo, 5" or 7"].
Contents: AG include in panel discussion on the wisdom of madness.

F21a *The World's Great Poets Reading at the Festival of Two Worlds, Spoleto, Italy: American Poets: Ginsberg, Berryman, Corso.* Applause Productions, Lp No. SP 412 M, New York, NY, 1968. Produced by Vincent R. Tortora. 33 1/3 rpm, 12". Matrix side 1: EC 68018A.
Contents: AG reads "Highest Perfect Wisdom [mantra] — Message II — Cafe in Warsaw — Who Be Kind To — Portland Coliseum — First Party at Ken Kesey's with Hell's Angels — Uptown — To the Body — Small Spoleto Mantra".
F21b *The World's Great Poets, vol. 1, America Today! Allen Ginsberg, Gregory Corso, and Lawrence Ferlinghetti.* CMS, Lp No. 617, New York, NY, 1971. Produced by Vincent R. Tortora. 33 1/3 rpm, 12" mono. Matrix side 1: CMS 617 A.
Note: Reissue of Applause Lp No. SP 412 M, includes a prose blurb on the back cover by AG.

F22 *The World's Great Poets Reading at the Festival of Two Worlds, Spoleto, Italy: Italian Poets: Ungaretti, Luzi, Gatto, Risi, Sereni. Vol. 1.* Applause Productions, Lp No. SP 414MA-(A), New York, NY, 1968. Produced by Vincent R. Tortora. 33 1/3 rpm, 12". Matrix side 1: EC 68020A.
Contents: AG reads the English translation of *Il Taccuino Del Vecchio* by Giuseppe Ungaretti.

F23 *Allen Ginsberg and the Daily Planet.* Produced for Random House by EMR Enterprises, Ltd., New York, NY, 1969. Written and produced by Jerry Levin. Executive producer, Robert L. Walter. 33 1/3 rpm, 12". Matrix side 1: YB-391-P1, matrix side 2: YB-392-P1.
Contents: AG reads excerpts from "Pentagon Exorcism — [mantras] — The Little Black Boy (by William Blake) [excerpt] — Little Lamb (by William Blake) [excerpt] — Laughing Song (by William Blake) [excerpt] — [interview quotes] — First Party at Ken Kesey's with Hell's Angels — Uptown".

F24a *Allen Ginsberg/William Blake: Songs of Innocence and Experience*, by William Blake, tuned by Allen Ginsberg. MGM Records, Verve Forecast, Lp No. FTS3083, New York, NY, 1969. Produced by Miles Associates. 33 1/3 rpm, 12" stereo. Matrix side 1: FTS-3083 S-1 MGS-2112, matrix side 2: FTS-3083 S-2 MGS-2113.
Contents: AG introductory comments and sings the following songs by William Blake "The Shepherd — The Echoing Green — The Lamb — The Little Black Boy — The Blossom — The Chimney-Sweeper — The Little Boy Lost — The Little Boy Found — Laughing Song — Holy Thursday — Night — Nurses Song — The Sick Rose — Ah! Sun-Flower — The Garden of Love — London — The Human Abstract — To Tirzah — The Grey Monk".

F24b *Archetypes.* MGM Records, Lp No. M3F-4591, Hollywood, CA, 1974. 33 1/3 rpm, 12" stereo. *Note:* Reissue of MGM Records, Lp No. FTS3083, this issue includes a sheet of AG's original annotated description of each of Blake's poems.

F25 *Ginsberg's Thing.* Douglas Recording Corp., Lp No. SD 801, New York, NY, 1969. 33 1/3 rpm, 12" stereo. Matrix side 1: W4RS-2033-2C, matrix side 2: W4RS-2034-2.
Contents: AG reads "Highest Perfect Wisdom [mantra] — Message II — Cafe in Warsaw — Who To Be Kind To [Who Be Kind To] — Portland Coliseum — First Party at Ken Kesey's with Hell's Angels — Uptown — To the Body — Small Spoleto Mantra — [translation of poems by Giuseppe Ungaretti]".

F26a *Spoken Arts Treasury of 100 Modern American Poets Reading Their Poems, Sampler.* Spoken Arts, Lp No. H-2396 A-B, New Rochelle, NY, Dec. 1969. Produced by Arthur Luce Klein. 33 1/3 rpm, 7" square clear plastic flexible record, mono. *Note:* This was a pre-publication sampler, not for sale, publication date of the series is Jan. 15, 1970. No matrix.
Contents: AG reads "Uptown".

F26b *Spoken Arts Treasury of 100 Modern American Poets Reading Their Own Poems, vol. 16: Merrill, Creeley, Ginsberg, Wagoner, Bly, Kinnell.* Spoken Arts, New Rochelle, NY, 1970. 33 1/3 rpm, 12".
Contents: AG reads "Who Be Kind To — Uptown".

F27 *The Spoleto Festival.* Mercury Record Corp., Lp No. SR 2-9133, Chicago, IL, March 1969. Produced by Vincent Tortora. 33 1/3 rpm, 12" stereo, 2 record set. Matrix side 1: SR 90513-A-M1.
Contents: AG reads "Small Spoleto Mantra — Portland Coliseum".
Note: Issued in a box with booklet of 36 pages entitled *Spoleto Festival*, which includes "Small Spoleto Mantra — Portland Coloseum" on pp. [10-11].

F28 *The Fugs: Tenderness Junction.* Reprise Records/Warner Bros. Records, Lp No. RS 6280, Burban, CA, 1969. 33 1/3 rpm, 12" stereo. Matrix side A: RS 6280 A.
Contents: AG chants "Hare Krishna" with Maretta Greer and the Fug Chorale with Gregory Corso on harmonium.

F29 *Cream.* ISKCON, Columbus, OH, 1970. 6 hrs, 3 3/4 ips, 1800 feet, 4-track or 3600 feet 2-track tape.
Contents: AG introduces Swami Bhaktivedanta.

F30 *Contemporary American Poets Read Their Works: Allen Ginsberg.* Everett/Edwards, tape no. 161, Deland, FL, 1971. 1 audio cassette, 29 min., 1 7/8 ips, 2-track mono.
Contents: AG reads "Havana 1953 — Malest Cornifici Tuo Catullo — Describe: The Rain on Dasaswamedh Ghat — Kral Majales — Carmel Valley".

F31 *John Sinclair Freedom Rally.* Rainbow Records, No. 22191, Detroit, MI, 1971. 45 rpm, 7". Matrix side B: 22191-B.
Contents: AG and Peter Orlovsky read "Prayer for John Sinclair".

F32 *Cold Turkey/Klacto Presents.* Cold Turkey Press, Lp No. 6802 944, Rotterdam, The Netherlands, June 1972. 33 1/3 rpm, 12".
Contents: AG reads "Kral Majales".
Note: Issued with a booklet including the text of "Kral Majales", ll. 15-16. The cover and text both contain AG's autobiographic precis.

F33 *The Dial-A-Poem Poets.* Giorno Poetry Systems, Lp No. GPS 001-002, New York, NY, 1972. 2 record set, 33 1/3 rpm, 12" stereo. Matrix side 1: GPS-001 SIDE 1, matrix side 2: GPS-001 SIDE 2, matrix side 4: GPS-002 SIDE 4.
Contents: AG reads "Vajra Mantra — Green Automobile — Merrily We Welcome in the Year [by William Blake]".

F34 *Panjandrum, no. 1.* Panjandrum Press, no. 1, San Francisco, CA, 1972. Produced by Dennis Koran. 33 1/3 rpm, 12" mono. Matrix side 1: DK-1, matrix side 2: DK-2.
Contents: AG reads "Guru Om".
Note: Issued in a box and accompanied by a loose leaf booklet which includes "Guru Om" and other contributors' works.

F35 *Sing Out!* Eva-Tone Soundsheets, New York, NY, 1972. 33 1/3 rpm, 7" microgroove. Matrix side 1: EV-411722AXT.
Contents: AG sings "September on Jessore Road".
Note: Included in *Sing Out!*, vol. 21, no. 2 (Jan./Feb. 1972).

F36 *Yevtushenko, in Readings from His New York and San Francisco Poetry Concerts.* Columbia, Lp No. S-31344, New York, NY, 1972. 33 1/3 rpm, 12" stereo. Matrix side 2: MBL-31344-1A.
Contents: AG introduces Yevtushenko and reads translations of "The City of Yes and the City of No — Question of Freedom" by Yevgeny Yevtushenko.

F37 *Ginsberg, DiPrima, Waldman Reading.* Naropa Institute Archives Project, #001, Boulder, CO: July 30, 1974. 2 cassettes.
Contents: AG comments and reads "Manifesto — To Dulles Airport — Energy Vampire — Tear Gas Rag — Returning to the Country for a Brief Visit — Mind Breaths — Stay Away from the White House — Jaweh and Allah Battle — Gaté".
Note: This is the first of a series of tapes produced by the Naropa Institute Archives Project to preserve important readings and discussions at the Jack Kerouac School of Disembodied Poetics where Allen Ginsberg was co-founder. Many of the tapes were released shortly after the readings, some as soon as the next day. Some were not released commercially for years. Actual release dates for the

cassettes were not generally available and so tapes are entered according to the date of the reading recorded.

F38   *"Art of Poetry" with Ginsberg, Waldman, Trungpa, etc.* Naropa Institute Archives Project, #072, Boulder, CO, 1974. cassette.
Contents: AG panel discussion comments and reading "Energy Vampire — First Thought Is Best".

F39   *Allen Ginsberg Interview for Radio.* Naropa Institute Archives Project, #073, Boulder, CO, 1974. cassette.
Contents: AG interviewed.

F40   *The Best of 1974 — Ginsberg, Waldman, Trungpa, DiPrima.* Naropa Institute Archives Project, #082, Boulder, CO, 1974. cassette.
Contents: AG comments and reads "First Thought Best Thought — Jaweh and Allah Battle — [improvisation] — Returning to the Country for a Brief Visit".

F41   *Disconnected: The Dial-a-Poem Poets.* Giorno Poetry Systems, Lp No. GPS 003-004, New York, NY, 1974. 33 1/3 rpm, 12" stereo, 2 album set. Matrix side 1: GPS-003A, matrix side 3: GPS 004A.
Contents: AG reads "I'm a Victim of Telephones [I Am a Victim of Telephone] — Jimmy Berman [Jimmy Berman Rag]".

F42   *The Pequod Selected Readings.* Robert R. Marino Co., Waterville, ME, 1974. 33 1/3 rpm, 7". Matrix side 2: EV-26743BXT.
Contents: AG reads "On Neruda's Death — Broken Bone Blues — Returning to the Country for a Brief Visit — Ah [mantra]".
Note: Issued as a black square plastic flimsy phonorecording.

F43   *Poetry International 1973.* Rotterdamse Kunststichting, Siegro Studio's Rotterdam, Lp No. 6810 459, Rotterdam, The Netherlands, 1974. 33 1/3 rpm, 12" stereo. Matrix side 1: AA 6810 459 1Y1 670 111.
Contents: AG reads "Please Master — Gaté".
Note: Accompanied by a 23-page booklet entitled *De Rotterdamse Kunststichting* which contains a translation by Simon Vinkenoog of "Please Master ‖ Alstublief Meester", pp. 9-12.

F44   *Burroughs and Corso Reading.* Naropa Institute Archives Project, #003, Boulder, CO, June 11, 1975. Cassette.
Contents: AG introductory comments.

F45   *Ginsberg and Whalen Reading.* Naropa Institute Archives Project, #004, Boulder, CO, June 18, 1975. Cassette.
Contents: AG reads "Regalia in Immediate Demand (by Philip Whalen) — Cyanide Water in Pittsburgh — Reading the Newspapers Can Drive You Mad — Freedom of Speech — Fragments from a Weekly Newsmagazine — Chicago Futures [Written on Hotel Napkin: Chicago Futures] — End Vietnam War — Can't Find Anyone [Guru Blues] — It Was a Lazy Fairy — Swallowing Poison — Midnite Dream".

F46   *Ed Sanders Poetry Reading.* Naropa Institute Archives Project, #006, Boulder, CO, July 9, 1975. Cassette.
Contents: AG introductory comments.

F47   *John Ashbery and W. S. Merwin Reading.* Naropa Institute Archives Project, #007, Boulder, CO, July 12, 1975. Cassette.
Contents: AG introductory comments.

F48a *Beauty and the Beast.* Naropa Recordings, Boulder, CO, Aug. 9, 1975. Cassette.
Contents: AG reads "Howl".
F48b *Ginsberg and Waldman Reading.* Naropa Institute Archives Project, #010, Boulder, CO, Aug. 9, 1975. Cassette. *Note:* Reissue of *Beauty and the Beast* (Naropa Recordings).
Contents: AG reads "Gaté — Howl — Thursday (by William Carlos Williams)".
F48c *Beauty and the Beast.* Watershed Tapes, Encore Series, No. C238, Washington, DC, 1990. Produced by Alan D. Austin. Cassette. *Note:* Reissue of *Beauty and the Beast* (Naropa Recordings).

F49 *William Burroughs Interview.* Naropa Institute Archives Project, #074, Boulder, CO, 1975. Cassette.
Contents: AG joins in the interview discussion.

F50a *Bard and Muse.* Naropa Recordings, Vajaradahtu Recordings, Boulder, CO, April 2, 1976. Cassette.
Contents: AG comments and reads "Gaté — Ayers Rock Uluru Song — Conscience Hypocrisy Ballad — We Rise on Sun Beams and Fall in the Night — Chögyam Trungpa's Crazy Wisdom Lectures [haiku] — Cabin in the Rockies — Rolling Thunder Stones — Gospel Noble Truths — Guru Blues — Rolling Thunder Stones (continued) — Sickness Blues — Come All Yea Brave Boys — Reading French Poetry — Don't Grow Old [Old Poet]".
F50b *Ginsberg and Waldman Reading.* Naropa Institute Archives Project, #012, Boulder, CO, April 2, 1976. Cassette. *Note:* Reissue of *Bard and Muse.*

F51 *Robert Duncan and Helen Adams Reading.* Naropa Institute Archives Project, #013, Boulder, CO, June 9, 1976. 2 cassettes.
Contents: AG introductory comments.

F52 *Allen Ginsberg and M. McClure Reading.* Naropa Institute Archives Project, #014, Boulder, CO, June 16, 1976. 2 cassettes.
Contents: AG comments and reads "Howl [excerpt] — My Alba — Sakyamuni Coming Out from the Mountain — The Green Automobile — On Burroughs' Work — Love Poem on Theme by Whitman — Song [The Weight of the World] — Malest Cornifici Tuo Catullo — Dream Record: June 8, 1955 — A Strange New Cottage in Berkeley — Sather Gate Illumination — Tears — Don't Grow Old [Old Poet] — I Came Out in My Business Suit — Guru Blues — Gospel Noble Truths".

F53 *Diane Wakowski [sic: Wakoski] Reading.* Naropa Institute Archives Project, #015, Boulder, CO, June 30, 1976. Cassette.
Contents: AG introductory comments.

F54 *Waldman, Ginsberg, CTR [Chogyam Trungpa Rinpoche] Reading.* Naropa Institute Archives Project, #020, Boulder, CO, Aug. 7, 1976. Cassette.
Contents: AG reads "Ayers Rock Uluru Song — We Rise on Sunbeams and Fall in the Night — Hospital Window — Cabin in the Rockies [haiku] — Reading French Poetry — Don't Grow Old [Old Poet] — Father Death Blues"

F55 *Fagin, Gallup, Whalen, Clausen.* Naropa Institute Archives Project, #021, Boulder, CO, Aug. 10, 1976. Cassette.
Contents: AG introductory comments.

F56 *Ginsberg, Rowan, Orlovsky, Whalen, etc.* Naropa Institute Archives Project, #023, Boulder, CO, Aug. 13, 1976. Cassette.
Contents: AG comments and reads "Rolling Thunder Stones — Father Death Blues — Talking Asshole (by William S. Burroughs)".

F57 *Allen Ginsberg Live at St. Mark's.* S Press Tonbandverlag, SP48, Düsseldorf, W. Germany, 1976. 41 min., cassette.
  Contents: AG reads "Mantra for the Purification of Speech — Flying to Fiji — Siratoka Beach Croon — Bus Ride Ballad Road to Suva — Returning to the Country for a Brief Visit — Mind Breaths — Flying Elegy — D.C. Mobilization — Stay Away from the White House — On Reading Dylan's Writings — Jaweh and Allah Battle".

F58 *Totally Corrupt, The Dial-a-Poem Poets.* Giorno Poetry Systems Institute, Lp No. GPS 008-009, New York, NY, 1976. 33 1/3 rpm, 12" stereo. 2 records.
  Contents: AG reads "Please Master".

F59 *John Ashbery Reading.* Naropa Institute Archives Project, #024, Boulder, CO, 1976. Cassette.
  Contents: AG comments.

F60 *Potpourri of Poetry, 1.* Naropa Institute Recordings, Vajradhatu Recordings, Boulder, CO, 1976. Cassette.
  Contents: AG reads "Thursday (by William Carlos Williams) — Ego Confession".

F61 *Allen Ginsberg and Anne Waldman Reading.* Naropa Institute Archives Project, #025, Boulder, CO, April 10, 1977. Cassette.
  Contents: AG reads "Junk Mail — Father Guru — What's Dead? — Ballade of Poisons — Lack Love — I Take Your God — Western Airlines Boat [From Journals] — Don't Grow Old [Old Poet] — Drive All Blames into One — Haunting Poe's Baltimore — Contest of Bards — I Lay Love on My Knee".

F62 *Allen Ginsberg and Peter Orlovsky Reading.* Naropa Institute Archives Project, #026, Boulder, CO, June 22, 1977. 2 cassettes.
  Contents: AG comments and reads "Nurse's Song (by William Blake) — Lay Down Yr Mountain — The Rune — Contest of Bards — The Rune".

F63 *Michael McClure Reading.* Naropa Institute Archives Project, #028, Boulder, CO, July 27, 1977. Cassette.
  Contents: AG comments.

F64 *Allen Ginsberg and Anne Waldman Reading.* Naropa Institute Archives Project, #030, Boulder, CO, Aug. 3, 1977. Cassette.
  Contents: AG comments and reads "Gaté — Teton Village — Don't Grow Old [Old Poet] — Drive All Blames into One — Hearing Lenore Read Aloud — Punk Rock Your My Big Crybaby — Kidney Stones Traum [Kidneystone Opium Traum] — I Lay Love on My Knee — Love Replied — Gospel Noble Truths".

F65 *Black Box, no. 12.* Watershed Foundation, Washington, DC, 1977. Editorial Director: Alan Austin. 2 stereo C-60 cassettes. 2 hrs.
  Contents: AG reads "CIA Dope Calypso — Don't Grow Old [Old Poet] — Father Death Blues — Rolling Thunder Stones".

F66 Cohen, Leonard. *Death of a Ladies' Man.* Warner Brothers, BS-3125, Hollywood, CA, 1977. Produced by Phil Spector. 33 1/3 rpm, 12" Lp.
  Contents: AG sings in the background to "Don't Go Home with Your Hard On".

F67 *Ken Kesey.* Naropa Institute Archives Project, #31, Boulder, CO, July 18, 1978. Cassette.
  Contents: AG introductory comments.

F68 *William Burroughs and K. Kesey Reading.* Naropa Institute Archives Project, #034, Boulder, CO, July 19, 1978. Cassette.
  Contents: AG introductory comments.

F69 *Diane Di Prima and A. Baraka Reading.* Naropa Institute Archives Project, #036, Boulder, CO, July 26, 1978. Cassette.
Contents: AG introductory comments.

F70 *Anne Waldman Reading.* Naropa Institute Archives Project, #037, Boulder, CO, Aug. 2, 1978. Cassette.
Contents: AG introductory comments.

F71a *L.S.D. Colloquium.* New Dimensions Radio Tapes, #1220, San Francisco, CA, 1978. 3 hrs. *Note:* All tapes are 'made to order' from master tapes.
Contents: AG interview comments.

F71b *L.S.D.—A Generation Later.* New Dimensions Radio Tapes, #1184, San Francisco, CA, 1978. 2 hrs. *Note:* Edited 2 hour version of tape #1220.

F71c *L.S.D. Interviews and Opinions.* New Dimensions Radio Tapes, #1221, San Francisco, CA, 1978. 1 1/2 hrs. *Note:* Edited 1 1/2 hour version of tape #1220.

F72 *Ginsberg, Sakaki, and Kesey Reading.* Naropa Institute Archives Project, #040, Boulder, CO, July 4, 1978. 2 cassettes.
Contents: AG comments and reads "A Crazy Spiritual — National Poem (by Jack Kerouac, Gregory Corso and AG) — Independence Day-America II — Rose Tree [My Pretty Rose Tree] (by William Blake) — The Tyger (by William Blake) — Dope Fiend Blues — I Can't Find Anyone [Guru Blues] — Everybody Sing — Where the Years Have Gone".

F73 *Plutonium Ode.* Poetry London/Apple Magazine, SFI 489 A&B, London, England, Autumn 1979. 33 1/3 rpm, 7" Flexi-disc. *Note:* Issued in *Poetry London/Apple Magazine,* vol. 1, no. 1 (Autumn 1979). Matrix side 1: A.
Contents: AG reads "Plutonium Ode [Plutonian Ode]".

F74 *The Nova Convention.* Giorno Poetry Systems Institute, GPS 014-015, New York, NY, 1979. Produced by John Giorno, James Grauerholtz and Sylvere Lotringer. 33 1/3 rpm, 2 - 12" Lp stereo. Matrix side 4: GPS 014-015 Side 4. *Note:* Also issued as 2 cassettes GPS 016-017.
Contents: AG reads "Punk Rock Your My Big Crybaby — Old Pond — Feeding Them Rassberies to Grow (by Peter Orlovsky) — Nurses Song (by William Blake)".

F75 *Ginsberg, Waldman, Orlovsky Reading.* Naropa Institute Archives Project, #043, Boulder, CO, Feb. 15, 1980. Cassette.
Contents: AG introductory comments and reads "I Sing of a Mayden [anon. 15th century song] — After 53 Years, I Still Cry Tears — Ruhr Gebiet — Tubingen-Hamburg Schlafwagen — Maybe Love — Love Forgiven".

F76 *Gaté.* Loft, #1001, Munich, W. Germany, April 15, 1980. 33 1/3 rpm, 12" stereo. Matrix side 1: ST L 1-A, matrix side 2: ST L 1-B.
Contents: AG reads "Gospel Noble Truths — My Pretty Rose Tree (by William Blake) — Put Down Yr Cigarette Rag — Everybody Sing — Don't Grow Old — Father Death Blues — Tyger (by William Blake) — Jimmy Berman Rag — Guru Blues — Sickness Blues — Gaté".
Note: Includes 4 pages with poems and translations by Michael Köhler and Wolfgang Mohrhenn as follows: "Gospel Noble Truths || Gospel Edle Wahrheiten — My Pretty Rose Tree || Mein Schöner Rosenstock — Put Down Yr Cigarette Rag — Everybody Sing — Don't Grow Old — Father Death Blues || Vater Tod Blues — The Tyger || Der Tiger — Sickness Blues || Krankheits-Blues — Jimmy Berman Rag — Guru Blues || Guru Blues (in German)".

F77 *First Blues.* S Press Tonbandverlag, Düsseldorf, W. Germany, April 15, 1980.   45
min., cassette.
Contents: AG reads "Gospel Noble Truths — My Pretty Rose Tree (by William
Blake) — Put Down Yr Cigarette Rag — Sickness Blues — Don't Grow Old —
Father Death Blues — Tyger (by William Blake) — Jimmy Berman Rag — Guru
Blues — Everybody Sing — Gaté". *Note:* This is the same recording as Loft
#1001 but the order of the poems is slightly revised.

F78 *Ginsberg, Whalen, and Clausen Reading.* Naropa Institute Archives Project, #046,
Boulder, CO, July 23, 1980.   2 cassettes.
Contents: AG comments and reads "Guru Blues — I Sing of a Mayden [anon. 15th
century song] — Love Forgiven — Nagasaki Days — Las Vegas: Verses
Improvised — Love Continued [Some Love] — A Tall Student [haiku] —
Tubingen-Hamburg Schlafwagen — Verses Written for Student Anti Draft Rally
1980 — Red Cheeked Boyfriends — Gospel Noble Truths — Reflections at Lake
Louise — The Rune".

F79 *Burroughs and Norse Reading.* Naropa Institute Archives Project, #048, Boulder,
CO, Aug. 13, 1980.   Cassette.
Contents: AG introductory comments.

F80 *Sugar, Alcohol, & Meat: The Dial-a-Poem Poets.* Giorno Poetry Systems Institute,
Lp GPS 018-019, New York, NY, 1980.   Produced by John Giorno.   33 1/3
rpm, 2-12" stereo records.   Matrix side 3: GPS017A.
Contents: AG reads "CIA Dope Calypso".

F81 *Allen Ginsberg Reading.* Naropa Institute Archives Project, #049, Boulder, CO,
June 24, 1981.   Cassette.
Contents: AG reads "Birdbrain — Grim Skeleton — Reflections at Lake Louise —
Thundering Undies (by AG and Ron Padgett) — Put Down Yr Cigarette Rag — I
Don't Like the Government Where I Live — Prayer Blues".

F82 Gluons.   *Birdbrain!* Alekos Records/Wax Trax Records, Denver, CO, 1981.   33 1/3
rpm, 7".   Matrix: 33-7-12811539.
Contents: AG reads "Birdbrain".

F83a *First Blues: Rags, Ballads and harmonium Songs.* Folkways Records, FSS 37560,
New York, NY, 1981.   Produced by Ann Charters.   33 1/3 rpm, 12" Lp stereo.
Matrix side A: FSS 37560 A, matrix side B: FSS 37560 B.
Contents: AG reads "4 AM Blues — New York Blues — NY Youth Call
Annunciation — Come Back Christmas — Macdougal Street Blues — CIA Dope
Calypso — Put Down Yr Cigarette Rag — Slack Key Guitar — Siratoka Beach
Croon — Bus Ride Ballad Road to Suva — Prayer Blues — Dope Fiend Blues".
Note: Issued with 4 pages containing the following: "Explanation of *First Blues*
[prose] — 4 AM Blues [with music notation] — New York Blues [with music
notation] — CIA Dope Calypso [with music notation] — Prayer Blues [with
music notation]".
F83b *First Blues.* Smithsonian Folkways Records, #37560, Washington, DC, 1991.
Cassette. *Note:* Reissue of Folkways FSS 37560 and also includes the 4 page
liner notes.

F84 *A Treasury of American Jewish Poets, vol. vi.* Spoken Arts, Inc., SAC 1150, New
Rochelle, NY, 1981.   Produced by Arthur Luce Klein.   Cassette.
Contents: AG reads "Kaddish".

F85   *The World Record: Readings at the St. Mark's Poetry Project 1969-1980.* Poetry Project, WR 1/2, New York, NY, 1981. Edited by Bill Berkson and Bob Rosenthal. 33 1/3 rpm, 12" Lp, 2 record set. Matrix side 2: PP-100-B.
Contents: AG reads: "Popeye and William Blake Fight to the Death [by Kenneth Koch and AG]".

F86   *German Tour: Allen Ginsberg, Peter Orlovsky, Steven Taylor.* S Press Tonbandverlag, SP 1079, Wuppertal, W. Germany, 1981. Cassette.
Contents: AG reads: "Ruhr Gebiet — Punk Rock — Ode to Failure — Dope Fiend Blues — Song of the Shrouded Stranger — Pull My Daisy — Don't Grow Old/Father Death Blues — Resigned — Love Forgiven".

F87   *Ginsberg Remembers.* New Dimensions Foundation, No. 1634, San Francisco, CA, 1981. 62 min., cassette.
Contents: AG interview comments.

F88   *Ginsberg, Sakaki, Orlovsky Reading.* Naropa Institute Archives Project, #050, Boulder, CO, April 28, 1982. Cassette.
Contents: AG comments and reads "Green Valentine Blues — Airplane Blues — Things I've Got to Do — You Want Money? — Homage to Philip Lamantia — Front Porch Haikus [Porch Scribbles] — Old Thoughts — The Black Man — That Tree — Homage Vajracara — Why I Meditate — Capitol Air — Do the Meditation Rock".

F89   *Blake's Greatest Hits.* Blue Moon Records, M112857, Kansas City, MO, 1982. Produced by J. N. Fleeman. 33 1/3 rpm, 7". Matrix side 1: M112857A 40187, matrix side 2: M112857B 40187.
Contents: AG reads "Nurse's Song (by William Blake)".
Note: Accompanies the book *Sparks of Fire,* also available separately.

F90   The Clash. *Combat Rock.* Epic Records, CBS Inc., FE 37689, FMLN 2, New York, NY, 1982. 33 1/3 rpm, 12" stereo. Matrix side 1: PAL-37689-1A, matrix side 2: PBL-37689-1A.
Contents: AG reads "Car Jamming (written with the assistance of AG) — Ghetto Defendant (vocal by AG) — Death Is a Star (written with the assistance of AG)".
Note: Also available as Epic Stereo Cassette PET 37689 and as Compact Disc EK 37689. Sleeve notes include words to songs on the phonodisc and compact disc, but not the cassette format.

F91   *A Little Bit of Awareness.* S Press Tapes, SP 1048, Wuppertal, W. Germany, 1982. 60 min., cassette.
Contents: AG reads "Ah [mantra] — Prayer Blues II, for John Lennon — The Rune — Howl".
Note: Cover sheet contains the lyrics for "Prayer Blues II, for John Lennon".

F92   *On the Road/The Jack Kerouac Conference.* Wind over the Earth, Inc., Naropa Institute, Boulder, CO, 1982. *Note:* A set of 70 cassette tapes of every program presented at the 10-day symposium organized by Allen Ginsberg under the auspices of Naropa Institute, July 23-Aug. 1, 1982. Every day the tapes were made and offered for sale on the day following the program. Each cassette containing AG's voice is listed with AG's contribution noted.

   Tape 231. *Conference Opening.* Ginsberg, Ven. Chögyam Trungpa, Rinpoche. [taped July 23, 1982].
   Contents: AG welcoming comments, questions during Trungpa's speech, comments and remarks.
   Tape 242. *Symposium on Texts I.* Coolidge, Creeley, Tallman. [taped July 24, 1982].
   Contents: AG closing announcements and comments.

Tape 243A & B. *Political Fallout of the Beat Generation.* Panel: Burroughs, Ginsberg, Hoffman, Leary, Krassner. [2 tapes made July 24, 1982].
Contents: AG comments and closing announcements.

Tape 246. *Workshop: Ginsberg.* [taped July 24, 1982].
Contents: AG workshop discussion and reads "On My Feet in the Ballroom on Stage".

Tape 251A & B. *Kerouac in Denver.* Brierly, Holmes, Ginsberg, Goldman, White, Livornese. [2 tapes made July 25, 1982].
Contents: AG comments and questions.

Tape 252. *Kerouac in the 80's.* Leary, Ginsberg, DiPrima. [taped July 25, 1982].
Contents: AG comments and announcements.

Tape 256. *Workshop: Ginsberg.* [taped July 25, 1982].
Contents: AG workshop discussion.

Tape 261. *Jack and Jazz.* Charters. [taped July 26, 1982].
Contents: AG closing comment.

Tape 262. *Kerouac's Biography.* Panel: Charters, McNally, Ziavras [sic: Jarvis], Nicosia, Walsh. [taped July 26, 1982].
Contents: AG announcements.

Tape 263B. *How the 50-60-70's Led to the 80's.* Hoffman [continued]. [taped July 26, 1982].
Contents: AG announcements.

Tape 271. *Kerouac and Women, the Beats & Women.* Panel: Cassady, Johnson, Parker, Pivano, Walsh, McClure. [taped July 27, 1982].
Contents: AG comments from the audience.

Tape 272B. *Jazz Concert: Amram, Granelli, Peacock, Priester, Landesman, Ginsberg, Gail, et al.* [taped July 27, 1982].
Contents: AG reads from "Mexico City Blues (by Jack Kerouac)".

Tape 279. *Reading: Burroughs, Holmes, Huncke.* [taped July 27, 1982].
Contents: AG introductions and comments.

Tape 282. *Recollections and Gossip.* Panel: Amram, Corso, Ginsberg, Holmes, Orlovsky, Parker, Pivano. [taped July 28, 1982].
Contents: AG comments and reminiscences.

Tape 289B. *Reading: DiPrima, McClure, Waldman.* [taped July 28, 1982].
Contents: AG announcements.

Tape 292. *Kerouac, Catholicism, and Buddhism.* Panel: Ginsberg, Holmes, Arguelles, Tendezin, Nicosia. [taped July 29, 1982].
Contents: AG introduction and comments.

Tape 293B. *Kesey & Babbs Present Cassady.* [taped July 29, 1982].
Contents: AG announcements.

Tape 300. *Micheline & Solomon Reading.* [taped July 31, 1982].
Contents: AG introduction.

Tape 302. *Censorship and the Beats.* Panel: Ginsberg, McClure, Landesman, Burroughs, Ferlinghetti. [taped July 30, 1982].
Contents: AG announcements and comments.

Tape 306A & B. *Workshop: Ginsberg.* [2 tapes recorded July 30, 1982].
Contents: AG workshop.

Tape 309A. *Reading: Bremser, Corso, J. Kerouac, Orlovsky, Johnson.* [taped July 30, 1982].
Contents: AG announcements.

Tape 312A & B. *Symposium on Texts II.* Charters, Holmes, McClure. [taped July 31, 1982].
Contents: AG comments from audience.

Tape 316A & B. *Workshop: Ginsberg.* [2 tapes recorded July 31, 1982].
Contents: AG workshop and includes excerpts of some of his poems.

Tape 319A & B. *Reading: Ferlinghetti, Ginsberg, Kesey.* [taped July 31, 1982].
Contents: AG comments and reads "On Neal's Ashes — Memory Gardens — Returning to the Country for a Brief Visit — Homage to Philip [Lamantia] — The Black Man — Those Two — Trungpa Lectures — Why I Meditate — Old Love Story — A Public Poetry — When Young I Drank Beer — What You Up To? —

He Was a Blue Eyed Baby — Jack Was the Creator of a World of Darkness — I Drove Out to the Airport — Do the Meditation Rock".

Tape 401A & B. *Oracles: An Agenda for the "Found Generation".* Berrigan, Bremser, Burroughs, Coolidge, Corso, DiPrima, Ginsberg, Knight, McClure, Micheline, Orlovsky, Waldman, et al. [2 tapes recorded Aug. 1, 1982].
Contents: AG comments and announcements.

F93 *Polyphonix !, Premiere Anthologie Sonore.* Multhipla Records, M20138, Milan, Italy, 1982. Produced by Cramps Records: Association Polyphonix, Giorno Poetry Systems. 33 1/3 rpm, 12" Lp stereo. Matrix side 1: M20138-A.
Contents: AG reads "I Sing of a Mayden [anon. 15th century song]".

F94 *Allen Ginsberg: Poetics and Meditation.* Ojai Foundation, Ojai, CA, 1982. 3 cassettes.
Contents: AG seminar.

F95 *S Press Sampler 1.* S Press Tonbandverlag, Wupertal, W. Germany, 1982. Cassette.
Contents: AG reads "Everybody Sing [from *First Songs* SP1080] — Punk Rock [from *German Tour* SP1079]".
Note: Issued in a limited edition of 50 copies for advertising only.

F96 *First Blues.* John Hammond Records, W2X 37673, New York, NY, Feb. 14, 1983. Produced by John Hammond. 33 1/3 rpm, 2-12" Lp stereo. Matrix side 1: W-38401-AS-1D, matrix side 2: W-38401-BS-1A, matrix side 3: W-38402, matrix side 4: W-38402-DS-1A.
Contents: AG reads "Going to San Diego — Vomit Express — Jimmy Berman Rag — NY Youth Call Annunciation — CIA Dope Calypso — Put Down Yr Cigarette Rag — Sickness Blues — Broken Bone Blues — Stay Away from the White House — Hardon Blues — Guru Blues — Everybody Sing — Gospel Noble Truths — Bus Ride Ballad to Suva — Prayer Blues — Love Forgiven — Father Death Blues — Dope Fiend Blues — Tyger (by William Blake) — You Are My Dildo (by Peter Orlovsky) — Old Pond — No Reason (by Steven Taylor) — My Pretty Rose Tree (by William Blake) — Capitol Air".
Note: Included with the records is a single sheet of photographs and an 8 page newspaper-format songsheet, entitled *The Ginsberg Gallimaufry* (Spring edition 1983) CW2X 37673. Includes "Going to San Diego — Vomit Express — Jimmy Berman Rag — NY Youth Call Annunciation — CIA Dope Calypso — Put Down Yr Cigarette Rag — Sickness Blues — Broken Bone Blues — Stay Away from the White House — Hardon Blues — Guru Blues — Everybody Sing — Gospel Noble Truths — Bus Ride Ballad Road to Suva — Prayer Blues — Love Forgiven — Father Death Blues — Dope Fiend Blues — The Tyger (by William Blake) — You Are My Dildo (by Peter Orlovsky) — Old Pond — No Reason (by Steven Taylor) — My Pretty Rose Tree (by William Blake) — Capitol Air — Holy Soul Jelly Roll [prose] — First Blues Hammond Sessions 1976 [prose]".

F97 Start. *Look Around.* Fresh Sounds, Inc., FS 203, Lawrence, KS, 1983. 33 1/3 rpm, 12" Lp stereo. Matrix side 2: 301024X-B.
Contents: AG reads "Little Fish/Big Fish".

F98 Allen Ginsberg & Het Mondriaan Quartet. *September on Jessore Road.* One World Poetry for Vinyl Records, Amsterdam, The Netherlands, 1983. 33 1/3 rpm, 7" black plastic flexidisc. Matrix SHOL 3377 A.
Contents: AG reads "September on Jessore Road [excerpt]".
Note: Issued as an insert in *Vinyl,* vol. 3, no. 24 (April 1983).

F99 *Allen Ginsberg with Still Life.* Local Anesthetic Records, LA LP-001, Denver, CO, 1983. Produced by Mike Chappelle. 33 1/3 rpm, 12" Lp. Matrix side A: E302X45-A, matrix side B: E302X45-B.
Contents: AG reads "The Warrior — Movement (AG reads excerpts from several poems) — Capitol Air — Pythagorean Spaghetti — Birdbrain".

F100 *You're a Hook.* Giorno Poetry Systems Institute, GPS 030, New York, NY, 1983. Produced by John Giorno and Gregory Schifrin. 33 1/3 rpm, 12" Lp stereo. Matrix side 2: GPS-030 B [crossed out is FW-39198-B GPS-030-B].
Contents: AG reads "Father Death Blues".

F101 *Amiri Baraka Reading.* Naropa Institute Archives Project, #060, Boulder, CO, July 28, 1984. Cassette.
Contents: AG announcements.

F102 *Something's Happening: Allen Ginsberg on KPFK.* Sound Photosynthesis, A0196-85, Mill Valley, CA, 1985. 90 min. cassette.
Contents: AG reads "I've Been Thinking about Plutonian — Hum Bom — Little Fish Devours the Big Fish — World Karma — Those Two — Written in My Dream by William Carlos Williams — Birdbrain — [interview comments] — Birdbrain (another version) — September on Jessore Road".

F103 *1985 Summer Poetry Series.* Allen Ginsberg, Philip Whalen, Eric Mottram. Sounds True, NP-2, Boulder, CO, 1985. Cassette.

F104a *Allen Ginsberg Reading.* Naropa Institute Archives Project, #063, Boulder, CO, May 22, 1986. Cassette.
Contents: AG reads announcements and "Gospel Noble Truths — Airplane Blues — Do the Meditation Rock — On the Conduct of the World Seeking Beauty — African Spirituality Will Save the Earth — You Don't Know It — Velocity of Money — Sphincter — Who's Gone? — Spot Anger — I Went in My Room in the Boarding House — Bob Dylan Touring with Grateful Dead — Nurses Song (by William Blake) — Porch Scribbles — Happening Now — 221 Syllables [at Rocky Mountain Dharma Center] — Fighting Phantoms [Fighting Phantoms] — Sunday Prayer — Student Love — In My Kitchen in New York — Memory Cousins — After Antipater — Cadillac Squack — Jumping the Gun on the Sun — Guru".

F104b *1986 Summer Poetry Series. Allen Ginsberg.* Sounds True, NP-7, Boulder, CO, May 22, 1986. Cassette. *Note:* Reissue of *Allen Ginsberg Reading* (Naropa Institute Archives Project, #063).

F105 *Jim Carroll Reading.* Naropa Institute Archives Project, #064, Boulder, CO, July 3, 1986. Cassette.
Contents: AG introductory comments.

F106 *1986 Summer Poetry Series. Allen Ginsberg, Steven Taylor, Andy Clausen.* Sounds True, NP-13, Boulder, CO, July 12, 1986. Cassette.

F107 *Made Up in Texas.* Paris Records, Dallas, TX, 1986. Produced by Les Michaels and Dennis Lowe. 33 1/3 rpm, 12" Lp. Matrix side A: PAR-001A-5H1, matrix side B: PAR001B.
Contents: AG reads "Airplane Blues — Nurses Song (by William Blake)".

F108 *The 20th Anniversary of the Summer of Love: 1967-1987.* Shimmy-Disc, Shimmy-001, New York, NY, 1987. Produced by Kramer. 33 1/3 rpm, 12" Lp. Matrix side B: SHIMMY 001-B.
Contents: AG reads "Dear M".

F109 *Hobo Blues Band and Allen Ginsberg: Üvöltés.* Krem, SLPM 37048, Budapest, Hungary, 1987. 33 1/3 rpm, 12" Lp stereo. Matrix side A: SLPM 37048A, matrix side B: SLPM 37048B.
Contents: AG reads "Gospel Noble Truths — Tear Gas Rag — Guru Blues — Come Back Christmas — Cafe in Warsaw — Sickness Blues — Howl".

F110 *New Letters on the Air: Allen Ginsberg.* New Letters Magazine, No. 040188, Kansas City, MO, 1988. Interview by Rebekah Presson and Robert Stewart in Sept. 1987. 29 min., cassette.
Contents: AG interview comments.
Note: This was broadcast on National Public Radio after the initial transmission on April 1, 1988.

F111 *Poetry Performance: Allen Ginsberg, Anne Waldman, Steven Taylor.* Sounds True, NP-24, Boulder, CO, 1988. Cassette.

F112 *Selections from Howl.* Eva-Tone Soundsheets, Clearwater, FL, 1988. Black floppy phonorecording. Matrix side 1: EV 104623-1AT, matrix side 2: EV 104623-1BT.
Contents: AG reads "Howl".
Note: This square plastic record appeared between pp. 16 & 17 in *Chicago History,* vol. 17, no. 1-2 (Spring-Summer 1988).

F113 *Philip Agee on the CIA & Covert Action.* Ram's Horn Productions, Haledon, NJ, 1988. Edited by Stuart Hutchison. 3 hrs., 2 cassettes.
Contents: AG reads "CIA Dope Calypso".
Note: Recorded at Wm. Paterson College on April 26, 1988 and first broadcast on National Public Radio on Oct. 27, 1988.

F114 *Allen Ginsberg, Reading His Own Works.* Albert Hofman Foundation, #103, Santa Monica, CA, March 1989. Cassette.
Contents: AG comments and reads "CIA Dope Calypso — A Western Ballad — Song [The Weight] — Sunflower Sutra — Kaddish [excerpt] — Wales Visitation — Jaweh and Allah Battle — Do the Meditation Rock — White Shroud — Written in My Dream by W. C. Williams".

F115 *The Lion for Real.* Great Jones/Island Records, Inc, CCD 6004, New York, NY, Nov. 11, 1989. Produced by Hal Willner. Compact disc. Also issued as cassette #ZGJ 6004 with contents as the CD but without the poem "C'Mon Jack". Also issued as phonorecording #GJ 6004, matrix side A: GJ 6004-A-RE1, matrix side B: GJ 6004-B-RE1 with contents the same as the cassette issue.
Contents: AG reads "Scribble — Complaint of the Skeleton to Time — Xmas Gift — To Aunt Rose — The Lion for Real — Refrain — The Shrouded Stranger — Gregory Corso's Story — Cleveland, The Flats — The End — Stanzas: Written at Night in Radio City — Sunset — Hum Bom! — Kral Majales — Guru — Ode to Failure — C'Mon Jack".
Note: Issued with liner notes which include the words to all the poems plus a brief description of each poem by AG. Second and subsequent pressings make no reference to Great Jones and is listed only as Island Records.

F116 *Tuli Kupferberg: Tuli & Friends.* Shimmy Disc, Shimmy 020, New York, NY, 1989. Produced by Kramer at Noise. 33 1/3 rpm, 12" Lp. Matrix side B: Shimmy 20B. Also available as a cassette.
Contents: AG reads "Go Fuck Yourself with Your Atom Bomb".

F117 *We Magazine,* no. 11 (June 1989) audio cassette format.
Contents: AG reads "White Shroud".

F118   *Allen Ginsberg: Live and Lively Accompanied by Don Was.* Sound Photosynthesis, A 0601-90, Mill Valley, CA, 1990. 90 min., cassette.
Contents: AG reads "CIA Dope Calypso — Do the Meditation — Europe Who Knows? — Gospel Noble Truths — Hard Labor — Drive All Blames in One — Cosmopolitan Greetings — On the Conduct of the World Against Government — Personals Ad — May Days 1988 — Father Death Blues — Airplane Blues — Don't Smoke — Grandma Earth's Song — I Went to the Movie of Life — Nurse's Song (by William Blake)".

F119   *Speak Up,* vol. 6, no. 66 (Sept. 1990) Milan, Italy. Cassette.
Contents: AG interview comments and reads "Father Death Blues".
Note: Issued with the magazine *Speak Up,* vol. 6, no. 66 (Sept. 1990) which is published for Italians learning to speak English.

Related Item: *Phil Ochs: There & Now: Live in Vancouver, 1968.* Rhino/Archives, R2 70778, Los Angeles, CA, 1990.
Contents: AG plays finger-cymbals on one cut "The Bells".

F119X   *Tonite Let's All Make Love In London.* See For Miles Records, SEE CD 258, Ashford, England, 1990. Compact disk.
Contents: AG reads "Tonite Let's All Make Love In London".

F120   *Catullus, Selected Poems Read by Allen Ginsberg.* Spring Audio, Inc., New York, NY, 1991. 35 min., cassette.
Contents: AG reads poems by Gaius Valerius Catullus as translated by Jacob Rabinowitz.

F121   *The Dharma Bums by Jack Kerouac, Read by Allen Ginsberg.*   Audio Literature, CP 147, Berkeley, CA, 1991. 3 hrs., 2 cassettes. Serial number on tape #1: CP 147 1 1112, serial number on tape #2: CP 147 293.
Contents: AG reads *The Dharma Bums* (by Jack Kerouac).

F122   *Fear, Power, God: Birth of Tragedy Magazine.* CFY Records, Stanford, CA, 1991. 33 1/3 rpm, white vinyl 12" Lp. Matrix side 2: CFY 004 B1.
Contents: AG reads "A Song [Europe Who Knows?] — Dream about William Carlos Williams [Written in My Dream by W. C. Williams]"

F123   *Poets in Person: Allen Ginsberg.* Modern Poetry Association for Poetry Magazine, Chicago, IL, 1991. 30 min., cassette.
Contents: AG interview comments.
Note: Recording of a National Public Radio broadcast series entitled 'Poets in Person' in July 1991. The set of 14 programs were not available individually until 1992.

F124   *The Beat Generation.* Rhino Records, R2 70281, Santa Monica, CA, 1992. 3 CD set. Also available as a 3 cassette set, #R4 70281.
Contents: AG interview comments and reads "America".

F125   *The Museum Inside the Telephone Network: InterCommunication '91.* Nippon Telegraph and Telephone Corp., No. 1C 91-001, Tokyo, Japan, 1992. 2 CD set.
Contents: AG reads "American Haikus".

F126   *September on Jessore Road.* Soyo Records, CD 0001, Amsterdam, The Netherlands, 1992. Produced by Benn W. Posset. Compact disc.
Contents: AG reads "September on Jessore Road".

F127   *Utopia Americana.* New Tone, #NT 6707, San Germano, Italy, 1992. Compiled by Renzo Pognant Gros. Compact disc.
Contents: AG reads "Hum Bomb — Father Death Blues".

F128 Glass, Philip. *Hydrogen Jukebox.* Libretto by Allen Ginsberg. Electra Nonesuch, #79286-2, New York, NY, 1993. Compact disc.
Contents: AG reads "Iron Horse (excerpt) — Jaweh and Allah Battle (excerpt) — To P.O. (excerpt) — Wichita Vortex Sutra (excerpt) — Howl (excerpt) — Nagasaki Days (excerpt) — Throw Out the Yellow Journalists (excerpt)".
Note: Includes printed libretto and liner notes which contain the following: "Philip Glass and I [prose] — Iron Horse (excerpt) — Jaweh and Allah Battle — To P. O. — Crossing Nation (excerpt) — To Poe: Over the Planet, Air Albany Baltimore (excerpt) — Wichita Vortex Sutra (excerpt) — Howl (excerpt) — Cabin in the Woods (excerpt) — Nagasaki Days (excerpt) — To Aunt Rose — The Green Automobile (excerpt) — N.S.A. Dope Calypso — Ayers Rock/Uluru Song (excerpt) — Throw Out the Yellow Journalists (excerpt) — Father Death Blues

F129 *Howls, Raps & Roars: Recordings from the San Francisco Poetry Renaissance.* Fantasy Records, 4 FCD-4410-2, Berkeley, CA, 1993. 4 CD set.
Contents: AG reads "Howl — Footnote to Howl — A Supermarket in California — Transcription of Organ Music — America — In Back of the Real — Strange New Cottage in Berkeley — Europe! Europe! — Kaddish, pt. 1 — Sunflower Sutra — Patna-Benares Express — May 22 (1962) Calcutta".

F130 *Omphalos.* White Fields Press, #DIDX 019485, Louisville, KY, 1993. Compiled by Richies Lemon and Herb Media. Compact disc.
Contents: AG reads "Put Down Your Cigarette Rag".

F131 *Allen Ginsberg: Holy Soul Jelly Roll—Songs and Poems (1949-1993).* Rhino Records, PRCD 7068, Los Angeles, CA, 1994. 1 CD [promotional issue]
Contents: AG reads and sings "Pull My Daisy — The Green Automobile — Howl [pt. 2] — Pacific High Studio Mantas — Kral Majales — Capitol Air — Nurse's Song (by William Blake)".
Note: Although designated as not for sale many of these advance CD's were in fact available at $15.00 each during the Naropa Conference for Allen Ginsberg in July 1994.

G

Film, Radio and Television Appearances by Allen Ginsberg

FILMS:

G1 *Pull My Daisy.* Directed and produced by Robert Frank and Alfred Leslie. G-String Productions; New York, NY. 1959. 29 min., black and white, 16 mm.
Contents: AG appears as himself without dialogue.
Note: Filmed between Jan. and April 1959, based on a free adaptation of the 3rd act of Jack Kerouac's unpublished play "The Beat Generation" and narrated by Jack Kerouac. Premiered at The Cinema 16 (New York, NY) program 2, season 13, Nov. 10/11, 1959.

G2 *Guns of Trees.* Directed and produced by Jonas Mekas. New York, NY. 1962. 75 min., black and white, available in 35 mm & 16 mm.
Contents: AG reads part of "Death to Van Gogh's Ear — Sunflower Sutra — The Fall of America".
Note: Spoken in the film's soundtrack, some by AG personally, are excerpts from the above poems and improvisations. Folksongs by Sarah and Caither Wiley and Tom Sankey.

G3 *Couch.* Directed by Andy Warhol. New York, NY. 1964. 58 min.
Contents: AG appears as himself.

G4 *Allen for Allen.* Directed and produced by Barbara Rubin. New York, NY. 1965. 20 min., black and white, 16 mm.
Contents: AG reads "Who Be Kind To — The Change — Mantras".
Note: Filmed June 11, 1965 at Royal Albert Hall, London. Premiered at The Film-Makers' Cinematheque.

G5 *Wholly Communion.* Directed and produced by Peter Whitehead. Lorrimer Films, Ltd., London, England. 1965. 35 min., black and white, 16 mm.
Contents: AG reads "International Poetry Incarnation [England! Awake! Awake!] — Who Be Kind To — The Change".
Note: Filmed at Royal Albert Hall, London. Premiered at the Academy Cinema (London), April 1966.

G6 *Galaxie.* Directed and produced by Gregory J. Markopoulos. 1966. 90 min., color, 16 mm.
Contents: AG appears briefly.
Note: Premiered in New York in 1966.

G7 *Hare Krishna.* Directed and produced by Jonas Mekas. New York, NY. 1966. 4 min., color, 16 mm.
Contents: AG chants "Hare Krishna".
Note: This included in full in the longer *Walden: Reel Two.*

G8a *Walden: Reel Two.* Directed and produced by Jonas Mekas. New York, NY. 1966. 40 min., color, 16 mm.
Contents: AG chants "Hare Krishna".
Note: This includes all of the film *Hare Krishna* (1966).

G8b *Walden.* Directed by Jonas Mekas. Film-Maker's Coop; New York, NY. 1969. 185 min., color.
Contents: AG appears as himself.

G9 *U.S.A. Poetry (No. 2): Allen Ginsberg and Lawrence Ferlinghetti.* Produced by Richard Moore. Produced and directed by KQED Film Unit, San Francisco for National Educational Television and Radio Center, New York, NY. 1966. 30 min., black and white, 16 mm.
Contents: AG interviewed and reads "Howl — Who Be Kind To — Kral Majales — New York to San Fran — Guru".
Note: Filmed on July 18, 1965 and Dec. 14, 1965. TV broadcast premiere on WNET-TV (New York, NY) the week of March 7, 1966. An audio-video TV filmscript was mimeographed and stapled with the cover title: *U.S.A.: Poetry/Allen Ginsberg and Lawrence Ferlinghetti.*

G10 *The N.E.T. Outtake Series: Ginsberg.* Produced by Richard O. Moore. American Poetry Archive and the Poetry Center, San Francisco, CA. 1966. 55 min., black and white, videotape.
Contents: AG interviewed and reads "Kral Majales — Guru — The Moments Return" — [conversation with Neal Cassady and Peter Orlovsky].
Note: Filmed on July 18, 1965 and Dec. 14, 1965. Contains all footage of AG not used in *U.S.A. Poetry (No. 2): Allen Ginsberg and Lawrence Ferlinghetti.*

G11 *America's Wonderful.* Directed by Bob Giorgio. 1967. 7 min., color, 16 mm.
Contents: AG appears as himself.

G12 *Be-In: 1967.* Directed by Jerry Abrams. 1967. 7 min., color, 16 mm.
Contents: AG appears as himself.

G13 *Chappaqua.* Directed and produced by Conrad Rooks. Universal, New York, NY. 1967. color.
Contents: AG chants the mantra "Bopala Gopala Devaki Nandana Gopala".
Note: Filmed in 1966 with cameraman, Robert Frank. Premiered at Sutton Theater (New York, NY) Nov. 5, 1967.

G14 *Don't Look Back.* Directed by Donn A. Pennebaker. Produced by Leacock Pennebaker, Albert Grossman, and John Court. New York, NY. 1967. 96 min., black and white, 16 mm. blown up to 35 mm. and available on video cassette after 1981.
Contents: AG appears as himself, with no dialogue.
Note: Filmed in April-May 1965. Premiered at Presidio Theater (San Francisco, CA) May 17, 1967.

G15 *Farm Diary.* Directed by Gordon Ball. New York, NY. 1967. 64 min., color, Std. 8 mm., silent.
Contents: AG appears as himself.

G16 *Herostratus.* Directed by Don Levy. Produced by Don Levy and James Quinn. I Films Ltd. with the British Film Institute Production and Board and BBC TV Enterprises, London, England. 1967. 142 min., color, 35 mm.
Contents: AG appears in excerpts taken from *Wholly Communion.*
Note: Premiered at the I.C.A. (London) July 1967.

G17 *Joan of Arc.* Directed and produced by Piero Heliczer. New York, NY. 1967. 30 min., color, 8 mm., silent.
Contents: AG appears in a police uniform.

G18 *Maha Mantra: Ginsberguru.* Directed by Gregg Barrios. Texas Underground, The Gulf-Coast Film-Makers Cooperative, 1967.
Contents: AG appears as himself.
Note: Premiered in June 1967 at the Film-Makers' Cinematheque.

G19 *Screen Tests: A Diary.* Directed by Andy Warhol. Produced by Andy Warhol, Gerard Malanga and Lita Hornick. Kulchur Press, New York, NY. 1967. 3 min., black and white, 16 mm., silent.
Contents: AG appears as himself.

G20 *Camera Message No. 3: Summer Happenings U.S.A. (1967-8).* Directed by Takahiko Iimura. Sound by Akiko. 1968. 27 min., 16 mm.
Contents: AG dialogue on soundtrack of film.

G21 *Me and My Brother.* Directed by Robert Frank. Produced by Helen Silverstein. Screenplay by Sam Sheppard and Robert Frank. New Yorker Films; New York, NY. 1969. 91 min., color and black and white segments.
Contents: AG appears as himself and chants mantras.
Note: Filmed in 1964. Premiered at New Yorker Theater (New York, NY) Feb. 2-8, 1969.

G22 *Breathing Together: Revolution of the Electric Family.* Directed by Morley Markson. Edited by Morley Markson and J. N. W. Smith. New Line Cinema; New York, NY. 1971. 83 min., black and white.
Contents: AG appears as himself.
Note: Premiered at Whitney Museum on April 16, 1971.

G23 *Ciao! Manhattan.* Produced by Robert Margouleff, John Palmer and David Weisman. Screenplay by John Palmer and David Weisman. Court Productions Inc.; A Sugarloaf Films Inc. release. 1973. 90 min., color with black and white segments.
Contents: AG appears briefly in a party scene filmed ca. 1967 in black and white.

G24 *Emunah.* Directed by Pamela Badyk. Produced by Barbara Rubin. City College; New York, NY. 1973. 18 min., color and black and white, 16 mm. Sound on 1/2" track mono 7 1/2 ips.
Contents: Tape soundtrack made by AG.

G25 *Pickup's Tricks.* Directed and produced by Gregory Pickup. Inner City Reels, Inc.; San Francisco, CA. 1973.
Contents: AG appears dressed as a 'Jewish Mother'.
Note: Premiered at the Palace Theatre (San Francisco, CA) Nov. 9, 1973.

G26 *The Writer's Forum: Poets on Video Tape: The Poetry of Allen Ginsberg.* Produced by Francis R. Filardo. New York State University at Brockport; Brockport, NY. 1974. 58 min. Available in 1" ampex, 2" ampex, 1/2" EIAJ-1, U-Matic videocassettes.
Contents: AG comments and reads "Wales Visitation — The Trembling of the Veil — A Western Ballad — Mantra to Shiva — Little Lamb (by William Blake) —

The Nurse's Song (by William Blake)" — [and passages from Poe, Shelley, Dante, Kerouac — includes an interview with AG by William Heyen and Allen DeLoach].
Note: Filmed in 1970.

G27   *The American Poetry Archive, First Series: Allen Ginsberg/Louis Ginsberg.* The Poetry Center, San Francisco State University; San Francisco, CA. 1975. Color, 1/2" reel-to-reel videotape, 3/4" videotape cassette.
Contents: AG reads "Flying Elegy — Pentagon Exorcism — Jaweh and Allah Battle — Stay Away from the White House — Teton Village — On Neruda's Death — The Great Father — What Would You Do If You Lost It? — Mantra".

G28   *A Film about Allen Ginsberg.* Directed and produced by Michael F. Cassidy and Richard Reeder. St. Cloud State College; St. Cloud, MN. 1976. 10 min., black and white, 16 mm.
Contents: AG comments and reads "Can't Find Anyone [Guru Blues] — Gaté — Sakyamuni Coming out from the Mountain".

G29   *Crow Dog's Paradise.* Produced by Mark Elliott. Centre Productions, Inc.; Boulder, CO. 1978. 28 min., color, 16 mm. or 3/4" video cassette.
Contents: AG narrates the film.
Note: Taped on April 13, 1978.

G30   *Renaldo & Clara.* Directed by Bob Dylan. Lombard Street Films; New York, NY. 1978. 292 min.
Contents: AG appears as himself.
Note: Filmed in the Fall 1975, edited in 1977 and premiered Jan. 25, 1978. An edited, 2 hour version was released in the Fall of 1978.

G31   *Fried Shoes, Cooked Diamonds.* Directed by Costanzo Allione. Produced by Carmina Cinematografica S.R.L.; Santhia, Italy. 1979. 55 min., color, videocassette. [later on VHS-B109 by Mystic Fire Video (New York, NY)]
Contents: AG interview comments and reads "Father Death Blues — Plutonian Ode".

G32   *Poet and His Place: William Carlos Williams' 'Paterson'.* Directed and produced by Richard Atnally. William Paterson College; Wayne, NJ. 1979.
Contents: AG appears.

G33   *The Beats: An Existential Comedy.* Directed by Philomene Long. Produced by Jay D. Kugelman. Venice of America Films; Venice, CA. 1980. black and white.
Contents: AG comments.
Note: Premiered on May 24, 1980 at Fox Venice (Venice, CA).

G34   *The Living Tradition: Ginsberg on Whitman.* Centre Productions Inc.; Boulder, CO. 1980. 1 filmstrip (120 frames), color, 2 cassettes.
Contents: AG narrates and reads "Ginsberg on Whitman (11 min.) — Ginsberg Reads Whitman (13 min.)".
Note: This is a full-color sound filmstrip with an additional cassette.

G35   *Plutonium Ode.* Directed by G. P. Skratz and Linda Lemon. 1980.
Contents: AG reads "Plutonian Ode".

G36   *Buddha Bellies.* Directed by Sheila Carr. 1981. 8 min., black and white.
Contents: AG script and narration.

G37 *Amiri Baraka: In Motion.* Produced by St. Clair Bourne. Chamba Organization; Franklin Lakes, NJ. 1982. 58 min., color. Available in 3/4" or 1/2" video cassette.
Contents: AG comments.
Note: TV broadcast premiere on June 28, 1983 on WNET-TV (New York, NY).

G38 *Guerre a la Guerre.* Directed by Francoise Mimet. Produced by Jean-Jacques Lebel. UNESCO; Paris, France. 1982. Video cassette.
Contents: AG appears.
Note: Premiered on June 23, 1983 in Italy.

G39 *Poetry in Motion.* Directed and produced by Ron Mann. Sphinx Productions in association with Giorno Poetry Systems; Toronto, Canada. 1982. Also available in 1985 on video cassette from Voyager Press (Los Angeles, CA) and in 1989 as 1 videodisc, digital sound.
Contents: AG interview comments and reads "Birdbrain — Do the Meditation Rock — Capitol Air".
Note: Premiered at Bloor Cinema (Toronto, Canada) on Sept. 17, 1982.

G40 *Allan 'n' Allen's Complaint.* Directed by Nam June Paik. Produced by Nam June Paik and Shigeko Kubota. Send Video Arts; San Francisco, CA. 1983. 30 min., color, 1/2" cassette, VTG-101, VHS or Beta.
Contents: AG appears as himself.

G41 *Back to Wuppertal.* Produced by Joachim Ortmanns and Wolfgang Mohrhenn. S Press Video; Wuppertal, W. Germany. 1983. 90 min., color, videocassettes: VHS, Betamax, Video 2000.
Contents: AG reads "Back to Wuppertal — Gospel Noble Truths — America — Homework — Punk Rock Your My Big Crybaby — The Warrior — Dope Fiend Blues — Everybody Sing — Ruhr-Gebiet — Lower East Side — Don't Grow Old [Wasted Arms] — Father Death Blues" and sings Blake songs.
Note: Videocassette is packaged in a box with the booklet: *Allen Ginsberg on Tour Feb. 16, 1983.*

G42 *Burroughs: The Movie.* Directed by Howard Brookner. Produced by Alan Yentrob and Howard Brookner. Citifilmworks; New York, NY. 1983. 86 min., color.
Note: Available as a VHS or Beta videocassette in 1985 from Giorno Poetry Systems (New York, NY).
Contents: AG interview comments.

G43 *Before Stonewall.* Directed by Greta Schiller. Co-directed by Robert Rosenberg. Produced by Robert Rosenberg, John Scagliotti and Greta Schiller. Before Stonewall Inc. and the Center for the Study of Filmed History released through David Whitten Promotions; New York, NY. 1984.
Contents: AG comments.
Note: Premiered in New York at the Waverly Theatre, June 27, 1985.

G44 *Dedicated to Jack Kerouac/This Song for Jack.* Directed and produced by Robert Frank. New York, NY. 1984. 30 min., black and white.
Contents: AG interview comments.
Note: Premiered at S.W.A.T. Theater (New York, NY) on Jan. 5, 1984. Filmed at the 1982 On the Road Conference in Boulder, CO.

G45 *Kerouac.* Directed by John Antonelli. Produced by John Antonelli and Will Parrinello. Kerouac Inc.; San Francisco, CA. 1984. 90 min., color.
Contents: AG interview comments.
Note: Premiered at Roxie Cinema (San Francisco, CA) on July 2, 1985.

G46 *Manhattan Poetry Video Project.* Directed by Karoly Bardosh. Produced by Rose
Lesniak. Out There Productions; New York, NY. 1984. 5 min. Also available
as a videocassette.
Contents: AG reads "Father Death Blues".
Note: Premiered at the Public Theater (New York, NY) on Sept. 16, 1984.

G47 *What Happened to Kerouac?* Directed by Richard Lerner and Lewis MacAdams.
Produced by Richard Lerner. Written by Malcolm Hart and Lewis MacAdams.
Overseas Filmgroup; Los Angeles, CA. 1984. 96 min., color, 35 mm.
Contents: AG interview comments.
Note: premiered at One World Poetry Festival (Amsterdam, The Netherlands) in
1984. Theatrical premiere at Cinema Studio 2 (New York, NY) May 23, 1986.

G48 *It Don't Pay to Be an Honest Citizen.* Directed by Jacob Burckhardt. Naropa
Poetics Program; Boulder, CO. 1985.
Contents: AG appears as himself.
Note: Premiered at Naropa Institute (Boulder, CO) on April 24, 1985.

G49 *The Beat Generation: An American Dream.* Directed and produced by Janet
Foreman. Renaissance Motion Pictures. 1987. 90 min., color.
Contents: AG appears as himself.
Note: Premiered at the Berlin Film Festival (Berlin, Germany) on Feb. 21, 1987.
Theatrical premier at the Roxie Cinema (San Francisco, CA) on Dec. 2, 1987.

G50 *The First American Poetry Disc, vol. 1: An Introduction to Poetry* and *vol. 2:
Contemporary American Poetry.* County College of Morris; Randolph, NJ.
1987. Available in VHS, Beta, 3/4" and Laserdisc formats.
Contents: AG reads.

G51 *Meditation, Clear Seeing & Poetics.* Dharma Communications; Mt. Tremper, NY.
1988. 70 min., color. VHS cassette, speed: SP.
Contents: AG reads "A Western Ballad — Going to the World of the Dead — CIA
Dope Calypso — Visiting Father and Friends — Sphincter — Spot Anger —
Cosmopolitan Greetings — Graphic Winces — I Went to the Movie of Life — On
Cremation of Chögyam Trungpa Vidyandara — Brain Washed by Numerous
Mountain Streams — Tompkins Park — Proclamation — When Dull Roots Write
Laws in Sweden or New York — Salutations to Fernando Pessoa — May Days
1988 — Fifth Internationale — Europe, Who Knows? — I Was Traveling on the
Subway — Jaweh and Allah Battle — Gospel Noble Truths".

G52 *Gang of Souls.* Directed by Maria Beatty. Giorno Video Pak; New York, NY.
1989. 60 min. VHS video cassette.
Contents: AG reads "Fifth Internationale".
Note: Filmed in New York City in 1988.

G53 *Growing Up in America.* Directed and produced by Morley Markson. Cinephile
Pictures. 1989. 81 min.
Contents: AG appears as himself.
Note: Premiered at Santa Monica 4-Plex (Santa Monica, CA) on Jan. 2, 1989.

G54 *Heavy Petting.* Directed by Obie Benz. Skouras Pictures. 1989. 86 min. Later
available on VHS video cassette.
Contents: AG interview comments.

G55 *Lannan Literary Series, no. 9: Allen Ginsberg.* Directed and produced by Lewis
MacAdams and John Dorr. Lannan Foundation in association with Metropolitan
Pictures and EZTV; Los Angeles, CA. 1989. 87 min. VHS video cassette.
Contents: AG interview comments and reads "A Western Ballad — Do the
Meditation Rock — Airplane Blues — Fifth Internationale — May Days 1988 —

Spot Anger — Cosmopolitan Greetings — A Supermarket in California — America — Sunflower Sutra — Kaddish [excerpt] — Guru — On Neal's Ashes — Father Death Blues — Put Down Yr Cigarette Rag".

G56 *Play It Again, Nam.* Directed by Nam June Paik. Produced by Jean-Paul Fargier. Ex Nihilo, Canal + Centre Georges Pompidou; Paris, France. 1990. 29 min., color. VHS video cassette, NTSC.
Contents: AG appears as himself.

G57 *A Moveable Feast: Profiles of Contemporary American Authors.* In Our Time Arts Media, Inc., Atlas Video, VHS 2142. 1991. 8-videocassettes (ca. 30 min. each) sound, color, 1/2 in.
Contents: AG appears as himself.

G58 *The Life and Times of Allen Ginsberg.* Produced by Jerry Aronson. Edited by Nathaniel Dorsky. 1992. 83 minutes.
Contents: AG interview comments and reads "Song (The Weight of the World) — Tears — Howl (excerpt) — Kaddish (excerpt) — Kral Majales (excerpt) — Wales Visitation (excerpt) — Plutonian Ode (excerpt) — Don't Grow Old (Old Poet) — Father Death Blues — Broken Bones Blues".

G59 *The American Poetry Review Presents Allen Ginsberg.* Philadelphia, PA: American Poetry Review, 1993. 103 min., color, VHS cassette.
Contents: AG comments and reads "Dream Record June 8, 1955 — Howl (excerpt) — A Supermarket in California — Ode to Walt Whitman (by Federico Garcia Lorca) — Sunflower Sutra — Kaddish (excerpt) — Don't Grow Old (Wasted Arms) — Do the Meditation Rock — To Aunt Rose — Wales Visitation — Birdbrain — Priimiitittiii (by Kurt Schwitters) — Hum Bom! — Tyger (by William Blake) — Infant Joy (by William Blake) — My Pretty Rose Tree (by William Blake) — The Sick Rose (by William Blake) — The Sunflower (by William Blake) — The Nurse's Song (by William Blake) — The Lamb (by William Blake) — Written in My Dream by William Carlos Williams — To Elsie (by William Carlos Williams) — Ode to the West Wind (by Percy Bysshe Shelley)".

G60 *New York Post Wave.* High Frequency Wavelengths, Inc.; New York, NY, 1993. Produced and directed by Marilynn P. Danitz. 19 min., color, VHS cassette.
Contents: AG reads "September on Jessore Road".

SELECTED HIGHLIGHTS
OF RADIO AND TV BROADCAST APPEARANCES

GG1 *Poetry: Allen Ginsberg.* KPFA Radio; Berkeley, CA. 1956. 25 min. Radio broadcast: Oct. 25, 1956; re-broadcast: Aug. 26, 1961 and Dec. 1, 1962.
Contents: AG reads "Howl — A Supermarket in California — In Back of the Real".

GG2 *Beatniks at the University.* KPFA Radio; Berkeley, CA. 1959. 33 min. Radio broadcast: Aug. 31, 1959.
Contents: "Sakyamuni Coming Out From the Mountain — Epithalamium — A Strange New Cottage in Berkeley — Fragment 1956 — Short Line Improvisation — Ignu".
Note: This is a recording of the University of Chicago reading.

GG3 *Under Discussion: The Poet Looks at the Twentieth Century.* Produced by Joann Goldberg. Moderated by Heywood Hale Broun. Metromedia, Inc.; Metropolitan

382 Film, Radio and Television Appearances

Broadcasting Television Division for WNEW-TV; New York, NY. 1964. 90 min. TV broadcast: Sept. 13, 1964.
Contents: AG as panel member.

GG4 *Third Programme: Poetry of Allen Ginsberg.* Hosted by Eric Mottram. Interviewed by Philip French. BBC; London, England. 1965. 30 min., TV broadcast: Dec. 14, 1965.
Contents: AG interview comments and reads "Magic Psalm".

GG5 *Tonight: 4th June, 1965.* Produced by Derrick Amoore. BBC; London, England. 1965. 35 min. TV broadcast: June 4, 1965.
Contents: AG interview comments.

GG6 *What Do You Want Me To Say?* KQED-TV; Berkeley, CA. 1965. 60 min. TV broadcast: Dec. 3, 1965.
Contents: AG acts as interview for Bob Dylan.

GG7 *Alan Burke Show.* Hosted by Alan Burke. Radio broadcast: Sept. 10, 1966.

GG8 *Video Sutra.* Produced by Sandra Gardner. KQED-TV; Berkeley, CA. 1966. 55 min. TV broadcast: Aug. 2, 1966.
Contents: AG reads "Wichita Vortex Sutra — Mantra".

GG9 *Changes.* KPFA Pacifica Radio; Berkeley, CA. 1967. Radio broadcast: Feb. 1967.
Contents: AG panel discussion.

GG10 *Merv Griffin Show.* Hosted by Merv Griffin. Anthony Productions. TV broadcast taped: June 22, 1967.
Contents: AG interview comments.

GG11 *The Mind Alchemists.* Directed and produced by Michael Tuchner. BBC-TV; London, England. 1967. 45 min., black and white, 16 mm. TV broadcast: Aug. 18, 1967.
Contents: AG comments.

GG12 *Father & Son, pt. 1 & 2.* KPFA-Radio: Berkeley, CA. 1968. 150 min. Radio broadcast: May 11-12, 1968.
Contents: AG and Louis Ginsberg interview comments.

GG13 *Firing Line: The Avante-Garde.* Hosted by William F. Buckley, Jr. New York, NY. 1968. 60 min. TV broadcast: Sept. 24, 1968.
Contents: AG interview comments.

GG14 *David Frost Show.* Hosted by David Frost. Group W Productions; Los Angeles, CA. 1969. TV broadcast: Aug. 8, 1969.
Contents: AG interview comments.

GG15 *Dick Cavett Show.* Hosted by Dick Cavett. New York, NY. 1969. TV broadcast: July 29, 1969.
Contents: AG interview comments.

GG16 *Merv Griffin Show.* Hosted by Merv Griffin. 1970. TV broadcast taped: May 13, 1970.
Contents: AG and Louis Ginsberg interviewed.

GG17 *Free Time: Allen Ginsberg & Friends.* Produced by Fern McBride. PBS-TV and WNET-TV; New York, NY. 1971. 90 min. TV broadcast: Nov. 16, 1971.
Contents: AG reads "Nurse's Song (by William Blake) — A Dream — Mantra — September on Jessore Road".

GG18 *Blake Films.* ABC-TV; New York, NY. 1972. TV broadcast: Jan. 16 & 23, 1972.
Contents: AG reads as the voice of William Blake.

GG19 *Dick Cavett Show.* Hosted by Dick Cavett. New York, NY. 1972. TV broadcast: Jan. 27, 1972.
Contents: AG interview comments.

GG20 *Speaking Freely.* Hosted by Edwin Newman. NBC-TV; New York, NY. 1975. 60 min. TV broadcast: May 24, 1975.
Contents: AG interview comments.

GG21 *Sunday Morning.* Hosted by Charles Kurault. CBS-TV; New York, NY. TV broadcast: Oct. 28, 1979.
Contents: AG interview comments.

GG22 *Good Morning, Mr. Orwell.* Directed by Nam June Paik. Produced by Sam Paul. WNET-TV; New York, NY. 1984. 60 min., color. TV broadcast: Jan. 1, 1984.
Contents: AG reads "Do the Mediation Rock — Feeding Them Rassberries to Grow (by Peter Orlovsky)".

GG23 *David Letterman Show.* Hosted by David Letterman. NBC-TV; New York, NY. 1986. 60 min.
Contents: AG interview comments.

GG24 *All Things Considered.* Hosted by Andrei Codrescu. National Public Radio; New York, NY. 1988. 15 min. Radio broadcast: March 3, 1988.
Contents: AG interview comments.

GG25 *American Radio Theater.* Hosted by Garrison Keillor. National Public Radio; New York, NY. 1992. 120 min. Radio broadcast: May 30, 1992.
Contents: AG reads poems by Walt Whitman.

GG26 *Charlie Rose Show.* Hosted by Charlie Rose. PBS-TV; New York, NY. 1994. 60 min. TV broadcast: Feb. 15, 1994.
Contents: AG interview comments.

Titles and First Lines Index

I've had this finger and that [see...Mr Sharpe the Carpenter from Marysville]

I've known Eliot Katz for about ten years, and I've seen his [prose], B205

Jack Kerouac Est Mort Le 21 Octobre 1969, B81

Jack Kerouac's interest in Buddhism began [see...Kerouac's Ethic]

Jack was the creator of a world of darkness, F92

Jai Guru Jai Sarawati [see...Saraswati's Birthday]

Jan. 1, 1960 Sunrise [see...Sunrise]

Jan. 9. 63 [poem], C171, C211

Jan. 13 [see...The complete fire is death]

January N.Y. 1961 [see...Journal Night Thoughts]

January 19, 1968 [see...Are You Prepared for the Atom Bomb]

January 1972: if zaniest apocalyptic left [see...On the new cultural radicalism]

Jaweh and Allah Battle, A37, A48, B109, C654, C659, C693, E296, E323, F37, F40, F57, F114, F128, G27, G51

Jaweh with Atom Bomb [see...Jaweh and Allah Battle]

Jerry Rothenberg's followed upon a choice variety of studies that no [prose], B224

Jew Song, A35

Jimmy Berman Newsboy Gay Lib Rag [see...Jimmy Berman Rag]

Jimmy Berman Rag, A33, A44, C561, F41, F76, F77, F96

Joe Blow has decided [see...The Archetype Poem]

John, A63

John had AIDS [see...John]

John Lennon came right up to his household door [see...Prayer Blues II]

John Wieners speaks with Keatsean [prose], B176

Journal Entry on Visit to Timothy Leary's House in Boston, Dec. 1960 [see...Police]

Journal Night Thoughts, A15, A48, AA2, B45, C232, C251, F5

Journals Nov. 22, '63 [see...The black and white glare blink in the inky Air Force night]

Julian was a monster of aesthetics [prose], C1090

July 4, 1969 [see...Independence Day]

July 6, 1962 Calcutta 12 pm [see...Any Town Will Do]

Jump in time [see...Siesta in Xbalba]

Jumping the Gun on the Sun, A50, E335, E357, F104

Junk Mail, A41, A48, C847, F61

'Junky' Restored [prose], B125, C745

Just Say Yes Calypso, A63, C1151, C1153, C1160, C1162, C1167

Kaddish, A4, A48, A59, B10, B11, B12, B157, B235, C80, C89, C98, C103, C104, C156, E17, E55, E84, E96, E236, E239, F2, F7, F84, F114, F129, G55

Kali Ma tottering up steps to shelter tin roof, feeling her way to [see...Describe: The Rain on Dasaswamedh]

Kali Yuga we really are in it, heavy metal Age [see...Swami Bhaktivedanta Chanting God's Song in America]

Kansas City to Saint Louis, A26, A48, C330, C428

Karel Appel had taken the initiative, old Cobra [see...Playing with Appel]

Kenji Miyazawa, A32, A37

Kenneth Rexroth [prose], C972, C1062

Kenneth Rexroth was born in South Bend, Indiana on [see...Kenneth Rexroth]

Kerouac [prose], A31

Kerouac, a seminal poet in 1950s seeded the inspiration of young [prose], E300

Kerouac on Ayahuasca, A35

Kerouac's Ethic [prose], B207, C1179

Kerouac's Haiku Conception Is, C1223

Kheer, A19

Kidneystone Opium Traum, C813, F64

King of May [see...Kral Majales]

Kiss Ass, A26, A44, A48

Kissass is the Part of Peace [see...Kiss Ass]

Kissinger Dream I [prose], A57

Kissinger Dream II [prose], A57

A knock, look in the mirror, C930

The Knower — in the emptiness — is me which knows inside [see...Ayahuasca IX]

Knowing that the nod [see...Leda]

Kral Majales, A15, A44, A48, AA3, B38, B48, B157, C252, C405, C407, C413, C484, C974, F5, F30, F32, F115, F131, G9, G10

Kunming Hotel, I vomited greasy chicken sandwiched [see...Black Shroud]

Kyoto-Tokyo Express [see...The Change: Kyoto-Tokyo Express]

Lack Love, A44, A45, A48, C822, C834, F61

The Lama sat [see...Everyday]

Land O' Lakes, Wisc., A37, A48

Land O' Lakes, Wisc. Seminary, A39

My favorite Aunt Elanor always had a rheumatic heart [see...After Whitman & Reznikoff]

My Free Bill of Rights [prose], C434

My God!, A35

My High School English Teacher [prose], B223, C1026

My intention was not to provoke aggression but [see...They Hurt Me Too]

My love has come to ride me home [see...Do We Understand Each Other?]

My Mother's Ghost, A35

My Mythic Thumbnail Biography of Gary Snyder [prose], B218

My Neighborhood [see...After Whitman & Reznikoff]

My Old Desk, A35

My own aesthetic, basically, is subjective. I wrote a short sort [see...Poetry for the Next Society]

My own Voice rose to Heaven in elation [see...Rolling Thunder Stones]

My poetry has been broadcast uncensored for thirty years, particularly the poems [see...Statement on FCC Censorship]

My Sad Self, A6, A48, C113, C135

Myths Associated with Science [prose], A31

N.S.A. Dope Calypso, A63, F128

N.Y.C. Blues [see...New York Blues]

N.Y. '52 [see...Up From My Books]

NY Youth Call Annunciation, A33, B106, C623, C705, F83, F96

Nagasaki Day Peace Protest [see...Nagasaki Days]

Nagasaki Day Peace Protests Arrests [see...Nagasaki Days]

Nagasaki Days, A41, A45, A48, B142, B144, C788, C799, C822, C838, C918, E148, E272, E296, E323, F78, F128

The Nameless Gives Names, A35

The Names, A21, A36, A41, A44, A48, C251, C774, E65

The Names of Cities Above, a Poem of Peter, A35

Nanao, A63, E274, G51

The Nap, C58

Narcotics Agents Peddling Drugs [prose], A31

Naropa Hot Tub [see...American Sentences]

Nashville April 8, C310

A National hallucination [see...The Dope Fiend Menace in America Is a National Hallucination]

National Poem, F72

"Native Son" Makes Good! [prose], C1

Neal Cassady was my animal [see...Many Loves]

Neal's Ashes [see...On Neal's Ashes]

Near the Scrap Yard My Father'll Be Buried [see...Don't Grow Old]

Negative Capability: Kerouac's Buddhist Ethic [see...Kerouac's Ethic]

The New Consciousness [prose], A43

A New Cottage in Berkeley [see...A Strange New Cottage in Berkeley]

New Democracy Wish List, C1185, C1189, C1190, C1193, C1198

New England in the Fall: Autumn Gold [see...Autumn Gold: New England Fall]

A new moon looks down on our sick sweet planet [see...Death on All Fronts]

The New Right's a creepy pre-Fascist fad [see...Industrial Waves]

New Year's Eve Poem [see...December 31, 1978]

New Years Greeting, C1200

New York Blues, A33, C623, C696, E99, F83

New York to San Fran, A12, C240, G9

New York Youth Call Annunciation [see...NY Youth Call Annunciation]

News Bulletin, A41, A48, C710, C778

News Stays News, A63

A nice day in the Universe on Broad Street — sun shines [see...Laughing Gas]

The Night-Apple, A5, A48

Night at the Burning Ghat [prose], B42

The night cafe — 4 AM [see...Havana 1953]

Night Gleam, A37, A44, A48, B112, B124, C675, C713

Night gloom, Kleig lights on grass [see...Ah, Wake Up!]

A Night in the Village, B129, C6

Night meat lights [see...Police State Blues]

The 1937 Marijuana Tax Act [see...Preface on Marijuana]

The 1966 published studies on the Warren [prose], C283

1984 Now [Red tanks in Prague], AA32

1984 Now [Tanks in Afghanistan], AA32

Nixon, C877

Nixon has a pillow in his mouth in the kitchen [see...Nixon]

No Fuss Is Necessary, C566

No Hope Communism No Hope, C925

No hyacinthine imagination can express this clock of meat bleakly [see...Hymn]

No Longer [see...Prophecy]

General Index

Ungaretti, Giuseppe, C450, F22, F25
Unger, David, B172
United Artists [New York, NY], C853, C865, C886
Unity Press, E166
University of Wisconsin, Milwaukee Ballroom Reading, E195
University Review [New York, NY], C437, C585, C609
Unmuzzled Ox [New York, NY], C559, C582, C743, C847, C1002, C1057, C1102
Unspeakable Visions of the Individual [California, PA], C520, C641, C698, C699, C700, C771, C772, C773, C884, C913, C914, C1003, D9, D11, D15
The Untold Tradition, E206
Updike, John, B105, B177
Upper India Express, May 1, 1963 [see...Patna-Benares Express]
Uptown N.Y., E45
Uranus [Beloit, WI], C918
The Urban Reader, B77
Utopia Americana, F127

V-Letter, by Karl Shapiro, C15
Vagabond [St. Louis, MO], C1136
Vajradhatu Sun [Boulder, CO], C863, C864, C869, C897, C979, C1011, C1022, C1073, D33
Valley Advocate [Springfield, MA], C941
Van Buskirk, Alden [see...Buskirk, Alden Van]
Van Doren, Mark, B238, C700
Vanity Fair [New York, NY], C1004, C1156, C1216, D24
Vanwyngarden, Bruce, B189
Variegation [Los Angeles, CA], C40, C44, C46
Veitch, Tom, B121
Venture [New York, NY], C112
Venue [Charleston, WV], C1091
The Verdict Is In, B239
Verses Written for Student Anti Draft Rally 1980, E153
The Vestal Lady on Brattle, B2
Village Voice [New York, NY], C62, C64, C99, C130, C255, C273, C279, C314, C332, C341, C391, C392, C803, C805, C815, C1111, C1112
Village Voice Reader, B17
Villager [New York, NY], C610, C729
Vinkenoog, Simon, B42, F43
Vinson, James, B70
The Visionary Poetics of Allen Ginsberg, B133, E131
Visions of Cody, B94, D137, E360

Visions of Kerouac, Film Northampton at the Arts Centre, E219
The Visions of the Great Rememberer, A30, D8
Visions: Reflections of Jack Kerouac, D61
Visiting Father & Friends, A60
Visual Dharma Seminar, E137
Vogue [New York, NY], D41
Vogue Italia [Italy], D130
Voice [see...Village Voice]
Voices [Portland and Vinalhaven, ME], C38, C42
Vosnosensky, Andre [see...Voznesensky, Andrei]
Voznesensky, Andrei, A41, A48, A63, B135, C859, C1149, D132, F4

W.C. Williams, E237
WFMT Chicago Fine Arts Guide [Chicago, IL], C119
WPFW 89.3 FM Poetry Anthology, B237
Waddell, Eric, B207
Wagner Literary Magazine [Staten Island, NY], C76
Wagoner, David, F26
Waiting for Godot Books, E312, E352
Wakoski, Diane, B70, F53
Walden, G8
Walden: Reel Two, G8
Waldman, Anne, B83, B137, B138, B215, B222, C602, C784, C1074, D33, D54, D69, D101, E227, E362, F37, F38, F40, F48, F50, F54, F61, F64, F70, F75, F92, F111
Waldman, Ginsberg, CTR Reading, F54
Wales, A Visitation, A13
Wales Visitation, A13
Wallace, Amy, B245
Wallace, Irving, B134
Wallechinsky, David, B134, B245
Walls, Karen, B193
Walsh, Alice, C343
Walsh, Joy, F92
Walt Whitman, the Measure of His Song, B156
Walter, Robert L., F23
War Poems, B52
Ward, Lynd, AA26, E134
Warhol, Andy, B199, E20, G3, G19
Waring, James, C64
Warmbier, Dieter, E178
Warner, Patrick, D101
Warsh, Lewis, C886
Was, Don, F118
Washington, Jerome, E173
Washington Bulletin [Washington, DC], C276

About the Author

BILL MORGAN is a librarian and archival consultant in New York City. He has published several other works on Ginsberg and the Beat Poets.

Recent Titles in
Bibliographies and Indexes in American Literature

Bibliography of the Little Golden Books
Dolores B. Jones, compiler

A Chronological Outline of American Literature
Samuel J. Rogal, compiler

Humor of the Old Southwest:
An Annotated Bibliography of Primary and Secondary Sources
Nancy Snell Griffith, compiler

Images of Poe's Works: A Comprehensive Descriptive
Catalogue of Illustrations
Burton R. Pollin, compiler

Through the Pale Door: A Guide to and through the American Gothic
Frederick S. Frank

The Robert Lowell Papers at the Houghton Library,
Harvard University
Patrick K. Miehe, compiler

Bernard Malamud: A Descriptive Bibliography
Rita N. Kosofsky

A Tale Type and Motif Index of Early U.S. Almanacs
J. Michael Stitt and Robert K. Dodge

Jerzy Kosinski: An Annotated Bibliography
Gloria L. Cronin and Blaine H. Hall

James Fenimore Cooper: An Annotated Bibliography of Criticism
Alan Frank Dyer, compiler

Ralph Waldo Emerson: An Annotated Bibliography of Criticism,
1980–1991
Robert E. Burkholder and Joel Myerson, compilers

John Updike: A Bibliography, 1967–1993
Jack De Bellis, compiler

ISBN 0-313-29389-9

90000>

9 780313 293894

HARDCOVER BAR CODE